Ralph Waldo Emerson's dictum "The corruption of man is followed by the corruption of language" belongs to a long tradition of writing connecting political disorders and the corruption of language that stretches back in Western culture at least to Thucydides' *History of the Peloponnesian War*. *Representative Words*, which gives an account of the tradition from its classical and Christian origins through the Enlightenment, is primarily a study of how and why Americans renewed and developed it between the ages of the Revolutionary and Civil wars.

Drawing upon a wide range of materials from politics, linguistics, literature, history, rhetoric, and law, this study focuses on the quest by statesmen and writers from John Adams and Noah Webster to Emerson and Lincoln to oppose the corruption of words or to establish a more representative language – a quest, Gustafson argues, that was at the heart of revolutionary politics and American Renaissance literature. By studying the history and dynamics of the relationship between fears of corruption and efforts at conservation and renewal in language – a relationship embedded in Emerson's reflections on language in *Nature* – *Representative Words* establishes an important context for understanding the connections between the classical rhetorical and republican traditions and the ideology of the Declaration and the Constitution as well as between the politics and the literature of antebellum America. The American Revolution, the Civil War, and works by such writers as Brackenridge, Cooper, Melville, and Stowe are viewed in part as arising from a crisis of linguistic as well as political representation that Gustafson terms the "Thucydidean moment" – a time when words are perceived to be not a representative sign of ideas but a sovereign, duplicitous force.

Combining extensive historical investigation in grammars, rhetorics, political pamphlets, and journal essays with the perspectives provided by contemporary literary theory on the politics of representation and interpretation, this study offers a comprehensive examination of the language of politics and the politics of language in the early history of what Washington Irving called the American "logocracy."

CAMBRIDGE STUDIES IN AMERICAN LITERATURE AND CULTURE

Representative Words
Politics, Literature, and the American Language, 1776–1865

Continued on pages following the Index

Representative Words
Politics, Literature, and the American Language, 1776–1865

THOMAS GUSTAFSON
University of Southern California

CAMBRIDGE
UNIVERSITY PRESS

Published by the Press Syndicate of the University of Cambridge
The Pitt Building, Trumpington Street, Cambridge CB2 1RP
40 West 20th Street, New York, NY 10011-4211, USA
10 Stamford Road, Oakleigh, Victoria 3166, Australia

First published 1992

Printed in the United States of America

Library of Congress Cataloging-in-Publication Data
Gustafson, Thomas, 1953–
Representative words : politics, literature, and the American
language / Thomas Gustafson.
p.   cm. – (Cambridge studies in American literature and
culture)
Includes bibliographical references and index.
ISBN 0-521-39512-7 (hardback)
1. American literature – 19th century – History and criticism.
2. Politics and literature – United States – History – 19th century.
3. English language – Political aspects – United States.   4. Rhetoric –
Political aspects – United States.   5. Politicians – United States –
Language.   6. Political oratory – United States.   I. Title.
II. Series.
PS217.P64G8   1992
810.9′358′09034 – dc20   91-41045

A catalog record for this book is available from the British Library.

ISBN 0-521-39512-7 hardback

Contents

v

Part IV. From Logomachy to Civil War: The Politics of Language
in Post-Revolutionary America

Acknowledgments

Representation in scholarship as well as in politics requires the accumulation of large debts to a number of constituencies. Let me begin to repay in these notes my debt to several key contributors. My interest in the language of American politics and literature must have its deepest origin in a ritual from my childhood: instead of having me recite prayers at night, my father had me memorize passages from the speeches of Franklin Roosevelt and William Jennings Bryan and a stanza from William Cullen Bryant's "To a Waterfowl." The participation of my parents in the local government of Brookside, New Jersey, also gave me an early appreciation of what I would later learn to call civic humanism. Along with my brother, Gregory Gustafson, several teachers from high school, college, and graduate school have had a lasting influence in shaping my interests and the concerns of this book: Fred Fayen, Tony Roberts, David Brion Davis, Max Byrd, and George Dekker. My biggest debt of scholarly gratitude is to Jay Fliegelman, who taught me by precept and example. As my tutor, he renewed my interest in American literature, and his scholarship has been my guide. A more enlightened tutor and a more encouraging friend for this project I could not imagine. I would also like to thank Carolyn Dewald, Al Gelpi, and my two readers for Cambridge University Press for their editorial suggestions and Joseph Dane at USC for his collegial support. Mark Schoenfield provided a most helpful reading of much of this book that saved me from many embarrassments. Jane Van Tassel copyedited the manuscript with a patience, care, and ear for language that improved its style and accuracy in countless ways. The faults that remain are very much mine because I did not always heed their advice. My wife, Meg, has performed the hardest work for this book: she has given me, at no small cost to herself, the time to write it and the reason to finish it. My three children – Sarah, Britta, and Elisabeth – were born during the course of working on this study, and Sarah ended up helping me to spell-check and proofread it. I hope some day they will understand why I took the longest turns playing on the computer.

An early version of this book won the Raymond Alden Dissertation Prize in the English Department at Stanford University in 1986, and I thank the Alden family for their generosity in establishing this award. An NEH Summer Stipend grant enabled me to complete additional research.

Abbreviations and Editions Cited

AD	Cooper, James Fenimore, *The American Democrat*, ed. George Dekker and Larry Johnston (Baltimore: Penguin, 1969).
AJL	*The Adams–Jefferson Letters*, ed. Lester J. Cappon, 2 vols. (Chapel Hill: University of North Carolina Press, 1959).
AP	Whitman, Walt, *An American Primer*, ed. Horace Traubel (Boston: Small, Maynard, 1904).
AR	Howe, Samuel Gridley, *Eighteenth Annual Report of the Trustees of the Perkins Institution and Massachusetts Asylum for the Blind* (Cambridge, Mass.: Metcalf and Co., 1850).
BB	Melville, Herman, *Billy Budd, Sailor*, ed. Harrison Hayford and Merton M. Sealts, Jr. (Chicago: University of Chicago Press, 1962).
BFA	Franklin, Benjamin, *The Autobiography of Benjamin Franklin*, ed. Leonard Labaree, Ralph L. Ketcham, Helen C. Boatfield, and Helene H. Fineman (New Haven, Conn.: Yale University Press, 1964).
BP	Melville, Herman, *The Battle-Pieces of Herman Melville*, ed. Hennig Cohen (New York: Thomas Yoseloff, 1963).
CAF	*The Complete Anti-Federalist*, ed. Herbert J. Storing, 7 vols. (Chicago: University of Chicago Press, 1981).
DA	Tocqueville, Alexis de, *Democracy in America*, trans. Henry Reeve, ed. Arthur B. Fuller, 2 vols. (New York: Random House, 1945).
DC	Hobbes, Thomas, *De Cive, or The Citizen*, ed. Sterling P. Leonard (New York: Appleton-Century-Crofts, 1949).
DEL	Webster, Noah, *Dissertations on the English Language* (Boston: Isaiah Thomas, 1789).
DRH	Ramsay, David, *History of the American Revolution*, 2 vols. (New York: Russell and Russell, 1969; repr. of 1789 edition).
DSC	*The Debates in the Several State Conventions on the Adoption of the Federal Constitution*, ed. Jonathan Elliot, 5 vols. (Philadelphia: Lippincott, 1936).

DWW Webster, Daniel, *The Writings and Speeches of Daniel Webster*, 18 vols. (Boston: Little, Brown, 1903).

ED Adams, John, *The Earliest Diary of John Adams*, ed. L. H. Butterfield, Wendell D. Garrett, and Marc Friedlaender (Cambridge, Mass.: Belknap Press, 1966).

ELA Emerson, Ralph Waldo, *Essays and Lectures*, ed. Joel Porte (New York: Library of America, 1983).

EWW Whipple, Edwin P., "Words," *American Review*, 1 (1845).

FBW Bacon, Francis, *The Works of Francis Bacon*, ed. James Spedding, 8 vols. (New York: Garrett, 1968).

FLA Franklin, Benjamin, *Writings*, ed. J. A. Leo LeMay (New York: Library of America, 1987).

FP *The Federalist Papers*, ed. Clinton Rossiter (New York: New American Library, 1961).

HLA Hawthorne, Nathaniel, *Tales and Sketches*, ed. Roy Harvey Pearce (New York: Library of America, 1982).

HTJ Thoreau, Henry David, *The Journal of Henry D. Thoreau*, ed. Bradford Torrey and Francis H. Allen, 14 vols. (Boston: Houghton Mifflin, 1906).

HTW Thoreau, Henry David, *Reform Papers*, ed. Wendell Glick, The Writings of Henry D. Thoreau (Princeton, N.J.: Princeton University Press, 1973).

ILA Irving, Washington, *Washington Irving*, ed. James W. Tuttleton (New York: Library of America, 1983).

JAW Adams, John, *The Works of John Adams*, ed. Charles Francis Adams, 10 vols. (Boston: Little, Brown, 1850–6).

JLA Jefferson, Thomas, *Writings*, ed. Merrill D. Peterson (New York: Library of America, 1984).

JLW Lowell, James Russell, *Works of James Russell Lowell*, 10 vols. (Boston: Houghton Mifflin, 1890).

JML Madison, James, *Letters and Other Writings of James Madison*, 4 vols. (New York: R. Worthington, 1884).

JMN Emerson, Ralph Waldo, *The Journals and Miscellaneous Notebooks of Ralph Waldo Emerson*, ed. William H. Gilman, Ralph H. Orth, et al., 16 vols. (Cambridge, Mass.: Belknap Press, 1960–).

L Hobbes, Thomas, *Leviathan*, ed. C. B. MacPherson (Baltimore: Penguin, 1968).

LE Locke, John, *An Essay Concerning Human Understanding*, ed. Alexander Campbell Fraser, 2 vols. (Oxford: Clarendon Press, 1894).

LLA Lincoln, Abraham, *Speeches and Writings*, ed. Don E. Fehrenbacher, 2 vols. (New York: Library of America, 1989).

LR Adams, John Quincy, *Lectures on Rhetoric and Oratory*, 2 vols. (Cambridge, Mass.: Hilliard and Metcalf, 1810).

MC   Brackenridge, Hugh Henry, *Modern Chivalry*, ed. Claude M. Newlin (New York: American Book, 1937).

ML   Marsh, George P., *Lectures on the English Language* (New York: Scribner, 1859; rev. 1882).

MLA   Melville, Herman, *Pierre. Israel Potter. The Piazza Tales. The Confidence-Man. Uncollected Prose. Billy Budd*, ed. Harrison Hayford (New York: Library of America, 1984).

MP   Webster, Noah, *Miscellaneous Papers, on Political and Commercial Subjects* (1802; repr. New York: Burt Franklin Research and Source Works, 1972).

NFC   Madison, James, *Notes of Debates in the Federal Convention of 1787 Reported by James Madison*, ed. Adrienne Koch (New York: Norton, 1969).

NHW   Hawthorne, Nathaniel, *The Centenary Edition of the Works of Nathaniel Hawthorne*, ed. William Charvat, Roy Harvey Pearce, and Claude M. Simpson, 20 vols. (Columbus: Ohio State University Press, 1965).

NV   Taylor, John, *New Views of the Constitution of the United States*, (Washington, D.C.: Way and Gideon, 1823).

NW   Webster, Noah, *On Being an American: Selected Writings, 1783–1828*, ed. Homer D. Babbidge, Jr. (New York: Praeger, 1967).

NWL   Webster, Noah, *The Letters of Noah Webster*, ed. Harry M. Warfel (New York: Library Publishers, 1953).

PAR   *Pamphlets of the American Revolution*, ed. Bernard Bailyn (Cambridge, Mass.: Belknap Press, 1965).

PLA   Poe, Edgar Allan, *Poetry and Tales*, ed. Patrick F. Quinn (New York: Library of America, 1984).

PS   *Political Sermons of the American Founding Era*, ed. Ellis Sandoz (Indianapolis: Liberty Press, 1991).

REW   Emerson, Ralph Waldo, *The Complete Works of Ralph Waldo Emerson*, ed. Edward Waldo Emerson, 12 vols. (Boston: Houghton Mifflin, 1903–4).

SAW   Adams, Samuel, *The Writings of Samuel Adams*, ed. Harry Alonzo Cushing, 4 vols. (New York: Putnam, 1904–8).

SJW   Johnson, Samuel, *Works of Samuel Johnson*, ed. Arthur Murphy, 12 vols. (London: Luke Hanford, 1806).

THW   Hobbes, Thomas, *The English Works of Thomas Hobbes*, ed. Sir William Molesworth, 11 vols. (London: John Bohn, 1840).

TJW   Jefferson, Thomas, *The Writings of Jefferson*, ed. A. Lipscomb, 20 vols. (Washington, D.C.: Thomas Jefferson Memorial Association, 1903).

TLA   Thoreau, Henry David, *A Week on the Concord and Merrimack Rivers. Walden; or, Life in the Woods. The Maine Woods. Cape Cod*, ed. Robert F. Sayre (New York: Library of America, 1985).

TPW   Paine, Thomas, *The Complete Writings of Thomas Paine*, ed. Philip S. Foner, 2 vols. (New York: Citadel, 1945).

WLA   Whitman, Walt, *Poetry and Prose*, ed. Justin Kaplan (New York: Library of America, 1982).

WMW   Mathews, William, *Words; Their Use and Abuse* (Chicago: S. C. Griggs, 1876).

It is by words and the defeat of words,
Down sudden vistas of the vain attempt,
That for a flying moment one may see
By what cross-purposes the world is
    dreamt.

Richard Wilbur, "An Event"

Introduction

Representative – misrepresentative

Nathaniel Hawthorne, *American Notebooks*

In 1845 Edwin Whipple, an eminent New England literary critic, published in the *American Review* a remarkable essay on the power and duplicity of words in which he declares at the outset, "Words . . . exercise such an untrammeled influence [in the concerns of the world], that it is unjust to degrade them from sovereigns into representatives." He adds, "The true ruler of this big, bouncing world is the Lexicon. Every new word added to its accumulated thousands is a new element of servitude to mankind."[1] For Americans today Whipple's words should sound a familiar note of alarm, for in the past two decades, and especially as we approached 1984, we were frequently reminded of George Orwell's vision of the tyranny of Newspeak. It appeared to many citizens that in the era of Vietnam, Watergate, and Nukespeak we were enduring in our own state a long reign of linguistic and political misrepresentation that threatened the pursuit of life, liberty, and happiness. The words of our political leaders not only cloaked indefensible actions with the semblance of virtue but seemingly led us to commit them: in Southeast Asia, we made a wasteland of villages and called it pacification; in Nixon's White House, the term "national security" sanctioned criminal break-ins; and at Reagan's urging, MX missiles were funded as Peacekeepers, a term applied in nineteenth-century America to the Colt .45 pistol.[2]

Alarmed by the deployment of doublespeak in the political discourse of the United States and foreign countries, English teachers and political commentators have often turned in defense to Orwell's classic essay "Politics and the English Language." Frequently assigned as reading in high school and college, this essay has become a primer for

1

introducing students to the politics of language and educating them about the way words and politicians misrepresent reality – or govern our perceptions of it.[3] But if we use Orwell's essay to ward off the advance of Newspeak that seemed to threaten us with the "double-think" of Big Brother several decades before 1984, we should also note that it belongs to a long tradition of writing connecting political disorders and the corruption of language that stretches back in Western culture at least to Thucydides' observations in his *History of the Peloponnesian War*.[4] My work, which provides an account of the tradition, is primarily a study of how and why Americans renewed and developed it between the ages of the Revolutionary and Civil wars. It thus seeks to examine and explain a quest that has often been at the heart of American politics and literature – a quest to end the corruption and tyranny of words or to establish a more representative language – and it places that quest in the wider context of classical, Enlightenment, and modern concerns about political and linguistic misrepresentation.[5]

"For if the word has the potency to revive and make us free, it has also the power to blind, imprison and destroy," declares Ralph Ellison, and in the United States the quest for representative words has been in large part an attempt to constitute or reconstitute the words of the English language and the words of America's governing texts – the Declaration and the Constitution – so that those words would free and unite rather than blind, imprison, and destroy.[6] But the essence of that quest is captured by John Dos Passos as the attempt to keep ourselves and our nation from being beaten by those "who have turned our language inside out who have taken the clean words our fathers spoke and made them slimy and foul."[7] Between the Revolution and the Civil War, this quest took a variety of forms and was engaged in by a host of figures from poets and politicians to ministers, schoolmasters, and philosophers. It includes projects to guard or renovate the language that range from John Adams's proposal for an "American Academy for refining, improving, and ascertaining the English Language" and Noah Webster's labors on his spellers and dictionary to Ralph Waldo Emerson's condemnation of "rotten diction" in *Nature* and the efforts of James Fenimore Cooper in *The American Democrat* and of Abraham Lincoln to rectify the meaning of such key political words as "liberty" and "equality." For John Quincy Adams, the pursuit of liberty demanded the recognition that the "words our fathers spoke" and wrote down in the Constitutional Convention were themselves "slimy and foul." During his defense of the slaves who had revolted on the *Amistad*, Adams noted that the framers had hid the sin of slavery under the fig leaf of a circumlocution – "person held to service" – and he sought, as did Frederick Douglass and William Lloyd Garrison, to rip off the veil of words covering the country's original sin and to perform the Adamic task of calling things – and people who had been reduced to things – by their right names.[8] Compelled not only by a sense of "wonder" before the "fresh, green breast of the new world" but as witnesses to corruption hidden by "rotten diction" in the American city of words, writers and political activists working in the American grain have labored to name things correctly.[9]

The American quest for representative words can also be considered to include not just attempts to guard or renovate the words of the English language and the governing texts of America, but to change Americans themselves – to convert, reform, or inspire them – so that their actions would be guided by the Word of God or by the words of the Declaration and the Constitution. Americans have conceived of themselves as the "people of the Word," and whether that word is understood as the Word of God or the words of the founding fathers, it has been their calling to rise up and live out the meaning of those words. And typically in political discourse as well as in literature, Americans have affirmed that vocation, the country's calling by the Word, while criticizing the errant flesh: the failure to be faithful in acts to those words. It is a failure that seemingly bankrupts those hallowed words, leaving them specious, hollow, counterfeit – not "apples of gold in pictures of silver" but mere sounding brass. But while this form of criticism – the lament of American Jeremiahs – denounces the differences between word and deed, saying and doing, letter and spirit in America, it upholds the promise of their future correspondence and calls upon the people to suit their actions to their words so that the country can be held up truly to the world as a "city on a hill" or as a shining reflection of "laws of nature and nature's God."[10] To renew the words, to make them representative, to redeem their value, from this perspective people must perform anew the acts of liberty, revolution, sacrifice, brotherhood, charity underwritten by the rhetoric of America's first revolution. Only then when the words of the Declaration and the Constitution are backed by the bullion of deeds will people enjoy the full cash value of those promissory notes: "the riches of freedom and the security of justice."[11] Only then when those words become flesh will America cease being a land of false prophets and appear instead as the "political Messiah."[12] This call for words redeemed by action in an America that has substituted rhetoric for action is the call that Thoreau makes in his essays, that Fuller addresses in her letters from Italy, that Lincoln embodies in his Gettysburg Address, and that Dos Passos summons up in his tribute to Sacco and Vanzetti in *The Big Money*: "hear the old words of the haters of oppression made new in sweat and agony tonight."[13] But as we have been reminded by Sacvan Bercovitch and others, this call is deeply problematic given what the words of the Revolution and Constitution underwrote and sanctioned, and given how that call transforms dissent into a ritual of consensus and how the language of the Revolution has been exploited by merchandisers of the word to sell middle-class goods.[14] Ever since the first settlement in Massachusetts, when the Puritans, in William Carlos Williams's words, used the "jargon of God" as the "dialect by which they kept themselves surrounded as with a palisade," Americans have continued to fortify and expand their construction of a city on a hill within a circle of moral rhetoric that has been, since the beginning, in varying parts, a mixture of utopian vision, pragmatic action, "soul butter," and "hogwash."[15]

There has been another dialect, however, in which Americans have built (or remodeled) the words representing and sustaining visions of the country in which they live; and though this language has also worked to fortify the moral rhetoric or ideology of American political discourse, it has often done so by questioning that rhetoric or the uses to which it has been put by confidence men, demagogues, Indian haters, slave masters, lawyers, presidents, ministers, and other members of the word-slinging class. This discourse, this counterjargon, is the dialect of Huck Finn and the "polyphonic oratory of reality" of *Uncle Tom's Cabin* and *Moby-Dick*.[16] Representing or inspired by an American vernacular – the commonsense speech of the people or the "bold, nervous, lofty language" of their representatives in the forum and pulpit – these forms of dialectal speech are the styles that Americans developed in the nineteenth century to become revolutionary artists. Indeed, just as the Sons of Liberty in the Revolutionary era opposed a sovereign or corrupt discourse – the artifices of the king's ministers and the misrepresentations of Parliament – with the counterdiscourse of common sense and impassioned oratory in their quest for better representation, so too did artists of the American Renaissance seek to challenge sovereign lexicons or "rotten diction" with idiomatic expression and rhetorical argument grounded in the vox populi or the voice of nature in a quest for "new potentialities of speech" and representation; and in their triumph they created a place for themselves as founding fathers (or mothers) of what Ann Douglas calls "'the great American tradition' of the novel as rhetoric, talk, voice, language," a tradition that has its poetic equivalent in the language experiments of Lowell's *Biglow Papers* and Whitman's *Leaves of Grass*.[17]

At the forefront of this tradition are those works whose narratives are driven by a dialogical conflict between high and low voices, between, more specifically, grammatical characters and oral, ungrammatical ones – between, for instance, Captain Farrago and Teague O'Regan, Judge Temple and Natty Bumppo, Captain Vere and Billy Budd, Tom Sawyer and Huckleberry Finn.[18] This tradition also includes such later works as Zora Neale Hurston's *Their Eyes Were Watching God* and Norman Mailer's *Why Are We in Vietnam?*, sustained largely by the boundless vitality of a single voice as well as by works underwritten by a dialogue, in Douglas's words, "between the apparent and the actual, between one imaginary voice and another possibly more authentic one," such as occurs in Melville's *Benito Cereno* and *The Confidence-Man* and in the works of many of "his most interesting literary successors, from Twain to Mailer and Pynchon."[19] This dialogue or contest between voices demands from the reader, as does a legal trial, a checking and balancing of representations, a testing of one construction of language against another. The dialogue can work to emancipate us from any one circle of words, or, as in the conversations on board the *Fidèle* in *The Confidence-Man*, it can invite us to repose confidence in none of the voices nor in representation itself. Indeed, if the visionary end of the early American quest for representative words is a community of people faithful to words and of words faithful to nature, in *The Confidence-Man* the quest comes to an abrupt halt in a revelation about the apocryphal nature of words and the people of the Word. The novel does not guide us through a city of words into scenes of nature but instead leaves us lost in a cul-de-sac wherein we can only turn around and recognize that the place where we live is a city (or country) where words and things, words and deeds, words and people stand in no reliable connection or fidelity to one another. The moral rhetoric that was to sustain construction of a city on a hill – the invocation to charity – appears in this novel on the lips of the confidence man as the ideal mask of self-interest. Something further of the masquerade will always follow, because here we see not face to face or nature through a "transparent eye-ball"; here we see darkly through what James Madison called the "cloudy medium" of language; and here in this new world, as in the fallen old world, we are destined to meet Carwins, Claggarts, confidence men out to deceive us through the duplicitous possibilities of representation.[20]

In America, then, the quest to end the corruption and tyranny of words has followed three broad routes: the reform of language, the reform of people, and the reform of people's understanding of the potentials and liabilities of language. The tutelary spirit of the first route is the Schoolmaster; of the second, the Minister; and of the third, the Artist. These routes have, of course, run parallel, criss-crossed, and converged throughout American history, and each figure who has undertaken the quest has been guided or motivated by some combination of each mentor. But whatever form the quest took between the Revolutionary era and the Civil War, and whoever guided it, the underlying motivation was often the same: Americans fondly hoped – or fervently believed – that the advance of liberty and a more perfect union could be achieved through a reformed state of language. "NOW is the time, and *this* the country," Noah Webster declares, "in which we may expect success, in attempting changes favorable to language, science and government."[21] Here in this new world, it was envisioned, a purified and uniform language could overcome the babel of tongues that had plagued the old world; here people could free themselves from the artifices and false entitlements of aristocracy by naming things according to their nature; here in this new republic, it was assumed, eloquence would sustain liberty and liberty would sustain eloquence as it did in classical republics; and here a sovereign political language could be constituted whose words would represent not the dictates of a monarch but the common sense of the people and would act as a chart for guiding the ship of state safely between the Scylla and Charybdis of tyranny and anarchy. But perhaps more important, here too in this new world it was strongly believed – or deeply feared – that the misuse and misunderstanding of words could be, in Noah Webster's phrase, "*the efficient causes of our political disorders.*"[22] Here too the corruption of language could precipitate a fall into the strife and tyranny that marked the end of classical republics and England in the seventeenth century. Here too, that is, words could become not representative signs but a sovereign power or the instrument of the demagogue who would make people "First slave to words, then vassal to a name. / Then dupe to party."[23] Here too, in phrases drawn from Emerson and Shakespeare's *Troilus and Cressida*, old words could be "perverted to stand for things which are not" (ELA, 25), and ugly things could be given fine names (REW, XI, 259), so that "force should be right; or rather right and wrong . . . should lose their names, and so should justice too" (I.iii, 116, 118); and here especially, in this "LOGOCRACY," this "*government of words*," as Washington Irving labeled the American political system (ILA, 144), the ship of state could be wrecked by the indefiniteness of the Lexicon or be driven dangerously off course by those who would misconstrue or nominally follow the chart drafted by the founding fathers. For all of these reasons, fear of the word and its corruption was the beginning of political wisdom.

"We have only words against Power Superpower," Dos Passos declares in *The Big Money*, and in America the battle people have waged against the oppression and misrepresentation of Power Superpower – and against linguistic corruption itself – has been a persistent one fought with sporadic intensity and varying success.[24] The Puritan migration that first settled New England with Europeans had its roots in a protest against the "corruptions" of God's Word and the persecutions undertaken in His name – a protest that was repeated when Roger Williams proclaimed his dissent in *The Bloody Tenet of Persecution, for Cause of Conscience, in a Conference Between Peace and Truth* against those who had "under the name of Christ, etc." conducted "bloody, irreligious, and inhumane oppressions and destructions."[25] My account of the battle begins, however, when a vocal minority of colonists turned to sermons, speeches, and pamphlets primed with the language of evangelical religion and republican ideology to protest against (and later free themselves from) what they viewed as a long train of artifices and prevarications perpetrated by King George III and the British government to defend indefensible acts of tyranny and make them pay obeisance (and taxes) to a representative institution that did not represent them. And my account continues through the attempts of reformers in antebellum America to end what were in their view the misinterpretations of the Declaration of Independence and the contradictions of the Constitution that had turned the words representing the ideals of the Revolution into a misrepresentative Newspeak sanctioning slavery and other forms of inequality. "In the beginning of America," as Ralph Ellison declares, "was not only the word but the contradiction of the word."[26] The Declaration and the Constitution, the verbal fiats that spoke a country and wrote a government into existence, said the thing which was not. The words securing life, liberty, and the pursuit of happiness and establishing justice for We, the People, were not made flesh for blacks, women, and other people in the country whose labor helped provide the freedom the founders needed to pen those words. Thus, while American history can be read, in Ellison's words, as a history of the "idealistic action of the American Word as it goads its users toward a perfection of our revolutionary ideals," it can also be read as a history of the promulgation and citation of the American Word to secure not the blessings of liberty but the perpetuation of slavery, not the equal rights of We, the People, but the interests of a ruling class.[27] This study examines the history of American politics, literature, and language from both perspectives: as a history of Americans fighting, struggling, and conniving to make the dominant languages and shared texts of their culture – in particular the English language, the Declaration, and the Constitution – serve their ideals and their interests, and as a history of Americans reflecting upon their own use and abuse of the word.

In the early 1850s Nathaniel Hawthorne jotted down in a notebook two words connected by a dash that might have been such a reflection about language or politics in his age. The words were simply "Representative – misrepresentative."[28] Like the scarlet letter Hawthorne finds among the papers of Surveyor Pue, these words are "most worthy of interpretation." And like Hawthorne's own approach to the scarlet letter, my interpretation of these two words requires a reconstruction of the past, a telling of a story authorized and authenticated in part by documents from the custom house of European as well as American literature and political discourse. Only by telling that story can we appreciate more fully how Americans from the age of the Revolution through the Civil War confronted in their politics and explored in their literature all the hopes and fears that their Western forebears had expressed for language as an instrument of representation and misrepresentation, and why they so often conducted politics and literature in this period as a battle against the bewitchment of the understanding by language.

Part I of this four-part study develops two frameworks for approaching the nexus of word and act in America, or the ways in which the Actual and the Imaginary – the politics and the literature of the early republic – were each imbued with the nature of the other. In America, I argue, political and linguistic concerns have often merged in questions about the amount of confidence that can be placed in forms of representation and in the degree to which change can be permitted in the English language and the language of the law. Part II places this American nexus of word and act in a larger historical context that reaches back to the roots of democracy and rhetoric in Western culture. It briefly examines the classical and Christian origins of the tradition connecting political and linguistic corruption and then traces its development through the Enlightenment in order to show more fully, in Part III, how and why Noah Webster, Thomas Jefferson, and other early Americans welcomed revolutionary changes that would renovate not only their form of government but the constitution of the English language. In America, the pursuit of liberty and a more perfect union was inseparable from the quest for proper representation in both a political and a linguistic sense, or for a language as well as a government that would correspond to common sense or to the natural constitution of things. This part also describes how John Locke's contractual theory of language, and especially his ideas about remedying the imperfections and abuses of words, influenced early American linguistic speculation and helped Revolutionary Americans combat the "misrepresentations" of the British and construct a new political language: the Constitution. The Constitution itself is viewed here as the culmination of a transformation in political and linguistic theory which began in the seventeenth century whereby the people replace the monarch as the source of authority in both law and language. In America, that is, the divine right to name and give meaning becomes the right of humanity. In the beginning is the word of We, the People.

Part IV then examines how the early hopes Americans had for the reform of the English language in America – the prospect, for instance, that America could repair the curse of Babel – gave way in the mid nineteenth century to increasing fears of its corruption and to the conviction of many statesmen and writers that the political disorders of the period – including the Civil War – were caused in large part by the misuse and misunderstanding of words or by their omnipotence. It was a time when, it seemed, "political double-dealings naturally grew out of verbal double meanings," words quoted by Oliver Wendell Holmes, and when language appeared to be the source of a new tyranny, a power exercising "'a sovereign sway and masterdom' over the whole domain of thought and emotion," in Edwin Whipple's words.[29] The great political questions of the day, from the debate over the tariff and the charter of the national bank to the extension of slavery into the territories, resolved themselves, as Tocqueville observed, into judicial questions, and those judicial questions further resolved themselves into rancorous quarrels and grandiloquent debates about the definition and interpretation of words in the Constitution.[30] Like the Bible in seventeenth-century England, America's fundamental law became the battleground for a war of words, and the fighting among political parties, branches of government, and outspoken individuals over its proper construction helped shape the age's understanding of the way words govern people and people govern the meanings of words. The legal controversies and political debates of this period, which often centered on acts of interpretation and turned on acts of oratory, not only provoked violent confrontations but spurred concern about the power and duplicity of words and the values and dangers of linguistic change which manifested itself in the literature and language theory of the American Renaissance.

In the last part of this study I argue, in fact, that the unease many American writers expressed about the unsettled state of the American language and their consequent attempts to preserve its purity and uniformity, their protests over the corruption of words and their corresponding desire for a language grounded in nature, and their warning about the dangers of mistaking words for things and representations for reality must be seen in a political context. More specifically, that unease and those fears and warnings must be seen in conjunction with the unease Americans felt about the unsettled state of words in American law and political discourse, their protests over the corrupt interpretations of the Constitution and its lack of grounding in the laws of nature, and their fears that the people were being deluded by false politicians and fake philanthropists – what Margaret Fuller termed "word-Catos" and "word-Christs" – invoking such terms as "liberty" and "union" and party names like "Republican" and "Democrat" for purposes that contradicted the ideals of the Revolution.[31] The heightened skepticism about language and the pervasive concern about its ambiguity in this period, which stemmed at least in part from the constitutional controversies, are developments reflected in the experiments of American Renaissance writers with the "possibilities of symbolism" and their ventures into a "rhetoric of ambiguity" such as we find in those two great novels written at the height of the constitutional crisis: *The Scarlet Letter* and *Moby-Dick*.[32] The "obliquity of signs," the contrasting planes of discourse, and the multiple interpretations of symbols aboard the *Pequod* and in Hester Prynne's Boston mirror a political world, like the United States in the 1850s, that is united by a text but divided over its interpretation.[33] It is a world of contradictory voices deaf to its own contradictions, a world where people insist passionately, vehemently – indeed, monomaniacally – on the truth of their own interpretation of a symbol or of the letter of the law and can see or admit of no other interpretation because of ideological blindness or ideological fervor – or because they possess a theory of language that assumes that words have a "natural" or "proper" or "determinate" meaning.

Perhaps in an effort to transcend (or challenge) the ideology of party politics and reform movements wherein each party claimed to possess the natural and proper meanings of words and made "truthclaims" for their own diction or perhaps were just sickened by what Fuller termed the pomp and strife of words, some writers in the period questioned the concept of a proper meaning and an objective interpretation, contending instead that the difference between true representation and misrepresentation, plain sense and corrupt sense, false interpretation and correct interpretation was fundamentally one of perspective or political party.[34] From this vantage point, the "poetics of indeterminacy" that scholars have commented on in works by Emerson, Hawthorne, and Melville can be seen as less the product of an escape from history into aesthetics and more as an aesthetic response – or symbolic challenge – to a politics of determinacy or to the efforts of politicians and reformers to affix a determinate meaning to the letter of the law and to claim for their interpretation the validity of logic or a faithful interpretation of the will of the founding fathers. But by the end of the 1850s, the ambiguities of the Constitution and of a nation half free and half slave could no longer be tolerated (much less appreciated) in a liberal spirit of compromise and pluralistic truth: one interpretation, one side of the house divided had to dominate by force of law or law of force. "A general massacre of all who have not thought in a certain way has proved a very effective means of settling opinion in a country," observed Charles Sanders Peirce, who spent the decades following the Civil War seeking philosophic or semiotic methods of a different caliber to fix beliefs and make our ideas clear.[35]

This book, then, is a study of the language of politics and the politics of language in Revolutionary and post-Revolutionary America. Its method draws upon the work of J. G. A. Pocock in the history of political discourse in the republican tradition and on his theoretical statements about the practice of studying the history of political thought as a history of the interactions of *langue* and *parole*, of confining discourses and innovative speech acts, and of paradigms of discourse extended, modified, or challenged in the context of social and political change.[36] But my aim is not so much to study transformations in the language of politics in the context of social change as to examine transformations in attitudes toward language in the context of political change. To chart those changes, I draw upon many of the canonical texts of early American culture and upon a large body of writing about language theory and practice contained in journal articles, grammars, popular books, legal texts, and political essays of the period. I examine the relationship between political and linguistic concerns in these texts by focusing on the political metaphors Americans used to describe language and linguistic processes and on the linguistic metaphors they used to describe political processes. That focus leads me to investigate the parallels that Americans perceived (or that their writings suggest) between political and linguistic representation, between rules of grammar and the laws of the land, between definitions and contractual government, and between political revolution and linguistic change. These parallels in general have received much attention in modern literary criticism, and that criticism informs my discussion of early American investigations into – or confrontations with – the politics of language and interpretation. My main concern, however, is not to reveal how this speculation about language anticipates modern theories; it is rather to place that speculation in its political and cultural context.

Several recent studies of American language theory and practice undertaken from different perspectives by Philip F. Gura, Dennis E. Baron, David Simpson, Kenneth Cmiel, and Michael P. Kramer have made a significant contribution to such a contextual study.[37] But what needs to be investigated more closely is what Americans learned from and what they contributed to the dialogue about the relationship between politics and language that began in classical antiquity and continued strong through the Enlightenment. That dialogue is an integral part of the classical rhetorical tradition and of the literature of eighteenth-century England that played such a crucial role in the formation of republican ideology. The dialogue treats such subjects of particular concern to early Americans as the relationship between liberty and eloquence, force and persuasion, political and linguistic reform, the corruption of words and a corrupt body politic, misrepresentation and tyranny, and freedom of speech (in its broadest sense) and democracy. Early Americans were keenly aware of these relationships from studying the political and historical works of classical and Enlightenment authors and from reading their poems, plays, philosophy, and fiction. Indeed, they would not have doubted what John Adams declared in 1780: "It is not to be disputed that the form of government has an influence upon language, and language in its turn influences not only the form of government, but the temper, the sentiments, and manners of the people."[38] This study could be considered an attempt to document Adams's assertion. It seeks to reveal in particular how political events and a republican form of government helped shape linguistic theories and practices in America; how theories of language and fears about the power and duplicity of words influenced political thought and the form of American goverment; and how language came to be seen by Americans as a political instrument that possessed many of the advantages and disadvantages of government itself: an instrument, that is, which could, on the one hand, help preserve order and liberty, but also an instrument which could, on the other hand, become a source of tyranny and corruption, a power that could mislead the people, confound their ideas of virtue and vice, and exercise a profound influence – indeed, a sovereign sway – over their hearts and minds.

The sovereign sway of words was what Edwin Whipple feared when he declared in 1845, "The true ruler of this big, bouncing world is the Lexicon."[39] This statement, remarkable in 1845, has now become a cliché. We are governed, ruled, constituted by discourse; we are caged in a prison house of language; the word is my master. I write not to honor this cliché or bury it but to historicize it, or to suggest when and why such early Americans as Whipple felt compelled to come to this conclusion and to challenge the Lexicon when opposing the sovereign power or ruling interest of the day (e.g., the king, the parliament, the "slave power," the people). It is a story of people fearing imprisonment in what Thomas Paine called the "Bastille of a word" and seeking their freedom by asserting what John Locke called "man's inviolable liberty" to make "words stand for whatever ideas he pleases" or acting upon Horace Bushnell's belief that "we have our freedom, as our fathers had, and as good a right to use words with new meanings, certainly, as to have new thoughts."[40] But as Bushnell (and Locke) recognize, this inviolable liberty gives us the freedom to fall into the confusion of Babel. "To settle the meaning of a word," Bushnell writes, "is often a matter even of the highest consequence to the welfare of society. Most especially is this true of words that are used with a standard reference to great moral and political distinctions."[41] This conflict between the need to settle the meanings of words to maintain order, community, and communication and the need to unsettle them to pursue liberty, independence, and self-expression is a conflict lying at the heart of politics and literature in America, and while this conflict is by no means particular to this country, it has been exacerbated by the contradictory imperatives of the revolutionary and constitutional traditions. The revolutionary tradition with its emphasis on liberty demands resistance to an inherited language and reverence for the sovereignty of the vox populi and vox Dei, while the constitutional tradition with its emphasis on union demands compliance with an inherited language or reverence for the sovereignty of a text written by the founding fathers and guarded by the priests of America's "civil religion" (the justices of the Supreme Court).[42]

The drama of American democracy, which sets the word of one text or one representative voice or agency against the word of another, can be scripted in the terms of recent criticism as a power play of differences or as a conflict between order and liberty and the rulers and the ruled that is engaged in by people playing language games, stealing symbols back and forth, working the loom of language to reweave the fabric of imperatives, locking up or unlocking power by turning "keywords," countering Power Superpower with words made new, and defending against Newspeak with old words recalled.[43] Much of the same drama could probably be told for every country and culture, and here I seek not to emphasize America's uniqueness but to present Revolutionary and mid-nineteenth-century America as case histories of a people seeking to prevent and then fearing they are caught in the confusion and violence of what I term the Thucydidean moment: that moment when, as occurs in Thucydides' famous description of the *stasis* at Corcyra, political and linguistic disorders – the corruption of people and language – become one and the same.[44]

The concept of a Thucydidean moment seeks to complement J. G. A. Pocock's notion of the Machiavellian moment, which he describes as "the moment in conceptualized time in which the republic was seen as confronting its own temporal finitude, as attempting to remain morally and politically stable in a stream of irrational events conceived as essentially destructive of all systems of secular stability. In the language which had been developed for the purpose, this was spoken of as the confrontation of 'virtue' with 'fortune' and 'corruption'."[45] I use the term "the Thucydidean moment" to describe the moment that succeeds the failure of the Machiavellian moment: it is the moment when fortune or necessity or corruption defeats virtue, or when moral and political stability – and the code of language that sustains that stability – collapses into confusion and the muteness of violence. Railing against this collapse, the poet's voice articulates the conditions of this chaos, this fall of words. In the crucible of the Thucydidean moment, under the pressure of competing voices, from the heat of clashing interests, "words strain, crack and sometimes break." Under this burden, or from the tension of shrieking, scolding, mocking, chattering voices, in T. S. Eliot's words, or from "the desire of riches, of pleasure, of power, of praise," in Emerson's phrase, words "slip, slide, perish"; they are "perverted to stand for things which are not"; they "Decay with imprecision, will not stay in place, / Will not stay still."[46]

This decay of words can no more be avoided than the dropping of leaves and fruit, but in the soil of politics, as well as in the verses of poetry, an unsettling of words, their turning and troping, even their uprooting, can yield something other than rotten diction: it can help produce new growth, new leaves of grass, new conceptions of liberty.[47] In America, when people have perceived words cracking, breaking, and decaying in the dirt of political machination, when they have felt themselves caught in the semantic confusion and violence of the Thucydidean moment, they have not just suffered it in silence or sought an escape in nature. Writers and political activists, for instance, have responded with radical or underground efforts to cultivate the language in more productive and exemplary ways, sometimes seeking to conserve the root meanings of words, sometimes transplanting them to new ground, sometimes exposing the decay of "rotten diction" wherever they have smelled it; at other times just uncovering the contra-dictions. Standard dictionaries and "devil's dictionaries"; sermons, pamphlets, and speeches; composition texts; "inarticulate" heroes, unreliable narrators, and self-reflexive novels have been some of the tools. This relationship between perceptions or fears of linguistic decay and efforts at conservation, growth, and renewal in language – a relationship embedded in Emerson's seminal reflections on language in *Nature* – is a relationship whose history and dynamics can be studied to help us perceive the thematic connections if not causal links between the language of American politics and the politics of language in American literature, and I hope such a study will enable us to learn more fully how Americans have succeeded in criticizing and improving their forms of political and linguistic representation so we ourselves can pursue the essential tasks of representative politics with more insight.

Today we commonly acknowledge that we are inevitably caught in the confusion, violence, and power of language, and history is now written from this perspective as an archaeology of sovereign discourses.[48] In the writing of American history, for instance, the language of republican ideology, the rhetoric of the jeremiad, the persuasions of Jefferson and Jackson, and the lingua franca of parent–child relationships have been regarded as universes of discourse or constellations of meaning under whose controlling influence and revolving meanings move the thoughts and actions, the perceptions and behavior of earthly, word-bound humans.[49] The sovereign power of each of these discourses, however, has been challenged by the recognition that historical actors can at times choose their roles from competing scripts or be fluent in some and thus mastered by none. My study of the politics of language in Revolutionary America and afterwards offers more of a Whig than a Tory interpretation of the sovereignty of discourse, because while it recognizes how Americans have been constituted and governed by the languages of their state and culture and by the social forces upholding and deriving power from such languages, it privileges the acts (and presumes the capacity) of a people to assert and develop the right to question, amend, and change the words, the laws, the languages, and the political agents who represent or constitute them as a people, and it maintains that the creation and development of these rights and capacities – and the formation of public spaces and arenas of the imagination where they can be exercised – are essential and interrelated aspects of the enduring pursuit of liberty and a more perfect union.

I

The American Logocracy:
The Nexus of Word and Act

1

Political and Linguistic Representation: Confidence or Distrust?

"Distrust is a stage to confidence."
"I have confidence in distrust."

Herman Melville, The Confidence-Man

Besides, to distrust words, and indict them for the horrors that might slumber unobtrusively within them – isn't this, after all, the true vocation of the intellectual?

Václav Havel, "Words on Words"

Call it misrepresentation: "Indian," the name given to Native Americans; "America," a name still appropriated to denominate the United States; "Lake George," a name imposed on a lake "robbed," Cooper writes, of "its original appellation of 'Horican'"; "We, the people," an inclusive term that excluded more people than it included; "person held to service," the euphemism for a slave in the Constitution.[1] The names of a people, the names on the land, the words of the Constitution all testify to a nature "disturb'd" by names and to the hold that the word has had over fact in a country invented by a declaration, governed by a constitution, and defended, in the words of Washington Irving's Mustapha Rub-a-Dub Keli Khan, "*vi et lingua*, that is to say, by *force of tongues*" (ILA, 144).

In several of the *Salmagundi* letters attributed to Mustapha and in *The History of New York*, Irving probes the nexus between word and act, language and violence, misrepresentation and tyranny in the American logocracy. Every man who has "the *gift of the gab*" in this state becomes "a soldier outright" (ibid.). The offensive and defensive measures of "SLANG-WHANGERS" (politicians and editors) are enforced by "*wordy battle*" and "*paper war*" (ibid.). In *The History of New York*, the loquacious European settlers in America conquer first by "dint of argu-

19

ment" and afterwards by the "RIGHT BY GUNPOWDER" (ILA, 414, 419). Later the "grand palladium" of the country – the "*liberty of speech*" – becomes in the narrator's eyes "the right of talking without ideas and without information – of misrepresenting public affairs; of decrying public measures – of aspersing great characters, and destroying little ones" (ILA, 494). Politics is little else but war conducted by the word. A loquacious and sometimes vicious people exercising their liberty of speech become victims of that liberty: "Have we not within but a few years released ourselves from the shackles of a government, which cruelly denied us the privilege of governing ourselves, and using in full latitude that invaluable member, the tongue? and are we not at this very moment striving our best to tyrannise over the opinions, tie up the tongues, or ruin the fortunes of one another?" (ILA, 495). Irving here stands at the forefront of a tradition in American literature. The force of the tongue and the hold of the word over fact (and opinion) in the United States becomes not just a source of personal concern and artistic investigation for Irving but for a number of his successors in the tradition of American literature who also fostered a self-consciousness about the act of naming and the politics of representation, such as Herman Melville foregrounds in the opening of *Moby-Dick*, which begins not with the narrator's invocation of a name but with a section of etymology offering multiple perspectives on the naming of the whale and a cross section of extracts drawn from the world of books and whose authenticity we are advised to doubt by a narrator calling himself a commentator on the subsublibrarian who supplied the extracts.

In an essay entitled "Nature and the Linguistic Moment," J. Hillis Miller employs the term "the linguistic moment" to describe this moment in literature when "language as such, the means of representation in literature becomes problematic, something to be interrogated, explored or thematized in itself." He adds, "In the work of many prominent Victorian writers . . . this linguistic moment becomes explicit enough and prolonged enough so that it can displace Nature or human nature as the primary focus of imaginative activity."[2] Critics of American Renaissance literature, such as F. O. Matthiessen, Charles Feidelson, Philip Gura, and Tony Tanner, have similarly argued that the work of Emerson, Hawthorne, Melville (and others) in the mid nineteenth century participates in such a linguistic moment when language itself becomes a primary focus of imaginative activity or is self-consciously interrogated, explored, and thematized.[3] Tanner in his most recent work locates this linguistic moment even earlier than the American Renaissance, maintaining that "the American writer, after the War of Independence, experienced the ambiguities, the ambivalences, the anguishes, involved in the relation between nature and language, thing and name, scene and sign, with a quite unprecedented acuteness." He adds that this is "why it can be said that almost from the start American (i.e., post-colonial) literature was unavoidably 'modern' – whatever we care to mean by that term – in that it encountered and confronted the cultural, political, and onto-logical problematics of language in a way which was quite new, certainly in the history of the western world."[4]

Tanner has been a pathfinder in exploring the ways American writers have encountered the "problematics of language," but in this study I argue in mild dissent that American writers encountered the problematics of language in many of the same ways as did their European forebears in the old world. I also believe that if postcolonial American writers manifest a particular acuteness or "modernity" about the problematics of language, this acuteness derives in part from their confrontation with the problematics of representation and inter-pretation arising from the highly linguistic nature of their own system of government, and that those problematics were exacerbated by the war of words over slavery and by other political issues that embroiled the United States before the Civil War. Between the Revolution and the Civil War, language itself – as the means of representation in politics and the material basis of the Constitution – became highly problematic, an instrument that was interrogated, explored, and thematized extensively in the political and legal discourse of the age as well as in its literature and language theory. If, after the ratification of the Constitution, the government of the United States was not "a pure unadulterated LOGOCRACY or *government of words*," the centrality of a written text and of representation in American politics did make the practice and criticism of interpretation and representation central political activities for its citizens (ILA, 144). Indeed, the very nature and function of government as a representative democracy built upon a written text ruled by the vox populi nourished the fears Americans inherited from their classical and Enlightenment forebears about the cheat of words and the ways texts could be constructed and mis-construed to serve personal and party interests. If, then, as Tanner argues in *City of Words*, "American writers seem from the first to have felt how tenuous, arbitrary, and even illusory, are the verbal con-structs which men call descriptions of reality," this should not surprise us once we consider how American politics continually offered Amer-ican writers a lesson in the arbitrariness of words and the illusory nature of verbal representation.[5] And if, in Michael Rogin's words, "politics made accessible the material from which the American Romantics made art," then constitutional debate and representative politics made accessible the material from which the American Romantics and their precursors in American literature constructed their language theories.[6]

Political leaders and writers in America from James Madison and James Fenimore Cooper to the present have been quick to point out that representation is the "vital principle" of the American Republic, the very pivot on which its system of government moves.[7] In almost the same breath, they have been sure to mention that the gravest danger to the republic is the ease with which false representation can masquerade as true representation. Political candidates can win the confidence of the electorate with promises to serve the public interest and then betray that confidence by serving their private ends. The very words "republican," "democrat," "liberty," and "freedom" can be a cloak for the pursuit of riches, pleasures, and power. Thus Cooper advises readers in *The American Democrat* (1838), a book of essays in which he defined political terms in order to combat cant: "Men are the constant dupes of names, while their happiness and well-being mainly depend on things. The highest proof a community can give of its fitness for self government is its readiness in distinguishing between the two; for frauds, oppression, flattery and vice, are the offspring of the mistake."[8] In 1836 the author of an article entitled "Theory of Political Representation" in the *American Quarterly Review* similarly points out: "The evil which threatens most the usefulness if not the purity of the franchise in a republican government does not come in the shape of bribery or ignorance; it arises from the overwhelming influence of popular names, and the artful obtrusion of them by every aspirant who is in search of suffrages. Such names are like the red cross on the collar or sleeves of the crusaders, – they cover and conceal every political enormity. . . . The suffrage which is given to a mere name is the suffrage of a slave."[9] The bond between a representative and a constituent, which is the soul of representative government, can be forged through bribery. But a more dangerous form of corruption, in this author's view, is the bondage between a representative and a constituent that arises from the suffrage given to a mere name: then the bond is not voluntary but constrained. Through verbal misrepresentation, a link in the process of free government becomes a manacle of slavery. In the American logocracy, consent by "the People" to the words of the founding fathers authorized the United States, and consent to the words of orators authorized more compromises with slavery. Writers in the republic were not unwilling to probe all that made consent to words less than voluntary and informed.

In America, the pursuit of republican ideals has always been accompanied by attacks against false representation and fears of the people becoming the dupes of artful words and demagogues. The jeremiad in America, which Sacvan Bercovitch has shown to be such a typical American literary form, is at once a castigation of America as a home of false representation – a place where people backsliding from their covenant have broken their word with God and each other – and an exhortation for Americans to heal that discrepancy between their professions and practices by rededicating themselves to the national errand.[10] "We must realize our rhetoric and our rituals," demands Emerson.[11] Only through such a reform could America fulfill its promise as the "Israel of our time"; only then could the country become the representative of God's Word: a "political Messiah."[12] And through the ritual of the jeremiad with its rhetoric of distrust, Americans crusaded westward, "civilizing" the wilderness.[13]

Excessive fear of false representation also keynoted the paranoid style in American politics – a virulent strain in our politics that has bred upon the suspicion, never completely exorcised from the national psyche, that somewhere out there, lurking behind signs, manipulating appearances, is a sinister force – a Catholic, a communist, a capitalist – whose end is subversion.[14] From the cant of conquest over the Indians to the cant of conquest over communists in Vietnam and beyond, American leaders have campaigned against figures of duplicity, summoning the people to practice what Melville calls in *The Confidence-Man* the "metaphysics of Indian-hating." But these campaigns have provoked some to spot duplicity not in evil empires but in language itself or in the rhetoric of freedom, democracy, and manifest destiny.

The extreme distrust of representation that characterizes the paranoid style has seemed to be a safer alternative, however, than the innocence of Billy Budd, who has never heard of the "too fair-spoken man."[15] There is no doubt about Billy's Achilles' heel: "To deal in double meaning and insinuations of any sort was quite foreign to his nature" (BB, 49). The narrator suggests, in contrast, that "an undemonstrative distrustfulness" is essential for survival in a world where there is "unobstructed free agency on equal terms" (BB, 87). "Unless upon occasion," the narrator adds, a person "exercises a distrust keen in proportion to the fairness of the appearance, some foul turn may be served him" (ibid.). Cooper applies this same point directly to politics when he warns in *The American Democrat*, "In discriminating between candidates, it should be remembered that there are 'wolves in sheep's clothing,' in character, as well as in other things."[16] Not without cause, Americans have cried wolf when they have spotted fleecy words and lamblike persons. "Through the arts of conspirators," Melville laments in "Supplement" in his volume of Civil War poems, ". . . the most sensitive love of liberty was entrapped into the support of a war whose implied end was the erecting in our advanced century of an Anglo-American empire based upon the systematic degradation of man."[17] Emerson also spotted characters as duplicitous as John Claggart operating in history. "All the great cities, all the refined circles, all the statesmen, Guizot, Palmerston, Webster, Calhoun," he asserts, "are sure to be found befriending liberty with their words, and crushing it with their votes" (REW, XI, 240). John Taylor of Caroline offered, in striking terms, an early version of this warning: "The hooks of fraud and tyranny, are universally baited with melodious words." He then counsels: "There is edification and safety in challenging political words and phrases as traitors, and trying them rigorously by principles, before we allow them the smallest degree of confidence. As the servants of principles, they gain admission into the family, and thus acquire the best opportunities of assassinating their masters, should they become treacherous."[18] This image of a word, like Macbeth, betraying the highest of confidences and turning bloody advises us to take alarm at the equivocal status of representative signs. Stand at the gate, challenge all political words: the innocent servant may be an evil usurper. But the quintessential warning about the duplicity of words is from the Bible: "An enemy speaketh sweetly with his lips" (Ecclesiasticus 12:16). Not surprisingly, this maxim is quoted by a character in *The Confidence-Man*.[19]

The problem that lies at the heart of Melville's novel of masquerade is our paradoxical need for confidence and distrust in the words of our fellow citizens, a problem brought to the fore not only by the dynamics of the economic marketplace but by the structural principle of American government. At the center of representative politics is a fundamental paradox: citizens must place confidence in political representatives to speak for them, and yet they must distrust what they say. "Representative organs" always tend "to become corrupt and perverted," explains Jefferson.[20] Representative government is "government by fiction," claims Edmund Morgan.[21] Representation itself is necessarily a distortion; it can never be a presentation of the thing itself; the representative's voice is not the voice of the people. Political representatives thus stand in relation to their constituents as language does to the world. The classical ideal is mimesis: The "representative assembly," John Adams asserts, "should be an exact portrait of the people at large" (JAW, IV, 195). The reality of representation, however, is not the sameness of an echo but the difference of a new voice.

Political representatives can no more be equated with their constituents than a word can be equated with the thing it stands for. Just as a word replaces the presence of a thing, so too do political representatives replace the presence of the people. Or, as a Pennsylvanian wrote in 1728, there is "no *transsentiating* or *transsubstantiating* of being from people to representative."[22] Representation is, inevitably, misrepresentation.

Jean-Jacques Rousseau presents the leading case against representation in *The Social Contract*. The moment "a people allows itself to be represented," he writes, "it is no longer free: it no longer exists."[23] The people become enslaved when they sign away their authority to representatives and become obedient to the scriptors of the law. Representative government works by synecdoche: a part stands for the whole. For Rousseau, the synecdoche of representation dismembered the body politic into separate parts. A representative assembly is a tongue speaking or a hand writing laws for an absent body. With their tongue and hands severed from their body, the people are reduced to participating in government by waving their bloody stumps (or contributing funds). Rousseau demands a participatory democracy that would join together in the flesh all parts of the body politic. "The moment a people is legitimately assembled as a sovereign body, the jurisdiction of the government wholly passes, the executive power is suspended, and the person of the meanest citizen is as sacred and inviolable as that of the first magistrates; for in the presence of the person represented, representatives no longer exist."[24] When the people appear together, they regain their sovereign power. Democracy heals the division between tongue and heart, head and hand.

Rousseau's critique of representative government as a sovereign power masquerading as a servant raises a question similar to one asked about language in Lewis Carroll's *Through the Looking-Glass* and one that Americans in the late eighteenth century had the opportunity to answer. The question is who is to be the master: the sign or the signifier, the representative or the represented? And where should our confidence be placed? As Gordon Wood has explained, in creating the American republic the founding fathers placed confidence and mastery neither in the people nor in their representatives. Distrust of representation led to confidence in the people, but distrust of the people led to confidence in representation.[25] Debates over the nature of representation occupied center stage during the political conflict between the Colonies and England, and after the war the debate continued among Americans. The quest for "proper" representation in the 1760s and 1770s led to the demand that representatives should be bound more closely to their constituents. The reigning system of "virtual" representation had to be replaced by "actual" representation. But after the war doubts about the Articles of Confederation and, more specifically, fears about the "licentiousness" of the many led some of the "worthy" to propose a reform in the government.[26] These proposals led to the deliberations in Philadelphia and the creation of a new order of government in which confidence is placed in a system of distrust or in a constitutional process that establishes a set of checks and balances among several forms of representation. In this government, political authority is theoretically centered in the people, and the people are sanctioned in political rhetoric as sovereigns over their representatives. In practice, however, central political authority is divided among the three branches of the federal government, and the people exercise whatever sovereign power they possess on election day.[27] "The people, after this species of division of power," writes John Taylor of Caroline, "retain the importance and sovereignty of Lear, after he had divided the kingdom among his three daughters."[28]

Convinced that representatives tied to their constituents by no firmer bond than an election at infrequent intervals would betray their interests, the Antifederalists opposed the Constitution as a government that would moor representatives too far away from the people – the fountainhead of legitimate authority. Convinced, on the other hand, that the streams of power flowing from the people tended to be muddy and turbulent, the Federalists supported a system of representation that would channel and filter these streams. Indeed, the constitutional scheme of representation devised by the founders grants representatives more distance from their constituents than the Antifederalists desired. It enables representatives to enjoy in the houses of Congress a relatively free play of differences apart from the control of the theoretical center of power: the sovereign people. John Adams envisioned a representative assembly as a faithful portrait of the people, and though the Federalists paid lip service to this ideal of mimesis, what they preferred to see in practice was a less faithful picture: a portrait of the people removed of the warts and blotches.

Cast in the terms of Jacques Derrida's contemporary reflection about representation in language, the separation of representatives from their constituents guarantees a *différance* between the voice of the people and written law. Rather than merely transcribing the will of the people into law as if they were scriveners, representatives possess the space to differ from their constituents and the time to deliberate among themselves before authoring a law. Representation thus provides a mechanism of delay that decreases the dangers of demagogic oratory, the Achilles' heel of classical republics, for as Madison and others read ancient history, democracies degenerated into spectacles of turbulence and contention through the quick spread of communication and concert sparked by fiery speeches. Unlike a democracy, a representative government creates firebreaks: it largely confines speech (except during election campaigns) within the walls of a legislative assembly. When representation is spread over an extensive territory, Madison argues, "factious leaders" "may kindle a flame within their particular States but will be unable to spread a general conflagration through the other States" (FP, 10.84). The *différance* between representatives and constituents also defers legislative decisions from the people to a chosen body, a deferral the Federalists welcomed because of their distrust of the people and because of their hope that deference would be paid to a virtuous elite. But the play of differences between representatives would not be unconstrained. It was to be confined by a political grammar: the Constitution.

In the American republic, the people do not write the laws that govern them but are granted the opportunity to select through elections the authors of their laws, and they retain through elections a form of editorial approval that suggests that a people need not forever be governed by the same laws and the same representatives (who are bound to become corrupt). Thus what William Whitney, the foremost American linguist in the nineteenth century, says of language and words can be applied to political representatives (as his own imagery suggests): "Every language must prove itself able to signify what is in the minds of its speakers to express; if unequal to that, it would have to abdicate its office; it would no longer answer the purposes of a language."[29] He later points out, "But it is the customary office of a word to cover, not a point, but a territory, and a territory that is irregular, heterogeneous, and variable."[30] The implicit analogy Whitney makes between a word and a political representative is suggestive, and it can be developed further if we consider how John Locke explained linguistic representation in his *Essay Concerning Human Understanding* and how James Madison envisioned political representation in *The Federalist*. Words, according to Locke, represent objects at different levels of generality depending on the complexity of the idea (or the simplicity of the object) to be represented. The more complex or heterogeneous the referent, the more abstract is the word. Madison argues in *The Federalist* for the merits of a representative covering an extensive territory and heterogeneous constituency, stressing that it would make the representative less likely to serve a faction. The representative covering a heterogeneous territory would be more obligated to form his ideas in a fashion similar to the way a general idea is formed in Locke's linguistic philosophy. The representative would collect sense impressions from a diversity of constituents and then abstract or refine these impressions into general ideas. In contrast, the representative covering a less extensive and more homogeneous territory could confine his or her concerns to a particular idea or special interest.

But just as Tocqueville recognized the "great imperfection" as well as the "great merit" of abstract terms in the American language, so too did Madison recognize the imperfections as well as the merits of abstraction in the American system of political representation (DA, II, 74). Like abstract terms in Tocqueville's analysis of democratic language, representatives covering an extensive territory "enlarge" but also "obscure the thoughts they are intended to convey" (ibid.). Put simply, the price of abstraction in language and politics is a loss of specifics. Put differently, the price of abstraction is a loss of minority interests. Political representation for a heterogeneous territory produces not so much a detailed, mimetic portrait of the people as an abstract, cubist portrait with some features exaggerated, others skewed, and some left out. For Madison, one remedy for that "imperfection" was frequent elections: a change of politicians could lead to improvement in representation or to the better covering of a heterogeneous territory, a remedy similar to a point made by Whitney that "the general object attained by additions to language is obviously the extension and the improvement of expression, supply of representative signs for new knowledge, amendment in the representation of old knowledge."[31]

Whitney's language of "representative signs" and "amendment" hints of an analogy between political and linguistic representation that can be drawn out more by observing the connections Americans posited (or presumed) between the virtues of political and linguistic change. Indeed, the quest in the early republic for faithful politicians and representative men was matched by the revolutionary call of Jefferson and Whitman for "new words, new phrases" and "new potentialities of speech" (JLA, 1296).[32] In language and politics, they recognized, change could be an antidote for corruption and tyranny. Just as Madison believed that a "succession of new representatives" in Congress could restore a corrupt government to its "pristine order," so too did Jefferson, Whitman, and other Americans believe that the introduction of new words and meanings into the custom house of language – or the restoration of old ones – could be a beneficial revolution in the linguistic and perhaps even in the political order of things (FP, 63.388). Thus Whitman's demand for "new law-forces of spoken and written language" and his assertion "I think I am done with many of the words of the past hundred centuries – I am mad that their poems, bibles, words, still rule and represent the earth, and are not yet superseded" (AP, 12). Ralph Ellison gives the most succinct expression to this belief that the writer, by developing the representative capacity of the American language, performs a task correspondent to the citizen's responsibility for maintaining the representativeness of government: "Just as there is implicit in the act of voting the responsibility of helping to govern, there is implicit in the act of writing a responsibility for the quality of the American language – its accuracy, its vividness, its simplicity, its expressiveness – and responsibility for preserving and extending the quality of the literature."[33]

Comparisons between the epistemology of political and of linguistic representation can also be turned around to cast the action of political representation in the mold of linguistic theory. Just as Americans have upheld as an ideal an honest, direct language that corresponds faithfully to nature or the soul, so too have they championed the ideal of political representatives, such as Andrew Jackson, who would be signifiers directly motivated by the will of their constituents or natural symbols of nature.[34] The American Revolution itself can be seen as a quest to replace forms of political representation that had degenerated into corruption with ones that would more faithfully reflect the concerns of the Colonies. English representatives appeared to be too self-interested or too undifferentiated from the court of England to represent the country interests of the Colonies. The colonists recognized that the only bond that could be trusted to unite political representatives and their constituents was the same bond that could be trusted to unite words and their representative ideas: the bond of sympathy. That is the bond which holds together Tristram Shandy's family in Jefferson's favorite novel, and at the conclusion of his original draft of the Declaration of Independence he calls upon the colonists to affirm that bond of affection against a parent country that has betrayed it. Communication between members of the Shandy family repeatedly breaks down because family members, possessing different interests, interpret words in disparate ways. But because of their shared sympathies, the family can come together. The colonists possessed different ideas about what was meant by liberty, equality, and the pursuit of happiness, but, thanks to the activities of rabble-rousers, enough of them shared a feeling of fear and enmity toward England and affection for each other to enable the Colonies to unite as Sons of Liberty behind the words of the Declaration. The American Revolution, as Garry Wills reminds us, was in part a "sentimental journey" to independence.[35]

Parallels between political and linguistic representation can be extended to include what Leslie Fiedler called the "peculiar and intimate connections" between the novel and America.[36] Mikhail Bakhtin's writings on the novel suggest how these intimate connections can be seen to include correspondences between the form of the novel and America's constitutional government. According to Bakhtin, the novel is the "genre of becoming," and its language is composed of a "living mix of varied and opposing voices" that denies "the absolutism of a single and unitary language" and depends upon an "active polyglossia" or a struggle among "socio-linguistic points of view" where one point of view, one evaluation, or one accent is opposed to another.[37] Bakhtin's "dialogical" novel is grounded in a conflict of representations, and it orchestrates the conflicting voices of the social world. The American form of government can also be considered dialogical because its structure is grounded in a conflict of representational modes and because it seeks to orchestrate the many and conflicting voices of the body politic. There is, however, a crucial distinction. The dialogical novel maintains an unresolvable conflict of representations, while America's constitutional government seeks to resolve those conflicts in acts of voting, legislation, or judicial review. But this distinction needs to be qualified, because the structure of American government precludes the finality of any resolution. The consensus of the vote, of legislation, and of judicial review is temporary; it yields to new campaigns, new debates, new cases. The American government invites conflict, and it recognizes its fallibility. The Constitution authorizes its own reinterpretation and amendment. The conflict between what Bakhtin calls the centripetal forces of monoglossia and the centrifugal forces of heteroglossia, or between centralizing forces seeking a unitary language and decentralizing forces seeking diversity in language and thought, is written into the very fabric of American government in the conflict between federal and state governments and between the state and the individual.[38] The "enlightened votaries" of America, Madison argues, "must perceive the necessity of such a modification of power as will not only divide it between the whole & the parts, but provide for occurring questions as well between the whole & the parts as between the parts themselves."[39] Whitman concurs with Madison: "There are two distinct principles – aye, paradoxes – at the life-fountain and life-continuation of the States; one, the sacred principle of the Union, the right of ensemble, at whatever sacrifice – and yet another, an equally sacred principle, the right of each State, consider'd as a separate and sovereign individual, in its own sphere. . . . The problem is, to harmoniously adjust the two, and the play of the two" (WLA, 1051). Whitman's own poetry offers us, as Kerry Larson argues, a "drama of consensus" or an

incarnate vision of how to "gather together without artificially dicho-
tomizing 'opposite equals'" in a "forum of exchange."[40]

One yet many, diversity within unity: the paradox of the United
States is the paradox of the novel. The nation's motto, *E pluribus unum*,
presents the United States as the resolution of this paradox; the novels
of the American Renaissance, and the American novels that have
taken race as a central concern, have often represented the irresolu-
tion of this paradox. The novel and the nation-state, it has been
argued, arose in tandem from the ashes of a Christendom fragmented
by religious and political conflict. No longer after the Reformation
was there a community of people harmoniously bonded together by
the Word of God and by Latin. The nation-state and the novel are
newly imagined communities, invented and drawn together in part by
the strength of emergent vernacular tongues and the force of an
emergent press.[41] Freed more than ever from the Christian demand
that the word of man serve and represent the Word of God, language
in the Renaissance becomes a sovereign force in the creation of new
worlds of the imagination or of those fact–fiction worlds of the novel
and the nation. Though united, these composite communities of the
word are still fractured by diverse dialects and idioms (reflections of
divisions of class and ethnicity) and by diverse modes of standardized
print (e.g., newspapers, the law, the book). The printing press and the
vernacular voice become primary forces in creating the imagined life
of the nation and of the novel, and these two forces remain in as much
conflict and consensus in the nation invented by the Declaration,
sustained by the Constitution, and authorized by a vox populi as do
Don Quixote and Sancho Panza in *Don Quixote*.

Among the rise of the novel, the development of vernacular languages and the press, and the origins of the Declaration and the
Constitution there is, indeed, an intertextuality. If the epic, as Bakhtin
argues, is governed by the "absolutism of a single and unitary language," the United States, like the novel, has its roots in revolution,
and it is governed by a language – the Constitution – that frames a
multiplicity of voices: the vox populi. Walter Reed argues, for instance, that the novel is revolutionary because it "frees the classical
imagination from its own imperial tendencies" and "puts forward the
insubordinate claims of more popular forms." *Don Quixote*, Reed
writes, set a "precedent for the unprecedented"; it established a
"charter for the innovations of a type of literature that repeatedly
declared its independence from literary tradition."[42] *Don Quixote* does
not just declare independence from medieval romance; it constitutes
the structure of the novel that Fielding and subsequent novelists would

adopt. What Fielding sought in *Tom Jones*, in Leo Braudy's words, is what the founding fathers sought as well: "a form for uncertainty, a structure for spontaneity, a pattern for contingency," and, we could add, a structure that would contain a multiplicity of voices within a unity.[43] And just as the founding fathers, who distrusted political representatives as unprincipled, developed a system of government that depends upon several forms of representation to check and balance each other, so too did American writers, who recognized that words were imperfect representatives, develop and employ literary forms, particularly the novel, which rely on multiple forms of representation to check and balance each other.[44] To represent the United States in literature, to write the Great American Novel, it requires, it seems, a structure akin to its system of political representation: a structure that orchestrates a checking and balancing between a range of representative modes and voices. Juxtaposing multiple discourses in *Moby-Dick*, Melville thus represents the heterogeneity of the white whale and of the *Pequod*. The novel convenes a congress of representative voices and draws upon a wide range of textual extracts to debate the significance of the whale and counter the force of Ahab's single-minded representation.

The relationship between the representative system of the novel and the American government can also be suggested if we recall a political metaphor Henry Fielding employs in *Tom Jones* to characterize his power as author. In Book II, Chapter 1, Fielding declares that he is the "founder of a new province of writing" wherein he is "at liberty to make what laws" he pleases and where the readers are his subjects "bound to believe in and obey" the laws he creates for "their own good."[45] Fielding emphasizes that he is not a *jure divino* tyrant and his readers are not slaves, but he does stress that he is "set over them," and he suggests that it is the reader's duty to consent to his laws. Extending Fielding's metaphor to characterize the political form of the Constitution, we could call its framers the founders of a novel province of written law wherein the people are the readers of that text who are bound to obey the written law for their own good. But the Constitution no more claims to enslave its readers than does Fielding in *Tom Jones*. Through the powers of the Supreme Court, the Constitution leaves a space for select readers to collaborate with the original authors to produce the meaning of the text. And through the processes of popular elections and amendment, the people can choose new authors who can write new chapters or revise old ones for their approval.

Just as a novel frames the vox populi, or constructs the speaking and plots the action of characters, so too does the Constitution frame a vox populi; it constructs political bodies who speak for the people, and it plots the structural relationship of those bodies. The characters who speak for the people (or as the people) in law are the bodies of the federal government – the executive, the legislature, the judiciary – and the representative assemblies of the state. Throughout much of American history, the distillations of the electoral process have left us, by and large, with white men representing and not necessarily speaking for a diverse constituency, just as the distillations of American literature, as defined by the canon (circa 1964), left us, by and large, with white men representing the United States and framing the voice of minorities, such as Chingachgook, Babo, Pip and Jim. But the oral has been a resource for amending or reconstructing the written in American politics as well as in literature. In every national literature, Gayl Jones asserts, "the voices of the less powerful group, 'the other,' always must free themselves from the frame of the more powerful group, in texts of self-discovery, authority and wholeness." "To liberate their voices from the often tyrannic frame of another's outlook," writes Jones, "many world literatures continue to look to their own folklores and oral modes for forms, themes, tastes, conceptions of symmetry, time, space, detail, and human values."[46] Just as literary genres have been revitalized by drawing on and incorporating oral modes, the Constitution has been amended by drawing on oral modes or by incorporating the speech of the people who were outside government and whose rights were outside the protection of law. The written frame provides for its own reconstruction, and during the pressure of civil rights movements it has been reconstructed by such liberating voices as those represented by Frederick Douglass and Elizabeth Cady Stanton.

There is another parallel between American systems of political and linguistic representation that I wish to discuss which will return us to the problem I presented at the beginning of this chapter: the problem of confidence or distrust in representatives and representative signs. From Brockden Brown to Melville, a range of writers in post-Revolutionary America invited their readers to discover for themselves the unreliability of narrators and of representation itself. Just as we can find in this period an antipolitical politics, a politics that called upon voters to distrust government as a constriction of their freedom and a source of corruption, so too can we find an antilanguage literature, a literature that called upon its readers to distrust language as an instrument of false representation that could turn into a dangerous sovereign power. American novelists from the beginning have made distrust of words as much a part of their story as politicians in pursuit of office have made distrust of a competitor's campaign rhetoric a part of their speeches.[47]

But while such writers in post-Revolutionary America as Brown and Melville generated suspicion about the power of words and even subverted the authority of their own texts, their commitment to fiction reflects a hope, if not a confidence, that their representations could provide a challenge – perhaps even a corrective – to the representations of other word slingers: to the representations deployed, for instance, by the Steadfast Dodges of the newspaper industry, by the Aristabulus Braggs and Judge Pyncheons of the business and legal communities, by the scribbling tribes of popular women writers scorned by Hawthorne and Melville's Pierre, and by the William the Testys, Stony Phizzes, and Brevet Brigadier G. Smiths of the political world. Harriet Beecher Stowe thus invokes the power of the word in *Uncle Tom's Cabin* to represent antislavery sentiment and give voice to the slaves after Daniel Webster had betrayed that representative role when he used his grand powers of eloquence to support the Compromise of 1850.[48] Her novel, like Melville's *Moby-Dick*, is a congress of voices engaged in a debate that both mirrors and challenges the range of voices who were doing battle on the floor of the Senate and the House in antebellum America. By opening ears to voices unheard in the houses of the federal government, by seeking to redeem the language corrupted by Webster – the language of the Declaration of Independence and the Word of God – and by fashioning an eloquence that stirred hearts and awakened consciences, she entered the political forum and altered the course of the debate more movingly than many antebellum politicians.

In the tradition of Stowe and Whitman, American writers have reposed confidence in the word to renew faith in the pursuit of liberty and a more perfect union, and in the tradition of Melville they have engaged in a dialectical debate and performed language experiments to renew distrust in words. No matter the party affiliation, writers have been united in their attempt to give us insight into how and why people have used – or been used by – words that blind, imprison, and destroy. And these writers have sought instead to use language more charitably, more faithfully, more resourcefully, as do Melville in *Moby-Dick* and Stowe in *Uncle Tom's Cabin* and Dos Passos in *U.S.A.* and Ellison in *Invisible Man* and Mailer in *The Armies of the Night* and Reed in *Mumbo Jumbo*, to orchestrate the rich colloquy of tongues that compose and have composed the USA and thus address our ears through the music of their art with the representative voices of invisible men and women made famous – castaways, renegades, immigrants, sharecroppers, blues people – and through their art give us the hope that some day fact can come closer to imitating the ideal of fiction or the American dream that "the jangling discords of our nation" can be transformed "into a beautiful symphony of brotherhood."[49] "Imaginative literature," to heed Warner Berthoff's monitory words, ". . . does not commonly issue direct forensic challenges to the dominant beliefs and fixed ideas of the age – unless, of course, it is directly forensic literature. . . . Instinctively on the side of plenary truths and unafraid of vernacular inconsistency, it concentrates its efforts on forms of statement outside the scrutiny of system-keepers but already secure in the pleasure and acceptance of some unconscripted audience, high or low, which it finds its own pleasure in getting on good terms with."[50] Yet before we insist on the need for art to offer statements that transcend politics and the givens of the system keepers, let us listen to Horace Bushnell's vision in 1837 of what American literature was to become, for what he offers is a standard by which to measure that literature's success in becoming a form of cross-examination as vital to the life of a people pursuing liberty and justice as any courtroom case on record:

> And as our history is to be a struggle after the true idea and settlement of liberty, so our literature will partake in that struggle. It will be the American mind wrestling with itself, to obtain the true doctrine of civil freedom; overwhelming demagogues and factions, exposing usurpations, exploding licentious opinions, involved in the fearful questions which slavery must engender, borne, perhaps, at times, on the high waves of revolution, rejoicing at peace in the establishment of order and justice, and deriving lessons of wisdom from the conflicts of experience.[51]

On the occasion of winning the National Book Award in 1953, Ellison offers his judgment that the "classical nineteenth-century novelists" provided such a cross-examination: "Their works were imaginative projections of the conflicts within the human heart which arose when the sacred principles of the Constitution and the Bill of Rights clashed with the practical exigencies of human greed and fear, hate and love."[52]

Just as novelists sought to refract the vox populi of America into a spectrum of sounds beyond the range acknowledged or represented by other social and political forces, so too have they fashioned in words sovereign representations that seek to transcend rather than reflect the world of history. Like the separation of representatives from their constituents, the separation of words from their referents opens a space for deception, but it also opens a space that allows writers (as well as legislators) to transcend the world as given and create new worlds of the imagination. Representation can be valued in fiction and politics precisely because it does not correspond to facts, to things as they are, to the actual voices of the people. Representation can create a romance world that does not "rigidly subject itself to laws," as Hawthorne says the novel must in his preface to *The House of the Seven Gables*, a romance world, that is, where the "wrong-doing of one generation" can be overcome by successive generations, thus making whole a house divided (NHW, II, 1–2). Or it can create a new world of abstract values, a world where people can hold to be self-evident the idea that all men are created equal. As Ralph Ellison explains,

> Fiction is but a form of symbolic action, a mere game of "as if," [and] therein lies its true function and its potential for effecting change. For at its most serious, just as is true of politics at its best, it is a thrust toward a human ideal. And it approaches that ideal by a subtle process of negating the world of things as given in favor of a complex of manmade positives.
>
> So if the ideal of achieving a true political equality eludes us in reality – as it continues to do – there is still available that fictional *vision* of an ideal democracy in which the actual combines with the ideal and gives us representations of a state of things in which the highly placed and the lowly, the black and the white, the Northerner and the Southerner, the native-born and the immigrant are combined to tell us of transcendent truths and possibilities such as those discovered when Mark Twain set Huck and Jim afloat on the raft.[53]

Ellison's argument bears emphasis: American fiction at its most serious, like American political discourse at its best, has been committed to both realist and romance imperatives, to both a representation and a critique of the historical world out there and a sovereign vision of "a world elsewhere."[54]

2

Language and Legal Constitutions: The Problem of Change and Who Governs

> Touching construction of a pact,
> A paper pact, with points abstruse
> As theologic ones – profuse
> In matter for an honest doubt;
> And which, in end, a stubborn knot
> Some cut but with the sword.
>
> Herman Melville, *Clarel*

Language and law share a power and a paradox. By providing the rules that govern speech and action, by defining values, by specifying a sense of what is right and wrong, just and unjust, they make possible communication and community – those systems of ordered liberty and rule-governed freedom that distinguish us as the social animal who speaks. Rules of grammar and the laws of the state are undeniably repressive; they structure or seek to structure our words or actions. We ignore or violate them at the risk of being misunderstood, shamed, punished, or exiled. But in a paradox resembling the Christian belief that freedom is found in obedience to the Word, obedience to grammar and law can be considered liberating. Grammar frees us from the confusion of babble, and law frees us from social chaos. "Strange as it may seem," Whitman declares, "we only attain to freedom by a knowledge of, and implicit obedience to, Law" (WLA, 1073). Through language and law, we gain citizenship in a city of words, a moralized realm of linguistic positives (e.g., justice, freedom) built upon a foundation of negatives (e.g., "Thou shalt not . . ."). The cost is exile from the world as given – the state of nature or chaos – and the threat that the structures of law and language may become too repressive, demanding a "No" – or, better yet, an "ain't" – in thunder.

A long lineup of characters in American literature voice this protest. They are "grammar-breakers" who violate what Whitman

37

called the "little laws" of language "to enter truly the higher ones" (AP, 6). Many of these "ungrammatical" characters, most notably Natty Bumppo and Huck Finn, break the laws of state almost as forthrightly as they violate grammar. They speak in terms of a more natural-seeming language, and they act in terms of a more natural-seeming law. When Cooper, Stowe, Twain, and other pioneers of the vernacular voice in American literature dramatize conflicts between civil disobedients in the realm of language and law and those who enforce those codes, they are participating in a debate conducted prosaically in grammars and legal texts about the act of taking liberties with words or about the problem of change in the constitution of the English language in America and in the language of the Constitution.

Americans frequently made comparisons between the rules of grammar and the laws of the land and, more broadly, between language and political constitutions. In the same year the Constitution was ratified, Noah Webster argues, for instance, that no individual has the prerogative to dictate the "laws of language," because those laws should be based on the "unanimous consent of a nation" and a "fixed principle interwoven with . . . the language" (DEL, 29). Thomas Jefferson in "An Essay on the Anglo-Saxon Language" calls for a revolution in the study of the Anglo-Saxon language that will "renovate the vigor of the English language, too much impaired by the neglect of its ancient constitution."[1] Richard Grant White in *Words and Their Uses* asserts that "usage" is not the "absolute law of language" and recommends that criticism should instruct the "framers" and the "arbiters" of "linguistic law."[2] And Whitman, taking a more radical stance than White with the same analogy, insists in *An American Primer* that the English language "spurns laws, as the greatest tongue must" (AP, 30).

This analogy between the laws of grammar and of the state was also turned around to compare law to language. Thomas Paine declares in *The Rights of Man* that the "American Constitutions were to liberty, what a grammar is to language: they define its parts of speech, and practically construct them into syntax" (TPW, I, 300). When Daniel Webster refutes John Calhoun in an 1833 speech, he calls the Constitution "our American political grammar" and calls Calhoun's principle of nullification a solecism in that grammar.[3] During the Nullification crisis, Edward Mansfield published a textbook on American government entitled *The Political Grammar of the United States*, which begins with a set of definitions for political terms. Later in the 1850s, Joseph Bartlett Burleigh designed a primer, *The American Manual*, which required students to develop their language skills by studying the Constitution and the Declaration of Independence.

Such analogies between language and law were a common feature of eighteenth-century English linguistic theory, and its roots can be traced as far back as Plato's assertion that the first name-givers were the first lawgivers and Horace's dictum of "jus et norma loquendi."[4] In the United States, the analogy was put to new uses befitting a country ruled at once by a written grammar and a spoken idiom: the Constitution and the vox populi. These analogies illustrate not only that language was conceived of in political terms but also that the schoolmasters of the language were not eager to embrace democratic rule in their province. Though grammarians in the new republic generally consented to the principle that "common usage" should rule language just as We, the People, ruled the country, few were willing to give common usage unlimited sovereignty. Instead most preferred to see the people led by an elite in linguistic usage as well as in political practice, and they countered the claims of majority rule with the principle that the laws of language should be founded in reason, guided by analogy, or judged by the supreme court of a language academy. The advocacy by early republican language reformers of correct standards in speech and writing needs to be considered in conjunction with the advocacy in the United States of laws grounded in reason and nature and the preference for something more fixed than the vox populi to govern the people. Long before the debate in the early 1960s over the lexicographical principles of *Webster's Third New International Dictionary*, Americans confronted in matters of language what they confronted in their politics: opposition to majority rule and the efforts of the few to legislate for the many what was proper and correct (all done in the name of an impersonal authority – e.g., law, grammar, reason, custom).[5]

In policies of language as well as in politics, the United States was divided into parties. Radicals sought to republicanize the language by embracing popular usage. Conservatives wanted to preserve purity by outlawing "Americanisms." Unionists desired a standard language for the country. Advocates of liberty defended vernacular variations. Transcendentalists envisioned a correspondence between language and nature. Contractualists considered language a social institution that was as fallible or corrupt as the people who spoke it. These party labels, however, are misleading. Most citizens of the republic of letters who joined the debate about language were as complex or shifty in their politics as Benjamin Franklin, whose support for radical changes in the phonetics of the English alphabet was moderated, as Christopher Looby explains, by conservative concerns about preserving social order.[6]

Of all the linguistic issues debated in the early republic, the one that raised the most questions about who should govern the language was the issue of neologisms. Which changes in the constitution of the English language were necessary and proper, and who should judge them? John Gardiner in 1801 pleaded the conservative (and Anglophile) position when he protested that the adoption of "colloquial barbarisms" could only please those who believed that "to coin new words, or to use them in a new sense, is incontrovertibly, one of the unalienable rights of freemen; and whoever disputes this right, is the friend of civil tyranny, and an enemy to liberty and equality."[7] The terms of Gardiner's remark suggest how in judging the validity of new words Americans had to confront the rights and limitations of popular sovereignty. Should the court of public opinion be allowed to elect or veto neologisms, or should a language academy be established to decide questions of linguistic law, just as the Supreme Court ruled on questions of constitutional law?

Compounding the problems associated with neologisms was the recognition that while the right to coin new words appeared inalienable in a republic founded on revolution, the creation and maintenance of a common language seemed crucial to the preservation of union and political order. "Our political harmony," Noah Webster declared in 1789, ". . . is concerned in a uniformity of language" (DEL, 20). In 1789, Americans had a new reason to consider their political harmony endangered by linguistic change. A written text, the Constitution, had begun to rule, and people feared that if its words were too loose, the political edifice it supported would crumble. "Questions involving the meaning of political words," comments one writer in 1833, "lie at the very foundation of political society, and accordingly as they are settled in one way or another, the whole fabric must assume a different shape and character." The author adds that "a mistake in regard to the proper definition of a word may have an important bearing on the happiness of millions."[8] Theodoric Beck succinctly posed the problem surrounding neologisms when he remarked in 1829, "Believing then that reason as well as patriotism conspire to teach the importance of a certain degree of stability to a language, it remains to inquire how far innovation, or, if we please, improvement, is proper – Whether the introduction of new words is proper – the revival of obsolete ones, or the remodelling of present ones."[9]

To answer such questions, William Cardell in 1820 helped organize the American Academy of Language and Belles Lettres, whose stated purpose was to "determine the use of doubtful words and phrases" and establish a "correct, fixed, and uniform" language throughout the country.[10] Cardell seemed to envision the academy as a supreme court of language: two of the vice-presidents elected in June 1821 were Supreme Court justices, Brockholst Livingstone and Joseph Story, and the constitution of the academy, which possessed seven articles (the same number as the U.S. Constitution), began with a preamble modeled on the form of the Constitution. Cardell also sought endorsements for the academy from a number of statesmen, including Chief Justice John Marshall and James Madison, and both Madison and Marshall responded with highly favorable letters in which they stressed the importance of establishing a national language and of providing for its "purity" and "stability."[11] Thomas Jefferson, however, offered a strong dissenting opinion against the academy. When asked in 1821 to become its honorary president, he declined the office and explained to the corresponding secretary that it was fortunate such an academy was not formed "in the days of our Saxon ancestors, whose vocabulary would illy express the science of this day." "Judicious neology," he adds, "can alone give strength and copiousness to language, and enable it to be the vehicle of ideas."[12] Defending in a different letter the right of the people to rule the language, Jefferson similarly argues: "Had the preposterous idea of fixing the language been adopted by our Saxon ancestors, of Pierce Plowman, of Chaucer, of Spenser, the progress of ideas must have stopped with that of the language. On the contrary, nothing is more evident that as we advance in the knowledge of new things, and of new combinations of old ones, we must have new words to express them" (TJW, XIV, 463–4). Let the people judge, Jefferson concluded.

By a resounding voice vote, the people sided with Jefferson, choosing to neologize freely. The schoolmasters preferred to defend the opposing position. George Marsh, a professor of English at Columbia College who also served Vermont as a legislator, presents the case of the schoolmasters when he explains in *Lectures on the English Language* (1859) the hazards posed by linguistic change in America:

> In free states, ecclesiastical and political institutions are of themselves in so mutable a condition, that any voluntary infusion of disturbing ingredients is generally quite superfluous, and under most circumstances not a little hazardous. Intimately connected with the changes of opinion on these great subjects are the changes constantly going on in language. . . . Fluctuations in language are not merely a consequence, they are yet more truly an indication, and a cause of corresponding fluctuations in moral and intellectual action. Whoever, therefore, uses an important word in a new sense, is

contributing to change the popular acceptation, and finally the settled meaning, of all formulas in which that word is an element. Whoever substitutes for an old word of well understood signification a new vocable or phrase, unsettles, with the formulas into which it enters, the opinions of those who have habitually clothed their convictions in those stereotyped forms, and thus introduces, first, doubt, and then, departures from long received and acknowledged truth.[13]

Marsh then draws upon the law to support his case for a settled language:

Experience has taught jurists that in the revision or amendment of statutes, and in sanctioning and adopting by legislative enactment current principles of unwritten law, it is a matter of the first importance to employ a phraseology whose precise import has been fixed by a long course of judicial decisions, and it has been found impossible in practice to change the language of the law, for the purpose of either modernizing or making it otherwise more definite, familiar or intelligible, without at the same time changing the law itself. Words and ideas are so inseparably connected, they become in a sense so connatural, that we cannot change the one without modifying the other. (ML, 637–8)

Besides linking the value of conservation in law and in language, Marsh equates the duties of the theologian and the philologist as guardians of the word:

Whatever theories . . . may be entertained respecting the evils of a rigorous national conformity to particular symbols – whatever views may be held with regard to the growth, progress and fluctuations of language – both the theologian and the philologist will admit, that a certain degree of permanence in the standards of religious faith and of grammatical propriety is desirable. (ML, 621)

In 1861, Nathaniel Hawthorne comes close to adopting Marsh's opinion when he writes to thank Joseph Worcester, one of his old teachers, for sending him a copy of Worcester's dictionary:

Of all lexicographers, you seem to me best to combine a sense of the sacredness of language with a recognition of the changes which time and human vicissitude inevitably work upon it. It will be ominous of anarchy in matters moral and political, when our Dictionaries cease to be mainly conservative; and for my own part, I would not adopt a single new spelling, unless it were forced upon me by the general practice of the age and country; – nor willingly admit a new word, unless it brought a new meaning along with it.[14]

For Marsh and Hawthorne, a certain conformity to the usages and symbols of a linguistic community is necessary to sustain political and moral stability. Language, they suggest, holds us together by housing us in common meaning, and thus the loss of shared significance through verbal fluctuations means difference, discord, diversity – a house divided. And throughout the first half of the nineteenth century the debates that threatened to divide the Union centered on the liberties Americans took when they created certain neologisms associated with constitutional issues – e.g., "nullification," "secession," "states' rights" – and when they sought to give new meanings to various words in their political grammar, beginning with the phrase "We, the People," including in particular a clause in the middle, "necessary and proper," and continuing through the concluding line of the Bill of Rights in which nothing was necessarily concluded: "The powers not delegated to the United States by the Constitution, nor prohibited by it to the States, are reserved to the States, respectively, or to the people."

Called upon to govern the Constitution that governed them, Americans confronted the same type of problem they confronted when governing their language: Which changes in the law were necessary and proper, and who should judge them? Should the Supreme Court be the final authority in settling the meaning of the Constitution, or should the states receive or reject new constructions and possess the right to develop their own dialects in law? Could change be permitted in the language of the Constitution, or would change corrupt its purity? Could a judge sanction a departure from the American political grammar by claiming allegiance to a "higher law," just as Whitman believed that writers could break the "lower laws" of grammar? To what degree should the vox populi be subordinate to the written law and the written law be open to change by new pronunciations of the majority?

Problems of constitutional law became so knotted together with problems of language in the early republic that the two strands could not be separated. No one tussled with the knot more frequently than did James Madison. "If the meaning of the text [the Constitution] be sought in the changeable meaning of the words composing it," Madison writes in 1824, "it is evident that the shape and attributes of the government must partake of the changes to which the words and phrases of all living languages are constantly subject" (JML, III, 442). To maintain the stability of the Constitution and the government it structured, Madison acknowledges that the English language had to be maintained in its purity and uniformity. But in trying to preserve the original meaning of the Constitution, Americans battled not only the inevitability of linguistic change but the inevitability of differences in interpretation and the difficulty, if not impossibility, of recovering the "original intent" of a written text. After the deaths of Thomas Jefferson and John Adams on July 4, 1826, and of Madison in 1836, the problem became more manifest, leaving the people in the predicament of the three sons in Jonathan Swift's *Tale of a Tub*: a will to interpret but no voice of the father to provide guidance. No longer beholding the fathers face to face, the sons were left to construe the intent of the will primarily through the words of the Constitution that seemed to grow more dark as the debate over slavery became more impassioned, presaging the storm to come.

Raoul Berger contends in *Government by Judiciary: The Transformation of the Fourteenth Amendment* that "the Constitution was written against a background of interpretive presuppositions that assured the Framers their design would be effectuated."[15] Madison, however, writes in *Federalist* No. 37 that "all new laws," because they are penned in an imperfect human language, "are considered as more or less obscure and equivocal, until their meaning be liquidated and ascertained by a series of particular discussions and adjudications" (FP, 37. 229). He also explains that the "cloudy medium" of language makes it difficult, if not impossible, to "discriminate and define" the boundaries between the legislative, executive, and judicial branches and between the federal and state governments (FP, 37. 228–9). And though Madison was dismayed by the Marshall court's "latitudinary mode of expounding the Constitution" in the case of *McCulloch v. Maryland*, he counsels Judge Spencer Roane in a letter, "It could not but happen, and was foreseen at the birth of the Constitution, that difficulties and differences of opinion might occasionally arise in expounding terms & phrases necessarily used in such a charter."[16] Given the framers' philosophy of language as represented by Madison, Berger's opinion must be revised. The Constitution was written within an epistemological framework that assured the founders that their design would forever be obscured by language and endangered by new construction.

For John Taylor of Caroline, a leading figure among Jeffersonian Republicans and the author in 1814 of an eccentric but brilliant critique of Adams's *Defence of the Constitutions of Government of the United States*, the decisions of the Marshall court were the handwriting on the wall that revealed all too clearly an ominous power inhabiting the house the fathers had built: the force of judicial construction, or what Taylor called "The power imperial of a court, / Supremely fixing right and wrong / By constitution of the tongue."[17] In 1823, he made what he might have termed a modest proposal in *New Views of the United States Constitution*, a long pamphlet he penned as a scathing critique of the Marshall court. An early advocate of states' rights (and a slaveholder), Taylor argued that the decisions of the Marshall court, particularly *McCulloch v. Maryland*, were creating by judicial construction a political enormity – a consolidated nation – that violated the original intentions of the founding fathers. He concludes his critique with the observation that "whether we shall have a concentrated power, invested with local supremacy or a limited federal government, is again to be decided, not by a solemn appeal to the people, but by Judge Construction, into whose mouth the parties interested can put whatever words they please" (NV, 289). The modest proposal he makes is to recommend that the advocates of national consolidation and supporters of Chief Justice Marshall distribute a hundred thousand copies of a work that would never have been found in the reading curriculum of any law student in the new republic but one that Taylor believed would serve as a "complete prolegomena for explaining their [the Marshall court's] constructions of the constitution" (NV, 289). The work was Jonathan Swift's *Tale of a Tub*. Moreover, Taylor develops in the last chapter of *New Views* an extended interpretation of *A Tale of a Tub* as a prophecy of America's experience in construing its Constitution.

Taylor's outrageous construction of Swift's satire as a political prophecy was unique, but his view of the relevance of Swift's work was shared by others in the early republic. In 1834, William Leggett, a newspaper editor who was one of the intellectual leaders of the Jacksonian Democrats, complains in one of his editorials that there is "a clause in the Constitution [the "necessary and proper" clause], which is . . . somewhat like the old gentleman's will in the Tale of a Tub. . . . It admits of a wonderful latitude of construction, and an ingenious man can find no great difficulty in interpreting it to suit his own particular interests."[18] And a year later, in 1835, in the wake of the Nullification crisis, Cooper combines allusions to *A Tale of a Tub* and *Gulliver's Travels* in *The Monikins* in order to provide an extensive satire on contemporary constructions of the Constitution. In the novel, some characters engage in Gulliver-like travels to unknown countries, including a land called Leaplow, which is a thinly veiled United States. In the capital city of Leaplow, these voyagers watch legislators do exactly what Swift complained that lawyers do: they turn black into white, or, more precisely, they twist and turn and torture a constitution (which is called the "Great and Sacred National Allegory") in order to overturn Article IV, Clause 6, which reads "The Great National Council shall, in no case whatever, pass any law, or resolution, declaring white to be black."[19] After observing the legal shenanigans, one character concludes that "words had no just value," a statement which answers the question posed earlier: Is the ship of state of Leaplow "to be mast-headed . . . according to the book?"[20]

Throughout the first half of the nineteenth century, Americans shared with the voyagers to Leaplow a similar feeling. They feared that if the words in their Constitution had "no just value" or if the American ship of state was unguided by the book written by the founding fathers, the Union would be a ship forever tossed about by new waves of construction and left to drift without anchor on the fluency of language. "You, my countrymen," Noah Webster warned in a pamphlet on the French Revolution, "if you love liberty, adhere to your constitution of government. The moment you quit that sheet-anchor you are afloat among the surges of passion and the rock of error; threatened every moment with shipwreck."[21] In 1823, John Taylor of Caroline also employed a nautical metaphor to offer a similar caution: "The constitution was not turned afloat to be carried hither and thither by the winds and waves of forensick and geographical constructions; of prepossession, avarice, and ambition" (NV, 253). But Taylor's vision of a Constitution that would be sailed in a steady direction or be less troubled by the "winds and waves" of party politics was a pipe dream if we listen to Emerson, who comments in "Politics" that "in our license of construing the Constitution, and in the despotism of public opinion, we have no anchor" and that (quoting Fisher Ames) "a republic is a raft, which would never sink, but then your feet are always in water" (ELA, 565). No matter what is done legally to prevent it, he also points out, "property will, year after year, write every statute that respects property" (ELA, 563). Or, as Edwin Whipple phrased it, "written constitutions, by a process of interpretation, are always made to follow the drift of great forces; they are twisted and tortured into conformity with the power dominant in the State."[22]

The framers took little heed to protect the Constitution from the power of property, but they did seek to protect property from the vox populi with a fence of written words. Indeed, the founders, according to Sidney George Fisher in *The Trial of the Constitution* (1862), when drafting the Constitution were much troubled by "the proverbial instability of popular opinion," and Fisher too turns to a nautical metaphor to illustrate his point:

> Hamilton, Washington and others, regarded democracy as a very doubtful experiment. They made the Constitution as conservative as they dared to make it, but they knew well it was a fragile bark,

freighted with a precious cargo, and launched on the waves of a
treacherous and tempestuous sea. They looked in vain for the elements that give strength and endurance to the British Government,
the Church, the aristocracy, the throne, each connected with the
past and the future, each presenting bulwarks like rocks to the surges
of popular passion.[23]

Just as Hawthorne and James compose catalogues of the old-world
institutions that America lacked, Fisher lists the institutions of the old
world missing in the United States to explain the absence of materials
that could provide a stable foundation for law in the new republic.
Given this lack, Fisher argues that the judiciary must be regarded as
the source of stability for democracy in America. Since that branch
was not elected by the people, it "could not . . . be affected by the
fluctuating tides of party power, or by the wild sallies of popular
sentiment."[24] Tocqueville, who along with Fisher suffered disquiet
about the force and mobility of public opinion in America, offered
counsel about how to mitigate the tyranny of the majority: "Federal
. . . Judges must be statesmen, wise to discern the signs of the times,
not afraid to brave the obstacles that can be subdued, nor slow to turn
away from the current when it threatens to sweep them off, and the
supremacy of the Union and the obedience due to the laws along with
them" (DA, I, 157).

When these commentators on the law turned to nautical metaphors
to articulate their political concerns, they were drawing upon (and
elaborating) a dominant trope in antebellum political rhetoric: the
Union as a ship of state. When Cooper and Melville turned to writing
sea fiction, they too could draw upon this trope. The *Red Rover*, the
Neversink, the *Pequod*, the *San Dominick*, and the *Bellipotent* are micro-
cosms of the social order wherein the conflict between the authority
of the captain (backed by naval law) and the rights (or licentiousness)
of the sailors (or the human cargo in *Benito Cereno*) mirror the larger
conflicts in the Union between the claims of communal order and the
claims of personal liberty, or the conflict between master and slave.[25]
Captain Vere in *Billy Budd*, for instance, is a man whose "settled
convictions" are represented as a "dike against . . . invading waters of
novel opinion, social, political, and otherwise, which carried away as
in a torrent no few minds in those days" (BB, 62). And when Billy is
executed, a murmur begins to rise among the sailors that is compared
to "the freshet-wave of a torrent suddenly swelled by pouring showers
in tropical mountains," but before this "murmur had time to wax into
a clamor," a "strategic command" is given, dissipating the "ominous
low sound" (BB, 126). Captain Vere, like the judge praised by Tocque-

ville and Fisher, resists the current, the waves, the torrent. But the murmur of the abolitionist movement, which would not cease at the bidding of any judge or statesman or any gag law or any compromise, waxed into a clamor.

The abolitionists were apostles of a novel opinion who led something of a mutiny against a government mastheaded by the book of the founding fathers. No dike, not even the bulwark of the Constitution, would stand in the way of their revolutionary opposition to slavery. Just as the guidebook from Redburn's father's library proves "a miserable cicerone" for Redburn in Liverpool, the guidebook of the founding fathers was all too fallible for the abolitionists who shared Redburn's perception, arrived at in Liverpool, where the principal commerce had been the African slave trade, that the "struggle between sordid interest and humanity had . . . estranged sons from sires" and that the old guidebook, "stripped of its reputation for infallibility," "could not guide the son" (but Redburn refuses to treat with "contumely or disdain those sacred pages which had once been a beacon to my sire").[26] A Constitution fixed by its original meaning, Garrison protested, had fixed a hideous birthmark upon the republic – the blot of slavery, which had been poorly covered up by the euphemism "person held to service." When John Quincy Adams defended the "captured" slaves' claim to freedom in the *Amistad* case, he ridiculed this euphemism: "The words slave and slavery are studiously excluded from the Constitution. . . . Circumlocutions are the fig-leaves under which these parts of the body politic are decently covered."[27] Adams demands no cover – verbal or legal – for the original sin of the fathers. Emerson offers a general-purpose condemnation of "rotten diction" in *Nature*, and after the passage of the Fugitive Slave Law in 1850, that condemnation becomes more specific as he focuses criticism on the rottenness of a Constitution whose false basis of representation perverts black men into things which they are not: three-fifths of a white man. Just as Emerson demands a closer correspondence between language and nature to end the corruption of words, he also demands a closer correspondence between the laws of the state and the laws of nature to end the corruption of politics. "This time," he writes in the middle of the Civil War when envisioning a new basis for the nation, "no compromises, no concealments, no crimes that cannot be called by name shall be tucked in under another name, like 'persons held to labor,' meaning persons stolen, & 'held,' meaning held by hand-cuffs, when they are not under whips" (JMN, XV, 302). Thoreau advances the same argument in *Walden*: "Let us settle ourselves, and work and wedge our feet downward through the mud and slush of opinion, and prejudice, and tradition, and delusion, and appearance, that alluvion which covers the globe . . . till we come to a hard bottom and rocks in place, which we can call *reality*, and say, This is, and no mistake; and then begin, having a *point d'appui* . . . a place where you might found a wall or a state" (TLA, 400). Thoreau locates such a *point d'appui* for the state in "Slavery in Massachusetts" when he calls upon people to obey "that eternal and only just CONSTITUTION, which He, and not any Jefferson, or Adams, has written in your being."[28] Only if America reconstructed its political language on the solid ground of the laws of nature and nature's God could it free itself from the original sin of the fathers. Only then could the American ship of state become something less than a pirate craft carrying contraband cargo disguised as "persons held to service" and something more of an ark bearing the rights of man.

"We are launched on the ocean of an unchained democracy," Wendell Phillips declared. For Phillips, an ardent abolitionist, the sheet anchor that would provide safety for the republic and guide the abolition of slavery was not to be found in the judiciary or in the text of the Constitution but within the people: "in those laws of gravity which bind the ocean in its bed – the instinctive love of right in the popular heart – the divine sheet anchor, that the race gravitates toward right, and that the right is always safe and best."[29] By addressing the popular heart in his oratory, Phillips sought to affect the currents of the ocean so that the slave ship, with no captain but an overruling Providence, would be guided to a port of freedom.

The Constitution was the fundamental instrument for sustaining the Union in antebellum America. But as people insisted on adhering to the Constitution as strictly as Shylock insists upon following his bond with Antonio in *The Merchant of Venice*, its ambiguities, gaps, and silences became more apparent. The text became not the source of union but the scene of division, not a crystal ball providing answers but a glass mirroring the opposing visions of a divided country. Even the abolitionists were riven in two. Douglass insisted that the Constitution was antislavery because nowhere was slavery "nominated in the bond," but Garrison maintained a proslavery interpretation of the document.[30] Closer scrutiny of the text just magnified the political crisis.

The divisiveness of the debate over the Constitution gave rise to deeper reflection on the part of commentators on the law to the rules for interpreting the law. Vainly, lawyers, politicians, ministers, and ex-slaves proclaimed and defended principles of interpretation that would make constitutional exegesis correct or bound by a greater rule than sway of self or party.[31] Joseph Story's *Commentaries on the Constitu-*

tion of the United States (1833), which became the preeminent treatise on
the Constitution in the nineteenth century, contains a long chapter,
"Rules of Interpretation." A professor of law at Harvard who served
on the Supreme Court, Story hoped his exposition of rules would
provide a "fixed standard" for constitutional construction.[32] But,
ironically, there is no greater testament to the baseless fabric of his
dream of fixing the Constitution than a passage in the *Commentaries*
wherein he makes a Lockean observation about language that contradicts any hope he had that the words of the Constitution would reign
as a sovereign over the people and the judiciary. "Words," Story
declares, "from the necessary imperfection of all human language,
acquire different shades of meaning, each of which is equally appropriate, and equally legitimate; each of which recedes in a wider or
narrower degree from the others, according to circumstances; and
each of which receives from its general use some indefiniteness and
obscurity, as to its exact boundary and extent." He adds:

> We are, indeed, often driven to multiply commentaries from the
> vagueness of words in themselves; and perhaps still more often from
> the different manner, in which different minds are accustomed to
> employ them. They expand or contract, not only from the conven-
> tional modifications introduced by the changes of society; but also
> from the more loose or more exact uses, to which men of different
> talents, acquirements, and tastes, from choice or necessity apply
> them.[33]

No poststructuralist, I daresay, could articulate more judiciously the
arbitrariness of the sign or the problem of textuality. The word, in
Story's view, is elastic; its meaning can expand or contract, and each
meaning is "equally appropriate, and equally legitimate." This is an
extraordinary opinion from the bench. The judge's office is to determine the interpretation of a word or text that is more legitimate.
Story himself claims that his objective in this chapter is to explain the
rules that will provide a "fixed, uniform, permanent construction" for
the Constitution.[34] Who can deconstruct Story's claim more effi-
ciently than he does himself?

The quest for a method of constitutional interpretation that would
provide a sheet anchor to constrain the will of judicial captains
persists, and the terms (and metaphors) of the current debate can help
us understand the politics and linguistics of the antebellum debate. In
the 1980s, Owen Fiss maintains in "Objectivity and Interpretation"
that legal rules of interpretation can "constrain" the freedom of
interpreters.[35] He argues that a judge "is not free to assign any
meaning he wishes to the text," because he "is disciplined by a set of

rules that specify the relevance and weight to be assigned to the material (e.g., words, history, intention, consequence), as well as by those that define basic concepts and that establish the procedural circumstances under which the interpretation must occur" (744). He then suggests that the "disciplining rules" of legal interpretation "operate similarly to the rules of language, which constrain the users of the language, furnish the standards for judging the uses of language, and constitute the language" (755). "The disciplining rules of the law may be understood," he adds, ". . . as a professional grammar" (755). But what Fiss does not address and what antebellum legal practice clearly reveals is that just as consensus can be difficult to attain regarding what is grammatical in language and who should rule the rules of grammar, so too consensus may be impossible to achieve on which rules of interpretation should apply and who participates in the codification of that grammar. In addition, just as an artist possesses the poetic license to violate rules of grammar, a judge possesses – or judges have exercised – a legal license to break precedent and follow a higher grammar, as Robert Cover argues in *Justice Accused*.

Cover offers a variation on the analogy between rules of law and the rules of grammar to insist upon the legitimacy of a judge violating the rules of "law-language," an argument that can be read in line with Whitman's brief in *An American Primer* for the legitimacy of the ungrammatical.[36] Cover writes: "A great speaker or writer of the language ordinarily acts according to the rules but knows when and how to ignore them as well. Often as not, when the articulate user of language consciously departs from the rules, he creates changes in the rules themselves. . . . If the departure becomes sufficiently widespread, the rule may change despite the protestations of the acknowledged masters of the language" (127). This "process of change," he adds, ". . . is not only tolerated in language, it is an integral part of the language. A language that does not grow in this way is a language continually in the process of becoming obsolete" (127). Cover argues that the judge also must make departures if the law is to grow. He points out that there are judges "who speak law-language poorly – whose departures from the law will not live. . . . Others – the vast majority – speak according to the rules. . . . They depart occasionally, usually inadvertently. Then there are prophets and masters who move the law more than their democratic, *per-capite* share" (128). He concludes that a departure in "law-language" need not be "simply bad law" but can be "eloquence," just as a departure from grammar can be the best style (128). When antebellum judges were called upon to render justice in trials of the Constitution and its fugitive-slave clause, Cover believes that, like Captain Vere in *Billy Budd*, they forfeited a chance for eloquence, or by stuttering worse than Billy they allowed the strong arm of a cruel law to rule.

Captain Vere appeals to the laws of the king to maintain order on board the *Bellipotent*. Antebellum Americans appealed to the Constitution as the "measured form" of law to maintain the Union. The text would guide the ship of state and settle it in a storm. But a Constitution composed in a changeable language and interpreted by a changeable people could not steer the Union in a steady direction even if the people agreed that their destination was a more perfect union and the tranquillity of justice. In 1839, Francis Lieber, a friend of Story's, also wrote a guidebook on interpretation entitled *Legal and Political Hermeneutics, or Principles of Interpretation and Construction*. A German immigrant who was trained in the higher criticism of the Bible, Lieber believed his critical theory could be applied to address the political problems of the United States, for those problems were hermeneutical. But in the midst of the Civil War, Lieber acknowledges the futility of his earlier effort to guide construction of the Constitution when he writes in terms that recall Dr. Johnson's confession of his doomed dreams as a lexicographer: "Laws are . . . like languages. That tongue would not be a living language which could not expand and adapt itself to new relations, things, and wider or minuter thoughts. The lexicographer who thinks that, by his dictionary, he can shut the gate upon his language and imprison it . . . [is] presumptuous. A law, a constitution, however important, remains a means, as government and the state themselves . . . are means, to obtain things still higher."[37] So often exalted before the Civil War as a sacred text, the Constitution becomes for Lieber a pragmatic instrument, the tool of the state, a means to attain a higher end.

The Civil War demanded the reconstruction of constitutional ideology. The abolitionist rule of interpretation that regarded the Declaration as the apple of gold and the Constitution its frame of silver was no longer a minority opinion. The Gettysburg Address founds the beginning of the nation not in 1787 or 1789 but in 1776, a rewriting of history that helps assure the reconstruction of the Constitution. Before the Civil War, the Constitution had been the sepulcher of the fathers – a text to be preserved inviolate in honor and memory of a prophetic wisdom that could be revered but not reconstructed. But once the battlefields of the Civil War became the sacred ground, the Constitution became less a sacred ground and more of a battlefield. After 1865, that is, the Constitution became more in theory what it had been in practice: the field on which a people could war with words for principles or for property. Appropriately, a Union soldier wounded grievously in the Civil War, Oliver Wendell Holmes, Jr., becomes a leading advocate of this pragmatic vision of law as nothing sacred, but an agency of social power that emerges from a history of conflict and the "felt necessities" of the time. Joseph Story, however, undermines any easy formulation of legal history. He presents a vision of the Constitution as a battlefield years before the Civil War, in the time of the Nullification crisis:

> In the interpretation of constitutional questions alone, a vast field is open for discussion and argument. The text, indeed, is singularly brief and expressive. But that very brevity becomes of itself a source of obscurity; and that very expressiveness, while it gives prominence to the leading objects, leaves an ample space of debatable ground, upon which the champions of all opinions may contend, with alternate victory and defeat. Nay, the very habits of free inquiry, to which all our institutions conduct us, if they do not urge us, at least incite us, to a perpetual renewal of the contest.[38]

This passage should serve as the epigraph for every textbook on constitutional law. The Constitution is the field of battle, words are the chosen weapons, the Supreme Court is the referee, and may the best argument win – and may the conversation continue about what constitutes the best argument.

The arbitrariness of the linguistic sign, the multiple commentaries and irreconcilable judgments that arise because of such arbitrariness, the way readers shape rather than discover the meaning of the texts that they arbitrate – these beliefs are not the fashionable discoveries of poststructuralism, but old hat. Between 1789 and 1865 much was said to the contrary about law and interpretation. Rufus Choate articulates this idealized vision of law when he describes it as "almost up to the nature of an independent, superior reason, in one sense out of the people, in one sense above them."[39] But if the founders hoped, as Michael Warner writes, that "ecriture would save the republic," the sons learned that the Constitution could no more save the Union from the violations of lynchings (and secession) – those local incarnations of a vox populi pronouncing itself – than grammar books could save the English language from Americanisms.[40] After the ratification of the Constitution, and especially in the midst of the constitutional crises over nullification in the 1830s and slavery in the 1850s, Americans confronted in their politics and explored in their literature the benefits and liabilities that arise from the freedom of words from a fixed sense. Just as Hester Prynne consents to wear the letter of the law but adorns it uniquely and transforms its significance in the eyes of her beholders, Americans in the new republic adhered to the Constitution, but many recognized that there was ample room for speculation and debate. The text, because it was language, was subject to interpretation, and interpretation, because people are people, was subject to the play of power politics.

Suspicious of the Federalists before Jefferson's victory, Abraham Bishop comments in 1800, "The constitution is perhaps as well wrought as language would admit; but language is very elastic." He adds, "The men, whose interest it is to stretch it to the extent are, or have made themselves, the judges of it."[41] "You cannot separate the law from the construction of the law," Judge Hopkinson remarks in 1809, especially when "scarcely a word in our language has a single, fixed, determinate meaning."[42] In 1815, Hugh Henry Brackenridge, a lawyer, writes in *Modern Chivalry*, "A constitution is like a nose of wax; it is twisted by the party that is predominant."[43] Concerned that the Supreme Court was pushing America into consolidation, Jefferson complained in 1819 to Judge Spencer Roane: "The constitution . . . is a mere thing of wax in the hands of the judiciary, which they may twist and shape into any form they please" (JLA, 1426). During and after the Nullification crisis, Jefferson's complaint becomes more of a litany. In 1836, Robert Rantoul, Jr., a lawyer and Jacksonian democrat, declares, "The judge makes law, by extorting from precedents something which they do not contain. . . . The law, then, is the final will or whim of the judge."[44] Alexander Bryan Johnson, a banker and author of *A Treatise on Language* (1836), writes in an 1851 essay on the constitutionality of a proposed public improvement: "Every verbal proposition is like a mirror. It reflects the lineaments of the man who looks into it."[45] Characters in *The Scarlet Letter*, completed by Hawthorne a year earlier, reveal their lineaments through their commentary on Hester's letter, just as characters in *Moby-Dick*, published in 1851, mirror themselves in their interpretation of Ahab's doubloon. The commentaries on the scarlet letter and the doubloon are so contradictory that the reader has little choice but to recognize that something beyond interpretation of a common text is needed to produce the consensus that sustains union.[46] Disgusted by legal trials and legislation that continued to sanction slavery, Emerson proclaims in 1854: "And in this country one sees that there is always margin in the statutes for a liberal judge to read one way and a servile judge another" (REW, XI, 225). And in 1857 Theodore Sedgwick asserts in *A Treatise on the Rules Which Govern the Interpretation and Application of Statutory and Constitutional Law*: "It is plain that differences will arise in the construction of written laws. The history of private discussions and of public controversies, of contracts and of treatise, and more than all the religious annals of our race, show the feebleness and imperfection of language, and the sad facility with which it lends itself to the various interpretations put upon it by ambition, fraud, or even honest difference of judgment."[47] The dominant rhetoric of antebellum constitutional hermeneutics represented the judge as the servant of the law who found the proper or correct meaning. But for these commentators on the law, and perhaps for Hawthorne and Melville as well, judicial practice revealed what theory denied: the judge is not a servant, but a sovereign reader; not a passive recipient of meaning, but a shaper of it. The judicial order cannot long abide ambiguity or polysemy. Indeed, judges do not create meaning. They kill competing meanings so that one can live. Fortunately, literature can serve a different end.

"If illogicality is . . . the constitutive feature of literary language, why," Barbara Foley asks, "was this trait discovered only in the crucible of the United States of the 1850s?" Though this trait was not in fact discovered in the 1850s but just made abundantly manifest by American Renaissance writers, Foley's question is apt, and it can be answered in part by recognizing the degree to which the Constitution became more manifestly illogical in the 1850s. The quarrels over the Constitution unclothed the emperor, exposing it to those not blinded by myth and not afraid to witness the father's sins to be a plural, multivoiced, open-ended text full of clauses irreducible to a single meaning, a text that was a bundle of conflicting values that could not have a final, infallible, unified interpretation for a number of political, philosophical, and historical reasons.[48] The Constitution had no single author; it delegates no sovereign interpreter; it was written by a committee that disagreed among itself; it was ratified by state conventions that were divided; it was interpreted by a Supreme Court whose judgments are rendered as opinions; and its ostensible ruler was that unstable and multivoiced entity the vox populi. The conflict of voices that constituted the Constitution could be quieted but not suppressed. When Madison's *Notes of Debates in the Federal Convention* was published in 1840, it was clear for all to see that the unanimity of the framers was partly a matter of compromise and partly myth. John Marshall, when he became chief justice, resorted to a legal fiction to maintain the clarity of the voice of law: he ended the practice whereby each justice delivered his opinion and substituted the protocol of the "Court" or the "unanimous Court" rendering judgment through the voice of a single member, usually himself. But no legal cover-up – and no paper pact by itself – could suture the Union. In 1833, a reviewer of Story's *Commentaries on the Constitution* argues that the word of the fathers, from the beginning, was not univocal: "From the hour of the promulgation of our Federal Constitution to the present day, a continued controversy has been carried on by our statesmen and politicians to fix or unfix the meaning of certain essential parts of it. We have had an unceasing war of constructions, and every clause and word of it has been subjected to the closest scrutiny."[49] Emerson thus concludes in 1845: "The constitutional argument is ever trivial for the *animus* of the framers is not a fixed fact but a Proteus. . . . In such a case, nothing avails but morals & might." (JMN, IX, 180).

Confronted with this war of constructions, Americans sought some means besides might or some end besides war to resolve its ambiguities and the sectional conflict over slavery that was becoming irrepressible. Closure was sought in Supreme Court decisions, and commentators turned to texts beyond the Constitution to clarify the Constitution. They appealed beyond the letter of the law to the spirit of '76 incarnate in the Declaration and to the spirit of Christianity incarnate in the Bible. But as Emerson notes in disgust in an 1854 essay on the Fugitive Slave Law, the Declaration and the Bible proved just as protean:

> I fear there is no reliance to be put on any kind or form of covenant, no, not on sacred forms, none on churches, none on bibles. For one would have said that a Christian would not keep slaves; – but the Christians keep slaves. Of course they will not dare to read the Bible? Won't they? They quote the Bible, quote Paul, quote Christ, to justify slavery . . .
>
> These things show that no forms, neither constitutions, nor laws, nor covenants, nor churches, nor bibles, are of any use in themselves. The Devil nestles comfortably into them all. (REW, XI, 234)

Emerson resisted despair by offering his own "fundamental law of criticism": "'Every scripture is to be interpreted by the same spirit which gave it forth'. . . . A life in harmony with nature, the love of truth and of virtue, will purge the eyes to understand her text" (ELA, 25). People, and not the text, needed moral reconstruction. But for Herman Melville, the text of nature, like the Constitution for Alexander Bryan Johnson, was a narcissistic mirror; it reflected not the law of God but the opinion of man. "Say what some poets will," Melville writes in *Pierre*, a work subtitled *The Ambiguities*, "Nature is not so much her own ever-sweet interpreter, as the mere supplier of that cunning alphabet, whereby selecting and combining as he pleases, each man reads his own peculiar lesson according to his own peculiar mind and mood."[50] Nature's own voice is a silent, indecipherable alphabet that echoes what people proclaim and desire to hear. Augustine St. Clair, a slaveholder in *Uncle Tom's Cabin* who opposes slavery, consolidates the conclusions of Emerson and Melville: "Planters, who have money to make by it, – clergymen, who have planters to please, – politicians, who want to rule by it, – may warp and bend language and ethics to a degree that shall astonish the world at their ingenuity; they can press nature and the Bible, and nobody knows what else, into the service."[51] For Stowe, only God and His evangelical disciples could redeem the Word from this abuse. "To interpret Christ," Emerson asserts, "it needs Christ in the heart" (REW, XI, 234). To interpret the law of man and God and end slavery, Stowe places Uncle Tom in our hearts.

In 1821 James Madison observed, "The Gordian knot of the Constitution seems to lie in the problem of the collision between federal & State powers, especially as eventually exercised by their respective Tribunals." He then warned, "If the knot cannot be untied by the text of the Constitution it ought not, certainly, to be cut by any Political Alexander."[52] But neither the text of the Constitution nor the Supreme Court nor appeals to nature, to the Declaration, to the Bible, or to Madison's intentions could untie the knot and bring a verbal resolution of the conflict. All the attempts to resolve the "points abstruse" of the paper pact were no more successful, finally, than Captain Delano's attempt to interpret the knot thrown to him as a sign by a sailor on board the *San Dominick* in Melville's *Benito Cereno*. Swords had to arbitrate instead. John Brown and Jefferson Davis are figures of the "Political Alexander" Madison feared. After secession, Lincoln reciprocated with his own swift sword.

Writing after the Civil War, Hermann Von Holst, a German historian, observed in *Constitutional and Political History of the United States* that the malleability of words in the Constitution was not a danger but a political safety valve: "The Constitution afforded such a field for a war of words . . . that . . . the erroneous view began to obtain currency in the third decade of this century that all difficulty would end in a war of tongues. . . . The extraordinary dilatibility of the boundaries postponed the moment of the breach."[53] For Von Holst, the elasticity of the words of the Constitution made possible a tug of politics. Few were willing to let go of the rope, and no party and no section could pull its antagonists completely to the side of antislavery or slavery, but war was thus conducted by other means. James Russell Lowell, however, reached a less benign conclusion about the verbal play of differences in an 1866 essay: "We hoped to hear less in future of the possible interpretations by which the Constitution may be made to mean this or that. . . . It was by precisely such constitutional quibbles, educating men to believe they had a right to claim whatever they could sophistically demonstrate to their own satisfaction . . . that we were interpreted, in spite of ourselves, into civil war."[54] Lowell's statement may seem farfetched. Could the constitutional quibble be the fatal Cleopatra for which the Union was lost? We must remember that much of the passion and most of the power struggles over the national bank, the tariff, and slavery were funneled into the arena of constitutional debate, thus reducing politics to quibbling over words. Words such as "liberty" were deployed to claim legitimacy for opposing policies: the right of slaveholding and secession versus the right of emancipation and a war to end secession. For Lowell, the quibbling was a paltering in double senses that ended in a bloody betrayal of America's king: the Constitution.

Constitutional choices, Laurence Tribe explains, are "channeled by a constitutional text and structure and history, by constitutional language and constitutional traditions, opening some paths and foreclosing others."[55] To extend this metaphor, the judicial system and the Supreme Court can be envisioned as one of the three primary channels within the federal government designed to control (with a series of locks) the torrent of public opinion and filter the mud stirred up by the passions and prejudices of the people. But political forces can alter the course of the channel. The Supreme Court itself, argues John Hart Ely, must seek to keep clear "the channels of political change" and keep open "the channels of political participation and communication."[56] In 1866 James Russell Lowell blasted "the theorists of the Virginia school" of constitutional interpretation for damming those channels of change that Ely calls upon the Supreme Court to keep open. The Virginia theorists, Lowell writes, "would have dammed up and diverted the force of each State into a narrow channel of its own, with its little saw-mill and its little grist-mill for local needs, instead of letting it follow the slopes of the continental water-shed to swell the volume of one great current ample for the large uses and needful for the higher civilization of all" (JLW, V, 299).

The forces of politics that opened and closed the locks of change, dilating the boundaries of the Constitution, making its words shifty, led at least in part to the intensified quest for a science of law in the years that followed the Civil War, a quest which Christopher Columbus Langdell helped to advance as dean of the Harvard Law School. Langdell's emphasis on legal science, Lawrence Friedman explains, "exalted the prestige of law and legal learning; at the same time it affirmed that legal science stood apart, as an independent entity, distinct from politics, legislation, and the man on the street."[57] Legal science would thus perform a saving procedure, quarantining law from the diseases of politics, a severance imagined a bit differently in a dream described by James Bradley Thayer, a student (and later a colleague) of Langdell's. The dream is a vision of a language purged of ambiguity that would be "a lawyer's Paradise where all words have a fixed, precisely ascertained meaning; where men express their purposes not only with accuracy, but with fullness; and where, if the writer has been careful, a lawyer, having a document before him, may sit in his chair, inspect the text, and answer all questions without raising his eyes."[58] Less lyrically, Oliver Wendell Holmes, Jr., rendered a concurrent opinion in "The Path of the Law": "I often doubt whether it would not be a gain if every word of moral significance could be banished from the law altogether, and other words adopted which should convey legal ideas uncolored by anything outside the law."[59]

Langdell's legal science would separate law from politics; Holmes's vision of language would separate law from morality. But the Constitution will always be read through a prism that refracts the meaning of its words within a spectrum of ideology whose colors are constituted by a range of political, cultural, and personal beliefs and experiences. That prismatic vision can be regarded, however, not as a sign of an exile from a lawyer's paradise but as a fortunate fall that insures that there will always be debate about the meaning of the text. The words of the Constitution read solely in the white light of the founders' vision, if that vision could be attained, would lose the richness they have gained by being read through the prisms of different ages and by being tossed and turned in the kaleidoscope of debate. The founders' words, remembered and recalled, will remain an important part of any conversation about the law, but we cannot be confined by the political dictionaries of the past (though we may be ruled by the law's grammar).

The Constitution belongs to the living; it is the grammar that structures the conversation, the debate, the disputes among the voices of the people, and that grammar can generate new legal experiments.[60] The Declaration derives its authority from truths held self-evident by a We and from the laws of nature and nature's God. The Constitution derives its authority as an incarnation of the vox populi. "Ironically," Sanford Levinson writes, "the American Revolution . . . made in the name of the fundamental law . . . presaged a future in which popular sovereignty, rooted in will rather than in a common moral order, was to become the motif of the new American polity."[61] Although the Constitution (with the Bill of Rights) was designed to constrain and check the majority will as expressed by the state legislatures, through the amendment process and elections a structure was provided that allowed the people to revise more or less indirectly their fundamental written law. The governing vocabulary and the rules of grammar of the Constitution are open to revision. The degree to which the vox populi can change the written law through amendment and representation and the degree to which the representatives of the people – the executive, the legislature, and the Supreme Court – should listen to the vox populi present a problem similar to the one that faced Samuel Johnson and Benjamin Franklin as reformers of the language: to what degree should the orthography of words be correspondent to their pronunciation? And just as Johnson discovered during his work on the dictionary that "sounds are too volatile and subtile for legal restraints" and that "to enchain syllables, and to lash the wind" are the "undertakings of pride, unwilling to measure its desires by its strengths," so too have Americans discovered, often to their dismay, that the written Constitution could not fetter the vox populi (or the voice of property).[62]

For Samuel Johnson, change in language was a form of corruption, and he observed that such change could not be prevented: "Tongues, like governments, have a natural tendency to degeneration" (SJW, II, 64). Madison similarly observes that "all living languages are constantly subject" to change and that the words and phrases of the Constitution must necessarily partake of that change (JML, III, 442). For Johnson, a language was like a government because both instruments of the social order were capable of change or threatened by corruption. But for Madison the link between language and government was not just one of analogy but identity, because the Constitution was a written text. And Madison, like Lieber, sounds much like Dr. Johnson, the disillusioned lexicographer, when he writes as follows in a letter to Converse Sherman, who had sent him the prospectus for Noah Webster's dictionary:

> Whilst few things are more difficult, few are more desirable than a standard work, explaining, and as far as possible fixing, the meaning of words and phrases. All languages, written as well as oral, though much less than oral, are liable to changes, from causes, some of them inseparable from the nature of man and the progress of society. A perfect remedy for the evil must, therefore, be unattainable. But as far as it may be attainable, the attempt is laudable; and next to compleat success, is that of recording with admitted fidelity the state of a language at the epoch of the record. In the exposition of laws, and even of Constitutions, how many important errors may be produced by mere innovations in the use of words and phrases, if not controulable by a recurrence to the original and authentic meaning attached to them! (JML, III, 519)

For Madison, as well as for Dr. Johnson, we must palliate what we cannot cure, and for Madison even more than for Dr. Johnson, the struggle to preserve the government became one with the struggle to preserve the established meaning of words. The vox populi had to pronounce itself according to the orthography and the grammar of the written law, and the written law had to be stabilized by the dictionary.

But the voices that the standard of the written Constitution repressed – the voice of the slave, the Native American, the woman, the unpropertied – would return in a different written frame: the frame of American novels by Cooper, Melville, Stowe, Twain, and others. Just as Robert Cover argues that sacred narratives can serve as "narratives of judicial resistance" or as narratives that constitute "a ground for judicial commitments" that can supplement (or challenge) the traditions of positive law, so too, as Brook Thomas argues, a range of American literary narratives can be read to offer resistance to (as well as affirmation of) legal practice and ideology; these texts can help us recognize both what was left silent by legal discourse and what remains untold.[63] Figures of the oral in American literature and politics – Patrick Henry, declaring for liberty or death; Natty Bumppo, breaking grammar and the law of Templeton; Margaret Fuller, leading her "Conversations"; Garrison, burning first the Fugitive Slave Law, then a court decision, then the Constitution while addressing a crowd in 1854; Davy Crockett, rendering judgments that were never appealed from, he boasted, though he had never read a page in a lawbook; Huck Finn, tearing up the letter he wrote that would turn Jim in as a fugitive slave; the invisible man, breaking away from the script of the Brotherhood to address an audience in Harlem in his own terms; Martin Luther King, Jr., departing from his written text at the end of the "I have a dream" speech – these figures brush up against and bother the frames of the written, the frames guarded by the powers of politics, property, and print. Sometimes they loosen the hold of the written, but more often they are defeated, at least temporarily. The language and literature of the United States have drawn strength and extended their range by incorporating the oral, and the Constitution, designed in part as a bulwark against the demagogue and the mob, has also been loosened and enriched by the orality of protest. The opposition of the oral to the written, of the pronunciations of the vox populi to the orthography of dictionaries, of slang to standard language, of oratory to print, and of the vernacular voice of revolution to the grammar of written constitutions are oppositions that assure transformations in the language, and these oppositions and the demand for variation by the oral – a demand won by the Revolution and legitimated by the Constitution – are invariants in our culture.

"The American people have wanted some anchorage, some link with the invariant," and they have turned to the Constitution for that anchor, declared Max Lerner in a 1937 law review article entitled "The Constitution and Court as Symbols."[64] But because of the license we possess to construe the Constitution and because of the fluctuating voice of the people and the fluid state of language itself, the American ship of state, as Emerson remarked, has no anchor. The threat of wind and rain or of torrents and currents – the images so often deployed to figure the power and passion of popular opinion – made the prospect of an anchorless ship a source of fear and trembling for many antebellum commentators on the law. But Benjamin Cardozo, a Supreme Court justice from 1932 to 1938, offers a different response in *The Nature of the Judicial Process* (1921) as he provides a log of his own experience as a judge:

> I was much troubled in spirit, in my first years upon the bench, to find how trackless was the ocean on which I had embarked. I sought for certainty. I was oppressed and disheartened when I found that the quest for it was futile. I was trying to reach land, the solid land of fixed and settled rules, the paradise of a justice that would declare itself by tokens plainer and more commanding than its pale and glimmering reflections in my own vacillating mind and conscience. I found "with the voyagers in Browning's 'Paracelsus' that the real heaven was always beyond." As the years have gone by, and as I have reflected more and more upon the nature of the judicial process, I have become reconciled to the uncertainty, because I have grown to see it as inevitable. I have grown to see that the process in its highest reaches is not discovery, but creation; and that the doubts and misgivings, the hopes and fears, are part of the travail of mind, the pangs of death and the pangs at birth, in which principles that have served their day expire, and new principles are born.[65]

Exiled from a paradise of plain words and settled rules, Cardozo becomes a voyager, and he reconciles himself, poetically, to uncertainty and creation, and he draws his faith, as Lincoln calls upon us to do in the Gettysburg Address, from a vision of birth and death and rebirth in the life of the word of American law. James Boyd White similarly suggests that the discovery that the law has no objective meaning need not be a cause for despair: "When we discover that we have in this world no earth or rock to stand and walk upon, but only shifting sea and sky and wind, the mature response is not to lament the loss of fixity but to learn to sail."[66] Or, as Bushnell remarks in his ruminations on interpreting the Bible: "The second, third, and thirtieth senses of words – all but the physical first sense – belong to the empyrean, and are given, as we see in the prophets, to be inspired by. . . . We learn to embark on them as we do when we go to sea; and when the breeze of inspiration comes, *we glide.*"[67] "Sail forth – steer for the deep waters only / . . . O farther, farther, farther sail!" concludes Whitman in "Passage to India" (WLA, 539–40).

Sailing away from the "slavish shore," from the comfort of port, from the safety and succor of home, as Melville reminds us in *Moby-Dick*, is a necessity if the soul is to maintain an "open independence" and if shipwreck is to be avoided in a storm. Yet the voyage of the *Pequod* shows how dangerous the journey of landless intrepid souls can be. Ahab casts a blind eye and cold heart on his family and the shore; he abandons his quadrant; he forgoes conversation; he disguises his intentions by maintaining the "nominal purpose" of the voyage; he hides a special strike force against an "evil" thing in the bowels of his ship. His deviousness, born from a monomaniacal reading of Moby-Dick, subverts a contract and a constitutional process. But Ahab, so magnificent in his oratory, is defeated as the most powerful voice in American literature by Huck Finn, a grammar-breaking juvenile who tries to steal a slave to freedom by piloting a raft against the current of law. And just as Ahab, who bears a likeness in his oratory to John Calhoun and Daniel Webster and who may be a figure of one or a composite of both, is defeated as a model of American language by Huck Finn, so too in history Calhoun and Webster are defeated as models of oratory by Lincoln, the Mark Twain of our politics.[68]

The indeterminacy of the law can be a challenge, as the raft piloting of Lincoln and Huck Finn suggests, not just to our deviousness but to our virtue and charity and to our aspirations. "The simpler words, – we do not know what they mean, except when we love and aspire," counsels Emerson (ELA, 413). Let us, Thoreau advises in *Walden*, conjecture from the words of our heroic books "a larger sense than common use permits out of what wisdom and valor and generosity we have" (TLA, 403). The simpler words from the Preamble to the Constitution – "establish Justice," "promote the general Welfare," "secure the Blessings of Liberty" – can speak to us not just about political rights but about the need for economic security that Franklin Roosevelt advanced with the New Deal in the 1930s. "Liberty," "justice," and the "general welfare" can be defined, that is, not just as the quest to preserve free speech and assembly and so on, but as the right to food, shelter, and health. We can, in short, supplement the letter of the law and thus remedy what H. Jefferson Powell calls the Constitution's "failure explicitly to acknowledge society's affirmative obligations to the poor, the elderly, the disadvantaged."[69] Or, as Lerner concludes his article, written in the midst of the Depression but certainly not dated: out of fear, he says, we can cling to old symbols, looking toward the past, or out of hunger and hope we can look forward to new economic and political constructions, reshaping old symbols, shaping new.[70]

The ideology of legal theory is reflected in its metaphors; change the metaphor, expose its contradictions, elaborate its implications, and challenge the ideology. The Constitution can be not just a bulwark, fortifying rights against the passion of public opinion and the power of a demagogue, but a channel for what Hamilton called the "streams of national power" that "ought to flow, immediately from that pure, original fountain of all legitimate authority": "THE CONSENT OF THE PEOPLE" (FP, 22. 152). Indeed, as Whitman suggested shortly before the Civil War, the danger opposing the torrent of public opinion is stagnant water or the blocked channel that allows scum to remain on the top: "I know that underneath all this putridity of Presidents and Congressmen that has risen at the top, lie pure waters a thousand fathoms deep. – They make the real ocean, whatever the scum may be on its surface."[71] The Constitution can also be figured as not just a sheet anchor but the chart we use to guide the republican raft past the Scyllas and Charybdises of the political world – tyranny on the port, and mob rule on the starboard, side. The amended Constitution can also be, as Justice William J. Brennan, Jr., asserts, a "lodestar for our aspirations."[72] As a chart, it maps old ground; as a sheet anchor, it can stay the course in a crisis; as a lodestar, it can help us find our way to explore new oceans and find new riches of liberty, justice, and equality. By following a lodestar and sailing away from a strict interpretation of original intent, by taking different constitutional tacks, the ship of state has, like the devious-cruising *Rachel* in *Moby-Dick*, picked up outcasts and renegades or Ishmaels disinherited in the original will of the founding fathers. Only by deviating from the original intent of the founding fathers did Washington, D.C., become something besides the home of a dead-letter office: the home, that is, of a law whose letter was killing the rights of "persons held to service." In Cooper's *Monikins*, legislators in an imaginary world overturn Article IV, Clause 6, in the "Great and Sacred National Allegory" in order to turn black into white. Ironically or prophetically, two decades after the publication of *The Monikins*, the United States Congress reconstructs its own Constitution by declaring black to be white. American legislators overturn Article IV, Section 3, containing the notorious fugitive-slave clause, and add Amendment 14, which guarantees equality and due process of law to all citizens, both black and white. Only by sailing on new waves of construction did lawmakers rise in this moment above the forceful undercurrent of racial prejudice that drew the country into the maelstrom of the Civil War.

"Your Constitution is all sail and no anchor," Lord Macaulay remarked to an American in 1857.[73] But the words on parchment, though they may seem as insubstantial at times as breath in the wind, remain as solid as the rock Dr. Johnson kicked to refute the philosophical idealism of Bishop Berkeley; indeed, they remain a stumbling block or, better yet, a touchstone for any metaphysical construction that prefers the spirit to the letter. "The word beats all the speakers & definers of it, & stands to their children what it stood to their fathers," notes Emerson (JMN, XI, 232). At the conclusion of the *Phaedrus*, Plato comments that when a written composition "is ill-treated and unfairly abused it always needs its parent to come to its help, being unable to defend or help itself," and we can turn to the words of the Constitution and of its parents for such help.[74] By reviewing the meanings of the words in history as well as by revising their meanings in the present, we can build upon those words, as if they were basalt beneath sand, the bridge that can offer us an alternative to sailing without an anchor. On its span we can travel freely and safely between our history on the one side and on the other bank our visions of a future land that will be more just than our past.[75] But James Russell Lowell suggests that any attempt to ground the Constitution permanently, like a bridge, in a shoreline of politics, even the one bulwarked by the rock of the founders, will provide a stability that is bound to frustrate:

> That there should always be a school who interpret the Constitution by its letter is a good thing, as interposing a check to hasty or partial action, and gaining time for ample discussion; but that in the end we should be governed by its spirit, living and operative in the energies of an advancing people, is a still better thing; since the levels and shore-lines of politics are no more stationary than those of continents, and the ship of state would in time be left aground far inland, to long in vain for that open sea which is the only pathway to fortune and to glory. (JLW, V, 299)

Literature's gift to law lies not in its claims to a special morality or to a higher political vision – the poet can be as specious as any acknowledged legislator – but in its creation of those metaphors that can help us clarify and amend our constructions of the law.

II

Political and Linguistic Corruption:
The Ideological Inheritance

3

The Classical Pattern:
From the Order of Orpheus
to the Chaos of the Thucydidean Moment

"With mankind," he would say, "forms, measured forms, are everything; and that is the import couched in the story of Orpheus with
his lyre spellbinding the wild denizens of the wood."

Herman Melville, *Billy Budd*

. . . read Thucydides without horror?
words lost their significance

Ezra Pound, Canto LXVII
(citing John Adams, *A Defence of the Constitutions*)

In "The House-top," a haunting poem about the draft riots in New
York City in the summer of 1863, Herman Melville gives form to a
moment that is the antithesis of form: the dismemberment of law.
"The Atheist roar of riot," which resounds through New York in the
dog days of July, murders sleep and stifles the sound of sense. During
the riots, which culminated in the massacre of blacks, inhabitants of
the city shed their humanity and return to a savage nature, a state of
bellum omnium contra omnes.

> The Town is taken by its rats – ship-rats
> And rats of the wharves. All civil charms
> And priestly spells which late held hearts in awe –
> Fear-bound, subjected to a better sway
> Than sway of self; these like a dream dissolve,
> And man rebounds whole aeons back in nature.
>
> (BP, 89)

The rats infesting the city bite through the cords – the political and
religious bonds – that have subjected them to a better sway than sway
of self. The scourge of Draconian law and Calvin's creed must be
wielded again. The Melville who wrote "The House-top," as opposed

69

to the Melville who wrote *White-Jacket* – his 1850 novel that registers
dissent against Draconian law, represented by the scourge of flogging
– would probably have little reservation seconding Captain Vere's
reported declaration in *Billy Budd*: "'With mankind,' he would say,
'forms, measured forms, are everything; and that is the import
couched in the story of Orpheus with his lyre spellbinding the wild
denizens of the wood'" (BB, 128).[1] Vere, who sacrifices Billy Budd to
maintain the laws of state against the threat of anarchy on board the
Bellipotent, falls victim himself to the atheist roar of riot when he is in
battle with the *Athée*, a warship from Revolutionary France, a state
that epitomizes for Vere the "disruption of forms." In another Civil
War poem, "The Armies of the Wilderness," Melville alludes again to
Orpheus:

> The fight for the city is fought
>   In Nature's old domain;
> Man goes out to the wilds,
>   And Orpheus' charm is vain.
>   (BP, 100)

For Melville, the Civil War is a fight for the city and for the law and
for Unity; it is a fight to preserve all that Orpheus was represented to
have founded through the sound of his lyre (a figure in some tellings of
the myth for the word, for poetry, or for law).[2]

Orpheus, the archetypal poet and legislator, was divinized by the
ancients of Greece and Rome, and the myth of Orpheus preserves a
story of transformation by "forms" that suggests the incomparable
value attributed to speech in classical culture. In the beginning there
was wildness. But Orpheus, with his lyre, charms the denizens of the
woods, or rude and savage men, to a gentler way of life, calling them
together in one place, teaching them to build cities, to keep laws, and
to embrace virtue. This transformation from chaos to civility is a
moment when language and law, poetry and politics combine to
create and celebrate the founding of the polis. The advent of the word
brings, in Georges Gusdorf's phrase, "an overturning of the conditions
of existence, a reworking of the environment for the establishment of
man," and it is this belief in the word as the agency of political
transformation that Renaissance humanists celebrated in their myth of
Orpheus, and it is this power of the word that American orators and
poets would often dream of recovering.[3] "The supreme value of
poetry," writes Emerson, "is to educate us to a height beyond itself,
or which it rarely reaches;– the subduing mankind to order and virtue.
He is the true Orpheus who writes his ode, not with syllables, but
men" (REW, VIII, 65–6).[4] "I do not wonder," Emerson remarks

elsewhere, "at the miracles which poetry attributes to the music of Orpheus, when I remember what I have experienced from the varied notes of the human voice. They are an incalculable energy which countervails all other forces in nature, because they are the channel of supernatural powers" (ELA, 155). Walt Whitman, who called for a "revolution in American oratory" and who sought to draw his powers from the varied notes of the human voice, also possessed Orphic aspirations. Found in his manuscripts is the following note: "To inflate the chest, to roll the thunder of the voice out from the ribs and throat, / To make the people rage, weep, hate, desire, with yourself, / To lead America – to quell America with a great tongue."[5] To dream of the poet or orator as an acknowledged legislator of mankind is to remember Orpheus. But as Emerson and Whitman reveal through the force of their verbs – "subdue," "countervail," "lead," "quell" – the Orphic dream of transforming a savage wilderness into the order of culture through the word – a dream, as Eric Cheyfitz argues, that has often preoccupied the imagination of the West and the foreign policy of the United States – is a dream fraught with the nightmare of conquest and empire.[6]

The antithesis of the Orphic transformation from a state of disorder to the sustaining language and law of the polis is what I call the Thucydidean moment, a moment when, as occurs in Corcyra in Thucydides' account of the Peloponnesian War, the social contract – the bond of faith, affection, and compromise sustaining harmony between man and man – is broken by political strife and linguistic duplicity. In this moment, the order of Orpheus is dismembered: civil charms and priestly spells give way to their sinister double – the word as the most potent form of political violence – and to the violence of war itself. From the perspective of commentators on politics in the early republic, this transformation from the order of Orpheus to the chaos of the Thucydidean moment threatened to occur at various times and did occur as dreams of a *novus ordo seclorum* vanished in the face of an uncompromising pursuit of self-interest that culminated in civil war. To understand more fully American fears of this transformation and of the corruption of language that accompanied it, we need to examine some key texts from the classical rhetorical and republican traditions that tutored Americans about the dangers and virtues of democracy and the word.

In Western culture, the tradition of connecting linguistic and political disorders begins at least as far back as ancient Greece, and it arises in large part because of the transformations in classical politics that placed language squarely at the heart of human affairs in the developing polis. Speech became not just the medium for the allocation of power, property, and prestige; it was the raison d'être of the city. Man lives in a polis, Aristotle explains in the *Politics*, because he alone of all the animals possesses *logos*, the power of speech. Aristotle's famous definition of man as a political animal (*zoon politikon*) must be understood in conjunction with his other definition of man as a language animal, a living being capable of speech (*zoon logon ekhon*).[7] For Aristotle, *logos* is not merely a capacity for speech; it is the capacity for rational discourse that enables humans to distinguish and express what is advantageous and harmful, just and unjust, good and bad. Through speech, that is, man alone has a common sense of right and wrong, and it is this community of understanding, Aristotle insists, that constitutes every human association from the family to the polis.[8]

Aristotle's fundamental theorem that man is a social animal whose political community and moral relationships are constituted and enhanced by the development of a shared language has remained at the core of the humanist tradition. A classic American formulation of this theorem is by Henry James in *The Question of Our Speech*:

> All life therefore comes back to the question of our speech, the medium through which we communicate with each other. These relations are made possible, are registered, are verily constituted, by our speech, and are successful . . . in proportion as our speech is worthy of its great human and social function; is developed, delicate, flexible, rich – an adequate accomplished fact. The more it suggests and expresses the more we live by it – the more it promotes and enhances life. Its quality, its authenticity, its security, are hence supremely important for the general multifold opportunity, for the dignity and integrity, of our existence.[9]

A more succinct formulation of Aristotle's theorem regarding the constitution of the human and ethical realm by the word belongs to N. Scott Momaday: "There is no way in which we can exist apart from the morality of a verbal dimension."[10] James and Momaday express so well what has often been thought: humane existence hinges on the word.

This classical formulation of the interdependence between humanity and language is also a point that has been developed extensively by recent biologists, philosophers, and sociologists who insist that language constitutes man, the speaking subject, as much as man-the-ruler constitutes language. "We speak, therefore I am," is the contemporary *dicemus* to replace Descartes's *cogito*: "I think, therefore I am."[11] This reciprocal relationship between language and humanity that delimits a person's autonomy and necessarily makes people political beings subject to the language of others is captured in Fénelon's aphoristic phrase "For the Greeks, everything depends on the people, and the people depend on speech."[12] The implications of this phrase can be drawn out in several directions, but one important corollary is that the inhabitants of the Greek polis who were denied the opportunity to speak in public or who were prevented from developing the faculty of rational argument (*logos*) and participating in cooperative action (*praxis*) were not considered fully human or not fully Greek or not fully free, and they were certainly not the people who governed; they were slaves, women, children, and aliens. Confined to the households or to the fields or excluded from the city walls, these people could not deliberate in public regarding the advantageous, the good, and the just.[13] Political liberty in the Greek polis consisted first and foremost in the opportunity to participate in the public speech and action of the polis. The city exists, Aristotle declares, "for the sake of noble action" and for the "sharing of deeds and words."[14] The Greek polis offered its citizens something more than a liberal protection of life and property. It provided them, as Hannah Arendt argues, with a public space for developing and displaying the qualities that separate humankind from the animals and distinguish persons from each other – the *logos*, or skill in speech and reason.[15] Theseus in Euripides' *Supplices* bears witness to this version of freedom when he asserts: "Being free is this: Whoever wishes to bring useful advice before the public may do so. In this way, whoever longs for eminence can shine – while the man lacking this desire remains silent. What could be more equitable in a city than this?"[16] To speak, to shine, to serve the city: this is the pursuit of life, liberty, and happiness to the citizen celebrated in the culture of Greek democracy.

The revolutionary achievement of the Greek polis was to transplant the field of political action from the battlefield to the forum and thus provide a space where speech could reign and where man could fulfill his quest for glory and excellence – for *arete* – not through physical conquest over the body of another warrior but through the conquest of the minds of a multitude with the power of the tongue. With that transformation, the ground was prepared for the Greek citizen to declare, as Emerson would remark at the beginning of his ministerial career, "For I have hoped to put on eloquence as a robe, and by goodness and zeal and the awfulness of Virtue to press and prevail over the false judgments, the rebel passions and corrupt habits of men."[17] In the polis, the heroic ideal of military excellence, appropriate to the feudal and aristocratic society of the Homeric era, grew musclebound and gave way to a new ideal – verbal excellence – and to a new discipline: rhetoric as taught by the Sophists. Within the polis, in short, training in rhetoric replaced training in arms, the word replaced the sword, speech replaced action or became another form of action, and the cultural hero became the rhetor, the man who possessed, as Emerson said he did, "a passionate love for the strains of eloquence" and who burned with Emerson for the "'aliquid immensum infinitumque' which Cicero desired."[18] In *The Human Condition*, Arendt summarizes this transformation in the Greek polis: "To be political, to live in a polis, meant that everything was decided through words and persuasion and not through force and violence. In Greek self-understanding, to force people by violence, to command rather than persuade, were prepolitical ways to deal with people characteristic of life outside the polis."[19] While Arendt's vision of the Greek polis is colored by a fond remembrance of things past that is politically charged – she reads Greek history to uphold a political ideal of liberty in an age shocked by World War II and too familiar with totalitarianism – such an idealization of the politics of persuasion in the polis is itself an essential part of the classical rhetorical and civic humanist traditions that seeks to persuade us of the nonviolent and transformative powers of speech. Speech, of course, was part of politics in the Homeric era before the formal invention of rhetoric, and violence was part of politics in the Greek polis after the invention of rhetoric. Yet something did change in the Athenian polis. A new political space – the forum of democracy – was constructed not just as a rhetorical ideal but as a physical space for collective action, and within that space, the public exercise of the most human of all human faculties – the power of speech – became at once the sign of liberty and the means of fulfilling one's humanity. The art of rhetoric was itself born, according to Aristotle, after the fall of the tyrants in Sicily in 456 B.C. when Corax sought to teach citizens how to use the tongue in courts of law to recover the property the tyrants had illegally confiscated.[20] The significance of this rise of rhetoric in the classical republic remained crucially alive in the mind of John Quincy Adams, who pointed out in his inaugural address as the first Boylston Professor of Rhetoric and Oratory at Harvard, that in Athens and Rome the "talent of public speaking" was not just a source of liberty but "the key to the highest dignities; the passport to the supreme dominion of the state."[21] To unlock the doors to power, it seems, one just had to turn skillfully the tongue, and in *Heroes and Hero-Worship* Thomas Carlyle describes the potential of the tongue as man's most democratic power and the dependence of democracy on that power: "Whoever can speak, speaking now to the whole nation, becomes a power, a branch of government, with inalienable weight in lawmaking, in all acts of authority. It matters not what rank he has, what revenues or garnitures: the requisite thing is, that he has a tongue which others will listen to; this and nothing more is requisite. The nation is governed by all that has tongue in the nation; Democracy is virtually there."[22] For Carlyle, the tongue is truly man's most democratic instrument, the power that allows the common man without rank, revenues, or garnitures to become the uncommon leader, the power that arms every person with the potential to become a participant in government and even a ruler or a sovereign force. It is the power that makes the right of every citizen to speak and be heard the necessary and sufficient ground of democracy, and it is a power whose loss can mean a forfeiture of the rights of man and a return to violence. *Billy Budd* is our testimony.

Only if a democracy seeks to keep its political arteries open for those who wish to speak can the health of the body politic be sustained. Billy, of course, cannot speak when called to defend himself, and that failure leads to his fall. Captain Vere can speak, but he chooses to repress his inner voice – the conscience that tells him Billy is an angel of God who should not hang – and he silences the murmurs on board the *Bellipotent* in order to preserve the links in his chain of command. The silencing by Vere and his resort to the force of law and his institutional authority must be weighed in the balance with Billy's own silence and resort to force. Billy's act of force is judged criminal; Vere's act of force is draped in the legitimacy of law. But the killing of Claggart is not the tragic crime of *Billy Budd*. Vere's self-imposed silencing of himself and others is the tragedy of criminal justice on the *Bellipotent*. The fate of Billy, who was born the year Thomas Jefferson appealed to the laws of nature and nature's God to sanction revolutionary violence against the King of England, is a testament to what Robert Cover calls the "jurispathic office" of the judge who, in confronting the luxuriant growth of a multitude of legal traditions, must "assert that *this one* is law and destroy or try to destroy the rest."[23]

The commanding role envisioned by the Greeks for speech in the drama of social and political life is perhaps best suggested by Isocrates. Convinced that a transformation in educational practices could transform the social order, Isocrates maintained that training in the art of discourse was not simply a technique for attaining power. Consistently, he celebrates the word as the primary source of knowledge available to people and as the one political force capable of unifying all of Greece. But one passage from his *Antidosis*, the great oration of his old age, stands out as an expression of the classical verbal ethic that identifies language, in Max Byrd's phrase, "as our greatest collective activity, our unmistakably human way of creating community, the city we live in."[24]

> For in the other powers which we possess . . . we are in no respect superior to other living creatures; nay, we are inferior to many in swiftness and in strength and in other resources; but, because there has been implanted in us the power to persuade each other and to make clear to each other whatever we desire, not only have we escaped the life of wild beasts, but we have come together and founded cities and made laws and invented arts; and, generally speaking, there is no institution devised by man which the power of speech has not helped us to establish. For this it is which has laid down laws concerning things just and unjust, and things honourable and base; and if it were not for these ordinances we should not be able to live with one another. It is by this also that we confute the bad and extol the good. Through this we educate the ignorant and appraise the wise; for the power to speak well is taken as the surest index of a sound understanding, and discourse which is true and lawful and just is the outward image of a good and faithful soul. With this faculty we both contend against others on matters which are open to dispute and seek light for ourselves on things which are unknown; for the same arguments which we use in persuading others when we speak in public, we employ also when we deliberate in our own thoughts; and, while we call eloquent those who are able to speak before a crowd, we regard as sage those who most skilfully debate their problems in their own minds. And, if there is need to speak in brief summary of this power, we shall find that none of the things which are done with intelligence take place without the help of speech, but that in all our actions as well as in all our thoughts speech is our guide, and is most employed by those who have the most wisdom.[25]

Isocrates offers a virtual codification of the classical rhetorical view of the reciprocal relationship between man and language that forms the core of the humanist tradition. It is a view of man as a rhetorical creature who constitutes and governs the human world through the word.

Yet while the "measured forms" of language were granted an extraordinary power to enfranchise people and sustain politics in the classical rhetorical tradition, it was also feared that the corruption or misuse of language could disrupt every human endeavor and threaten a return to prepolitical ways of life. This fear has often been expressed in literature – it is at the center of Ulysses' speech on degree in Act I, Scene 3, of Shakespeare's *Troilus and Cressida*, and it forms the apocalyptic conclusion to Pope's *Dunciad*. But it is Thucydides who provides the *locus classicus* for any investigation into the connection between the corruption of language and the decline and fall of the city of man. In a passage describing the incredibly bloody internal struggle that took place between democratic and oligarchic factions in Corcyra beginning in 427 B.C., Thucydides gives us the antithesis of Isocrates' vision, a nightmarish look at the failure of language as an instrument of deliberation and peace and its frightening success as an instrument of power. Here is the passage in a translation John Adams used in his preface to *A Defence of the Constitutions of Government of the United States of America*:

> The contagion spread through the whole extent of Greece; factions raged in every city; the licentious many contending for the Athenians, and the aspiring few for the Lacedaemonians. The consequence was, seditions in cities, with all their numerous and tragical incidents. . . . Words lost their signification; brutal rashness was fortitude; prudence, cowardice; modesty, effeminacy; and being wise in every thing, to be good for nothing; the hot temper was manly valor; calm deliberation, plausible knavery; he who boiled with indignation was trustworthy; and he who presumed to contradict, was ever suspected. Connection of blood was less regarded than transient acquaintance; associations were not formed for mutual advantage, consistent with law, but for rapine against all law; trust was only communication of guilt; revenge was more valued, than never to have suffered an injury; perjuries were master-pieces of cunning; the dupes only blushed, the villains impudently triumphed.
>
> The source of all these evils was a thirst for power, from rapacious and ambitious passions. The men of large influence, some contending for the just equality of the democratical, and others for the fair decorum of aristocratical government, by artful sounds, embarrassed those communities, for their own private lucre, by the keenest spirit, the most daring projects, and most dreadful machinations. Revenge, not limited by justice or the public welfare, was measured only by such retaliation as was judged the sweetest; by capital condemnations, by iniquitous sentences, and by glutting the present rancor of their hearts with their own hands. The pious and upright conduct was on both sides disregarded; the moderate citizens fell victims to both. Seditions introduced every species of outrageous wickedness into the Grecian manners. Sincerity was laughed out of countenance; the whole order of human life was confounded; the human temper, too apt to transgress in spite of laws, now having gained the ascendant over law, seemed to glory that it was too strong for justice, and an enemy to all superiority. (JAW, IV, 285–6)[26]

What Thucydides draws for us here is a stark portrayal of people falling prey to party, to power, and to their passions; of people ruthlessly pursuing their self-interest against all claims of family and state; of people breaking the bonds of justice and morality that are too intrinsic to life to unloose; of people with a will to power botching up words to defend the indefensible. Ambition, revenge, avarice, power, greed, self-interest, fear – these are the passions that reign in this portrait of political chaos. Plotting, deceit, imposture – or what Locke calls artifice, prevarication, and the abuse of words and what Orwell terms Newspeak – these are the strategies of power that will be regarded as cleverness and cunning or politics itself by those who prevail. And this, in Thucydides' words, is what "happens and always will happen while human nature is what it is" (3.82). The moment in history that Thucydides describes here, and the moment he knows will always return in the course of human events, is that moment when first principles and founding words are hallowed in speech but violated in deeds, when an individual "I" claiming to speak for a collective "we" traduces the republican political grammar that subordinates "I" to "we," when rhetoric becomes a debased form of political action – deceit or flattery – and when even a dialogue of deceit and flattery collapses into discord and separate monologues, and, finally, when eloquence or *logos* becomes not the alternative to violence and the very power that distinguishes humans from the beasts but the inciter to or legitimator of immoral violence – the power that lowers us below beasts into the rungs of hell.

"War is a violent teacher" (3.82), Thucydides writes, and what his portrayal of the *stasis* at Corcyra teaches by the darkness of a negative example are the ease with which false representation can stalk the forum in the guise of true representation and the constitutional need to form and keep verbal pledges so as to avoid the civil disorders that break out when words lose their established value and moral values lose their established hold as stays against confusion.[27] Civil war is presented as nothing less than a betrayal of the social value of language and of the shared values of the city that language ideally stabilizes. In the *stasis*, the corruption of language does not just follow the corruption of man, as Emerson writes in *Nature*; the two processes are reciprocal. And, indeed, the reciprocal relationship identified in this passage between political instability and linguistic change, between fraudulent representation and the misuse of power, between the failure of words and outbreaks of violence, and between breaches of those invisible bonds that connect people in partnerships of family and community – bonds, I would say, of mutual obligation, faith, and affection – and breaches of the equally intangible bonds that connect a word with its meaning is something that writers have continued to describe in moments of political crisis ever since Thucydides.

Romans after the collapse of their republic, French writers during the civil strife of the sixteenth century, British writers in the seventeenth and eighteenth centuries, and Americans in the early republic not only quoted the passage from *The Peloponnesian War* cited above; they applied Thucydides' commentary to an analysis of politics in their own countries. For instance, when Cato, the Roman patriot who would be the archetype of virtue for American revolutionaries, denounces the conspiracy of Catiline in Sallust's *Bellum Catilinae*, a work modeled in part on Thucydides' *History*, his denunciation of corruption in Rome rings with the sounds of Thucydides' exposure of verbal fraud in Corcyra: "But in very truth we have long since lost the true names of things. It is precisely because squandering the good of others is called generosity, and recklessness in wrongdoing is called courage, that the republic is reduced to extremities (52.4)."[28] In the midst of the French Wars of Religion, Montaigne recalls Thucydides to condemn the verbal fraud of his own age: "We are experiencing what Thucydides says of the civil wars of his time, that men baptized public virtues with new milder names to excuse them, adulterating and softening their true titles" (1.23.87).[29] The first work Thomas Hobbes published was a translation of Thucydides' *History*, which he undertook in the late 1620s during the conflicts that initiated the Puritan migration to America largely because he believed his contemporaries could learn from Thucydides' counsels about the dangers of democracy and demagogues. Thomas Gordon in his translation of Sallust's writings includes as part of his commentary the passage from Book III on the *stasis* at Corcyra and supplies a translation that equates the verbal fraud at Corcyra with Satanic seduction: "Such was the Blindness, as well as Fury, of this Civil Rage, that Good and Evil lost their Names and Application. Good was Evil; Evil was Good; just as Men, in seeing or doing either, were inspired by their Possessions."[30] John Adams cites a long passage from Thucydides' *History* on the *stasis* in the preface of *Defence of the Constitutions*, which he published a year before the calling of the Constitutional Convention to warn Americans about the dangers of faction and illustrate the need for a system of checks and balances in their republican institutions. Deeply disturbed again by party politics, he remarked in an 1812 letter to Jefferson (who was another avid reader of Thucydides) that when he reads Thucydides (and Tacitus) "I seem to be only reading the History of my own Times and my own Life."[31] In December 1844, Rufus Choate, a Whig lawyer, notes in his diary that he has begun reading a "great work" – Thucydides' *History* – because he sought "political lessons for his country," and he writes that a translator of Thucydides would add to "his means of counselling the people on the things of their peace" and "would have learned more of the uses and dangers of liberty, and the uses and dangers of union."[32] Nine months later he began such a translation. Francis Lieber, a professor of political philosophy, cites in his *Manual of Political Ethics* (1839) a passage from Thucydides on the *stasis*, and on the eve of the Civil War he notes in a letter to his son, who would later die fighting for the Confederacy while he supported the Union cause: "It sometimes has occurred to me that what Thucydides said of the Greeks at the time of the Peloponnesian War applies to us. The Greeks, he said, did not understand each other any longer, though they spoke Greek. Words received a different meaning in different parts."[33] Lieber never mailed the letter to his son. Oliver Wendell Holmes, Jr., who was wounded in the Civil War and who turned to the strictures of law as the certain force that would counter the forces that dismember order in "The House-top," could not abide Thucydides: "It isn't the kind of thing I like to read – just as I hate to read of our Civil War."[34]

The awfulness of Thucydides' portrait of the *stasis* at Corcyra needs no preface and no conclusion to make it more stark, but there is a preface – Pericles' Funeral Oration – that enables us to approach Thucydides' *History* as Hobbes and Adams approached it and as Melville approached the Civil War – to look upon it as a "great historic tragedy" that can "instruct . . . through terror and pity" (BP, 202). Just as Melville's view of the Civil War as tragedy depends on his keeping an eye fixed on the founding vision of the United States as a *novus ordo seclorum*, so too we can read the account of the *stasis* at Corcyra with an eye on the vision of the Athenian state that Pericles presents in the Funeral Oration, a speech that resounds with the very principles of a republic that would be limned in many American orations and in Lincoln's own memorial address at Gettysburg. Providing in his oration what could be called a grammar of republican principles, Pericles gives tribute to the ancestors of the Athenians whose courage, virtue, and sacrifice bequeathed to the present generation a free country. He reminds the citizens that their constitution, which reposes sovereignty in the "whole people" and guarantees every person equality before the law, is a model for other states. He points out that people are appointed to positions of public responsibility on the basis of merit, not class position, and that they respect and obey written and unwritten laws, especially "those which are for the protection of the oppressed" (2.36–8). He also reminds the people, after celebrating the freedom and openness of public and private life in Athens, that their success as an empire has depended on the courage and adventurous spirit of their citizens and on their willingness to participate in public affairs and subordinate their self-interest to the public good to the point of sacrificing their lives. And in a crucial passage Pericles declares, "We Athenians, in our own persons, take our decisions on policy or submit them to proper discussions: for we do not think that there is an incompatibility between words and deeds; the worst thing is to rush into action before the consequences have been properly debated" (2.40). At the center of this passage and, as Adam Parry argues, at the heart of Thucydides' *History* as a whole, governing its narrative strategies, is a relationship between *logos* and *ergon*, or variously between word and deed, theory and practice, thought and actuality.[35] The triumph of Athens in general, and of Pericles in particular, is the synthesis of *logos* and *ergon*. His policies are developed or guided by *logos*, and through the dynamic harmony of *logos* and *ergon* Athens has become a magisterial empire: "an education to Greece" (2.41).

But what Thucydides reveals soon after Pericles' oration, first in his account of the plague (2.47–53) and then in the *stasis* at Corcyra (3.82–4) and afterwards throughout the *History*, is a breakdown of that unity of word and deed. The correlation between human action and *logos* that occurred when the Athenians subjected themselves to a better sway than sway of self is shattered, for instance, when the successors of Pericles "adopted methods of demagogy" and "with an eye to personal ambition and private gain, . . . shaped policies for themselves" (2.65). Brutal assertion of an imperial self – the sovereign interests of Athens – against all claims to pity, to diplomacy, to decency, or to a discourse that respects others outside Athens similarly characterizes Cleon's final solution in his debate with Diodotus regarding the treatment of Mytilene, a city which had just surrendered to Athens (3.40). Soon thereafter, in the fallen world of the *stasis* at Corcyra, people manipulate words to suit the action, as opposed to Periclean Athens where actions are suited to words; in the *stasis*, that is, *ergon* – deeds of power, of *dynamis* – triumph over or subvert a transcendent *logos*. No longer is there a state where citizens impose an intellectual order, a city of words, on the world outside them, as did Orpheus with his music and as did Athene at the end of Aeschylus's *Oresteia*, wherein a cycle of violence is broken by the institution of legal proceedings and the subordination of *bia* (force) to *logos*, a subordination that occurs as the Eumenides are courted into submission by the *peitho* of Athene.[36] Now the force of things, the power of chance, the claims of necessity and of man's own atavistic nature intervene and dismember the order of language and law: ". . . these like a dream dissolve, / And man rebounds whole aeons back in nature." Now, in short, the aspiration to fulfill a *logos* or to constitute an order shaped in language and guided by the highest resources of the intellect is overcome by a frantic or self-interested resort to *logos* as the weapon of the war of all against all.

Thucydides' portrayal of a state of political and linguistic crisis in Corcyra and the use that Americans made of the passage can be better understood if we review a remarkably similar passage in Book VIII of Plato's *Republic* that John Adams also comments on in *A Defence of the Constitutions* and if we also gain an understanding of what Plato meant by the word *anatrope*, a term that describes the semantic and ethical inversion of values that occurs during the Thucydidean moment. Plato composed his dialogues in the aftermath of the Athenian debacles in the Peloponnesian War and the collapse of its democracy. Close relatives of his were leaders of an oligarchic or antidemocratic faction that participated in struggles for power in Athens. Often considered the model of a detached philosopher pursuing the transcendent truth, Plato (at least in his political philosophy) needs to be read in part as a footnote to Thucydides, for only then can we appreciate how and why he gave us, in John Adams's opinion, "the most accurate detail of the natural vicissitudes of manners and principles, the usual progress of the passions in society, and revolutions of government into one another" (JAW, IV, 448). Like many great works of political philosophy, *The Republic* can be conceived of as both a diagnosis and cure for the Thucydidean moment, or, in Garry Wills's words, *The Republic* is another example that the "great breakthroughs in political theory have often been gigantic efforts at talking people into order when society has taken on the logic of a barroom brawl." Wills suggests, for instance, that Plato, Hobbes, Locke, and Rousseau were each driven in the midst of political crisis "to make newer, deeper arguments for resuming mutual obligations, patching up the intestine quarrels that society has become in their darkest vision."[37] Just as these four political philosophers explored means for resuming the mutual obligations between man and man in a political society, so too did they explore means as theorists of language for founding on a new or more authentic basis the relationship between a word and its referent. For them, as for Thucydides, the breakdown of a political community was at once political, moral, and linguistic, and thus the constitution of a more perfect republic required in their view a reconstruction of linguistic as well as political theory and practice. *The Republic* thus needs to be read in relation to Plato's critique and rehabilitation of rhetoric in the *Gorgias* and the *Phaedrus*.

In Book VIII Plato establishes a chain of correspondences between the moral nature of man and the political principles of his society as his dialogue treats the processes that threaten to subvert the stability of the ideal society. The links that Plato forges among "the progress of the passions," "revolutions of governments," and the insidious trickery of rhetoric in Book VIII are the links that connect together in Adams's mind (and in the minds of many of his contemporaries, including the authors of *The Federalist*) the dangers of democracy and rhetoric and confirm in their minds the need to sustain a republic through the creation of a constitution for the state and the soul that is capable of counterbalancing demagoguery with deliberation or rhetoric with dialectic.

For Plato, there are five types of political constitution, and there is a type of individual soul or inner constitution that corresponds to each political constitution. According to him, the best type of political constitution is government by the best, a natural aristocracy in which the rulers or guardians of the city are philosopher-kings, and the best type of individual soul is the good and just man, the man in whom reason and truth reign. In Book VIII Plato chronicles a series of political and psychological transformations in which the city and its citizens decline from the best type of constitution to the worst, a decline that begins because of what Adams also feared and what Madison sought to neutralize: factions within the body of ruling citizens. In descending order, the ideal city and its citizens degenerate from the just man (a seeker of the good) to the timocratic man (a seeker of honor), the oligarch (a seeker of wealth), the democrat (a seeker of unrestrained liberty), and the tyrant (a seeker of power). This degeneration is Plato's version of the world turned upside down: the citizens depose the natural *aristoi* and are themselves deposed by the tyrant; analogously, the "lawless passions" depose reason and are themselves subjected to the rule of force. Plato uses the term *anatrope* to describe this process of social and moral inversion. As John Wild explains in *Plato's Theory of Man*, "the expressive noun *anatrope* (inversion) or the corresponding verb . . . (to invert)" involves the "complex, dynamic confusion which lies at the root of moral and evil sin." For Plato, Wild adds, the word *anatrope*, which literally means to turn upside down or to turn over, and is often used of ships capsizing, refers to "the miscarriage of human action involving misapprehension of the hierarchical structure of means and ends."[38] In his discussion of Plato's conception of *anatrope*, Wild emphasizes the fundamental importance in Plato's work of the contrast between the true, upward way of life – the ascent toward the light and the idea of the good – and the downward way: the descent into the cave that appears to be an ascent. No man, Plato points out, would choose to go down simply for the sake of going down, for men by nature seek the good. But since the good and the bad (e.g., liberty and licentiousness) are closely linked, even though they are opposites, they are readily confused. Not just the delusive powers of the imagination and the lawless passions, but words themselves as imitations twice removed from the real, can trip us up and make us mistake the bad for the good and down for up.

In the later sections of Book VIII, when the city and the individual soul degenerate from oligarchy into democracy, the process of social and moral inversion occurs as a corollary of verbal inversion: virtue is mistaken for vice and vice for virtue because of a reversal in the meanings of words. Terms are turned upside down, emptied of their own content, and filled with a new meaning that contradicts the old one. Or, to borrow words from John Dos Passos that recall the process of inversion as Plato describes it, "slogans and phrases that yesterday pointed steadily toward the lodestar of good today spin waveringly round the compass and tomorrow may have taken on meanings opposite from the meaning they started with. A moral judgment will turn inside out on you overnight."[39] In the heat of the Thucydidean moment, words change their valences: terms with a negative value, like "equality for the masses," can become positive if equality is reconceived as a natural right, and a positive term, such as "liberty," can become negative if liberty is reconceived to signify not the right to participate in government but merely the sanction to pursue one's self-interest. The passage in *The Republic* chronicling this moral, social, and verbal inversion must be examined closely. It provides an etiology for the type of political and linguistic corruption Thucydides describes during the upheaval in Corcyra. Here again, as in Thucydides, the warring factions that turn words and the world upside down are the oligarchic and democratic parties.

Plato begins by portraying the conflict between the oligarchic and democratic factions in Book VIII as a revolutionary battle inside the individual soul of a young man, a battle that begins in large part because of the father's "illiberal and niggardly" education of the youth.[40] For Plato, the battle between the oligarchic and democratic factions is also an internal strife between necessary and unnecessary desires. During the strife, the youth's father and his kin attempt to rescue him, and they succeed at one point in expelling the democratic desires. But owing to the "father's ignorance of true education" their victory is short-lived; the democratic desires, "stealthily nurtured," eventually "seize the citadel of the young man's soul, finding it empty and unoccupied by studies and honorable pursuits and true discourses, which are the best watchmen and guardians in the minds of men who are dear to the gods" (788; 560b–c). Left unguarded because of an improper education and weakened within by democratic desires, the citadel of the soul is an easy target for a sneak attack. There is no

Hector-like "true discourse" within the walls to come to the defense of the youth and oppose words as treacherous as a Trojan horse and as boisterous as Ajax. "And then false and braggart words and opinions charge up the height and take their place and occupy that part of such a youth" (788; 560c). As the occupation succeeds, the situation turns hopeless for the youth's kin, and the revolution continues within the youth's soul. "And if any support comes from his kin to the thrifty element in his soul, those braggart discourses close the gates of the royal fortress within him and refuse admission to the auxiliary force itself, and will not grant audience as to envoys to the words of older friends in private life" (789; 560d). With the lines of communication to the outside cut, the victory of the revolution is sealed. The triumphant force in this logomachy between "braggart words" and "true discourses" gains both the power to purge the defeated and the power to define or the power to change the charge on words from positive to negative and vice versa: "And they [braggart discourses] themselves prevail in the conflict, and naming reverence and awe 'folly' thrust it forth, a dishonored fugitive. And temperance they call 'want of manhood' and banish it with contumely, and they teach that moderation and orderly expenditure are 'rusticity' and 'illiberality,' and they combine with a gang of unprofitable and harmful appetites to drive them over the border" (789; 560d). This purge and exile are the antithesis of Plato's banishment of the poets from his ideal republic in Book X. There the true banish the false; here the false banish the true. There the philosophers banish a rhetorical force; here a rhetorical force banishes reason. After the takeover and purge, the exiled democratic desires are invited to return.

> And when they have emptied and purged of all these the soul of the youth that they have thus possessed and occupied, and whom they are initiating with these magnificent and costly rites, they proceed to lead home from exile insolence and anarchy and prodigality and shamelessness, resplendent in a great attendant choir and crowned with garlands, and in celebration of their praises they euphemistically denominate insolence "good breeding," license "liberty," prodigality "magnificence," and shamelessness "manly spirit." (789; 560e)

The transformation in the youth from "the restriction to necessary desires" to the "liberties and release of his unnecessary and harmful desires" occurs in part through the confusion caused by misrepresentation and euphemisms. Good ideas are branded with bad names and are exiled; hallowed names are retained but are given a new content that opposes all they had represented. The democratic revolution within the youth combined with the confusion from bestowing fair

names on vices and foul names on virtues destroys his ability to
distinguish true from false and good from bad, a loss that leads to a
dangerous reign of equality: "And he does not accept or admit into the
guardhouse the words of truth when anyone tells him that some
pleasures arise from honorable and good desires, and others from those
that are base, and that we ought to practice and esteem that one and
control and subdue the others, but he shakes his head at all such
admonitions and avers that they are all alike and to be equally es-
teemed" (789; 561c). When all things are equal, there are no differences, and with the death of differences comes the birth of violence
and chaos, as René Girard explains in *Violence and the Sacred* and as
Ulysses argues in Shakespeare's *Troilus and Cressida*:

> O, when Degree is shaked . . .
> Force should be right, or rather right and wrong –
> Between whose endless jar justice resides –
> Should lose their names, and so should justice too.
>   (I.iii.101, 116–18)

"The cultural order," Girard asserts, "is nothing more than a
regulated system of differences," a system of distinctions established
or at least confirmed by our words.[41] Language divides into parts – it
articulates – an undifferentiated whole, and the shared understanding
of those distinctions constitutes the foundation of a social order. When
in the Thucydidean moment the customary distinctions are muddled
or transgressed as words are stretched casuistically beyond their established boundaries – when, for instance, the word "justice" is deployed
to sanction a brutal act of revenge or to describe a show trial or when
war is peace and freedom is slavery – then beckons the breakdown of
community. Consensus yields to ambiguity or to a conflict of contradictions, a polarization between an oldspeak (justice as due process of
law) and a newspeak (justice as revenge or the mask of power). The
mix-up between what was once held in opposition and the mimetic
rivalry between opposing parties fighting to possess the same concept
(e.g., justice, freedom) may be resolved only through violence.
    The word, as Bakhtin reminds us, is a primary scene of political
conflict; its multiple definitions are a microcosmic incarnation of
debate between parties or factions in the political forum. This duplicity or equivocality of the word – what Bakhtin calls the "*inner dialectic
quality* of the sign" – is muted in periods of ideological consensus, but it
becomes manifest in times of revolutionary struggle and in the Thucydidean moment.[42] The openness of the word to contradiction becomes
in this moment a political, linguistic, and moral crisis that cries out for
resolution. Yet the confusion of this moment can lead to enlighten-

ment and liberation. The recognition of an incongruity between word and action, a perception of corrupt naming or of verbal duplicity, can foment moments of sustained reflection, of fundamental questioning and redefinition. If this act called just is not just, then what is justice? Such questions can cultivate the ground for a new or reconstructed vision of a republic – the place where Plato conducts us after Book VIII and the place where Aeschylus leads us in the *Oresteia*. His trilogy reminds us that justice as due legal process was once a newspeak countering an oldspeak of justice as revenge. The transformation from old law to new law in the final scene is itself facilitated by the persuasive newspeak of Athene, a benevolent Big Sister. The unfastening of words in the Thucydidean moment – or the exposure of a word's equivocality – can be the prelude to a new order of the ages. As people become more self-conscious about the politics of naming because of verbal duplicity, they may act collectively to overcome *stasis* through redefinition. More ominously, however, the unsettling of an old vocabulary can provoke nostalgia for the return of the old order and thus portend the reign of the tyrant who will impose rule by force of arms and the fraud of euphemism ("Force should be right" etc.). The topsy-turvy world of the Thucydidean moment, like the antistructure worlds of the carnival and *communitas* described by Bakhtin and Victor Turner, is never one of unlimited duration.[43] Nor does a social order long sustain the equal value of contradictory voices. Authority resists the claims of equivocation, and while the fate of Macbeth and Ahab manifests the dangers of such resistance, the vision of a time when equivocality (or multivocality) yields to univocality – the state of *e pluribus unum* – remains a powerful ideal (or the ideal of the powerful).

From Thucydides and Plato to Orwell and beyond, we can find writers commenting upon (or constructing) a pattern of political and linguistic corruption: words lose their original meaning and become a means of deception and domination. Fine words decoy political machinations. The very gift of speech that enabled Orpheus and Amphion to build the walls of the city turns traitor and opens a breach in the walls it had helped to build. The city falls victim to verbal Trojan horses – to words as hollow and deceitful as gifts bearing Greeks. In the aftermath, the gift of speech is recognized to be a tool of power. The language that constructs the walls of the city becomes a prison.[44]

In Western culture, verbal skepticism and fear about the tyranny of words have often come to the center of cultural politics in the midst or aftermath of war and civil strife. Major works of linguistic and rhetorical criticism have arisen during the darkness of the Thucydidean moment. This is when Hermes has so often taken flight, guided by the owl of Minerva. Consider, for a moment, the period that followed World War II. The postmodern critique of the word has many roots, and this is not the place to historicize it, but here I call to witness some testimony drawn primarily from American sources in order to provide an additional vantage point – a reverse angle – for viewing the development in the early United States of the classical paradigm regarding political and linguistic corruption.

Addressing the situation of the writer in 1947, Jean-Paul Sartre in *What Is Literature?* describes a "crisis of language" fomented in part by the linguistic machinations of politics that Plato describes. "Each party," he writes, "shoves them [words] forward like Trojan horses, and we let them enter because they make the nineteenth-century meaning of the words shine before us. Once they are in place, they open up, and strange, astounding meanings spread out within us like armies; the fortress is taken before we are on guard." Sartre's response is to call upon writers to clean their instrument, "call a spade a spade," and "re-establish language in its dignity."[45] In England, George Orwell responds to his own vision of a crisis of language in Western politics with an essay and a novel that popularized the reciprocal relationship between corruption and tyranny in politics, language and thought. When "Politics and the English Language" appeared in 1946 and *1984* two years later, the battle against the bewitchment of the understanding by language was given a new terminology; it became a war against Newspeak and Doublethink, and under Orwell's leadership, an allied force of critics, semanticists, and commentators has continued to fight propaganda and save a declining English language. On the Continent, under the leadership of Foucault and Derrida, the weapons of criticism have been modernized with state-of-the-art jargon, but the fight remains much the same: the power that has invaded the realm of discourse/knowledge must be resisted and the capitulators exposed.[46]

The classic American counterpart to Sartre's and Orwell's critique and treatment of political discourse in the aftermath of World War II is Kenneth Burke's *A Rhetoric of Motives*. Written in 1950 as a companion work to *A Grammar of Motives*, which took as its motto "Ad bellum purificandum" (Toward the purification of war), Burke's *Rhetoric* is often highly reminiscent of Thucydides' description of the *stasis* at Corcyra in its analysis of the rhetoric of human relations. As a form of logotherapy for that logomachy, it draws upon the methods of Platonic dialectic. Just as Plato's *Republic* seeks to lead citizens from the corruption of the city and soul typified in Book VIII to a vision of the just state and a transcendence of the pursuit of honor, wealth, sensual desire, and power in pursuit of the Good, the end of Burke's philosophy of rhetoric is a dialectical understanding of language itself – and the transcendence of war in a vision of more perfect forms of communion and communication.[47] The first step of his study is a descent into the cave: he directs our attention to the rhetoric and imagery of the kill. The *Rhetoric*, he explains, "must lead us through the Scramble, the Wrangle of the Market Place, the flurries and flare-ups of the Human Barnyard, the Give and Take, the wavering line of pressure and counterpressure, the Logomachy, the onus of ownership, the War of Nerves, the War."[48] War for Burke is, in its essence, a "perversion of communion," a consequence of diseased cooperation and communication, and whichever way he looked in 1950 – whether toward the past of capitalist imperialism, Hitler's *Mein Kampf*, and World War II, or toward the future of the Cold War – he saw signs of that corruption. The "order of killing, of personal enmity, of factional strife, of invective, polemic, eristic, logomachy," he asserts, are all "aspects of rhetoric that we are repeatedly and drastically encountering, since rhetoric is *par excellence* the region of Scramble, of insult and injury, bickering, squabbling, malice and the lie, cloaked malice and the subsidized lie" (19). Burke's diagnosis of this corrupt rhetoric confirms the earlier opinions of Thucydides and Plato; it is a symptom of "the presence of strife, enmity, faction" rankling within the body politic. In the sobering tone of Thucydides, he then advises, "We need not close our eyes to their almost tyrannous ubiquity in human relations; we can be on the alert always to see how such temptations to strife are implicit in the institutions that condition human relationships" (20). War – and Marx's analysis of the class war – is Burke's sternest teacher. Confronted with this war and the rhetoric of the human barnyard, he offers an antidote. He juxtaposes a discourse whose motives are rooted in resources of appeal ranging from "sacrificial, evangelical love, through the kinds of persuasion figuring in sexual love, to sheer 'neutral' *communication* [i.e., the sheer pleasure of talking together]" (19). This discourse, like Whitman's poetics of union, is a rhetoric of cooperation and identification, a rhetoric grounded in love, a rhetoric, we might say, of evangelical inspiration whose transcendent goal is a fulfillment of the possibilities of the word as a counter to the world as given and as the agency of a people acting together to attain unity in difference, a union built not through exclusion but inclusion. "For genuine peace today could be got only by such a dialectic as risked 'contamination' by the enemy. Or rather, by such a dialectic as sought deliberately to give full expression to the voice of the enemy, not excluding it, but seeking to assign it an active place in an ultimate order" (263). Burke, however, does not leave us finally in an optative mood about attaining such a bipolar union or transcendence of opposites: "In sum: On every hand, we find men, in their quarrels over property, preparing themselves for the slaughter, even to the extent of manipulating their profoundest grammatical, rhetorical, and symbolic resources of human thought to this end" (264).

A dozen years later, at the height of the Cold War, Edmund Wilson writes a literary history of a people who, in the midst of a quarrel over property, are goaded in the name of the profoundest rhetorical resources of its culture – the Declaration, the Constitution, and the Bible – to slaughter each other in patriotic gore. Evidently deeply troubled in 1962 about how Americans "have been adding such terms as 'the American dream,' 'the American way of life' and the 'defense of the Free World' to other forms of warlike cant," Wilson argues in the introduction to *Patriotic Gore* that the country had forgotten the Mexican War and tried to forget the lessons of the Civil War. His great study of Civil War literature thus seeks to remind us that "the difference . . . between man and the other forms of life is that man has succeeded in cultivating enough of what he calls 'morality' and 'reason' to justify what he is doing in terms of what he calls 'virtue' and 'civilization.' Hence the self-assertive sounds which he utters when he is fighting and swallowing others: the songs about glory and God, the speeches about national ideals, the demonstrations of logical ideologies." In a comment that further captures the semantic inversion and confusion that occur in the Thucydidean moment, Wilson adds, "These assertions rarely have any meaning – that is, they will soon lose any meaning they have had – once a war has been got under way." Convinced as were Jeremy Bentham and Friedrich Nietzsche that moral terms are the *agents provocateurs* and special strike force of the will to power, Wilson at the end of his introduction offers counsel for chastening the rhetoric of United States foreign policy: "I want to suggest – headed as we seem to have been, for a blind collision with the Soviet Union – we ought to stop talking in terms of 'oppressors' and 'criminals,' our old patter of 'right' and 'wrong' and punishing the guilty party."[49]

For many Americans, the defense of the indefensible by supporters and critics of the Vietnam War and the specious morality of Watergate confirmed and deepened the distrust of political and moral rhetoric captured in Wilson's introduction to *Patriotic Gore*. Beginning in the mid 1960s, concern – even fear and paranoia – on the left for what Herbert Marcuse termed the "closing of the universe of discourse" became widespread; and it was soon matched by trepidation on the right that America was becoming the death of the English language.[50] The culprits charged with abusing the language were legion: politicians, the media, ad men, the Establishment, the youth movement. Marcuse's manifesto of 1969, *An Essay on Liberation*, condemns (as does Sallust's Cato) the semantic inversions of the oligarchical party while it offers (in the manner of Plato) a guide to "linguistic therapy" or "the effort to free words (and thereby concepts) from the all but total distortion of their meanings by the Establishment."[51] Dedicated to students seeking to liberate themselves from what he calls the "rules and regulations of a pseudo-democracy in a Free Orwellian World," his essay is an attempt to penetrate the "armor of the Establishment" – their "political linguistics" – and aid the radical opposition in developing a new language of freedom (x, 73). Arguing that the one-dimensional order sustains its hegemony by monopolizing the discourse of law and ethics (and thus coercing our perceptions of right and wrong, just and unjust), he calls upon readers to smash "the ideological context" in which "words are employed and defined" and place "them in the opposite context – negation of the established one" (35). The charged verbal missiles fired from behind the barricades to disperse the dissent of the unruly must be hurled back like tear-gas cannisters to disrupt the masked violence of the establishment's law and language. "Obscenity," Marcuse argues, for instance, "is not the picture of a naked woman who exposes her pubic hair but that of a fully clad general who exposes his medals rewarded in a war of aggression; obscene is not the ritual of the Hippies but the declaration of a high dignitary of the Church that war is necessary for peace" (8).

Of all the critiques of political linguistics in the late 1960s, perhaps none is more inspired than Norman Mailer's *Armies of the Night*, his account of the 1967 March on the Pentagon. This book, which follows Mailer's *Why Are We in Vietnam?* in challenging the obscenity of "burning unseen women and children in the Vietnamese jungle" with the noble obscenity of the vernacular voice, could be regarded in part as the *Dunciad* of the sixties; it is at once a satire on mobs and tyrants and a jeremiad against all the forces of the deadening letter who were killing the spirit of the Word in America and bringing on the armies of the night.[52] Just as in Book VIII of *The Republic*, the psyche of an individual and the state of the republic mirror each other. The landscape of Mailer's mind, like the darkling plain around the Pentagon, is a staging ground for the drama of democracy which proceeds, as Ellison reminds us, through "a warfare of words and symbolic actions by which we seek to advance our private interests while resolving our political differences."[53] Indeed, inside Mailer's mind and outside in Washington, D.C., there is a *stasis*: a conflict of desires, a raging battle of interests, a civil war of representations and misrepresentations between the left and conservative parties. Locked in competition, struggling on a common ground, seeking to occupy the hearts and minds of the people are the divergent voices of the republic, and Mailer is willing to do battle against them all in his own representative quest for liberty. Almost as caustic as his protest against the Vietnam War is Mailer's protest against the oppressive rhetoric of politicians and protesters, the Establishment and the new left. Like Brackenridge's *Modern Chivalry*, *Armies* is at once a stylistic and a political critique of the excesses and foibles of American democracy. Mailer gives us complaint upon complaint and scene after scene of minds infiltrated or drugged into dullness by the wordslingers of the United States. But against the bullshit of LBJ's "Upper Rhetoric" (i.e., "the Rhetoric . . . located three inches below and back of Erogenous Zone Clitoric"), which he elsewhere calls "totalitarian prose," and against the logorrhea running from the mouth of the media and middle-class liberals, Mailer juxtaposes the "noble shit" of the vernacular, the poetry of Robert Lowell and the erogenous-zone rhetoric of his own fantasized and consummated speechmaking: a rhetoric of words on fire with love and passion for the America of romantic and revolutionary dreams, the "tormented lovely girl" who might "deliver a babe of a new world brave and tender, artful and wild" but who has now become an "awful deadening programmatic inhuman dowager of a nation, corporation, and press" (320, 133).[54] If Mailer is as vehement as Pope in his scorn for the uncreating word, he is as passionate as Whitman in his dream for an erotics of speech – an evangelical rhetoric – that will draw upon what he calls the "incommensurable resources" of the American language to create a more perfect union by stimulating in a divided country a shared vision of love for the will of God and the will of the people: ". . . for the will of the people – if the locks of their life could be given the art to turn – was the will of God" (62, 320). But "liars controlled the locks" (320). Mailer's own art of words is keyed to turn the locks; it must rescue the people from the liars – the cave of misperception and misrepresentation. In this book, as in works penned by Stowe and Melville in the 1850s, the corruptions and confusions of the Thucydidean moment must be countered by a dialectics of speech which will clarify the country's vision of itself and of its grounding in the often muddied and now perverted language of the founding fathers and the Word of God. "You see, dear fellow Americans, it is Sunday, and we are burning the body and blood of Christ in Vietnam. Yes, we are burning him there, and as we do, we destroy the foundation of this Republic, which is its love and trust in Christ" (239). "And if it [the written word] is ill-treated or unfairly abused it always needs its parent to come to its rescue," counsels Socrates in Plato's *Phaedrus* (275e). Mailer, enacting the role made famous by Abraham Lincoln, plays the memorialist and the heroic son in the drama of American democracy: he pays tribute to the marchers who, in an "echo of far greater rites of passage in American history," manacled themselves until the dawn of Sunday to a "painful principle" (311), and he comes to rescue the word of the father by seeking to grow its seeds in ground manured by the "noble shit" of the vernacular and cultivated by what Plato called the "art of dialectic" – the art that "plants and sows" seeds of truth and knowledge "from which fresh truths spring up in other minds" (277e) and which Emerson describes in his chapter on Plato in *Representative Men* as "the Intellect discriminating the false and the true" through "the observation of identity and diversity" (ELA, 645).

Plato's own experience of worldly politics, like Mailer's in 1967 (or Melville's in the year of *The Confidence-Man*), must have reinforced if it did not form his conviction that the sensible world was one in which the words of representative media clouded perception of the truth and where opinion passed for knowledge and thus a world in dire need of logotherapy. In *The Republic*, Socrates asserts that the multitude have only heard "the forced and artificial chiming of word and phrase" and have never been "seriously inclined to hearken to fair and free discussions whose sole endeavor was to search out the truth at any cost for knowledge's sake," and he adds that such discussions "dwell apart and salute from afar all the subtleties and cavils that lead to nought but opinion and strife in courtroom and private talk" (734; 499a–b). Plato's retreat from the forum and the courtroom to the philosophical academy was a retreat from the temporal, the relative, and the probable – the world of democratic politics – to a haven for "fair and free discussions" whose end would be to understand the Idea of the Good, the Beautiful, the Just, and other eternal concepts that could not be manipulated. "For surely," Socrates remarks, ". . . the man whose mind is truly fixed on eternal realities has no leisure to turn his eyes downward upon the petty affairs of men . . . but he fixes his gaze upon the things of the eternal and unchanging order" (735; 500c). But for the Sophists, no such retreat was possible. The world of man, the speaking animal, was a rhetorical world: a community of speech in which citizens create for themselves rather than discover the Good, the Beautiful, the Just. The discourse of the Sophists, Eric Havelock asserts, "is social or it is nothing; its topics and problems are by definition common ones, group notions; the words of men act on other men and vice versa. There is an exchange of opinion, discovery of common opinion, consensus and decision. It is not a discourse carried on in the private soul." In the political world of the Sophists, he points out, "there cannot be any question of going outside current discourse to discover the language of justice, nor of transcending current opinion in order to define its sources."[55] But for Plato the discourse of the Sophists was the discourse of the agora or of a marketplace where words are exchanged solely for profit and self-interest.

Plato, in opposition to the Sophists, retreats from the politics and rhetoric of the agora for the realm of contemplation and the dialogue of reason. Rather than to flatter the populace and cater to their desires, as he accused the Sophists of doing, his goal – and the goal he sets forth for the ideal statesmen – is to give "those desires a different direction instead of allowing them free scope, by persuading and compelling citizens to adopt courses that would improve them" (*Gorgias*, 298; 517c). Plato's model of discourse (and of politics) is educative, not economic; the purpose of discourse in a philosophic symposium (or in a political congress) is to challenge rather than serve what Emerson called our "secondary desires" – "the desire of riches, of pleasure, of power, and of praise."[56] The philosopher as a teacher has to cultivate in the city of man a dialogue counter to the prose of the world that would at once weed out false discourse and plant within the soul what Socrates calls in the *Phaedrus* the seeds of "words founded on knowledge" from which "new words" could "grow up in other characters" (522; 277a). Indeed, the mission of the historic Socrates, and of Plato the philosopher, as Brian Vickers describes it, was to point out to fellow citizens "their corruption of values, to set philosophy against politics and against rhetoric, its tool and medium."[57] Through the discipline of a philosophic education with its training in the analytic power of dialectic and the revisioning of words, Plato believed that the *anatrope* or inversion of the city of man that occurs in Book VIII could be avoided. Education in his eyes could be both revolutionary and conservative; it could turn the soul from the downward to the upward path, from the dark to the light, from the "prevalence of secondary desires" to the "sovereignty of ideas," and it could fortify the soul with studies, honorable pursuits, and true discourses, the guardians the soul needs to prevent false discourse from entering the royal fortress while securing safe passage for the true. The first line of defense was to expose discourse itself in its duplicity, in its double aspects as not just an imperfect representative tool but as a sovereign force.

The Sophist Gorgias, who figures as an opponent of Socrates in one of Plato's dialogues, captures in a word some of the dual aspects of discourse when he calls language in his "Encomium on Helen" a *pharmakon*, a remedy and a poison, a drug that can induce health or sickness and give pleasure or "bewitch the soul."[58] In this address, which exists only in fragments, Gorgias also calls speech "a great power, which achieves the most divine works by means of the smallest and least visible form; for it can even put a stop to fear, remove grief, create joy, and increase pity."[59] But if speech is divine, it is also demonic or all too human; it can seduce, ravish, and rule. "Persuasion by speech is equivalent to abduction by force," Gorgias asserts, and the art of rhetoric, one recent critic writes, "lies in concealing this equivalence, turning rape into seduction."[60] Plato, as a prosecutor of the Sophists, seeks to expose this equivalence and banish their rhetorical practice. But he also advances the prospect of rehabilitating rhetoric. In his reconstructed city, the tyrannical power of rhetoric would be governed and its bewitching force rationalized by rhetoric's being subordinated to the love of wisdom – to philosophy.[61] For Plato, that is, eloquence had to be ruled by the virtue of knowledge, just as the passions had to be ruled by reason and just as the people had to be ruled by a philosopher-king. But the politics of the Greek polis nurtured a different approach to language that militated against Plato's hierarchy. The spirit of democratic politics demands, as Benjamin Barber points out, a community of speech within which the power to determine the meanings of the words of that community is dispersed and shared among equals rather than commanded by an elite. "If the definition of democracy as popular sovereignty has any meaning, then it is sovereignty over language – over talk fashioned by and for the talkers themselves."[62] But while the Greeks sought to make speech the alternative to force, they also recognized that speech was the equal of force. "In the life of man," says Odysseus in Sophocles' *Philoctetes*, "it is the tongue and not the act, that governs all."[63]

In a fascinating study of Christopher Marlowe's *Tamburlaine* and the origins of Elizabethan tragedy, Michael Roberts suggests most succinctly how the changing political contexts of the classical world shaped attitudes toward language and rhetoric when he points out that not only Greek drama but "rising Attic culture as a whole, had been premised at least in part upon an attitude towards language as itself a mode of action, forceful, vital, and expressive" and that "an active and largely democratic oratory which had an essential role to play in the maintenance of the Greek city-state served to keep this approach to language alive."[64] He continues:

> But when ultimately occasions for oratory diminished during the Hellenistic centuries (as once again at Rome when basic freedoms began to be lost under the Caesars) lip service inevitably arose and a kind of formal rhetoric which in practice reduced language to the

level of ornament and the ideal of eloquence itself to a virtuosity
divorced from life. Rhetoric, in short, now became an art, and it was
this late and greatly confined rhetorical study, cut off as it was from
the vital functions of persuasion, which must be said to have colored
the attitude towards expressive language throughout the post-classi-
cal period.[65]

The importance of Roberts's discussion to a study of the relationship
between politics and language in the United States should be obvious
and suggestive. He describes a connection that was a fundamental
equation of early republican politics and culture between the rise of
republics, where persuasive speech reigns as political power, and the
flourishing of a "bold, nervous, lofty language." Conversely, if arms
or cash or any other form of coercion or manipulation replaces open
political debate as the medium of politics – if power, in other words, is
detached from the activity of speech in the forum – then language
becomes not potent but flaccid, not virtuous but corrupt, while the
rhetorical discipline retreats, in Terry Eagleton's words, from
"market place to study, politics to philology, social practice to semiotics."[66] This connection between forms of government and qualities
of linguistic practice was an essential truism of the political literature
and literary criticism of the Neoclassical period in England and America: the dark side of the connection underlies Pope's argument in *The
Dunciad* that with the advent of tyranny comes the death of the
creating word, and the bright side appears in a letter John Adams
wrote in 1780 advocating the establishment of an "American Academy
for refining, improving, and ascertaining the English language." "As
eloquence," he begins, "is cultivated with more care in free republics
than in other governments, it has been found by constant experience
that such republics have produced the greatest purity, copiousness, and
perfection of language" (JAW, VII, 249).[67] He then comes to the
almost inevitable conclusion of a classical scholar and a republican
patriot: "The admirable models which have been transmitted through
the world, and continued down to these days, so as to form an essential
part of the education of mankind from generation to generation, by
those two ancient towns, Athens and Rome, would be sufficient,
without any other argument, to show the United States the importance to their liberty, prosperity, and glory, of an early attention to
the subject of eloquence and language" (ibid.). Convinced, as is
Adams, that a republic is "the orator's natal soil," a speaker at the
graduation of the Harvard Class of 1794 goes beyond Adams to declare
an exalted destiny for eloquence in America. In a commencement
address that Caleb Bingham included in his *Columbian Orator*, the

speaker asks, "And when did Greece or Rome present a fairer field for eloquence than that which invites the culture of enlightened citizens of Columbia?" The answer is a patriotic one: "Never had eloquence more ample scope" than here in this country where "*real merit* is . . . required as a qualification for the most dignified offices of state" and where Americans "cannot fail in time to raise Columbian eloquence 'above all Greece, above all Roman fame.'"[68] The lessons of *The Columbian Orator* were not lost on Frederick Douglass, who achieved his literacy partly through the study of this text and who offered his own life as a text that taught the inextricable connection between the pursuit of eloquence and liberty.

What the speaker of this address on oratory never mentions, however, and what John Adams does not address in his 1780 proposal, but what his son, John Quincy Adams, would confront in his lectures on rhetoric and oratory at Harvard and what the authors of *The Federalist* could never forget is that if eloquence is the child of liberty, it can also be, as Plato and Tacitus warned, the parent of sedition and tyranny. "No; the great and famous eloquence of old," counters Tacitus in his *Dialogue on Oratory*, "is the nursling of the license which fools called freedom; it is the companion of sedition, the stimulant of an unruly people, a stranger to obedience and subjection, a defiant, reckless, presumptuous thing which does not show itself in a well-governed state."[69] Just as oxygen nourishes life, eloquence nourishes liberty, or so John Adams and his son assert, but Madison and Hamilton feared that in nourishing liberty eloquence could ignite the passions of a people into a conflagration of mob action or hasten the moment when one voice consuming all the air would suffocate the dialogue among the plurality of voices that was so necessary for a democracy. "In the ancient republics, where the whole body of the people assembled in person, a single orator, or an artful statesman, was generally seen to rule with as complete a sway as if a scepter had been placed in his single hand," Hamilton observes in *Federalist* No. 59 (FP, 59. 360). Convinced that an overly large representative assembly would breed the same diseases that infected and killed ancient republics, Hamilton adds that in such an assembly "ignorance will be the dupe of cunning, and passion the slave of sophistry and declamation" (ibid.). Indignant at the eloquent detractors of eloquence who contend that upon "every breeze her breath wings the pestilence of sedition, or kindles the flames of unextinguishable war" and that it is "an insidious appeal to the passions" and "the weapon of faction," John Quincy Adams calls upon his students to silence the detractors with a "great and overpowering truth": "Say, that by the eternal constitution of things it was ordained, that liberty should be the parent of eloquence; that eloquence should be the last stay and support of liberty" (LR, I, 63, 72). The experiment of the American republic and the trial of the Civil War would test, among other things, the self-evidence of this truth and require in the end a reconstruction of this "eternal constitution." More than one writer was provoked in mid-nineteenth-century America to repeat or echo Tacitus's famous condemnation of the Romans for expanding their empire through the meanness of force and justifying their imperialism through the meanness of rhetorical fraud: "To spoil, to slaughter, and to commit every violence; and then call the manoeuvre by a lying name, – government; and when they have spread a general devastation, – call it peace."[70] Eloquence, paired so often as the bride of liberty in the classical rhetorical tradition, must also be figured as the whore of empire.

4

The Christian Typology:
From Eden to Babel to Pentecost

On this Western hemisphere all tribes and people are forming into one federated whole; and there is a future which shall see the estranged children of Adam restored to the old hearth-stone in Eden. . . . Then shall the curse of Babel be revoked, a new Pentecost come.

Herman Melville, *Redburn*

For Henry James, the Civil War was a "great convulsion" that brought about the loss of an innocent new world in America, and for Herman Melville the conflict between North and South challenged the "Founders' dream" that America could begin and build a government founded on a higher power than force. "The Civil War," James declares, "marks an era in the history of the American mind. It introduced into the national consciousness a certain sense of proportion and relation, of the world being a more complicated place than it had hitherto seemed, the future more treacherous, success more difficult. . . . The good American, in days to come, will be a more critical person than his complacent and confident grandfather. He has eaten of the tree of knowledge."[1] In one of his Civil War poems, "The Conflict of Convictions," Melville also turns to biblical (and Miltonic) imagery to portray the war as "man's latter fall" from grace.

> Return, return, O eager Hope
>   And face man's latter fall.
> Events, they make the dreamers quail;
> Satan's old age is strong and hale.
>   (BP, 37)

In the last stanza, Melville describes the probable loss of another vision of paradise:

99

> Power unanointed may come –
> Dominion (unsought by the free)
>   And the Iron Dome,
> Stronger for stress and strain,
> Fling her huge shadow athwart the main;
> But the Founders' dream shall flee.
>
>   (BP, 40)

The increase in federal power needed to restore the Union and give freedom to the slaves is an increase that threatens the founders' dream that government would derive its sole sanction from the consent of the vox populi and from the laws of nature's God. In *Daisy Miller* and *Portrait of a Lady* James retells the story of a fall from innocence and an initiation into experience, as does Melville in *Billy Budd*. The fatal mistake of Daisy and Billy and the mistake of Isabel Archer arise in large part from their inability to distinguish good from evil, false discourse from true, or from their blindness to duplicity.

Like many Americans, James and Melville learned from the Bible as well as from the classics and the events of their own history the deceits of rhetoric and the dangers of double meanings, and they well knew that the good American and the good reader needs to be more critical than complacent and more distrustful than confident, for the prince of darkness can appear as an angel of light or as a "lamb-like" man. In his own Bible Melville underscored a verse from the book of Isaiah that offers a Christian version of the Platonic condemnation of the confusion of moral terms that is part of the Thucydidean moment: "Wo unto them that call evil good, and good evil; that put darkness for light, and light for darkness; that put bitter for sweet and sweet for bitter!" (Isaiah 5:20).[2] This verse condemns with God's wrath the verbal deceiver, but it also offers a caution to the guileless who may be deceived by a transvaluation of terms. And so this verse was cited in the Revolutionary era by Benjamin Franklin and the patriot minister Andrew Lee to warn colonists against the verbal misrepresentations of the British, who were, in their eyes, justifying tyranny as government and liberty as slavery and branding the colonists who were tenacious for their rights as factious and rebellious.[3] So it was cited by William Lloyd Garrison to vilify attempts to justify the evil of slavery as a republican good and by Horace Mann to condemn those who in their confusion called abolition rather than slavery an evil warring against liberty.[4] So it was cited by Abiel Livermore to protest the pretence that the Mexican War was anything but "violence, fraud, murder, and a temporary repeal of every commandment of the King of kings."[5] And so the verse might have been cited by

Dansker to warn Billy about the sinister dexterity of Claggart. From Genesis and Isaiah and from other sources in the Bible Americans derived lessons about the power of the word and the dangers of "evil communication," and they applied and reworked these biblical passages in the context of their own history to advance that education and their own prophecies.

For early Americans, the biblical story of corruption that began with the seduction of Adam and Eve by a double-tongued deceiver and continued through the collapse of the tower of Babel was probably more influential than classical literature in shaping a distrust of rhetoric and in forging links between political and linguistic corruption. No one has ever written a book entitled *The American Satan* to complement R. W. B. Lewis's *The American Adam*, but the figure of Satan is at least as prevalent as Adam in American fiction and more prevalent in American political discourse. In literature, for instance, there is the diabolism of Carwin, Claggart, and the Confidence-Man and of George Lippard's Devil Bug and Mark Twain's Mysterious Stranger; and in early American politics there is a veritable coven of devilish plotters ranging from the "Black Regiment" of patriot ministers denounced by Loyalists and the cabal of British ministers denounced by the patriots to the satanic apparitions of Nat Turner and John Brown in antebellum America. From the confidence games of conspiring figures in American politics and the plotting of sinister characters in the fiction of Brown, Cooper, Melville, and others, there emerges a common archetype – the devil or demagogue – and a common stratagem: the subversion of things by names or the seduction of the mind by the duplicitous voice.[6] And just as literary critics have tended to highlight the figure of the American Adam over the voice of an American Satan, so too historians have written more about America's messianic vision of itself as a new Eden or a redeemer nation than they have commented on America's unmessianic vision of itself as a new Babel.[7] We will never forget Lincoln at Gettysburg representing the death of soldiers as a redemptive sacrifice for the nation, but just as typically (if not more so), Edward Everett, in the keynote address, portrayed the "rebellion" of the South led by Jefferson Davis as "an imitation on earth of that first foul revolt of 'the Infernal Serpent.'"[8] Christian history closely links together the sin of man with the seductive powers of rhetoric and the imperfection or multiplicity of languages, and a brief review of key passages in that history can remind us of the framework through which Americans so often viewed threats to their liberty and their union and how they interpreted their own success or failure in reforming their language (and their country) as a sign that they were redeeming or repeating the fall of man and the curse of Babel.

In the beginning of Christian history is the Word of God, who calls the world into being. God speaks, and things are; Adam then speaks, and nature is named: "And whatsoever Adam called every living creature, that was the name thereof" (Genesis 2:19). The creation of the world by the Word and the naming of nature by Adam establish a book of nature and an original language that could be read without confusion. The words of that language correspond perfectly to things or to what God – the perfect Author – intended them to signify. It was a language that could not be misinterpreted or glossed; it could only be understood and obeyed. But Adam and Eve, commanded by God to respect his Word, listen instead to the false words of Satan, who puts evil for good and bitter for sweet, and they are seduced into sin. The perfect correspondence between the Word and nature, God and man is lost. Exiled from the garden, Adam and Eve enter into a fallen world wherein man's tongue inherits a diabolic potential: "But no human being can tame the tongue – a restless evil, full of deadly poison" (James 3:8). Christian history becomes thereafter a series of disobediences in which the original transgression is repeated. The building and collapse of the tower of Babel perpetuate the fall of a people forgetful of the divine Word. The episode accounts for the loss of a transcendent community but sustains it as an ideal: "And the whole earth was of one language, and of one speech" (Genesis 11:1). But God, in order to punish the excessive pride of the manmade project to scale the heavens, visits upon the people a confusion of tongues. The shared language of creation succumbs to the diversity of tongues. People become strangers to one another. "Because the Lord did there confound the language of all the earth; and from thence did the Lord scatter them abroad over the face of all the earth" (Genesis 11:7–8). For a mid-nineteenth-century American, the lesson of Babel was a fundamental one:

> How impotent is a man when he would war with the Omnipotent! Their language was confounded – for Adam's tongue had been until then universal; they were no longer united – like the disciples, when the voice of their Lord fell no longer upon their ears, they went 'each to his own,' and the labor of their hands became the Babel monument of human impotency.[9]

The tower of Babel, however, is far from the last chapter in the biblical history of language. After Christ's crucifixion, in the revelation of Pentecost, the Holy Spirit descends upon the apostles and gives them the gift of tongues: "And there appeared to them tongues as of fire, distributed and resting on each of them" (Acts 2:3). The Apostles are also empowered to speak so that each person understands their words in his or her own tongue or tribal language. Thus, the early dispersal into multiplicity is compensated for by a miraculous gift for recovering the communion of a diverse people. People of all nations can now share in the spirit of the Word. A unity can be achieved through a multiplicity of tongues that overcomes (but does not end) diversity.

The Book of Jeremiah provides another portrait of a people who are mired in forms of political and linguistic corruption after forsaking the law of God and disobeying His voice. When the backsliding Israelites break their covenant with the Word, every tongue turns into a weapon of deceit and every neighbor becomes an enemy, thus provoking the wrath of God.

> They bend their tongue like a bow; falsehood and not truth has grown strong in the land; for they proceed from evil to evil and they do not know me, says the Lord. Let every one beware of his neighbor, and put no trust in any brother; for every brother is a supplanter, and every neighbor goes about as a slanderer. Every one deceives his neighbor, and no one speaks the truth; they have taught their tongue to speak lies; they commit iniquity and are too weary to repent. Heaping oppression upon oppression and deceit upon deceit, they refuse to know me, says the Lord. Therefore says the Lord of Hosts: Behold, I will refine them and test them, for what else can I do, because of my people? Their tongue is a deadly arrow; it speaks deceitfully; with his mouth each speaks peaceably to his neighbor, but in his heart he plans an ambush for him. Shall I not punish them for these things? says the Lord; and shall I not avenge myself on a nation such as this? (Jeremiah 9:3–9)

Just as frightfully as in Thucydides' description of the *stasis* at Corcyra, people beat their tongues into swords and sever bonds of love and friendship. The Lord, however, will wield his scourge against this unruly people and their unruly tongue.[10] Yet the chosen people of Israel are not condemned eternally: God promises them a new covenant.

Just as Christian history can be read as a history of a people oscillating between the fallen speech of Babel and the redeemed speech of Pentecost (and between broken and renewed covenants), so too have Americans read their own history as a movement toward or away from the dream of a new Edenic tongue (and state) and the nightmare of an old Babel. And, as many early Americans recognized, if America was to recreate a version of Eden it had to reverse or at least control the linguistic consequences of Babel. Communion through the agency of the word becomes the task not just of ministers but of linguists. "To disorganize and disunite mankind," writes an American in 1855, "it was necessary to confound their language: to harmonize and reunite them, we must look for a common tongue."[11] Only when the marplots of the Fall and Babel were cured would the country be safe for the rights of man and American Adams like Billy Budd. Only then would the garden of America be protected.

Sealing the American garden against counterfeiters, ventriloquists, and other duplicitous seducers of the mind was, as Jay Fliegelman shows, a preeminent concern in post-Revolutionary America that reached its formal realization in the passage in 1798 of the Alien and Sedition Acts.[12] John Adams suggests why he committed his administration to the passage of those acts when he declares in an address printed in the *Gazette of the United States* that "the delusion and misrepresentation which have misled so many citizens must be discountenanced by authority as well as by the citizens at large."[13] Whereas Adams sought to silence the deluders, Abraham Bishop, a Connecticut minister and ardent Jeffersonian republican, preferred to educate public opinion and to hope that vigilant citizens and an unfettered press would counter delusion when people had become the dupes of "artful manoeuvres." In Bishop's eyes, the seditious misrepresentations that endangered America were not those of a "licentious" press but those perpetrated by the founding fathers and the ruling elite of the country. When Bishop looked back in an 1802 pamphlet at the original promise of America, he observed, "At the peace of 1783 . . . [we] were far distant from the kingdoms of Europe, those theatres, where religion and humanity had been always outraged by civil and ecclesiastical tyrants," and we "had an extended country, to which we might invite the oppressed of the world."[14] But in an 1800 oration entitled "The Extent and Power of Political Delusion" he describes not an innocent but an already fallen or at least corrupted America, and the oration itself offers a fascinating early example (which prefigures Ambrose Bierce's *Devil's Dictionary*) of an attempt to defend against the serpents in the American garden by calling attention to the linguistic stratagems of the devil's avatars and the typology of humankind's first fall into corruption. Bishop warns in the opening of his oration that since Satan "practised his deceit on our federal mother," new practitioners of delusion have bedeviled the world, and the agents of that delusion are "the great, the wise, rich and mighty men of the world" and their subject "the laboring and subordinate people throughout the world." He adds, "Not more opposed to religion are the world, the flesh and the devil than are, the subtlety, avarice and pride of the *one tenth* to the rights of the *nine tenths* in society." This ruling class, he explains, succeeds largely through a form of verbal cunning that depends on putting evil for good and sweet for bitter. When the deluders "would enslave the people, they present to them pictures of liberty; when they would impoverish them, they present pictures of wealth; when they would lead them to war, they present pictures of peace and security," and with "subtle arguments well directed and eloquently enforced" they can "prove conclusively that a national debt is a blessing or a curse; that an army destroys or cherishes freedom; that the friends of government are the guardian angels of liberty, and that the opposers are a part of Satan's chosen legion."[15] Here, in short, the Christian typology of the fall from liberty into slavery provides the terms for a critique of words and ruling-class actions that would be applied to the same period by the Progressive historian Charles Beard and to later periods by Populist and New Left critics.

But while Adams and Bishop share an appreciation for the dangers of verbal duplicity and the difficulty in countering the consequences of the fall of man in post-Revolutionary America, others mitigated those fears with a glorious, even messianic, hope of countering the consequences of Babel. Soon after the drafting of the Constitution, in the year of its ratification, Noah Webster, who spent a large part of his life seeking to establish a uniform language for the country, envisioned a time when, through the spread of a common tongue in America, "the people of one quarter of the world, will be able to associate and converse together like children of the same family" (D, 21). Later in his life Webster, discouraged with American politics but motivated by deep religious convictions, labored delusively to repair Babel by recovering the root meanings of words from their traces in existing languages. Like Webster in 1789, Edward Everett anticipates in an 1824 address before the Phi Beta Kappa Society that America will soon write a new chapter in the history of language and politics:

> Instead of that multiplicity of dialect, by which mental communication and sympathy between different nations are restrained in the Old World, a continually expanding realm is opened to American intellect, by the extension of one language over so large a portion of the Continent. . . . In Europe, the work of international alienation, which begins in diversity of language, is consummated by diversity of race, institutions, and national prejudices. . . . While, on the other hand, throughout the vast regions included within the limits of our own republic, not only the same language, but the same national government, the same laws and manners, and common ancestral

associations prevail. Mankind will here exist and act in a kindred mass, such as was scarcely ever before congregated on the earth's surface.[16]

The dream that America could restore linguistic unity is a profoundly political dream. It is the dream that the country could avoid the confusion of tongues and people that befell the old world and become instead the home of a single language that would unite citizens in a state of political and religious harmony unknown since Babel. It is the dream that a common language could help erase the differences of race, class, and locality that had divided Europe. It is the dream, in short, of *e pluribus unum*, and it has been one of the defining goals of American politics. "Let us, then, fellow-citizens, unite with one heart and one mind," declared Jefferson in his First Inaugural Address after a bitter election contest in 1800. "Let us restore to social intercourse that harmony and affection without which liberty and even life itself are but dreary things" (JLA, 493). The farther America has deviated from the ideal of harmonious conversation, the farther it has deviated in its own mind from the "road to happiness & to glory," a road Jefferson helped to map out and called upon Americans to traverse in his Declaration and First Inaugural Address (JLA, 23).[17]

Disturbed by the conflict of voices surrounding the drafting of a new political language in the Constitutional Convention, Benjamin Franklin feared that without the "concurring aid" of God the committee members "shall succeed in this political building no better, than the builders of Babel: We shall be divided by our little partial local interests; our projects will be confounded, and we ourselves shall become a reproach and bye word down to the future ages."[18] But near the end of the convention, Franklin expresses his faith that the sun is rising in America and that the finished product of their labors "will astonish our enemies, who are waiting to hear with confidence that our councils are confounded like those of the builders of Babel" (NFC, 653–4).[19] Joel Barlow, in the conclusion of his epic *The Vision of Columbus*, published the year of the Constitutional Convention, echoes Franklin's bright hopes for America when he contrasts the "tumultuous discord" "when impious Babel dared arise" with the voice of Heaven's vision of "nobler joys to come" in America: "The tongues of nations, here, harmonious blend, / Till one pure language thro' the earth extend."[20] Wellingborough Redburn, the priggish narrator of Melville's *Redburn*, proclaims even more optimistically: "On this Western hemisphere all tribes and people are forming into one federated whole; and there is a future which shall see the estranged children of Adam restored to the old hearth-stone in Eden. . . . Then shall the curse of Babel be revoked, a new Pentecost come."[21] In an 1855 essay in the *Democratic Review*, the author reminds his readers, "While half a million of men are isolated from their fellows by a peculiar tongue, their prejudices, their affinities, their passions, and their jealousies can never be assimilated: they are a family of Ishmaels, at variance with the human family, and without the bond of language can never be reduced into homogeneity."[22] He then adds a more hopeful, indeed a pentecostal, counterpoint: "As tongues were confused only when the design of man had become impious and intolerable, it is not impossible, at least, that a common language should be restored to us, in order the better to universalize the one true faith of Christianity."[23] The title of the essay is "Our Language Destined to Be Universal." Figuring forth the full significance of the prospect of a new Pentecost as an article of faith in America's civil religion, Reverend Dimmesdale in *The Scarlet Letter* pronounces from his pulpit an Election Sermon that converts the atmosphere into "words of flame" as it celebrates a "glorious destiny for the newly gathered people of the Lord" in the new world (NHW, I, 248–9). In this pentecostal moment, Dimmesdale resolves his ambiguous relationship to the community that has affixed the letter of the law to Hester's breast, a letter that elicits a babel of interpretations from a community which becomes increasingly willing and able to entertain diverse interpretations. The community, however, remains fixed in its vision of its own destiny. The scarlet letter as text is replaced by the Election Sermon. Violation (i.e., corruption) of the Word gives way to its future fulfillment. The sermon, which tells of that destiny, evokes a "mighty swell of many voices, blended into one great voice by the universal impulse which makes likewise one vast heart out of the many" (NHW, I, 250). The movement of the story from multiplicity to unity, from adulteration of the letter to purification of the spirit, from dissent to consensus, from declarations of independence to constitutions of a more perfect union, from Babel to Pentecost, recapitulates, as Sacvan Bercovitch argues, the visionary narrative of America's ideology in antebellum America – and beyond.[24]

Undaunted by the broken promises of the past, Martin Luther King, Jr., one hundred years after the signing of the Emancipation Proclamation, sounds the same mystic chord of a redeemed future wherein corruptions of the word will cease when he dreams that one day "we will be able to transform the jangling discords of our nation into a beautiful symphony of brotherhood."[25] T. S. Eliot, retracing Franklin's movement from dismay to faith in the Constitutional Convention, opens *Four Quartets* with images of the "Word" assailed by shrieking, scolding, mocking, chattering voices, but then concludes, "All shall be well / When the tongues of flame are in-folded / Into the crowned knot of fire / And the fire and the rose are one."[26] But at the end of *The Crying of Lot 49*, Thomas Pynchon leaves Oedipa Maas, the heroine charged with executing the will of her ex-lover Pierce Inverarity, awaiting the "crying" of "Lot 49," the pentecostal moment that will endow her with the special linguistic abilities needed to bring Inverarity's will – a will somehow bound up with the meaning of America – into "pulsing, stelliferous meaning."[27] Oedipa, who awakes in the story to a world that has "lost the direct, epileptic Word, the cry that might abolish the night," is perhaps now on the verge of finding that Word or a way to end the confusion of signs, symbols, and tongues that composes her America, or instead she just might be left in the auction room, as Pynchon leaves us as readers, reflecting in the mind's ear on what can be learned by searching out and listening to the diversity of sounds and silences in the disorder of things.[28]

Frequently in America, then, writers have counterpointed the discordant sounds of Babel with the dream of Eden or Pentecost, but more than a few have left us at the end listening neither to the consensus that Franklin acclaims nor to the symphony of love that King envisions nor to a lyrical silence before the purified word that Eliot reverences but to all too present cacophonies. Two decades after the ratification of the Constitution, in the midst of Jefferson's second administration, Washington Irving pens a letter for his *Salmagundi* in the name of Mustapha Rub-a-dub Keli Khan that suggests that while the architects of the Constitution may have avoided building a new tower of Babel, one of the houses they planned had become nothing less than a new Pandaemonium: "This is a blustering windy assembly where every thing is carried by noise, tumult and debate; for thou must know, that the members of the assembly do not meet together to find out wisdom in the multitudes of counsellors, but to wrangle, call each other hard names and hear *themselves talk*. . . . Unhappy nation – thus torn to pieces by intestine talks! never, I fear, will it be restored to tranquility and silence" (ILA, 147–8). In 1848, as part of James Russell Lowell's condemnation of the actions and big talk of Manifest Destiny that led to the Mexican–American War, Homer Wilbur, A.M., the purported editor of *The Biglow Papers*, offers an annotation on the Babel story that confirms Irving's satire in *Salmagundi* and extends its critique of the American logocracy. By "speech-making," Wilbur observes, we make ourselves "unintelligible, to our fellows," and "Babel was the first Congress, the earliest mill erected for the manufacture of gabble" (JLW, VIII, 87).

For John Adams, however, it was not just the forums of politics but the language of politics itself that reflected the confusion of a people torn apart by differences – or by the exercise of their liberty. In *Defence of the Constitutions* he points out that "in the science of legislation . . . there is a confusion of languages, as if men were but lately come from Babel. Scarcely any two writers, much less nations, agree in using words in the same sense" (JAW, V, 452). In the nineteenth century the multiple meanings of political terms, which Adams vainly sought to control through his own definitions, became for some an irrepressible problem of catastrophic dimensions, a problem that was contributing, in Daniel Webster's view, to the destruction of the house that the founding fathers had built. Combating the nullifiers in one of his key speeches, "The Constitution Not a Compact Between the Sovereign States," Webster declares, "If we are to receive the Constitution as the text, and then to lay down in its margins the contradictory commentaries which have been, and which may be, made by different States, the whole page would be a polyglot indeed. It would speak with as many tongues as the builders of Babel, and in dialects as much confused, and mutually as unintelligible" (DWW, VI, 196). In Webster's eyes, the states of the Union, though federated along one keel, were speaking in as many dialects as the "Isolatoes" on board the *Pequod*. "The builders of Babel," Melville writes in *Moby-Dick*, ". . . intended to rear the loftiest mast-head in all Asia," but he believed, along with Webster, it seems, that the "Great Washington" who stood aloft "on his towering main-mast in Baltimore" could best "descry what shoals and what rocks must be shunned" if the country was to avoid a Babel-like disunion perpetrated by the monomaniacal schemes of an Ahab or a John Calhoun, who in Webster's view was faultily constructing from the words of the Constitution the building blocks of a new political theory – the doctrine of nullification – that threatened to collapse the Union into splintered wood and rubble.[29]

A few years after Webster helped engineer the Compromise of 1850 that was designed to prevent the Union's collapse, Melville completes "The Bell-Tower," the story of the "great mechanician," Bannadonna, who constructs for a republic a tower "like Babel's" whose base "was laid in a high hour of renovated earth" (MLA, 819). But this tower also crashes into rubble. At one o'clock, when Talus, a mechanical (or perhaps human) slave who serves as part of the clock's mechanism, is designed to "sever" the "loved clasp" of the hands of two figures on the clock, Una and Dua, Bannadonna is struck and killed by the swing of Talus. Then when the bell of the tower is rung at his funeral, as the Liberty Bell was rung at the funeral of John Marshall and on the birthday of George Washington (two slaveholders from Virginia), the tower collapses. The fall is ascribed to pride and to Bannadonna's mistake in casting the bell with a fatal flaw. He had killed a worker, whose blood was mixed with the metal composing the bell. The homicide is not punished by the republic, and Bannadonna conceals the "blemish," but the weakness from where "man's blood had flawed it" proves disastrous (MLA, 833). The collapse of the bell tower ends the "jubilant expectations" of a race who had soared "into Shinar aspirations" (MLA, 819). Melville's reprise of the Babel story rings with the overtones of political as well as religious allegory. Published two months earlier than *Benito Cereno*, in *Putnam's Monthly* in 1855, the story can be read as a parable of slave revolt and as an omen, in Carolyn Karcher's words, of the "extinction that threatened the American republic if it failed to repair its moral flaw and make good its pledge of freedom to all mankind."[30] It might also allude to the dangers associated with severing the connection between the Una and Dua of the federal and state governments and warn against an exalted pride in the work of the great mechanics, the founding fathers, who constructed, in James Russell Lowell's words, a "machine that would go of itself" – the Constitution – whose workings also incorporated and concealed the expenditure of slaves' blood (JLW, VI, 207). The epigrams Melville included in the version printed in *Putnam's Monthly* invite such a political construction of the story: "Like negroes, these powers own man sullenly; mindful of their higher master; while serving, plot revenge. . . . Seeking to conquer a larger liberty, man but extends the empire of necessity" (MLA, 819). "And so pride went before the fall," concludes Melville in "The Bell-Tower" (MLA, 833). In 1862, Sidney George Fisher comes to a similar conclusion in *The Trial of the Constitution*. Contemplating alternatives for repairing the Union rent by civil war, he writes, "It seems, indeed, as if, for our presuming in attempting to raise our tower of empire so high, we had been struck with confusion of tongues, and had ceased to be intelligible to each other."[31]

In the middle of the Civil War, Stephen Pearl Andrews, an abolitionist and utopian reformer, developed his own plan to restore a more perfect union. In 1864 he announced and introduced in the *Continental Monthly* "the most stupendous discovery to which the human intellect is capable of attaining": a new "scientific and universal language" "for the remedy of the confusion and great evil of Babel."[32] This language, he explains, is to be "elaborated from the fundamental laws of speech existing in the constitution of the universe and of man," and in a detailed synopsis of the language he published in 1870 he adds that it "shall be in its structure the Rectified and Clarified Transcript of the Universe" and will serve "as the Vernacular of the Unitized

Humanity or Grand Planetary Nation of the Future." Through this scientific language, Andrews asserts, we may recover "from a Lingual Paradise Lost . . . to a Lingual Paradise Regained in literal fulfillment of the promise of prophecy that all the nations of the earth shall be of one speech."[33]

Andrews's plan for a universal language presents a grandiose manifestation of the dream of establishing a universe of signs that would faithfully represent the universe of fact, thought, and feeling. This same desire (or logocentric delusion) manifested itself in more modest but also more problematical forms in the social and political world of nineteenth-century America. At the end of the nineteenth century, James Bradley Thayer chided a fellow lawyer for still dreaming of "that lawyer's Paradise where all words have a fixed, precisely ascertained meaning."[34] Thayer's comment, like Andrews's scheme, can remind us that the ideal of an Edenic language of fixed meanings was not merely contemplated in reverie but sought with vigor as a means of establishing political and religious harmony in nineteenth-century America. Ironically, however, it was the dream of recovering or establishing a language wherein words have a fixed meaning or a perfect correspondence to things that helped provoke violent opposition to contradictory interpretations and opposing voices. To believe in the ideal of such an Edenic language is to condemn all change in language as a corruption. To believe that people were once united by a common language is to consider all differences of language a curse. To defend the "natural" or "proper" meaning of the words constituting the texts of America's creed and to regard the Supreme Court as an infallible interpreter is to condemn all opposing interpretations as heretical: the product of a sinful disobedience rather than the exercise of an "inviolable liberty." The dream of a common language is no utopian vision but a nightmare for those who fear, as did George Fitzhugh in *Cannibals All!* (1857), that an overriding of linguistic differences – an imposed unilingualism – is the beginning of tyranny.[35] Against the reign of a Big Brother who silences differences of dialect and definition, a babel of tongues is freedom – a fortunate fall. To overcome Babel or to universalize a particular language is an imperious quest fraught with danger, as the fate of Ahab's federation of diverse voices into a single mission for the *Pequod* suggests. Aliens or subjects who are taught the master's tongue may have some revenge beyond the cursing of a Caliban. The master who mutes different voices creates a deafness that may prove mortal.

Stephen Andrews's plan for a new universal language may strike us as bizarre – it is a plan that deserves to be forgotten – but his vision in the time of the American Civil War of a lingual paradise regained, like the language planning of John Wilkins in the aftermath of the English Civil War, speaks to a deep disquiet about the social world. In stark contrast to the linguistic inventions of Andrews – and to the patriotic (or imperialist) claims made for the manifest superiority of the English language by such figures as Walt Whitman – lies the work of William Whitney, an American pioneer in the science of language who first presented his work as a linguist in six lectures on the "principles of linguistic science" delivered at the Smithsonian Institution in 1864. A contemporary of Andrews and Whitman, Whitney concludes his chapter "Local and Class Variation of Language Dialects" in *The Life and Growth of Language* with the advice that we should recognize that "the dream, of a time when one language may be spoken all over the earth" may be "Utopian" and that the words "language" and "dialect" are "only two names for the same thing, as looked at from different points of view."[36] He adds, "The science of language has democratized our views on such points as these; it has taught us that one man's speech is just as much a language as another man's; that even the most cultivated tongue that exists is only the dialect of a certain class in a certain locality."[37] For Whitney, differences of speech are not the product of sin or moral degeneration but the result of social and geographical factors, and no speech of any one class or locale is better than another. Whitney's linguistic science thus bears a resemblance to the medical science of Oliver Wendell Holmes, who maintained that "if for the Fall of man, science comes to substitute the Rise of Man, . . . it means the utter disintegration of all the spiritual pessimisms which have been like a spasm in the heart and cramp in the intellect of man for so many centuries."[38] By replacing a religious concept of the fall of an Edenic language with a scientific study of the rise of dialects, Whitney helped to free the study of language from the religious or racial bias that had cramped the intellect and hardened the heart as it classified forms of speech and entire languages as signs of moral depravity or inherent social inferiority. With his principle of prejudice toward none and a charitable respect for all languages and "dialects," Whitney offered a model of a reconstructed linguistic science, and Ferdinand de Saussure, who commented extensively on Whitney's work, praised him as the beginner of the "Neogrammarian trend" in linguistics.[39] Saussure was particularly impressed by a passage from *The Life and Growth of Language* wherein Whitney concludes "that language is nothing more than a particular case of the sign, unable to be judged by itself."[40] The word is an arbitrary sign because its meaning is subject to arbitration, to judgment, and in the aftermath of the Civil War, Whitney probably would have had few doubters in the classroom when he argued as a professor at Yale that language is not "of divine origin" and not an "integral system of natural and necessary representatives of thought . . . but, on the contrary, a body of conventional signs, deriving their value from the mutual understanding of one man with another," and when he recognized how difficult it could be at times to reach mutual understanding or a common judgment: "Nay, who knows not that verbal disputes, discussions turning on the meaning of words, are the most frequent, bitter, and interminable of controversies?"[41]

The following chapters will examine more closely how views of language were democratized and secularized in America. It is a study of how a religious conception of speech as a gift of God gave way to a political conception of language as a product of consent or, more precisely, of how the divine right to name and give meaning that God gave to Adam was assumed by monarchs and then by the people and how it was finally recognized that it was the people themselves who gave the right to God. Man, that is, created God in his own image: He is a power who constitutes the human world with his words. Emerson for one did not shy away from that power: he looked upon himself as an "Adam in the garden" whose purpose was to "new name all the beasts in the field & all the gods in the Sky," and he also envisioned the divine gift of Pentecost as a human capability (JMN, VII, 271).

"Yet let us enjoy the cloven flame whilst it glows on our walls," comments Emerson in "Circles" (ELA, 408). The pentecostal moment he is referring to is one that encompasses not a nation but merely the participants in a conversation, and the moment is short-lived: "The parties are not to be judged by the spirit they partake and even express under this Pentecost. To-morrow they will have receded from this high-water mark" (ibid.). Emerson describes conversation as a "game of circles," and it seems the game is lost or ends if the participants remain enclosed in the circle of yesterday. Conflating religious and political imagery, he champions the moment when "each new speaker strikes a new light, emancipates us from the oppression of the last speaker, to oppress us with the greatness and exclusiveness of his own thought, then yields us to another redeemer," and in this moment "we seem to recover our rights, to become men" (ibid.). The voice of the redeemer, who speaks the "initiative, spermatic, prophesying, man-making words" that Emerson summons for his own muse, breaks the circle of consensus, but that fissure does not produce an infernal confusion of tongues (JMN, VIII, 148). It yields to a higher consensus, to the tongues of flame of Pentecost. If Babel is the story of the failure of man to surmount the distance that separates heaven and earth, its antitype is the Incarnation and the new gift of Pentecost, those moments when the Word or the Holy Spirit descends in humility and glory to connect flesh and spirit, man and God. But while Emerson makes this divine act of transcendence a human possibility – "Let them, then, become organs of the Holy Ghost" – the redemption is not eternal (ELA, 412). There is no final word to end the conversation. The silence of shared understanding, of transcendent illumination, will dissipate and be broken by new speech which can return us to new silence that will dissipate and be broken by new speech, and the cycle will continue until thy kingdom come.

Emerson in "Circles" is the voice of pentecostal aspiration, but he also must be recognized to be at the same time, paradoxically, a Babel builder. He expresses no trepidation for that moment when "all that we reckoned settled shakes and rattles; and literatures, cities, climates, religions, leave their foundations, and dance before our eyes" (or crash) (ELA, 408). "The only sin is limitation" (ELA, 406). "In the thought of to-morrow there is a power to upheave all thy creed, all the creeds, all the literatures, of the nations, and marshal thee to a heaven which no epic dream has yet depicted" (ELA, 405). Build therefore your own tower. Be eccentric, be extravagant, outcircle the last speaker, confound old representations. Emerson's vision of the conversational process is a dialectic of dissensus and consensus, Babel and Pentecost, the many and the one wherein old representations yield to new representative voices. The dialectic is neither a matter of mere process where the game is played to keep the conversation going nor solely a matter of Socratic progress where the end of the game is to defeat error or champion the truth; it is a process with the bipolar telos of liberty and union, emancipation and community. Emersonian conversation, on the one hand, is the Christian typology of redeeming linguistic corruption through the advent of the new Word secularized; on the other hand, it is Jefferson's faith in the winnowing process of free speech and of Madison's vision of the filtering process of representative government transcendentalized.[42]

"The faith has always been," says Benjamin Barber of America, "that from the clash of opposites, of contraries, of extremes, of poles, will come not the victory of any one but the mediation and accommodation of them all." From that clash of voices on the anvil of debate, he adds, would also come, according to this faith, the "American version of truth and unity, if there was to be one."[43] Babel, in short, would yield to Pentecost. Ralph Ellison has upheld as an essential task of the American writer the attempt to forge order out of chaos or from the "rich babel" of idioms that swirl around in our streets and through our history by constructing an art that embraces the democratic ideal of unity in diversity and oneness in manyness while never forgetting the violations of that ideal. Yet he discusses in his criticism the very difficulty of transcending in art as well as in life the social, cultural, and biological differences that underlie the "rich babel" of our speech and thus of achieving an "American version of truth and unity."[44] He also offers us an eloquent portrait of a society that is for the most part neither a Pentecost, where diverse tongues are orchestrated into symphonies of brotherhood, nor a Babel, where tongues confound and war against each other, but something in between (though closer here to Babel):

> The whole [of American society] is always in cacophonic motion. Constantly changing its mode, it appears as a vortex of discordant ways of living and tastes, values and traditions; a whirlpool of odds and ends in which the past courses in uneasy juxtaposition with those bright, futuristic principles and promises to which we, as a nation, are politically committed. In our vaguely perceived here and now, even the sounds and symbols spun off by the clashing of group against group appear not only alarmingly off-key, but threatening to our inherited eyes, ears, and appetites. Thus, in our intergroup familiarity there is a brooding strangeness, and in our underlying sense of alienation of a poignant – although distrusted – sense of fraternity.[45]

Listening to the principles and promise of the United States as if to the leitmotifs of a musical score, Noah Webster and Edward Everett heard the beginning of the end of Babel; listening to the clashing of group against group in antebellum America, watching an America raise its tower of empire, fearing the cacophony of the civil strife to come, Whitman and Melville became "speakers of tongues." Whitman embraced an English language in America that could contain multitudes of dialects and absorb the riches of all other tongues: "I like well our polyglot construction-stamp," he notes (WLA, 1075).[46] Melville displays in Ishmael a similar liking or a spirit that enables him to embrace a Queequeg and seek communion with foreign tongues. Each writer in his own way was an apostle of a pentecostal spirit.

While the babel of tongues that swirled in antebellum America – the diverse idioms of class, race, religion, and political party – confronted Union statesmen with a threat that intensified all their efforts to instruct the nation in the grammar and vocabulary of a particular tongue that claimed universality (e.g., the Constitution, the language of nature), this babel was, in effect, a fortunate fall for the American Renaissance writer who incorporated this confusion of tongues in the works of art that we now praise and privilege, for we share Roland

Barthes's preference: "The text of pleasure is a sanctioned Babel."[47] The English language, as James Russell Lowell suggests in 1868, was enriched by Babel. "The English-speaking nations," he writes, "should build a monument to the misguided enthusiasts of the Plain of Shinar; for, as the mixture of many bloods seems to have made them the most vigorous of modern races, so has the mingling of divers speech given them a language which is perhaps the noblest vehicle of poetic thought that ever existed" (JLW, III, 1–2). As the English language spread westward, following the course of the American empire, it incorporated in its grasp a diverse range of tongues. The result was for Lowell (and Whitman) a noble vernacular: a rich and diverse but still unified tongue, a tongue "brawny enough and limber and full enough," in Whitman's words, to befriend "the grand American expression" – a tongue that "shall well nigh express the inexpressible" (WLA, 25). But Lowell, through Homer Wilbur in *The Biglow Papers*, provides something of a heretical commentary on Pentecost and Babel that suggests how Lowell recognizes, as part of his argument that the war with Mexico was a poor excuse to extend the empire of slavery, that the expansion of the American tongue into new space could be a curse and Babel a blessing. After learning that a deacon in his congregation had received a first installment of the gift of tongues, Wilbur confesses: "I could not reconcile it with my ideas of the Divine justice and mercy that a single wall which protected people of other languages from the incursions of this otherwise well-meaning propagandist should be broken down" (JLW, VIII, 88). "The curse of Babel," W. H. Auden suggests, "is not the fact that there are many diverse languages – diversity in itself is a good – but the idolization by each linguistic group of its own tongue."[48]

5

Eloquence, Liberty, and Power: Civic Humanism and the Counter-Renaissance

Potentissima belli; *pacisque machina*; *Oratio*. Eloquence, the mightiest Engin [both of war and peace] in the world.

Gabriel Harvey, Marginalia

The ferment and germination even of the United States to-day, dating back to, and in my opinion mainly founded on, the Elizabethan age in English history, the age of Francis Bacon and Shakespere.

Walt Whitman, "A Backward Glance o'er Travel'd Roads"

At the end of the Middle Ages in Italy, Dante contemplated in *De Vulgari Eloquentia* a people divided among themselves by their diverse tongues – a consequence, in his mind, of man's disobedience in building the tower of Babel. Italy alone, he noted, had "at least fourteen vernaculars, all of which have variations within themselves," and it was his quest to establish "one illustrious vernacular" in his country that had been divided by dialects, by rival city-states, and by factions within city-states such as the one in Florence that drove him into exile.[1] Dante chose to write *The Divine Comedy* in the vernacular, the language of temporality, change, history – of fallen man. He chose to write *On Monarchy* in Latin, the sacred language that united citizens of the City of God. Not long after Dante's death, at the advent of the *renaissance des lettres*, Petrarch, who did much to inaugurate that movement, composed letters to his favorite classical authors and dreamed of recovering their eloquence, just as he dreamed that Italy could be restored to the glory and grandeur of ancient Rome. For Petrarch, and later for Machiavelli, the glory that was Rome served as a reproach to the Italy of their own day, and while Machiavelli in *Discourses on Livy* and *The Prince* offered political advice for recovering that glory, Petrarch, who would support the ambitions of a prototype of Machia-

117

velli's prince, Cola di Rienzo, campaigned by word and deed for a
different strategy – a recovery of classical letters and learning. It is
this strategy of politics by the word which is at the heart of Renaissance humanism, and it is this tradition that needs to be investigated
more closely as a prelude to studying the American Revolution. Not
just the City of God but the City of Words of Cicero became a city
whose gates the humanists wanted to enter. Not just imitating God's
Word and acting as God's scribe but imitating Cicero's word and
acting as the orator became their pursuit of happiness. Not just a new
Jerusalem but a new Rome or a new Florence was the end of the
American Revolution. The humanists, led by the archphilologist
Lorenzo Valla, and the reformers of the church, led by Martin Luther,
came to conclude that medieval Latin – or the official language of the
Catholic Church – was not an eternal, sacred language but a language
as temporal, changeable, and corrupt as man himself. The Renaissance
and the Reformation as well can be seen as movements to restore the
purity of the word or the uncorrupted language of classical and
Christian texts, and it is that battle of liberation and restoration
fought against the corruption of the Dark Ages that would precede
and help create the structural dynamics for two more revolutions – the
scientific revolution and the American Revolution. Both of these
revolutions, which helped usher in modernity, can also be seen as
attempts to recover an uncorrupted text: the language of nature and
nature's God.[2]

John Adams, John Dickinson, Joel Barlow, Hugh Henry Brackenridge, Daniel Webster, Ralph Emerson, Edward Everett, Walt Whitman, Frederick Douglass: these statesmen, poets, and essayists, though
as diverse in their style of eloquence as in their politics, were animated
by the same ideal – the classical ideal of the orator that was reani-
mated in the Renaissance. Indeed, they often envisioned themselves as
civic humanists who had to turn, as did Cato and Cicero, to rhetoric to
combat conspiracies that threatened to rob them of their liberties, and
they hoped that with the revival of a republic and a truly representative government in America there would come a new revival of
eloquence and a more representative tongue. But while resurrecting
all the hopes that classical orators and Renaissance humanists had
expressed for language as a form of political action, they also resurrected the fears of Plato and Thucydides.

The colonists and later Americans, like the Puritans before them,
were both rhetorical and antirhetorical. Their antirhetoric itself was
rhetorical: they preached against false preaching (in the name of God),
they orated against oratory (in the name of plain common sense), and
they rejected words for acts against corrupt representation, but those

acts received much rhetorical justification (e.g., the Declaration of Independence). For early Americans, eloquence was liberty but also power – and a potentially tyrannical power. And whether eloquence was looked upon more as an agent of liberty or of tyranny – a question that was very much at the center of the ancient quarrel between rhetoric and philosophy – is a question whose answer was determined, to some degree at least, by the political moment. In 1776 the judgment was in favor of eloquence, but not in 1787. The confidence of rebellious colonists in eloquence was the faith of the Renaissance. The distrust of Publius in *The Federalist* for eloquence was the distrust that marks the end of the Renaissance. This chapter and the next one will review some of the past stagings and restagings of the opposition between the liberating power of a critical rhetoric and the enslaving power of a specious rhetoric as they helped influence the American performance of this drama of distrust and confidence in the era of the Revolution and before the Civil War. The colonists' quarrel with England and the abolitionists' quarrel with the slaveholder participated in the larger ancient quarrel between rhetoric and philosophy, or between the sovereign power of words and the power of representative ideas grounded in nature. During these quarrels, Americans drew upon both the weapon of the eloquent pen and tongue that the Renaissance humanists wielded against the Dark Ages and the weapon of the pure Word – the uncorrupted text of the Bible – that the leaders of the Reformation wielded against the forces of popery.

At the basis of the remarkable confidence in the powers of language that distinguishes the Renaissance from the ages that surround it is a deep belief, as Michael Roberts explains, "in the value of style as a progressive and formative influence in the life of man."[3] For Augustine, the Word of God was the sole power capable of converting people from vice to virtue, and his rhetorical theory dominates the Middle Ages. But at the beginning of the Italian Renaissance, Petrarch claims, "how much eloquence is able to accomplish in the shaping of human existence is known both from the reading of many authors and from the experience of everyday life." He adds, "How great is the number of those we recognize in our own day, to whom even examples [of virtue] were of no help, who have been aroused and turned suddenly from a most wicked manner to a perfectly ordered one simply by the sound of others' voices."[4] And it is this conception of the power in the word that animates the semantic faith of the Renaissance and places the pursuit of eloquence squarely at the heart of its life and affairs.[5]

What the humanists reclaim for eloquence and letters is nothing less than the Orphic power to civilize or the God-like power to bring order out of chaos. Thomas Wilson, an English humanist of the mid sixteenth century, in his recapitulation of the Orphic myth regards eloquence, for instance, as the first cause of human civilization:

> Whereas men lived brutishly in the open fields, having neither house to shroud them in, nor attire to clothe their bodies, nor yet any regard to see their best avail, these [orators] appointed by God called them together by utterance of speech and persuaded them what was good, what was bad, and what was gainful for mankind. And, being somewhat drawn with the pleasantness of reason, and the sweetness of utterance, after a certain space they became of wild, sober: of cruel, gentle: of fools, wise: and of beasts, men.[6]

And wherever we look in Renaissance literature – if we turn to moral treatises, rhetorical handbooks, orations, or defenses of poetry – we can find Orpheus deified as the poet and orator who refashioned human life and transformed culture through the sound of his voice, an apotheosis that offers Renaissance humanists – and American statesmen and poets – an ideal image of themselves as orators.[7]

At the very heart of the enthusiasm for eloquence in the Renaissance, as Michael Roberts argues, lay "a fundamental faith in the irresistible power of words," and while many may have mistrusted the application of this power, fine-sounding defenses made for rhetoric as virtue's weapon seemed to counter this fear. But the coercive powers of the human art of persuasion were never covered up: "Such force hath the tongue," Wilson declares, "and such is the power of eloquence and reason, that most men are forced even to yield in that which most standeth against their will."[8] And for Henry Peacham, the "true Orator" might be described as "in a maner the emperour of men's minds and affections, and next to the omnipotent God in the power of persuasion."[9] Thus, as Roberts explains, "in contrast to the abstract and 'mythic' powers in language" as presented by Wilson earlier, "which by emphasizing the characteristically human and humanizing qualities of speech offered to raise mankind and his culture as a whole above the level of the beasts, this dynamic conception of oratory was of its very nature before all else an individual power technique, transforming the Renaissance's conscientiously humanized world of words into an arena for the exercise of private aspiration and paving the way indeed for the superior orator to raise himself by his skillful eloquence uniquely over the ranks of his fellows."[10] Eloquence, in short, promised power, and it came to be seen in the Renaissance as a virtual equivalent to arms and action. Aeneas Silvius (later Pope Pius II) thus counsels his friend Adam Mulin, Keeper of the British Privy Seal: "Persevere therefore, friend Adam, my master;

hold fast and increase the eloquence you possess; consider it the most honorable thing possible to excel your fellows in that in which men excel other living creatures. For great in truth is eloquence and nothing so much rules the world."[11] For the Renaissance humanist, an uninterrupted path seemed to lead from the schoolroom – or wherever eloquence was taught – to the highest places of power in the state. John Adams and his son when he conducted lectures as the first Boylston Professor of Rhetoric and Oratory at Harvard would be among the foremost of a line of classical scholars in America to resurrect the same conviction and remind citizens that in earlier republics the "talent of public speaking was the key to the highest dignities; the passport to the supreme dominion of the state," and that the same would be true in the United States.[12] Emerson confirmed their prophecy: "If there ever was a country where eloquence was a power, it is the United States" (REW, VIII, 132).

From its inception, rhetoric had been considered an instrument of political sway in the ancient city-states. "Its aim," as Henri Marrou says, "was to arm the strong character, to prepare him for political strife so that he would succeed in imposing his will on the city."[13] The ancient orator "was always arming himself for the fight of eloquence," Edward T. Channing explains in his inaugural address as the Boylston Professor of Rhetoric and Oratory in 1819.[14] Again in the Renaissance language offered itself as the tool of power: aspirants for influence and fame first in the Italian city-states and then in the courts of Europe were delighted with the prospect that a training in rhetoric would whet the tongue for success in the verbal swordplay of politics. Yet for the pursuit of eloquence to be sustained as a cultural ideal – and as the mark of the gentleman courtier – the orator's power had to serve something beyond self-interest, and here is where the full range of liberal arts, the *studia humanitatis*, came into play. Their study would fashion the orator into the good man and eloquence into the "instrument of society," or, as Roger Ascham, an early humanist educator in England, maintained, a study of "God's holie Bible" joined with "Tully in Latin, Plato, Aristotle, Xenophon, Isocrates, and Demosthenes in Greek, must needs prove an excellent man."[15] And therefore Henry Peacham clothes his naked look at oratory as the "emperour of men's minds" with the asseveration "Honest and eloquent orators are props to uphold a State and the onely keyes to bring in tune a discordant Commonwealth."[16] Channing, who taught Emerson and Lowell and served as the Boylston professor from 1819 to 1851, countered Adams's dream that the United States would revive an eloquence that would match the ancients' power for power by claiming that the oratory most appropriate for the country would be less powerful, less passionate, and thus less likely to rabble-rouse the public than the oratory of the ancient demagogue, who "would draw the attention of the discontented to some foreign enterprise, or fix it upon a victim at home, and tempt the rabble to waste their irritation upon an unpopular benefactor, or upon some harmless neighbor whose liberty gave offense."[17] Channing seeks to defang a rhetoric of power by holding forth the ideal of the civic humanist that was developed in Renaissance Florence.

In the Italian city-state where humanism was first bred and nourished – the Florence of Coluccio Salutati and Leonardo Bruni – rhetoric was repeatedly championed as the power that could serve the state. There rhetoric became what it had been for Cicero and what it would be for American revolutionaries: the instrument for advancing civic liberty. Pocock has argued in *The Machiavellian Moment* that American revolutionaries were the civic humanists of their day fighting for liberty against tyranny and for virtue against corruption. The civic humanists of Florence recognized that this fight could be won with the power of the word, and it is the connection between eloquence and liberty which the revolutionaries rehabilitated and helped transmit to America, where, as a young man in the Colonies planning his studies and plotting his career, John Adams asked himself in his diary, "Of what use, to a lawyer is that part of oratory, which relates to moving of the passions?" His answer is classic: "It may be used to raise . . . an Admiration, and Esteem of the wise, human, equitable and free Constitutions of Government we are under. It may be used to rouse in the Breasts of the Audience a gallant Spirit of Liberty, especially when declaiming upon any Occasion, on any Instance of arbitrary Conduct in an Officer or Magistrate."[18]

Republican virtue demanded the subordination of self-interest to the public good, and in Quattrocento Florence there appeared to be a time, as there would appear to be in Revolutionary America, of a reciprocity of interests between the individual and the community: a time when the humanist, the man of letters, pursued happiness by pursuing public service. The personal rewards of that service – riches, pleasure, power, praise – were not negligible, and they were not overlooked, but they were regarded, in Emerson's terms, as "secondary desires" whose fundamental pursuit, as Emerson argues in *Nature*, would corrupt language (ELA, 22). "There is nothing more glorious in this life, nor more excellent, nor more sacred," declared one Florentine, "than in administering the common weal, to discharge one's filial duties to one's country and render it service."[19] A commitment to the public was at the heart of Florence's republican glory, according to

Leonardo Bruni in *Oration for the Funeral of Nanni Strozzi*, and what sustained this commitment, Bruni explains in terms that recall Pericles' praise for Athens in the Funeral Oration was a conviction that free and equal access to positions of public service were open to all.

> The constitution we use for the government of the republic is designed for the liberty and equality of indeed all the citizens. . . . Our liberty is equal for all, is limited only by the laws, and is free from the fear of men. The hope of attaining office and of raising oneself up is the same for all, provided only one put in effort and have talent and a sound and serious way of life. Virtue and probity are required of the citizens by our city. Anyone who has these two qualities is thought to be sufficiently well-born to govern the republic. . . . This is true liberty, this is fairness in a city: not to have to fear violence for injury from any man, and for the citizens to be able to enjoy equality of the law and a government that is equally accessible to all.[20]

"For Bruni," as Nancy Struever writes, "the central motif of Florentine history is the formation of a public sphere where freedom as virtuosity can appear, the creation of a sphere of good faith where one can debate without fear of intimidation or constraint, in which men talk and act in real *libertas*."[21] The creation of such a space must be seen as one of Jefferson's highest ideals. This was the space jeopardized, Jefferson believed, by the Alien and Sedition Acts of 1798, which he strenuously opposed, and the recovery of such a space is what he proposes in his First Inaugural Address: "Let us restore to social intercourse that harmony and affection without which liberty and even life itself are but dreary things. And let us reflect that, having banished from our land that religious intolerance under which mankind so long bled and suffered, we have yet gained little if we countenance a political intolerance as despotic, as wicked, and capable of as bitter and bloody persecutions" (JLA, 493). Bruni expounded further on the value of such a free space: "And when a free people are offered this possibility of attaining offices, it is wonderful how effectively it stimulates the talents of the citizens. When shown a hope of gaining office, men rouse themselves and seek to rise; when it is precluded they sink into idleness. In our city, therefore, since this hope and prospect is held out, it is not at all surprising that talent and industriousness should be conspicuous."[22]

The talent that republican freedom most encouraged, and the talent that became the means of access to public office, or so the humanists declared, was the talent of talk. "Who but our citizens," Bruni asks, "brought back to light and into practice this art of public speaking

which had been completely lost?" Bruni then concludes his oration
with a tribute to Florence that embraces the credo of humanism – that
the restoration of liberty is followed by a renaissance of letters:
"Who, if not our city, recognized the value of Latin letters, which had
been lying abject, prostrate, and almost dead, and saw to it that they
were resurrected and restored? . . . [W]hy should this city of ours not
. . . be called the parent of the Latin language for restoring it to its
splendor and dignity from its recent state of ruin and corruption?"[23]
Like Bruni, Pius II praised Florence for using a verbal measure when
selecting its chancellors. The city did "not seek out lawyers, as most
states do, but those skilled in oratory and what is called the *studia
humanitatis*."[24] Not just in Florence but throughout Renaissance Italy
princes, popes, and prelates vied with each other in seeking to draw
the best writers and orators into their courts, because the humanist's
talent, his ability to deliver an eloquent formal speech or compose a
state paper, was regarded as of utmost importance in political affairs.
Domenico Bandino of Arezzo reports, for instance, "The splendor of
Coluccio's eloquence became with time so brilliant that his almost
countless prose letters show how kings, prelates and emperors tried to
persuade him by incredible rewards to enter their service."[25] The
eloquence of Salutati and Bruni was more than an exercise in classi-
cism. Their speeches were pronounced amid the tumult of the public
square; their letters were directed at enemy chiefs of state; and their
eloquence was seen to convince assemblies of a course of action or
change the course of foreign policy. Pius II reports that Salutati's
eloquence "was such that Galeazzo, the ruler of Milan who waged a
terrible war against Florence . . . was often heard to say that a
thousand Florentine knights did him less harm than Coluccio's pen."[26]
In the war against Milan, Hans Baron argues, the humanists of Florence deployed the power of the pen and cited the classics to defend
their liberties.[27] They fashioned with their words a myth of Florence
as heir of the old Roman republic and convinced citizens to become
new Ciceros and new Catos fighting the advance of tyranny just as
John Adams and a host of other writers who took classical names were
persuaded that their fight against Britain was the fight that their
bookish study of Catiline's conspiracies against liberty had prepared
them for. And after 1783 the myth of American liberty won by the
word would be perpetuated so often as to obscure, consciously and
unconsciously, the blood spilt by the sword.

So convinced were the humanists of the importance of eloquence to
the preservation of liberty that in their eyes the free practice of speech
was the goal of political development and the measure of liberty.
Bruni and other humanists echo the assumption of many classical

orators that eloquence thrives in a state of liberty and declines in a tyranny. The assumption was so paradigmatic that it governed their reading of history and contemporary events. The central thesis of Bruni's *Laudatio of the City of Florence* is the conviction that the "vanishing of brilliant minds" in imperial Rome was due to the baneful effects of despotic rule on the character of the Roman people, and Poggio Bracciolini, the humanist chancellor who succeeded Bruni, structures an account of Roman history upon the same correlation: "From the words of Seneca in which he states that brilliant minds had been born in the age of Cicero, but later had declined and deteriorated; and from the testimony of Tacitus who asserts that those brilliant minds disappeared after power had been concentrated in one hand; it is quite obvious how great a damage Roman letters suffered by the loss of liberty." Poggio adds, "Caesar was the parricidal murderer of the Latin language and the literary arts as much as of his *patria*, because after the destruction of the republic, Latin eloquence collapsed."[28] With the lesson of the fate of eloquence and liberty in imperial Rome indelibly in their minds, Bruni and Poggio were convinced, Nancy Struever argues, that open deliberation in good faith and the cultivation of eloquence would expose the path to greatness for the Florentine city-state.[29] The candor that was not part of Caesar's Rome or George III's England was, Jefferson suggests, the glory of the colonists, who in 1776 could pledge, in the words of his draft of the Declaration, "a faith yet unsullied by falsehood" and who would sustain what an imperial England had murdered: "a communication of grandeur & of freedom" (JLA, 20, 23).

But because of mid-fifteenth-century developments in which Cosimo Medici was seen to advance a tyranny under a facade of liberty, the reciprocity of interests between the humanist and the city-state was disrupted. Lauro Martines explains in a study of the social world of the Florentine humanists that in the first half of the fifteenth century the humanists saw a "close relationship between the civic life that actually existed and the sort of life they wanted," which was a harmony between the active and contemplative life. Thus "men like Salutati, Bruni, Poggio and Manetti were as much at home with philological and literary questions as with political and historical ones." "But in the second half of the century," Martines writes, "when interest in political and historical reflection could no longer draw on the resources of a vigorous civic life, . . . the *studia humanitatis* became more thoroughly literary, or much more concerned with idealistic and abstract question."[30] When equal access to public office was denied, when the arteries that led from the heart of the forum to the head of state were closed, when eloquence was cut off from political action, when what was said in politics made no difference to what was done, the civic humanist became merely the humanist. After Bruni the position of the chancellor changed as the figure lost all political influence and became ornamental. The citizen-orator was reduced to a ceremonial orator, and rhetoric, devoid of its vital function of political persuasion, was reduced to mere rhetoric – panegyric or the philology of the library. Or else it became simply a power technique, the weapon of *virtù*. In the early sixteenth century Pietro Aretino, "the Scourge of Princes," stands forth as the antithesis of the civic humanist, an inversion of the legendary Salutati warring with words against enemies of his city. "With goose-quill and a few sheets of paper," Aretino boasts, "I mock myself of the universe."[31] With his pen as his sword, Aretino becomes a condottiere in the republic of Italian letters. He identifies himself proudly as no noble; he flatters (and sometimes threatens) princes, popes, and patrons; and he makes a fortune and a name for himself, receiving in tribute from Francis I a gold chain on which was written "His tongue speaketh a lie." Aretino marks the death of republican Venice and its transformation into the pseudo-republican Venice of intrigue and masquerade whose affairs Cooper examines in *The Bravo* (1831). Aretino, who courts the powerful with lies and flattery and who deploys the press to serve his interest, is an ancestor to Dodge and Bragg, the Aretinos of Templeton.

Inherent in the rhetorical discipline was always the danger that the orator might deploy words as did Aretino, solely for personal rather than public ends, making the orator no civic humanist but a demagogue or tyrant. Cicero for one realized that since eloquence "can impel" an audience whithersoever it inclines its force, it is necessary that "it should be united with probity and eminent judgment," because "if we bestow this faculty of eloquence upon persons destitute of these virtues, we shall not make them orators, but give arms to madmen."[32] Juan Luis Vives echoes Cicero's concern in an image that should remind us of the fears expressed in antebellum America of a ship of state driven off course by a spellbinding orator: "The tongue is the cause of great benefits and mischiefs depending on its use. . . . James the Apostle compares it properly to the rudder of a ship" because "roping must be thrown on it and drawn tight, so that it neither hurts others, or itself."[33] In order to bridle the power of language and foster the wise discipline of the complete orator, Cicero demands that the orator become a philosopher, just as Emerson in each of his two essays on eloquence counters his opening paean to the power of the word with a closing injunction that the orator must love

the word. Consistently in the *Essais* he measures the disproportion that divides words from their referents on a mature reckoning, and he condemns the essential superfluity, or even deceitfulness, of eloquence that the division manifests. For Montaigne, rhetoric is little else than the art of deceiving and flattering; like cosmetics, it is used to deceive "our judgment," and it corrupts "the essence of things."[39] Countering the beliefs the humanists held so dear, or so paradigmatically, he argues that eloquence was not invented to replace arms or to advance peace and liberty but "to manipulate and agitate a crowd and a disorderly populace," and he asserts that eloquence flourished most at Rome not when the city was at its political height but "when affairs were in the worst state and agitated by the storm of civil wars" (222). Yet while Montaigne, like Edward Channing, views the power of words to sway the mind as more of a curse than a blessing – a power that had to be defused – he also recognizes the fundamental importance of language to the maintenance of a civil community and thus the dangers that arise when the word is abused: "Since mutual understanding is brought about solely by way of words, he who breaks his word betrays human society. It is the only instrument by means of which our wills and thoughts communicate, it is the interpreter of the soul. If it fails us, we have no more hold on each other, no more knowledge of each other. If it deceives us, it breaks up all our relations and dissolves all the bonds of our society" (505). For Montaigne, the social world is sustained by the verbal contract, and he acknowledges that persuasion itself depends not just on the ability or character of the speaker but on the consent of the listener, or what Montaigne calls "the stupidity and facility that is found in the common people, which makes them subject to be led by the ears to the sweet sound of this harmony without weighing things and coming to know their truths by force of reason." (222). A favorite story of the humanists, which Montaigne alludes to here, was the story of Hercules Gallicus, a figure of eloquence whose words were so powerful that legend represents him (and artists illustrate him) drawing listeners wherever he so willed by a chain that leads from his mouth to their ears, a chain that according to Montaigne is forged not by the orator alone but by the ignorance of the audience. Montaigne argues, in short, that the force and meaning of a word depend not just on the will of the speaker but on the opinions of the people who form its audience. This perspective is the necessary and sufficient foundation for a contractual theory of language such as would be further developed in the seventeenth century by Locke. But we must also note how Montaigne, in his observations on the "sweet sound" of the harmony of words, recognizes what Locke, who was no poet, does not explain but what the orator in America would play upon to enforce (or bypass) the "rational" or contractual sense of a word: its tone.

Like Plato before him and Hobbes afterward, Montaigne in the *Essais* provides a diagnosis of the Thucydidean moment when, in the midst of civil strife, people break the verbal contracts that have sustained a community by baptizing, in Montaigne's words, "public vices with new milder names to excuse them, adulterating and softening their titles" (119). Caught in the civil wars that prompted several of his contemporaries to cite Thucydides' description of the *stasis* at Corcyra, Montaigne responds to these events as something more than an essayist exploring and recording the movements of his own mind. He was a lawyer and a public official whose meditations are prompted not just by a close reading of the twists and turns of his own meditations and of his favorite books but by a reading of the disputes and betrayals of contemporary politics, which must have inclined him to some degree to take his antirhetorical stance and to proclaim, as he does in "The Apology for Raymond Sebond," that "our speech has its weaknesses and its defects, like all the rest." He adds: "Most of the occasions for the troubles of the world are grammatical. Our lawsuits spring only from the debate over the interpretation of the laws, and most of our wars from the inability to express clearly the conventions and treaties of agreement of princes. How many quarrels, and how important, have been produced in the world by doubt of the meaning of that syllable Hoc!" (392). Three hundred years later similar statements would be made by Americans who concluded that the troubles that led to the Civil War were grammatical controversies over the meanings of such words as "necessary and proper" and "We, the People." Opposed to the verbal betrayals and fanaticism of his age, Montaigne offers his readers, partly as an antidote, a prose faithful to the supple workings of his own mind, a prose that Emerson would admire for its ability to capture life in words: "Cut these words & they would bleed; they are vascular & alive; they walk & run."[40] The suppleness of Montaigne's *Essais*, wherein words seem to follow the meanderings of a mind, becomes a model for Emerson. The word should not channel thought: language must follow the course set by nature.

The transformation in linguistic attitudes which Montaigne signals from the verbal reliances of humanism to the verbal skepticism of the seventeenth century can be traced in the literature of Renaissance England. Spenser, Marlowe, and Shakespeare, for instance, mirror in their own works through their continuing reflection upon language the whole cultural metamorphosis in verbal attitudes from a bright, nearly magical confidence in words that marks the beginning of the Renaissance to the dark fears of the Jacobean period and the antirhetorical empiricism of the so-called Age of Reason. Spenser, who it seems had originally hoped that the courtiers of England could be refashioned into more courteous gentlemen in as long a time as it took them to read *The Faerie Queen*, concludes his poem not with the visionary politics and prophetic history he had outlined in his early books but with the rampage of the Blatant Beast, the backbiting monster armed with a thousand tongues who is a virtual incarnation of the unbridled tongue Erasmus describes in *Lingua*. Marlowe in his first play creates his great hero, Tamburlaine, who scourges princes and conquers the world with "high astounding terms" and "working words" that fulfill on the stage all the powers the humanists had ascribed to eloquence in the theater of the world. But then, in *Dr. Faustus*, Marlowe's seemingly omnipotent scholar – a magus of words – is damned by his illusions about the "virtues" in "heavenly words": no spell can spare him from the call of Mephistopheles. Finally, in *Edward II*, Marlowe depicts a hardened political world wherein rhetoric's only power is to divert, deceive, or describe. A young man seeking to make his way in the courtly world is given a bit of advice in *Edward II* that counters the thesis of every rhetorical handbook in the Renaissance but fits him for the world of intrigue and plots that became the drama of politics in Jacobean England. Unlike Polonius's advice to Hamlet, this counsel is to the point: "You must cast the scholar off / And learn to court it like a gentleman. . . . You must be proud, bold, pleasant, resolute, / And now and then stab, as occasion serves" (II.i.31–2, 42–3).

In Shakespeare's drama, the intoxicating wordplay of *Love's Labour's Lost* becomes more troublesome in the equivocal world of the problem plays and tragedies. Hamlet, like Faustus, is a scholar who loves to play with words, but he recognizes their futility to suffice for action and their facility at covering up deeds in a corrupt world where power is determined not by words but by the sword and poison. In the end not Horatio, the windbag of *oratio*, but Fortinbras, the strong arm of action, is left to rule. In *King Lear*, a king's discovery of the impotence of his own language and the falsity of his daughters' declarations of love leads to disgust with words, words, words. After the opening scene, the play records Lear's grudging but progressive acknowledgment that the world will not conform to his will or be altered by the fiat of a king's sentence. When he enters into the wilds of nature and strips himself of his clothes, he realizes that the words of his two eldest daughters, like his robes, have clothed him only in the appearance of a king and that he is truly just another "bare forked animal." Lear demands a naked confrontation with nature, and out on the heath he senses that such words as "justice" and "adultery" and even the title of king are arbitrary designations, the attempts of humanity to clothe nature with a fabric of meaning – and those garments can hide sin as much as protect those who are more sinned against than sinning. Lear must learn what always remains difficult for a man accustomed to power to learn: how not to define things in his own terms, how not to listen to flattery, and how to listen to the weak, the powerless, and the mad – to his Fool and to Cordelia.

Walt Whitman suggests in a piece entitled "What Lurks Behind Shakespeare's Historical Plays?" that "it is possible a future age of criticism, diving deeper, mapping the land and lines freer, completer than hitherto, may discover in the plays named the scientific (Baconian?) inauguration of modern Democracy" (WLA, 1150). Elaborating upon the connection Whitman posits, we could say in our current age of criticism, alert as it is to the connections between discourse and power, that what Shakespeare helps inaugurate in his history plays (and in his tragedies) and what Bacon (and the American Revolution) continues to develop is a contractual understanding of linguistic power that anticipates or coincides with the development in the seventeenth century of democratic (or at least republican) concepts of political power. More precisely, Shakespeare's drama of the power and limitations of kingship and language in such plays as *Richard II* and *King Lear* leads to the conclusion that the power and meaning of a word, like the power of a king, is sustained not by any sovereign nomination or right relation of the word (or king) to nature, but by the force of consent, by public opinion, or by the power to enforce an opinion.

The lesson Lear learns on Dover plain is one that the seventeenth century was determined not to forget: to trust in the correspondence of language and nature is to risk madness or to become a Quixotic dupe of language.[41] At almost the same time that *King Lear* and *Don Quixote* were being written, Francis Bacon begins his revolutionary epistemological reforms in *The Advancement of Learning* by attacking the verbalism of past methods of learning and by advocating a new method that would surmount or replace the vulgar terms of common understanding – the "Idols of the Market-place." Soon afterwards René Descartes begins a similar attack and reform in his *Discourse on Method* and issues the same warning about the way words distort the perception of reality. The conclusion reached at the end of *King Lear* and *Don Quixote* about the nature of language and the lack of correspondence between words and things was to be further developed by philosophers and linguists over the next two centuries: the only bond between a word and its referent is a contractual bond, a bond that can be sealed by the affection of a Cordelia or broken by the design of an Edmund.[42] In those years, as Gerald Gillespie writes, Bacon and his followers seek "to deconstruct language itself as an unreliable instrument, and to reconstruct a linguistic counterpart for the natural philosophy of the age, on the grounds that the consideration of the truth of ideas could not proceed without strictly controlled definitions."[43] Not just the Royal Society of England but the *philosophes* of the American Revolution would follow Bacon in this regard.

No one revealed the unreliability of language in the seventeenth century more imaginatively than did Cervantes in *Don Quixote*. But his novel leaves us wondering whether we can or whether we should overcome all aspects of the madness that so confuses and so inspires Quixote. We long to participate in worlds created by words. Desire is shaped by the word, and the word offers a seductive vision of romance – a vision of the world, for instance, where justice triumphs, where the low are exalted, where people are entitled to the pursuit of liberty and a more perfect union. Teague O'Regan, related closely in spirit to Sancho Panza, will pursue such desires (and other desires) in *Modern Chivalry* against the constraints of Captain Farrago. Cervantes also offers something of a new method for learning about the nature of the world that Brackenridge follows. Through the novel, the reader enters into a diverse marketplace of language. Vocabularies are in competition, challenging each other, offering a range of goods. One voice offers a particularly important perspective: the vernacular voice of Sancho Panza, who irrepressibly challenges the vision of his master, Don Quixote, an aristocrat and something of a scholar who, all too typically, constructs a vision of the world that conforms to the books he has read.

Shakespeare and Rabelais, like Cervantes, serve a great feast of languages, and everyone seems to attend and contribute. The high and the low, fools and monarchs, servants and nobles, arrive and mix it up in everything from slang to stately verse. Mikhail Bakhtin has enabled us to understand more fully the social and political implications of the remarkable play with language that distinguishes Rabelais's work and that of other Renaissance writers. Bakhtin argues that the "literary and linguistic consciousness" of the Renaissance was formed in the crucible of "a complex intersection of languages, dialects, idioms and jargons," and he argues that this "active plurality of language" led to the "exceptional linguistic freedom" of the Renaissance and to the cultural defeat of "the influence of the century-old hidden linguistic dogmatism on human thought."[44] The Renaissance was a dialectic revolution. Just as the authority of medieval Latin was undercut by the recovery of classical Latin and by the legitimation of vernacular tongues of the humanist movement, so too was the authority of the Catholic Church in religion and of Aristotle in science challenged by, respectively, the dissenters of the Reformation and the scientific revolution, who chose to speak a different language. Humanists and reformers in religion and science declared their right to purify the language of classical and Christian texts or to interpret the Book of Nature and the Book of God free from the dictates of authority – an assertion that could and did lead to persecution. New powers arose to govern language and people, and old ones remained; but still, it seems, the tongue became more unbridled in the Renaissance – or that was the way it appeared to such writers of the American Renaissance as Melville and Whitman, who drew inspiration for their own language experiments from what Jefferson called Shakespeare's "free and magical creation of words" (TJW, XIV, 464).

For Lowell, Shakespeare was no solitary genius but a representative man because he was a phenomenon of a special moment in the life of the English language. Shakespeare arrived, Lowell writes, "at the full development of his powers at the moment when the material in which he was to work – that wonderful composite called English . . . – was in its freshest perfection" (JLW, III, 1). The "mingling of divers speeches" in the Renaissance, Lowell argues, had transformed the English language into "perhaps the noblest vehicle of poetic thought," just as "the mixture of many bloods" made the English "the most vigorous of modern races" (JLW, III, 1–2). Whitman expresses the same pride (i.e., chauvinism) in the English language, calling it the "chosen tongue" and embracing its assimilation of different languages: it is "the accretion and growth of every dialect, race, and range of time, and . . . the free and compacted composition of all" (WLA, 1165). Lowell as the poet of *The Biglow Papers* and Whitman as the poet of *Leaves of Grass* would draw upon their perception of multiplicity within the unity of the language in imitation, in part, of Shakespeare's own practice. In Shakespeare's day, Lowell adds, the language was established but not yet "fetlocked by dictionary and grammar mongers," and "no arbitrary line had been drawn between high words and low; vulgar then meant simply what was common; poetry had not been aliened from the people by the establishment of an Upper House of vocables, alone entitled to move in the stately ceremonials of verse" (JLW, III, 8–9). For Lowell and Whitman, the low vocable as well as the high had an inalienable right to citizenship in the language of literature, and by defending that right and by representing the low vocable in their own work, Lowell and Whitman helped to champion a democratic idiom against what Lowell called the "Universal Schoolmaster, who does his best to enslave the minds and memories of his victims to what he esteems the best models of English composition, that is to say, to the writers whose style is faultily correct and has no blood-warmth in it" (JLW, VIII, 159). The lesson that Shakespeare offers to Lowell becomes the lesson he teaches in *The Biglow Papers*: "A literate dialect grows ever more and more pedantic and foreign, till it becomes at last as unfitting a vehicle for living thought as monkish Latin," but "our popular idiom is racy with life and vigor and originality" (ibid.). Lowell and Whitman and other writers in the literary era that Matthiessen aptly entitled the American Renaissance construct a Shakespeare and a *renaissance des lettres* (and an image of the vox populi) that nourish their own love of a people's speech and aid them in their battle against the schoolmasters who had been trying to fetlock and bridle the tongue, it seems, ever since the beginning of the seventeenth century. Indeed, Whitman's interpretation of three classic writers demands a democratization of the muse. He argues that it is "foolish talk" to say that "Dante, Shakespeare, [and] Luther . . . created their languages anew. . . . Great writers penetrate the idioms of their races, and use them with simplicity and power."[45]

What began to be lost in the seventeenth century in England and what Lowell and Whitman would fight to regain is the conviction that the language of the marketplace – the vernacular tongue – is a source of eloquence and that language itself is a medium that could faithfully represent the world and "well nigh express the inexpressible" (WLA, 25). While language was for the humanists of Renaissance England one of the greatest gifts God had given man, for Bacon language was an all too human instrument, prey to error, corruption, and deceit. Thus whereas the humanists praised eloquence as the necessary catalyst for making wisdom active in the world, Bacon asserts that it is the very reaction to words in the understanding that has rendered "philosophy and the sciences sophistical and inactive."[46] And whereas Roger Ascham in *The Scholemaster*, a major humanist treatise on education in Tudor England, warns, "Ye know not what hurt ye do to learning, that care not for words, but for matter; and so make a divorce betwixt the tongue and the heart," Bacon maintains that "the first distemper of learning, [is] when men study words and not matter" (FBW, III, 284).[47] Bacon's fears became commonplace concerns, and the commonplaces of the humanists became trivial. But here, before moving on to study Bacon's rhetoric of antirhetoric, let me recall in tribute to the Renaissance pursuit of eloquence an additional part of Ascham's critique of the corruption that occurs in the affairs of the heart and soul when we care not for words but for matter and leave "fair

Rhetoric," in Pope's words, "languish'd on the ground." "For mark all ages," Ascham counsels,

> look upon the whole course of both the Greek and Latin tongues, and ye shall surely find, that, when apt and good words began to be neglected, and properties of those two tongues to be confounded, then also began ill deeds to spring; strange manners to oppress good orders; new and fond opinions to strive with old and true doctrine, first in philosophy, and after in religion; right judgment of all things to be perverted, and so virtue with learning is contemned, and study left off.[48]

The radical interdependence of word and thought, virtue and good letters that Ascham develops here is at the heart of the humanist vision, but here, as in Pope's *Dunciad* and Orwell's "Politics and the English Language," the connection is stressed in negative terms, presenting us with a sorrowful reminder of the treason, heresy, strife – or, in a word, chaos – that arise as part of the Thucydidean moment when the compact of the *logos* or the union of *res* and *verba* is broken.[49]

Writing on Shakespeare in 1868, Lowell cites Ascham's caution about making a "Divorce betwixt the Tongue and the Heart" (JLW, III, 7). Near the outbreak of the Civil War, Lowell condemned the country's politicians for making such a divorce: they neglected the "vital and formative principle" of the country – the Declaration – for the rule of "dead formula" (JLW, V, 36–7). After the Civil War, Lowell offers Shakespeare as the example of a poet who could teach a people how to reconcile life and language, the tongue and the heart, word and thought (JLW, III, 6–7). Indeed, just as Lowell in 1866 endorsed a Constitution governed not by the letter but the spirit, so too he praises Shakespeare in the late 1860s as the poet who proved his argument that "no language is ever so far gone in consumption as to be beyond the great-poet-cure" (JLW, III, 307).

6

The Enlightenment Project:
Language Reform and Political Order

> ... but I leave it to be considered, whether it would not be well for mankind ... that the use of words were made plain and direct; and that language, which was given us for the improvement of knowledge and bond of society, should not be employed to darken truth, and unsettle people's rights; to raise mists, and render unintelligible both morality and religion?
>
> John Locke, *An Essay Concerning Human Understanding*

Led by Bernard Bailyn, Gordon Wood, and J. G. A. Pocock, scholars of colonial American history have developed the argument (often referred to as the "republican synthesis") that the ideas, beliefs, fears, and perceptions of the "Commonwealthmen" or "Real Whigs" were "the primary elements of American politics" in the eighteenth century because they formed the political assumptions and expectations of the colonists and furnished "not merely the vocabulary but the grammar of thought, the apparatus by which the world was perceived."[1] The most important argument of the republican synthesis consists in the claim that the political thought of the Revolution was not primarily rooted in the Lockean tradition of liberalism but in the language of civic humanism developed in the classical and Renaissance city-states and elaborated in the dissenting literature of the English Civil War and in the opposition literature of the eighteenth-century Commonwealthmen. Though the language of republicanism shared the public stage of Revolutionary America with other idioms, the classic texts of the republican tradition provided the colonists with a highly developed discourse for understanding and protesting those actions of a government or the diseases of a state that signified in their minds the advance of corruption against virtue and of tyranny against liberty. The specific causes for alarm include unchecked ministerial influence, the placement of worthless men in public posts, infringements on the liberty of the press, the advance of luxury, the growth of professional, or standing, armies, and taxation without proper consent. These forms of abuse have been studied as the acts of corruption and tyranny that the colonists protested and that Jefferson enumerated in the Declaration of Independence. But what has not been emphasized enough is that writers in the republican tradition were alarmed that linguistic misrepresentation itself could be a tyrannical political abuse and that literary texts as well as political treatises served as Paul Reveres to summon people against the threat.

Dissenting against the "linguistic turn" in the study of the American Revolution, John Diggins asserts that "it is difficult to see how we can reenact the eighteenth-century mentality by using the conceptual knowledge of the twentieth century mind [e.g., the anthropological theories of Geertz or the language philosophy of Wittgenstein]." He adds, "For thinkers of the eighteenth century politics was real, not symbolic, for politics was about the struggle for interests and power and not merely the use of rhetoric and the acting out of roles."[2] Just as wrongheadedly, in my opinion, Thomas Pangle asserts that the "treatment of the Founders' political thought in terms of Wittgenstein 'language games'" is a method as "unsympathetic to the Founders' claims to truth" and as "unwilling to engage the Founders' arguments with serious respect" as "the approach employed by reductionist historians under the spell of Marx or Beard."[3] To engage the founders' arguments with serious respect, however, we must reconstruct the eighteenth-century mentality regarding the power of words in politics. We must recognize that the colonists shared with Locke, Thomas Gordon, Jean-Jacques Rousseau, and many other Enlightenment writers a sophisticated awareness about how the struggle for interests and power was conducted through verbal means and how people could be governed, manipulated – indeed, tyrannized over – by words as well as by the rule of force and about how politics thus had to be conducted in part as literary criticism or even as a language game that could be won by those most skilled in opposing the abuse of words. Indeed, from their reading in Enlightenment literature, the colonists understood the imperfections of language as well as they understood the imperfections of government; and they were particularly aware of the liability of all languages to revolve in cycles of progress and decay, purity and corruption, and for the representative signs of language to become sovereign forces that could enslave the mind and incite the passions, leading people into tyranny and chaos. When Locke himself justified revolution in *Two Treatises of Government*, he singled out "Prevarications" and "Artifices" as well as "Abuses" as signs of tyranny that had to be resisted.[4] Locke, the Commonwealthmen, and the colonists inherited their distrust of the word from classical philosophers and Christian forebears, but this distrust was exacerbated by the corrosive verbal skepticism that was the legacy of Francis Bacon and René Descartes in their revolt against the verbalism of past methods of learning. To gain perspective on the eighteenth-century mentality regarding words, we can begin with Bacon's new science and his attack on the reign of the schoolmen and the humanist mentality.

Ending the Tyranny of Words: Francis Bacon

Nearly two centuries before the American Revolution, Bacon declared his independence from the verbalism of the past. His grievance: words "plainly force and overrule the understanding, and throw all into confusion, and lead men away into numberless empty controversies and idle fancies" (FBW, IV, 55). His antidote: study nature, a prescription that would become the raison d'être of the Royal Society and a cure that would be translated into political terms in America, most notably by Paine and Jefferson, and into cultural terms by such figures as Emerson. Opposed to a long train of artifice, prevarication, and contentious verbal wrangling, which Bacon claimed was the science of the schoolmen, he inaugurates a scientific revolution.

The significance of Bacon's revolt against words was quickly and widely recognized. In the mid seventeenth century in England a chorus of praise began to swell for Bacon as he was hailed as a liberator and as the founding father of a new method of science whose aim was, in Bacon's own view, to free philosophy from sterile verbal controversy and "commence a total reconstruction of sciences, arts, and all human knowledge, raised upon the proper foundations" (FBW, IV, 8). Abraham Cowley's praise for Bacon in "Ode to the Royal Society" is representative: "*Bacon*, like *Moses*, led us forth at last" from a land of false idols. He asserted a liberty from the ancients – the guardians of knowledge who had turned usurpers – and thus made possible the discovery of a "blest promis'd land": a purer knowledge of God's book of nature.[5] "From words," Cowley writes, "which are but Pictures of the Thought / (Though we our thoughts from them perversely drew) / To Things, the Minds right Object, / He [Bacon] it brought." Similarly, James Thomson lauds Bacon as "the great deliverer" who "led forth true philosophy," which had long been held "in the magic chain of words and forms / And definitions void," from the "gloom / Of cloistered monks and jargon-teaching schools."[6] Thomas Jefferson and a number of other early Americans share the same reverential respect for Bacon. Jefferson includes Bacon along with Locke and Newton in his trinity of demigods; John Adams writes that in "Metaphysicks, Mr. Locke, directed by my Lord Bacon, has steered his course into the unenlightened Regions of the human Mind, and like Columbus, discovered a new world"; Madison praises him for lifting "the veil from the venerable errors which enslaved opinion"; and Emerson, who delivered an early lecture on Bacon, refers to him in his journal as an "intellectual giant who has been the instructor of the world and must continue to be a teacher of mankind till the end of time" (JMN, II, 180).[7] In an age of discovery and reform, Bacon was a pioneer, and among revolutionaries in America he was looked upon as a teacher and a guide.

Bacon conceived of himself as a discoverer in the world of nature and a voyager in the intellectual realm; he was one who was charting a path and leading the expedition past the "few received authors" who "stand up like Hercules' Columns, beyond which there should be no sailing or discovering" (FBW, III, 321). Despite his strong support of the English monarchy – he dedicated *The Advancement of Learning* and *Great Instauration* to James I and rose to become a powerful lord chancellor – the founding fathers had good reason to consider him a fellow revolutionary. Like those Americans who viewed their own revolution as a conservative restoration of the laws of nature and nature's God, Bacon declared that his task was to end the tyranny of the ancient authors, such as Aristotle, "who have usurped a kind of dictatorship in the sciences" and to promote a liberty of examination whose end was to restore the sovereignty of the laws of nature (FBW, IV, 15–16). He demanded the overthrow of the vulgar terms of common understanding, which he considered one of four "Idols of the Mind," because, like the words of the ancients, they corrupted and usurped "Ideas of the divine" and the "true signatures and marks set upon the works of creation as they are found in nature" (FBW, IV, 51). What Bacon advanced, in short, was a method for liberating the mind, and, as Locke and leaders of the Revolution in America understood so well, the fight for independence of the mind had to be won if political independence and self-government were to be achieved.

Though Bacon championed progress, the ultimate end of his advancement of learning was a recovery of an origin, a return to a beginning, an instauration. In *Valerius Terminus* he asserts that "the true ends of knowledge" are a "restitution and reinvesting (in great part) of man to the sovereignty and power (for whensoever he shall be able to call the creatures by their true names he shall again command them) which he had in his first state of creation" (FBW, III, 222). Emerson later would want to name the elements anew; Bacon wants to recover the old names. The state they both hold forth as an ideal is an Edenic state where there will be a faithful marriage between the mind and the world, language and nature. Bacon pictures man as sovereign, but he also suggests that man's sovereignty arises, paradoxically, only from his willingness to obey God's words which compose the book of nature. Bacon rejects any imposition of human names: he wants to transcend language, to become, in Emerson's phrase, a "transparent eye-ball" so he can be a scribe copying from "the volume of Creation": "For this is that sound and language which went forth into all lands, and did not incur the confusion of Babel; this should men study to be perfect in, and becoming again as little children condescend to take the alphabet of it into their hands, and spare no pains to search and unravel the interpretation thereof" (FBW, V, 132–3). He also describes that lost original state as a time of marriage between Pan and Echo, who in his interpretation stand for the world and discourse, and he adds that Echo should always be chosen for the world's wife, "for that is the true philosophy which echoes most faithfully the voices of the world itself, and is written as it were at the world's own dictation" (FBW, IV, 327). But instead of hearkening to the voice of the world, man began to impose his own names on nature and substitute his law for God's law in acts of idolatry. Though they will hold different culprits responsible, Americans will continue Bacon's critique, making a protest against a nature disturbed by names one of the most common refrains of American literature. And this refrain began long before Natty Bumppo and Emerson. Listen, for instance, to Alexander Hamilton when, in the midst of a confusion of laws arising from the colonists' dispute with England, he echoes Bacon's faith that there is a book beneath the book that no one dare abuse by ignorance or arrogance: "The sacred rights of mankind are not to be rummaged for among old parchments or musty records. They are written, as with a sunbeam, in the whole *volume* of human nature, by the hand of Divinity itself, and can never be erased or obscured by mortal power."[8]

More than once Bacon insists in his work that what Adam began, Aristotle, the alchemists, the schoolmen, and the humanists continued: they perpetuated the divorce between God and man, language and nature. Early in his career, in 1592, Bacon announced in a letter to the lord treasurer that he had "vast contemplative ends," for it was his desire to purge the province of knowledge of "two sorts of rovers, whereof the one [the schoolmen] with frivolous disputations, confutations, and verbosities: the other [the alchemists] with blind experiments and auricular traditions and impostures, hath committed so many spoils."[9] "The one never faileth to multiply words," he comments, "and the other ever faileth to multiply gold."[10] Just over a decade later, Bacon began to enact his "vast contemplative ends" with

The Advancement of Learning, the first major strike in his purge of usurpers in the realm of knowledge. Near the beginning he offers an account of the development in the Renaissance of a passionate affair with eloquence. He suggests that the multiplication of words begun by the Greeks had increased manyfold in his day because Martin Luther's attack against the "degenerate traditions of the church" prompted a return to classical texts and languages, which stimulated an admiration for ancient authors and a "delight in their manner of style and phrase" (FBW, III, 282, 283). Provoked also by hatred for the schoolmen, this "affectionate study of eloquence and copie of speech" "grew steadily to an excess; for men began to hunt more after words than matter" (FBW, III, 283, 282). Bacon condemns this affection as a vain romance that will be as barren as "Pygmalion's frenzy" because it can never beget the fruitful works and knowledge that could arise from a true marriage of words and sense, Pan and Echo (FBW, III, 284). "That wisdom," Bacon writes, "which we have derived principally from the Greeks is but like the boyhood of knowledge, and has the characteristic property of boys: it can talk, but it cannot generate; for it is fruitful of controversies but barren of works" (FBW, IV, 14). To advance from the sterility of boyhood to an adulthood that will give birth to new inventions, we must advance from words to things. Verbalism must give way to an embrace of the world. Not a masturbatory love for eloquence but a direct engagement with the facts of life must be pursued.

Just as frequently and perhaps more tellingly than in the sexual metaphors, Bacon resorts to political metaphors to describe speech and eloquence. In an aphorism in *New Organon* that recalls Plato's imagery of the mind as a fort in Book VIII of *The Republic*, Bacon conceives of his program to advance learning as an attempt to purge the mind of false words and the other usurpers who have forcibly possessed the mind and barricaded the entrance against the truth. These usurpers of the mind are called by Bacon the Idols of the Tribe, the Cave, the Theater, and the Marketplace. The word "idol" (or *idolum*) in Bacon's writings is most likely derived, as Charles Whitney indicates, from both Plato's myth of the cave in *The Republic*, where shadows are taken for reality, and Jeremiah's and Ezekiel's attacks on false prophets, idolators who "speak a vision out of their own heart, and not out of the mouth of the Lord" (Jeremiah 23:16).[11] To Bacon the idols of the mind are false gods, and against the power of words and the worship of other idols Bacon wields the weapons of his new science: the method of induction and experiment. With these tactics Bacon fights to free people from their bondage to the words of the past, but he also seeks to free people from their bondage to the words of the present: the language of everyday life. In an early work, *Valerius Terminus*, he calls words the "idols of the Palace" (FBW, III, 242). Perhaps the court world first appeared to him as the locus of deception. For whatever reason, he later switches to the term "Idols of the Market-place," and his effort to topple them becomes an attack on the people who have usurped "the Ideas of the divine," the "true signatures and marks set upon the works of creation" (FBW, IV, 51). The countermajoritarian thrust of Bacon's program of restoration is further suggested in *Valerius Terminus*, wherein he complains that the "state of knowledge is ever a *Democratie*," because "that prevaileth which is most agreeable to the senses and conceits of the people" (FBW, III, 227). In his view, language enshrines these false conceptions of reality, for the words that have been constituted by the "tacit agreements" of the vulgar make distinctions where there should be none, or draw faulty lines rather than representing the true divisions of nature. And if an "acute intellect" seeks to introduce more faithful distinctions, words, which serve as the representatives of democratic knowledge, rebel (FBW, IV, 55). Bacon continually portrays words as a dangerous power in political terms: they are rebellious and ungovernable; they "force and overrule the understanding" (ibid.); they "lead men into empty controversies" (ibid.); they "throw all [things] into confusion" (ibid.); they "forcibly disturb the judgment" (FBW, IV, 434); they "shoot back upon the understanding" like a "Tartar's bow" (FBW, III, 396); and they are "full of trickery and deceit" (FBW, IV, 51). Even "learned men" who seek "to guard and defend themselves" by definitions fool themselves, for to believe that "reason governs words" is to ignore experience and reason itself (FBW, IV, 55, 61).

For Bacon, the beginning of wisdom is the distrust of words. His attack on the Idols of the Marketplace reinvigorated for the seventeenth century the Platonic critique of words, and it became the forerunner of Lockean epistemology and the Ideologue movement in the Enlightenment, which had at its center, in Kenneth Minogue's words, "a kind of psychology whose purpose was to reform thought and language on the basis of sensation and experience."[12] Bacon himself was not unwilling to prescribe remedies for the defects of words and to hope that they could become what they once were: "footsteps and prints of reason" (FBW, III, 401). He suggests that the "setting down" of definitions and the use of "technical terms" "after the prudent course of mathematicians" "may avail to correct the perverted acceptations of terms," but he knows that since definitions are words, they merely beget more words (FBW, IV, 434). Thus a stronger remedy is needed. He also advises that a grammar could serve as "an antidote against the curse of the confusion of tongues" (FBW,

IV, 440–1), and he speculates about developing a philosophical grammar that would inquire into "the analogy between words and reason," and examine "the power and nature of words as they are footsteps and prints of reason" (FBW, III, 401). He mentions in one of his works the existence in China of "Characters Real, which express neither letters nor words in gross, but Things or Notions," and while he never seemed to contemplate creating such a language in England, John Wilkins would develop such a proposal in 1667 (FBW, III, 399). Indeed, with these comments and suggestions, Bacon set forth the plans and began to lay down the foundation that scientists, philosophers, and linguists would build upon over the next century in their efforts to reform the language in order to advance the cause of learning and political order. What was needed was a new constitution of language that would correspond to nature and reason and would be governed not by the people but by the philosopher or scientist.

In the decades that followed Bacon's death in 1626, his epistemological concerns were confirmed and deepened by the political and religious controversies that embroiled the seventeenth century. A common diagnosis of these controversies was that they were due in large part to the abuse of words or to their overruling power. This diagnosis, which can be found in a number of the major political and literary works of the period, received one of its most important elaborations in the work of Thomas Hobbes, who forged some of the tightest links in the so-called Age of Reason between the quest for a new or reformed language and reform of the political state.

Ordering Discourse and the Commonwealth: Thomas Hobbes

In the late 1620s, Hobbes, who had served as an amanuensis for Francis Bacon and translated some of his essays into Latin, began working on translations of two classical works profoundly concerned with the origins of war: Homer's *Iliad* and Thucydides' *History of the Peloponnesian War*. At the time, England was becoming deeply engaged in the political and religious conflicts that sent the first wave of Puritans to America in 1620 and Charles I to the chopping block in 1649. Hobbes wrote his translation of Thucydides' *History*, he later explained in his *Autobiography*, because Thucydides was in his eyes the one classical author who could counter the favorable impressions of democracy that Englishmen had received from studying the works of Greek and Roman authors. Hobbes's translation was as much the act of a troubled citizen as of a classical scholar; it was an attempt to prevent a recurrence in England of a moment of civil collapse such as Thucydides describes in his account of the *stasis* in Corcyra, a moment when, among other things, "the received value of names imposed for signification of things, was changed into arbitrary" (Hobbes's translation).[13]

In 1651, two years after the execution of Charles I, Hobbes published another work "occasioned by the disorders of the times": *Leviathan*.[14] In this work Hobbes does not just offer counsel about the dangers of democracy and a diagnosis of the causes of civil war. He offers a cure: the establishment of a sovereign authority with the power to change arbitrary significations into absolute ones, a sovereign, that is, who could end the Thucydidean moment in England and transform a people, as Orpheus was said to have done, from a brutish condition to a humane one, from a condition of war to a state of peace.

For Hobbes, as for many of his contemporaries, the ordering of discourse was inseparable from the establishment of a more orderly commonwealth. The first theorem of the political science Hobbes sought to teach his contemporaries was that multiplicity of meaning equals political confusion. He notes in *Human Nature: or the Fundamental Elements of Policy* "how *unconstantly* names have been settled, and how subject they are to *equivocation*, and how *diversified* by *passion* (scarcely any two men agreeing what is to be called good, and what evil; what liberality, what prodigality; what valour, what temerity)."[15] This is the arbitrariness that a sovereign power had to resolve if people were to advance from confusion to certainty in knowledge and from confusion to order in a commonwealth.

Hobbes's conception of the relationship between political and linguistic disorders, like that of early Americans, was shaped significantly by the biblical tradition. In Chapter 4 of *Leviathan*, "Of Speech," Hobbes briefly reviews the Christian story connecting rebellion against a sovereign authority – God – and linguistic disorder. "The first author of Speech," he writes, "was *God* himself, that instructed *Adam* how to name such creatures as he presented to his sight. . . . But all this language gotten, and augmented by *Adam* and his posterity, was again lost at the tower of *Babel*, when by the hand of God, every man was stricken for his rebellion, with an oblivion of his former language" (L, 100–1). For Hobbes, the remedy for the linguistic confusion (and rebellion) of Babel is not, as it was for Bacon, a matter of recovering a divinely authorized language that corresponds to the nature of things. Since that language was lost, the sole solution lies in the creation of a sovereign power whose arbitrary naming will be enforced as authoritative.

While Hobbes often cites scripture to support his call for an absolute monarch and an authoritative language, he also cites the classics against a classical tradition that honored democracy and eloquence. Educated at Oxford in a humanist course of study, Hobbes derives from the classics an understanding of man as a language-using animal who creates but who can also destroy the political and ethical world with words. With Isocrates and Aristotle, Hobbes asserts (in *Leviathan*) that before there was language, "there had been amongst men, neither Common-wealth, nor Society, nor Contract, nor Peace, no more than amongst Lyons, Bears, and Wolves" (L, 100). Without names, man exists in a state of nature, and for Hobbes "the natural state of men" is "a war of all men against all men," a state wherein "there is a dominion of passions, war, fear, poverty, slovenliness, solitude, barbarism, ignorance, cruelty."[16] In society, however, there is or can be the "dominion of reason, peace, security, riches, decency, society, elegancy, sciences, and benevolence" (DC, 114). The advent of the word makes possible the advancement of humanity, a transfiguration from a state of civil war to Orphic order. Through language, people can establish distinctions between mine and thine and thus fashion laws and a commonwealth.

But Hobbes emphasizes that language is not an entire blessing. "The tongue of man," he declares in *De Cive*, "is a trumpet of war and sedition" (66). It can incite the passions and foment factions; it can dethrone reason and monarchs. Because man possesses the "benefit of *words* and ratiocination," he not only exceeds "*brute beasts* in knowledge" but exceeds "them also in *error*: for *true* and *false* are things not incident to beasts" (THW, IV, 25). Only man can mistake the true for the false, the good for the bad, because these distinctions, Hobbes asserts, "are the attributes of Speech, not of Things" (L, 105). And because words derive their meaning from the will of men, their meanings can be changed by the will of men or abolished, and because men are passionate and very willful – because they strive for power and pleasure, because they are diverse in their desires and their constitutions, and because there is no authoritative standard beyond the will of men to define the meanings of words – there is inevitable turmoil in the realm of ethics and law.

In his analysis of the causes of civil disorders, Hobbes provides an updated version of Thucydides' and Plato's own discussion of the link between the misuse of words and the onset of political chaos. For Hobbes, the state of war is akin to Plato's condition of *anatrope*; it arises from a confusion "concerning *meum* and *tuum*, just and unjust, profitable and unprofitable, good and evil, honest and dishonest, and the like, which every man esteems according to his own judgment" (DC, 74). Plato appealed to a "realm of Ideas" as a standard to make these distinctions. But for Hobbes, the very nature of language and the very nature of man resist the attempt to turn language into a dialectical instrument, a tool for knowing. Words in general and ethical terms in particular, he explains, do not so much represent a common world of ideas as the "nature, disposition, and interest of the speaker" or "their own affections, as love, hatred, anger, and the like" (L, 109; DC, 88).

Given the arbitrariness of words and the biases of judgment, it seems next to impossible that man could advance from confusion to certainty and from anarchy to order, especially because, in Hobbes's opinion, the arbitrariness of words and errors of judgment are aided and abetted by the practice of oratory. In a familiar ploy of the rhetorical tradition, Hobbes distinguishes in *De Cive* between two types of eloquence. The praiseworthy form of eloquence is "an elegant and clear expression of the conceptions of the mind, and riseth partly from the contemplation of things themselves, partly from an understanding of words taken in their proper and definite significations" (138). The other and more dangerous form of eloquence is "a commotion of the passions of the mind . . . and derives from a metaphorical use of words fitted to the passions" (ibid.). The end of the first type of eloquence, Hobbes says, is truth; the end of the second, victory. The art of the first he calls logic; the art of the second, rhetoric. Logical eloquence, grounded in reason, seeks to represent "things as they are"; rhetorical eloquence, grounded in the will and directed at the passions, seeks to make "good and evil, profitable and unprofitable, honest and dishonest, appear to be more or less than indeed they are; and to make that seem just which is unjust" (DC, 123). The distinction, as Emerson would later develop it in an essay on eloquence, is between an eloquence that clings to facts and a too artful eloquence, which confounds fact, making "the great small and the small great" (REW, VII, 98).

Writing on eloquence, Emerson cites the complaint (made by Daniel Webster), that "the curse of this country is eloquent men" (REW, VII, 75). Hobbes complains similarly but more bitterly. Countering the hopes the Italian humanists placed in a republic to foster eloquence and in eloquence to foster the good of the republic, Hobbes maintains that democracy is the best forum for the triumph of the unscrupulous orator's art and the excitation of the passions of the multitude. Rather than advancing the cause of liberty, eloquence, in Hobbes's view, was an agent of tyranny, and he even condemns democracy as "no more than an aristocracy of orators, interrupted sometimes with the temporary monarchy of one orator" – an opinion that John Adams would second in a private letter: "What are demagogues and popular orators but aristocrats? John Cade and Wat Tyler were aristocrats" (THW, IV, 141; JAW, IX, 508). For Hobbes (and Adams), eloquence and folly are the necessary and sufficient grounds for political disorder. As proof, he cites Sallust's remark that Catiline, the author of the greatest sedition in Rome, had *"eloquentiae satis, sapientiae parum; eloquence sufficient,* but *little wisdom"* (THW, IV, 209). Hobbes's remedy for the troubles of the state that arise from the arbitrariness and power of the word is the appointment of a sovereign whose arbitrary words will be considered authoritative in meaning and absolute in power.

Hobbes's sovereign, as Sheldon Wolin explains, is first and foremost a definer who can enforce the definitions and interpretations he arbitrarily makes.[17] To escape the anarchy of meanings that perpetuates civil conflict, Hobbes insists that the multitude have to "contract one with another, that the will of one man, or the agreeing wills of the major part of them, shall be received for the will of all" (DC, 71). One definition, one judgment has to become standard. The sovereign will "make some common rules for all men . . . by which every man may know what may be called his, what another's, what just, what unjust, what honest, what dishonest, what good, what evil, that is summarily, what is to be done, what to be avoided in our common course of life" (DC, 74). What needs to be emphasized is that the definitions and interpretations of the sovereign would have no grounding in nature: they would be merely an imposition, an act of power. Civil laws, Hobbes maintains, are "the commands of him who hath the chief authority in the city, for direction of the future actions of his citizens" (DC, 75). Hobbes's sovereign wears no robes that would disguise his sword, for "Covenants, without the Sword, are but Words, and of no strength to secure a man at all" (L, 223). Civil law, Hobbes explains, will be like "Artificiall Chains" which the people themselves "by mutuall covenants, have fastened at one end, to the lips of that Man, or Assembly, to whom they have given the Soveraigne Power; and at the other end to their own Ears" (L, 263–4). The figure Hobbes alludes to here is that of the mythical orator Hercules Gallicus, whose words of power become for Hobbes an ideal image of sovereign authority. In effect, Hobbes's sovereign is the supreme orator, the orator whose words are actions and swords, the orator whose words are irresistible, and his audience is the constituency of the commonwealth composed of the common people, whose minds, Hobbes says, are (or should be like) "clean paper, fit to receive whatsoever by Publique Authority shall be imprinted in them" (L, 379). Here and elsewhere Hobbes, who often declares his desire to repress rhetoric and metaphor, resorts to rhetoric and metaphor, and one could say of course that *Leviathan* as a whole is an attempt to convince people that what they are reading is not rhetoric but logic, or not political oratory but political science. In the 1760s and 1770s colonists in America would reveal how specious

Hobbes's metaphors could be when during the Stamp Act crisis they began to resist the attempt of the sovereign power in England to imprint a stamp on their paper and imprint an interpretation of the law and a definition of the word "tax" on their minds. The artificial chains of English law began to break in America under the stress of equivocation about the meanings of such words as "tax" and "representation."

Hobbes's relevance to a study of American politics and language theory extends beyond the Revolution, for if the American Revolution seemed to be a time when, contrary to Hobbes's belief, the practice of eloquence and the pursuit of liberty dovetailed, many Americans in the Confederation period began to have grave doubts about the virtue of the American people and began to adopt something of a Hobbesian view of humanity and a Hobbesian fear of demagogues, democracy, and oratory and began to call, as did Hobbes, for a sovereign power who could enforce the words of a covenant with a sword. And, as we shall see, equivocation about the meaning of the Constitution that was created at the end of the Confederation period – or lack of agreement about the sovereign power that was to define its meaning – seemed to return people, as Hobbes had predicted, to the state Hobbes always sought to counter: civil war.[18]

Verbicide and Regicide: The Fall of Words and Kings

Oliver Wendell Holmes in *The Autocrat of the Breakfast-Table* cites an account of the fate of the pun in Tudor and Stuart England provided by "the historian": "The gravest wisdom and the highest breeding [during the reign of Queen Elizabeth] lent their sanction to the practice [of punning]. . . . The fatal habit became universal. The language was corrupted. The infection spread to the national conscience. Political double-dealings naturally grew out of verbal double meanings. The teeth of the new dragon were sown by the Cadmus who introduced the alphabet of equivocation. What was levity in the time of the Tudors grew to regicide and revolution in the age of the Stuarts."[19] The historian may be spurious and the anecdotes that support the account apocryphal, but Hobbes would not have doubted its lesson. Treason speaks the discourse of equivocation in *Macbeth* and in the political theory of Hobbes and in the writings of contemporaries of Shakespeare and Hobbes (and of Holmes).[20] Indeed, Hobbes was not alone when he demanded in *Leviathan* that language should be "snuffed" by "exact definitions" and "purged from ambiguity" not only to advance the cause of reason and science but because, as Hobbes argues, "reasoning upon" "Metaphors, and sensless and ambiguous words . . . is wandering amongst innumerable absurdities; and their end, contention, and sedition, or contempt" (L, 116–17). This declaration by Hobbes is but one in a long series of explanations of how the "foolish fires" of metaphors, hard words, "fantastick phrases," and "enthusiastical" preaching ignited the conflagration of the Civil War years in England. Samuel Butler similarly begins his extremely popular poem *Hudibras* (1663) with the lines "When *civil* fury first grew high, / And men fell out they knew not why; / When hard words, *Jealousies* and *Fears* / Set Folks together by the ears . . ."[21] Clarendon writes in *The History of the Rebellion* that terms such as "Religion, Law, Liberty, and Parliaments, (words of precious esteem in their just signification)" were at the heart of the conflict.[22] Thomas Sprat notoriously declares in his *History of the Royal Society* (1667) that "*eloquence* ought to be banish'd out of all *civil Societies*, as a thing fatal to Peace and good Manners."[23] Samuel Parker in *Discourse of Ecclesiastical Politie* (1670) points out that "the Nation" was "shattered into infinite factions with senseless and phantastick phrases" and recommends that "had we but an Act of Parliament to abridge Preachers the use of fulsome and luscious Metaphors, it might perhaps be an effectual cure for all our present distempers."[24] Joseph Glanvil in "An Essay Concerning Preaching" complains that there "is a bastard kind of eloquence that is crept into the Pulpit, which consists in affectations of wit and finery, flourishes, metaphors and cadencies," and that such eloquence, or "mysterious, notional preaching," "hath put many conceited people upon meddling with what they can never well understand, and so hath fill'd them with air, and vanity, and made them proud, phantastical, and troublesome; disobedient to their Governours, and contemptuous to their betters."[25] And John Wilkins in *An Essay Toward a Real Character, and a Philosophical Language* (1668) believes his design for a new language will "contribute much to the clearing of some of our Modern differences in Religion, by unmasking wild errors, that shelter themselves under the disguise of affected phrases," and he adds that such a language "in these days" is "well worth a mans pain and study, considering the Common mischief that is done, and the many impostures and cheats that are put upon men, upon the disguise of affected and insignificant phrases."[26] But no act of parliament, no plea for plainness, no newly invented language would avail to counter the rhetorical figurations of a people's discourse if we listen to the words of a figure Samuel Shaw creates in *Words Made Visible* (1679): "Rhetorick governs all the World; and Tropes and Figures . . . carry all before them. They talk of plain, simple, literal, ingenious, cordial, real and I know not what; but the plain truth is, there is nothing plain nor true amongst men; but the whole life of man is a Tropical Figurative Converse, and a continual Rhetorication."[27]

In 1686 Robert South, an Anglican divine who served as a chaplain to Charles II, delivered a series of four sermons entitled "The Fatal Imposture and Force of Words." Just as Shaw acknowledges that language is irreducibly figurative, South's sermons acknowledge that language is unimpeachably political: a force inheres in moral terms that makes them weapons of war. Thus William Mathews, an American professor of literature who delivered a series of lectures in the 1850s called "Words, – Their Significance, Use and Abuse," quotes extensively from South's sermons in a chapter on the "morality in words" in a book that grew out of those lectures.[28] More important than any direct line of influence to American writers, South's sermons (which were reprinted in 1844 by a Philadelphia publisher) provide historical referents for the concerns about the "cheat" of words that Hobbes and Locke address more abstractly or more philosophically in their writings on language. The biblical text for the four sermons was the same verse from Isaiah that Melville underscored in his Bible: "Woe unto them that call evil good, and good evil," and the primary lesson South seeks to draw from his commentary is "what a fatal, devilish, and destructive effect the misapplication and confusion of those great governing names of *good* and *evil*, must inevitably have upon the societies of men."[29] In the first sermon South declares that "the generality of mankind is wholly and absolutely governed by words or names" and that "there is nothing in which they are so remarkably and powerfully governed by them as in matters of good and evil" (I, 173, 175). From this thesis, he develops the argument that words in general are "a dangerous and dreadful weapon," especially in the mouth of an "expert demagogue" or "rabble-driver" who can manage a multitude by noises and cries as if it were a drove of sheep (I, 174). But it is not only the "vulgar" who are subject to the force of words, because, South says, there "is hardly any rank, order, or degree of men, but, more or less, have been captivated and enslaved by words" (ibid.). To account for their power, he suggests that there is a "certain bewitchery" or "magic" in words that "makes them operate with a force beyond what we can naturally give an account of," and as a result of that "enchantment" "the greatest affairs and most important interests of the world are carried on by things, not as they are, but as they are called" (I, 174–5).

In his next three sermons, South describes a number of the "rabble-charming words" which have spread destruction in England in order to "lay open the true meaning and design of them" and snuff out the "wildfire wrapt up in them," the same task of verbal criticism that would spill much ink from the pens of Loyalists and Sons of Liberty during the war of words that preceded the Revolution (II, 546). In his second sermon, entitled "The First Grand Instance of the Fatal Influence of Words and Names Falsely Applied, in the Late Subversion of the Church of England by the Malicious Calumnies of the Fanatic Party, Charging Her with Popery and Superstition," South discusses the "direful and mischievous effects" on the Church of England "of calling good evil and evil good." In his opinion, the "treacherous cant and misapplication" of the words "*popery, superstition, reformation, tender conscience, persecution, moderation,* and the like" effectively burnt the church down to the ground (II, 543). He explains that the "great seducers" – Cromwell and his "fellow-rebels" (II, 539) – falsely called the "religion of the Church of England" by the evil name of "popery," and those evil and "schismatic deserters" mislabeled themselves "true protestants" and the subversion of the church a "reformation," and they branded the "execution of the laws in behalf of the church" "persecution" (II, 539–41). He adds that the word "popery" served as "an effectual engine to pull down the monarchy to the ground" and that the word "reformation" cost "this kingdom about a hundred thousand lives" (II, 539). South rhetorically asks in the end, "Was it not high time . . . to tie up the tongues of those seducers, who could arm mere cant and nonsense to such a formidable opposition to the government, as to make one despicable word, villainously misapplied, and sottishly misunderstood, a fatal 'besom of destruction,' to sweep away all before it, civil or sacred, legal or established, both in church and state?" (II, 543). For South, it seems, Spenser's Blatant Beast has returned to England in the person of Cromwell and his fellow "pulpit impostors" who, with their ungovernable tongues, have ruined the peace of England and who could, like the Devil, cite scripture to seduce men into "the most violent and outrageous courses" (ibid.).

In his third sermon, entitled "The Second Grand Instance of the Mischievous Influence of Words and Names Falsely Applied, in the Late Overthrow of the English Monarchy, Compassed Chiefly Hereby, in the Reign of King Charles I, and Attempted Again in the Reign of King Charles II," South expresses his fear that what happened earlier in the century was about to happen again because several new words, whose power would be recharged in the colonists' controversy with George III, were being used to confuse good and evil: "*arbitrary power, evil counsellors, public spirits, liberty, property, and the rights of the subject*" (II, 546). He specifically complains that the enemies of the "mildest government" were traducing "the best of monarchies" "by the odious name of arbitrary power" and misrepresenting "the ablest friends" as "*evil counsellors*" (ibid.). These enemies, who falsely labeled themselves "*public spirits*" and "*patriots*," were also couching their "malicious and ambitious designs under the glorious cover of *zeal for liberty and property, and the rights of the subject*," a tactic that provoked South to label these terms "mouth granadoes" uttered by incendiaries who were threatening to "throw the whole frame of government into tumult and confusion" (ibid.). The fourth sermon treats the evil effects of slander, and therein South remarks, "All or most of our miseries and calamities which afflict mankind, and turn the world upside down, have been conceived in, and issued from, the fruitful womb of this one villainous artifice" of robbing a man of his innocence by calling him wicked (II, 559).

When South was a student at Westminster School in 1649, he was within earshot of the shout and groan that met the execution of Charles I, whose honor he would later defend and protect in an anniversary sermon. Just as he damned the usurpation of Cromwell, South in these sermons damns the "absurd empire and usurpation of words over things" (I, 175), and he gives what he considers irrefutable proof of how the misuse of words can lead to that time when people mistakenly pursue evil because it has been called good and avoid the good because it has been called evil, a mistake that leads to the moral inversion and political upheaval of a world turned upside down. In 1750 Jonathan Mayhew preached a sermon on the anniversary of Charles I's execution wherein he defended Cromwell as a patriot and excoriated Charles I as wicked. This was one of the opening shots in a rhetorical battle against unlimited submission to the monarchy in England that would conclude on the battlefield at Yorktown, where the British troops played the song "A World Turned Upside Down."

The strong conviction that South shared with other seventeenth-century English writers about how the terms of political and religious discourse could serve as agents of conspiratorial rebellion was a product if not the cause of what Melvin Lasky has termed a "verbal counterrevolution which, in poetry, was associated with the Restoration's neoclassicism and, in general, with an intellectual aversion to the exorbitance of prevailing forms of feeling and emotion." This verbal counterrevolution, called by George Williamson a "revolt against enthusiasm," was characterized by a reiteration of Bacon's demand that words be rigorously subordinated to things and by an attempt to insure that rhetoric's only function in the pulpit and the forum would be, in Bacon's words, "to win the Imagination from the Affection's Part, and contract a confederacy between Reason and Imagination against the Affection" (FBW, IV, 80).[30] But rather than calling it a revolt against enthusiasm, it might be better to call it a "restoration of reason," for the writers, scientists, and ministers associated with this cause in the later seventeenth century sought to restore reason to the throne, just as Charles II had been restored, and they sought to end the usurpation of words over things, just as Cromwell's usurpation had been ended. Language in their plans would not only represent but preserve the old order of things. On October 14, 1662, Charles II himself addressed a directive to the archbishop of Canterbury wherein he asserts that "the extravagance of preachers has much heightened the disorders, and still continues to do so, by the diligence of factious spirits."[31]

What political directives could not accomplish, schoolmasters sought to achieve through other devices. Plans conceived in groves of academe and ivory towers of the mind for reforming the language and style of Englishmen were not few. Thomas Sprat and the Royal Society vigorously encouraged a new "plain style" that would put an end to what Sprat called "this trick of *Metaphors*, this volubility of *Tongue*, which makes so great a noise in the World" and return language back "to the primitive purity, and shortness, when men deliver'd so many *things*, almost in an equal number of *words*"[32] When Sprat called for "Mathematical plainness" in language, it must be emphasized that he was not only seeking to advance the cause of learning; for Sprat envisioned that such stylistic reforms, like the Royal Society itself, would advance the cause of peace. A scientific language, like a scientific academy, in his view, would be a model of consensus, a means of countering the wranglings of the forum and of defusing its "mouth granadoes" – the incendiary rhetoric that South describes. It would help create a garden court of reason in the midst of a babel of tongues; as Sprat points out, "In the *Royal Society* the *Scotch*, the *Irish*, the *English* Gentry do meet, and communicate, without any distinction of *Countries*, or affections. From hence no doubt very much *Political*, as well as *Philosophical* benefit will arise." He also notes that "the contemplation [of nature] . . . never separates us into moral Factions"; instead it "gives us room to differ without animosity; and permits us, to raise contrary imaginations upon it, without danger of a *Civil War*."[33]

Calls for stylistic reform and plans for a language academy were matched in this era by projects for a new scientific or universal language that would faithfully represent the world. John Wilkins, Cave Beck, Thomas Urquhart, George Dalgarno, Seth Ward, Robert Boyle, and Isaac Newton are just some of the men who either proposed a reformed or universal language or commented on its desirability.[34] Whether these plans for a new language and the calls for a "plain style" were motivated by the new science and a desire to continue Bacon's recommendation for the advancement of learning, as R. F. Jones argues, or whether they were part of an anti-Ciceronian movement or a Puritan reaction to Anglican preaching or an Anglican reaction to Puritan preaching, as others have argued, is secondary.[35] Their ultimate goal is almost invariably the same: to end the confusion between people and their exile from nature by recreating an Edenic language in which the relationship between words and things, language and nature, intention and expression will not be problematical. What was desired, in short, was what Thoreau searched for in his own philological researches: a language whose representative authority would derive its just powers from reason or nature.[36] For these reformers, language in the state of Eden was like a flawless mirror reflecting every thought and thing, and that clear glass became the standard of perfection and the desired panacea in the later seventeenth century. For instance, John Wilkins writes in the Epistle Dedicatory to his plan for a "Real Character, And a Philosophical Language," "He that knows how to estimate that judgment inflicted on Mankind in the Curse of the Confusion [of tongues], with all the unhappy consequences of it, may thereby judge what great advantages and benefit there will be, in a remedy against it."[37] George Dalgarno in *Ars Signorum* encapsules in a few phrases the primary goal of the language reformers when he describes his desired end as "that primitive and Divine, or purely rational Sematology, taught by Almighty God or invented by Adam before the Fall."[38] And he writes in *Didascalocophus* (1680) that his plan shows "a way to remedy the difficulties and absurdities which all languages are clogged with ever since the confusion, or rather since the fall."[39]

The confusion and fall Dalgarno refers to here are the confusion of tongues after Babel and the fall of man in the garden of Eden. But many of the language reformers in the seventeenth century associated the corruption of language with another confusion and fall: the fall of Charles I's head in the execution of 1649 and the confusion of the Civil War years. Indeed, the common diagnosis of the sickness causing so many of the political and religious controversies of the age was a diseased language whose pathology includes senseless, hard, or ambiguous words, metaphor, and "Enthusiastick Jargon" or overheated rhetoric, and it is a diagnosis that persists in the eighteenth century. Jonathan Swift, for instance, in his "Proposal for Correcting, Improving and Ascertaining the English Tongue," traces the corruption of the English language directly to the Civil War and also to the "Licentiousness" of the Restoration:

> The Period wherein the *English* Tongue received most Improvement, I take to commence with the beginning of Queen *Elizabeth's* Reign, and to conclude with the Great Rebellion in Forty Two. . . . From

the Civil War to this present Time, I am apt to doubt whether the Corruptions in our Language have not at least equalled the Refinements of it; and these Corruptions very few of the best Authors in our Age have wholly escaped. During the Usurpation, such an Infusion of Enthusiastick Jargon prevailed in every Writing, as was not shook off in many Years after. To this succeeded that Licentiousness which entered with the *Restoration*, and from infecting our Religion and Morals, fell to corrupt our Language; which last was not like to be much improved by those who at that Time made up the Court of King *Charles* the Second; either such who had followed Him in His Banishment, or who had been altogether conversant in the Dialect of those *Fanatick Times*. . . . The Consequence of this Defect, upon our Language, may appear from the Plays, and other Compositions, written for Entertainment within Fifty Years past; filled with a Succession of affected Phrases, and new, conceited Words, either borrowed from the current Style of the Court, or from those who, under the Character of Men of Wit and Pleasure, pretended to give the Law.[40]

For Swift, the age of Shakespeare and the King James Bible marked the height of the English language, an opinion later shared by Noah Webster and James Russell Lowell, and the strength and quality of the language in that seemingly pre-Babel age before the Civil War had great emotional and nostalgic appeal. That appeal was both for a less corrupt language and a more innocent or more orderly age, and that connection between the state of the language and the state of England underlies the assumption prevalent among language reformers of the seventeenth and eighteenth centuries that a reconstituted language was a necessary condition for a restoration of political and social order and religious peace. The same basic assumption animated the quest of Noah Webster (and other language reformers in the early United States) to diffuse a uniform and purified language throughout the country, and it also lay behind the linguistic concerns of the philosopher who had perhaps the greatest influence on early American linguistic speculation: John Locke.

Language and the Social Contract: John Locke on the Use and Abuse of Words

In the early 1800s John Adams remarked in a letter to John Taylor of Caroline that though "Mr. Locke's chapter 'on the abuse of words' . . . contains nothing but what daily experience exhibits to all mankind," it "ought, nevertheless, if he had never written anything else, to secure him immortal gratitude and renown" (JAW, VI, 455). Similarly, in 1833 an American writer using the name "Rhetor" published in the *New England Magazine* an essay entitled "The Abuse of Words" in which the author advises at the end, "Let every one, who is conscious of a liability to disgrace the English tongue, diligently peruse Locke on the Human Understanding, which should rather have been called Locke on the Abuse of Language, and the Diversions of Purley."[41] What Adams and "Rhetor" recognize, as did others in the eighteenth and nineteenth centuries, is that Book III of Locke's *Essay*, "Of Words," was an essential if not the crucial part of the *Essay*, which was one of the most widely read books in early America. Henry F. May and David Lundberg found in their survey of libraries in the period 1776 to 1790 Locke's *Essay* was included in 62 percent of the libraries and continued to be very popular in later years.[42] The *Essay* was also the most widely read or best-known philosophical book in the eighteenth century, and while it shaped Enlightenment psychology of the mind (Locke was the Freud of his century), it also shaped and embodied the predominant theory of language in the Enlightenment. Its influence on Jonathan Swift, Henry Fielding, Laurence Sterne, and Samuel Johnson has been widely discussed, and through its influence on Condillac, as Hans Aarsleff argues, it significantly influenced the linguistic thought of eighteenth-century French writers.[43] Perry Miller can thus claim, "For two or three generations after 1690 practically all theorizing upon language attempted by English or colonial American writers, and much of that on the Continent, was a reworking or reinterpretation of Locke." He adds, "Vast differences slowly began to emerge, but the starting points remained, into what we call the romantic era, those of Book III; perhaps these are even yet the tacit assumptions of schools that are hostile to the Lockean temper."[44]

If the United States was founded on a Lockean theory of government, it was also founded on a Lockean theory of language, for it was in a Lockean linguistic framework that Americans would construct, debate, and battle over the Constitution. Close paraphrases of Locke on language can be found in three of the most important texts that shaped a liberal interpretation of the Constitution: *The Federalist*, Chief Justice Marshall's decision in *McCulloch v. Maryland*, and Justice Joseph Story's *Commentaries on the Constitution*. Key figures in early American politics from Franklin, Jefferson, and John Adams to Daniel Webster announced their admiration and indebtedness to Locke, and not just the Locke of *Two Treatises of Government*, but also the Locke who explored the limits of understanding. John Adams, for instance, reveals why he valued Locke's work on language so much when he explains in a letter written in 1819 to a correspondent who proposed writing a dictionary of political terms, "I have always been convinced, that abuse of words has been the great instrument of sophistry and chicanery, of party, faction, and division in society." He adds that any project that might help remedy such abuses as the "pursuit of correct definitions" would receive his highest endorsement (JAW, X, 377). Joseph Collet, a London pepper merchant living in Sumatra, suggests further how Locke was valued for his writings on language when he writes in 1714 to Richard Steele: "The Bible has the first place in my Study, as teaching me the whole Compass of Duty. Mr. Lock, who first taught me to distinguish between Words and Things, has the next."[45] This is the lesson that many early Americans learned, by and large, directly or indirectly, from Locke, and this lesson helped them to perceive and to counter the designs of power.

For all its influence, Book III of Locke's *Essay* was something of an afterthought, or so Locke declares. He confesses in Chapter 9 of Book III that when he began his study of the understanding he "had not the least thought that any consideration of words was at all necessary to it" (LE, II, 118). But then he discovered that the "extent and certainty of our knowledge . . . had so near a connexion with words, that, unless their force and manner of significance were first well observed, there could be very little said clearly and pertinently concerning knowledge" (LE, II, 119). Like Bacon and Hobbes, Locke realized that words "interpose themselves so much between our understandings, and the truth . . . that . . . [their] obscurity and disorder do not seldom cast a mist before our eyes, and impose upon our understandings" (ibid.). And, like Hobbes, Locke understood that this "imposition" and "disorder" were not just an epistemological problem but a political liability. After confessing his original disregard of words, he concludes the paragraph with the declaration, "But I am apt to imagine, that, were the imperfections of language, as the instrument of knowledge, more thoroughly weighed, a great many of the controversies that make such a noise in the world, would of themselves cease; and the way to knowledge, and perhaps peace too, lie a great deal opener than it does" (LE, II, 119–20). For Locke, the act of studying and warning readers about the imperfections and abuses of words was an essential act of political reform, a means of establishing a more perfect order, if not a way of preserving the liberties of citizens.

When Locke began his first draft of the *Essay*, which he completed in 1671, he was not so naive about the way words impose on the understanding as he later maintains. In one of his earliest manuscripts, published in 1967 as *Two Tracts on Government*, he notes that a confusion about the meaning or a misuse of two words – "liberty" and "authority" – has led to anarchy and tyranny: conditions antithetical (but related) to the meanings the words should represent. " 'Tis not without reason that *tyranny* and *anarchy* are judged the smartest scourges can fall upon mankind, the plea of *authority* usually backing the one and of *liberty* inducing the other: and between these two it is, that human affairs are perpetually kept tumbling."[46] Locke develops in this early work an understanding of how words can foment and perpetuate the confusion of the Thucydidean moment:

> Indeed [I have] observed that almost all those tragical revolutions which have exercised Christendom these many years have turned upon this hinge, that there hath been no design so wicked which hath not worn the vizor of religion, nor rebellion which hath not been so kind to itself as to assume the specious name of reformation, proclaiming a design either to supply the defects or correct the errors of religion, that none ever went about to ruin the *state* but with the pretence to build the *temple*, all those disturbers of the public quiet being wise enough to lay hold on religion as a shield which if it could not defend their cause was best like to secure their credit, men finding no cause that can so rationally draw them to hazard this life, or compound for the dangers of a war as that which promises them a better.[47]

He adds that in this moment, when good and evil are utterly confounded,

> all things sacred as well as profane are held as nothing and so long as they march under the banners of liberty and conscience, those two watchwords of wonderful effect in winning support, they assert that each may do what he will. And certainly the overheated zeal of those who know how to arm the rash folly of the ignorant and the passionate multitude with the authority of conscience often kindles a blaze among the populace capable of consuming everything.[48]

Locke reveals in these passages that he shares with South the conviction that it was the fatal imposture and force of such words as "liberty," "conscience," and "reformation" that helped provoke the disorder of the English Civil War. In that moment, when words acted as weapons and banners, they stirred the passions of the multitude, they deceived the understanding, and they held up a false religion as a true religion. Those words, from Locke's perspective, were not representative signs of ideas but sovereign forces, not the instruments of knowing but the agents of delusion.

Locke designed his *Essay*, as Neal Wood argues, as something more than philosophy divorced from the concerns of the forum: it was an effort to guide Englishmen "in the great practical concerns of religion, morality, politics, and law, and in normal intercourse." Wood stresses Bacon's influence on Locke: he was a member of Bacon's "'party' of liberty and mild social reform against the defenders of authority, tradition, and the old order of things.''[49] Locke's famous image of the mind at birth as a *tabula rasa* is itself Baconian. Bacon calls the mind "a fair sheet of paper with no writing on it" (FBW, IV, 26–7); Locke terms it "a white Paper, void of all Characters" (LE, I, 121). Locke built from this view of the mind his convictions regarding the fundamental importance of education in shaping the child.[50] Children will receive the imprint of the ideas of the family members, social group, sect, or party that encircle their world and circumscribe their experience as they mature, a conviction that endowed a child's circle of relations with great power and danger.

> Who is there almost that has not opinions planted in him by educa-
> tion time out of mind . . . which must not be questioned, but are
> then looked on with reverence, as the standards of right and wrong,
> truth and falsehood; where perhaps these sacred opinions were but
> the oracles of the Nursery, or the tradition and grave talk of those
> who pretend to inform our childhood, who receive them from hand
> to hand without ever examining them? By these and perhaps other
> means opinions came to be settled and fixed in men's minds, which,
> whether true or false, there they remain in reputation as substantial
> material truths . . . and if they happen to be false, as in most men the
> greatest part must necessarily be, they put a man quite out of way in
> the whole course of his studies. Men take up prejudice to truth
> without being aware of it, and afterwards feed only on those things
> that suit with and increase the vicious humour.[51]

Every person begins imbibing true and false ideas or an ideology from the moment of birth, and the only way to free oneself from the limitations of that legacy – from a nurture which conforms the understanding to the dictates of authority, fashion, tradition, party, and sect rather than to reason and revelation – is a process of education that emphasizes critical reflection: the logical analysis of words, the checking and balancing of ideas against experience, the testing of the strength of a persuasion in the give-and-take of conversation. Locke's *Essay* and *Some Thoughts Concerning Education* advocate methods for developing that critical reflection: they are self-help books that promise liberty and self-government as their goal.

In "Epistle to the Reader," which opens the *Essay*, Locke declares his intention to remove "some of the rubbish that lies in the way to knowledge" (LE, I, 14). That rubbish, in his view, is largely composed of what Emerson would term rotten diction and what Locke calls "vague and insignificant forms of speech" and "hard or misapplied words": language unrooted in nature or bearing no correspondence to true ideas (LE, I, 14). Like Bacon and Hobbes, Locke believes that in his own day *ratio* has been supplanted by *oratio*, and he plans to "break in upon the sanctuary of vanity and ignorance" and purge it of empty verbalism. Locke's project, then, recalls Plato's account in *The Republic* of the mind as a fortress that has been taken over and barricaded by false words that must be defeated to restore reason and the "real constitution of things."

The social program behind Locke's *Essay* becomes more apparent in Book IV when he expresses his fervent wish that "men would sincerely, and with freedom of mind, employ all that industry and labour of thought in improving the means of discovering truth, which they do for the colouring or support of falsehood, to maintain a system, interest, or party they are once engaged in" (LE, II, 246). Writing against partisan politics, he recalls his earlier protest in *Two Tracts on Government* about the abuse of political and religious terms: "Some confused or obscure notions have served their turns; and many who talk very much of *religion* and *conscience*, of *church* and *faith*, of *power* and *right*, of *obstructions* and *humours*, *melancholy* and *choler*, would perhaps have little left in their thoughts and meditations, if one should desire them to think only of the things themselves, and lay by those words with which they so often confound others, and not seldom themselves also" (ibid.). The "vague and insignificant forms of speech" and "hard or misapplied words" Locke would like to see remedied belong, it seems, to the parties and sects whose interests he opposes.

Locke, then, devoted Book III of the *Essay* to a study of the uses and abuses of language for much the same reason that Hobbes treated language in *Leviathan* (and for much the same reason that Wilkins devoted time to his scheme for a new scientific language): by stabilizing the linguistic contract, they hoped to improve the social contract. Locke opens Book III with the statement that God has designed man to be "a sociable creature" and has furnished him with language as "the great instrument and common tie of society" (LE, II, 2). But Locke recognizes that because of the nature of language and the understanding, language does not necessarily fulfill its God-given intentions as "the great bond of society." Book III thus seeks to study and treat the defects of language that render words an instrument of faction and misunderstanding.

Locke explains in Book III that language's defectiveness as an instrument of representation arises because words bear no "natural connexion" (LE, II, 8) to ideas and do not represent the particular "*reality of things*" (LE, II, 11). Instead words are formed by a "voluntary imposition" that "arbitrarily" designates a "sensible sign" to be a mark of an idea which is itself an "invention of the understanding made for its own use" (LE, II, 8, 11). Words do not designate the world but the mind, not things but ideas, which are formed when the mind refines particular sensations into simple ideas and simple ideas into abstract or "complex ideas" (LE, II, 17). Because general ideas are separated from "the circumstances of time and place" (ibid.), the words that designate them and the ideas themselves are removed from reality and can thus easily lead the mind into a realm of deceptive appearances. But this process of abstraction and representation has its advantages as well as defects. Unlike Wilkins, Locke claims that "*a distinct name for every particular thing would not be of any great use for the improvement of knowledge*" (LE, II, 15). By and large, representation by the word is virtual and not actual representation: individual things are spoken for by abstract terms. Knowledge, Locke explains, "enlarges itself by general views," and this process would be inhibited if "words and thoughts [were] confined only to particulars" (LE, II, 15, 31).

Madisonian political philosophy recapitulates Lockean faculty psychology. Locke's model of linguistic representation and the justification he provides for it will be imitated, that is, by Madison's model of political representation and the justification he provides for it in *Federalist* No. 10. Madison argues for the advantages of a form of political representation in which a limited number of representatives would "enlarge" their views by representing the general interests of diverse particular territories rather than having an overwhelming number of representatives represent the particular interests of many small territories – a process that would confine their views to serving special interests. Particular or special-interest representation would be more mimetic, but it would also be as cumbersome as Wilkins's "Real Character," and it would inhibit the formation and communication of general or complex ideas. The general term that represents a complex idea, such as justice, in Locke's scheme becomes the basis for clarifying relationships among the different ideas people possess. Language as a whole thus becomes for Locke, in John Richetti's words, "a political solution for both the variety of minds and inexhaustible particularity of the world," just as Madison's form of political representation becomes for the founders a solution for reconciling the diversity and particularity of political interests with a scheme that will work to create unity from diversity, or consensus out of Babel.[52] Just as the mind serves as the scene in Locke's faculty psychology where particular sensations are refined into complex ideas and general words, Congress in Madison's scheme of representation becomes the scene wherein those particular interests – the general ideas of each representative (which are themselves refinements from the particular voices of constituents) – are compared and refined again to reach a consensus that will produce common laws for a diverse people.

Locke's concept of language is most directly analogous to Locke's concept of civil government. He believes that language, like civil government, is the result of a contract among individuals. Like government, language is created not by God but by man, and the meaning of a word is not determined by divine imposition or by a sovereign authority. No one, Locke says, not even "the great Augustus himself," could impose a new usage or "arbitrarily appoint what idea any sound should be the sign of, in the mouths and common language of his subjects," for "no one hath the power to make others have the same ideas in their minds that he has, when they use the same words that he does" (LE, II, 12–13). Instead the meaning of the word is created by the people, and it gains its authority from their continuous consent. "It is true," Locke asserts, that "common use, by a tacit consent, appropriates certain sounds to certain ideas in all languages, which so far limits the signification of that sound, that unless a man applies it to the same idea, he does not speak properly" (LE, II, 13). Just as individuals form contracts to limit their natural liberty for their own good and to protect their property, so too do people form contracts that limit the meaning of a word for the good of communication and to designate what is proper and what is not.

Locke recognizes, however, that the contractual status of language does not insure the stability of language or the stability of the social contract. Common use, as the lawgiver of language, may "regulate the meaning of words pretty well for common conversations," but those laws are anything but settled in matters of "Philosophical Discourses" and "controversial debate," because "every man has so inviolable a liberty to make words stand for what ideas he pleases" (LE, II, 108, 12). Just as the state of nature Locke envisions in *Two Treatises of Government* defends man's natural right to freedom, the state of nature defends a principle of linguistic freedom: "The same liberty . . . that Adam had of affixing any new name to any idea, the same has any one still" (LE, II, 96). Note that Locke's Adam is not the first sovereign who imposes his names on the universe, but instead the first man to exercise his "inviolable liberty" to annex his own names to ideas and things. Adam's liberty is not without its dangers: people are free to break linguistic covenants and disobey the laws that sustain a social order designed to protect rights and property. Locke informs readers of their linguistic liberty, but then counsels: "In places where men in society have already established a language amongst them, the significations of words are very warily and sparingly to be altered" (LE, II, 96–7).

Just as strongly as Jefferson affirms self-government and Emerson affirms self-reliance, Locke affirms the "inviolable liberty" of defining for oneself: the right of the individual to create new words and to transfer old words to new objects, a right that Jefferson and Emerson also advocate. But Locke counters his own liberalism: he is deeply troubled by a vision of individuals pursuing their liberty unconstrained, and he is troubled by the exercise of linguistic liberty in the realm of political and religious discourse. And just as Locke sought to compromise the liberty of the individual with the benefits of consent to the authority of law, he sought to curtail linguistic liberty by consent to common usage. When Locke analyzes and condemns the "abuse of words," that is, "*wilful* faults and neglects which men are guilty of . . . whereby they render . . . signs less clear and distinct in their signification than naturally they need to be" (LE, II, 122), he gives special prominence to the vice of "applying old words to new and unusual significations; or introducing new and ambiguous terms, without defining either; or else putting them so together, as may confound their ordinary meaning" (LE, II, 126). For Locke, those "abuses" threaten a breakdown of the social contract, and such abuse, or the "art" of confounding the "known significance" of words, have already "obscured and perplexed the material truths of law and divinity; brought confusion, disorder, and uncertainty into the affairs of mankind; and if not destroyed, yet in great measure rendered useless, these two great rules, religion and justice" (LE, II, 130–1). Thus he rhetorically asks "whether it would not be well . . . that the use of words were made plain and direct; and that language . . . should not be employed to . . . unsettle people's rights; to raise mists, and render unintelligible both morality and religion?" (LE, II, 131). Like Hobbes, Locke believes that words had to be legislated by strict definitions to settle a people's rights and mitigate conflict in law and religion. But he was more willing to repose the sovereign authority to govern the language in the people, as opposed to a monarch; by consenting to common usage, the people ratify a constitution of language that becomes, in effect, a second nature. This constitution determines what is proper and right and thus compensates for the absence of a "settled standard anywhere in nature existing, to rectify and adjust them [names] by" (LE, II, 106). To abuse this linguistic contract is to make words less clear and distinct than they "naturally" need to be, Locke writes, even though he argues that a word has no "natural" signification.

Locke never identifies in any lineup of abusers the practitioners of the "art" who had confounded the words of religion and law, but in his chapter "Of the Abuse of Words" he criticizes, as does Bacon, the schoolmen for spinning an "unexplicable web of perplexed words," and he adds that "in these last ages" "this artificial ignorance, and learned gibberish" "hath invaded the great concernments of human life and society" and have "prevailed mightily . . . by the interest and artifice of those who found no easier way to that pitch of authority and dominion they have attained, than by amusing the men of business, and ignorant, with hard words, or employing the ingenious and idle in intricate disputes about unintelligible terms, and holding them perpetually entangled in that endless labyrinth" (LE, II, 128). He also maintains that at one time "unlearned men well enough understood the words white and black, etc.," but then "there were philosophers found who had learning and subtlety enough to prove that snow was black; i.e. to prove that white was black," and as a result "they had the advantage to destroy the instruments and means of discourse, conversation, instruction, and society" (LE, II, 129). The word turns inside out and becomes its opposite. This example and this complaint are familiar ones. Swift would have Gulliver lambaste the lawyers of England for confounding black and white, and Cooper (perhaps the most Lockean of antebellum American writers) would have one of his voyagers to the land of the Monikins observe politicians in the "Great National Council" pass a law declaring white to be black. Against the philosophers whose disputations have rendered law and religion unintelligible, Locke juxtaposes "unscholastic statesmen" to whom "the governments of the world owed their peace, defence, and liberties" (LE, II, 128). Although Locke never specifies whom he means by "unscholastic statesmen," the context suggests what he might mean. Such statesmen would discuss matters of law and religion without disputation or without striving to impose their own sense on words; they would use words settled in their meaning or define their terms; and they would doubt their own infallibility in matters of interpretation, just as Benjamin Franklin recommended the framers of the Constitution should do when passing judgment on their own work. Indeed, "unscholastic statesmen" might be those who would, like Franklin, seek to avoid a habit of "a Positive assuming Manner," which he says in his *Autobiography* "seldom fails to disgust, and tends to create Opposition, and to defeat every one of those Purposes for which Speech was given to us, to wit, giving or receiving Information, or Pleasure."[53] Perhaps it is no coincidence that Franklin began to rid himself of his habit of disputation, which he says he "caught . . . by reading my Father's Books of Disputes about Religion," at about the same time that he read "Locke on Human Understanding."[54]

The confusion Locke finds in public discourse does not arise, in his view, solely from the willful abuse of words. The complexity of ideas that the words must represent is also responsible. Locke notes in the chapter "Of the Imperfection of Words" that the more complex the idea is, the more abstract the word will be and the more liable it is to be used in eccentric and unusual senses. Scarcely any name "of any very complex idea," he writes, ". . . may not be made the sign of far different ideas" (LE, II, 108), and this problem arises particularly in "controversial debate, or familiar discourse, concerning honour, faith, grace, religion, church, &c." "And hence," he adds, "we see that, in the interpretation of laws, whether divine or human, there is no end; comments beget comments, and explications make new matter for explications; and of limiting, distinguishing, varying the signification of these moral words there is no end" (LE, II, 109). Locke never develops to the same extent as Hobbes the notion that interpretation of words will always be colored by our interests and passions and that conflicts about the meaning of a word are, on a deeper level, conflicts of interest and wills, or political rather than verbal conflicts. But he does recognize that interpretation cannot be objective or conclusive. Given man's inviolable (and irrepressible) linguistic liberty, the play of interpretative freedom will never end. When Locke drafted his "Fundamental Constitutions" for the government of Carolina, he inserted a clause reading "Since multiplicity of comments, as well as of laws, have great inconvenience, and serve only to obscure and perplex, all manner of comments and expositions on any part of these fundamental constitutions, or on any part of the common or statute laws of Carolina, are absolutely prohibited."[55] This clause extends into law one of the fundamental principles of Locke's linguistics: once consent has been established, it must be maintained for the sake of the social contract. At the end of his chapter on the imperfection of words, Locke offers a remedy different from legal fiat for conflicts of interpretation. He concludes with the fond hope that, given the "common and natural obscurities and difficulties incident to words," people will be "less magisterial, positive, and imperious, in imposing our own sense and interpretations" on divine and human law ?nd more "careful and diligent in observing" "the precepts of Natural Religion," which are "plain, and very intelligible" (LE, II, 121). Here, then, Locke advocates what Paine, Emerson, and Thoreau (and Natty Bumppo) would also advocate as a solution to the problem of political and religious interpretation: study and interpret the book of nature written by the divine Word rather than books written in an "imperfect" or "corrupt" language by fallible men.

In the final chapter of Book III, "Of the Remedies of the Foregoing Imperfections and Abuses," Locke also proposes that to limit the arbitrariness of words one should do such things as annex clear ideas to words, apply words in common uses, declare ideas by synonymous terms, study the history of the idea, and use the same word constantly in the same sense. Yet he recognizes the vanity of believing that his own prescribed remedies could be followed to the letter and the foolishness of pretending that anyone could attempt "the perfect reforming [of] the language of the world." No such reformation will occur until people become "very knowing and very silent" (LE, II, 148).

Condemnations of rhetoric became *de rigueur* in the Enlightenment, and the condemnations did little to reduce the rhetoric of other condemnations. Locke includes in Book III his own condemnation of rhetoric: to him, it is the art of fallacy, and figurative speech is designed "for nothing else but to insinuate wrong ideas, move the passions, and thereby mislead the judgment" (LE, II, 146). He also ends the *Essay* with a continuation of the Restoration revolt against enthusiasm: he attacks enthusiasm, or what he calls "the unguarded fancies of man's own brain," for ignoring the restraint of reason and revelation and the check of reflection. Perry Miller, who recognized that Locke's *Essay* was "a weapon against enthusiasm, incantation and priestcraft," claims that Locke's cautions and remedies worked to bring a respite from "acrimonious theological pamphleteering" in England.[56] But even if Locke's *Essay* did not have this effect, it did by and large supply the terms and analysis – indeed, the conceptual framework – that would be used by eighteenth-century Englishmen and early Americans in their protests against the abuse of words and passion-stirring rhetoric in political and religious discourse.

When Locke attacks Robert Filmer in *Two Treatises of Government*, he himself shows how his analysis of the abuse of words can be used in a political argument. In Book III of the *Essay* he notes that

> there is no such way to gain admittance, or give defence to strange and absurd doctrines, as to guard them round with legions of obscure, doubtful, and undefined words. Which yet make these retreats more like the dens of robbers, or holes of foxes, than the fortress as of fair warriors: which, if it be hard to get them out of, it is not for the strength that is in them, but the briars and thorns, and the obscurity of the thickets that they are beset with. For untruth being unacceptable to the mind of man, there is no other defence left for absurdity but obscurity. (LE, II, 128)

In *Two Treatises*, Locke approaches Filmer as if he were the fox of this passage and the *Patriarcha* a den of doubtful and undefined words barricaded by a thicket of rhetorical nonsense. His task, as he announces in the preface, is to strip away Filmer's "Flourish of doubtful expressions," expose his "Contradictions dressed up in a Popular Stile," and reduce his words to "direct, positive, intelligible Propositions," which will prove that they are nothing but "glib Nonsence" (171–2). Elsewhere Locke complains that Filmer makes such a "medley and confusion" out of "doubtful and general terms" that to show his mistakes it is necessary to examine the "several Senses, wherein his Words may be taken," and he protests that Filmer has treated the "Words and Sense of Authors" as Procrustes treated his guests, lopping off or stretching them to fit his notions (190, 221). In *Two Treatises*, Locke puts his remedies for the abuses of words into action. He insists that he is countering nonsense with reason, rhetoric with logic, convoluted English with plain English, misrepresentations with the truth. There is nothing surprising about this insistence: it replays the Platonic trope of good words having to assault a fortress usurped and defended by a legion of false words. Literary criticism allies itself or becomes one with political criticism. What may surprise us, however, is that in the final chapter of *Two Treatises*, "Of the Dissolution of Government," linguistic abuse becomes one with political abuse as a justification for revolution – and the detection of such abuse becomes incumbent on the pursuers of liberty. Locke maintains that citizens are justified in dissolving a government "if a long train of Abuses, Prevarications, and Artifices, all tending the same way, make the design visible to the People" (463). Two of the words – "Prevarications" and "Artifices" – clearly designate an abuse of words and the third word – "Abuses" – could also in this period (according to the *OED*) have indicated an abuse of words. Undoubtedly Locke believed, as did John Dickinson, Thomas Paine, and other colonial leaders of the opposition to Britain, that linguistic misrepresentation was a dangerous political act to be remedied by words or, that failing, resisted by swords. The American revolution against corrupt representation draws its battle cry and tactics from Book III of Locke's *Essay*.

Real Whigs vs. Ruling Words: Cato's Letters and the Dissemination of Lockean Linguistic Politics

Locke's ideas about the abuse of words and its remedies were transmitted to America directly through the widespread popularity of his *Essay* and through the development and application of Lockean notions about language in works of literature and politics. A number of the works of the Real Whig tradition, particularly John Trenchard and Thomas Gordon's *Cato's Letters* and various works by eighteenth-century English writers who were widely read in the Colonies, such as Pope, Swift, Addison, Richardson, and Sterne, share with Locke's *Essay* an acute awareness of how easily people can be deluded by the words, artifices, and prevarications of a Lovelace, a Jonathan Wild, or a Robert Walpole and how easily words can be abused to fit the designs of corrupt men.[57] Conspiracies, plots, artifice, hypocrisy, deceit, masquerade, conspiracies against conspiracies, designs within designs – this is the stuff, as Gordon Wood argues, that people perceived everywhere in the eighteenth century; this is the stuff knaves perpetrated and fools never detected in eighteenth-century literature; and this is the stuff Trenchard and Gordon warn about persistently in *Cato's Letters*.[58]

Just the titles of four of the letters Trenchard and Gordon wrote in the early 1720s should suggest the degree to which they were students of Locke and masters at reading the language of politics and the politics of language: "The Arts of Misleading People by Sounds," "Of the Abuse of Words," "Of the Proper Use of Words," and "Of Eloquence, Considered Politically." Trenchard, who was the senior partner in the collaboration, and Gordon, who published translations with commentary of works by Sallust and Tacitus that were also favorites of American revolutionaries, shared with Tacitus an understanding that the political process, in the words of Peter Gay, "is the collision of force and fraud, the arena of persuasion, enthusiasm and violence, of the attempts by charismatic, clever, or unscrupulous leaders to control and exploit multitudes afraid of ghosts and greedy for food, shelter, and entertainment."[59] In their own words, "it is the Characteristic of Society, it is the Nature of Man, to guide, and to follow; to dictate, and to obey; to deceive, and to be deceived," and it was their aim to educate their readers about how to gain or preserve their liberties in such a society. The world they describe seems to be perpetually in the throes of the Thucydidean moment; it is a world where the war of all against all is conducted by fraud rather than force – by the "pious imposture" of foxes rather than the brute strength of lions. In the midst of this corruption, they become gadflies, stinging people into an awareness of what they call the "ridiculous Force and Witchcraft attending Names" and "big Words" proceeding from "preposterous Education."[60]

Trenchard and Gordon, like other Whig writers, could be as critical of the people as any Tory satirist. Common people are represented in their writings as being at times a mob of dunces governed by their ruling passions, particularly self-love, and by a host of forces that usurp the reason and manacle the mind: by the sound of words rather than their sense, by prejudice rather than truth, by superstition rather than religion, by titles rather than the character of men, by custom and received system – by forces, in short, that secure the "Servitude of the Body" by the "Servitude of the Mind" and fortify "Oppression" "by Delusion."[61] Yet Trenchard and Gordon were also deeply sympathetic to the plight of the common people and hostile to the powers that oppress them: "You are called the Mobb, the Canaille, the stupid Herd, the Dregs and Beasts of the People, and your Interest is never thought of by those Men, who thus miscal you . . . Men whose Insolence and Sauciness are owing to Wealth, which they have plundered from you" (III, 11). Instead they praise the people as "our *Alpha* and *Omega*, our first and last Resource," and they contend in Real Whig fashion that "when your Virtue is gone, all is gone" (ibid.). They also call upon the people to "shew that you are Men" (ibid.). Indeed, it is their mission, as it would be Emerson's in "Self-Reliance," to "free and manumit Mankind from the many Impositions, Frauds and Delusions, which interrupt their Happiness" and to educate "Narrow Minds, which, locked up in received Systems, see all Things through false Mirrors, and as they are represented by strong Prejudices, prevailing Customs, and very often by Corruption and Party-Interest . . ." (III, 90; II, 177). Only when those mind-forged manacles are broken can the pursuit of liberty and happiness hope to succeed.

Emerson's statement "The corruption of man is followed by the corruption of language" is a familiar refrain of Real Whig writers who examine, critically and compulsively, the fall into corruption (ELA, 25). Emerson ascribes the fall into corruption to the pursuit of riches, power, pleasure, praise. Sallust describes Rome's fall from liberty into corruption and tyranny as beginning, in Gordon's translation, with a "Lust of Money," next a "Passion for Place and Sway," then "Reigning Ambition [which] generally forced people to be deceitful, to conceal their real Meaning; to profess, what they meant not," and finally "Luxury, Voraciousness, and Pride . . . [which] captivated the Minds" of the Romans.[62] People "are naturally Innocent," write Trenchard and Gordon, "yet [they] fall naturally into the Practice of Vice" (I, 239). But, like Sallust and Thucydides, they recognize that the fall into corruption is also hastened and perpetuated by corrupt politicians and the corruption of good words, which are "wrested first by Design, and afterwards by Ignorance and Custom, from [their] Original and virtuous Signification" (II, 18). When words fall from virtue, they can do as much mischief as any tyrant, as Trenchard and Gordon write in a letter that closely recalls Locke's analysis of words in Book III of the *Essay*.

> I have often thought, that most of the Mischiefs under which Mankind suffers, and almost all their polemick Disputes are owing to the Abuse of Words. If Men would define what they mean by the Sounds which they make use of to express their Thoughts, and then keep to those Definitions, that is, annex always the same Ideas to the

same Sounds, most of the Disputes in the World would be at an End:
But this would not answer the Purposes of those who derive Power
and Wealth from imposing upon the Ignorance and Credulity of
others. And therefore, till the World can agree to be honest, and to
buy and sell by the same Measure (which they do not seem in Haste
to do), I doubt this Evil is likely to go on. (IV, 96)

Writing in the aftermath of the South Sea Bubble, Trenchard and
Gordon suggest that the marketplace of ideas is a bazaar where words
of no fixed value are bought and sold in exchanges that benefit those
deserving the least credit. Concerned that people could be bubbled out
of their liberty as easily as they had been bubbled out of their money,
they offer a warning about confidence men and the duplicitous power
inherent in moral terms:

> Even in Countries where the highest Liberty is allowed, and the
> greatest Light shines, you generally find certain Men, and Bodies of
> Men, set apart to mislead the Multitude; who are ever abused with
> Words, ever fond of the worst of Things recommended by good
> Names, and ever abhor the best Things, and the most virtuous
> Actions, disfigured by ill Names. One of the great Arts, therefore,
> of cheating Men, is, to study the Application and Misapplication of
> Sounds – A few loud Words rule the majority, I had almost said, the
> whole World. (I, 83)[63]

Language operates not as the "great bond of society" but as an
instrument of power, or how Bernard Mandeville describes language
in *The Fable of the Bees.* Just as Mandeville challenges the assumptions of
contemporary moralists by arguing for the social benefits of vice, he
challenges the moral assumptions of the many seventeenth- and eighteenth-century writers on language who located its origin in a gift
from God and its function as the communication of ideas. Instead,
Mandeville proclaims, the "first design of Speech was to persuade
others to give Credit to what the Speaking Person would have them
believe; or else to act or suffer such Things, as he would compel them
to act or suffer, if they were entirely in his power."[64] Mandeville's
cynicism about speech is to the polite world of the eighteenth century
what Nietzsche's verbal nihilism is to Victorian morality.

Trenchard and Gordon, however, resist Mandeville's conclusion
that language is solely an instrument of power or self-interest. They
argue that words possess an "honest" or "virtuous" sense, which is
their "common sense" signification, and that words can unite people.
What they condemn most severely is the abuse of the "common sense"
of words that confuses virtue and vice and leads to the moment
wherein "the worst Things that Men do, called by a good Name, pass

for the best; and the best, blackened by an ill Name, pass for the worst" (II, 113–14). Words can be so easily abused to create this confusion, they explain, because "there is scarce a Virtue but borders upon a Vice, and, carried beyond a certain Degree, becomes one" (III, 296). For example, they point out, "Courage soon grows into Rashness; Generosity into Extravagancy; Frugality into Avarice; Justice into Severity; Religion into Superstition" (ibid.). Like Pope and Swift, who were their contemporaries, Trenchard and Gordon seek to clarify how the misapplication of sanctifying terms or an ignorance of their "true" definition can lead to the moment of *anatrope* or enable "Tyranny, which is the extirpation of Government" to call itself "Government," and for "Rogueries" to pass as "Majesty's Measures," and for people "to reverence Butchers, Robbers, and Tyrants under the reverend Name of Rulers" and "to adore the Names and Persons of Men, though their Actions be the Actions of Devils" (III, 225; I, 83; IV, 221). When virtue is called vice, when fair names are speciously applied to foul acts, the maneuver is not quite deception by a euphemism: the conscience, or what Jefferson called the moral sense, is attracted by the word, but it gets drawn in the wrong direction. The heart falls for the word, the mind consents to it, the person gets bamboozled.

To counter a people's sliding into corruption as a result of words slipping from virtue into their bordering vice, Trenchard and Gordon seek to define the meaning of virtuous terms so as to maintain the borders between vice and virtue. For instance, they explain, "the Government of One for the Sake of One, is Tyranny; and so is the Government of a Few for the Sake of Themselves: But Government executed for the Good of All, and with the Consent of All, is Liberty; and the Word *Government* is prophaned, and its Meaning abused, when it signifies any Thing else" (I, 179–80). Another defense against the abuse of good words and against tyranny itself that they recommend is for subjects never to take their rulers' "Words about the Motives of their Designs, but to judge of their Designs by the Event" (I, 86). "This," they add, "is the Principle of a *Whig*, this the Doctrine of Liberty," and this is the defense that American revolutionaries would adopt against the abuses and designs of the British (ibid.). A people jealous of their liberties will never trust words: confidence can only be gained by acts that deliver the goods promised by the words. The paranoid style of colonial American politics arose at least in part from a rational or at least a Lockean understanding of the power of a "few loud Words" to "rule the Majority."

Though counseling a jealous distrust of words, Trenchard and Gordon, unlike Locke, are not willing to renounce eloquence. The only power, they believe, that can resist the "dictatorial Art of speaking" is the dictatorial art of speaking. In a cleverly ambiguous sentence they assert, "If we enquire into the Use and Purposes of Eloquence, and into the Good and Evil which it has done, we must distinguish between Eloquence and Eloquence" (III, 320). On the one hand, they explain, there is a type of eloquence that is "every where useful and commendable," and that is "good Sense, put into good Words" (ibid.). And when Rome was confronted by "many publick Mischiefs," Cato turned to this eloquence, and to frustrate the tyrannical designs of Caesar, Cicero turned to it (III, 316). But there is another type of eloquence that has "done some Good, and infinite Mischief" (III, 320). This is "the Art of Flattering and Deceiving," and they add, "It fills the Mind with false Ideas; and by raising a Tempest in the Heart, misleads the Judgment: It confounds Good and Evil, by throwing false Colours over them; and deceives Men with their own Approbation: And it has in many Instances unsettled all good Order, and thrown flourishing States into Pangs and Desolation" (III, 321). Their hope, of course, is that in a state of liberty and virtue the first type of eloquence will prevail, and their fear is that if "Virtue" is vanquished by "irresistible Gold," as eventually occurred in the "free states of *Greece* and *Rome*," then orators, "finding their Souls and their Voices saleable," will become "Slaves of Ambition" (III, 315). Then "the Art of Flattering and Deceiving" will gain a monopoly over truth.

Because of the warnings they offer about the second type of eloquence, one passage by Trenchard and Gordon on eloquence stands out as remarkable for both the morally neutral tone in which they describe the sublime power of words and for the way they tap that power in their own prose as they delight the ear and impress the mind with a rhythmical set of rhetorical questions. "How vastly prevailing," they ask, must be the force of sound and gesture

> when it comes arrayed and heightened by a swelling and irresistible Tide of Words, enlivened by the most forcible and rapid Ideas, and bears down all before it? When the Orator attracts your Eyes, charms your Ears, and forces your Attention; brings Heaven and Earth into his Cause, and seems but to represent them, to speak their Sense, and to contend for their Interest? When he carries your Passions in his Hands, suspends or controuls all your Faculties, and yet persuades you that your own Faculties guide you? When he lessens great Things, magnifies little Things, and disguises all; his very Gesture is animated, and every Muscle persuades; his Words lighten, and his Breath is on Fire; every Word glows, and every Image flames; he fills, delights, kindles, and astonishes your Imagination; raises a Storm in your Heart, and governs you in that Storm; rouzes all that is human in you, and makes your own Heart conspire

> against you! – In this magical and outrageous Tempest, you are at the
> entire Mercy of him who raised it. (III, 328)

The orator becomes the governor who persuades us that we are
governing ourselves when we obey his words. The orator's words *seem*
to represent heaven and earth. But the orator can disguise all. The
distinction that Trenchard and Gordon draw between a safe and a
dangerous rhetoric, or between an eloquence of liberty and an eloquence of power, collapses in this passage, or it becomes not an
aesthetic or moral distinction between "good sense, put into good
words" and the "Art of flattering and deceiving" but a political
distinction between whether the tempest is stirred up to support or
oppose one's cause. Here in this passage Trenchard and Gordon revolt
against the revolt against enthusiasm, and they provide a glimpse of
the rhetoric of sensation that George Whitefield would bring to life to
help kindle the Great Awakening and that the orators of the American
Revolution would recover to fight their battles; it is also the rhetoric
that Locke counsels against and that would be blamed for igniting
the conflagration of America's Civil War. This orator, a figure of the
power attributed to Orpheus, could also be seen as a figure of the
rhetoric of the founding fathers: we are governed by words that
persuade us we are governing ourselves. The words seem to represent
the laws of earth and heaven (of nature and nature's God) – and the
rhetoric disguises its distortions.

Written Legislation for Language: The Dictionary of Samuel Johnson

By the mid eighteenth century, fervor for a radically new
scientific language and for the recovery of an old Edenic tongue had
died down. The English language was now not to be overthrown in
favor of a universal language or restored to a pre–Civil War or pre-
Babel condition. It was to be reformed. Plans such as John Wilkins's
"Real Character" were once a *desideratum* of the Royal Society; in
Gulliver's Travels, Swift subjects them to his satire. While the ideal of a
language as logical and as faithful in its representative capacities as the
language of the Houyhnhnms (a fully rational language that has no
words for love or for lying) persisted through the eighteenth century,
what was accepted as part of the human condition was a language as
imperfect as Gulliver and as corruptible as the text of the will
bequeathed to the three sons in *A Tale of a Tub*. But even Swift pressed
for reform. He advocated, as did Daniel Defoe, the creation of an
academy for governing the English language. Swift's satiric pieces,
though remorseless in their criticism, can also be considered acts of

reform. Whereas Bacon sought to battle words with science and Hobbes called for a sovereign authority to purge language of its ambiguity, and whereas Sprat resolved that "*eloquence* ought to be banish'd out of all *civil Societies*," Swift turns language against itself. In *A Tale of a Tub*, "The Battle of the Books," and "A Discourse Concerning the Mechanical Operation of the Spirit," books battle books, jargon ridicules jargon, enthusiastic oratory pleads against enthusiastic oratory, the abuse of words abuses the abuse of words, and textual criticism criticizes textual criticism.

Lesser writers than Swift, however, tried the remedies for the abuses and imperfections of words that Locke prescribes in Book III of the *Essay*. Writers also turned to enacting the legislation of grammars and dictionaries as a means of codifying usage and mitigating verbal corruption and disorder. Although the tactics of these schoolmasters of the language differed from those tried by philosophers and divines in the seventeenth century, they share the desire to wrest control of the language from what Bacon called "the will of the generality." Indeed, while these reformers consented to Locke's position that language should be governed by custom, they used that position to affirm some form of elite control over the language, a practice that many American language reformers, such as Noah Webster, would follow.

Ben Jonson, who composed one of the first English grammars, makes a seemingly paradoxical remark about language in *Timber; or, Discoveries* that captures a fundamental position English writers took in the seventeenth and eighteenth centuries concerning the question of who should govern the language. "Words are the Peoples," he declares, "yet there is a choise of them to be made." "*Custome* is the most certaine Mistresse of Language," he adds, but he stresses that what he means by custom is not "the vulgar Custome" but the "consent of the Learned."[65] Language belongs to the people, but the words that are to be chosen to serve as representatives in literature are not to be selected by the people, but by the learned. According to James Russell Lowell, after Shakespeare's time the schoolmasters of the language began to rule. The English language was "fetlocked by dictionary and grammar mongers": an "arbitrary line" was drawn between "high words and low," alienating poetry from the people by establishing "an Upper House of vocables, alone entitled to move in the stately ceremonials of verse" (JLW, III, 8–9). Lowell's conclusion may be overstated, but his imagery is apt. Throughout the seventeenth and eighteenth centuries English writers made comparisons between the laws of good English and the laws of the land and conceived of their language as a constitution that should be governed – and could be corrupted – by the same forces that governed and corrupted their political constitution. John Barrell, who examines these comparisons extensively in "The Language Properly So-Called: The Authority of Common Usage," points out that the canons of common usage were described in terms of common law. The English language, like the English constitution, was said to breathe a spirit of liberty; and "all men were understood to be governed by the laws of language, which, like the laws of the land, were claimed to have been established by 'the public free Consent,' but some members of the language community were enfranchised, and could use their voice in making the laws which bound them, and some were not."[66] Just as William III's title was said to reside in the "consent of the people," whereas in fact it resided in the convention parliament (which represented only enfranchised owners of property), so too it was said that custom and usage were sovereign in matters of language, but the customs of the vulgar were granted no authority in determining correct usage.[67] James Greenwood makes this policy explicit in *Practical English Grammar*: "custom" is "a very dangerous and bad Influence" if "it should take its Name from the Practice of the Majority. . . . In Discourse, if there be any thing that has corruptly prevail'd among the Multitude, we must not receive or embrace that for the Rule or Standard of Speech. . . . I therefore call the Custom of Speech, the Agreement of the Learned."[68] This account of custom was the accepted doctrine of grammarians: the majority have no legislative voice in language. In language theory as well as political theory, custom became a "legal" principle whose authority ruled against extension of power to unlearned, common people.

Style may mirror the man; speech codes mirror the class. Speak that I may see thy refinement. Correct speech becomes a key mark of social distinction for the gentleman of the eighteenth century. Lord Chesterfield, whose *Letters to His Son* offered a model of how the cultivation of good letters could facilitate the development of a gentleman, called for a "lawful standard" for the English language in a letter he wrote to the *World* on November 28, 1754. Chesterfield also announces in the letter his support for the forthcoming publication of Samuel Johnson's dictionary. Casting his praise for the project in political metaphors and analogies, he complains "that our language is at present in a state of anarchy," and he declares:

> Good order and authority are now necessary. But where shall we find them . . . ? We must have recourse to the old Roman expedient in times of confusion, and chuse a dictator. Upon this principle I give my vote for Mr Johnson to fill that great and arduous post. And I hereby declare that I make a total surrender of all my rights and

privileges in the English language, as a free-born British subject, to the said Mr Johnson, during the term of his dictatorship. Nay more; I will not only obey him, like an old Roman, as my dictator, but, like a modern Roman, I will implicitly believe in him as my pope, and hold him to be infallible while in the chair; but no longer.[69]

To end the anarchy, Chesterfield is as willing as Hobbes to resign his natural rights in the English language to a sovereign authority whose decrees would be absolute and infallible. Like Hobbes, he too does not just conceive of linguistic authority as analogous to political authority; he believes that a "fixed" language could be a crucial instrument of political authority. In an earlier letter to the *World*, dated December 6, 1753, Chesterfield expresses an opinion about the connection between political and linguistic disorders that suggests why Johnson's dictionary appealed to him.

> The uninformed herd of mankind are governed by words and names, which they implicitly receive, without either knowing or asking their meaning. Even the philosophical and religious controversies, for the last three or four . . . [hundred] years, have turned much more upon words and names, unascertained and misunderstood, than upon things fairly stated. The polite world, to save time and trouble, receive, adapt, and use words, in the signification of the day; not having leisure nor inclinations to examine and analise them: and thus often misled by sounds, and not always secured by sense, they are hurried into fatal errors, which they do not give their understandings fair play enough to prevent.
>
> In explaining words, therefore, and bringing them back to their true signification, one may sometimes happen to expose and explode those errors which the abuse of them both occasions and protects.[70]

The common people are governed by words because of their ignorance; polite society misunderstands words because of their haste. Chesterfield divides society into two and hopes Johnson's dictionary will conquer both.

At the end of his "Plan for an English Dictionary," Johnson reveals that he himself conceived of his task as a lexicographer to be something like that of a dictator: "like the soldiers of *Caesar*" about to invade the new world of Britain, he hoped that even if he could not "complete the conquest" of the English language, he could "at least discover the coast, civilize part of the inhabitants, and make it easy for some other adventurer . . . to reduce them wholly to subjection, and settle them under laws" (SJW, II, 29). The inhabitants he hopes to colonize through law are the words of the language, but there is an implicit suggestion that a greater degree of linguistic order would bring a greater degree of Orphic order to the actual inhabitants of Britain. The order will be imposed, however, not by a sovereign voice but by the stability of the written word.

Scott Elledge notes a tension running through Johnson's "Plan" between two aspects of his role as a lexicographer: he presents himself as both a discoverer who will describe what he finds and as a colonizer who will legislate and prescribe; the one role is passive – describing, observing, recording – and the other is active – guarding, purifying, fixing, perpetuating.[71] In the active role he proclaims law, and in the other role he collects precedents and ultimately discovers or judges what is and what should be. The same tension between legislating and judging a language runs throughout the history of lexicography as the debate between prescriptive and descriptive linguistics. When Johnson later describes his aims and frustrations as a lexicographer in "Preface to the English Dictionary," this tension reappears, as does a conflict between the instability of the voiced and the stability of the written, and a review of the language in which he presents these conflicts and his effort to resolve them can help us understand how for Johnson (and later for Noah Webster) the acts of a lexicographer could participate in a struggle to preserve from corruption not just the English language but also the political constitution.

In the "Plan" Johnson announces that his primary intent is to "fix the *English* language," by which he means that he seeks to regulate the pronunciation and orthography of words and settle their meaning so that the "fundamental atoms of our speech might obtain the firmness and immutability of the primogenial and constituent particles of matter" – a project that depends upon Johnson's belief that words possess a "natural and primitive signification" and that "all change is of itself an evil" (SJW, II, 12, 17, 20, 11). But while Chesterfield was willing to let Johnson dictate the laws needed to end the anarchy of the English tongue, and while Johnson himself seems willing at times to assume the absolute power needed to "secure our language from being over-run with cant" and "from being crowded with low terms," he prefers to present himself not as a dictator or as a legislator but as a judge who will discover the law rather than proclaim it: "I shall therefore, since the rules of style, like those of law, arise from precedents often repeated, collect the testimonies on both sides, and endeavour to discover and promulgate the decrees of custom, who has so long possessed, whether by right or by usurpation, the sovereignty of words" (SJW, II, 16, 23). Johnson does not oppose his own power to the power of custom or precedent. His task as a judge, however, is hindered by his recognition that there are no general or natural laws of language that can be followed or enforced. "It is not in our power," he points out, "to have recourse to any established laws of speech," and he notes: "Speech was not formed by an analogy sent from heaven. It did not descend to us in a state of uniformity and perfection." Instead "language is the work of man," a being from whom "permanence and stability cannot be derived," and thus Johnson must determine the verbal precedents that have arisen from human folly and affectation and by accident (SJW, II, 19, 16).

When Johnson resurveys the state of the English language in the "Preface," he again notes a language in an anarchic and corrupt condition: it has "spread, under the direction of chance, into wild exuberance," and it has been corrupted by "ignorance, and caprices of innovation" and tyrannized over by "time and fashion" (SJW, II, 32). Confronted with a language in this state, Johnson forms a party of opposition: he seeks to depose the tyranny of "time and fashion" and reinstate precedent; he combats the anarchy of "chance" with the order of rules derived from experience and analogy; and he fights the corruption caused by ignorance and caprice with the labor of his mind and with examples drawn from what he calls (quoting Spenser) "*the wells of English undefiled*" – the classic writers of English before the Restoration (SJW, II, 52). The campaign that Johnson wages is not an easy one, for he must make choices "without any established principle of selection" and detect adulteration "without a settled test of purity" (SJW, II, 32). The principle that he adopts to guide his work is a "scholar's reverence for antiquity, and a grammarian's regard to the genius of our tongue" (SJW, II, 36). In practice, this principle means that Johnson prefers the precedents and even the irregularities that have been established by the classic writers of the English tongue to what may be more reasonable and certainly prefers them to the "corruption of oral utterance" (ibid.). In language as well as in law, he asserts, there is "in constancy and stability a general and lasting advantage, which will always overbalance the slow improvements of gradual correction." Thus Johnson maintains that he is unwilling "to disturb, upon narrow views, or for minute propriety, the orthography of their fathers," and he upholds the written language as the standard to which the spoken must conform (ibid.). In the "Plan" Johnson remarks that a "great orthographical contest has long subsisted between etymology and pronunciation," and that contest is, in effect, between a party of memory led by writers of the language and a party of the present led by its speakers (SJW, II, 10). Johnson supports the party of memory, and his preference for the orthography of the fathers and for the written language, as opposed to the "boundless chaos of living speech," is closely related, as John Barrell suggests, to the deference to the wisdom of political forefathers that Edmund

Burke champions in his resistance to innovations in law and to Burke's own contention that customary usage does not mean the practice of the present generation but the hereditary practice of several generations – "the deliberate election of ages and generations."[72] Johnson's ideal, then, is a language that will be stabilized, if not fixed, by a written account of customary usage as he judges it, and he hopes that his definitions, spellings, and pronunciations will form something of a linguistic contract that will be unimpeached by innovators or by the sounds of the people arising from the street or marketplace. The contest Johnson describes and participates in between etymology and orthography will be renewed by different parties in the United States: to serve the needs of the present, Franklin invents a new phonetic alphabet and slights concerns that it will obscure etymology; to counter a popular voice that had betrayed past ideals and "corrupted" words, Thoreau recalls through etymology and puns their "original" or root meaning.

Johnson observes in the "Preface" the same diseases he earlier diagnosed in the "Plan," but the "Preface" evinces a profound doubt about his ability – or anyone's ability – to remedy those diseases. Refuting his own ideal of permanence, Johnson admits the stubborn fact of linguistic change: a fact so stubborn that the more he kicks at it, the more he refutes his own idealism. His earlier hopes of purifying and fixing the language are but "the dreams of a poet doomed at last to wake a lexicographer" (SJW, II, 56). The lament of the lexicographer, however, approaches the lyricism of a poet: "Words are hourly shifting their relations, and can no more be ascertained in a dictionary, than a grove, in the agitation of a storm, can be accurately delineated from its picture in the water" (SJW, II, 47). He similarly points out that "sounds are too volatile and subtile for legal restraints; to enchain syllables, and to lash the wind, are equally the undertakings of pride, unwilling to measure its desires by its strengths" (SJW, II, 61). Given this rebellious state of language, the lexicographer as governor must become the historian of language who marks the "progress of its [a word's] meaning, as . . . [it passes] from its primitive to its remote and accidental signification" or who records the changes that take place as people exercise their liberty to annex their own ideas to words. And at last, he notes, the "pen must at length comply with the tongue" (SJW, II, 48, 63).

C. H. Knoblauch argues that Johnson was "pugnacious in the Plan about interpreting linguistic change as degeneration," but that by 1755, the date of the "Preface," "this attitude had been perceptibly colored by the poet's admiration for a positive vitality of language in the face of any mechanical effort to shackle it within rules."[73] But while Johnson comments in a neutral tone on "the exuberance of signification" in language, he still persists at times in interpreting linguistic change as corruption, and he does not forgo moral disapproval of a licentious language. Thus, though he remarks that no one should be so vain as to imagine that a dictionary can "embalm" a language and "secure it from corruption," the emphasis falls on his desire to accomplish these impossible feats and his struggle to do what is possible in this regard: "It remains that we retard what we cannot repel, that we palliate what we cannot cure" (SJW, II, 60, 64). But Johnson in the "Preface" willingly recognizes that some changes in the language are more natural or less corrupt than others, for they are caused not by the folly and ignorance of man but by the advancement of knowledge, the "cultivation of various sciences," and the "levity" of man. Near the end of the "Preface" Johnson also advances the notion that change in language is not corruption but part of a creative evolution when he turns to an organic metaphor (borrowed from Horace) to explain the limitations of lexicography: "No dictionary of a living tongue ever can be perfect, since, while it is hastening to publication, some words are budding, and some falling away" (SJW, II, 65).

The organic metaphor that Johnson evokes to describe the process of linguistic change becomes in the nineteenth century an integral part of a theory of language (associated with Romanticism) that supplants another theory of linguistic change that Johnson delineates more fully (and with more allegiance) in the "Preface." The central postulate of this theory, simply expressed, is that language at some point in the past – usually in some form of golden age – was plain and expressive, but as civilization matured it became more complex and corrupt. Johnson writes, for instance, that "it is incident to words, as to their authors, to degenerate from their ancestors" and that "every language has a time of rudeness antecedent to perfection, as well as of false refinement and declension" (SJW, II, 41, 52). Linking classical political theory with linguistics, Johnson also remarks that "tongues, like governments, have a natural tendency to degeneration," a conviction that leads him to recruit members for his party of linguistic conservation: "We have long preserved our constitution, let us make some struggles for our language" (SJW, II, 64). Several decades later, after Americans had struggled to preserve and reform their constitution, Noah Webster would propose his own method for reforming the constitution of the English language and defend himself by arguing "that to believe the *ipse dixit* of a Johnson . . . has the force of law" and that "to contradict it, is rebellion" is to surrender our "right to private judgment" to "literary governors" (DEL, 168). If Chesterfield had ever written to his son about the American Revolution, he might have advised him that the dispute between Britain and America arose in part because of the unruly unwillingness of the colonists to heed the "true significations" of words as defined by their political and literary governors and by their rude willingness to be misled by the sounds of their own demagogues. From the perspective of Noah Webster and other colonists, Americans were not about to be colonized by the *ipse dixit* of a Johnson or a Grenville.

The Sovereign Voice: Joseph Priestly, Thomas Sheridan, and the Revolt Against Artificial Languages

Every revolution demands a transformation of the established language. The American Revolution itself can be said to participate in a larger transformation in linguistic attitudes that helps mark the passage from the classic to the Romantic phase in literary history. This shift is not abrupt and cannot be schematized too sharply, but it can be distinguished in part both by a growing willingness to regard linguistic change not as a corruption of language but as part of a natural revolution and to believe that the original language of humankind was not plain and rational but passionate and metaphorical – a language of the heart, not the head. What writers in the second half of the eighteenth century sought to recover was an ancient constitution of language that had not been corrupted by artifice, a language of sincere emotion and honesty that would be the natural voice of a people of virtue standing close to nature. The Revolution of 1776 gave impetus to this willingness to find in the language of the common people a source of virtue rather than corruption and to regard change in language as positive and necessary. Joseph Priestley and Thomas Sheridan were two harbingers of this change.

Known for his discovery of oxygen, Priestley was a nonconforming minister whose radical views provoked hostility against him in England and led him to seek refuge in America, where he maintained a friendship with Jefferson and Franklin. A supporter of the American and French revolutions, Priestley also embraced the principle of revolution in language. When he was a tutor in languages and belles-lettres at the dissenting academy of Warrington in the early 1760s, he published three works on language: *The Rudiments of English Grammar* (which went through nine editions from 1761 to 1833), *A Course of Lectures on the Theory of Language and Universal Grammar*, and *A Course of Lectures on Oratory and Criticism*. Noah Webster and Jefferson were both familiar with Priestley's work on language, and Jefferson's own embrace of linguistic change bears close resemblance to the positions Priestley advanced. Instead of criticizing change in language as a corruption and seeking to halt it by fixing the language, Priestley treats change as a natural process and discusses it not only in organic imagery but in terms of liberty, innovation, and revolution. "Languages," he writes in *Lectures on the Theory of Language*, ". . . cannot be expected to continue long in the same state [since] . . . they have a kind of *regular growth, improvement,* and *declension*" which proceed "from the necessity of giving names to new objects, new ideas and new combinations of ideas."[74] He adds, "No internal constitution can preserve" a language from its "general revolutions," and he advises that it is "absurd . . . to set up the compositions of any person or persons whatsoever as the standard of writing," because in language as well as in custom and laws "the body of a people who, in this respect, cannot but be free, will certainly assert their liberty, in making what innovations they judge to be expedient and useful" (169, 184). Priestley also asserts in *The Rudiments of English Grammar* that "we need make no doubt but that the best forms of speech will, in time, establish themselves by their own superior excellence: and, in all controversies, it is better to wait the decisions of Time, which are slow and sure, than to take those of Synods, which are often hasty and injudicious."[75] What Priestley rejects is what Johnson supports: a language of authority based upon custom or precedent. While Johnson attacks innovations in language in terms similar to Burke's attack on the innovations of the Constituent Assembly in Revolutionary France, Priestley praises innovations in language in terms similar to those in which Paine and Jefferson would praise the American Revolution. For Priestley (and Jefferson), linguistic innovation asserts the inalienable right to introduce rational changes in the established language without respect to past generations and without deference to the wishes of an elite or authorized body, a right that Burke and Johnson challenge in the name of custom. Priestley's approach to language is laissez-faire: he is willing to wait for the decisions of "time," which means that he is willing to trust the decisions that the "body of the people" make regarding their language. He also distrusts any authoritative interference in the process of linguistic change, because he believes that "since all men, and all bodies of men, are fallible," the "interposition of their authority is in danger of contributing to establish phrases and constructions, which the more mature judgment of after ages would see reason to correct" (181). Free the language, Priestley counsels, from literary governors and language reformers; they are more liable to corrupt it than the people.

At times, however, Priestley expresses his desire for something beyond the people to give law to language: a natural law that would provide a standard of appeal to decide questions of usage. He writes, for instance, that "were the language of men as uniform as the works of nature, the grammar of language would be as indisputable in its principles as the grammar of nature."[76] But he adds that "since good authors have adopted different forms of speech" and because "one authority may be of as much weight as another" and because what is considered "good usage" is merely the forms of speech that have "the most powerful advocates," there can be no standard but that of "all-governing custom." Yet he also asserts that recourse can be had to "the analogy of language," by which he means the forms of language that ought to apply on the belief that one can derive some fundamental principles of language from the study of custom.[77] While Johnson and Priestley both maintain that custom should rule in language, they differ in their understanding of custom, and their differences would remain alive in America as reformers of the English language embraced different strategies to govern, reform, or revitalize its constitution.

Language reform holds a mirror up to social and political fears: the forces reformers perceive corrupting the language are the forces they perceive, by and large, as a threat to their social and political values. Language is their battleground for meeting an enemy that they are unable or unwilling or indisposed to meet elsewhere. Consistently writers in the Real Whig tradition second Cato's conviction (reiterated by Emerson in *Nature*) that lust for money is at the root of political corruption and social malaise. Not uncommonly, poets in the second half of the eighteenth century, such as Thomas Gray, William Collins, and Oliver Goldsmith, develop a similar lament that the growth of cities and trade are manifestations of a commercial spirit – the lust for money writ large – that is portending England's descent into the luxury and corruption that marked the decline and fall of the Roman Empire, which Edward Gibbon masterfully narrated in a history published in 1776. Language, the poets recognized, participated in the fall. When Goldsmith, for instance, depicts the damaging effects of luxury and "trade's unfeeling train" in "The Deserted Village," a poem that was a favorite of its age, he depicts a reciprocal loss of community and communication. The desertion of the village is marked by a deep diminishment of the word's persuasive power. The poet remembers the village preacher who "prayed, and felt for all" and the schoolmaster who was "skill'd to rule" and argue for many things, but especially for their commanding eloquence (lines 160, 195).[78] "Truth" from the parson's lips "prevailed with double sway," and "fools who came to scoff, remained to pray," while the teacher, with "words of learned length, and thundering sound, / Amazed the gazing rustics ranged around" (lines 179–80, 213–14). At the pub good cheer and congenial talk flowed as swiftly as the beer until it was time for the "woodman's ballad" to "prevail" (line 244). The Auburn of memory is united by the harmonies of eloquence, talk, song. But discord is the only note heard on the docks where the community is dispersing. Most are silent. Even before they board ship, the "poor exiles" have lost their desire to communicate. Except for some weeping, they stand speechless, resembling the "silent bats" that "in drowsy clusters cling" (line 350). Goldsmith calls in the poem for a poetry whose "voice prevailing over time" could with its "persuasive strain" "Aid slighted truth" and "Teach erring men to spurn the rage of gain" (lines 421, 424–5). But that poetry, it seems, is something he can only summon up in a remembrance of things past rather than enact in the present, because poetry is "first to fly where sensual joys invade" (line 408). Goldsmith bids farewell not just to the community of Auburn but to this virtuous poetry whose persuasive power he would love to recover. What he does not imagine, however, is that in the near future the exiles who leave for the Colonies will one day seek to recover and preserve their own virtue against the threat of a Britain consumed by unfeeling trade and deaf to the voice of "justice and consanguinity." The deserted village of Auburn will be regathered in colonial towns where the voices of preachers and schoolmasters will prevail with double sway.

In an essay entitled "Of Eloquence" that appeared in the *Bee*, Goldsmith suggests where the lost charm of poetry and the power of eloquence could be found:

> It has been remarked, that the lower parts of mankind generally express themselves most figuratively, and that tropes are found in the most ordinary forms of conversation. Thus, in every language, the heart burns: the courage is roused; the eyes sparkle; the spirits are cast down; passion enflames; pride swells, and pity sinks the soul. Nature, everywhere, speaks in those strong images, which, from their frequency, pass unnoticed.[79]

The belief that the "lower parts of mankind" express themselves more figuratively and passionately than the upper parts had become a platitude by the later eighteenth century. The farther one descended in the social hierarchy and the farther one retreated in history (until the time before Babel or Adam's fall), it was assumed that the more passionate and figurative was the language. Intellectual and cultural advance was marked, conversely, by the disavowal of figurative language or its relegation to a special use – poetry. William Warburton thus asserts in *The Divine Legation of Moses* (1741) that metaphor was an original defect due to "rusticity of conception."[80] The proper language was precise, literal, temperate. Bacon, Hobbes, and Locke agree that the advance of knowledge and the maintenance of the social order could best be promoted if language was refined of its metaphorical elements. Metaphor was an insinuation of the passions, hence a threat to reason, and therefore best set off as clearly as possible from regular discourse.

When philosophers reconsidered the origins of language in the mid eighteenth century and as poets and critics in England began to reassess their literary heritage, they began to regard the language of the "lower parts of mankind" in a different light: that language was forceful, virtuous, honest; their own language was artificial, weak, corrupt. This reevaluation of language, as W. J. Bate argues, was part of a deeper and widespread conviction in later-eighteenth-century culture about the burden and glory of the past: a burden that prompted some poets to cast off the present and turn to the presumed spirit of an earlier poetry.[81] "Does it not sound something like Treason in *Apollo's Court*," asks Thomas Blackwell in *Enquiry into the Life and Writings of Homer* (1735), "to say that a *polished Language* is not fit for a great Poet? . . . Let me only observe, that what we call *Polishing* diminishes a Language."[82] Fascination with cultural primitivism with its "treasonous" preference for a more demotic language helped sponsor the popularity of Bishop Percy's *Reliques of Ancient English Poetry* and create the atmosphere for Chatterton to invent Rowley and for Macpherson to "discover" Ossian, an epic poet from the distant past whom Jefferson admired without knowing that the poet was Macpherson's forgery. This turn to the past was engendered, at least in part, by the belief that Homer and the great poets of the English tradition, as well as the Celtic and Hebrew bards, were unaffected by the progress of civilization. Unencumbered by society and unbothered by the dictates of critics, their imaginations, their emotions, and their language were more forceful and truthful. "It was therefore an advantage to the Father of poetry [Homer]," writes Robert Wood in 1769, "that he lived before the language of Compact and Art had so much prevailed over that of Nature and Truth."[83] Homer never knew Locke; he never consented to any social contract: he was a founding father who possessed an original relationship to nature, and his sovereign voice stands as a rebuke to the poetasters of a later age.

When the poets and critics of the later eighteenth century compared their own language with that of the past, it struck them that something desirable had been lost. The poetry of Chatterton and Macpherson, and some of the poetry of Gray, Collins, Smart, and Burns – the bardic poetry, the songs, *Jubilate Agno* – must be regarded as more than mere nostalgia: they are experiments, some more successful than others, with new yet presumably older versions of language. Indeed, when poets and critics began to explore the springs of English and classical poetry (the reassessment of Homer, Shakespeare, and Spenser; the study of Hebrew and Runic poetry, Celtic literature, and the medieval English tradition) and when Lord Monboddo and James Harris (along with others) began to study the origin and progress of language, it was largely a search for a more natural and representative language – a language, that is, in which metaphors were bold and poetry sublime.[84] The quest took them back through etymology, critical research, and philosophical speculation to the roots of words and to the ancient constitutions of languages.

In 1772 Johann Herder announces in "Essay on the Origin of Language" the past existence of such a language, and he suggests its potential for rebirth:

> There is, then, a language of feeling which is – underived – a law of nature. . . . A refined, late-invented metaphysical language . . . such a language, the child of reason and of society, cannot know much or anything of the childhood of its earliest forebear. But the old, the wild languages, the nearer they are to their origin, the more they retain it. . . . Open at random an Oriental Dictionary, and you will see the urge to express! How these inventors tore ideas away from one feeling to use them in the expression of another! How they did this borrowing most extensively from the heaviest, coldest, keenest senses! How everything had to turn into feeling and sound before it could turn into expression! Hence those powerful bold metaphors in the roots of the words. . . . But beware of calling this spirit of metaphors Asian. . . . It is alive in all unpolished languages.[85]

Contained in essays on the origin of language by Herder and Rousseau and continuing in the work of Romantic poets is the conviction that humankind's original or most natural language is, as Rousseau declares, "vital and figurative"; for, as he explains, "man's motives for speaking were of the passions," and thus "the first expressions were tropes."[86] "As we go back in history," Emerson similarly insists in *Nature*, "language becomes more picturesque, until its infancy, when it is all poetry" (ELA, 22). Opposed to the artifice and arbitrariness of a conventional language governed by the head, there is a more fundamental language that springs from the sentiments and a close correspondence with nature, and what such Romantic poets as Wordsworth and Shelley seek to do is revitalize poetry by returning language to its more natural condition in order to express more fully the nature of the world and people's experience of it. Wordsworth, for example, asserts in "Preface" to *Lyrical Ballads* that he is striving to depict men of "humble and rustic life" whose speech is said to be "real" and "natural" rather than artificial and civilized, and Shelley's ideal language is that mythic Orphic song "Which rules with Daedal harmony a throng / Of thoughts and forms, which else senseless and shapeless were."[87] And when Wordsworth speaks in the "Preface" of the corruption of language by modern poetasters and of the need to return to a more primitive stratum of language in rustic society, he states a version of the theory of linguistic decay that Samuel Johnson limned in his "Preface," but he advocates a radically different means to overcome it: a resurrection of the language of common people. And when Jefferson declares in "An Essay on the Anglo-Saxon Language" that a "revolution" (which, he says, some may consider a "rebellion") must be able to "renovate the vigor of the English language" that has been "too much impaired by the neglect of its ancient constitution," he too is advocating a means to reverse the corruption of the English language (TJW, XVIII, 391). Just as Rousseau's politics sought to recover, as E. J. Hundert argues, "the lost, primal eloquence of communities before their rhetorical fall, a mode of speaking which could command the affections without appealing to interest," so too did Jefferson and his compatriots.[88] Indeed, when the colonists turned to a rhetoric of sensation and enthusiasm to enforce their claims for liberty and awaken the colonists to the dangers posed by English authority, they were recovering what very many poets in the second half of the eighteenth century thought had been lost in their age and what they too were seeking to recover. William Wirt argues in *Letters of the British Spy* that for a man to be eloquent he has to overcome "a habit of artificial and elaborate decorum" derived from civilization and recover "the primitive simplicity of the patriarchal age."[89] In these letters, as well as in his best-selling biography of Patrick Henry, he presents Henry as such "an orator of nature" who spoke in the "extemporaneous effusions of a mind deeply convinced, and a heart inflamed with zeal for the propagation of those convictions."[90] Henry is the Romantic bard of the American Revolution.

Though Henry may have been tutored by nature, Wirt and other orators of the Revolutionary era acquired a fondness for a more natural-seeming eloquence not just from Henry and from the example set by evangelical ministers in the Great Awakening. Thomas Sheridan, a founder of the elocutionary movement in England, helped teach Jefferson and other Americans (including Whitman) how to go beyond the language of compact (and the theories of Locke) to recover a natural language of the heart: an honest, primal eloquence. Just as Priestley challenged Locke's (and Johnson's) preference for stability in language by sanctioning the innovations made by "the body of people," Thomas Sheridan challenged Locke's distrust of rhetoric by leading the elocutionary movement in Britain, which quickly spread to America, where Noah Webster paid him a tribute that suggests his high regard among Americans: "Sheridan, as an improver of the language, stands among the first writers of the British nation" (DEL, 176). The son of a classics professor and the godson of Jonathan Swift, Sheridan promoted a transformation in educational and linguistic practices whose end was nothing less than a revival of oratory in Britain that would match the splendor of Greek and Roman eloquence. Such a revival of oratory, Sheridan believed, could advance the public good in moral and political matters as well as provide a way for achieving what Swift desired: a refinement of the English tongue.

Beginning in the early 1750s, Sheridan advocated his transformation of rhetorical practice in a series of lectures and a set of works whose influence was wide-ranging.[91] His major publications include *British Education* (1756), *A Course of Lectures on Elocution* (1762), *A Plan of Education* (1769), *Lectures on the Art of Reading* (1775), and *A Rhetorical Grammar of the English Language* (1781). The main argument of these works is suggested in the full title of his first book: *British Education: Or, The Source of Disorders of Great Britain, Being an Essay towards proving, that the Immorality, Ignorance, and false Taste, which so generally prevail, are the natural and necessary Consequences of the present defective System of Education. With An Attempt to shew, that a Revival of the Art of Speaking, and the Study of Our Own Language, might contribute, in a great measure, to the Cure of those Evils. In three parts. I. Of the use of these Studies to Religion, and Morality; as also, to the Support of the British Constitution. II. Their absolute Necessity in order to refine, ascertain, and fix the English Language. III. Their Use in the Cultivation of the Imitative Arts: shewing, that were the Study of Oratory made a necessary Branch of the Education of Youth; Poetry, Musick, Painting, and Sculpture, might arrive at as high a Pitch of Perfection in England, as ever they did in Athens or Rome.*[92] As this title suggests, the fundamental premise of the rhetorical tradition shaped Sheridan's hopes for his elocutionary program; he was convinced that Greece and Rome owed their success in developing the splendor of their culture and the glory of their liberty to the care with which the people cultivated, refined, and guarded their language, and he feared that neglect of speech could only lead to a return to barbarism. He thus encouraged the British people to develop the same care for the arts of language, particularly oratory. In the classical republics, he points out, "the tongue of an orator could do more than the sceptre of a monarch, or the sword of a warrior."[93] Oratory arms the man of virtue with his most potent weapon for preventing and redressing evil, and Sheridan points out elsewhere that both Britain and the ancient states "have councils, senates, and assemblies of the people (by their representatives) whose deliberations turn upon matters of as much moment, where oratory has fields as ample, in which it may exert all its various powers, and where the awards and honours, attendant on eloquence are equal."[94] He also insists that development of a uniform system of pronunciation would end the "odious distinctions between subjects of the same king, and members of the same community, which are ever attended with ill consequences," and thus insure that natives from Ireland, Scotland, and the Americas would possess the same chance as the English for distinguishing themselves in the public councils of the realm.[95] Underlying his emphasis on pronunciation is thus a vision of achieving through the reform of language an end to linguistic differences that reflected social differences of class and region which translated into acts of prejudice against those who spoke in accents different from the members of the British court. A uniform language in Britain would not, in his view, centralize power or sustain a hierarchy. It would distribute throughout the realm the privileges of those who spoke the standard language.

The strong appeal of the elocutionary movement in Britain in the later eighteenth century – an appeal that would cross the Atlantic and continue in America through the middle of the nineteenth century – was sustained by more than its principle of reviving the ancient art of oratory and its emphasis on pronunciation and delivery as integral elements of the oratorical art.[96] What distinguishes Sheridan's program is that although he begins with Lockean principles of language and extends Locke's quest to remedy "the abuses of words," he also challenges Locke's principles in the development of his own linguistic theory and practice. He champions the study of language and the cultivation of the art of speaking because he insists that language is more than an instrument of the understanding created by convention; it is an affective force grounded in nature whose mastery could promote a more perfect social union or be, in his words, "the most effectual way to check the force of that sordid principle, selfishness, the nourisher of every vice; and to give vigour to that noble one of benevolence, the source of every Christian virtue" (186). What Sheridan offered, in short, was a rehabilitation of oratory as a virtuous power that could accomplish the most important of political ends by moving the passions.

Though Sheridan differs from Locke, his starting point is Locke's *Essay*. Sheridan, for instance, praises Locke in the introductory discourse to *The Course of Lectures on Elocution* for discovering the dependence of abstract thinking on abstract terms and for showing that "most errors in thinking" and "most controversies and disputes" arise from "an abuse of words" or from the failure to affix "clear and precise ideas" to terms (vi–vii). He maintains, however, that Locke's discoveries have been of little benefit to mankind because he failed to develop practical remedies for the problems he so acutely diagnosed. Disorders of language persist, Sheridan asserts, because the "study of our own language has never been made part of the education of our youth" (vii). Sheridan advocates several related changes as his own remedy: "mankind" must be "taught from their early days, by proper masters, the precise meaning of all the words they use," and more time in school should be devoted to the study of the English language rather than to the "dead" classical tongues (viii). He also develops a form of linguistic practice to treat vital aspects of the human mind besides the understanding that Locke ignored: the passions and the imagination. Just as the understanding can be better regulated through the analysis of words and ideas that Locke advocates, so too does Sheridan declare that the passions and the imagination can be regulated through the development of another form of language – the "language of nature" – which for Sheridan is the language of tones, sounds, and gestures (xiii). This "spoken language," he argues, is the "gift of God," whereas written language is the invention of man, and by cultivating God's language, or by following this language of nature as did the ancients, he believes people can recover a language of sublime force that can be used to suppress passions dangerous to society and promote, as did Orpheus, "those of the nobler and social kind" (xiii). Locke, according to Sheridan, merely examined the nature of words as "symbols of our ideas" and rejected the "nobler branch of language, which consists of the signs of internal emotions" (97). In *The Course of Lectures on Elocution* and his other works promoting the elocutionary movement, he makes up for that neglect by giving instruction in what he refers to as the "fixed, self-evident, and universally infallible" language of the affections and the passions (101). This language is composed of tones and gestures that evoke our sympathies and express our feelings of sorrow, connection, mirth, joy, hatred, anger, love, and pity, and it is this language of nature that would figure so large in theories of rhetoric that gained favor in America between the era of the Revolution and the Civil War. Indeed, it is this language of nature addressed to the heart that John Adams began studying in 1758, when he noted in his diary that an "Orator to gain the Art of moving the Passions, must attend to Nature, must observe the Sounds in which all sorts of People, express the Passions and sentiments of their Hearts, and must learn to adapt his own Voice, to the Passions he would move," and when he asked himself, "And has Language Power to charm, and shall I not avail myself of that Power?" (ED, 74, 77). And it is in this language that other colonists began addressing each other and charming the people in protesting the "unfeeling" acts of the British, and it is this language that Jefferson himself probably had in mind when he accented a draft of the Declaration of Independence with diacritical marks in preparation for his address to be read aloud, perhaps in those "self-evident" tones that would help win assent to the sentiments and self-evident truths he advanced to justify the cause of independence.[97]

After the Revolution, the elocutionary vision of a natural language continued to leave its mark on American letters. Just enter the wilderness of James Fenimore Cooper's *Last of the Mohicans* and listen and watch as Chingachgook and Uncas or the Mohican women at the funeral of Uncas speak and gesture in the "arts of native eloquence." Opposed to the dissimulations of the French and to the "cold and artificial manner" of speaking which Cooper says characterizes the Anglo-Americans (including Hawkeye) when they are unexcited, the native eloquence is warm, musical, natural, "governed by the emphasis and tones," and at times highly metaphorical and enthralling. Just as the names of Cooper's Native Americans are more reasonable and resembling of nature than those of the French and English, their voices are more likely to be an accurate transcription of their sentiments. The native eloquence becomes the standard by which to measure the "corruption" of civilized tongues.[98] Enter as well the notebooks of Whitman and observe how the American rough studied to master the vocal tones and gestures of the elocutionists. The voice of Whitman's bard, like the voice of the Revolutionary orator, claims to be derived from nature, but it was tutored by the elocutionary principles of the rhetorical culture it was seeking to transcend.

To combat the corruption and disorder that the British were perpetrating with their words and acts, the colonists turned, then, not just to Lockean analyses of the abuse of words but to the Orphic powers of a language of nature to protect their liberties and unite citizens in bonds of union. First in the Great Awakening and then during the Revolutionary period, colonial preachers and orators recovered and exploited what Locke sought to suppress – a language of enthusiasm – and with this rhetoric they roused colonists to unite and fight for the words and ideas that were being defined with Lockean analysis by the lawyers who helped lead the resistance to Britain.

III

The American Language of Revolution and Constitutional Change

7

The Language of Revolution: Combating Misrepresentation with the Pen and Tongue

> Indeed we ought firmly to believe, what is an undoubted truth, confirmed by the unhappy experience of many states heretofore free, that UNLESS THE MOST WATCHFUL ATTENTION BE EXERTED, A NEW SERVITUDE MAY BE SLIPPED UPON US, UNDER THE SANCTION OF USUAL AND RESPECTABLE TERMS.
>
> John Dickinson, *Letters from a Farmer in Pennsylvania*

In *The Professor at the Breakfast-Table* Oliver Wendell Holmes makes a series of seemingly offhand remarks about language in general and the language of the Revolutionary era in particular that should be taken more seriously than Holmes's jocular style suggests. He writes:

> Language! – the blood of the soul, Sir! into which our thoughts run and out of which they grow! We know what a word is worth here in Boston. Young Sam Adams got up on the stage at Commencement, out at Cambridge there, with his gown on, the Governor and Council looking on in the name of his Majesty, King George the Second, and the girls looking down out of the galleries, and taught people how to spell a word that wasn't in the Colonial dictionaries! *R-e, re, s-i-s, sis, t-a-n-c-e, tance. Resistance!* That was in '43, and it was a good many years before the Boston boys began spelling it with their muskets; – but when they did begin, they spelt it so loud that the old bedridden women in the English almshouses heard every syllable! Yes, yes, yes, – it was a good while before those other two Boston boys got the class so far along that it could spell those two hard words, *Independence* and *Union*! I tell you what, Sir, there are a thousand lives, aye, sometimes a million, go to get a new word into a language that is worth speaking. We know what language means too well here in Boston to play tricks with it. We never make a new word till we have made a new thing or a new thought, Sir! When we

195

shaped the new mould of this continent, we had to make a few. When, by God's permission, we abrogated the primal curse of maternity, we had to make a word or two. The cutwater of this great Leviathan clipper, the OCCIDENTAL, – this thirty-masted wind-and-steam wave-crusher, – must throw a little spray over the human vocabulary as it splits the waters of a new world's destiny![1]

In this passage Holmes figures the American passage from colonial dependence to revolutionary independence and national union as a language-learning lesson: the people in a reciprocal process create and are taught a new vocabulary. The first word that Sam Adams spells out for the class in defiance of the British authorities is "Resistance," a word that could not be found in colonial dictionaries because a lexicon governed by English authority would have incorporated what Sam Adams meant under the definition of a different word: rebellion. Then two more "Boston boys" – perhaps John Adams and Daniel Webster – taught the class two more words: Independence and Union.

Holmes's discussion of Revolutionary linguistics in this passage should remind us of Karl Marx's celebrated metaphor in the opening of *The Eighteenth Brumaire of Louis Bonaparte* which argues that revolutionary movements must function like those who successfully learn a second language and speak in that language without recourse to translation from the mother tongue. Marx first explains that all too often in revolutionary crises the dead generations of the past weigh too heavily on the brain of the living, for just when people "seem engaged in revolutionizing themselves and things, in creating something that has never yet existed, precisely in such periods of revolutionary crisis they anxiously conjure up the spirits of the past to their service and borrow from them names, battle cries and costumes in order to present the new scene of world history in this time-honored disguise and this borrowed language."[2] For Marx, retreat to the past transforms a potentially authentic revolutionary moment in which a new order of things would be created into bad theater – an unoriginal drama of rehearsed action and prescribed words – that threatens to become farce. Marx then compares the difficulty of breaking through inherited representations and of forging a new language in the revolutionary moment wherein words will suit the actions to the difficulty of gaining fluency in a new language: "In like manner a beginner who has learnt a new language always translates it back into his mother tongue, but he has assimilated the spirit of the new language and can freely express himself in it only when he finds his way in it without recalling the old and forgets his native tongue in the use of the new."[3] Holmes's passage suggests that Americans succeeded in doing exactly what Marx claimed revolutionaries must do and what he understands is so difficult: learn to speak differently or think in a new revolutionary language rather than in the old native tongue. Indeed, Holmes claims that in abrogating the primal curse of their maternal bond to Britain, the colonists had to reject their mother tongue and make a word or two, and that the new ship of state they created would continue to "throw a little spray over the human vocabulary" as it cuts a path to fulfill its destiny. It is important to note here that Holmes explains that this creation of a new vocabulary was not the work of just leaders of the Revolution, but of the people. The acceptance of a new word in the vocabulary of a tongue is a democratic process. A neologism that is offered in the forum or the marketplace will be cast aside unless it receives support from the majority. It is a struggle, a fight – sometimes "a thousand lives, aye, sometimes a million, go to get a new word into a language that is worth speaking."

To develop further Holmes's image of the Revolutionary era as a time of language learning and verbal innovation, this study examines in Part III how colonists such as Sam Adams fought in word and deed to revise the vocabulary and representational system of the British, and how the founding fathers violated the grammar of classical political discourse to create a new political grammar which was the Constitution, and a new political system – the United States – that could not be denominated with the words "monarchy," "aristocracy," and "democracy" or even solely with the word "national" or "federal." We shall consider, then, how Americans in the Revolutionary era enacted the demand Whitman later made to perform language experiments to "give the spirit, the body, the man, new words, new potentialities of speech."[4] We shall also examine how far we can apply Holmes's metaphor about language – "the blood of the soul, Sir! into which our thoughts run and out of which they grow!" – to a study of the American language of revolution; for at the heart of much current debate about the Revolution is how much the language of republicanism governed the thoughts and expectations of the colonists and how much they governed that language to advance their political, religious, and economic interests. To what degree, that is, did their thoughts run into and grow out of that language (and out of other political languages in their culture)? To what degree, in other words, did the colonists become consenting (or unconsenting) subjects – or masters – of the languages that constituted them as a people?

Americans did exactly what Marx said happens in a revolutionary crisis. They borrowed the language and donned the costumes of their classical, Christian, and British forebears to justify their protests and stage their revolution. Those who wrote and spoke out most loudly in public rummaged through the attic of antiquity; they mined the resources of the republican tradition; they relied on a shared understanding of the Word of God. From these sources (and others) they chose scripts, they assumed roles, they taught people lines, they directed action – and they improvised. Town meetings, courts of justice, presses, and every fireside – all these became, in John Adams's words, "theatres of politics."[5] These scenes of debate and dialogue were occasions for the people to act as critics, masters, and teachers of the languages that governed them, "spreading and distributing far and wide," in Adams's phrase, "the ideas of right and sensations of freedom."[6] Here too the colonists practiced and developed the art of counterdiscourse, the Lockean strategy of opposing misrepresentations and the abuse of words by redefining or clarifying the meanings of terms. This battle for the hearts and minds of the colonists climaxed in a rejection of the King's English for a new discourse that claimed to be more faithful to common sense and the language of nature. And when the drama of the Revolution concluded, the process of language learning and linguistic experimentation continued: Americans began drafting the plans for a novel political form that required them to create new meanings and collectively formulate representative ideas for the words that had become and would remain sovereign forces in American politics – "liberty," "union," "the people," "equality." It required, ultimately, the toppling of a mother tongue – classical political discourse – to achieve a new science of politics.[7]

Gordon Wood writes in his essay *Representation in the American Revolution* that "of all the conceptions of political theory underlying the momentous developments of the American Revolutionary era, none was more important than that of representation."[8] He continues:

> Nearly all of the great debates of the period, beginning with the imperial controversy in the 1760s and ending with the clash over the new Federal Constitution in the 1780s, were ultimately grounded in the problem of representation. Indeed, if representation is defined as the means by which the people participate in government, fulfillment of a proper representation became the goal and measure of the Revolution itself, "the whole subject of the present controversy," as Thomas Jefferson put it in 1775.[9]

Wood's assertion, to my mind, cannot be challenged, but it can be supplemented if we are willing to add that the problem of representation was not just a matter of political representation but also of linguistic representation. Indeed, the quest for proper representation in the Revolutionary era was at once a quest to restore and maintain a meaningful correspondence between political representatives and their constituents and a quest to restore and maintain a meaningful correspondence between words and their representative ideas. The American Revolution, that is, can be seen as an attempt to replace a system of linguistic as well as political representation that had degenerated into corruption with one that would be vitally responsive to the voice of nature and the ideas of the people. Just as Americans protested that they had been betrayed by their virtual representatives in Parliament, so too did they protest that they had been betrayed by the virtual meanings of words in the King's English. Under the pretence of regulating trade, their property had been unjustly seized; in the name of law, their liberties were being destroyed; or so they argued. The notion of virtual representation itself, claimed Daniel Dulany, was a "mere cobweb, spread to catch the unwary and entangle the weak."[10] Refusing to be imposed upon any longer by artful misrepresentations, the colonists demanded a radical change in the way they were represented: they became Sons of Liberty and began to spell "resistance" with their muskets and define "liberty" in their deeds.

"Revolution at one level," writes Tony Tanner, "is nothing more or less than a disappropriation of the signs hitherto owned by a privileged class, or a challenging of what Lacan calls 'the master words of the city' – les maîtres-mots de la cité)."[11] By 1776 the colonists were more than willing to challenge the master words of a governing order: the words of King George III and Parliament that sanctioned their privileges and defended their policies. In effect, the colonists acted upon Locke's belief, which he expresses in Two Treatises of Government, that "a people" can rise up in revolution "if a long train of Abuses, Prevarications, and Artifices, all tending the same way, make the design visible to the People, and they cannot but feel, what they lie under, and see whither they are going" (463). Jefferson similarly argues in the Declaration of Independence that "when a long train of abuses & usurpations pursuing invariably the same object, evinces a design to reduce them under absolute despotism, it is their right, it is their duty to throw off such a government" (JLA, 19). Scholars generally agree that this statement by Jefferson justifying revolution is indebted to Locke. But Jefferson's version has led scholars to overlook what the colonial opposition understood so well: prevarications and artifices as well as abuses of the kind listed in the Declaration were dangerous political acts that had to be resisted. Thus, when John Adams looked back in the early 1800s at the Revolution, he emphasized how "the lords, as well as the commons, of Great Britain, by continued large majorities, endeavored by finesse, tricks, and stratagems, as well as threats, to prevail on the American colonies to surrender their liberty and property to their disposal." He adds,

"These failing, they attempted to *plunder* our rights by force of arms. We feared their arts more than their arms" (JAW, VI, 424–5). To oppose these "arts," the colonists not only sniffed the approach of tyranny in every breeze and every imperial breath from England; they challenged these arts with an outpouring of verbal criticism and counterrepresentation. "Common people are not incapable of discerning the motives and springs of words and actions," John Adams noted in his diary, and we must see how the effort to foster this critical ability was an essential task of the leaders of the Revolution who wrote and spoke against the designs of the British (JAW, II, 64). It was their effort to oppose British propaganda or the false signs of an ideology in the Marxist sense with the science of studying signs which the philosophes termed ideology.[12] This challenge reached its height in Paine's attack on the master words of the British in *Common Sense*, and it culminated in the Declaration of Independence. This challenge, of course, has long roots, and this chapter will examine several of the crucial texts from the Revolutionary era in which verbal criticism – a study of the use and abuse of words – became political action of the highest sort. The American Revolution, like the scientific revolution led by Francis Bacon, was partly an attempt to topple the "Idols of the Market-place" that had forced and overruled the understanding of people, or a struggle to free the colonists from what Paine called in *The Rights of Man* "the Bastille of a word" and replace a language of artifice with a language of nature (TPW, I, 287). "From the outset," as Gordon Wood writes, "the colonists attempted to turn their decade-long controversy with England into a vast exercise in deciphering and applying the philosophy of the age."[13] Or, as the truism goes, the American Revolution is the Enlightenment program put into action. But what needs to be emphasized is how the colonists operated within the linguistic philosophy of the age and how they applied that philosophy to decipher and combat the "misrepresentations" of the British and formulate their own representative ideas.

Jonathan Mayhew and Symbolic Redefinition: From Rebellion to Resistance

Oliver Wendell Holmes praised Sam Adams for teaching the colonists the significance of resistance, but that honor should go first and foremost to Jonathan Mayhew, who in 1750, on the anniversary of Charles I's execution, preached what is regarded as one of the most famous sermons in pre-Revolutionary America and the "first salvo" of that struggle.[14] Reprinted within a few months of its initial appearance and again in 1775, it was, according to John Adams, "read by everybody, celebrated by friends, and abused by enemies."[15] The anniversary of Charles I's execution had become in England the occasion for Tory, High Church, and Jacobite orators to revive the theory of the divine right of kings, and as the anniversary approached in the Colonies, Mayhew noted in the pronouncements of British Anglicans a "strange sort of frenzy . . . preaching passive obedience, worshipping Charles I, and cursing the dissenters and puritans for murdering him" (*PAR*, 206). In direct challenge to the hagiography and martyrdom of Charles I and to the absolutist doctrine of the divine right of kings, Mayhew delivered three sermons on the subject of obedience and disobedience to higher authorities, and in the last, his *Discourse Concerning Unlimited Submission and Non-Resistance to the Higher Powers*, he took up the mantle of John Milton's *Eikonoklastes* and demanded that people see Charles I for what he was in truth rather than in title: not a king, but a tyrant; not a saint, but a "*royal sinner*"; not an authority to be obeyed passively, but a "lawless" man to be resisted actively (*PAR*, 246, 243).

The rhetorical strategy of the sermon depends in part on two tactics that had been deployed repeatedly by Whig opposition writers and would be used frequently in the pamphlet war with Britain. The first tactic is an attempt to limit the claims of British power by delimiting the meanings of the words that the government used to justify its power, and the second is a radical insistence on seeing beyond names and titles to observe people as they really are rather than as they are represented, a demand that owes much of its intensity, as Jay Fliegelman points out, to the empiricism that Bacon and Locke championed.[16] Indeed, just as Locke repeatedly warns about the dangers of mistaking words for things and being misled by sounds, so too does Mayhew (as did Milton, Algernon Sidney, and Trenchard and Gordon) caution people about mistaking the title of a man for his character, and he urges people to judge men not by their professions or offices but by their actions.[17] Mayhew, for instance, argues that when the Apostle advocates the duty of submission to "*higher powers,*" he does not favor "submission to all who bear the *title* of rulers in common, but only to those who *actually* perform the duty of rulers by exercising a reasonable and just authority for the good of human society" (*PAR*, 226). Thus, he adds, to call a king who is a tyrant and an oppressor a minister of God is blasphemy, and since Charles I's actions were those of a tyrant, "it must be said," Mayhew continues, that "*Cromwell* and his adherents were not, properly speaking, guilty of *rebellion* because he whom they beheaded was not, properly speaking, *their King* but a *lawless tyrant*" (*PAR*, 243). Charles I, that is, "*unkinged*" himself, and consequently to represent Cromwell and his followers in "the blackest colors" as "schismatics" and as "traitors and rebels" is to misrepresent them (*PAR*, 242, 246). To possess the authority of a king, it is not enough to be called a king; one must fulfill the definition of a king – as Mayhew defines it. Rulers, in his view, must exercise a "reasonable and just authority for the good of human society," and if they "rob and ruin the public instead of being guardians of its peace and welfare," then they "immediately cease to be the *ordinance* and *ministers of God* and no more deserve that glorious character than common *pirates* and *highwaymen*" (*PAR*, 226, 228). And from this principle Mayhew derives his thesis that opposition to Charles I cannot be defined as sinful rebellion but must be considered to be "a most righteous and glorious stand made in defense of the natural and legal rights of the people against the unnatural and illegal encroachments of arbitrary power" (*PAR*, 241).

The biblical text Mayhew glosses to defend his definition of kingship and the duties of subjects is Romans 13:1–8, and here Mayhew, in effect, turns Saint Paul into a disciple of Locke. In addition to converting Saint Paul into a believer in a Lockean social contract, Mayhew reveals a Lockean rather than a Hobbesian understanding of language and interpretation. When Hobbes contended for the absolute authority of the sovereign in *Leviathan*, he also contended that the sovereign must possess an unlimited power to establish the terms of the linguistic contract that sustains the social contract. In contrast, Mayhew contends that the words from the Bible used to justify the divine right of kings – "Let every soul be subject unto the higher powers" – cannot be understood in an absolute sense but must be limited by "common sense" (*PAR*, 223). "Nonresistance to the *higher powers*," he asserts, "cannot be argued from the absolute unlimited expressions" which Saint Paul uses, because "no one puts such a sense upon these expressions, however absolute and unlimited" (*PAR*, 225, 224). Those "absolute and unlimited terms" cannot be taken literally, because "common sense shows that they were not intended to be so understood" (*PAR*, 223). For Mayhew, then, the meaning of the biblical text is not to be determined by a single authoritative voice but by common understanding. The hermeneutic principle that Mayhew adopts in his sermon is thus an application of Mayhew's Lockean belief, expressed in 1748, that truth "as it relates to words and propositions is nothing but the right use of certain arbitrary signs, having a meaning annexed to them by common consent."[18] To fix "the exact limits of submission" to a ruler, then, Mayhew strives to fix and limit the meaning of the words that rulers use or abuse to claim unlimited submission. When people begin to define their rights, as Edmund Burke commented, it is "a sure symptom of an ill-conducted state."[19] That process of definition that Mayhew illustrates in his sermon would continue almost unabated in the Colonies after the Stamp Act, and the success of the colonists in conducting their language-learning exercises is suggested by George Washington when he remarked in 1783 that "the foundation of our empire was not laid in the gloomy age of ignorance and superstition; but at an epoch when the rights of mankind were better understood and more clearly defined, than at any former period."[20]

Sam Adams: Rhetorical Gadfly

Jonathan Mayhew declared in the preface to his *Discourse Concerning Unlimited Submission* that he was "engaged on the side of Liberty, the *BIBLE*, and Common Sense, in opposition to Tyranny, PRIESTCRAFT, and Nonsense" (*PAR*, 213). When Samuel Adams took his M.A. degree at Harvard in 1743, he argued the affirmative of the proposition "Whether it be lawful to resist the Supreme Magistrate, if the Commonwealth cannot otherwise be preserved," and although there is no record that he delivered his argument at the commencement, the argument marks the beginning of Adams's long career fighting with his pen and tongue for the same principles as Mayhew: liberty, the Bible, and common sense. "Without the character of Samuel Adams," John Adams maintained, "the true history of the American Revolution can never be written. For fifty years, his pen, his tongue, his activity, were constantly exerted for his country without fee or reward" (JAW, X, 263–4). Considered by some historians to be the leading propagandist of the American Revolution, Adams was looked upon in his own day by such Tory writers as Peter Oliver as at best a Machiavellian and at worst a "serpentine demagogue" who "could turn the minds of the great Vulgar . . . into any cause that he might chuse" and who ingratiated himself with John Hancock "in the same manner that the Devil is represented seducing Eve, by a constant whispering at his Ear."[21] Oliver pictures Adams in Miltonic terms as a disciple (or reincarnation) of Satan seducing the colonists into sinful rebellion with insinuating address; but the way Adams pictures himself is as if he were haranguing the colonists to save them from the fate of characters not in *Paradise Lost* but in Pope's *Dunciad*. "I know very well," he writes, "that to murmur, or even to *whisper* a complaint, some men call a riotous spirit. But they are in the right of it to complain, and complain ALOUD. And they *will* complain, till they are either redress'd, or become poor deluded miserable ductile Dupes, fitted to be made the slaves of dirty tools of arbitrary power."[22] The works of Milton and Pope were widely read in the Colonies, and the two poets were quoted in the political writings of the colonists as frequently as Locke and Trenchard and Gordon. *Paradise Lost* and *The Dunciad* are themselves classic representations of the two fundamental ways the colonists perceived themselves losing their liberty and virtue to the British threat: innocence could be seduced and ignorance deluded. Indeed, both poems confirm the lesson of Locke and Trenchard and Gordon that the fall of man from liberty into licentiousness and tyranny can be perpetrated by the abuse of the word. In *Paradise Lost* the most effective weapon of the archrebel, Satan, is verbal misrepresentation, and in *The Dunciad* the favorite stratagem of the tyrant is to make men "First slave to Words, then vassal to a Name, – Then dupe to Party" (IV, lines 501–2) and to "Give law to Words, or war with Words alone" (IV, line 178). In a footnote to this line, Scriblerus remarks "that the words *Liberty* and *Monarchy* have been frequently confounded and mistaken one for the other by the gravest authors."[23] In the 1760s and 1770s Adams was not about to let the colonists be confused about the difference between liberty and monarchy or be led into slavery by losing a war of words with the British. And he was certainly not about to let them be lulled to sleep.

Like Pope, Adams believed that the innocent and virtuous as well as the ignorant could be deluded and thus enslaved by the art and intrigue of arbitrary power. He also believed that "when designs are form'd to rase the very foundation of a free government, those few who are to erect their grandeur and fortunes upon the general ruin, will employ every art to sooth the devoted people into a state of indolence, inattention and security, which is forever the fore-runner of slavery" (SAW, II, 287). Thus he prayed, "May God preserve the Nation from being greatly injured if not finally ruin'd by the Vile Insinuations of wicked men *in America*" (SAW, I, 249). And Adams, as much as any other colonist, wrote and argued to keep alive the interpretation of British words and actions as a conspiracy against the liberties of the colonists, an interpretation that by and large shaped the colonial response to British policies from the Stamp Act crisis through the Revolution, as Bernard Bailyn argues in *The Ideological Origins of the American Revolution*. In a letter to the *Boston Gazette*, Adams declared that "*at present* there are good grounds to apprehend a settled design to enslave and ruin the colonies; and that some men of figure and station in America, have adopted the plan, and would gladly lull the people to sleep, the easier to put it in execution" (SAW, II, 148). For Adams, the colonists' fear of conspiracy was not a baseless vision or a paranoid response but a most rational conclusion that could be reached not only by observing the consensus of the people but by believing, as every rational man could, that "men . . . may . . . for a wedge of gold, detach themselves from the *common* interest . . . and triumph, in the ruins of their country" (SAW, II, 149); that "power, especially in times of corruption, makes men wanton" (SAW, II, 150); and that "Governors of a province" will "misrepresent and abuse the people even to the Ear of Majesty itself" (SAW, I, 338). Given these conditions, the response of the "*true* patriot," Adams asserts, must be to "stir up the people" and "*incessantly* to complain of *such men*, till they are either reform'd, or remov'd" and "enquire into the causes of the *fears and jealousies* of his countrymen; and if he finds they are not *groundless* . . . he will by all proper means in his power *foment* and *cherish* them" (SAW, II, 149–50). This is exactly how Adams defined and acted his part.

Ironically, members of the British administration and American Tories were just as fearful that the colonists were conspiring against their constitution as the colonists were fearful of them. Indeed, the British believed themselves to be the victims of Sam Adams and other subversives who cloaked their designs, as King George III proclaimed to Parliament in 1775, under "vague expressions of attachment to the parent state and the strongest protestations of loyalty" while in truth "they were preparing for a general revolt."[24] In British eyes, the colonists' complaints of being enslaved, their incessant protests about luxury, corruption, and tyranny, and their zealous devotion to liberty were rhetorical claims with no substantiation – a propaganda ploy designed to manipulate people and disguise their ambitious pursuit of power and profit. Countering this claim, Adams declares in a letter to the *Boston Gazette*, "The inhabitants of this continent are not to be duped 'by an artful use of the words *liberty* and *slavery*, in an application to their *passions.*' . . . They can distinguish between 'realities and sounds'; and by a proper use 'of that reason which Heaven has given them,' they can judge, as well as their betters, when there is danger of *slavery*" (SAW, II, 149).

When warning the colonists to be jealous of their liberties and watchful of the words of their rulers, Adams cites Roman history and the most famous of conspiratorial attempts that ended in tyranny: the rise of Julius Caesar. Like Milton's Satan, Caesar, in Adams's view, succeeded through the art of misrepresentation, or by confounding vice and virtue:

> By pretending to be the peoples greatest friend, he gain'd the ascendency over them: By beguiling arts, hypocrisy and flattery, which are even more fatal than the sword, he obtain'd that supreme power which his ambitious soul had long thirsted for: The people were finally prevail'd upon to *consent* to their own ruin: By the force of perswasion, or rather by cajoling arts and tricks always made use of by men who have ambitious views, they enacted their *Lex Regia* . . . that is, *the will and pleasure of the Prince had the force of law.* (SAW, II, 251)

The conclusion that Adams draws from this history, which is a lesson about the corruption of classical eloquence, is that it behooves the colonists "to awake and advert to the danger" they are in and recognize, as the Roman people failed to do, that their "enemies would fain have us lie down on the bed of sloth and security" and that they daily administer "the opiate with multiplied arts and delusions" (SAW, II, 252–3). And for Adams the best antidote for that dangerous opiate was the *pharmakon* of his own words and the words of fellow patriots:

> Let us converse together upon this most interesting Subject and open our minds freely to each other. Let it be the topic of conversation in every social Club. Let every Town assemble. Let Associations & Combinations be everywhere set up to consult and recover our just Rights. "*The Country claims our* active *AID* – let us roam; & where we find a Spark / Of Public Virtue, blow it into a Flame." (SAW, II, 337)

The frequent subject of critical gaze in eighteenth-century literature is the figure who becomes imprisoned in his or her own closed mind or caught in a realm of words impervious to the checks and balances provided by the give-and-take of conversation or by confrontation with the actual nature of things. The only dialogue, for instance, that Sterne's Walter Shandy, the Hack in Swift's *Tale of a Tub*, the pedants in Pope's *Dunciad*, the astronomer in Johnson's *Rasselas*, and Blake's Idiot Questioner seem to conduct is with their own delusions. Sam Adams functions in his setting as something akin to an eighteenth-century satirist: he is desperate to awake people from their delusions, to stoke up embers of virtue in a world grown corrupt, and to impel people into a remedial dialogue. A combination of conversation and raillery becomes for him, as it was for the Earl of Shaftesbury and very many other eighteenth-century writers, an antidote for linguistic dogmatism and political tyranny.[25]

The Stamp Act: Protesting Virtual Representation

In the decade that began with the Stamp Act crisis of 1765, several measures of the British Parliament and various pamphlets provoked the ire of the colonists and their searing complaint of taxation without representation. This grievance, as Richard Hofstadter remarks, "became the central issue, the focal symbol which expressed the entire American feeling of discontent."[26] Probably neither the burden of too much taxation nor the problem of too little (or no) representation could by itself have caused the colonists to respond as they did, but combined they provided the colonists with a volatile mixture of economic motivation and legal justification. The Stamp

Act crisis and the debate about representation also resonated, Jay
Fliegelman argues, with intellectual and moral implications that transcended questions of money and law: "the colonists' desire for 'actual'
rather than 'virtual' representation gave silent expression to the larger
cultural anxieties about the merely virtual representation of things by
language, of intentions by professions, of reality by appearances."[27]
He adds, "On a symbolic level the stamped paper Britain sought to
oblige colonists to buy stood in silent opposition to Locke's image of
the *tabula rasa*, that 'blank sheet' Paine declared America could write
its new government upon. The latter optimistically suggested freedom
from original sin and the power to create a new nation, the former
symbolically reflected a world of fixed values and fixed characters."[28]
The struggle of the colonists for actual political representation was
indeed closely linked to their concern about the virtual representation
of things by language; for that struggle was fought in part by the
colonists' demand that Britain supply representative ideas for their
words just as they called upon Britain to supply direct political
representatives for the constituency of the Colonies. In addition, the
colonists first petitioned to revise and then fought to erase the words
that the British had "improperly" affixed to their character or imprinted in their minds, just as they petitioned to remove the mark that
had been stamped on their paper. Sam Adams, for instance, was one of
several colonists to question the concept of virtual representation by
questioning the meaning of the word itself: "We have been told that
we are virtually represented, but we must desire an *Explanation* of this
vague Term, before we can give it serious Consideration" (SAW, I, 66).
And he and many others, in particular Benjamin Franklin, also protested vehemently that the colonists had been unjustly stamped with
"the odious names of traitors and rebels, only for complaining of their
grievances" (SAW, II, 359).[29]

Of all the millions of words that the Stamp Act provoked, "proba-
bly none were more widely read or more universally approved,"
Edmund and Helen Morgan write, "than those of a Maryland lawyer,
Daniel Dulany, in a pamphlet called *Considerations on the Propriety of
Imposing Taxes in the British Colonies, for the Purpose of Raising a Revenue, by
Act of Parliament.*"[30] In this pamphlet, which went through five editions
within three months of its initial appearance in 1765, Dulany was
responding directly to three British pamphlets, one of which was
Soame Jenyns's *Objections to the Taxation of Our American Colonies by the
Legislature of Great Britain, Briefly Consider'd*; and we first need to glance
at that pamphlet and a comment made by the English linguist Rowland Jones in his *Circles of Gomer* in 1771 to appreciate how the war of
words between Britain and the Colonies was in part a war about

words. In the midst of recommending a universal language that would reunite mankind, Jones asserts that

> to prove the confusion of knowledge to be the effect of that of language, we need only recur to our late altercations with respect to the American government, the right of the collective body, for want of a due conception of the first principles or original divine frame of which we might have been sufficiently furnished by a right definition of the terms of our laws and tenures and names of places and of things.[31]

Jones maintains that a proper understanding of political words and phrases would end the confusion of the colonists. Jenyns in his pamphlet proceeds upon the same assumption. In the opening paragraph he asserts that since the objections of the colonists to British taxation "are usually mixt up with several patriotic and favorite words such as liberty, property, Englishmen, etc., which are apt to make strong impressions on that more numerous part of mankind who have ears but no understanding," he believes it would not be improper to educate the colonists in the true meaning of those words.[32] Through such a process, he believes, the entire structure of the colonists' arguments will fall "at once to the ground, and like another Babel, [perish] by a confusion of words, which the builders themselves are unable to understand" (19). For Jenyns, the phrase that was the primary source of confusion because of its various significations is "the liberty of an Englishman," a term, he complains, that has been used for the past few years "as a synonymous term for blasphemy, bawdy, treason, libels, strong beer, and cyder" (20). Jenyns here repeats with some wit the familiar objection of British officials that the colonists were employing the term "liberty" in self-interested ways; their calls for liberty were but a cover for the pursuit of licentious desires. Rather than trying to define all that liberty can mean, a task that would have been in Jenyns's view as difficult as an attempt to define the bawdy meanings of the word "nose" in Sterne's *Tristram Shandy*, Jenyns limits himself to defining what it cannot mean: "an exemption from taxes imposed by the authority of the Parliament of Great Britain" (20). Keeping his tongue partly in his cheek, Jenyns also admits near the end of the pamphlet that he would be afraid of "the introduction of representatives from the several colonies into" Parliament, because he fears that given "the great powers of speech of which these American gentlemen are possessed . . . the sudden importation of so much eloquence at once, would greatly endanger the safety and government of this country" (22–3).

In striving to refute Jenyns's argument and the claim that parliamentary taxation of the Colonies was justified by their virtual representation in the House of Commons, Dulany in *Considerations* resorts to the same tactic as Jenyns: a critique of words. Dulany argues that the whole matter of whether "the imposition of the *stamp duties* is a *proper* exercise of constitutional authority" can be reduced "to the single question, whether the Commons of Great Britain are *virtually* the representatives of the commons of America or not" (*PAR*, 610). He answers that question in part by reducing the phrase "*virtual representation*" to what he feels it is: a verbal "cobweb, spread to catch the unwary and entangle the weak" (*PAR*, 611). He adds:

> Where have they defined or precisely explained what they mean by the expression *virtual representation*? As it is the very hinge upon which the rectitude of the taxation turns, something more satisfactory than mere assertion, more solid than a form of expression, is necessary. For how can it be seriously expected that men who think themselves injuriously affected in their properties and privileges will be convinced and reconciled by a fanciful phrase the meaning of which can't be precisely ascertained by those who use it or properly applied to the purpose for which it hath been advanced? (*PAR*, 611)

Here, in short, is a Lockean analysis of the abuse of words. The British have no more supplied a definite idea for the term "virtual representation" than they have supplied a definite representative for the Colonies, and he hopes that the colonists are not about to be duped by a fanciful phrase into giving up their rights and money. Throughout the pamphlet Dulany continues to examine "how unfair and deceptive" is the representation of the Colonies in a linguistic as well as a political sense. He warns, for instance, that by such "artifices and sophistry" as have been used in the debate over representation "ignorance [is] misled, credulity deceived, and prejudices excited," and the end result is a threatened return to the Thucydidean moment when vice passes for virtue, or, in Dulany's words, when "oppression gains the credit of equity, cruelty passes for moderation, and tyranny for justice, and the man who deserves reproach is celebrated by adulation and applauded by delusion for his wisdom and patriotic virtues" (*PAR*, 630). Near the end of the pamphlet Dulany protests against one of the most dangerous of all the misrepresentations when he objects as follows to the abuse of the word "Parliament":

> How awkwardly are the principles of the Revolution applied by some men! What astonishment would the promoters of that glorious measure, those patrons and friends of liberty, did they now tread the

stage of this world, express that a *word* by which they meant to assert the privileges of the subject and restrain despotic power should be relied upon to demolish the very principle by which themselves were animated, and after all their pains and hazards to establish the generous sentiments of liberty, that those who feel and enjoy the blessings of their successful struggles should not be able to raise a thought beyond the ideas affixed to systematic terms. (*PAR*, 636)

In Dulany's view, the very terms that animated the Glorious Revolution of 1688 were now being used to subvert the privileges and liberties that the revolution had won for the English, and he worries that the advance of despotic power will continue unless the heirs of that revolutionary legacy exercise their inviolable liberty and raise their thoughts beyond the ideas that have been improperly "affixed to systematic terms."

Soame Jenyns had some good reasons for expressing trepidation about American eloquence. Dulany's *Considerations* helped to make virtual representation a dead issue, and colonial pamphleteering and protests helped lead to the repeal of the Stamp Act of 1766. But the differences that had developed between England and the Colonies in their interpretation of the British constitution and the definitions of words could not be repealed. As Edmund and Helen Morgan write in their study of the Stamp Act crisis, "unfortunately, the repeal did not put back into the limbo of ambiguity the words which had been spoken so often in the preceding two years, 'the rights of Englishmen' and 'the authority of Parliament.' Grenville had given a meaning to one phrase, and the colonists to the other, which repeal of the Stamp Act could not erase."[33] Nor, in the opinion of Benjamin Franklin, could the Colonies be governed in 1766 "at the expence only of a little pen, ink and paper," as they had been in 1763.[34] The repeal of the Stamp Act did not lessen the fears of such colonists as Sam Adams and Silas Downer that the British were conspiring against their liberties. For them, as Pauline Maier writes, "repeal meant only an alteration, not an end, of the 'evil designs' of 1765."[35] Maier then quotes a letter Downer wrote to the New York Sons of Liberty in July 1765 in which he expresses his belief that "WHAT COULD NOT BE BROUGHT TO PASS BY AN UNDISGUISED AND OPEN ATTACK UPON OUR LIBERTIES IS INTENDED TO BE DONE BY SECRET MACHINATIONS, BY ARTIFICE AND CUNNING."[36]

John Dickinson: Penman Against the Thucydidean Moment

Less than a year after the repeal of the Stamp Act came the passage of the Townshend Revenue Act, a measure that revived colonial opposition and provoked John Dickinson to pen *Letters from a Farmer in Pennsylvania to the Inhabitants of the British Colonies*, which quickly became the most popular and the most influential piece of writing to appear in the Colonies before Paine's *Common Sense*. First published between December 1767 and February 1768 in the *Pennsylvania Chronicle*, Dickinson's letters were printed in nineteen of the twenty-three English-language newspapers published in the Colonies in 1768 and by 1789 had been issued in seven pamphlet editions. Praised by one colonist as containing "the great Axioms of Liberty" and "an American system of Politics," the letters renewed the efforts of Sam Adams and Dulany to awaken the colonists before they were, in the terms of a 1768 poem entitled "Liberty," "By Words delusive into Folly led."[37]

Although the letters were published serially, they were composed at the same time, and, as several scholars have noted, unified they take the form of a classical oration.[38] Their popular success has been attributed to the appeal of the farmer persona that Dickinson adopted, to his ability to apply Whig political theory to the crisis at hand, and to the facility with which he cites the lessons of history from ancient Greece to contemporary Ireland to criticize British policies. David Ramsay declared in his *History of the American Revolution* that Dickinson's letters, "being universally read by the colonists . . . universally enlightened them on the dangerous consequences likely to result from their being taxed by the Parliament of Great Britain," and he also claims that the letters sowed the seeds of the Revolution.[39] But though Dickinson outlined much of the strategy the colonists adopted to resist British taxation (particularly the tactics of petition and nonimportation), he was by no means an advocate of armed struggle or independence. Instead his purpose in writing was, as he declares, "to convince the people of these colonies, that they are at this moment exposed to the most imminent dangers; and to persuade them immediately, vigorously, and unanimously, to exert themselves, in the most firm, but most peaceable manner, for obtaining relief."[40] Dickinson's emphasis is on peaceable opposition as well as the colonists' exposure to the utmost danger. In his third letter he warns his countrymen against those who "may . . . endeavour to stir you up, under pretences of patriotism, to any measures disrespectful to our Sovereign and our mother country," and he urges people to "breathe a sedate, yet fervent spirit" (324). The colonists should be critical of rather than confident in both patriots and officials, and their actions should be prudent, not rash, for the cause of liberty should not be "sullied by turbulence and tumult" (324). What Dickinson truly fears is that moment when the pursuit of liberty degenerates into licentiousness and anarchy: the same moment that so deeply troubled Thucydides and Plato. It is the time when, in Dickinson's words, feuds reach a fatal point and "all considerations of reason and equity vanish; and a blind fury governs, or rather confounds all things" (327). Virtue is then misrepresented as vice and demagogues reign:

> The sway of the *Cleons* and *Clodius's*, the designing and detestable flatterers of the *prevailing passion*, becomes confirmed. Wise and good men in vain oppose the storm, and may think themselves fortunate, if, in attempting to preserve their ungrateful fellow citizens, they do not ruin themselves. Their *prudence* will be called *baseness*; their *moderation* will be called *guilt*; and if their virtue does not lead them to destruction, as that of many other great and excellent persons has done, they may survive to receive from their expiring country the mournful glory of her acknowledgment, that their counsels, if regarded, would have saved her. (327)

Dickinson describes here a transvaluation of terms and inversion of morals that recalls Thucydides' description of the *stasis* in Corcyra, and he echoes this passage for the same reason that John Adams would directly cite the passage in *A Defence of the Constitutions*: he seeks to tame the flattery of the passions that would displace the rule of the "wise and good" and turn the pursuit of liberty into an anarchic struggle for power and self-interest.

Dickinson's success in channeling colonial resistance into moderate or legal opposition cannot be judged, but he was successful in his own form of legal opposition. In the midst of the constitutional debate between Britain and the Colonies, he helped develop the distinction between taxation and duties for the regulation of trade. In his view, all duties not necessary for the regulation of trade were by definition taxes, and all taxation by Parliament was unconstitutional. Dickinson particularly objects to the underhanded attempt of Parliament to impose illegal taxation upon the Colonies under the guise of doing something legal: regulating trade. To combat this artifice, he begins, as Locke advises in his chapter on remedying the abuse of words, by setting forth the definite ideas he attaches to the meanings of words: "To the word '*tax*,' I annex the meaning which the constitution and history of *England* require to be annexed to it; that is – that it is *an imposition on the subject, for the sole purpose of levying money*" (328–9). And he counsels in his fourth letter, "Whenever we speak of '*taxes*' among *Englishmen*, let us therefore speak of them with reference to the *principles* on which, and the *intentions* with which they have been established. This will give certainty to our expression, and safety to our conduct" (330–1). The British attempt to legalize the illegal by calling a tax by a name that smells sweeter prompts Dickinson to add his voice to the chorus of Whig writers who cautioned people that the representative signs of language could become agents of oppression:

> It is true, that *impositions for raising a revenue*, may be hereafter called *regulations of trade*: But names will not change the nature of things. Indeed we ought firmly to believe, what is an undoubted truth, confirmed by the unhappy experience of many states heretofore free, that UNLESS THE MOST WATCHFUL ATTENTION BE EXERTED, A NEW SERVITUDE MAY BE SLIPPED UPON US, UNDER THE SANCTION OF USUAL AND RESPECTABLE TERMS. (346)

To illustrate his point, Dickinson, the consummate scholar, adds a short history lesson:

> Thus the *Caesars* ruined the *Roman* liberty, under the titles of *tribunical* and *dictatorial* authorities, old and venerable dignities, known in the most flourishing times of freedom. In imitation of the same policy, *James II* when he *meant* to establish popery, *talked* of liberty of conscience, the most sacred of all liberties; and had thereby almost deceived the dissenters into destruction.
>
> All artful rulers, who strive to extend their power beyond its just limits, endeavor to give to their attempts as much semblance of legality as possible. Those who succeed them may venture to go a little further; for each new encroachment will be strengthened by a former. "That which is now supported by example, growing old, will become an example itself," and thus support fresh usurpations. (346)

He concludes with a moral:

> A free people therefore can never be too quick in observing, nor too firm in opposing the beginnings of *alteration* either in *form* or *reality*, respecting institutions formed for their security. The first kind of alteration leads to the last: Yet, on the other hand, nothing is more certain, than that the *forms* of liberty may be retained, when the *substance* is gone. In government, as well as in religion, "The *letter* killeth, but the *spirit* giveth life." (347)

Any attempt to understand the language of politics and the politics of language in Revolutionary America must keep in mind these words from Dickinson's sixth letter. By sounding these warnings, by making these historical references, by giving this advice, Dickinson suggests why it is "not to be wonder'd" that people should resist any change that appears to hollow out the substance of liberty while retaining the form, and why they should "rouze themselves" to dissolve a government as Locke recommends if they have been subjected to "a long train of Abuses, Prevarications, and Artifices, all tending the same way."[41] When the dark purposes of the British became more and more visible, belying their representations, the colonists felt they had to act before the sanctifying terms of the Glorious Revolution became a sanction for tyranny. The pervasiveness of the colonists' concerns about the political dangers of verbal legerdemain indicates the extent to which they recognized that the struggle for liberty against power had to be waged with and against words. To free the minds and affect the hearts of the people, words had to be defended against, words had to be captured, and words had to become weapons.

James Wilson: Defending Virtue Against Its Misrepresentation

In January 1775, a few months before the battles of Lexington and Concord, James Wilson gave full expression to the American attempt to defend the colonists from the misrepresentations of the British and to demarcate the differences between vice and virtue, tyranny and authority, and liberty and licentiousness that the British, in his view, were confounding by their abusive words and actions. The occasion for Wilson's speech was the Pennsylvania provincial convention which was called to approve the work of the First Continental Congress. In his speech entitled "Vindication of the Colonies," Wilson, who had studied law in John Dickinson's Philadelphia office after coming to America from Scotland, maintained that if the king and Parliament violated the constitution, then Americans were within their rights – indeed, obligated – to oppose such violations. This assertion, which by 1775 had become a fundamental axiom for the colonists, establishes the ground for Wilson's opening protest against British practices of representation that had branded the colonists as unjust and rebellious.

> Whence, Sir, proceeds all the invidious and ill-grounded clamor against the colonists of America? . . . Why is their virtuous opposition to the illegal attempts of their governors, represented under the falsest colors, and placed in the most ungracious point of view? This opposition, when exhibited in its true light, and when viewed, with unjaundiced eyes, from a proper situation, and at a proper distance, stands confessed the lovely offspring of freedom.[42]

Wilson then proceeds to give an account of the transformation that took place in the hearts and minds of the colonists as an affectionate relationship with the parent country turned nightmarish:

> Our connection with our parent country, and the reciprocal blessings resulting from it to her and to us, were the favorite and pleasing topics of our public discourses and our private conversations. Lulled

> in delightful security, we dreamed of nothing but increasing fondness and friendship, cemented and strengthened by a kind and perpetual communication of good offices. Soon, however, too soon, were we awakened from the soothing dreams! Our enemies renewed their designs against us, not with less malice, but with more art. Under the plausible pretence of regulating our trade, and, at the same time, of making provision for the administration of justice and the support of government, in some of the colonies, they pursued their scheme of depriving us of our property without our consent. As the attempts to distress us, and to degrade us to a rank inferior to that of freemen, appeared now to be reduced into a regular system, it became proper, on our part, to form a regular system of counteracting them. (I, 69)

Wilson suggests that what the colonists discovered in addition to designs on their property was what Jefferson would later lament at the end of his draft of the Declaration of Independence: that "a communication of grandeur & of freedom" was below the dignity of the British. But Wilson announces that such a communication was precisely what the colonists were able to forge. In the Colonies citizens began to discuss their sentiments of liberty in district meetings, county committees, provincial conventions, and a continental congress, and "by this means," Wilson asserts, ". . . a chain of freedom has been formed, of which every individual in these colonies, who is willing to preserve the greatest of human blessings, his liberty, has the pleasure of beholding himself a link" (I, 70).

Besides praising their willingness to organize and speak out in protest, Wilson argues that the colonists were too knowledgeable about the law and too discerning to be deluded into losing their liberty. The conspiracy by artifice that so alarmed Sam Adams and Dickinson had been detected and would be defeated:

> Those who would blend, and whose crimes have made it necessary for them to blend, the tyrannic acts of administration with the lawful measures of government, and to veil every flagitious procedure of the ministry under the venerable mantle of majesty, pretend to discover, and employ their emissaries to publish the pretended discovery of such symptoms [of rebellion]. We are not, however, to be imposed upon by such shallow artifices. We know, that we have not violated the laws of the constitution. (I, 71)

Toward the end of the speech, Wilson forewarns his convention members how their own proceedings will be misrepresented when he predicts that their opponents will engage in the tactics and verbal abuses that foment the Thucydidean moment:

> I beg leave, here, to mention and to obviate some plausible but ill-founded objections that have been, and will be, held forth by our adversaries against the principles of the resolution now before us. . . . These objections will be displayed in their most specious colors; every artifice of chicanery and sophistry will be put into practice to establish them. . . . Those principles of our constitution, which were designed to preserve and to secure the liberty of the people, and, for the sake of that, the tranquillity of government, will be perverted on this, as they have been on many other occasions from their true intention, and will be made use of for the contrary purpose of endangering the latter and destroying the former. The names of the most exalted virtues on one hand, and of the most atrocious crimes on the other, will be employed in direct contradiction to the nature of those virtues and of those crimes; and in this manner those who cannot look beyond names will be deceived, and those whose aim it is to deceive by names will have an opportunity of accomplishing it. (I, 72–3)

But Wilson again expresses his confidence that the colonists are too sophisticated to be duped by any attempt to disguise illegal acts under the sanction of respectable terms: "But, sir, this disguise will not impose upon us. We will look to things as well as to names; and, by doing so, we shall be fully satisfied that all those objections rest upon mere verbal sophistry, and have not even the remotest alliance with the principles of reason or of law" (I, 73).

The way Wilson depicts the situation of the colonists in his speech can be compared to the predicament of Clarissa Harlowe in Samuel Richardson's *Clarissa*, a novel that had a considerable popularity in the Colonies and one that provides, as Jay Fliegelman explains, the "quintessential presentation of the inner drama that would inform the rhetoric and ideology of the American revolution against patriarchal authority."[43] For instance, just as Clarissa proclaims her innocence and virtue in letter after letter, so too did the colonists, as Wilson suggests, proclaim their virtue and good intentions in petition after petition to the king. When the petitions availed little, the colonists began to look upon themselves, as Terry Castle urges us to look upon Clarissa, as victims of hermeneutic violence.[44] Clarissa, Castle asserts, is victimized – indeed, she says "colonized" – by the collective rhetoric or patriarchal discourse of the Harlowes and Lovelace; they inscribe her with a range of oppressive meanings, calling her ungrateful, perverse, fallen; they continually interrupt and misrepresent her discourse; and eventually they deprive her of her instruments of correspondence – her pen and paper.[45] James Wilson and a number of colonial pamphleteers similarly maintain that the colonists had been wrongfully inscribed with a range of oppressive meanings – licentious, ungovernable, rebellious – and they too demanded, in Clarissa's words, "Let my actions, not *their* misrepresentations . . . speak for me."[46] And when their oppression continued, they no longer doubted that they too were victims of a "long train of Abuses, Prevarications, and Artifices" perpetrated by designing men bent upon robbing them of all that they valued – their liberty, their happiness, their morals, and their money. Unlike Clarissa, however, the colonists, as Wilson suggests, were well enough educated in the ways of the world – and in the duplicity of words – not to fall prey to the fraudulent discourse of a Lovelace, a Jonathan Wild, or a John Bull. They had studied their Locke and conned their novel lessons, and thus, rather than being imposed upon by artful misrepresentations, they unmasked hidden designs; and instead of submitting to the dictates of an unfeeling parent, they took arms against a sea of abuses. And unlike Clarissa, who is stripped of her pen and paper, the colonists were strong enough so that when confronted with a Stamp Act or a Boston Massacre, they were able to counter fraud with force and force with Committees of Correspondence.

The Loyalist Prosecution: Words as Stalking-Horses

The colonists who led the opposition to British policies were not the only ones who recognized that they were engaged in a hermeneutical struggle that was to be fought and won with words. British officials and American Tories were first as suspicious and then as convinced as the Sons of Liberty that they were becoming victims of a plot authored by designing word spinners, and they too recognized, as Thomas Hutchinson writes in *The History of the Colony and Province of Massachusetts-Bay*, that "the misapplication and abuse of words may be made to serve the cause of party as effectually as arguments supported by sound reason."[47] For Jonathan Boucher, the American Revolution "was not a war of conquest, or to repel insult or aggression, but merely a party contest," and "who does not know," he adds, "that misrepresentation and abuse are the usual weapons of the partisans of parties?"[48] For Boucher, that is, the conflict between the Colonies was more strictly political and ideological than social or economic, and in that struggle, Boucher continues, "each party made hardly less use . . . of the pen, than they did of the sword."[49] In his memoirs, *Reminiscences of an American Loyalist, 1738–1789*, Boucher also comments that Americans impressed him, in general, as being "eminently endowed with a knack of talking; they seem to be born orators."[50] Later in his memoirs he comments again on this constitutional facility of Americans, but now in a critical tone. He contemptuously regards the "two colleges of Philadelphia, and that at Princeton in the Jersies" as "chief nurseries" of a "frivolous and mischievous kind of knowledge" whose "chief and peculiar merit was thought to be in Rhetoric and the belles lettres." "Hence," he sneers, "in no country were there so many orators, or so many smatterers" (101–2). He also derides the preachers in the Colonies who delivered their sermons in a "light, flippant, and ordinary" manner, thus making themselves "pleasing and popular" (103). In the colleges and pulpits of the Colonies, as Boucher suggests, rhetoric was more than a method of adorning a speech or sermon: it was republicanized into an agent of popular arousal, and at the heart of his own explanation for the Revolution is his belief that in the Colonies, as in the "Great Rebellion in England," "much execution was done by sermons." "Those persons," he points out, "who have read any out of the great number of Puritan sermons that were then printed as well as preached, will cease to wonder that so many people were worked up into such a state of frenzy" (118). What Boucher shares, then, with other Tory commentators on the Revolution is Lord Chesterfield's opinion that "the uninformed herd of mankind are governed by words and names." They particularly felt that the colonists had been governed by the words and names applied to their passions by rabble-rousers such as Sam Adams. Boucher, for instance, comments in *A View of the Causes and Consequences of the American Revolution* that "popularity still does, in no ordinary degree, attach to those of them who, on the pretence of the liberties of the people, disturb the settled order of government – a pretence to which artful men in all ages and countries of time have always had recourse, and never without some degree of success."[51]

For Boucher and other Loyalists, the most dangerous word in the colonial lexicon was "liberty." In a pamphlet entitled *Some Further Observations on the Late Popular Measures*, published in 1774, John Drinker issued a vehement critique of the resistance movement in Philadelphia wherein he attacks the leaders for making "a notable stalking horse of the word LIBERTY."[52] He continues to condemn the "voice of the popular demagogues" by comparing it to "the wild jargon of Babel builders," and he later extends his critique to the colonists as a whole: "Though we bluster and say florid things of our great virtue, we are using the Words, LIBERTY and RIGHT *as sounding brass*; nay, we are wickedly making use of those high sounding names, and applying them as magic engines for the destruction of the substance."[53] Jonathan Sewall, a Loyalist in Massachusetts who had been a friend of John Adams's, similarly writes in a letter that "by the help of the single word, 'Liberty,'" demagogues in America "conjured up the most horrid Phantoms in the Minds of the common people, ever an easy prey to such specious Betrayers." The "Merchants," he adds, ". . . joined in Bubbling the undiscerning Multitude."[54] Sewall's account of the conflict recalls not only Pope's vision in *The Dunciad* of people being deluded by words and Trenchard and Gordon's commentary on the cheat of words but Swift's satiric critique of religious enthusiasm in "A Discourse Concerning the Mechanical Operation of the Spirit." In Swift's essay, cant and droning usurp the place of sense and reason as "the *Heat* of Zeal" works "upon the *Dregs* of Ignorance, as other *Spirits* are produced from *Lees*, by the Force of Fire."[55] Sewall writes, for instance, that "there is an Enthusiasm in politics, like that which religious notions inspire, that drive men on with an unnatural impetuosity, that baffles and confounds all Calculation grounded upon rational principles." And for Sewall the most intoxicating word that had stimulated the passions of the colonists was "liberty," a word, he says, "whose very Sound [among Englishmen] carries a fascinating charm." He continues, "The Colonists fancy this precious Jewel is in Danger of being ravished from them; and however ill-founded this Apprehension may be, while it continues, the Effect on their Minds is the same as moral Certainty would produce."[56] In Sewall's view, the colonists had failed to do exactly what Sam Adams and James Wilson praised them for being able to do: distinguish between realities and sounds, professions and intentions. Or they had failed to do exactly what Locke advised that people must do to counter the dangers of enthusiasm: rationally analyze the meanings of words.

In 1774 the nonimportation decrees of the Continental Congress, combined with what Samuel Seabury, rector of St. Peter's Church in New Rochelle, considered the abusive and deluded behavior of the colonists, provoked him to write in protest a series of four pamphlet letters under the name "A Westchester Farmer." Seabury's persona of the farmer, an act of false humility and seeming simplicity that was an unusual strategy in Tory literature, fit his design of speaking "plain English" to counter the misrepresentations of the colonists: "I must have the privilege of calling a fig, – a Fig; an egg, – an Egg."[57] But despite the presumed medium of a country farmer, Seabury's message is that of an Augustan satirist blasting with the vehemence of Pope or Swift "the *freedom* of America" as truly the "tyranny of a mob" and hurling back at colonial pamphleteers (specifically Alexander Hamilton) the abuse they had heaped on English officials: "You had no remedy but *artifice*, sophistry, *misrepresentation*, and *abuse*: these are your weapons, and these you wield like an old experienced practitioner" (104). The consequence for Seabury of the colonists' most obstreperous behavior – the consequence, that is, of their "Noise and blustering," of their "Loud cries of liberty" that had caught "the ignorant,"

and of "their passions, their prejudices, and their prepossessions" that
had warped their minds from judging "*realities*" – was the onslaught of
the final act of the Thucydidean moment: chaos (43, 85). "The American Colonies are unhappily involved in a scene of confusion and
discord. The bands of civil society are broken; the authority of government weakened, and in some instances taken away: Individuals are
deprived of their liberty; their property is frequently invaded by
violence" (43). For Seabury, in short, the colonists had been led by a
chain of misrepresentations from a true state of liberty back into a
cave of delusion and enslavement, or we could say that in Seabury's
vision they had been led forward into a time of Orwellian Newspeak
"when nothing is called FREEDOM but SEDITION! Nothing LIBERTY but
REBELLION!" (151).

Perhaps more than any of the other Tory spokesmen, Peter Oliver,
the chief justice of the Massachusetts Superior Court, in his *Origin &
Progress of the American Rebellion* depicts the Revolution as a triumph
of passion and plotting, of political enthusiasm and prevarication, of
people deluded and religion profaned – a triumph, in a word, of
propaganda. In this impassioned and embittered account, Oliver, like
Seabury, possesses the religious vocabulary of Milton, the spleen of
Swift, and the despair of the later Pope. For Oliver, the leaders of the
colonial opposition are demagogic devils who perpetrated "the sudden
Transition . . . from Obedience to Rebellion . . . to gratifye [their]
Pride, Ambition, & Resentment"; their speech is Billingsgate, their
councils are a Pandaemonium, their end is rebellion, their result is a
return to chaos or the establishment of a new form of government – a
"*Daemonocracy*" wherein "Hypocrisy, Falsehood & Prevarication"
reign (145, 84, 132). According to Oliver, the most devilish of the
demagogues are James Otis, whose life, he says, is a commentary on
Satan's declaration in Milton's *Paradise Lost*, "Better to reign in Hell
than serve in Heaven" (36); Sam Adams, who disguised himself as "an
Angel of Light" and who, "like the Cuddlefish, would discharge his
muddy Liquid & darken the Water" to confound and confuse others
(40-1); Samuel Cooper, whose "Tongue was Butter & Oil, but under
it was the Poison of Asps" (44); and Benjamin Franklin, a "*Printers
Devil*" who forced the press "to speak the Thing that was not" (79).
This cabal of demagogues, working in tandem with "the selfish Designs of the Merchants," in Oliver's view fomented the struggle and
uproar that beset the Colonies (65). But Oliver, like Sewall and
Boucher, blames the success of the rebellion not only on the propaganda of a conniving few but on the ignorance of the deluded many
and the bewitching power of one word in particular: Liberty. The
merchants, Oliver points out, "disguised their Private Views by mouth-

ing it for Liberty," and because the "generality of the People" in the
Colonies "were weak, & unversed in the Arts of Deception," when
the magic of the sound of "liberty" "echoed through the interior Parts
of the country . . . the deluded Vulgar were charmed with it – like the
poor harmless *Squirrel* that runs into the Mouth of the *Rattlesnake*, the
Fascination in the Word *Liberty* threw the People into the harpy Claws
of their Destroyers" (65, 145). Against the power of the word "liberty," the proclamations of the king and the Parliament were virtually
helpless. In the 1770s, however, Jeremy Bentham began experimenting
with proclamations of a different type as an antidote for the fevers
erupting in the body politic. His remedy was a dose of definition,
which he called "the grand prescription of those great physicians of
the mind, Helvetius and before him Locke."[58]

The "American dispute turns on words," Bentham jotted down in
one of his many manuscript notes.[59] Like John Horne Tooke, whose
Diversions of Purley he highly respected, Bentham was a student of
Locke's *Essay* who began his own career as a political and linguistic
reformer in the midst of radical opposition to the British government
in England and in the Colonies in the 1770s. The motto for much of
Bentham's prodigious work could be Tooke's own statement "Mankind in general are not sufficiently aware that words without meaning, or of equivocal meaning, are the everlasting engines of fraud and
injustice."[60] Bentham is now renowned for his critique of the French
Declaration of Rights, wherein he made his own declaration that
"natural rights is simple nonsense: nature and imprescriptible rights,
rhetorical nonsense, nonsense upon stilts."[61] But much earlier he had
fired a volley of rhetorical criticism at America's own declaration of
rights. In 1776 he collaborated as a silent partner with John Lind, a
pamphleteer for Lord North's policies, in drafting *An Answer to the
Declaration of the American Congress*, which both accused the colonists of
endeavoring "by a cloud of words, to throw a veil over their design"
of "subverting a lawful government" and exposed how the colonists
were betraying in their actions their rhetoric of an "inalienable right"
to "life, liberty, and the pursuit of happiness."[62]

Even less well known than this volley of criticism, which was barely
heard in the Colonies, is that Bentham had hopes that the "American
dispute," which turned in his view on the different meanings that
were being attached to such terms as "consent," "liberty," "representation," and "taxation," could be resolved not by colonists acting
upon the Lockean principle of justifiable revolution, but through the
more peaceable Lockean method of settling the meanings of words by
annexing clear ideas to them.[63] While engaged in the early 1770s in
preparing a *magnum opus* on jurisprudence, Bentham contemplated

writing a dictionary of moral and legal terms. His unpublished manuscripts reveal that he began defining and commenting upon fundamental political terms, such as "liberty," "power," "security," "law," "property," "privilege," and "duty," which he regarded as "so many fictitious entities" that had to be reduced to "real entities" or to what Locke termed "simple ideas." Definition and paraphrasis were his methods for accomplishing that reduction. James Streintrager reports that Bentham even believed "in one of his megalomanic moods" that the dispute between England and the Colonies could be prevented from erupting into war "if only he could complete his dictionary of moral and jurisprudential terms in time!"[64]

A note on one of Bentham's manuscripts suggests the underlying rationale for this vain hope: "A sober and accurate apprehension of the import of these fundamental words is a true key to Jurisprudence and the only effectual antidote against the fascinations of political enthusiasm."[65] In the privacy of his study, Bentham was doing what such Tory critics as Boucher and Sewall were doing more publicly: he was busy waging a linguistic war against the intoxicating charm of liberty and what he elsewhere called "passion-kindling appelatives."[66] When he penned these definitions and later when he promulgated his doctrine of utility, Bentham sought to sever what colonial pamphleteers and ministers were combining deliberately or inevitably when they discoursed upon the beauties of liberty: the heart and the head, emotions and ideas, passions and politics. In the words of Kenneth Burke, "Bentham hoped that by analyzing the nature of verbalization, he could militate against the tendency to elevate matters of public expediency to the impassioned and deceptive plane of heroism and indignation, where one's judgments are formed in advance."[67] Indeed, just as Plato developed his method of dialectical reasoning to oppose the Sophists and their rhetoric, which preyed upon the passions, so too did Bentham develop methods of linguistic analysis to combat logical and rhetorical "fallacies."[68] Beyond this, Bentham sought (as did Kenneth Burke in his rhetorical criticism) to alert readers not just to the combative nature of rhetoric but to the way, in Burke's words, that the "god-terms" of politics and ethics can goad us to the slaughter of each other. "Till men are sufficiently aware of the ambiguity of words," Bentham noted, "political discussions may be carried on continually, without profit and without end."[69] The American and French revolutions also convinced him that the debate about political terms could end in bloodshed.

Discourse upon the "rights of man" was itself for Bentham a "terrorist language," the stuff that the villainous dreams of an Iago could be built upon (269, 289). These words, he writes, "present a cloak for every conspiracy; they hold out a mask to every crime; they are every villain's armoury, every spendthrift's treasury" (289). The word "right" by itself, Bentham claims, is a "magic word," "as innocent as a dove: it breathes nothing but morality and peace" (287). But for him the word is truly a Trojan horse, an engine for subversion that makes possible the coup d'état of the city of the mind that Thucydides and Plato feared: "It is the shape that, passing in at the heart, it gets possession of the understanding; it then assumes its substantive shape, and joining itself to a band of suitable associates, plants the banner of insurrection, anarchy, and lawless violence" (287). "Alas!" Bentham cries out in his critique of the French Declaration, "how dependent are opinions upon sounds! What Hercules shall break the chains by which opinions are enslaved by sounds?" (288). With this question, Bentham projects his own role in the drama of revolutionary politics: he would cleanse the Augean stables of law and political discourse of all nonsense and thus insure that a reiteration of "passion-kindling appelatives" would never again produce the actions that transformed the last acts of the French Revolution into tragedy. The American Revolution provided Bentham with a dress rehearsal for this role.

In April 1776, when leaders in the Colonies were gathering in Philadelphia to debate the case for independence, Bentham published his first work, *A Fragment of Government*, which reveals his kinship, ironically, with the colonial pamphleteers who understood that to advance their case before the public they had to undeceive minds as well as win hearts. In short, they had to promote mental independence as a correlative to political liberty, and they adopted Lockean strategies to accomplish that task. Just as Locke maintains in the *Essay* that his aim of clearing away obstructions along the path to knowledge also required him to offer instruction about distinguishing words and ideas, Bentham similarly seeks to accomplish both tasks in the *Fragment*:

> [My mission is:] – To do something to instruct, but more to undeceive, the timid and admiring student – to excite him to place more confidence in his own strength, and less in the infallibility of great names: – to help him emancipate his judgment from the shackles of authority: – to let him see that the not understanding a discourse may as well be the writer's fault as the reader's: – to teach him to distinguish between showy language and sound sense: – to warn him not to pay himself with words: – to shew him that what may tickle the ear, or dazzle the imagination, will not always inform the judgment.[70]

Placed in conjunction with the activities of the Continental Congress, the *Fragment* can also be read as Bentham's advice to center the debate between England and the Colonies on an entirely different ground: talk of right, duty, and law in a moral sense and of such fictitious entities as a state of nature and original contract had to give way to a different form of discourse – to a scientific calculation about the "probable mischiefs of obedience and the probable mischiefs of resistance" or to a calculation about what would produce "the greatest happiness of the greatest number," a calculation whose sum would lastingly become for Bentham "the measure of right and wrong."[71] But, as Jefferson declares in his inspired letter to Maria Cosway, when the colonists weighed in the balance the calculations of the head and the sentiments of the heart, it was the heart that prevailed: "You [the head] began to calculate & to compare wealth and numbers: we [the heart] threw up a few pulsations of our warmest blood; we supplied enthusiasm against wealth and numbers; we put our existence to the hazard when the hazard seemed against us, and we saved our country" (JLA, 875). What Jefferson's "heart" does not explain, however, is how the pulsations of enthusiasm it supplied were stimulated by the word of the preacher and orator.

Evangelical and Elocutionary Oratory: Speaking to the Heart

The Tory critique of the American Revolution both elevates and reduces the power of the word. On the one hand, it elevates the word into a magic power, an elevation that should give critics and historians who have taken the "linguistic turn" pause because such an elevation of the word into the prime mover and shaker of people mystifies the degree to which religious concerns, economic fears, social injustices, and psychological needs can be the sources of discontent that motivate a people to rebel. Such belief in the magical power of words – or even belief in the power of paradigms of discourse – leaves us too much like characters in a fairy tale searching for the spell, the Rumplestiltskin name, the grammar that will give us control over the dynamics of historical action. On the other hand, the reduction of language to the medium that merely reproduces power relations, or to a cloak that covers a naked will to power or hides a predetermined economic self-interest, rationalizes away the degree to which the word can act as a catalyst to crystallize inchoate discontent and provoke new reactions, and it minimizes the degree to which sharing the word and acting together in its name can be a source of happiness and a motivation for the actions that sustain, reform, and revolutionize communities. Somewhere between mystifying the power of the word as magic and demystifying it as a medium for representing ideas or an ideology, there is a place for understanding the affective power of the word, and it was this affective power of the word to stir the passions and bind hearts – the power that so troubled Plato and Locke – that the colonists embraced with the commitment of a Romantic poet.

Since the 1960s, students of the American Revolution have recognized, thanks in large part to the scholarship of Alan Heimert, that the Tory interpretation of the American Revolution as an outbreak of political enthusiasm led by orators and preachers who appealed to the hearts – or to the passions and prejudices – of their listeners is a persuasive case, or at least has more validity than those who prefer to argue that the colonists were reasoned into revolution by enlightened gentlemen are willing to admit. In *Religion and the American Mind: From the Greak Awakening to the Revolution*, Heimert challenged many previous interpretations when he maintained that the "uprising of the 1770's was not so much the result of reasoned thought as an emotional outburst similar to a religious revival" and when he claimed in particular that the "'evangelical' religion, which had as its most notable formal expression the 'Calvinism' of Jonathan Edwards, . . . provided pre-Revolutionary America with a radical, even democratic, social and political ideology" – indeed, a rationale for revolution – and that it was the evangelicals or Calvinists (the New Lights) who inspired the American populace to fight for independence over the objections and reluctance of the liberals or Arminians (the Old Lights).[72] The 1770s, in this view, were a time when, as one observer noted, "the minds of the people are wrought up into as high a degree of Enthusiasm by the word liberty, as could have been expected had Religion been the cause."[73]

Heimert's claim did not go unchallenged, but what he, along with Sacvan Bercovitch, Emory Elliott, Donald Weber, and others, has valuably urged us to do is to study the Puritan roots of American Whig rhetoric and view the American Revolution, in Elliott's words, "as a political Great Awakening in which the people were reconverted to their national mission, expressed in an amalgam of religious and political terms."[74] Elliott argues that the rhetoric of colonial ministers and patriots was so successful because (to recall Marx's image) they turned the mother tongue of America – the language of the Puritan sermon – into a revolutionary language by supplying new referents for the highly charged and polarized terms of that language: God and Satan, saint and sinner, liberty and bondage.[75] In the context, that is, of political and economic conflict between the Colonies and Britain in the 1760s and 1770s, these terms took on new and more political or secular meanings (or they recovered the older meanings that were current during the English Civil War): "liberty," for instance, began to signify as a primary meaning not merely freedom from the tyranny of sin but freedom from the tyranny of a sinful Britain. In Kenneth Burke's terms, the word "liberty" acted as a "pontifical" word bridging religious and political realms: the "liberty wherewith Christ hath made us free" (Galatians 5:1) and the liberty wherewith a political revolution or constitution can make us free.[76]

The language of the Bible provided colonial ministers with an arsenal of verbal weapons that could be fired in the cannonade of a sermon to attack corruption not just in the heart of man but in the body politic of Britain. Perhaps no passage in the Bible was more powerful in this regard than the injunction from Galatians 5:1: "Stand fast therefore in the liberty wherewith Christ hath made us free." When, for instance, Simeon Howard, a Boston minister, preaches on this passage in 1773, his exegesis does more than unfold what is meant "by the liberty in which men ought to stand fast": he illustrates "what they may and ought to do in defence of it." Although at the end Howard is militant for Christ, reminding his parishioners that the most valuable kind of liberty to defend is the liberty that consists in being "free from the power and dominion of sins," through the course of the sermon he is militant in a more secular sense. He preaches that a "most desirable liberty . . . we should be ready to defend, is that of a well governed society," and he maintains that if this liberty is threatened, we are "first to try gentle methods . . . to reason with, and persuade the adversary to desist." But if this method fails, he adds, the principle of "self preservation" "allows for every thing necessary to self-defence, opposing force to force, and violence to violence."[77] Working the loom of language, shuttling into his sermon strands of liberty colored with the red dye of opposition politics, Howard reweaves the fabric of imperatives, justifying rebellion against tyrants. Similarly, when Levi Hart, a Connecticut minister, examines "the various significations" of liberty and bondage in a 1775 sermon, he too comments upon the passage from Galatians, and he too affirms by way of a rhetorical question at the end that the spiritual meaning of liberty had to be first and foremost in the minds of the colonists: "What is English liberty? What is American freedom? When compared with the glorious liberty of the sons of God?" But he too leads his audience in the course of his sermon, which contains a powerful protest against the slave trade, to a fuller understanding of the dimensions of civil liberty, arguing at one point for the "importance of intrusting those, and none but those, with the guardianship of our civil liberties who are themselves free, who are not under the dominion of this sordid selfishness and narrowness of soul by which they will betray their country, our dear Colony for a little private profit or honor to themselves."[78]

What these two sermons reveal (and what scholars of the Revolution have increasingly emphasized) is the rich complexity (or valuable vagueness) of such terms as "liberty" for colonial ministers and pamphleteers. In the crucible of colonial protest over the violation of constitutional rights, the word "liberty" and other key terms from political and religious discourse were recast and redeployed. The spiritual and secular senses of such words as "liberty" bonded together to form a two-edged sword enabling preachers, orators, and pamphleteers to cut against corruption in two directions and fight simultaneously for political and religious freedom. In Donald Weber's illuminating phrase, "during the charged rhetorical atmosphere enveloping the American Revolution the religious and political poles of the rhetoric of liberty, in a moment of creative potential, were connected."[79] And when these poles were connected, Weber further suggests, the language of the revolutionary pulpit mediated at once "the claims of residual yet still potent Puritan vocabularies and emergent political language to forge an enabling rhetoric that helped people act in history."[80]

A torrent of words coursed through the Colonies in the 1760s and 1770s in the form of sermons, orations, and pamphlets, culminating in 1776, when more sermons were preached than in any previous year. During this torrent, which made the Revolution a triumph of speech acts in a holy war as well as a testament to the powers of the press in a legal dispute, the boundaries of political protest were reshaped and even overflowed, while the meaning of such fundamental terms in religious and political discourse as "liberty" were deepened and expanded. Many preachers were as wary as John Dickinson about shifts in the meanings of words and their abuse. "Judge of all, and be careful not to carry liberty beyond its just bounds: – Not to use it for a cloke of maliciousness," advises John Tucker in a 1771 Election Sermon delivered in Boston.[81] Caught up in the squalls of political protest, ministers in the Colonies performed their ritual office: they exhorted, explained, instructed, chastized, and prophesied, using the Bible to chart a course that sought to guide the communities they piloted past the Scylla and Charybdis of licentiousness and tyranny to the temporal haven of civil liberty.

Sermon after sermon by religious radicals as well as conservatives, Old Lights and New Lights, warn the colonists, as did Tucker, about falling into licentiousness and rebellion in their pursuit of liberty and constitutional rights, reminding them, as Milton reminds readers in *Paradise Lost*, of the woe that comes not just to those who call "evil good, and good evil" but to those who, while listening, mistake the one for the other. The professed minister of God's Word may be in

truth "not of Christ, but of the devil, the father of falsehood, confusion and rebellion."[82] "By the blessing of the upright the city is
exalted, but it is overthrown by the mouth of the wicked," preaches
Gad Hitchcock in a 1774 Election Sermon, and he specifically points
out that "liberty and property, might be made an engine of . . .
destruction," for "under the pretext of pursuing constitutional measures," "rulers of evil dispositions" can "introduce general misery and
slavery." At the end of this sermon, which he delivered before
General Thomas Gage, the newly appointed governor of Massachusetts, Hitchcock offers a form of prayer: "But may we have that
wisdom which is profitable to direct, and distinguish between what
has, and what has not, a tendency to remove our burdens and prolong
our just rights and liberties."[83] By interpreting (or reinterpreting)
God's wisdom in such matters, and by awakening a people's enthusiasm for liberty, the ministers shared in directing the course that the
pursuit of rights would take, plotting in the eyes of the Tory critics a
devious-cruising path toward confrontation with the British Leviathan.

While scholars have followed Alan Heimert in emphasizing and
elaborating how in the 1760s and 1770s the colonial clergy politicized
the language of the Bible and sacralized the language of Whig politics,
some have also emphasized with Heimert that it was not just the
content and vocabulary of the evangelical sermon that were potentially revolutionary; it was the style. What ultimately and perhaps
most significantly divided the Calvinists and the Liberals, Heimert
asserts, were "the remarkable differences between their oratorical
strategies and rhetorical practices."[84] While the Liberals (and the
Tories) possessed a Lockean distrust of an eloquence that sought to
arouse people's wills as well as inform their minds, and while they
preferred to reach people primarily through the written word or
written speeches and sermons, the Calvinist clergy, led by the example of George Whitefield, engaged in what Donald Weber calls "a
stylistic revolt against the hegemonic formalism of the standing
clergy": they become confident masters of a more extemporaneous
style of preaching, speaking often from fragmentary notes, and they
redirected the rhetorical aim of the sermon itself, demanding that it
stimulate the affections as well as edify the understanding.[85] These
clergy practiced in their sermons what Charles Chauncy and Jonathan
Boucher preached against (and what Locke counseled against in the
Essay and what Swift satirized in "The Mechanical Operations of the
Spirit"): a rhetoric of enthusiasm. And by practicing and perfecting
this style, these ministers, according to Heimert, "inaugurated a new
era in the history of American public address" – an era in which the

affinities between speaker and listener, man and God, and an elect people and an elect nation would be sparked by what he calls "the peculiar potency of the spoken word."[86] Speech in the revolutionary period, in short, recovered its Orphic power as communal incantation.

To appreciate the revolutionary aspects of this rhetoric or to understand more fully how the epoch of revolutionary strife was not just, in Moses Coit Tyler's words, "a strife of ideas" and a "marshalling of arguments" in "a long warfare of political logic," we must, then, do what Heimert, Stout, Weber, and Rhys Isaac have urged us to do: we must look beyond the lines of written pamphlets and between the notations of manuscript sermons and try to hear or experience what people experienced in the oratorical world of the revival and the political assembly when they listened to Patrick Henry, Philemon Robbins, and others on the "sacred cause of liberty."[87] To aid us in hearing the incantatory power and enlivening spirit of speech in a world not yet dominated by the dead letter of print, we can be guided in part by the linguistic theories of Jean-Jacques Rousseau and Edmund Burke. By viewing revolutionary rhetoric in the perspective of their theories of language, we can continue Tyler's writing of a "literary history" of the Revolution, for if an essential strand of revolutionary rhetoric continues the stylistic revolt of the evangelical clergy that began in the Great Awakening, that strand is also entwined in the late Enlightenment (or early Romantic) challenge to Lockean linguistics.

Some twenty years after the colonists began responding to the heart-centered oratory of the Great Awakening and at about the same time as they began listening to the Sons of Liberty in public squares and political assemblies, Rousseau was writing *An Essay on the Origin of Language*, in which he argues that language is first and foremost a tool of the passions rather than of the reason and wherein he praises speech as the instrument of liberty. Rousseau maintains in this work that as a language advances along with civilization it becomes more "regular and less passionate. It substitutes ideas for feelings. It no longer speaks to the heart but to the reason. Language becomes more exact and clear, but more prolix, duller, and colder."[88] While Locke would have praised such an advance and sought to facilitate it in the *Essay*, Edwards, as Perry Miller shows, countered Locke in practice to fulfill a Lockean principle. To excite the same ideas in speaker and listener – the goal of Locke's model of communication – Edwards addressed the affections, the heart, the passions. "He reached," Miller writes, "into a wholly other segment of psychology, the realm of the passions, and linked the word not only with the idea but also with that from which Locke had striven to separate it, with the emotions."[89] In language theory as well as in social and political thought, then, Edwards was the American counterpart of Rousseau; for, as Heimert points out, there is an important connection between the language theory and the political thought of Edwards and other evangelicals that anticipates Rousseau: "The Calvinist political philosophy, which centered finally not on the consent of the governed but on the general will of the community, was sustained by the equally fundamental evangelical conception that the purpose of public discourse was to activate men's wills as well as inform their minds."[90] The language of the evangelical revival was as radically communitarian as its political or social thought. Aimed at the heart, the sermons sought to break down the differences between speaker and listener, idea and emotion, head and heart, and move people to action – to freedom from sin, to union. The evangelical sermon sought to do, in effect, what Derrida claims Rousseau advocated: end the "social distance, the dispersion of the neighborhood" which is the "condition of oppression, arbitrariness and vice."[91] In Derrida's words, Rousseau argues in his *Essay* that "the governments of oppression all make the same gesture: to break presence, the co-presence of citizens, the 'unanimity of assembled peoples,' to create a situation of dispersion, holding subjects so far apart as to be incapable of feeling themselves together in the space of one and the same speech, one and the same persuasive exchange."[92] Rousseau therefore links writing to political corruption because writing usurps the space of a people assembled and unified in the presence of speech. From Rousseau's perspective, then, the colonists began to experience in the revivals and then in the public squares and political assemblies of Revolutionary America a sense of co-presence and fraternity: a moment when they felt themselves bound together in a more perfect union by one and the same speech, by one and the same persuasive exchange – by the words of a preacher or patriot calling for their response – and it is a moment they would seek to perpetuate by establishing Committees of Correspondence and their own Continental Congress.

In the late 1740s, several years after Whitefield and Edwards kindled the Great Awakening, Edmund Burke, while a student at Trinity College, Dublin, began composing *A Philosophical Enquiry into the Origin of Our Ideas of the Sublime and Beautiful*, a treatise that provides in several regards a contemporary theoretical account for the rhetorical power of such figures as Whitefield and Patrick Henry. Burke concludes his *Enquiry* by seeking to explain the extraordinary dominion that words can exercise over the passions, and in so doing he presents a radical reformulation of Lockean linguistic theory that resembles in many respects the challenge to Locke presented both by the writings of the Scottish Common Sense philosophers and the elocutionary theorists – and by the rhetorical practices of Whitefield and Henry. Although Burke argues, following Locke, that there is a form of "clear expression" whereby words communicate by raising ideas in the minds of listeners, he emphasizes that there are also forms of "strong expression" whereby words do not raise "general" or "real ideas" but stimulate the heart or excite the passions and affections.[93] "No body," he points out, "immediately on hearing the sounds virtue, liberty, or honor conceives any precise notion of the particular modes of action and thinking, together with the mixt and simple ideas, and the general relations of them for which these words are substituted" (164). He later adds, "Many ideas have never been at all presented to the senses of any men but by words, as God, angels, devils, heaven and hell, all of which have however a great influence over the passions" (174). Instead of representing ideas or things, these words may "affect rather by sympathy," especially if they are accompanied by "a moving tone of voice, an impassioned countenance, an agitated gesture" (172, 175). Then, "by the contagion of our passions, we catch a fire already kindled in another." At this moment, the word becomes a sovereign force: "We yield to sympathy, what we refuse to description" (175). From the Great Awakening through the Revolution, the affective power of the word such as Burke describes remains a central concern in religious and political affairs, raising hopes, on the one hand, of a representative force that can awaken the people to "the sacred cause of liberty," and raising fears, on the other hand, of words that delude and rouse the rabble. To whose word would the sympathies of the colonists yield? To the Word of God or to the voice of the false prophet? To the patriot or to the demagogue? To the villainish seducer or to the virtuous lover? These are the questions that would be raised first by reluctant revolutionaries and then very often in the years following the Revolution, and these are the questions whose most troubling answers we can read in the fiction of the new republic by such authors as Washington Irving, Charles Brockden Brown, Hugh Henry Brackenridge, and Susannah Rowson.[94]

William Wirt in his famous biography *Sketches of the Life and Character of Patrick Henry* employs the very terms of Burke's *Essay* to characterize the difference between the "chaste – classical – beautiful" eloquence of Richard Henry Lee and the "wild and grand effusions" of Henry's sublime oratory.[95] Whereas Lee "'flowed on, like a quiet and placid river,'" Henry is "a cataract, like that of Niagara, crowned with overhanging rocks and mountains, in all the rude and awful grandeur of nature" (68). Plebian born, Henry develops his unique "species of eloquence," according to Wirt, not from studying the classics, as did Lee, but from conversing with people, from seeking to render himself intelligible to "plain and unlettered hearers," and from reading "the great volume of human nature" (28, 422). What he achieves is a "language of emotion" – an oratory that "burns from soul to soul," that paints "to the heart with a force that almost petrified it," that captivates hearers but so delights them that they follow "withersoever he led them" (28–9, 44, 46). The power of Henry's oratory is the sovereign power of an Orpheus or a Cicero – or of a tyrant; it is the power that the classical rhetorical tradition sought to discipline by demanding that the orator be a good or wise man who served the public. An education in the liberal arts would fashion that good man. But Patrick Henry, as constructed by Wirt, is the epitome of the unfashioned man. What guarantees his republican commitment is not a liberal education but a grounding in nature. Unlike Lee, Henry lacked "literary discipline"; he never became a master of the pen (131). But Wirt agrees that it was "fortunate for the revolution" that his "genius" was never curbed by composition, that it was "left at large, to revel in all the wildness and boldness of nature" (131).[96] This genius, schooled not by books but by nature, tutored not by classics but by commoners, enabled Henry "to infuse, more successfully, his own intrepid spirit into the measures of the revolution . . . and enabled him to achieve, by a kind of happy rashness, what perhaps had been lost by a better regulated mind" (131). While Wirt calls Lee the American Cicero, Henry is the American Demosthenes, a man who "belonged to the body of the people," a voice who spoke for what Thomas Gray called the "mute inglorious Miltons" (125, 52), and who now could be dubbed the rap artist of the American Revolution. Henry as constructed by Wirt (and Randolph) becomes the model of a Romantic philosophy of composition, just as Lee serves Wirt as the exemplum of the classical rhetorical tradition, and this opposition between the good old country boy speaking from the heart and the elite word man trained to speak from books would be soon met again in the presidential campaign between an Indian fighter from the West – Andrew Jackson – and an incumbent president who had been a professor of rhetoric from Harvard – John Quincy Adams. Training in the craft of rhetoric, reserved for an educated elite, would increasingly be challenged in post-Revolutionary America by the art of speaking honestly, the craft of democratic politics that could be mastered without fee or tutor by an Andrew Jackson, an Abraham Lincoln, or a confidence man; and this opposition would be constructed over and over again to meet the demands of the public for a representative voice and a language of truth in politics.

If Henry's sublime oratory thrilled Wirt, the dominion that his speech could exercise over the affections, making listeners captives of the word, struck into others, as did Whitefield's preaching, the fear of seduction. Wirt reports that "it became fashionable, in the higher circles, to speak of Mr. Henry as *a designing demagogue, a factious tribune*, who carried his points, not by fair and open debate, but by violent and inflammatory appeals to the worst passions of the multitude" (436). He also records how the "aristocracy" ridiculed "his vicious and depraved pronunciation, the homespun coarseness of his language, and his hypocritical canting in relation to his humility and ignorance" (72).[97] By defending Henry from this charge of demagoguery, by testifying how he annihilated "all the arts and *finesse* of parliamentary intrigue," and by accusing his critics of a snobbish and envious contempt for the style of eloquence that led the Revolution in Virginia, Wirt, a highly respected lawyer, becomes one of the first great champions of the vernacular voice in American letters, the voice that is heard stirringly in the country's literature of democratic protest from Harriet Beecher Stowe's *Uncle Tom's Cabin* and Twain's *Adventures of Huckleberry Finn* to Steinbeck's *Grapes of Wrath* and Walker's *Color Purple* (436). Looking backwards, however, we must also hear Henry's voice as the voice of the natural man, the primitive, the elocutionist sought for by Rousseau, by Goldsmith, by Sheridan – and the voice of the evangelical preacher.

In terms of oratory, as Patrick Henry's life suggests, the distance from the revival to the Revolution was not far. In the public square the colonists could hear a rhetoric of sensation applied to political topics by orators who had come of age during the Great Awakening. Edmund Randolph reports in his *History of Virginia* that Henry often listened to the dissenters from the established church "while they were waging their steady and finally effectual war against the burdens of that church, and from a repetition of his sympathy with the history of their sufferings, he unlocked the human heart and transferred into civil discussions many of the bold licenses which prevailed in the religions." Randolph adds, "If he [Henry] was not a constant hearer and admirer of that stupendous master of the human passions, George Whitefield, he was a follower, a devotee of some of his most powerful disciples at least."[98] Not depending upon what Randolph terms the "dead letter of written sermons," Henry and other orators in Revolutionary America, as Rhys Isaac explains, brought into the public square and into "the politics of the gentry world an adaptation of that popular oral form, the extempore sermon, that had been setting different parts" of Virginia ablaze ever since the Great Awakening of the 1740s.[99] Confident masters of "speaking from the heart," the orators also spoke to the heart in a sensational language that was the tabloid journalism of the day. Listen, for instance, to Joseph Warren on March 6, 1775, when during the annual public commemoration of the Boston Massacre he guides the sight and stirs the sentiments of his audience to evoke in them a lurid sense of ghastly events on a fateful day:

> Approach we then the melancholy walk of death. Hither let me call the gay companion; here let him drop a farewell tear upon that body which so late he saw vigorous and warm with social mirth – hither let me lead the tender mother to weep over her beloved son – come, widowed mourner, here satiate thy grief: behold thy murdered husband gasping on the ground, and to complete the pompous show of wretchedness bring in each hand thy infant children to bewail their father's fate – take heed, ye orphan babes, lest whilst your streaming eyes fixed upon the ghastly corpse, *your feet slide on the stones bespattered with your father's brains.*[100]

If Edwards presents us in his imprecatory sermons with terrifying images of sinners in the hands of an angry God, Warren presents an equally terrifying image of loving sons and fathers consigned just as suddenly from mirth to a living hell by the hands of angry sinners. The fall to be feared here is not backsliding into Satan's pit but a slide into blood drawn by the fire of British soldiers. But just as the evangelical appeal to the affections was greeted less than enthusiastically by the rationalist clergy trained in the old-school method of edifying the understanding, so too apparently was Warren's sensational rhetoric greeted with a mixed reaction. It was reported in *Rivington's Gazette*, a Tory journal, that Warren was "applauded by the mob, but groaned at by people of understanding."[101]

When John Adams presented the case for independence on the floor of the Continental Congress in June and July 1776, he too, by his own account, adopted something of the manner of an evangelical preacher, which he had once imitated as a schoolboy, for he later notes that on the occasion, at which he spoke with no written preparation, he had been "'carried out in Spirit' as Enthusiastic Preachers express themselves."[102] Denying later reports that he began his speech supporting a declaration of independence "by an Invocation to the God of Eloquence," Adams insisted instead that he began by saying, "This is the first time of my Life when I seriously wished for the genius and eloquence of the celebrated orators of Athens and Rome."[103] But if Adams had never wished for that talent before, he had dreamed about possessing it ever since he had been a student at Harvard, and what he could have summoned up on the floor of the assembly as his muse were his years of devoted study of what he termed the "prescious Remains of grecian and roman Eloquence" and of the "Talent, and Art of moving the Passions" by sounds – or of what Thomas Sheridan called the art of elocution.[104] What Adams's early diaries reveal clearly is that the theory of rhetoric whose practice helped work the changes in the "hearts and mind" and "religious sentiments" of the colonists regarding their "rights and duties," which Adams called the "real Revolution," stemmed from more traditions than the revival sermon (JAW, X, 282–3). Adams and other leaders of the Revolution who spoke and wrote so often from the Stamp Act crisis onwards translated into the action of eloquence the classic lessons they had learned in the classroom; they became Catos, Ciceros, Demostheneses inspiring virtue and declaiming against tyranny.

John Adams's diaries provide an extraordinary record of his quest to fulfill through the power of the word the claims of two masters: the self and the social order, or in Adams's own words, his desire for "Fame, Fortune, and personal Pleasure" and his desire "to defend Innocence, to punish Guilt, and to promote Truth and Justice among Mankind" (ED, 77). Cicero had argued centuries earlier that it was the office of rhetorical education to reconcile the claims of these two masters. The nascent orator, disciplined by a study of moral philosophy and history, would emerge as the statesman who would fulfill his ambition by serving the republic through the triumph of his rhetoric over the enemies of liberty and virtue. At times, the orator would enact the role of philosopher, contemplating wisdom and virtue in detachment from the commotions of the forum, but at other times, as an orator in the forum, he would seek to make wisdom and virtue active in the world through the catalyst of eloquence. After deciding upon a legal career in the late 1750s, Adams dedicates himself to the Ciceronian model, which would persist into antebellum America as the vocational model of the American lawyer.[105] "I find my self entering an unlimited Field," he writes a friend in 1758. "A Field in which Demosthenes, Cicero, and others of immortal Fame have exulted before me! A Field which encloses, the whole Circle of Science and Literature, the History, Wisdom, and Virtue of all ages" (ED, 65). Stepping into this field of study with at least one eye directed toward his own fame, Adams reads aloud Cicero's four orations against Catiline; he studies Rollin's *Method of Teaching and Studying the Belles Lettres; or, An Introduction to Languages, Poetry, Rhetorick, History, Moral Philosophy, Physics, &c.*; he takes notes on civil law, laboring to define the key words; he contemplates how eloquence moves the passions; he notes that "Sound is . . . a more powerful

Instrument of moving the Passions than Sense"; and he speculates that there is "a distinct peculiar sound" to every passion (ED, 74). "Of what use to a Lawyer," he asks, "is that Part of oratory, which relates to moving of the Passions?" His answer previews the very ways he would soon begin using that power: "It may be used to raise . . . an Admiration, and Esteem of the wise, humane, equitable and free Constitutions of Government we are under. It may be used to rouse in the Breasts of the Audience a gallant Spirit of Liberty, especially when declaiming upon any Occasion, on any Instance of arbitrary Conduct in an Officer or Magistrate" (ibid.).

The Tory critics of the colonial protest movement commented frequently and contemptuously about how the colonists were being governed by mere sounds. Adams, in his diaries, is not disgusted by or afraid of this power; he is fascinated by it. Though he describes himself in his diaries laboring in good Lockean fashion to form "distinct ideas" of such words as "law," "right," "wrong," "justice," and "equity," and while he labored to educate Americans in the sense of these words so they would not be governed by sounds, his diaries reveal his ambitious desire to master the sovereign power of words Locke sought to suppress. "An Orator to gain the Art of moving the Passions, must attend to Nature, must observe the Sounds in which all sorts of People, express the Passions and sentiments of their Hearts, and must learn to adapt his own Voice, to the Passion he would move" (ibid.). Adams resolves to attune his ear to the voices of all sorts of people, listening perhaps to frequencies of sound lower down on the social scale than other colonists, Whig and Tory, deigned to hear. Adams himself would be an American pioneer in using dialect to voice political dissent, in his Humphrey Ploughjogger letters to Boston newspapers. Even when he studies classical literature and "the greatest orators of Rome and Britain," he reads them not just for their content but to learn "what peculiar Sounds are used [to] express the different Emotions of the Mind" (ibid.).

In his diary entries, the education of a lawyer, the practice of a literary critic, the goals of the evangelical preacher, and the methods of the statesman all merge in Adams's quest to become a master of rhetoric, an American Cicero. In an extraordinary passage of self-examination and self-projection, Adams concludes by measuring his capabilities against his future desires: "[Oh Genius] . . . Oh Learning! Oh Eloquence! . . . may I dare to think I have the first? How shall I assume a Power to command the other two. Knowledge I can and will acquire, and has Language Power to charm, and shall not I avail my self of that Power?" (ED, 77). Often considered to be the epitome of the thinking revolutionary who marshaled the arguments of the Whig

opposition with the soberness of a Puritan, Adams is here a figure of
the rhetorical revolutionary, the student of the power of persuasion
who turns to the word not just to teach but to inspire and command.
Availing himself of that power, he becomes the "Atlas" of independence
on the floor of the Continental Congress, a "Colossus" who "came out
occasionally," Jefferson is reported to have said, "with a power of
thought and expression that moved us from our seats."[106] Arguing
against Dickinson's plea on July 1 to forbear declaring independence,
Adams carries the day. His triumph, and the successes on the battlefields
of eloquence of the other orators of the Revolution, such as Sam Adams
and Patrick Henry, can be classified as the triumph of neither revivalistic
enthusiasm nor legal rationality alone. It is a triumph of a double-
barreled politics of language. From the one barrel the orators fired the
strategy of Lockean linguistic analysis, and from the other they fired a
style of popular persuasion advanced by evangelicals and elocutionists
alike. Fired together in sermons and orations, these strategies triumphed
over proclamations from the king and Parliament. The words of the
orators sounded from the pulpit, from the bar, in the assembly, and on
the street helped to accomplish what Adams called for in his peroration
to *A Dissertation on the Canon and Feudal Law*: they spread far and wide
"the ideas of right and the sensations of freedom."

But in Adams's own view, as expressed in a letter to Benjamin
Rush, it was Jefferson's silent oratory of the pen that triumphed in
history. "Was there ever a *coup de théâtre* that had so great an effect as
Jefferson's penmanship of the Declaration of Independence?"[107] Several years after his defeat by Jefferson for the presidency in 1800,
Adams laments to Rush (as he frequently did) the course of politics in
the American republic, condemning the country and its leaders for
their vices and follies and offering a critique that contradicts the
fundamental thesis of the lectures his son, John Quincy Adams, had
begun to give at Harvard as the first Boylston Professor of Rhetoric
and Oratory. For the elder Adams, the age of oratory was over.
"Secrecy! Cunning! Silence!" had triumphed in its stead, becoming
the new mode of politics, "les grandes sciences des tempes modernes."
But Adams could no more stand the irrelevancy of oratory in a
republic than the irrelevancy of virtue. "The theory of rhetoric ought
not to be neglected in the seats of education," he advises. "Better
times may come."[108]

When John Adams himself was a student, the theory and practice of
rhetoric were undergoing renovation in the seats of education. From
the time of the Great Awakening through the Revolution, new opportunities for public speaking and new directions in rhetoric arose not
just outside the college in the field of religion and in the public space

of the revival but in the classroom. Before 1750, Gordon Bigelow explains, the study of rhetoric in the colleges had been pursued mainly in Latin and centered in the work of Peter Ramus, who regarded rhetoric in much the same way as did Bacon and Locke. Cutting rhetoric off from a vital relation to knowledge, Ramus treated it as merely ornament and style, a handmaiden to the science of logic. But after 1750, in Bigelow's words, "a number of important changes occurred: English replaced Latin; the great classical rhetoricians replaced Ramus; and a split occurred between the written and spoken phrases of rhetorical study, with 'elocution,' or the science of delivery, receiving more and more emphasis."[109] No longer in the colleges of the Colonies would rhetoric be the diminished thing of Ramus and Locke. In the 1750s William Smith, who had been trained at the University of Aberdeen at a time when the Scottish school system began to emphasize the importance of rhetoric and belles-lettres, became provost of the College of Philadelphia, and he soon instigated the same type of curriculum change by having the college offer more comprehensive instruction in rhetoric, composition, and literary criticism. Similarly, at Harvard, Yale, and William and Mary in the 1760s and 1770s instruction in rhetoric and the practice of public speaking became more central in the curriculum, and at Princeton a new president from Scotland, John Witherspoon, gave a distinguished series of lectures on rhetoric.[110] At these colleges and elsewhere, rhetorical education was becoming retooled, in effect if not in purpose, for a classical republican state wherein liberty would reign and persuasion would depose force and fraud as the true mode of politics. Just listen to the commencement oration of William Smith at the College of Philadelphia in 1757 as he advises the students (among whom were Francis Hopkinson and Jacob Duché) about how to employ the wisdom and talents of criticism and oratory they had garnered in the classroom:

> Should your *Country* call, or should you perceive the *restless Tools* of FACTION at Work in their dark Cabals, and "stealing upon the *secure Hour* of LIBERTY"; should you see the *Corruptors* or *Corrupted* imposing upon the Public with specious Names, undermining the *civil* and *religious* Principles of their Country, and gradually paving the Way to certain SLAVERY, by spreading *destructive Notions of Government* – then, Oh! then, be nobly rouzed! Be all Eye, and Ear, and Heart, and Voice, and Hand, in a Cause so glorious! *Cry aloud, and spare not,* fearless of Danger, regardless of Opposition, and little sollicitous about the Frowns of Power, or the Machinations of Villainy. Let the World know that LIBERTY *is your unconquerable Delight,* and that you are sworn Foes to every Species of Bondage, either of Body or of Mind!

These are Subjects for which you need not be ashamed to sacrifice your Ease and every other private Advantage – For certainly, if there be aught upon Earth suited to the native Greatness of the human mind, and worthy of Contention, it must be to assert the Cause of *Religion and Truth*; to support the *fundamental Rights and Liberties of Mankind*; and to strive for the Constitution of your Country, and a "Government of *Laws*, not of *Men*."[111]

What Smith provides is a précis of the counsel that would be sounded from so many republican rostrums in the years that followed 1757 and that would make so many of the colonists students of the rhetoric of liberty and law eager and able to defend their right against the corrupters and the corrupted. And this is the type of oration by a professor that might have convinced Jonathan Boucher that the "two colleges of Philadelphia, and that at Princeton in the Jersies" were "chief nurseries" of a "frivolous and mischievous kind of knowledge" whose "chief and peculiar merit was thought to be in Rhetoric and the belles lettres."[112]

College students in the Colonies also organized their own literary and debating societies, giving themselves further opportunities to transform rhetorical theory into practice. At Yale, the Linonia Literary and Debating Society reputedly began in 1753; at Harvard, there were the Hasty Pudding and Speaking clubs; and at Princeton, the Cliosophic Society and the American Whig Society. "The particular objects which these societies pursue," commented John Blair Linn in 1795, "are composition, verbal debates, and oratory," and he claimed that "the benefits" that students received from such societies "are considerable."[113] John Adams himself reports that he first began to contemplate a career in law because fellow members of a literary club praised his talent for public speaking. The debate and declamations in the college curriculum and in the clubs provided a form of dress rehearsal for the drama of Revolutionary politics. In 1769 students, for instance, debated the question "Whether Americans, in their present Circumstances, cannot with Good Policy, affect to become Independent States," and for Oliver Wendell Holmes, Sam Adams's address at Harvard in 1743 was the opening salvo in the war of words against British authority. At Harvard and Princeton, the two sets of literary clubs were themselves the staging ground for political as well as literary rivalries, preparing such students as James Madison, Philip Freneau, and Hugh Henry Brackenridge, who were fellow members of the American Whig Society, for roles they would continue to play in politics after their graduation.

In a list of proposals for future projects, Benjamin Franklin notes that "history will show the wonderful effects of ORATORY, in governing, turning and leading great Bodies of Mankind, Armies, Cities, Nations." He adds that "Modern Political Oratory" is "chiefly performed by the Pen and Press" and that "its Effects are more extensive, more lasting &c."[114] The oratory of the Revolution was a combination of this modern political oratory and the ancient oratory of the spoken word, and the lasting effect of that oratory, according to Benjamin Rush and David Ramsay, was the success of the Revolution itself. "We do not extol it too highly," Rush asserts, "when we attribute as much to the power of eloquence as to the sword in bringing about the American Revolution."[115] Ramsay concurs: "In establishing American independence, the pen and the press had merit equal to that of the sword. . . . To rouse and unite the inhabitants . . . this was effected in great measure by the tongues and pens of the well-informed citizens" (DRH, II, 319). No matter, then, whether their training in eloquence was classical or Christian, a product of the classroom or an extension of the revival, the orators of the Revolutionary era, claims Ramsay, were "inspired by a love of liberty, and roused by a common danger", they "laboured in kindling the latent sparks of patriotism. The flame spread from breast to breast, till the conflagration became general" (DRH, I, 60–1).

The more immediate effects of the oratory of the tongue were captured in a comment Jonathan Boucher made in 1773. He observed

> As though there were some irrefutable charm in all extemporaneous speaking, however rude, the orators of our committees and sub-committees, like those in higher spheres, prevail with their tongues. To public speakers alone is the government of our country now completely committed. . . . An empire is thus completely established within an empire; and a new system of government of great power is erected, even before the old one is abolished.[116]

Here is a transformation of the public sphere that fulfills Carlyle's claim in *Heroes and Hero-Worship* that "whoever can speak, speaking now to the whole nation, becomes a power. . . . The nation is governed by all that have tongues in the nation; Democracy is virtually there."[117] But Boucher is anything but pleased by this development. What he saw in the assemblies of the Colonies was not participatory democracy but an oligarchy of orators staging a usurpation. Looking at the same phenomena from a different perspective, James Wilson observed the creation of a chain of communication, a linking of citizens through acts of speaking, assembling, and corresponding that formed a chain of more inestimable value, he declared, than a chain of gold, for it was "a chain of freedom." In Hannah Arendt's terms, the colonists bound themselves together in voluntary associations based on discussion and public address to maintain a public space wherein citizens could speak openly – a place where they could assemble and represent themselves, a place where man the political animal is man the speaking animal. Here, in these places, is where a people of the Word came together to share the word and guard against its corruption, and here is where people of common sense and an uncommon talent for speaking or writing could rise and distinguish themselves by serving the cause of liberty through the "eloquence of the pen and tongue," those skills which, Jefferson asserts, insure distinction "in a free country" (JLA, 839).

Thomas Paine: Toppling Idols of the Marketplace

Just as eloquence nurtures liberty, liberty nurtures eloquence. This fundamental postulate of the classical rhetorical tradition is confirmed by David Ramsay when he observes in his *History of the American Revolution*:

> It seems as if the war not only required, but created talents. Men whose minds were warmed with the love of liberty, and whose abilities were improved by daily exercise, and sharpened with a laudable ambition to serve their distressed country, spoke, wrote and acted, with an energy far surpassing all expectations which could be reasonably founded on their previous acquirements. (DRH, II, 216)

One man whose writing talents the conflict with Britain summoned forth was the son of a poor corsetmaker in England. On November 30, 1774, this relatively undistinguished man, who had worked as a staymaker, teacher, and exciseman in England, arrived in America bearing a letter of introduction from Benjamin Franklin. He obtained employment with Robert Aitken, a Philadelphia printer, and in February 1775 he became the editor of the *Pennsylvania Magazine*, which Aitken had founded. Soon he began writing articles for the magazine, including an attack on slavery in America, a critique of titles, and an essay on unhappy marriages. And in January 1776 he published what Bernard Bailyn has called "the most brilliant pamphlet written during the American Revolution, and one of the most brilliant pamphlets ever written in the English language."[118] The success of the pamphlet exceeded all expectations, and it launched the career of a tireless foe of tyranny and injustice. The man, of course, is Thomas Paine, and the pamphlet is *Common Sense*. The fruit of Paine's labors was the most influential of all the colonial attempts to combat political and linguistic misrepresentation with the pen. Paine's thesis – independence, not reconciliation; his style – plain but often lyrical; his tone – one of outrage; his tactics – a fusion of religious, political, and economic arguments; his phenomenal success – 150,000 copies sold in the first three months, probably 500,000 copies sold in the year; and his legendary impact – a transformation in the terms of the political debate between Britain and the Colonies – have been ably and often discussed.[119] What I wish to focus on is how Paine in his pamphlet made the language of politics and the politics of language one and inseparable.

Rousseau writes in *Emile*, a treatise on education which addressed the politics of child rearing, that a child is born not free but dependent and subject to the power of others: "Your first gifts are fetters, your first treatment, torture." But he adds, "Their voice alone is free; why should they not raise it in complaint?"[120] When the colonists found themselves subject to the fetters and abuse rather than to the affection of their parent country, they began to raise their voices in complaint and seek redress of their grievances. When Paine surveyed America in the winter of 1775, he too found reason for the colonists to complain, but when he raised his voice in *Common Sense*, he called upon the colonists not to seek redress but to make their bodies as free as their voices – to contend for independence rather than dependence, to abandon a king whose claim to rule was a fraud and a constitution which was as corrupt as a whore, to escape the torture of a country that was not the benevolent parent it was considered to be, and to use their voices not to cry out for help but to call upon others to join them in building "an asylum for mankind" (TPW, I, 31). What Paine saw, in effect, when he surveyed the Colonies in the winter of their discontent was a people everywhere free but enchained by unmeaning names. The strongest of these mind-forged manacles were the false distinctions of kingship, which had been inscribed on the English constitution by force and fraud, and the mislabeling of England as the Colonies' parent country. And Paine understood that if America was to begin government at the right end – if it was to build that asylum in the springtime of a new age, if it was to make glorious the American promise and begin the world over again – it had to abandon its old, familiar mother tongue and learn a new language. In particular, the colonists had to abandon the "unmeaning name of king" and the "violated unmeaning names of parent and child" (TPW, I, 23), terms from their mother tongue that were lulling them into a dangerous sleep, and they had to learn to speak and translate into law the language that was their true inheritance, the language that was spoken by their first parent, Adam: the language of nature and nature's God. It was indeed the "weeping voice of nature" that was now crying out to them in distress, "'TIS TIME TO PART" (TPW, I, 21).

In the seventh number of *The Crisis*, the series of essays Paine wrote to bolster the morale of the troops and mobilize public opinion behind the war effort, he describes the sentiments of the colonists as he found them when he arrived from England in 1774:

> I found the disposition of the people such, that they might have been led by a thread and governed by a reed. Their suspicion was quick and penetrating, but their attachment to Britain was obstinate, and it was at that time a kind of treason to speak against it. They disliked the ministry, but they esteemed the nation. Their idea of grievance operated without resentment, and their single object was reconciliation. Bad as I believed the ministry to be, I never conceived them capable of a measure so rash and wicked as the commencing of hostilities; much less did I imagine the nation would encourage it. I viewed the dispute as a kind of law-suit, in which I supposed the parties would find a way either to decide or settle it. I had no thoughts of independence or of arms. The world could not then have persuaded me that I should be either a soldier or an author. . . . But when the country, into which I had just set my foot, was set on fire about my ears, it was time to stir. It was time for every man to stir. (TPW, I, 143–4)

When Paine did stir, he stirred a nation. By challenging the terms that had governed discussion of the political relationship between England and the Colonies, he broke apart the political presuppositions of the colonists that had congealed around the notions that their aim was to restore the balance of the English constitution and that their duty was to seek reconciliation with their parent country. And by opening the wounds of their grievances and rubbing them raw with some verbal vituperativeness, Paine helped turn esteem into resentment, resentment into bitterness, and bitterness into staunch opposition. "This animated piece," observed one contemporary, "dispels . . . the prejudice of the mind against the doctrine of independence and pours upon it . . . an inundation of light and truth."[121]

When Paine sought to enlighten the colonists to seek independence, he did so by aiming much of his rhetorical cannonade against the prejudices or received ideas that had been seemingly indelibly impressed upon the mind by the reigning vocabulary. Like his Enlightenment forebears, Paine recognizes in *Common Sense* that "men fall out with names without understanding them" (TPW, I, 16), and thus he proceeds in his pamphlet to educate readers in the sense or nonsense of words. He carefully examines the foundations of the words, or "idols of the marketplace," that were ruling or confusing people's understandings, topples them if necessary, and seeks to replace them with words representative of the natural constitution of things. He does not, for instance, merely call upon the inhabitants of America to cast off their "present denomination of British subject" so they will be "received" and "heard abroad" (TPW, I, 39); he protests that the very words that had defined the relationship between the Colonies and Britain had always been misapplications. That is, he understood what scholars have increasingly recognized: the relationship between the Colonies and Britain had always been discussed and debated in family terms.[122] The Colonies in this ideological paradigm were looked upon as children dependent upon the parent state, and the question was whether it was time for Britain to fulfill its role by ending its protection and granting the Colonies their independence or whether the Colonies were still obliged to be obedient. But in Paine's view the whole notion of Britain's paternal role was nonsense. "Europe, and not England, is the parent country of America," he declares (TPW, I, 19). Thus he emphasizes that the phrase "*parent or mother country*" when applied to Britain has no valid meaning. Instead, he writes, it "hath been jesuitically adopted by the king and his parasites, with a low papistical design of gaining an unfair bias on the credulous weakness of our minds" (ibid.). Besides, he argues, even if the presumed title of parent is true, how can Britain merit that name when not even "brutes" or "savages" make war on their young? In his view, England's claim of paternal protection is merely a mask for economic self-interest: "We have boasted the protection of Great Britain, without considering, that her motive was *interest* not *attachment*" (TPW, I, 18). Indeed, the putative parent of the Colonies was not a loving mother but a "cruel monster," not the home of "moral ideas" but an "empire of force." Thus Paine disdains "the wretch, that with the pretended title of FATHER OF HIS PEOPLE can unfeelingly hear of their slaughter, and composedly sleep with their blood upon his soul" (TPW, I, 25). "Wherefore," he concludes, "since nothing but blows will do, for God's sake let us come to a final separation, and not leave the next generation to be cutting throats under the violated unmeaning names of parent and child" (TPW, I, 23).

In the seventh essay in *The Crisis*, written in 1778, Paine returns to his argument in *Common Sense* that Britain should not be called the parent country of the Colonies in letter, because that title was "due to Europe collectively," or in spirit, because she had "destroyed by her conduct what she assumed in her title" (TPW, I, 154, 147). When he elaborates upon this point, he gives a brief treatise on the association of ideas and the magic of names that reveals how he recognized with Laurence Sterne and the Scottish Common Sense philosophers how words, for better or worse, react not only on the understanding but on the affections:

She [Britain] set out with the title of parent, or mother country. The association of ideas which naturally accompany this expression, are filled with everything that is fond, tender and forbearing. They have an energy peculiar to themselves, and, overlooking the accidental attachment of common affections, apply with infinite softness to the first feelings of the heart. It is a political term which every mother can feel the force of, and every child can judge of. It needs no painting of mine to set it off, for nature only can do it justice. (TPW, I, 147).

The mistake that Britain made was to disrupt this benevolent association of ideas and break the charm of words. "But has any part of your conduct to America corresponded with the title you set up?" (ibid.). Because of her conduct, there began a radical change in the affections of the colonists, and through the initiative of Paine's *Common Sense* they began to associate Britain's claim to parenthood with tyranny and the power of its empire not with "national honor" but with "bullying" and exploitation. Paine then adds his moral: "Had you been true politicians you would have seen all this, and continued to draw from the magic of a name, the force and authority of a nation. Unwise as you were in breaking the charm, you were still more unwise in the manner of doing it" (TPW, I, 148). Paine, who declared in an 1806 letter that "my motive and object in all my political works, beginning with *Common Sense* . . . have been to rescue man from tyranny and false systems and false principles of government, and enable him to be free" (TPW, II, 1480), was, in his terms, a "true politician," for he understood the degree to which words could participate in the creation and the destruction of "tyranny and false systems and false principles of government."

When Paine challenged Britain's claim to the title of parent country, he was challenging a metaphor that had governed much of the thinking about the relationship between the Colonies and Britain. But when he challenged the name of king as a false distinction, he was challenging an institution that had governed the bodies as well as the minds of the colonists. The basis of Paine's challenge is once again an appeal to nature and religion, and his aim is to reduce kingship to a metaphor and then prick the word that had bubbled people out of their rights and money. He begins by protesting that while male and female are distinctions of nature and while good and bad are distinctions of heaven, there is "no truly natural or religious reason" for the distinction of people into king and subjects (TPW, I, 9). That difference has been created by words and by words alone or by words enforced by fraud and brute force. In the beginning all men were equal, but false words, unjust deeds, and historical lies have covered up this truth of nature and nature's God. Now the equality of man is anything but self-evident. But if we just strip away the "dark covering of antiquity," lo and behold we shall discover that the first kings were "nothing better than the principal ruffian of some restless gang; whose savage manners or pre-eminence in subtilty obtained him the title of chief among plunderers: and who by increasing in power and extending his depredations overawed the quiet and defenceless to purchase their safety by frequent contributions" (TPW, I, 13). This ruffian may be called a "sacred majesty" and his plunder the royal revenue, but Paine asks us to do what Henry Fielding requires us to do in *Jonathan Wild*: recognize that virtuous words, such as "greatness," "goodness," and "honorable" have been applied to leaders rank with meanness and vice – a Jonathan Wild or a Robert Walpole. In *Jonathan Wild*, Fielding attributes a large measure of common sense to the "vulgar." He points out, for instance, in a shot of irony that gives the narrative its critical force, that what "GREAT men" sum up "in the collective name of policy, or politics, or rather pollitrics," "the vulgar call treachery, dissembling, promising, lying, falsehood, etc."[123] Paine, however, seems to be less confident of the ability of the common people to distinguish between greatness and goodness, a vile worm and a sacred majesty, but that is in large part because he feels they have not been just deluded but violently imposed upon. He protests, for instance, that the term "hereditary right" has been crammed "down the throats of the vulgar" (TPW, I, 14), and part of his tactic in *Common Sense* is to fill the people with such disgust for kings that they regurgitate those terms. Less blatantly, he strives to deflate the bubble of kingship and hereditary right through a strategy of verbal reduction that exposes a lowly referent skulking behind a highfalutin term. "A French bastard landing with an armed banditti and establishing himself king of England against the consent of the natives, is in plain terms a very paltry rascally original" (ibid.). Through the strokes of some coarse words and a small clause – "in plain terms" – Paine attempts to reduce what had been exalted to its "proper" level, and in the process he provides something of a devil's dictionary, or a revolutionary lexicon that defines revenue as plunder and translates making war and giving away places into impoverishing a nation and setting it together by the ears. Paine thus strips the emperor's clothes from George III for the eyes of the "vulgar," just as Fielding strips Wild (and Walpole) for his readers.

The success of Paine's pamphlet is the triumph of a rhetoric of radical simplicity. Opposed to an inflated, obfuscatory discourse that defends the indefensible, Paine affects to call a spade a spade. John Adams for one was not favorably impressed by the style of Paine's attacks on Britain and its king. He objects in his autobiography that the phrases "'the Royal Brute of England,' 'the Blood upon his Soul!' and a few other of equal delicacy" are "suitable for an Emigrant from New Gate." Yet he also comments that they "had as much Weight with the People as his Arguments" (JAW, II, 509). A vulgar tongue engages in battle with the King's English in *Common Sense*, but its victory for Paine is not the victory of vulgarity but of a vox populi that speaks the language of nature. Indeed, the rhetorical strategy of the pamphlet is to oppose courtly artifice to country truth, flattery to fact, duplicity to sincerity, and the long train of British prevarications to plain arguments and honest terms, and this effort marks a key advance in America of the championing of the honest common man and his homespun, straight-talking, "natural" speech that has its European counterpart in the fascination with cultural primitivism and the project of Wordsworth's *Lyrical Ballads* and that receives a further and influential development in William Wirt's biography of Patrick Henry as "the orator of nature."[124] If Henry is the "orator of nature," Paine is its penman. Together, as artisans of colloquial speech, they break precedent and decorum; like the sounds Dr. Johnson sought to enchain, their voices are too volatile for legal restraints.

Paine's insistent demand in *Common Sense* that readers draw a distinction between a title and a man (or country) is an application of the empiricist's injunction that people separate the knowledge of words from the knowledge of things, and indeed we could say that Paine adopts as his motto the motto of the Royal Society: *Nullius in Verbum* – "in the word of no one," a motto that was one of the battle cries of the scientific revolution. Paine's critique of titles in *Common Sense* is also an application of the argument that he makes in one of the first essays he published in America, a brief called "Reflections on Titles," which appeared in the *Pennsylvania Magazine* just a few weeks after the outbreak of hostilities at Lexington and Concord. Enraged at the indignity that bestows pompous titles on unworthy men, Paine begins the essay by uttering his contempt for the absurd habit of addressing a plunderer and murderer of mankind as "Right Honorable" (TPW, II, 33). He then explains the different effects that "high sounding names" have on different people. While "the reasonable freeman sees through the magic of a title, and examines the man before he approves him," titles "overawe the superstitious vulgar, and forbid them to inquire into the character of the possessor" (ibid.). "This sacrifice of common sense," Paine declares, "is the certain badge which distinguishes slavery from freedom: for when men yield up the privilege of thinking, the last shadow of liberty quits the horizon" (ibid.). For Paine, this "sacrifice of common sense" is the prologue to tyranny, and what he demands instead (to borrow a line from *The Rights of Man*) is that people bring titles to the altar and make "of them a burnt-offering to Reason" (TPW, I, 287). The connection Paine makes in this essay between freedom of the mind and political liberty and between the imposing force of words and slavery is at the heart of his political philosophy and literary practice. Political freedom depends upon the freedom of the mind, and one of the most dangerous threats to that freedom is the power of words, and one of the few defenses against that threat is to fight eloquence with eloquence, sovereign words with representative ideas, the voice of power with the voice of nature; and this is the fight Paine began with his essay on titles and one that he never stopped waging.

Paine concludes "Reflections on Titles" by pointing out that since "all honors, even that of kings, originated from the public," no man should personally assume a title, but he adds that since the "public may justly be called the fountain of true honor," it may justly grant "the title of *Honorable*" to a "body of men, who nobly disregarding private ease and interest for public welfare, have justly merited the address of The Honorable Continental Congress" (TPW, II, 34). The simplicity of this argument belies its importance. The right to name, as Hobbes recognizes, is the right to rule, and here in this passage Paine gives voice to a revolution in the grammar of politics that the Honorable Continental Congress would help translate into action. The voice of the third person plural – the "they" of the people – would now take precedence over the first person singular – the "I" of the king. No longer in theory, that is, would an "I" speak for a "they"; a "they" would speak as a "we." The public in this grammar would be at once the fountain of honor and the source of law.

Later, in *The Rights of Man*, Paine resumes his attack against titles, calling "duke," "count," and "earl" "senseless words" that are non-existent in the "vocabulary of Adam" and insisting that anyone who believes in these titles lives "immured in the Bastille of a word" (TPW, I, 287). To free people from this prison house of language, Paine performs a Lockean analysis. He explains that titles are words with no ideas associated with them and that it is common opinion alone that creates titles, and thus if society consents to ridicule them, as they should, people will be free of that chimera. Rank and dignity will then begin to "take the substantial ground of character, instead of the chimerical ground of titles" (ibid.). In *The Rights of Man* Paine also suggests how words themselves can be used to free people from the Bastille of a word. He explains that "there is often passing in the mind [of man] a train of ideas he has not yet accustomed himself to encourage and communicate," and he adds that it is "curious to observe how soon this spell [the imprisoning magic of a word] can be dissolved" (TPW, I, 421). He then asserts, "A single expression, boldly conceived and uttered, will sometimes put a whole company into their proper feelings, and whole nations are acted upon in the same manner" (ibid.). This passage could be said to explain the effect if not the intention of *Common Sense*. Paine sought to utter in this pamphlet not a single expression but a set of expressions for a train of ideas that the people were feeling at some level but had not yet accustomed themselves to encourage and communicate, and by acting upon the colonists in this manner, put them into their "proper feelings," which was for Paine a feeling of enmity toward England and an enthusiasm for independence.

In *Common Sense* Paine also challenges the reigning opinion about the British constitution by analyzing the words that had been used to explain it. In the first section of his pamphlet he maintains that to say "that the Constitution of England is an *union* of three powers reciprocally *checking* each other, is farcical," because "either the words have no meaning, or they are flat contradictions" (TPW, I, 7). Locke argues in the *Essay* that it is particularly difficult to describe complex ideas in words, and for Paine the British constitution is so complex that it "is too incomprehensible to be within the compass of description" (TPW, I, 8). Thus any attempt to denote the workings of the constitution will produce "words of sound only, and though they may amuse the ear, they cannot inform the mind" (ibid.). During the debate with Britain, the colonists had been reluctant to criticize the idea of the monarchy and the constitution; instead they maintained that the king had been deceived by his ministers and that the constitution was not corrupt in and of itself but merely corrupted by abuses that could be remedied. Paine, however, directly criticizes the very idea of the monarchy and the constitution, and even maintains that it "is somewhat difficult to find a proper name for the government of England" (TPW, I, 16). But while he challenges the entire set of received ideas on government, his purpose is to do more than abolish those ideas. In his *Dissertation on First Principles of Government*, he notes that the "moral principle of revolutions is to instruct, not destroy" (TPW, II, 587), and in *Common Sense* he begins to do what Marx says must be done in a revolution: he instructs the people in a new language that will replace their mother tongue. In the new language of government, "republic" will be a proper name, and the word "constitution" will have a standard signification affixed to it. And in that new language, Paine writes at the conclusion of *Common Sense*, the "names of Whig and Tory" will "be extinct." And "let none other be heard among us," Paine requests, "than those of a *good citizen*; an *open and resolute friend*; and a *virtuous supporter of the* RIGHTS OF MANKIND, *and of the* FREE AND INDEPENDENT STATES

OF AMERICA" (TPW, I, 46). Independence, Paine believes, will also guard Americans against a corrupt old tongue. By declaring independence, Paine writes, "our ears will be legally shut against the schemes of an intriguing, as well as cruel, enemy" (ibid.).

In *Common Sense* Paine manifests an acute sense of how easily the fortress of the mind can be invaded and reason deposed: "Our eyes may be dazzled with show, or our ears deceived by sound; . . . prejudice may warp our wills, or interest darken our understanding" (TPW, I, 6). In a letter to the Abbé Raynal, Paine develops a brilliant metaphor that describes the way in which the freedom of the mind can be impaired and lost through the growth of prejudice.

> There is something exceedingly curious in the constitution and operation of prejudice. It has the singular ability of accommodating itself to all the possible varieties of the human mind. Some passions and vices are but thinly scattered among mankind, and find only here and there a fitness of reception. But prejudice, like the spider, makes every place its home. It has neither taste nor choice of situation, and all that it requires is room. Everywhere, except in fire or water, a spider will live.
>
> So, let the mind be as naked as the walls of an empty and forsaken tenement, gloomy as a dungeon, or ornamented with the richest abilities of thinking, let it be hot, cold, dark or light, lonely or inhabited, still prejudice, if undisturbed, will fill it with cobwebs, and live, like the spider, where there seems nothing to live on. If the one prepares her food by poisoning it to her palate and her use, the other does the same; and as several of our passions are strongly characterized by the animal world, prejudice may be denominated the spider of the mind. (TPW, II, 242)

Paine understands that if people are to begin government at the right end and the world over again, they first must free themselves of the prejudices that infest the mind. He also understands that the spider of prejudice weaves its web through words, and in *Common Sense* he consistently seeks to destroy the web of prejudice by subjecting words to the purifying fires of nature and reason. But Paine also depends on something more than the voice of nature and reason to destroy prejudice and turn colonial opinion against the king of spiders in England. Unlike Plato, he believes that humans possess a guardian stronger than reason that cannot be overcome by the wordspinning of sophistry. He writes that "the Almighty hath implanted in us these unextinguishable feelings for good and wise purposes. They are the guardians of his image in our hearts. They distinguish us from the herd of common animals" (TPW, I, 30). Ultimately Paine in *Common Sense* appeals to these "feelings for good and wise purposes" to condemn Britain.

Reason may instruct us to reject the idea of monarchy and the British constitution, but it is our feelings that teach us that England has become a power which is "a reproach to the names of men and christians" (TPW, I, 41). The king, he asserts, "hath wickedly broken through every moral and human obligation, trampled nature and conscience beneath his feet," and has thus procured himself "an universal hatred" (ibid.), a hatred that Paine seeks to stir up with a rhetoric addressed to what he and Jefferson refer to as the moral sense. Testimony to Paine's success in appealing to this moral sense is provided by Abigail Adams. "I am charmed with the Sentiments of Common Sense; and wonder how an honest Heart . . . can hesitate one moment at adopting them," she declared in a letter to her husband. But for John, who expressed admiration for the "manly and striking" style of the pamphlet, the "Sentiments" that so impressed his wife posed for him the threat of seduction by a designing Lovelace. "Sensible men," he responded to Abigail, "think there are some Whims, some Sophisms, some artfull Addresses to superstitious Notions, some keen attempts upon the Passions, in this pamphlet."[125] The transparent language of the heart that Paine adopts (and Rousseau champions) as a counter to courtly artifice is for Adams merely another form of affectation: the ruse of the rake. For Edmund Randolph, the style of *Common Sense* itself was something of a revolutionary act in colonial pamphleteering, but the terms of his commentary confirm not merely the response of Abigail Adams but the suspicions of her husband. Paine, he writes, "poured forth a style hitherto unknown on this side of the Atlantic for the ease with which it insinuated itself into the hearts of the people who were unlearned, or of the learned, who were not callous to the feeling of man." It was a pamphlet, he adds, "pregnant with the most captivating figures of speech," and because of it, "the public sentiment, which a few weeks before had shuddered at the tremendous obstacles with which independence was environed, overleaped every barrier."[126] Insinuation and captivation: the words suggest that Paine, prophet of the "birth-day of a new world," belonged, as Blake said of Milton, to the party of the devil. And in the years that followed the Revolution, it was Paine's style of addressing the heart – or the passions – with abuse and insinuation that John Adams would seek to counter with the Alien and Sedition Acts of 1798 in an era when, as Jay Fliegelman explains, hearts were hardening against the power of sympathy, or against what Paine championed in America and France: sentimental fraternity.[127] In these years, sadly, Paine himself would become an exile from the hearts of the people. Impoverished at the close of his life and despised as an atheist because of *The Age of Reason*, he died in 1809 and was buried at his home in New Rochelle after his request for a Quaker grave site was denied.

In his letter to the Abbé Raynal, Paine declares that because of the American Revolution "our style and manner of thinking have undergone a revolution more extraordinary than the political revolution of the country. We see with other eyes; we hear with other ears; and think with other thoughts, than those we formerly used" (TPW, II, 243). He also believed that the Revolution would lead to a new style of language, because it was his conviction that a representative government, since it does not exist by "fraud and mystery" and "deals not in cant and sophistry," will inspire "a language, that, passing from heart to heart, is felt and understood" (TPW, I, 373). For Paine, the quality of a government is directly related to the quality of language it produces. A fraudulent language is the mark of monarchy, and an honest tongue is the sign and signifier of a representative government. In America, that is, political revolution would be accompanied by a linguistic revolution: a representative government would enable people to enjoy that "communication of grandeur & of dignity" that Jefferson said in his draft of the Declaration was beneath the capacity of the British.

"Let those flatter who fear; it is not an American art," maintained Jefferson in 1774 (JLA, 121). "But of all animals on earth that ever fell in my way, your trimmers, your double-tongued and double-minded men, your disguised folk, I detest most," complained John Adams in June 1776 (JAW, IX, 396). In July 1776 Jefferson and Adams were more than willing to dissolve the bands connecting the Colonies to an England rank with the "rotten diction" of courtly designs and mildewed in its royal ear, and it was left to the author of *A Summary View of the Rights of British America* – a petition penned, in Jefferson's words, in "the language of truth" divested of servility and with the "freedom of language and sentiment which becomes a free people claiming their rights, as derived from the laws of nature" – to compose the Declaration, the consummate gesture of colonial resistance to the king and to the "imperious breath of a body of men [the Parliament], whom they never saw, in whom they never confided, and over whom," Jefferson continued, "they have no powers of punishment or removal" – except the act of revolution (JLA, 105, 120–1, 111).

A Shandean Meditation on Jefferson's Declaration of Independence

Jefferson advised his nephew Peter Carr that "the writings of Sterne particularly form the best course of morality that ever was written" (JLA, 902). Sterne's *Tristram Shandy* also provides one of the best texts for understanding the dynamics of the relationship between gesture and emotion, sign and sentiment, utterance and response as those relationships were being reconceived by theorists of language in the later eighteenth century, and a historical recovery of these relationships can offer a perspective for envisioning what Jefferson sought to activate when he penned the words of the Declaration. In the middle of *Tristram Shandy*, Sterne invites us to meditate upon an eloquent gesture that strikes into the heart "one of your self-evident truths."[128] The gesture is the fall of a hat; the self-evident truth is our mortality ("Are we not here now, – and gone! in a moment?"); the occasion is the death of Bobby Shandy; the effect is to unify in grief the servants of the Shandy household, who are notorious for their inability to share a common train of thought. The author of the act is Corporal Trim. He stands in direct contrast as an orator to Walter Shandy, who also mourns Bobby's death. While Trim speaks to the heart, Walter speaks to the head, but he befuddles it. His oration on the death of Bobby is a long discourse on the decay and fall of kingdoms, provinces, towns, and cities that becomes so long that Bobby is forgotten. Sterne's narrator suggests, on the other hand, that the "preservation of our constitution in church and state . . . may in time come to depend greatly upon the right understanding of this stroke of the corporal's eloquence" (431).

Jefferson's Declaration is not as concise as Trim's drop of a hat, but, as Garry Wills suggests, a right understanding of Jefferson's eloquence as an appeal that ultimately aims, like Trim's eloquence, "strait forwards . . . to the heart" (429) – or to what Jefferson calls in his correspondence the moral sense and in the Declaration the "voice of justice & of consanguinity" – can help us better understand how the Declaration sought to ring the alarm bell for the fight for independence in all thirteen colonies at the same time and how it could unify in sentiment colonists who shared markedly different trains of thought or associations of ideas regarding the pursuit of liberty and happiness and how best to preserve the constitution of the state.[129] Jefferson, remarkably, cites no historical precedent for the colonists' case for independence. His appeal is to self-evident truths, to the laws of nature and nature's God, to the opinions of mankind, to the facts of British tyranny, and to the "agonizing affection" tormented by those facts. Yet a right understanding of Jefferson's Declaration must also build from his claim in an 1824 letter that the Declaration was not an effort to "find out new principles, or new arguments" but an attempt – on the order of Trim's gesture – to "place before mankind the common sense of the subject" and to harmonize the "sentiments of the day, whether expressed in conversation, in letters, printed essays, or in the elementary books of public right, as Aristotle, Cicero, Locke, Sidney, &c." (JLA, 1501). If the Revolution can be considered in Holmes's figuration as a language-learning lesson that began when Sam Adams, Jonathan Mayhew, and others began schooling a class of citizens in "the elementary books of public right," or in their rights and duties as British subjects, as Christians, and as people possessing a moral sense, and if this lesson was advanced by a host of Walter Shandys – lawyers, ministers, pamphleteers – who discoursed at length and repeatedly about the decline and fall of kingdoms and provinces, then the Declaration is the commencement address and Jefferson the valedictorian called upon to represent his class, or to express "the American mind, and to give to that expression the proper tone and spirit called for by the occasion" (JLA, 1501).

Yet the figuration of the Revolution as the culmination of an intensive language-learning lesson whose final session included a summary view of what Jefferson termed the "great principles of right and wrong . . . legible to every reader" is too tame and orderly to encompass the heat, the passion, the violence, and the reciprocity of Revolutionary rhetoric and action (JLA, 121). The metaphor simply suggests a hierarchy of an educated elite instructing a subordinate populace. The Revolution must also be considered as a vernacular revolt, a talking back of students (and teachers) to the King's English, a disobedience that began with throwing snowballs and erasers behind (or at) the principal's back and escalated into a takeover of classrooms and administration buildings or into the sacking of Thomas Hutchinson's house and a Boston Tea Party as well as into a Declaration of Independence. In the crucible of the 1760s and 1770s, discontent and disgust, fear and courage, avarice and virtue, envy and ambition, piety and patriotism – all of these motives (and more) which were stirred up by the actions of the British and the words of colonial rabble rousers took hardened form in the rituals and rhetoric of political protest, and these hard words and symbolic actions were themselves subject to metamorphosis by popular pressures. To the mixture of evangelical rhetoric, republican discourse, legal argument, and economic discontent in the colonial crucible we must add, if we are to explain these times, the sheer pleasure and pride (or is it the vindictiveness and sense of vindication?) that must come when, in Langston Hughes's phrase, "the folks with no titles in front of their names" rear up and talk back "to the folks called mister."

> Hell, no! It's time to talk back now!
> History says it's time,

And the radio, too, foggy with propaganda
that says a mouthful
and don't mean half it says –
but is true anyhow:

> LIBERTY!
> FREEDOM!
> DEMOCRACY!

True anyhow no matter how many
Liars use those words.[130]

The clarification of governing words made foggy by propaganda – the
opposition to a long train of artifice, prevarication, and abuse – the
rectification of names – the defeat of an oldspeak or newspeak –
the calling a spade a spade – the reconstruction or deconstruction of
the word – the transfer of old words to new objects and objectives:
call it what you will, this is a necessary act in the drama of revolution,
and if it is to be successful it must be played out in a theater of public
space and receive the acclaim of an audience.

If the colonists considered themselves as innocent, as virtuous, and
as abused as Samuel Richardson's Clarissa, this was an exaggeration.
Unlike Clarissa, they were never denied so formidably access to pen
and press, and from their own education in the grammar of republican
discourse, they were never so naive about the stratagems of power.
Their education had helped to teach them what Jefferson said was one
of the vital lessons to be learned from the study of history (which he
recommended as a primary subject in the first stage of education): "It
will qualify them as judges of the actions and designs of men; it will
enable them to know ambition under every disguise it may assume;
and knowing it, to defeat its views" (JLA, 274). Indeed, like Moll
Flanders after her first seduction, the colonists after the Stamp Act
crisis increasingly began to distrust the artifices of aristocrats and
measure the promissory notes of words by their fulfillment in the cash
of deeds. Though never as innocent as Clarissa, the colonists shared
her predicament: they feared more heartless subjugation to their
parent's will; they dreaded a corruption of their virtue; and they
experienced new schemes of abuse and misrepresentation that countervailed their appeals for a redress of grievances. In short, they
became convinced, perhaps a bit like Don Quixote, that what they
saw in their world corresponded to what they had read so avidly in
their favorite books; they detected a plot to corrupt and to enslave
them. But to appreciate the American Revolution as a triumph of the
republican (and Christian) word disseminated by the press and animated by the orator, we must go beyond the inculcation of lessons

from political grammars or beyond Holmes's figuration of the Revolution as a language-learning lesson (i.e., a pedagogy of the oppressed) and place its campaign of symbolic action in the perspective of a protest, which began necessarily as a conspiracy, against a more literal form of slavery and a more severe abuse of civil rights. Speaking in 1941 for twelve million black voices, Richard Wright declared:

> We stole words from the grudging lips of the Lords of the Land, who did not want us to know too many of them or their meaning. And we charged this meager horde of stolen sounds with all the emotions and longings we had; we proceeded to build our language in inflections of voice, through tonal variety, by hurried speech, in honeyed drawls, by rolling our eyes, by flourishing our hands, by assigning to common, simple words, new meanings, meanings which enabled us to speak of revolt in the actual presence of the Lords of the Land without their being aware! Our secret language extended our understanding of what slavery meant and gave us the freedom to speak to our brothers in captivity; we polished our new words, caressed them, gave them shape and color, a new order and tempo, until, though they were the words of the Lords of the Land, they became *our* words, *our* language.[131]

The rhetoric of the American Revolution can be psychoanalyzed, anthropologized, and new-historicized; it can be subjected to computer analysis, Marxist analysis, and deconstructive analysis; but it must also be read as a poetry of protest and prophecy. It must be read, that is, as the poetry (or signifying) of a people who caressed words, who gave them shape and color, a new order and tempo, new accents and inflections, who charged them with their longings and aspirations and discontents, who stole them from their masters as strong poets must, and who regarded the word itself as magic – or the agency of saving conversions (and seductive falls). We must, in short, take the Loyalists more at their word: it was through the art or the artful use of the language of liberty that the revolution in the hearts and minds of the colonists was accomplished. To study the rhetoric of the Revolution, that is, we must attend not just to the grammars of political and religious discourse in the era, but to styles of their expression and to attitudes toward language and style itself.

Jefferson himself gives remarkable testimony to the power of the word when he claims in an 1825 letter that the "style and manner" of David Hume's *History of the Stuarts* was so "bewitching" that "his readers were unwilling to doubt anything, swallowed everything, and all England became Tories by the magic of his art." He adds, "His pen revolutionized the public sentiment of that country more completely than the standing armies could ever have done, which were so much dreaded and deprecated by the patriots of the day" (TJW, XVI, 126). Can Jefferson be serious here? If we doubt him too much, however, we can recall the power ascribed by contemporaries to the style of Paine's *Common Sense* (and to Jefferson's pen) and note that John Adams expressed a similar opinion regarding Hume's *History of England* and that Jefferson in *Notes on the State of Virginia* had earlier commented on instances "where the judgment has been seduced by a glowing pen" (JLA, 189). We can also gain perspective on the style Jefferson himself deployed in the Declaration by comparing his commentary on Hume's writing to another letter he composed in 1825. Whereas, he claims, Hume "revolutionized public sentiment" through the "magic of his art" in a history in which he "suppressed truths, advanced falsehoods, forged authorities, and falsified records," Jefferson asserts in a letter written several months earlier that it was the aim of his Declaration "to place before mankind the common sense of the subject, in terms so plain and firm as to command their assent" (TJW, XVI, 125–6; JLA, 1501). Jefferson here presents his Declaration as eschewing the wit and antithesis, the metaphor and allusion of a Walter Shandy (and the tyrannical manipulation of a David Hume). His Declaration is instead a natural act governed by principle, grounded in the facts, and compelled by the heart and thus similar to the rhetoric of Trim's antirhetorical drop of his hat. Indeed, just as Plato sought to counter the rhetorical magic of the Sophists, Jefferson's philosophy as written in the Declaration, like Paine's *Common Sense*, can be regarded as a counterstatement to the style and sophistry of Tory literature as well as a counterplea against the abuses perpetrated by the king and Parliament. If the "whole art of government consists in the art of being honest," as Jefferson declares in *A Summary View of the Rights of British America*, the whole art of the Declaration, it seems, is the art of crafting the honest sentence, the stylistic achievement later perfected by Ernest Hemingway, who joined Jefferson in a quest to write words faithful to facts and to the felt experience of a moral sense (or ethical code) stabbed by the betrayals, the cruelties, and the falsehoods of man – a wounding that demanded in response an assertion of what Jefferson called in the Declaration "manly spirit" or the lighting out to freedom on less well-traveled roads, one of which might lead to the next (or last) good country (JLA, 121).[132]

Of course Jefferson's Declaration, like Plato's *Republic*, is also a crafty rhetorical persuasion that resorts to what Sterne describes in *Tristram Shandy* as the "highest stretch of improvement a single word is capable of": "a high metaphor" (484). From the "course of human events" to the departure on a new "road to happiness & to glory," Jefferson encircles his Declaration in images that illuminate the path of the Revolution as a necessary journey from dependence to independence. But it is in his correspondence that he more fully elaborates in metaphor the significance of what his "plain and firm" terms declare. Echoing imagery that can be traced back to Plato's *Republic*, he writes, for instance, in the last extant letter of his life that the Fourth of July must be seen as a light unto the world, or a signal "of arousing men to burst the chains under which monkish ignorance and superstition had persuaded them to bind themselves" (JLA, 1517). For Jefferson, the course of human events in the Colonies, which necessitated an insurrection against the violations of the laws of nature and nature's God, was but part of a larger course of revolutionary events that began with the "insurrection . . . of science, talents and courage" against the false entitlements of "rank and birth" – an insurrection advanced by the idol smashing of Bacon's method and which continued in France as *idéologues* stormed the "Bastille of a word" to liberate the mind and pursue a revolutionary trinity of values: *liberté*, *égalité*, and *fraternité* (AJL, II, 391). Near the end of that last extant letter, Jefferson also expresses, not now in "plain and firm" terms but in a striking metaphor, the self-evident truth that the Revolution declared to the world: "The mass of mankind has not been born with saddles on their backs, nor a favored few booted and spurred, ready to ride them legitimately, by the grace of God" (JLA, 1517). Here, then, in his correspondence, is a style able to counter the magic of any of Hume's Tory histories, and almost everywhere, it seems, in his correspondence, especially in the letters he exchanged with John Adams in the last decade of his life, we can find not just a style but a dignity, a generosity, a literariness, a *humanitas*, a faith, a hope, or, in a phrase, a "communication of grandeur & of freedom" that remains a resource that can perhaps enlighten the public sentiment of a people divided by what Jefferson and Adams themselves transcended in their letters: the party spirit with its abuse of affection and mutual respect. "I like the dreams of the future better than the history of the past, – so good night! I will dream on, always fancying that Mrs. Adams and yourself are by my side marking the progress and the obliquities of ages and countries" (AJL, II, 485).

If it was the triumph of patriot preachers and pamphleteers to ventriloquize the language of the Bible and Whig literature so as to make Isaiah, Cato, Locke, and other classical and Christian heroes speak for their particular cause, then it was the design and consummate achievement of the Declaration to orchestrate those voices and harmonize those sentiments so that a particular cause could seem a universal one: a cause capable of commanding the assent of the opinions of mankind. "The American Revolution," as Garry Wills asserts, "was not born from a Pentecost of mutual understanding, but from a Babel."[133] The scholars of the Revolution who have excavated the many layers of Revolutionary discourse and who have participated in the mapping of a "republican synthesis" and those who have examined the mechanics of political mobilization and who have turned to anthropology, psychology, and economics to illuminate the deep structure of transformational political grammars have enabled us to understand more fully how committees of correspondence and even a pentecost of mutual understanding could emerge from a babel of tongues in the thirteen colonies. To turn that babel into a pentecost (or just into consensus), more was needed, however, than shared vocabularies, economic aspirations, parliamentary provocation, and orators capable of Orphic or Trim-like eloquence: it required something of a Pentecostal spirit – a spirit born from a sense of shared sacrifice, a spirit that found in unmerciful self-interest and the unfeeling cruelty of a Pharoah (or a King George III) the greatest of sins, a spirit, in short, that was cultivated by evangelical preaching and tributes to republican virtue, by fast days and the remembrance of martyrs and even by the values of Enlightenment style and manners. "No man is a true republican that will not give up his single voice to that of the public," maintained a Pennsylvania pamphleteer in 1776.[134] The fundamental rule that had few exceptions in the grammar of republican discourse is this demand, that when "true republicans" speak and act in public, they must prefer to do so in the voice of the first or second person plural: a "we" must speak for an "I," a "you" for a "me."[135] Ambition had to be transmuted into emulation. The language of republican politics demanded, that is, not the assertion of self-interest or even the liberty of self-expression but the development of a representative voice or the freedom to engage in public conversation that would define and advance the concerns of the vox populi and that would be highly attentive to what the courtly ear of England was no longer willing or able to hear in Jefferson's opinion – "the voice of justice and of consanguinity." From the colonists' point of view, the court of England had first betrayed a decent respect to the opinions of mankind by failing to engage in what Jefferson called in a letter of advice to his grandson Thomas Jefferson Randolph the practice of "politeness," by which he meant "the practice of sacrificing to those whom we meet in society all the little conveniences and preferences which will gratify them, and deprive us of nothing worth a moment's consideration; it is the giving a pleasing and flattering turn to our expressions which will conciliate others, and make them pleased with us as well as themselves" (JLA, 1195). This habit of conciliation and consensus, this practice of self-effacement and rising above (or muting) contradiction, so often praised in the era of the Enlightenment – even Dr. Johnson and John Wilkes could engage in polite conversation – but so averse to a Romantic temperament less troubled by the voicing of natural (or ruling) passions, is in part the practice that facilitated Jefferson's and Franklin's own success in drafting for the invention of America the blueprints of a *novus ordo seclorum* that distilled from a babel of tongues "a communication of grandeur & of freedom."[136]

Here, in this Shandean meditation, I will ride my hobbyhorse a bit further and digress from the conclusion of the Declaration to its preamble in order to suggest how Jefferson's assertion of an inalienable right to the "pursuit of happiness" – a phrase that Bentham looked upon as nonsense – demanded in Jefferson's mind precisely what England had betrayed: a "communication of grandeur & of freedom." For Jefferson, the pursuit of happiness was neither a vague phrase nor a felicitous substitution for the third party in Locke's triumvirate: property. To unlock the significance of this phrase for Jefferson, we need to detour (as Jefferson sometimes did) around Locke and follow the path reopened by Garry Wills, a path which leads, ironically, to a work written by a student whom Locke tutored and which was seminal for the development of the moral sense school of philosophy and which Jefferson read early in his career: *Characteristics of Men, Manners, Opinions, Times*, by Anthony Ashley Cooper, third Earl of Shaftesbury.

Against Locke's insistence that our ideas of virtue and right are conventional, not innate, and against Hobbes's and Mandeville's dark view of a human nature devoid, in Shaftesbury's words, of "natural affection and wholly destitute of a communicative or social principle," Shaftesbury posits the presence of a moral sense, an intuitive faculty that makes possible a *sensus communis*, or a common sentiment regarding what is virtuous and just and right.[137] The development of this moral sense in social acts – in acts, for instance, of kindness and love, of sorrow and sympathy, of gratitude and generosity, of pity and succor, of grief and good humor, of converse and correspondence – was for Shaftesbury (and Jefferson) the exercise that more than any other defined a pursuit of happiness and enabled the creation of more perfect unions and the overcoming of the imperfections of language as the logical means to such unions. For Shaftesbury, in short, the "enjoyment of participation and community" derived from our engagement in a social world was "essential to our happiness" (I, 299). "We find," he asserts, that the exercise of "social affections and human sympathy, is of the highest delight, and affords a greater enjoyment in the way of thought and sentiment" than the indulgence of any other "sense and common appetite" (I, 297–8).

In Treatise IV of the *Characteristics*, entitled "An Inquiry Concerning Virtue or Merit," Shaftesbury examines the constitution of man and distinguishes between three parts of the soul that check and balance or rival each other for power during those inner dialogues of the soul that he always sought to encourage. In descending merit, he lists: (1) the "natural affections, which lead to the good of the public"; (2) the "self affections, which lead only to the good of the private"; and (3) the "unnatural affections," which lead to neither public nor private good (I, 286). Our "chief happiness," he explains, is to be derived "from the mental pleasures," and since "the chief mental pleasures" "are founded in natural affection, it follows 'that to have the natural affections is to have the chief means and power of self-enjoyment, the highest possession and happiness of life'" (I, 309). On the contrary, Shaftesbury argues, "whoever is unsociable, and voluntarily shuns society or commerce with the world, must of necessity be morose and ill-natured" (I, 315). He adds that "princes, monarchs, and those who seem by their condition to be above ordinary human commerce, and who affect a sort of distant strangeness from the rest of mankind" are particularly liable to this temperament. Indeed, what Shaftesbury denominates, in a revealing phrase, as the "tyrannical temperament" is denoted above all by a "bitterness, cruelty, and mistrust which belong to that solitary and gloomy state of uncommunicative and unfriendly greatness" (I, 316).

For Jefferson, it was King George III's uncommunicativeness and unnatural hard-heartedness, or more specifically his unfeeling willingness to disrupt through his acts not just a commerce of trade and an exchange of material goods but a commerce of affections and an exchange of mutual sympathies – his interruption, in the words of the Declaration, of "our connection and correspondence" – that defined his "character" as that of a "tyrant unfit to be the ruler of a people who mean to be free" and which demanded a formal dissolution of "political bands." For Shaftesbury, for Jefferson, for Paine, and for very many Enlightenment writers from Joseph Addison to Dr. Johnson, the antidote to this embargo on the natural affections – to the deafness to common sense that marked the tyrant as well as the madman or fanatic – was to submit oneself to the voice of public conversation (including its wit and raillery) or to engage in a free trade of communication with the opinions of mankind, a correspondence with the world such as Jefferson drafted for the Continental Congress in early July 1776 and such as he maintained throughout his career as an essential part of his own pursuit of happiness. The concluding words of this paragraph belong to Shaftesbury, but I believe they also speak for the Jefferson who wrote the parting words of the Declaration, which are so full, almost paradoxically, of regret and good riddance to "our British brethren": ". . . and besides the pleasure to be found in social entertainment, language, and discourse, there is so apparent a necessity for continuing this good correspondency and union, that to have no sense or feeling of this kind, no love of country, community, or anything in common, would be the same as to be insensible even of the plainest means of self-preservation, and most necessary condition of self-enjoyment" (I, 74).[138]

To talk back to an England grown insensible and corrupt, to fight the restriction on trade, the colonists found themselves talking together, taking occasion after occasion, whether they liked it or not (and John Adams for one did not always like it), to show off their taste for oratory, their talent at criticism, and their love of theater, and their facility at composition – the skills, in short, that made many of the colonists masters of rhetoric in an age that shaped (or enslaved) the school-bred to be rhetorical creatures. By talking or writing in caucus clubs, in committees of correspondence, in churches, and in the Continental Congress, the colonists engaged in what Benjamin Barber describes as the essential activity of politics: strong affective talk, or talk that seeks to develop a "we" from an assembly of "I's" by advancing mutual concerns and by breaking down the closed doors of exclusion and privilege.[139] Through this talk and in these forums, the colonists, in Jack Hexter's helpful metaphor, fashioned upon the loom of language a fabric of imperatives, which they wove and unwove and rewove as they awaited (more impatiently than Penelope awaiting the homecoming of Ulysses) the return of what Jefferson termed in 1775 their just rights (JLA, 749). They gathered many of the materials for their homespun fabric from the fields of republican discourse; they harvested some from the Bible; and, most important, in 1776 they were willing to dye a new fabric of imperatives with their blood. The final achievement of the Declaration was something akin to a communally sewn quilt of thirteen patches under which most were willing to sleep (though not necessarily together). To switch the metaphor, in the forges of public meetings, in the streets, in pamphlets, in parishes, wordsmiths melted down and recast and hammered out and tempered an enabling rhetoric which not only justified old actions and current desires but sanctioned and fostered new acts of independence. A British pundit was not amused by this smithing (and bellowing) of the Colonists. Complaining about an "increase in felonies," which he ascribed to the "puritanic petulance of the Americans," he composed an epigram in 1775 for the *Gazetteer* – "That some turn robbers, there's no doubt / Our Boston Saints have brought about" – and added a commentary: "While they [the colonists] from more sordid motives are forging forced meanings to the words *consent*, *representation*, etc. our manufacturers experience the meanings of the words *want* and *misery* in their full extent."[140] Another Tory supporter could only explain the phenomenal achievement of colonial protest in winning over the hearts and minds of the colonists by offering an explanation that recalls Sterne's revelations in *Tristram Shandy* about how such words as "nose" and "whiskers" can pick up associated ideas that defy logic and the definitions of a dictionary: "The words king, parliament, ministers, governors, *mandamus* councillors, revenue tea &c. carry the idea of slavery with them, while with as little color or reason the words congress, charter, patriots, delegates, charter councillors, independence, coffee &c. carry with them all powers of necromancy to conjure down the spirit of tyranny."[141] What finally emerged from the forge of the Continental Congress and particularly from Jefferson's personal act of republican synthesis is what Moses Coit Tyler describes in his grandiloquent literary analysis of the Declaration as "the most commanding and the most pathetic utterance, in any age, in any language, of national grievances and of national purposes; having a Demosthenic momentum of thought, and a fervor of emotional appeal such as Tyrtaeus might have put into his war-songs. Indeed, the Declaration of Independence is a kind of war-song; it is a stately and a passionate chant of freedom; it is a prose lyric of civil and military heroism."[142]

To associate as freely as Tyler (or Tristram Shandy), the invention of America as proclaimed in the Declaration can be regarded as the last riff of a jazz improvisation grounded in a legacy of blues experience and sustained by a gospel vision of liberation and the victory of God's Word; or it is a bricolage shaped by the materials, the technologies, and the languages at hand. The necessity that was the mother of this invention, the inspiration for the song, was at least in part a fiction of the imagination: the dream of a virtuous new world sustained and dignified by what Jefferson called in his Declaration a "communication of grandeur & of freedom." Here in the phrase we can recognize a vision that is perhaps more representative of the dream that has animated American artists than the more univocal vision of America as a city on a hill. It is the dream of a communication that would match in its eloquence and epic grandeur, in its liberty and honesty, the speech of a people committed to faith in the self-evident truths enunciated by the Declaration.

The striking out from Jefferson's draft of the Declaration the passage containing this phrase and the crucial removal of Jefferson's conflicted critique of the king's perpetuation of the slave trade, which begins with the condemnation "He has waged cruel war against human nature" but ends with a protest against the king's provocation of a slave revolt (i.e., a pursuit of liberty) against colonial masters (e.g., a Jefferson), are but the first diminishments of this dream which Jefferson committed to writing and the Colonies to enactment in the summer of 1776. The deep diminishment of this dream – its perversion in the nightmare of slavery and the recurring physical and psychic horror of that abuse – is the topic that Melville, Stowe, Twain, and Faulkner, for instance, were unwilling to edit from their writing as Jefferson himself did to some extent when he was unable to name slavery directly in a letter describing how "the momentous question" of the Missouri Compromise had, "like a fire bell in the night, awakened and filled" him with "terror." Confronting the terror defensively, Jefferson allowed "that there is not a man on earth who would sacrifice more than I would to relieve us from this heavy reproach [i.e., slavery] in any *practicable* way." Then, in a linguistic subterfuge he acknowledged but would not amend, he added, "The cession of that kind of property, for so it is misnamed, is a bagatelle which would not cost me a second thought, if, in that way, a general emancipation and *expatriation* could be effected" (JLA, 1434). On the subject of slavery, Jefferson could not write an honest sentence, it seems, except for a statement on slavery in *Notes on the State of Virginia*, which remarkably duplicates a passage from the second paragraph of the Declaration in its syntactical repetition of clauses beginning with "that" and in its chain of logic leading from the premise that our "liberties are of the gift of God" and that "they are not to be violated but with his wrath" to the conclusion justifying revolution against tyrants as obedience to God: "Indeed I tremble for my country when I reflect that God is just: that his justice cannot sleep for ever: that considering numbers, nature and natural means only, a revolution of the wheel of fortune, an exchange of situation, is among possible events: that it may become probable by supernatural interference!" (JLA, 289).[143] It was left to Nat Turner and John Brown (to some of their contemporaries supernatural apparitions of Christ or the Devil) and to Frederick Douglass in "The Heroic Slave" and to Herman Melville in *Benito Cereno* to develop the sequels to Jefferson's forebodings.

If the Declaration can be regarded as the charter of a newly incorporated (and monopolistic) power and light company whose primary resource of energy is the language itself, those words have continued to generate and conduct power (or hegemony) by calling forth in response the voices that were silent (or ignored) in the consensus of 1776. The phrase "We hold these truths to be self-evident, that all men are created equal" was for Lincoln in 1858 "the electric cord" that "links the hearts of patriotic and liberty-loving men together, that will link those patriotic hearts as long as the love of freedom exists in the minds of men throughout the world."[144] Beware of shocks, but tap into that electric cord and illuminate the darkness and the blackness of America and the infinite possibilities of every soul, Ralph Ellison seems to advise in *Invisible Man*, especially at the end when his narrator is reflecting upon the ambiguous last words of his grandfather: "Did he mean to affirm the principle, which they themselves had dreamed into being out of the chaos and darkness of the feudal past, and which they had violated and compromised to the point of absurdity even in their own corrupt minds? . . . Was it that we of all, we, most of all, had to affirm the principle, the plan in whose name we had been brutalized and sacrificed . . . ?[145] Dispossession by the word and repossession of the word are the typological acts at the heart of Ellison's novel, and this reciprocal action can be perceived as the systolic and diastolic movements sustaining the life of classic American narratives (both fictional and historical). Let me conclude this meditation with more counsel by Langston Hughes, who advises us in "Freedom's Plow" that to challenge the corruption of such words as "freedom," "liberty," and "democracy" we must keep plowing up the dirt as we nurture the seeds sown by Jefferson in the Declaration (and by Lincoln and Douglass).

A long time ago, but not too long ago, a man said:

ALL MEN ARE CREATED EQUAL . . .
ENDOWED BY THEIR CREATOR
WITH CERTAIN UNALIENABLE
    RIGHTS . . .
AMONG THESE LIFE, LIBERTY
AND THE PURSUIT OF HAPPINESS.

His name was Jefferson. There were slaves then,
But in their hearts the slaves believed him, too,
And silently took for granted
That what he said was also meant for them.
. . . .
ALL MEN ARE CREATED EQUAL.

NO MAN IS GOOD ENOUGH
TO GOVERN ANOTHER MAN WITHOUT
THAT OTHER'S CONSENT.

BETTER DIE FREE
THAN LIVE SLAVES.

Who said those things? Americans!
Who owns those words? America!
Who is America? You, me!
We are America!
To the enemy who would conquer us from without,
We say, NO!
To the enemy who would divide
And conquer us from within,
We say, NO!

FREEDOM!
BROTHERHOOD!
DEMOCRACY!

To all the enemies of these great words:
We say, NO!
. . . .
KEEP YOUR HAND ON THE PLOW!
HOLD ON![146]

To oppose the enemies of those words, we can become, in effect, what Jefferson himself was: a farmer of the word who cultivated not just a style of grace but a habit of turning words over in his mind, who developed schemes for improving the study of the English language and encouraged "new compositions of its elements" and a "free use of its faculties," who sought (as did Plato) to plant the seeds of "public right" in the soil of new fields and new souls, and who was willing, if necessary, to hold fast to freedom's plow by manuring those fields with the blood of tyrants, but who preferred to develop forums of education (including his own writings) that would open up minds to what Captain Vere mutes on the *Bellipotent* – the voice of the moral sense and the laws of nature and nature's God (JLA, 1299).[147] Jefferson's vision of America as an agrarian republic maintained by yeomen who possess and cultivate their own parcel of land is the dream of the past – a pastoral vision complicated by Jefferson's own acute awareness of the advance of the machine into the garden; but Jefferson's (and Hughes's) vision of a republic maintained by citizens each possessing a sense of property in the words of the Declaration and of a people committed to developing and enlarging that sphere of property not just for themselves but for new owners is the dream (and challenge) that can continue to court the industry of husbandmen and women in the future.[148]

The New Semiotic of Republican Politics

What Thomas Jefferson and the founders of the United States accomplished when they did what Thomas Paine urged them to do –

declare themselves independent from the rule of King George III and elect the law as their king – was to write a new chapter in what we could call the semiotics of politics: a story whose main plot is the conflict between the powers of a king's words – the efficacy of his sentences and his proclamations – and the voices of other people, whether those people were barons at Runnymede, aristocrats assembled in Parliament, colonists meeting in committees of correspondence, the vox populi embodied in customary law, or the "We, the people" that begins the Constitution, a "we" whose antonym is the royal "we" of a King George or a King Lear. It is the story of people circumscribing the powers of a king with smaller and smaller circles, reducing the crown to a symbol; more precisely, it is the story of people defining those powers (i.e., limiting the sway of a king's voice) in written documents, eventually erasing the royal prerogative and inking it over with the rule of law. The story is truly a drama, for at its basis is a conflict of interests and wills, a play of oppositions, a play of differences, a play we could entitle *The Word Against the Word*. The phrase is borrowed from Shakespeare's *Richard II*, a historical drama about the deposition of a king that is not unlike the action that occurs in the theater of American politics in July 1776. Indeed, what Shakespeare presents in *Richard II* as well as in *King Lear* (and in a number of his other plays) is the dynamic for understanding the development in the seventeenth century of a contractual theory of language and government that the American Revolution would help bring to fulfillment; for both developments begin in a decentering of authority from a divine or sovereign figure and its recentering or reconstitution in a more popular source: the people themselves or their representatives.

Monarchical authority in Tudor–Stuart England was premised on the idea that the monarch derived his or her authority not from the consent of the people but from God, and that the royal word, like God's creating Word, was omnipotent. A king's sentence or proclamation implied action; it brought about the state of affairs it named. In Shakespeare's *Richard II* and *King Lear* the strength of a king can be measured by the power of his words to command obedience, and his loss of power by a growing willingness on the part of others – and then on his own part – to recognize that kingship may not be a God-given or natural distinction but a title given to a "bare forked animal" and consented to by others. In the openings of both plays, each king possesses an unshakable belief in his ability to command, and their dictates do become fact. But then Richard collides with Bolingbroke and Lear with Edmund, Goneril, and Regan, characters who deny that a king's word has an inherent potency or absolute authority. Edmund, for instance, asserts that it is the plague of custom and not nature that

brands bastards as illegitimate and base, and Bolingbroke recognizes
that the power of a king is not derived from God but from the will of
the people or their willingness to bear arms for him, and that such
power can be gained by courting and winning powerful friends.
Bolingbroke may not be able to ascend the throne in God's name, but
he can ascend it in the name of an applauding populace and with the
force of twenty thousand armed men. Shakespeare thus creates a
world where such moral and political distinctions as kingship and
bastardy become fictions of the social imagination and where the
authority of a word does not derive from nature or from the sovereign
will of a king or an author; instead they are social determinations, a
product, in contemporary terms, of ideology and power relations, or a
matter, in Jefferson's terms, of what people are willing to hold in
common as truth or as self-evident.

In *King Lear* and *Richard II* the questioning and denial of a king's
authority go hand in hand with a questioning and denial of the verbal
authority of a sovereign will, and the answer that is given – that kingship, like the meaning of a word, is constituted by consent – is the
conclusion that John Locke and other Englishmen would reach in the
seventeenth century. As M. M. Mahood suggests, "In a process that
took some two centuries, the question [which Shakespeare asks]
'What's in a name?' was to destroy authority." She adds, "To doubt
the real relationship between name and nominee, between a word and
the thing it signified, was to shake the whole structure of Elizabethan
thought and society."[149] The question, however, did not destroy authority but reconstitute it, a process that can be glimpsed in a passage
from another Shakespeare play.

In Act IV, Scene 5, of *Hamlet* – a play that continually asks, "What's
in a name?" – a messenger rushes into court and informs Claudius that
the rabble have begun to cry, "Laertes shall be king!" In the an-
nouncement, the messenger also gives a short dissertation on the
collapse of one form of political and linguistic authority and locates its
new center.

> The rabble call him lord,
> And, as the world were now but to begin,
> Antiquity forgot, custom not known,
> The ratifiers and props of every word,
> They cry, "Choose we! Laertes shall be king!"
>
> (IV.5.106–10)

To ignore the authority of custom and antiquity – the ratifiers and
props of every word – is not merely to undermine the socially established meanings of words but the legitimacy of social distinctions and

the established order of things which words inscribe; this is the challenge that Hamlet makes throughout the play, and this is the challenge that rabble-rousers and rebels, such as Paine and Jefferson, would make in Revolutionary America. When Paine in *Common Sense* challenged the custom and antiquity that ratified and propped up the rule of kings in Britain, and when he and Jefferson sought to make common sense and the truths of nature held self-evident by a "we" the new ratifiers and props of government and its language, they were completing a process that began in the Renaissance: the authority of the sovereign to legislate and define is transferred to the rabble or to the representatives of the people. The vox populi replaces the voice of the king as the spokesman for the vox Dei. The people become the ultimate source of signification in both law and language; they gain the power to inscribe their words on the blank sheet of the world. Government and the world can begin anew. The divine right to name and give meaning become the right of humanity: in the beginning is the word of We, the People. In contractual political theory, that is, the people or constituency who had once listened to and obeyed the dictates of a sovereign authority becomes participants in the creation of authority and law, just as in contractual linguistic theory the reader who had once been conceived of as the passive recipient of meaning willed by a sovereign author becomes a participant in the constitution of that meaning. Long live the readers of the Constitution.[150]

8

The Grammar of Politics:
The Constitution

> The American Constitutions were to liberty, what a grammar is to language: they define its parts of speech, and practically construct them into syntax.
>
> Thomas Paine, *The Rights of Man*

Soon after the signing of the Treaty of Paris, which formally concluded the Revolutionary War, leading Americans began to discuss among themselves how to create a more perfect union that would secure the blessings of liberty and avoid the dangers of democracy that Shays's Rebellion portended. Their aim in part was to create a government that would restrict the potential for misrule by the demagogue and the mob – or by the majorities in the state legislatures – and provide a local habitation for such words as "liberty," which had, in their view, been corrupted by the British into an "airy nothing" and was now being misinterpreted by the American people. "The meaning of the word *liberty* has been contested," declares Alexander Hamilton in 1784. Opposed to the disenfranchisement of ex-Tories sponsored by the New York state legislature, Hamilton protests, "The name liberty applied to such a government" that makes a man "the innocent victim of the prevailing faction" "would be a mockery of common sense." He insists instead that the "true sense" of "liberty" must be "the enjoyment of the common privileges of subjects under the same government."[1] Others were no more sanguine that the "true sense" of liberty would prevail in the contests of the day. "It is really very curious to observe," remarks Edward Rutledge in a letter to John Jay in 1786, "how the people of this world are made the dupes of a word. 'Liberty' is the motto; every attempt to restrain licentiousness or give efficacy to Government is charged audaciously on the real advocates for Freedom as an attack upon Liberty."[2] Looking back at the era

270

between 1776 and 1787 in her *History of the Rise, Progress and Termination of the American Revolution,* Mercy Warren observes, "Few had yet formed any adequate ideas, and fewer indeed were sensible, that though the name of *liberty* delights the ear, and tickles the fond pride of man, it is a jewel much oftener the play-thing of his imagination, than a possession of real stability."[3]

But it was a band of poets – David Humphreys, John Trumbull, Joel Barlow, and Lemuel Hopkins – who cast some of the nastiest aspersions on the fate of liberty in America after the Revolution when they began publishing in October 1786 in the *New Haven Gazette, and the Connecticut Magazine* their mock-epic collaboration *The Anarchiad,* whose first of twelve installments ends in an ominous vision: "Thy constitution, Chaos, is restor'd; / Law sinks before thy uncreating word; / Thy hand unbars th'unfathom'd gulf of fate, / And deep in darkness 'whelms the new-born state."[4] The turbulent voices of chaos that drown out the voice of law in this satire spring from no other sources than "The giddy rage of democratic States, / Whose pop'lar breath, high-blown in restless tide, / No laws can temper, and no reason guide" and from the "wild demagogues" who lead "the factious crowd, / Mean, fierce, imperious, insolent and loud."[5] These concerns about how the people and the state legislatures were translating into practice abstract notions of liberty and republicanism testify to what Gordon Wood (following John Dickinson) has called the increasing fears of the "worthy" few about the "licentious" many, and it was this distrust of democracy in practice that played no small part in the call for a constitutional convention in Philadelphia and in the penning of a federal Constitution that would be the supreme law of the land.[6]

John Adams's *Defence of the Constitutions,* written in 1786 while he was serving as the first United States minister to Great Britain, captures more diffusely than *The Anarchiad* but just as desperately the darkening mood of the leaders of the Revolution, who were troubled by the dissipation of virtue in the new republic. "The passions and appetites are parts of human nature, as well as reason and the moral sense," Adams starkly observes, and in the three-volume *Defence of the Constitutions* he invokes Thucydides' portrait of the *stasis* in Corcyra and a wide range of political and historical works to teach his audience that the antidote to the excesses Thucydides describes – and that he (and others) feared at that moment in America – was a "well ordered constitution" (JAW, VI, 115, 219). "If men were angels, no government would be necessary," declares James Madison in *The Federalist* (FP, 51.322), and Adams strongly concurred in this sentiment. "In the institution of government, it must be remembered," he asserts, "that, although reason ought always to govern individuals, it certainly never did since the Fall, and never will till the Millennium" (JAW, VI, 115). "The virtues have been the effect of the well ordered constitution, and not the cause," Adams insists, and to create such a well-ordered constitution that would balance reason, virtue, and power against passion, prejudice, and liberty, he recognized, as did Madison, it would be necessary not just to counter the vices of fallen man but to counter the "confusion of languages" which exists "in the science of legislation . . . as if men were but lately come from Babel" (JAW, V, 452). "How is it possible," Adams asks, "that whole nations should be made to comprehend the principles and rules of government, until they shall learn to understand one another's meaning by words?" (JAW, V, 453). To oppose the extremes of anarchy and tyranny, and to remedy what Madison called in April 1787 the "Vices of the Political System of the United States," what was needed, they felt, is what they both studied history to develop and what Madison politicked for in 1786 and 1787: the advancement of a new science of politics whose reform of language would transform a state approaching chaos into a new order of the ages. Such a creation, drafted by the Constitutional Convention, helped inspire Joel Barlow to write not an amendment to *The Anarchiad* but an entirely new epic, *The Vision of Columbus*, later revised as *The Columbiad*.

For Thomas Paine, "the American Constitutions were to liberty, what a grammar is to language: they define its parts of speech, and practically construct them into syntax" (TPW, I, 300). The framers of the United States Constitution probably would not have been surprised by Paine's image of a constitution as a grammar; indeed, some of them were probably familiar with Condillac's assertion that a "science is a well-made language."[7] And they might well have conceived of their experiment in the science of politics as an attempt to do for that science what Antoine Lavoisier was doing for chemistry in 1787. In the year the delegates met in Philadelphia and drafted the Constitution, Lavoisier set forth his belief in *Méthode de nomenclature chimique* that a "well-made language adapted to the natural and successive order of ideas will bring in its train a necessary and immediate revolution in the methods of teaching, and will not allow teachers of chemistry to deviate from the course of nature; either they must reject the nomenclature or they must irresistibly follow the course marked out by it." "The logic of the sciences," he adds, "is thus essentially dependent on their language."[8] The founding fathers similarly sought to develop a well-made language adapted to the natural order of things (or to the nature of people) that would bring about a fundamental change in the method of conducting government. They based that language on their observations of human nature and of the fate of past republics, and they hoped that future generations would follow its nomenclature (or adapt it when necessary). The logic of American politics has been dependent on that language ever since. Or, as William Harris writes, what the logic of American constitutionalism manifests is "the radical bond of *word and power* – born together, and together generating order."[9]

Because the framers understood the imperfections of language as an instrument of science and logic, they did not ignore a point often glossed over in the years that followed the ratification of the Constitution: since the Constitution is written in a fundamentally imperfect human language, the text – and the political order it creates – possesses the fundamental imperfections of language itself. As Benjamin Franklin advised them, the framers of the Constitution should doubt their infallibility, and, he might have added, they should doubt the infallibility of the Constitution; and many of them, including James Madison and Patrick Henry, discussed the faults of the Constitution in terms of its imperfect and ambiguous language. And it was precisely the ambiguities they noted that would become the major fault lines along which the Constitution would fracture during the stress that preceded the Civil War. Unavoidably, the Constitution enshrines ambiguity; purposefully, the text quarrels with itself; necessarily, at times, but only for a time, the quarreling must stop: these moments, these stays against confusion, these judicial resolutions of conflict are acts of clarification – definitive opinions shaped in and for the present. Often, all too often, we prefer to believe, we prefer to argue, we pretend that these decisions are not opinions, or judgments of an arbitrary text (i.e., a text whose meaning must be arbitrated), or a selective choice from a range of competing political values, but discoveries or revelations – even the resurrection of an original intention from the dead letter.

During the battles over the Constitution in the new republic, the contending parties seldom acknowledged that their own side was doing anything different from what Edwin Meese, as the attorney general in Ronald Reagan's administration, urged courts to do: discover the "original meaning" of constitutional provisions and federal statutes. Meese maintains that there is "a danger in seeing the Constitution as an empty vessel into which each generation may pour its passion and prejudice."[10] Perhaps a greater danger arises, however, when we fail to understand or acknowledge how our Constitution, since its very beginning, has indeed been something of an empty vessel into which each generation has poured its passion and prejudice, a consequence that our founding fathers were not blind to, thanks in part to their reading of Enlightenment literature and philosophy. One day after adjourning the Constitutional Convention on September 17, 1787, George Washington mailed a copy of the Constitution to the Marquis de Lafayette. He added a note of apprehension, "It is now a Child of fortune to be fostered by some and buffeted by others."[11] Even more revealing, when Washington drew up his own final will, he included an elaborate arbitration provision designed, in the event of a dispute over the will's terms, to allow a determination of intentions "unfettered by law or legal construction."[12] Washington, it seems, was as wary of the constructions of lawyers as Locke and Swift, and in the generation that followed his presidency Americans were often convinced that the sons of the founding fathers were on the verge of tearing apart the political fabric of their country as they disputed the terms of the "will" of their fathers.

What Americans confronted from the beginning in their attempt to create and preserve a constitutional order in a country devoted to the pursuit of liberty was the conflict that Locke presents in Book III of his *Essay* between man's "inviolable liberty" to make a word stand for whatever ideas he pleases and the need to compromise that liberty if a society is to enjoy the benefits of political order. Like Locke, Americans in the era of the new republic understood how likely it was that words would be interpreted in "private and unusual senses," and they too were convinced that, in John Adams's words, the "latitude" for differences of definition in the language of legislation "allows a scope for politicians to speculate, like merchants with false weights, artificial credit, or base money, and to deceive the people, by making the same word adored by one party, and execrated by another" (JAW, V, 452). "The union of a people," he adds, is rendered impossible "because superstition, prejudice, habit, and passions, are so differently attached to words, that you can scarcely make any nation understand itself" (ibid.). These linguistic convictions, this wariness of merchants of the word and their buyers, helped lead the framers (and ratifiers) to consider very judiciously the meaning and implications of the words of the Constitution drafted in Philadelphia. A more perfect union demanded a more perfect linguistic contract. Adams, undeterred by his own logic, wrote *Defence of the Constitutions* to overcome a babel of tongues by supplying etymologies and definitions for such words as "republic." Similarly, the framers gathered in Philadelphia on May 14, 1787, to confront and transcend the dialects of liberty and republicanism in the state legislatures. Come September, the framers would prescribe a standard language, a grammar of political rules to structure the articulation of the vox populi and improve its pronunciation.

At times, however, in the middle of the summer, a more perfect union grounded in a common language seemed as impossible as Adams thought.

The Constitutional Convention: Crafting Linguistic Consensus

The records of the federal convention reveal that debates over the language of the document were numerous and that the framers made a concerted effort to do what Locke advised: annex clear ideas to their words. For instance, the provision giving Congress the power to negate "improper" state laws, the "necessary and proper" clause, and a provision concerning the removal of a president in case of a disability are criticized as too vague or indefinite. In addition, during the debates there were more than several objections that such terms as "states," "sovereignty," "national," "federal," and "revenue" were being used inaccurately, ambiguously, or deceptively (NFC, 152). The words "residence," "incompetent," "duties," "imposts" and "amend or alter" also became the subject of debate, prompting calls for more analysis of ideas and for exact definitions (NFC, 43–4, 217, 402–3, 406–7, 445–6, 466). Not surprisingly, Benjamin Franklin, who stresses in his *Autobiography* how he taught himself with the help of Locke to avoid the habit of "Contradiction and positive Argumentation" and who had once copied out extracts from John Wilkins's plan for a universal language, was dismayed by the constant disputes over phrasing and the different sentiments of the delegates on each issue. In an address to the convention, Franklin admitted that these disputes gave him "melancholy proof of the imperfection of the Human Understanding" (NFC, 209). Fearing that the framers would succeed in their political building no better than the builders of Babel, he called upon them to humbly apply to "the Father of lights to illuminate our understandings" (ibid.). Not divine inspiration, however, but down-in-the-mud give-and-take, or, in a word, compromise – combined with silence and the cover-up of contradiction – made possible the construction of a consensus. At the end of the convention, Franklin, an icon of pragmatism and Melville's epitome of the confidence man, stands forth as the model representative of this composing process: "Thus I consent, Sir, to this Constitution because I expect no better, and because I am not sure, that it is not the best. The opinions I have had of its errors, I sacrifice to the public good" (NFC, 654).

When it came to the problem of interpreting their own work, the framers understood that they could depend neither on divine illumination nor on the republican virtue of sacrifice of self-interest; instead they rested their hopes on the faith that the Constitution would be interpreted like other written legal documents in the common law tradition by privileging the meanings of its words as accepted by the ratifying parties. But from their own experience with the common law and from their own understanding of the nature of language, the framers accepted – usually very warily but sometimes with some wiles – the inevitability of construction of the Constitution that would be something more than or something less than or something different from a discovery of its contractual meaning. For instance, when a friend told Gouverneur Morris, a delegate from Pennsylvania, "You have given us a good Constitution," Morris replied, "That depends on how it is construed."[13] And Timothy Bloodworth simply declared in the North Carolina ratifying convention: "Gentlemen of the best abilities differ in the construction of the Constitution. The members of the Congress will differ too. Human nature is fallible."[14]

This acceptance of differences of construction, with its liabilities and potentials, is no more clearly revealed than in a discussion during the convention between two delegates, Pierce Butler, from South Carolina, and Nathaniel Ghorum of Massachusetts. At one point Butler complained that the vagueness of the word "incompetent" in the provision granting Congress the right "to legislate in all cases to which the separate States are incompetent," rendered it "impossible for any precise judgment to be formed" about the extent of that power (NFC, 298). Ghorum, however, countered Butler's objection with the observation "The vagueness of the terms constitutes the propriety of them. We are now establishing general principles, to be extended hereafter into details which will be precise & explicit" (ibid.). The comments of Ghorum and Butler suggest that the framers were by no means naive about the dangers of ambiguous words, and some were by no means naive about their virtues. Like Tocqueville, they understood that an abstract word was a box with a false bottom, and they guarded against any attempt by charlatans, demagogues, or lawyers to force their own ideas into that box or pull their own ideas out of it. But also, just as Tocqueville recognized that abstract words could be a "great merit" (as well as a "great imperfection") because they could enlarge thoughts, so too Ghorum and others saw that vague words could be a virtue because they could enlarge the potential for general agreement and suit the text to what John Marshall termed "the various *crises* of human affairs." Indeed, Ghorum's comments support the view of Leonard Levy that the framers had "a genius for studied imprecision or calculated ambiguity." It was the framers' design, Levy contends, to delineate the structure of American national government and to avoid the minute specifications of power that would become obsolete with change. Thus they tended to formulate abstract principles that would necessarily be particularized by future readers of the Constitution.[15] "Like every text worth reading," Justice William J. Brennan, Jr., observed during the bicentennial celebrations, "it [the Constitution] is not crystalline. . . . Its majestic generalities and ennobling pronouncements are both luminous and obscure. The ambiguity of course calls forth interpretation, the interaction of reader and text."[16]

It was also the framers' design, and their literary accomplishment, as Robert Ferguson contends, to achieve a linguistic consensus that sought to control and even conceal political differences.[17] Gouverneur Morris, the primary draftsman of the final version of the Constitution, remarked in an 1814 letter that, after having "rejected redundant and equivocal terms," he had composed a text that was "as clear as our language would permit," containing "unequivocal provisions and limitations." He expressed, however, no confidence that the "logical net" of words which was the Constitution could confine the "legislative lion" (DSC, I, 507). Unlike many opponents of the Constitution, Morris did not ascribe the weakness of that net to its language. Luther Martin, a delegate to the convention who later spoke against its ratification in the Maryland legislature, provides more damaging inside information about how the framers attained their linguistic consensus. The draftsmen did not merely edit the text for stylistic refinement; they artfully – or deceptively – crafted the text for reception by "We, the People." Martin reveals, for instance, that "they anxiously sought to avoid the admission of expressions which might be odious in the ears of Americans, although they were willing to admit into their system those things which the expressions signified." Rather than rejecting redundant and equivocal phrases for express terms, the framers added them to disguise their intentions. Martin also notes that the "word 'national' was struck out by them, because they thought the *word* might tend to alarm" (DSC, I, 362). Similarly, the word "stamp" was removed so as not to indicate precisely what powers were granted to Congress by the provision declaring that "Congress is to have power to lay and collect taxes, duties, imposts, and excises" (DSC, I, 368). Just as deceptively, or to salve their consciences, the framers resorted to a euphemism in a clause designed to prevent the general government from prohibiting the importation of slaves until at least 1808. Guarding against the explicit protection of slavery in a document whose declared intention was to "secure the blessings of Liberty," the framers rejected the word "slave" in Article I, Section 9, and referred instead to the "importation of such persons as any of the states now existing shall think proper to admit" (DSC, I, 372–3). "Centinel," the pen name of Samuel Bryan, whose Antifederalist essays appeared in the Philadelphia *Independent Gazetteer* and the *Freeman's Journal*, was equally scandalized that a people who had "asserted their own liberty by the sword" would then be so inconsistent as to violate the liberty of others by the word of law. He rebuked those framers who tolerated the phrasing in the Constitution that sanctioned an "odious traffic in the human species": "The words are dark and ambiguous; such as no plain man of common sense would have used, [and] are evidently chosen to conceal from Europe, that in this enlightened country, the practice of slavery has its advocates among men in the highest stations" (CAF, II, 160). Here then, as "Centinel" suggests, what the Constitution repudiates, in word and in effect, is Paine's revolutionary vision of a republican government conducting itself by neither force nor fraud and dedicated to preserving the rights of mankind and presenting "the noblest, purest constitution on the face of the earth" (TPW, I, 45).[18]

The Antifederalist Response: The Attack on Ambiguity

When the Constitution was proposed to the state conventions for ratification, the charge of ambiguity became a din among its critics: the Antifederalists saw none of the virtues but all of the dangers of vague or abstract terms. What these political opponents demanded in their literary criticism of the Constitution was a law whose language would be neither so complex nor so inexplicit that it could not be grasped by the common reader. "And where is the man," asked one such critic, "who can see through the constitution to its effects? The constitution of a wise and free people, ought to be as evident to simple reason, as the letters of our alphabet –" (CAF, V, 262). A delegate to the Massachusetts convention who opposed the ratification similarly maintained, "I think a frame of government on which all laws are founded, should be simple and explicit, that the most illiterate may understand it; whereas this appears to me so obscure and ambiguous, that the most capacious mind cannot fully comprehend it" (DSC, II, 160). The objections of William Manning, a New England farmer with but six months' schooling, were even more specific and just as defensive and typical of those, like Manning, who lacked the formal education characteristic of the framers. "The few have a grate advantage over the Many in forming & constructing Constitutions & laws, & are highly interested in haveing them numerous, intricate & as inexplicit as possable. By this they take to themselves the right of giving them such explanations as suits their interests, & make places for numerous lawyers & Juditial & Executive officers, which ads grately to their strength by numbers."[19]

Some Antifederalists detected in the language of the Constitution, because of its ambiguity, a conspiratorial attempt to destroy the blessings of liberty that were the legacy of the Revolution. Behind the closed doors in Philadelphia, in the aura of George Washington's presence, the framers, it was feared, had formulated with their pens what Washington had helped them destroy with their swords: a centralized despotism. As Gordon Wood explains, "the Antifederalists saw themselves in 1787–88 fighting the good old Whig cause in defense of the people's liberties against the engrossing power of their rulers."[20] Just as the Sons of Liberty fought the Whig battle against the artifices and misrepresentations of the British, so too did the Antifederalists take offense against the fraudulent words of the framers, or against what "Centinel" termed the "machinations of an ambitious junto, who, versed in Machiavellian arts, can varnish over with the semblance of freedom the most despotic instrument of government ever projected" (CAF, II, 192). By "ingenious sophisms," by the "refinements of falsehood," by misrepresenting "the unanimity of all concerns of America in favor of the new constitution," by writing "reams of letters to their tools in every direction," by making "the press groan and the whole country reverberate with their productions," by "the magic of great names" and the "suppression of information," by "personal abuse" and "consummate cunning and address," by "deceptive glosses," "specious reasoning," "bold assertions and mere declamation," by, in short, "the din of empty sound and the delusion of falsehood," conspirators were overpowering truth and liberty and betraying the rights of the people. Cloaked in the "suspicious garb of republicanism," "Centinel" cried out, is an attempt "to smuggle upon you" a "masqued aristocracy." Though presented as a "panacea for all the ills of the people," the plan for the new government struck him as more destructive of the people's liberties than the wooden horse deployed by the Greeks was to the city of Troy (CAF, II, 183, 196, 177, 197, 165, 183, 136, 163). What "Centinel" reveals by this harangue, in all its fury and desperation, is that the "conspirators" for the Constitution, like the conspirators for liberty in the Colonies, from the Tory perspective, had outcommanded – or abused – the resources of the word.[21]

Not just "Centinel" but a number of Antifederalists feared that a despotic central government would arise from the ashes of the Articles of Confederation as the Constitution was constructed by men all too skillful in the machinations of power. This fear stemmed in particular from the failure of the framers to draw lines sharply defining the boundaries between federal and state powers and circumscribing the judiciary. The ambiguous language of the Constitution established no bulwark strong enough to defend liberty against the grasp of power. Mercy Otis Warren in her "Observations on the New Constitution, and on the Federal and State Conventions" strenuously protests, for example, that "there are no well defined limits of the Judiciary Powers," but instead "they seem to be left as a boundless ocean." She also complains that the "Executive and the Legislative" powers "are so dangerously blended as to give just cause of alarm, and every thing relative thereto, is couched in such ambiguous terms – in such vague and indefinite expressions, as is a sufficient ground without any other objection, for the reprobation of [this] system" (CAF, II, 276). And Patrick Henry warned in the Virginia ratifying convention that when "power is given to this government" to suppress sedition and licentiousness, the "language it assumes is clear, express, and unequivocal; but when this Constitution speaks of privileges, there is an ambiguity, sir, a fatal ambiguity" (DSC, III, 46). Extending Henry's argument, "John DeWitt," the pseudonym of an unidentified Massachusetts Antifederalist, builds upon a Lockean linguistic premise a plea for a bill of rights as a defense against the fatal ambiguities of the Constitution. It was, he argues, not just the "insatiable thirst for unconditional controul over our fellow-creatures" but the "facility of sounds to convey essentially different ideas" that produced "the first Bill of Rights ever prefixed to a Frame of Government." The people who demanded this first Bill of Rights were "fully sensible that they reserved every tittle of power they did not expressly grant away." But because they were also "afraid that the words made use of, to express those rights so granted might convey more than they originally intended, they chose at the same moment to express in different language those rights which the agreement did not include, and which they never designed to part with, endeavoring thereby to prevent any cause for future altercation and the intrusion into society of that doctrine of tacit implication which has been the favorite theme of every tyrant from the origin of all governments to the present day" (CAF, IV, 22). To restrain the "legislative lion," to protect the people's rights, what was needed, in "DeWitt's" opinion, was more than one "logical net" of words. It required a second barrier, a precise enumeration of the rights reserved by the people. "Language is so easy of explanation, and so difficult is it by words to convey exact ideas, that the party to be governed cannot be too explicit," he reminded his audience (CAF, IV, 21).

Article I, Section 8, of the Constitution provoked the most concern about the implications of words during the ratifying conventions, and it also became the battleground of exegetical skirmishes during the first great constitutional struggle in the early 1790s, over the national bank and in Justice Marshall's opinion in *McCulloch v. Maryland*. This section, granting Congress "the power to lay and collect taxes, duties, imposts and excises, to pay the debts and provide for the common defence and general welfare of the United States" and "to make all laws which shall be necessary and proper for carrying into execution" the powers "vested by this constitution in the government of the United States," raised a chorus of opposition, conducted in the terms of Lockean linguistic analysis, about the boundaries, or more precisely about the lack of boundaries, limiting the authority of the proposed new government. The queries of a delegate to the New York convention are typical. "Are not the terms, *common defence and general welfare*, indefinite, undefinable terms? What checks have the state governments against such encroachments?" "Let us inquire also," he urged, "what is implied in the authority to pass all laws which shall be necessary and proper to carry this power into execution" (DSC, II, 338, 331). "Brutus," the author of a series of Antifederalist essays in the *New York Journal*, subjected the clauses to the same scrutiny and drew a similar conclusion. "What ideas are included under the terms, to provide for the common defence and general welfare? Are these terms definite, and will they be understood in the same manner, and to apply to the same cases by every one? No one will pretend they will. It will then be matter of opinion, what tends to the general welfare." "No terms," he points out elsewhere, "can be found more indefinite" than "necessary" and "proper." This language of Section 8 simply amounts in his view to "a power to make laws at discretion" (CAF, II, 397, 389). George Mason was just as troubled. "In my humble apprehension, unless there be some such clear and finite expression," he declared in the Virginia convention, the "general welfare" clause "will go to any thing our rulers may think proper" (DSC, III, 442).[22]

Distrustful of power, committed to the revolutionary principle of actual representation, the Antifederalists, in Cecelia Kenyon's formulation, were the "men of little faith."[23] The ambiguity of the Constitution, in their jealous, skeptical eyes, was no mere imperfection of language or an inevitable consequence of a complex plan of government, but a plot, a scheme, a device. "The Federal Constitution by a fair construction is a good one prinsapaly," William Manning maintained, "but I have no doubt that the Convention who made it intended to destroy our free governments by it, or they neaver would have spent 4 months in making such an inexplicit thing."[24] Just as the Antifederalists demanded a close, familiar attachment between political representatives and their constituents, so too did they demand a close bond between the words of the Constitution and the ideas they signified. The ambiguity of the Constitution, like the indirectness of virtual representation, obscured intentions, and it blurred the boundaries protecting the people's rights from the encroachments of power. "When I consider the effects which may happen to this country from its adoption," lamented a delegate to the Virginia convention, "I tremble at it. . . . [W]hen I find that the Constitution is expressed in indefinite terms, in terms which the gentlemen who composed it do not concur in the meaning of, – I say that, when it is thus, liable to objections and different constructions, I find no rest in my mind" (DSC, III, 637–8). A delegate to the New York convention voiced even more ominous reservations: "Ingenious men may assign ingenious reasons for opposite constructions of the same clause. They may heap refinement upon refinement, subtilty upon subtilty, until they construe away every republican principle, every right sacred and dear to man. I am, sir, for certainty in the establishment of a constitution which is not only to operate upon us, but upon millions yet unborn" (DSC, II, 338–9).

Madison's Defense: The Limitations of Language

Challenged by the Antifederalists' attack on the architects of the Constitution for their failure to create more safeguards against loose construction, the Federalists contended that such an attack ignored the limitations of language. Certainty was demanded, but certainty was impossible: we must live with doubt, ambiguity, interpretation. Theophilus Parsons of Massachusetts remarked, for instance, that "no composition which men can pen, could be formed, but which would be liable to the same charge of ambiguity" (DSC, III, 104). But the most philosophic, the most lengthy, and the most important defense against the Antifederalist charge of ambiguity can be found in Madison's *Federalist* No. 37. In this crucial paper, coming at the crossroads between his critique of the Confederation and his defense of the Constitution, Madison presents an essay on human misunderstanding. Like Book III of Locke's *Essay*, this paper confronts the inescapable fallibility of all human acts of discrimination and denomination due to the imperfections of the medium the human mind must depend upon in its encounter with the world: language.[25]

Madison begins his defense of the ambiguity of the Constitution by developing an analogy between the constitutional government and the constitution of the human mind and the natural world. Philosophers have never yet been able to define with precision the faculties of the mind, nor have the naturalists delimited the boundaries that separate the vegetable and animal empires. Much less, Madison argues, can we expect success in discriminating between the three great provinces of government – the legislature, the executive, and the judiciary – and between federal and state jurisdictions. Paraphrasing Locke on language, Madison then explains that a large part of the problem of definition stems from the point that no matter "how accurately objects may be discriminated in themselves . . . the definition of them may be rendered inaccurate by the inaccuracy of the terms in which it is delivered" (FP, 37. 229). No language, he points out, "is so copious as to supply words and phrases for every complex idea, or so correct as not to include many equivocally denoting different ideas" (ibid.). Madison then draws upon the highest authority to clinch his argument that an imperfect language is our unavoidable fate. He observes that even when "the Almighty himself condescends to address mankind in their own language, his meaning, luminous as it must be, is rendered dim and doubtful by the cloudy medium through which it is communicated" (ibid.). Locke makes a similar argument in Book III: "Nor is it to be wondered, that the will of God, when clothed in words, should be liable to that doubt and uncertainty which unavoidably attends that sort of conveyance, when even his Son, whilst clothed in flesh, was subject to all the frailties and inconveniences of human nature, sin excepted" (LE, II, 120). But while Locke turns this argument into a plea for humility, maintaining that we should be "less magisterial, positive, and imperious in imposing our own sense and interpretations" on God's Word (LE, II, 121), Madison deploys it to counsel patience: "All new laws, though penned with the greatest technical skill and passed on the fullest and most mature deliberation," must be "considered more or less obscure and equivocal, until their meaning be liquidated and ascertained by a series of particular discussions and adjudications" (FP, 37. 229). Madison's philosophy of language thus circumvents or reorients any quest to determine the express meaning of the letter of the law: the meaning of the Constitution must be produced in the future, not discovered in the past. As Garry Wills emphasizes, "if the distinctions in the Constitution remain, of necessity, uncertain; if they await future 'liquidation,'" then Madison "is arguing for a very adaptable and flexible instrument" or for the idea of the Constitution as "a 'living document' responding to society's needs" rather than "a text frozen in the first approximations of those who compromised it into being."[26]

Yet Madison, as an elder statesman, labored time and again to expound in his writings (primarily his correspondence) a canon of interpretation that would forestall what he knew could not ultimately be forestalled: "the silent innovations of time on the meaning of words and phrases" (JML, IV, 70).[27] "It is but too common to read the expressions of a remote period through the modern meaning of them," Madison laments in 1833 in the midst of the Nullification crisis. A year earlier he maintained in another letter his primary rule of construction in terms drawn from a classic canon of literary criticism:

Horace's advice to the poet. "We must be guided," Madison asserts, ". . . by the intention of those who framed, or, rather, who adopted the Constitution; and must decide that intention by the meaning attached to the terms by the '*usus*' which is the *arbitrum*, the *jus* and *norma loquendi*, a rule as applicable to phrases as to single words." He adds, "It need be scarcely observed that, according to this rule, the intention, if ascertained by contemporaneous interpretation, and continued practice, could not be overruled by any latter meaning put on the phrase, however warranted by the grammatical rules of construction were these at variance with it" (JML, IV, 242).[28] But before too long, the pro-Constitution wing of the abolitionist movement would begin appealing beyond the "usage" of the Constitution to a grammatical rule of construction that declared the law's sanction of slavery to be a solecism, an irregular usage in a document whose governing intention, defined in the Preamble, was to promote justice and secure the blessings of liberty. The victory of the North in the Civil War made possible, in regard to slavery, a victory of grammar over definition, structure over usage. To preserve and reconstruct the Union, Lincoln and the Reconstruction Congress changed the substance of the Constitution, redefining the meaning of "We, the People." This change in "*usus*," a defeat for the interpretative canon of the "Father of the Constitution," can be seen as the key precedent for the theory of judicial review that privileges structure, or grammatical principle, over definition by original intention. Madison himself suspected too much, he saw too clearly, he knew politics too well to believe that the interpretation of the Constitution would be guided by its intentions or by any one principle or theory of interpretation.

In an 1827 letter Madison provides an important supplement to his analysis in *Federalist* No. 37 to explain why, unhappily, it must be the case that different parties will give different interpretations to the Constitution, and that each will claim "paramount authority" and an understanding of its "true meaning." His explanation begins with reasons founded upon the theory of language he advanced in *Federalist* No. 37 and in his 1826 letter to Converse Sherman: the "imperfection of language" and "the change which the meaning of words inadvertently undergoes." But then he moves beyond the limitations of language and the human understanding to explain that "more frequent and formidable than either [linguistic] cause is the spirit of party or the temptations of interest." Politics, not language, is the culprit here. "Nor is the public good, real or supposed, without occasional effect in betraying honest minds into misconstructions of the Constitutional text." These last two "evils," Madison asserts, "cannot be altogether avoided"; the only consolation he takes from this observation – and it

is no small consolation – is that these "evils . . . are not to be compared with those inherent in arbitrary and undefined forms of Government" (JML, III, 565).

"American constitutional interpretation," William Harris writes,
"takes for granted the elemental preposterousness of its subject,
namely the presumption that a political world can be constructed and
controlled with words."[29] The quest of Madison, beginning most
concretely with his sketch for a new government that became the
Virginia Plan in the Constitutional Convention, and the quest that
united Federalists and Antifederalists, was to make this preposterous
presumption less preposterous. Madison's own hope for preventing
future unruly "misconstructions" of the Constitution was a faith that
its words would become not an imposition from without but an
internalized language, not a language subject to the manipulations of
party interest but a language that would be the object of mutual
affection and belief: "the gradual incorporation of the vital maxims of
free Government into the national sentiment, must tend to diminish"
the forces of misconstruction (JML, III, 565). The constitutional faith
of our founding fathers rests, ultimately, on the belief that it is better
to place confidence in the rule of words, however imperfect, than in
the rule of men, however noble, and that subjection to the power and
limitations of a constitution of "founded law and freedom defined" is
the sacrifice worth paying to avoid subjection to the "red meteor of
unbridled and unbounded revolt." The sacrifice to "freedom defined"
is the sacrifice Captain Vere makes in *Billy Budd*. With the execution
of Billy, the law of the state (as interpreted by Vere) prevails over the
threat of mutiny or "unbounded revolt." But Melville, distrustful of
anointed authority and fearful of unanointed power, had graver
doubts than Madison ever expressed that a political world could be
controlled by words and reason:

A Reasonable Constitution

What though Reason forged your scheme?
'Twas Reason dreamed the Utopia's dream:
'Tis dream to think that Reason can
Govern the reasoning creature, man.[30]

In writing and ratifying the Constitution, Madison and other supporters understood that they had no more overcome the imperfections
of words than they had overcome the imperfections of government;
but they did believe that by setting down the words on parchment
with common ideas annexed to them after much deliberation, debate,
and compromise, and by subjecting those words to the consent of the
people, they had taken steps to remedy both imperfections, and per-

haps had remedied them as well as anyone – including Locke – could have expected. By adding the possibility of amendments, the framers made sure that the Constitution could remedy the imperfections of its own words. The Constitution, that is, allows a space for appointed or elect readers to collaborate with the original authors to produce the meaning of the text. The framers penned a novel text which, though it does not have as many specified blanks to fill in as Sterne's *Tristram Shandy*, leaves room for amendment, revision, and reconstruction by its readers. The framers of the Constitution, however, never suspected how soon political representatives, competing to be the authors of new legislation, would appeal in their style not to the gentle reader of Sterne's or Fielding's figuration, but to a mass (or vulgar) audience, simplifying, sentimentalizing, vernacularizing political discourse as they sought not to educate but to pander to interests, not to lead tastes but to follow fashion, packaging their product for a commanding position in the marketplace of politics, turning the theater of politics into a stage for common melodramas with themselves as the defenders of virtue and their opponents as villainous seducers. The Federalists, however, were themselves masqueraders, the new republic's original confidence men.

The Triumph of the Federalist Persuasion: Artful Representation

The hiatus in American politics between ideology and motives, professions and intentions, begins, Gordon Wood argues, with the triumph of the Federalist persuasion. The rhetoric of the Revolution is redeployed to retard the Revolution. The spirit of '76 is killed by the letter of '76 coopted by the elite of '87. The so-called Federalists defeat federalism by denominating their antifederalism federalism and the real Federalists Antifederalists. They, the few, invoke "We, the People," the alpha of democratic radicalism, to inaugurate a Constitution that explodes in deed the center of power it installs in theory. The framers, that is, fragment a sovereign vox populi into multiple modes of representation. Aristocrats with no titles – or what Amos Singletary, a delegate to the Massachusetts ratifying convention, called the "lawyers and men of learning, and moneyed men, that talk so finely, and gloss over matters so smoothly, to make us poor illiterate people swallow down the pill" – these are the ones who presented the Constitution as a republican remedy for the diseases afflicting the body politic (DSC, II, 102). And it was their success, Gordon Wood writes, that "fixed the terms for the future discussion of American politics" – a discussion, Wood adds, that, in its ingenious disingenuity, in its ambiguous commitment to the garb of republicanism, in its failure to relate "differing ideas of politics" to "differing social interests," "has mitigated and often obscured the real social antagonisms of American politics," eventually "impoverishing later American political thought."[31] Ironically, despite their success, by addressing the people in a democratic rhetoric the founders scripted a role for the educated elite in the drama of republican government that consigned aspiring lead actors to the fate of playing the same role: the common man who voices solidarity with an egalitarian ethos. The demise of the Federalists, or conversely the democratization of leadership if not of the American mind, had begun.[32] The audience and not the director, the masses and not the elite, had (*pace* Marx) begun to mold the role of the political actor – and to control political ideology.

The theory of the Constitution that triumphs with the Federalist persuasion is indebted not just, or not primarily, to Locke and Country Party republicanism, but to Hume, and it also smacks of the antirhetorical and antidemocratic animus of Hobbes and Plato.[33] For Hume, as for Publius in *The Federalist*, the "instability, injustice, and confusion" of democracy (with its slangwhanging eloquence, or what Publius calls "the vicious arts by which elections are too often carried") are the "mortal diseases," and representation (with its refined deliberation) is the remedy (FP, 10. 77, 82). Repeatedly Madison and Hamilton recall the fall of classical republics into faction to teach a lesson from history: the need to curtail the politics (and the rhetoric) of a democracy.[34] Democracy in their view is, inevitably and disastrously, little else but an aristocracy of orators or an ungovernable mob. The larger the legislative assembly, Hamilton reasons in *Federalist* No. 59, "the greater will be the proportion of members of limited information and of weak capacities." "Now," he continues, "it is precisely on characters of this description that the eloquence and address of the few are known to act with all their force. In the ancient republics, where the whole body of the people assembled in person, a single orator, or an artful statesman, was generally seen to rule with as complete a sway as if a scepter had been placed in his single hand" (FP, 59. 360). Madison concurs: "In all very numerous assemblies, of whatever characters composed, passion never fails to wrest the scepter from reason" (FP, 55. 342). And in *Federalist* No. 10 he explains: "A society consisting of a small number of citizens, who assemble and administer the government in person, can admit of no cure for the mischiefs of faction. A common passion or interest will, in almost every case, be felt by a majority of the whole; a communication and concert results from the form of government itself" (FP, 10. 81). This comment is a revision of a note Madison made in April 1787 while, as a scholar of history, he prepared intensively for the oral presentation of a new plan for government at the Constitutional Convention: "If an enlargement of the sphere [or representation] is found to lessen the insecurity of private rights," it is because "a common interest or passion is less apt to be felt and the requisite combination less easy to be formed by a great than by a small number. Society becomes broken into a greater variety of interests, of pursuits, of passions, which check each other, whilst those who may feel a common sentiment have less opportunity of communication and concert."[35] Madison, an experienced politician in the Virginia state legislature, also notes in his preparatory study of the vices of American politics, "How frequently too will the honest but unenlightened representative be the dupe of a favorite leader, veiling his selfish views under the professions of public good, and varnishing his sophistical arguments with the glowing colours of popular eloquence?"[36]

To combat these vices, to contain faction and its *modus operandi* – demagoguery, the abuse of words, communication and concert – Madison champions a written constitution creating a system of representation that would counteract the forces Jefferson and others held responsible for the success of the Revolution: the stirring of common sentiments, the power of sympathy, even the agency of communication and concert, or the activities of political participation and correspondence.[37] Madison's written Constitution is, in a word, counterrevolutionary, or at least it is counterdemocratic (and counteroratorical). "What bitter anguish would not the people of Athens have often escaped if their government," Madison declares, had contained "so provident a safeguard against the tyranny of their own passions" as a "temperate and respectable body of citizens" (FP, 63. 384). "Had every Athenian citizen been a Socrates, every Athenian assembly would still have been a mob" (FP, 55. 342). Virtue is not enough to save a republic. One half of the constitutional solution is an extended republic: "Society itself will be broken into so many parts, interests and classes of citizens, that the rights of individuals, or of the minority, will be in little danger from interested combinations of the majority" (FP, 52. 324). The other half of the solution is creating a space for political deliberation among an elite apart from the marketplace. The rights of Socrates must be protected; the virtue of the people must be distilled; and the dialogue of reason, not passionate oratory, must be cultivated. Let us gather political philosophers, disinterested searchers for the public good, in a new political pantheon: a bicameral legislature (with a senate twice removed from the people). The ultimate solution remains a written constitution that will provide a standard, a touchstone, to try the representative actions of the forums and assemblies wherein speech prevails. Appropriately, in the Virginia ratifying convention, the great opponent of Madison (who was never proud of or known for his own speaking skills) was the orator – or the demagogue – of the Revolution in Virginia: Patrick Henry.

The specter of the demagogue and fear of oratory itself, so pronounced in *The Federalist*, has garnered, to my knowledge, relatively little notice in scholarly commentary on the text, which has focused on the problem of faction and its roots rather than on its *modus operandi*. This lack of attention is all the more surprising considering that the most appropriate contemporary analogue for Publius's distrust of oral representation is the current conviction, fanned by such jeremiads as Neil Postman's *Amusing Ourselves to Death: Public Discourse in the Age of Show Business*, that political debate in the United States has been corrupted by the art of television image making, an art of communication and concert by speech (and pictures) to which we can only imagine Publius's response. The very power ascribed to television reposes the questions debated by Plato and confronted frequently in the classical republican tradition: if the many are governed more by sound than sense, or more by the theatrics of words addressed to the passions than the analysis of ideas addressed to the reason, and if the few – the wealthy and the talented – have the most access to controlling what Trenchard and Gordon term the art of misleading the people by sounds, then what is the place of the image maker, the sophist, the media consultant, or the poet in a republic, or how might that art be disciplined and critiqued in a democracy?[38]

The faculty psychology of Publius, with its demand for a subordination of passion to reason and its fear of misrepresentation, recalls the analogy between faculty psychology and politics in Plato's philosophy.[39] The republican remedy of Publius for the political (and psychological) imbalances inherent in a democracy is in part the remedy of Plato's *Republic*: an escape from the forum, or the creation of a new forum of dialectical rhetoric, an insulated space for the philosopher-statesman as guardian. "When occasions present themselves," Hamilton argues, "in which the interests of the people are at variance with their inclinations, it is the duty of the persons whom they have appointed to be the guardians of those interests to withstand the temporary delusion in order to give them time and opportunity for more cool and sedate reflection" (FP, 71. 432). "If we are to take for the criterion of truth a majority of suffrages," Madison wrote to Benjamin Rush in 1790, "they ought to be gathered from the philosophical and patriotic citizens who cultivate their reason apart from every scene that can disturb its operations, or expose it to the influence of the passions" (JML, I, 510). If the representative assemblies become corrupt, if they are infiltrated by acts of false representation, then just as the parent was called upon to rescue the son in Book VIII of *The Republic*, Madison calls upon the people, the "pure, original fountain of all legitimate power," to flush out the assemblies: "A succession of new representatives would speedily restore all things to their pristine order" (FP, 22. 152; 63. 388). The Federalists' quest for a representative government that would favor the "disinterested gentlemen" who would distill the best or "true" interest of the people from all their expressions of self-interest is at the heart of their commitment to the Constitution, and in this sense, as Gordon Wood asserts, "the Constitution became a grand – and perhaps in retrospect a final desperate – effort to realize the great hope of the Revolution: the possibility of a virtuous politics."[40]

The constitutionalism of Madison and Hamilton is founded, however, not just on a faith that virtue could be refined but upon an axiom of the Enlightenment, expressed in Adams's *Defence of the Constitutions*, that "the multitude have always been credulous, and the few are always artful," and it proceeds to the conclusion that artfulness must be made to counteract artfulness in "schemes of representation" (JAW, IV, 292). Opposed to the Antifederalists, who upheld the principle that representation should be a mirror of the people, Madison's scheme of representation takes as its figure the filter. Representative government for an extended republic, he argues in *Federalist* No. 10, would "refine and enlarge the public views by passing them through the medium of a chosen body of citizens, whose wisdom may best discern the true interest of their country and whose patriotism and love of justice will be least likely to sacrifice it to temporary or partial considerations" (FP, 10. 82). The scum would stay below or behind; the virtuous would rise: their voices would clarify (or transcend) the vox populi. "Under such a regulation it may well happen that the public voice, pronounced by the representatives of the people, will be more consonant to the public good than if pronounced by the people themselves, convened for the purpose" (FP, 10. 82). The turbulent voices of a democracy – the shouting, the harangues, the accents of factious tempers, the passion-igniting orations, the dialects of local prejudices, the slang of direct expression of interests, the "vicious arts" of electioneering – all this is what stirred up the mud of politics in Madison's view, or this is what drowned out "the mild voice of reason, pleading the cause of an enlarged and permanent interest," and this is what he sought to screen out from the representative bodies in the federal government where calm, disinterested, candid deliberation would prevail, or so he wished (FP, 42. 268). For Publius, deliberation is the antithesis of faction. Deliberation listens to more than one voice; faction is deaf to all but its own voice. Deliberation seeks the enlargement of perspective; faction voices a narrow self-interest. Deliberation is the conversation of reason, candor, and conscience; faction is the monologue of passion-kindling, mind-deluding verbal abuse. Democracy breeds faction among the people; the Constitution creates spaces for deliberation apart from the people.[41] The "worst thing," Pericles declares in the Funeral Oration, "is to rush into action before the consequences have been properly debated," and just as Pericles praised the Athenians for submitting decisions to "proper discussions" and for sustaining a compatibility between words and deeds, Publius defends the Constitution for demanding political deliberation as the precaution to acts of state power. Fearful of passion and doubtful that reason would reign secure, Publius welcomes a politics that institutionalizes the prudence of deliberation and that demands, at various stages, the submission of the legislative voice to the act of writing.

Unlike the Antifederalists, and more like Hobbes and Hume, Publius is by no means hostile to the sovereign power of representation. Hamilton in particular is devoted to the art of political construction: the moral, heroic exercise of power – the activity of lawgiving that earned Solon and Lycurgus fame and honor as Orphic creators of a new order that secured peace, happiness, liberty, and property.[42] The Constitution, as a framework for virtual representation, stretches a canvas not just or not primarily for the work of the honest, imitative representative (the drone who serves local interests), but for the art of the statesman whose principle of representation is not the mirror of mimesis but the lamp of projection and invention – whose ideal, in other words, is the creation of masterpieces of legislation for the good of the common weal. The founders themselves, as political activists, create a new *logos* to transcend the forces of the Thucydidean moment: chaos, necessity, faction, fraud, force, or, in a word, *stasis*. Under the vigorous national government that the Constitution would institute, Hamilton argues in *Federalist* No. 11, "we might defy the little arts of little politicians to control or vary the irresistible and unchangeable course of nature" (FP, 11. 87). With the ratification of the Constitution, he envisions, as did Pericles for Athens, not just "an active commerce, an extensive navigation, a flourishing marine," but the prospect that the country "might make herself the admiration and envy of the world" (FP, 11. 87, 88). "The advantages of republicanism over democracy," in Publius's view, as Paul W. Kahn explains, "are found in the element of 'indirectness' which opens up a place for the art of political construction."[43] Eliminate that power of construction, prevent that indirectness, quell deliberation, and a space for political vision is foreclosed. Politics then succumbs to a mere reflection of base reality: it represents opinion, appetite, greed, fear, the voice of self-interest calling for protection or for more of the pie. It fails to entertain what the "men of little faith," the Antifederalists, never imagined: a romance vision of a *novus ordo seclorum* and of the Constitution as the transformational grammar for creating that new deal, that great society. The Federalist triumph over the Antifederalists is the triumph, in part, of Jay Gatsby over James Gatz: willfully unprovincial, they act (in the spirit of Ben Franklin) as entrepreneurs, inventors, risk takers, deceivers who, beating against a past, recreate a country in their imaginations and in their words.

The Politics of Interpretation in the New Republic

When the first Congress convened in the spring of 1789 to inaugurate the government created by the ratification of the Constitution, it found itself engaged in doing exactly what Madison said it must do: it began liquidating the Constitution's ambiguities. The debates over the establishment of the executive department, a protective tariff, and a national bank all involved the issue of determining the boundaries of federal authority as set forth by the Constitution. How would the more abstract words of the Constitution be defined in practice? More important, what principle – or policy – of interpretation would be used to make those definitions? Just as lexicographers define or make distinctions among the various meanings of a word by illustrating its use in sentences, so too did the first Congress help define the meaning of the Constitution by illustrating the words in the actions it took. But disputes arose at the very beginning about how the words were defined and about who had the right to judge or govern the meanings of those words. In the 1790s, the split in Washington's administration between Hamilton and Jefferson, a split that would soon develop into a division between Federalists and Republicans, was exacerbated if not defined by the controversy between a strict versus a broad interpretation of the Constitution. Federalists, as H. Jefferson Powell explains, found in the text the basis for an expansive view of federal power, while the Republicans warned that the "wiles of construction" could be controlled only by a narrow reading of the Constitution's language.[44]

With the victory of Jefferson over Adams in the contentious presidential campaign of 1800, the Republicans appeared to have every reason to feel confident that they had stemmed the tide of Federalist power. But though the Republicans controlled the presidency, the Supreme Court was led by the recently appointed chief justice, John Marshall, and for the next three and a half decades of his tenure, his nationalistic view prevailed on the court and left a deep and lasting imprint – and some bitter feelings. The judicial politics of the Marshall court, for instance, so outraged John Taylor of Caroline, an early strategist in the campaign for states' rights, that he declared that Swift's *Tale of a Tub* should be distributed throughout the United States to explain the workings of the Supreme Court. In Taylor's eyes, Marshall was doing exactly what Locke feared and Swift satirized: he was making words mean whatever he wanted them to mean.

In Marshall's key decision sanctioning a broad construction of the "necessary and proper" clause of the Constitution, *McCulloch v. Maryland*, he too turned to a Lockean conception of language to advance his argument. "Such is the character of human language," Marshall writes,

> that no word conveys to the mind, in all situations, one single definite idea. . . . Almost all compositions contain words, which, taken in their rigorous sense, would convey a meaning different from that which is obviously intended. . . . The word "necessary" is of this description. It has not a fixed character peculiar to itself. It admits of all degrees of comparison; and is often connected with other words, which increase or diminish the impression the mind receives of the urgency it imports. A thing may be necessary, very necessary, absolutely or indispensably necessary. To no mind would the same idea be conveyed, by these several phrases.[45]

He also points out, "It is essential to just construction, that many words which import something excessive, should be understood in a more mitigated sense – in that sense which common usage justifies."[46]

This passage, which immediately precedes the paragraph wherein Marshall makes his enduring claim that the Constitution was "intended to endure for ages to come, and, consequently, to be adapted to the various *crises* of human affairs," establishes, in the words of James Boyd White, "far more than the proposition that the word 'necessary' has a wide range of possible meanings. He defines the language of the Constitution, and hence the language of this opinion and of the law generally, as continuous with ordinary language and capable of the same richness, complexity and variation – indeed, of the same capacity for inconsistency."[47] His essential point, White adds, is that since the words of the Constitution, like all words, convey to the mind no single definite idea, the activity of interpretation cannot be limited to the interpretation of the text itself; instead interpretation must take into consideration "common usage." In his opinion, then, Marshall calls upon an authority that is not higher than the Constitution but prior to it: the language of which it is made. The language, he says, has been established by its "use" in the "common affairs of the world, or in approved authors"; or we could say it has its origins in the .people themselves. For Marshall, the Constitution as a law cannot be severed from the language of the people. The terms of the social contract participate in the rules and conventions of the linguistic contract. The Constitution, in a word, coexists – or lives – with the language of its culture.[48] Marshall in this decision is an ordinary-language legal philosopher.

Marshall's decision established a crucial precedent for a broad, or liberal, construction of the Constitution, but it did not end debate or even acrimonious disputes over the proper method of interpreting the text. Indeed, in the early republic much of the passion and most of the power struggles over such questions as the national bank, the tariff, and slavery were channeled into the forum of constitutional debate, and the words of the text were constructed and reconstructed by the various parties to support diverse and contradictory points of view. And in America there was no consensus about the sovereign center that was to end the infinity of interpretation, because the Constitution, in effect, had divided that center between the several branches of government and the states while theoretically locating it in that inherently diverse entity the vox populi. But while there was no consensus about the meaning of the words of the Constitution, there was a fundamental agreement until the crisis over slavery in the mid nineteenth century that the Constitution was the grammar that provided the rules for framing the articulation and resolution of differences between sources of authority and modes of representation in the American republic. Like language itself, the Constitution has the capacity to reconcile stability and liberty, order and change. It is a *langue* – a fundamental system of grammar, syntax, and vocabulary – that structures the process by which the vox populi articulates new *paroles*: new amendments, new political representatives. The Constitution's ability to sustain a tension between stability and liberty, mediating conflicts between the party of memory and the party of hope, was tested to the breaking point in antebellum America as the country began to fight a war of words over attempts to settle and reconstruct its language.

Retraction and Coda

I have argued so far that the language of the Constitution is ambiguous, that the framers designed it in part to be ambiguous, that the Antifederalists distrusted that ambiguity, and that Madison defended its ambiguity. But if we heed Walter Benn Michaels's argument in "Against Formalism: Chicken and Rocks," then I must retract part of my argument and maintain that the language of the Constitution is no different from the language of any text: it is not inherently ambiguous, nor is it inherently clear. Though we ascribe properties such as ambiguity and clarity to texts, these properties, Michaels asserts, do not belong to the text but are "functions . . . of the contexts in which texts are read."[49] An explicit text is, simply, a text whose meaning is not under dispute; and an ambiguous text is, conversely, a text whose meaning in contested. Read from a single perspective at a certain moment, the phrases "We, the People" and "freedom of speech" may appear as perfectly unambiguous as, say, the phrase "a pound of flesh" in Act I of *The Merchant of Venice*. But with a change of fortune or in a new context or viewed from more than one angle of vision, meanings proliferate, and ambiguity must be confronted: an ambiguity that reflects our attention back to the eyes (or the ideology) of the beholders. E. L. Doctorow switches our focus in this very way when he explains in a meditation on the Constitution as a text:

> All told, it is as if the enigmatic constitutional text cannot be seen through, but, shimmering in ambiguity, dazzles back at each generation in its own times and struggles. It is as if the ambiguity is not in the text but in us, as we struggle in our natures – our consciences with our appetites, our sense of justice with our animal fears and self-interests – just as the Founding Fathers struggled so with their Constitution, providing us with a mirror of ourselves to go on shining, shining back at us through the ages, as the circumstances of our lives change, our costumes change, our general store is transformed into a mile-long twenty-four-hour shopping mall, our trundle carts transmogrify into rockets in space, our country paves over, and our young republic becomes a plated armory of ideological warfare: a mirror for us to see who we are and who we would like to be, the sponsors of private armies of thugs and rapists and murderers, or the last best hope of mankind.[50]

The Constitution, in this reading, is a vessel for our passions and prejudices – and for our priniciples. The text, and its interpretations, however, have been more than a mirror representing our values. They have been sources of enlightenment, a lamp projecting values, shaping people to the order (and abuses) of the word and, more important perhaps, determining how we resolve – or seek to resolve – our clashes of values.

Now the coda. If rhetoric, as Yeats claims, arises from our quarrel with others, and poetry from our quarrel with ourselves, then the Declaration tends to rhetoric, and the Constitution to poetry. More than the Declaration, the Constitution is the ground of American Renaissance literature. The conflicts between union and liberty, freedom and slavery, the tyranny of the majority and the rights of the

individual, the protection of regional identity (states' rights) and the
quest for national identity (consolidation) and between property rights
and human rights: these moral and political conflicts, inscribed in the
text of the Constitution, take form first as the stuff of textual battles
in the constitutional crises of the nineteenth century and then, inscribed in the plots, as the stuff of American Renaissance literature.
Even the confrontation with slavery – the confrontation that demanded that American writers listen less to the courtly muses of
Europe and more to the principles of the Declaration – was first and
foremost (and finally) a constitutional crisis: a question of resolving
the ambiguity of "We, the People of the United States" and of
deciding whether or how to privilege one constitutional value, one
legal precedent, over and against another. The silences of the Constitution, the gaps in its articulation, its contradictions had to be overcome, and they came to be bridged not just by the voice of the law or
the voice of the political representative. When those voices failed,
when they stuttered, when they deceived, when the politicians and
judges bridged the gaps with the construction of moral compromises
(e.g., the Compromise of 1850 with its Fugitive Slave Law), they had
to be challenged or supplemented by the discourses of religion and
literature – the voice of the preacher, the essayist, the autobiographer,
the novelist, the poet, or so at least thought Garrison, Douglass,
Thoreau, Stowe, and Whitman. The voice of literature and religion
did its parrot's share of mimicking and reinforcing, in its own way, the
written law; the Constitution, like the Gag Rule of 1836, shaped, more
or less, what could be said in public regarding slavery and perhaps
even what could be thought in private. Even Whitman, for all his
rebellion against poetic form, for all his personal disgust with slavery,
for all his outspokenness, demanded obedience to the Constitution of
1789 and its sanction of slavery. But the Word of God, the book of
nature, and the Declaration became, at first and then more and more
in the North, alternative grammars of thought: a higher *langue* for
generating transcendental *paroles* and emancipation proclamations.

   The Constitution, if we consider it to be a grammar, possesses the
capacity – or we have made it possess the capacity in its history – to
incorporate in its workings more than one language. It can, that is,
construct or generate sentences from more words than its own dictionary of terms contained in the four corners of the text. "Is the
Constitution," Laurence Tribe asks, ". . . at war with its own pre-
mises?" "Perhaps," he responds, "it speaks in the words of Walt
Whitman: 'Do I contradict myself? Very well then, I contradict myself.
I am large. I contain multitudes.'"[51] The Constitution can speak in as

many tongues as Whitman sought to represent; it can listen to as many voices as Whitman heard (and more); it can be for new readers, as Whitman's children, a "chant democratic" that helps form, in the spirit of our bard, our most Orphic visionary, "a great aggregate Nation." "The founders have pass'd to other spheres – but what," Whitman asks, "are these terrible duties they have left us?" He answers: "I say we can only attain harmony and stability by consulting ensemble and the ethic purports, and faithfully building upon them" (WLA, 668, 976). In the past, of course, the chant of our law, in its jargon and in its practice, has worked not just to create ensemble but to exclude citizens from its circle.

Richard Wright observes in "How 'Bigger' Was Born," his introduction to Native Son, that since the civilization that had given birth to Bigger Thomas "contained no spiritual sustenance, had created no culture which could hold and claim his allegiance and faith," he had been left stranded, "a free agent to roam the streets of our cities, a hot and whirling vortex of undisciplined and unchannelized impulses." These observations made Wright feel "more than ever estranged from the civilization in which I lived, and more than ever resolved toward the task of creating with words a scheme of images and symbols whose direction could enlist the sympathies, loyalties, and yearnings of the millions of Bigger Thomases in every land and race." These words come in the midst of Wright's reflections on the rituals and symbols and oppressions of the Fascist movement in Nazi Germany. "What struck me with particular force was the Nazi preoccupation with the construction of a society in which there would exist among all people (German people, of course) one solidarity of ideals, one continuous circulation of fundamental beliefs, notions and assumptions."[52] The quest to create a scheme of representation – words, symbols, and rituals – that would lead without being demagogic, that would channel impulses without dictating, that would claim our allegiance without undue superstition, that would create structure without imprisoning, that would unite the many without oppressing the one, and that would enlist "the sympathies, loyalties, and yearnings" of a people driven by fear as well as hope and by self-interest as well as virtue, is, quite simply, the task of constitution making that challenged the framers in 1787, and it has continued to challenge the American writer. In 1940 it was Richard Wright's mission, as he suggests, to create an alternative (or amended) constitution for the dispossessed and disinherited Bigger Thomases who had lived "outside of the lives of men," like his lawyer, Max: "Their modes of communication, their symbols and images, had been denied him."[53] It was left to the anonymous (and dispossessed) narrator of Ellison's *Invisible Man* to figure out how to manipulate (rather than reject) the symbols that had been manipulated to exclude him.

Not just the breaking away from old covenants in acts of self-reliance (or violence) but the drama of projecting new covenants of community (or amending old ones) is part and parcel of the action in classic texts from the American Renaissance and beyond. American writers, that is, in their symbolic acts of protest and affirmation, in their forgings of new declarations of independence and visionary compacts, have taken as their model not just the spirit of '76 but the letter of '87, scripting visions of not just a more liberating but a more harmonious, a more inclusive, and a more constructive human colloquy: a more perfect union.[54]

IV

From Logomachy to Civil War:
The Politics of Language in
Post-Revolutionary America

9

The Unsettled Language:
Schoolmasters vs. Truants

> . . . for no language is so settled as not to undergo continual
> changes, if spoken by a nation in the full vigor of social and political
> life. Authority, in regard to language, will go far, but never can
> withstand for a long time the energies and wants of a free, indus-
> trious and thinking people.
>
> Francis Lieber, "Americanisms,"
> *Encyclopedia Americana*

"The new circumstances under which we are placed," Thomas Jefferson remarked in a letter to John Waldo in 1813, "call for new words,
new phrases, and for the transfer of old words to new objects" (JLA,
1295–6). For Jefferson, an unfixed relationship between words and
meanings and the unsettling linguistic process of neologization (his
word) were incumbent upon Americans if they were to hold the
mirror up to nature and suit their words to their actions. Creating the
American system of government alone demanded transformations in
political discourse. The framers of the Constitution borrowed from
the past, but they also recognized that their project required them to
formulate a new lexicon for politics, one that would accommodate a
neologism for a political system that could not be denominated with
the word "monarchy," "aristocracy," or "democracy" or even solely
with the word "national" or "federal." Much of the difficulty in
formulating the Constitution arose, as James Madison reports in *Federalist* No. 37, from a want of terms and the inadequacy of language, and
in 1824 Madison writes: "New ideas, such as presented by our novel
and unique political system, must be expressed either by new words,
or by old words with new definitions" (JML, III, 435).[1] The search for
terms to define what had been enacted became a long and problematical search. When Rip Van Winkle awakes after the Revolution, he is

bewildered by a "Babylonish jargon": "rights of citizens – election – members of congress – liberty – Bunker's hill – heroes of seventy-six . . ." (ILA, 779). The Revolution created new words or gave old words new meanings, but at mid century Whitman is still calling out for more, as if he recognizes with Karl Marx that a revolution could not be complete until the people were fluent in a new tongue:

> In America an immense number of new words are needed, to embody the new political facts, the compact of the Declaration of Independence, and of the Constitution – the union of States – the new States – the Congress – the modes of election – the stump speech – the ways of electioneering – addressing the people – stating all that is to be said in modes that fit the life and experience of the Indianian, the Michiganian, the Vermonter, the men of Maine – also words to answer the modern, rapidly spreading, faith, of the vital equality of women with men, and that they are to be placed on an exact plane, politically, socially, and in business, with men. (AP, 9)

For Jefferson and Whitman, in short, the people of the United States had to perform more linguistic experiments to advance the language beyond the range of inherited representations so as to explain their revolutionary achievements and to "give the spirit, the body, the man, new words, new potentialities of speech" (AP, 6).

Neologization and the transfer of old words to new objects became synonymous with America. The two linguistic processes throve in a world of invention, discovery, and social change – the world of democracy, the world of the frontier. Throughout the first half of the nineteenth century, Americans seemed to neologize freely if not always judiciously, as they democratized politics and pioneered the frontier. "In this country, in this 'wilderness of free minds,' new thoughts and correspondingly new expressions spring up spontaneously to live their hour or to be permanent," notes William Fowler, a professor of rhetoric and oratory at Amherst, in 1850.[2] New words, like new political candidates, were introduced to the public, and the representatives that won the hearts and minds of enough people became their new signifiers in the systems of language and government. Steadfast Dodge, a scurrilous self-promoter in Cooper's *Homeward Bound* (1838) who gives the people what they want to get what he wants, justifies a long list of new names for Dodge-town with the argument "It must be owned the people like change, or rotation in names, as well as in office."[3] What Dodge claims is what the American Revolution sanctioned: popular usage can replace old representatives with new ones, and the effort to legitimate the rule of popular sovereignty in language as well as in politics became not just a revolutionary engagement against Dr. Johnson and the King's English but a logomachy between Americans. Spellers, grammars, and dictionaries are the weapons of choice. Jefferson declares the theory for the linguistic revolution. Opposed to the notion that changes in the linguistic order were to be looked upon as corruptions unless introduced or approved by the consent of the learned or an elite, he champions the sometimes supported but usually discouraged principle that the free introduction of new words and new meanings into the custom house of language could be an enrichment rather than an adulteration of language: "I am no friend . . . to what is called *Purism*, but a zealous one to the *Neology* which has introduced these two words without the authority of any dictionary. I consider the one as destroying the nerve and beauty of language, while the other improves both, and adds to its copiousness" (JLA, 1295). Jefferson calls for an end to those artificial restrictions that prevent new words from advancing themselves on the force of their merits from positions of relative obscurity into the pages of a dictionary, just as he also calls for an end to those restrictions of birth and title that would prevent one of the natural *aristoi* from rising from obscurity to the halls of Congress. "In giving a loose to Neologism . . . uncouth words will sometimes be offered; but the public will judge them, and receive or reject, as sense or sound shall suggest, and authors will be approved or condemned according to the use they make of this license" (TJW, XIV, 464). Jefferson's principle for separating couth from uncouth words was the same as his principle for separating the pseudo-*aristoi* from the natural *aristoi*: Let the people judge.

In the nineteenth century numerous new words were brought before the court of public opinion. Some the people accepted, like "buncombe," "lobby," and "gerrymander"; some they voted out of office (alas), like "pollywog" (a professional politician) and "slang-whanger" (an abusive talker, the type who thrives in a negative campaign); some they disputed, like "nullifier" and "Manifest Destiny"; and some they had to reject or defend by force, like "concurrent majority," "secession," and "hygienic warranteeism" (a euphemism for slavery). Confronted with these neologisms, schoolmasters discovered that settling meaning and governing language in a "wilderness of free minds" was no easy task. William Fowler himself wrote the first Amerian textbook of English grammar designed for use in colleges. He feared, as did many others, that as Americans spread "westward across the continent" "in the use of their liberty" they would "break loose from the laws of language, and become marked not only by one, but by a thousand Shibboleths."[4] Fortunately, there weren't nothing much that Fowler or any other linguistic civilizer could do to catch all the

offenders. When pursued by pedants, folks either absquatulated, ske-
daddled, or just lit out for freer territory. Storytellers stuck around
and had fun trying to run the pedants out of town, as does Brom Bones
in Irving's "Legend of Sleepy Hollow."

With the defeat of the English at Yorktown, the American Revolution quit the battlefield. But soon after the signing of the Treaty of
Paris in 1783, the revolution against tyranny and corruption began to
be waged in the fields of linguistic theory and reform. Calls are made
for independence from the English language. Reformers seek to purify
the King's English of its corruptions. Demands are made for a republicanized language governed by the people or reconstituted by a philosophic grammar.[5] The Revolution brought popular sovereignty into
the marketplace of ideas with a vengeance, challenging the authority
of custom and the consent of the learned as the props and ratifiers of
words. The rhetoric of liberty and equality placed aristocracy on the
defensive: the revolution demanded transcendence of the past and its
false entitlements. "What, then, is the American, this new man?"
Crèvecoeur asks in *Letters from an American Farmer*, and he answers, "*He*
is an American, who, leaving behind him all his ancient prejudices and
manners, receives new ones, from the new mode of life he has
embraced, the new government he obeys, and the new rank he
holds."[6] In the new world, it seemed, people were as willing to forget
the origins of terms as their own origins as they sought to transcend
their past and make a new name for themselves, not on the basis of
who they had been or where they were from but on how they were
accepted and valued in society. "All significant transfer, growth of
new meanings, form-making," William Whitney argues, "is directly
dependent upon our readiness to forget the derivation of our terms, to
cut loose from historical connections, and to make the tie of conventional usage the sole one between the thing signified and its spoken
sign."[7] Conceived as an escape from the old world, America became
the home of linguistic as well as social transformation. The land
nurtured neologisms as well as the self-made man. In a footnote to the
word "gallied" in *Moby-Dick*, Melville, whose family fortunes slid
precipitously near the time Tocqueville was making his survey of the
United States, remarks on the fate of English words in America:

> To common land usages, the word [gallied] is now completely
> obsolete. When the polite landsman first hears it from the gaunt
> Nantucketer, he is apt to set it down as one of the whaleman's self-
> derived savageries. Much the same is it with many other sinewy
> Saxonisms of this sort, which emigrated to the New-England rocks
> with the noble brawn of the old English emigrants in the time of the
> Commonwealth. Thus, some of the best and furthest-descended

English words – the etymological Howards and Percys – are now democratised, nay, plebeianised – so to speak – in the New World.[8]

The early republic was not short of critics who expressed reservations about the linguistic behavior that a democracy encouraged or sanctioned. The people's unwillingness to be governed by anything but their own self and their scant deference to the guidance of an educated elite portended unwelcome changes, a mixing up of words as well as of classes. Englishmen were quick to lambaste the vulgarisms of the American dialect, and gentleman scholars in the United States often added their voices to that chorus of censure. It was a Frenchman, however, who provided one of the most discriminating examinations of the influence that democracy exercised on language in America. In the second volume of *Democracy in America* (1840), Tocqueville devotes an entire chapter to the topic: "How American Democracy Has Modified the English Language." The primary sources of modification in his analysis are the constant agitation in society due to competition, a love of change, a desire to rise in society, and a general ignorance of classical languages. He also notes that since "there is no common appeal [in democratic countries] to the sentence of a permanent tribunal that may definitively settle the meaning of the word, it remains in an unsettled condition" (DA, II, 71). For Tocqueville, the tendency of American democracy to provoke and then permit linguistic innovation is deplorable: it renders the meanings of words indeterminate. And because of the mixing of classes and styles in America, the origins of words, like the origins of individuals, are often lost. The result is "as much confusion in language as there is in society" (DA, II, 72). Tocqueville was more than a bit disturbed by the mobility of words and people in America. In a world of democratic equality where any word and any man could become anything, there seemed to be no possibility in his eyes for social order and the stability of truth.

Just as Tocqueville recognizes that the possibilities that a democracy offers for social mobility and self-transformation could be a mixed blessing, so too did the people discover that the mobility of words, or their freedom from a fixed sense, could be a source of danger as well as an invaluable liberty. In post-Revolutionary America the desire to preserve the purity and uniformity of language in America became the concerted effort of a number of schoolmasters who became wary of the "democratic" tendencies of language. Tocqueville carefully notes in *Democracy in America* the forces that tended to regulate individualism and mitigate the tyranny of the majority, but he does not consider the analogous attempts that were made in the United States to check linguistic freedom and mitigate the sway of popular usage. In 1780,

John Adams, for instance, recommended to the Continental Congress the formation of an "American Academy for refining, improving and ascertaining the English language." The language academies in France, Spain, and Italy convinced him that it would have "a happy effect upon the union of the States to have a public standard for all persons in every part of the continent to appeal to, both for the signification and pronunciation of the language" (JAW, VII, 249–50). Later, in the 1820s, William Cardell organized and promoted a short-lived Academy of Language and Belles Lettres that received the strong endorsement of James Madison (but not Jefferson). More important, the American schoolroom stressed training in spelling and grammar, the literacy skills that are most rule-bound; critics penned their own guidebooks to facilitate the proper use of language; and writers promoted literature itself as a means of guarding the language against the uncouthness of the people and the people against the couth of the demagogue. America's pioneer in language reform, Noah Webster, and one of its earliest novelists, Hugh Henry Brackenridge, turned, respectively, to the writing of grammars and of literature to govern the language in the democracy. A brief comment on *Modern Chivalry* and a review of Webster's work as linguistic reformer can suggest how the quest to settle the American language became for the two of them (and for others) a matter of politics conducted by other means.

Early Schoolmasters of the Language: Hugh Henry Brackenridge and Noah Webster

Modeled on *Don Quixote* and sharing affinities with Pope's *Dunciad* and Swift's *Tale of a Tub*, Brackenridge's *Modern Chivalry* is an innovator in American political humor. It makes us laugh, but like later classics of American literature – *The Confidence-Man, Invisible Man,* and *The Armies of the Night* – it also offers a profound commentary on the reciprocal relationship among political, social, and linguistic misrepresentation.[9] Brackenridge defends the novel in the preface not as art but as instruction: it is an attempt to do what "Dictionaries" and "Institutes" had failed to do – "fix the English language" (MC, 3). His novel will be, simply, a model of good style, and the ideal style is, simply, "proper words in proper places" (MC, 163). But the novel, published in installments between 1792 and 1815, offers an encyclopedic commentary on how democracy has modified America; it predates Tocqueville's survey of the United States by a generation, and it prepares us for the concerns he would express and the conclusions he would draw about the democratization of American politics. It is a world where neither people nor words remain settled in their proper places.

In *Modern Chivalry*, the republican ideal of the natural aristocrat is as much a breed threatened by extinction as the knight-errant in Don Quixote's Spain. What rules in *Modern Chivalry* (and in the modern world of democracy Tocqueville analyzes) is not deference but equality, not virtue but interest, not the good of the community but individualism, not the moral sense but the tyranny of the majority (or the mob). Captain Farrago, a republican man of letters, mixes it up in a series of adventures with his servant, Teague O'Regan, an incarnation of the democratic idiom, and both lose. Teague rises above his master to become, among other things, a candidate for Congress, a prospective minister, and a member of the American Philosophical Society, but he is not properly qualified for any of these positions. Captain Farrago, who tries to educate Teague for the positions, resorts to deceptive schemes of representation to delude Teague into relinquishing his ambitions as well as his gains.

The novel also incorporates the voice of the narrator as an enlightened commentator: it is the voice of education and correction set against the artifices, prevarications, and abuses of Farrago and Teague and of the demagogue and the mob. It is a voice that points out how Thucydides' *History* offers "a perfect model of a demagogue" in the person of Cleon and a warning against the excesses of democracy (MC, 525). "The demagogue," Brackenridge writes, "is the first great destroyer of the constitution by deceiving the people," but he knows better than John Adams not to cite classical texts in long quotations or choose the form of Adams's *Defence of the Constitutions* to counsel the people and defend the constitutions of government (MC, 507). *Modern Chivalry* is not addressed to "the legislature, or executive power of the government; but *to the people*" or to "Tom, Dick and Harry, in the woods" (MC, 471). He insists, "It is talk out of doors that I respect. And this is the fountain which is to be corrected" (MC, 449). Brackenridge is democrat enough to recognize that the vox populi is entitled to be sovereign; it is the legitimate fountain of power. He is also republican enough to recognize that the fountain can become muddy and in need of filtration: "It is therefore into this pool *that I cast my salt*" (ibid.). Brackenridge is a schoolmaster who seeks to instruct the people in the grammar of republican politics and law as well as in the grammar of the language and the art of good style. But his medium to reach Tom, Dick, and Harry will not be the official textbook – the political treatise, the grammar, or the sermon – but the "talk out of doors" of the picaresque novel. Incorporating the voice of the minister, the grammarian, and the judge (as well as the voice of the democrat and aristocrat), but subordinating them all to a vernacular mode, *Modern Chivalry* is a farrago of common sense. Just as Paine did in 1776 (and just as Twain will do in *Huckleberry Finn*, although Twain makes the truant the schoolmaster), Brackenridge vernacularizes political oratory in the medium of print and becomes one of the great pioneers in America of the novel as talk, rhetoric, debate. What is most modern about *Modern Chivalry* is its form: the novel is an oratorical forum of modern democracy. Though Brackenridge offers a representation of the languages of the forum, he writes as a voice independent of that marketplace, insisting that, unlike speakers in deliberative assemblies, he is no slave to his constituents (MC, 668). He will not flatter; he will not conciliate: he will ridicule and instruct. But the novelist must also court the public to be heard. Brackenridge's mission borders on that of Captain Farrago, and he invites the reader to investigate the closeness: "He is no democrat that deceives the people. He is an aristocrat. Have I deceived the people?" (MC, 507). Near the end of his last installment, he draws a distinct line of difference: "How shall we account for this eternal babbling in our public bodies, which delays and confuses business? . . . Something ought to be done to correct this logomachy, or war of words" (MC, 801). Against this war of words, he offers a comic novel of words that sometimes nears the seriousness of Pope's mock-epic *The Dunciad*.

What is missing from this account of *Modern Chivalry* is how the novel in its several installments was partly shaped and amended by Brackenridge's adventures (and misadventures) in politics as a statesman and lawyer and how its structure and evolution offer a commentary on what Gordon Wood terms "the democratization of the American mind."[10] Most succinctly, in Robert Ferguson's words, "Farrago represents the intellectual, gentlemanly, republican past; Teague, the ill-mannered, democratic future."[11] Though famous as a lexicographer, Noah Webster was a prolific writer who wrote much about language and much about other subjects besides language, and his own career as writer, which spans the period from 1783 to the early 1840s, can be read in large part as his own Farrago-like attempt to educate and refine a democratic voice.

In the early 1780s, Noah Webster, a young schoolteacher eager for fame, took a patriot's dislike to British primers, and he conceived of a plan to advance the interests of America and his own reputation. He began writing the textbooks that carried the War for Independence out of the battlefield and into the classroom. Only through a new system of education and a national language, he insisted, could America fulfill its revolutionary destiny and become an independent nation free from the corruption of the old world. In 1783 he published under the weighty title of *A Grammatical Institute of the English Language* part one of his new three-part plan for American education – a speller.

Known informally as "The Blue-Backed Speller," it underwent at least 385 editions in Webster's lifetime and became one of the best-selling books of the nineteenth century. The text was largely an adoption of two British works with some added information about United States geography and history, several changes in spelling and pronunciation, and fewer references to the Deity. What distinguishes it as American – and revolutionary in its ideology – is its preface, a stirring call for America's political and cultural independence:

> Europe is grown old in folly, corruption, and tyranny – in that country laws are perverted, manners are licentious, literature is declining, and human nature debased. For America in her infancy to adopt the present maxims of the old world would be to stamp the wrinkles of decrepid age upon the bloom of youth and to plant the seeds of decay in a vigourous constitution. American glory begins to dawn at a favourable period and under flattering circumstances. We have the experience of the whole world before our eyes; but to receive indiscriminately the maxims of government, the manners, and the literary taste of Europe and make them the ground on which to build our systems in America must soon convince us that a durable and stately edifice can never be erected upon the mouldering pillars of antiquity. It is the business of *Americans* to select the wisdom of all nations as the basis of her constitutions, to avoid their errours, to prevent the introduction of foreign vices and corruptions and check the career of her own, to promote virtue and patriotism, to embellish and improve the sciences, to diffuse an uniformity and purity of *language*, to add superiour dignity to this infant empire and to human nature.[12]

In this preface, which anticipates Madison's renowned comment in *Federalist* No. 14 that the framers of the Constitution did not allow "a blind veneration for antiquity, for custom, or for names, to overrule the suggestions of their own good sense, the knowledge of their own situation, and the lessons of their own experience" (FP, 14.104), Webster defines the goals of his career and his hopes for America: the young country could mature into an empire of reason if it adopted reforms in politics, education, and language and developed its own manners and literary tastes. Webster, an enlightened tutor, would help guide that development.

In 1784 Webster published a grammar and in 1785 a reader to complete parts two and three of *A Grammatical Institute of the English Language.* He based the grammar on Robert Lowth's *A Short Introduction to English Grammar* and differed most from Lowth in his willingness to accept general usage as a standard of correctness (he sanctioned such expressions as "it is me" and "them horses" and welcomed neologisms). In language, he recognized, the vox populi is sovereign; it can amend the rules of grammar. Webster, no matter how critical he became of American democracy in his later years, never renounced this radical linguistic theory. But no matter how much he was caught up in the flush of enthusiasm over the success of the Revolution at the outset of his career, he was never one to repose complete power or trust in the people. Though he maintained that the yeomanry of America spoke truer English than the aristocrats of England because they were less subject to the vagaries of linguistic fashion, he also appealed, as did Joseph Priestley, to analogies or to historical patterns of linguistic change as a rule of propriety.

To complete his plan for an elementary education that would inculcate American ways of speaking and thinking, Webster abridged versions of the speller, grammar, and reader for the youngest pupils. These were published as *The New England Primer, "Amended and Improved . . ."* (1789), a revised version of the popular colonial schoolbook without its rigorous Calvinism; *An Introduction to English Grammar* (1789); and *The Little Reader's Assistant* (1790), which included his "Federal Catechism," a simple explanation of the Constitution. These books are typical of Webster's career: an education in language will remain for him an occasion for political literacy, and he will give special attention to the education of youth because of his beliefs that the "only practicable method to reform mankind is to begin with children" and that the "impressions received in early life usually form the characters of individuals, a union of which forms the general character of a nation" (NW, 83, 78). Webster would reach Tom, Dick, and Harry before they got into the woods or while they were in the one-room schoolhouse. Webster shared faith in the formative power of education with his contemporaries and led them in translating it into programs of action to shape the character of the new nation.

In 1788, Webster published in the *American Magazine* a short essay entitled "A Dissertation Concerning the Influence of Language on Opinions and of Opinions on Language," which reiterated the concerns he developed in *Sketches of American Policy* (1785), a four-part political treatise that contained a plan for a stronger central government and ended with a vigorous plea for new cultural, as well as political, bonds of union. The title of the essay and much of its argument were borrowed from a work Johann David Michaelis wrote in 1759, which appeared in an English edition in 1769. Michaelis argues in a passage that Webster would later cite in *Dissertations on the English Language* that "language is a democratical state, where all the learning in the world does not warrant a citizen to supersede a received custom, till he has convinced the whole nation that this custom is a mistake."[13] For Michaelis, a language governed by the people is more conservative than radical: it serves as the best defense against the "innovations" of the "learned," whose "heads teem with them [errors] no less than the vulgar."[14] He fears that if everyone may "coin a new word," the established language will be broken into dialects, and the people will be threatened with a return to the "confusion" of Babel. In the late 1780s, the specter of disunity haunted Webster as it did Madison and other members of the Constitutional Convention, and just as the founding fathers developed a common political language based on democratic principles to control the dialects of state government and unite the worthy against the licentious, Webster believed, thanks in part to Michaelis, that a national language based on democratic principles could be a bond of union and an instrument for cultivating the habits of respect and obedience that were being broken, in his opinion, by the "licentious passions of men" (NW, 70). A national language would promote allegiance to a standard that transcended the "narrow views" and "illiberal prejudices" that produce "a selfish system of politics in each state" (NW, 45). Webster also concludes the essay with a statement that offers a clue to his convictions about his own self-importance: "If it can be proved that the *mere use of words* has led nations into errors, and still continues this delusion, we cannot hesitate a moment to conclude, that grammatical researches are worthy of the labor of men."[15]

When Webster supported the Constitution in a pamphlet published in 1787, he had already sought to prove to others how "some erroneous opinions respecting *freedom* and *tyranny*" had perpetrated delusion in the nation (NW, 51). To correct these errors, Webster becomes a lexicographer: he distinguishes between two definitions of "liberty" and insists that the one definition must not be confused with the other.

> Many people seem to entertain an idea that liberty consists in a *power to act without any control.* . . . But in a civil society political liberty consists in *acting comformably to the sense of a majority of the society.* In free government every man binds himself to obey the *public voice*, or the opinions of the majority, and the *whole society* engages to *protect each individual.* In such a government a man is *free* and safe. (NW, 51)

Just as people should respect the "public voice" in matters of spelling and pronunciation, so too must they respect the public voice in matters of law. Webster makes the same distinction in this passage that John Winthrop made in his address to the General Court in 1645, and he makes it for a similar reason: he too wants to harmonize the pursuit of liberty and the pursuit of order by defining liberty as obedience to the community. He offers a similar lesson in his 1828 dictionary. Though

he first defines liberty as "freedom from restraint," he points out that
this form of liberty is always "abridged by the establishment of
government." His subsequent definition is of civil liberty.

When Webster toured the states to promote his speller and the
cause of a stronger political union, he gave a series of lectures on
language and education. At the urging of Benjamin Franklin, he
published a revised version of his lectures on language in 1789 as
Dissertations on the English Language. This work reiterates the themes of
his textbook prefaces and sets forth the theoretical foundation for his
lexicography. But Webster also seizes the revolutionary – and the
constitutional – moment to fulfill at once a dream of the Enlightenment and a pressing political need: he will reform the language,
purging it of its corruptions, and through this reform he will promote
a "more perfect union": "America is in a situation the most favorable
for great reformations. . . . The minds of men in this country have
been awakened. . . . NOW is the time, and *this* the country, in which we
may expect success, in attempting changes favorable to language,
science and government. . . . Let us then seize the present moment,
and establish a *national language,* as well as a national government"
(DEL, 405–6). To justify his call for a national language, Webster turns
to the rhetoric of the American Revolution and draws upon its vocabulary of republicanism and its spirit of religious reform. Specifically,
he draws upon the link so often made in the eighteenth century
between political and linguistic degeneration when he argues that if
America is to free itself from English corruption, linguistic revolution
has to accompany political revolution. "Stile and taste, in all nations,"
he argues, "undergo the same revolutions, the same progress from
purity to corruption, as manners and government," and "in England
the pronunciation of the language has shared the same fate" (DEL,
177). Thus Webster demands that since "the taste of her writers is
already corrupted, and her language on the decline," we should
constitute our own system of language as well as government and end
our "astonishing respect" for its "arts and literature" and a "blind
imitation of its manners" (DEL, 20, 398). "To copy foreign manners
implicitly," he writes, "is to reverse the order of things, and begin our
political existence with the corruptions and vices which have marked
the declining glories of other republics" (DEL, 179). Webster also
argues, drawing directly upon Michaelis, that neither the scholar nor
anyone else has the right to dictate usage or compel people to defer to
linguistic innovations, for language "is a democratical state" (DEL,
167). To believe, then, that the "*ipse dixit* of a Johnson, a Garrick, or a
Sheridan, has the force of law; and to contradict it, is rebellion" is to
surrender our "right of private judgement" to "literary governors"

(DEL, 168). It is equally unjust, he points out, that English authors, in attempting to make the "practice of the court and stage in London the sole criterion of propriety in speaking," have abridged "the nation of its right," since "the *general practice* of a nation" is the "rule of propriety" (DEL, 24). Webster promulgates in the *Dissertations* a declaration of cultural independence that partakes of both the vocabulary of Paine's *Common Sense* and Emerson's later animus toward the "courtly muses of Europe."

Webster dedicates the *Dissertations* to Benjamin Franklin, whom he praises as a man who was "violently attached to no political party" and who labored "to reconcile contending factions in government" (DEL, v). The *Dissertations* can be considered part of Webster's attempt to accomplish through language what Franklin fostered through the statesman's deed as well as the writer's word: an overcoming of Babel, a transformation of diversity into social consensus. The Revolution had freed America from political dependence on England, but to avoid "losing the benefits of independence" Webster argues that citizens had to form "constitutions of government" to "secure freedom and property" and had to "embrace any scheme" that tended "to reconcile the people of America to each other, and weaken the prejudices which oppose a cordial union" (DEL, 36). Just as Franklin helped to devise a scheme – the Constitution – to secure freedom and property, Webster would devise schemes – spellers, grammars, readers, dictionaries – to facilitate a cordial union. A reform that would "make a difference between the English orthography and the American," he declares, "is an object of vast political consequence"; "a national language is a band of *national union*" (DEL, 397). Webster, like Whitman, promotes language as an adhesive force; the one does it by writing and promoting a poetic language that incorporates other voices but retains his personal accent, and the other by writing spellers, grammars, and dictionaries that promote a common language but retain the accents of Webster's voice and region. (Webster's 1828 dictionary never sold very well in the South.) But precisely why Webster considers a national language to be of vast political consequence is often ignored in this age, so alert to the politics of language and to the role played by a common language disseminated through print in the constitution of a nation as an imagined community. When Webster argues in an oft-quoted line, "Our political harmony is therefore concerned in a uniformity of language," he is worrying not about differences of meaning but differences of pronunciation (DEL, 20). What disunites a people is not thought but acts of pride, prejudice, ridicule, and provincialism that stem from those differences of pronunciation that "incline men to treat the [linguistic] practice of their neighbors with some degree of contempt" (ibid.). If all persons "of every rank" would speak "with some degree of precision and uniformity," he explains, "it would remove prejudice, and conciliate mutual affection and respect" (DEL, 397). Webster's friend is Teague O'Regan, the person whose nonstandard voice would subject him to contempt, and his enemy is the enemy of Jefferson's Declaration – a dissocial spirit that severs bonds of affection and respect: "Thus small differences in pronunciation at first excite ridicule – a habit of laughing at the singularities of strangers is followed by disrespect – and without respect friendship is a name, and social intercourse a mere ceremony" (DEL, 20). Webster's plan to restore to social intercourse what Jefferson called the "harmony and affection without which liberty and even life itself are but dreary things" is to insure that all people grow up speaking equally (JLA, 493).

Scarred by the differences of dialect and pronunciation that had befallen people ever since Babel, the people of the United States could overcome that curse by adopting republican principles to govern their language. To establish linguistic uniformity, the standard of propriety could be neither "the practice of any particular class of people" (DEL, 25) nor "local and variable custom" (DEL, 27). Just as the founding fathers reposed power in the people, Webster decides that in the democratical state of language, the rule of propriety must be "the *general practice of the nation*" (ibid.). But that practice, he adds in the same breath, must be tempered by the "*rules of the language itself*" (ibid.), by which he means "a fixed principle interwoven with the very construction of language, coeval and coextensive with it," which he compares to the "common laws of a land, or the immutable rules of morality, the propriety of which every man, however refractory, is forced to acknowledge, and to which most men will readily submit" (DEL, 29). According to Webster, language possesses natural or fundamental laws, an internal logic, that should determine how a people change their linguistic representatives. What Webster advocates is perhaps best explained by Dugald Stewart, a Scottish philosopher and a contemporary of Webster, who argues in *Political Economy* that the introduction of "a new word, or a new combination of words" by a writer "is not sufficient to justify the use of it." He adds, "It must be shewn that it is not disagreeable to the general analogy of the language, otherwise it is soon laid aside as an innovation, revolting, anomalous, and ungrammatical. It is much in the same manner that we come to apply the epithet unconstitutional to law."[16] The speech of the people in the present must be governed by the speech of the people from time immemorial. But Webster also argues that the fundamental rules of language can be amended by a form of unanimous consent in the present: "When a deviation from analogy has become the universal practice of a nation, it then takes place of all rules and becomes the standard of propriety" (DEL, 28). The constitution Webster prescribes for the English language is one that establishes both a principle of stability and a principle for accommodating change, and both principles are rooted in popular sovereignty.

Webster appended to his *Dissertations* a radical proposal for linguistic reform that extended even further the reign of the vox populi in his reconstitution of the English language. His plan was to render the "orthography of words correspondent to the pronunciation" (DEL, 391). Samuel Johnson insisted on the subordination of the oral to the written; Webster proposes the reverse. The word would directly represent sound. The voice would be sovereign. Webster never justifies his proposal to reform the orthography of the "AMERICAN TONGUE" by appealing to the precedent of the Constitution, nor does he discuss the degree to which his own efforts to diffuse a uniformity of language through the medium of printed grammars and spellers would subordinate the voice to the written. But he was more than willing to acknowledge publicly on one special occasion how political and linguistic reform could go hand in hand. In the New York procession honoring the ratification of the Constitution, Webster marched with the Philological Society of New York, whose armorial seal bore the figure of a woman representing the Genius of America. She held the Constitution in one hand and with the other pointed to the scroll of the Philological Society.[17] In the years that followed the ratification of the Constitution, the political grammar of the nation was as reverently respected as any schoolmaster could have desired, but Webster was troubled by the way the key words in that grammar were being abused. In 1802 he notes, for instance: "There is no exact standard of political right and wrong by which discordant opinions can in all cases be adjusted. Even the Constitution is not sufficiently explicit to furnish this standard" (NW, 126). What the country needed, it seems, was a political dictionary to accompany its political grammar.

In the late 1780s and the 1790s Webster became one of the country's leading political essayists and a prolific author. For the *American Magazine*, a general-interest monthly publication, the *American Mercury*, a daily newspaper, and the *Herald*, a semiweekly, he wrote essays on a wide range of subjects, including the Constitution, penal reform, slavery, banking, commerce, education, city planning, forest conservation, the French Revolution, and epidemic diseases. Not without controversy, he also promoted the policies of Washington's administration. One of the prime subjects of his editorial attacks was the growing party spirit in the country; a related concern, as Joseph Ellis notes, was the imprecision of political discourse.[18]

By 1794, when Webster wrote a long essay on the French Revolution, the theory he had expounded in 1788 to justify grammatical research – "the *mere use of words* has led nations into errors" – had in his estimation received incontrovertible proof. The French Revolution and American party politics convinced him and a number of other writers in the early republic that there was an inseparable connection between political and linguistic disorders.[19] Disturbed by the delusions perpetrated by the abuse of words, some pleaded for and others proposed verbal solutions, including a dictionary of political terms. In 1792, for instance, a writer in the *National Gazette* complains:

> The improper use of words, or the artful misapplication of names and epithets it is very evident, has had a great and dangerous influence upon the politics of this country. Has not every abuse of language, that can be thought of, been constantly practiced for a long time, to give the people false ideas, both of the government, and of its administration. . . . I wish some ingenious hand, would furnish the public with a short dictionary of those words, which, like many of the political leaders of our country; have changed their meaning since the year 1776.[20]

Webster's own lexicographical labors must be seen as arising in part from an era that witnessed a democratization of politics that fulfilled for the Federalists the state of the soul and the state of language that Plato associates with democracy in *The Republic*. Faction, the archnemesis in Thucydides' account of the *stasis* at Corcyra and of *Federalist No. 10*, is the nemesis of politics in Webster's 1794 analysis of the revolution in France. To describe the effects of the revolution in France and of all wars on people, Webster coins a new word, one of his two neologisms: "demoralizing."[21] The demoralization of the mind Webster preaches against is the state when people lose their virtue and usurp the empire of reason: "Men are always the same ferocious animals, when guided by passion and loosed from the restraints of law" (PS, 1294). During the factional strife that marked the French Revolution and that Webster saw as a threat to the national character of the United States, language itself is demoralized. The "language of the ruling faction in France" and the "language of party in all countries," Webster writes, is always the same: "'to rescue the state from tyranny – to destroy despotism – to exterminate traitors'" (PS, 1283). But these terms are mere pretexts for violence: they sanction ugly deeds; they defend the indefensible. The cant of Sulla and Marius in

Rome, of Cromwell in England, and of the ruling men in France –
betrayers all of liberty, in Webster's view – is the cant of the demagogue whose rise to power brings about the fall of the state and the
fall of words.

> The state must be saved, and to save it, our party must prevail;
> liberty must be secured; but to secure it, we must be absolute in
> power, and of course liberty is crushed. A republic must be estab-
> lished; but to do this, a few commissioners, with dictatorial power,
> seconded by an irresistable military force, must govern the country.
> Our government shall be a *republic, one and indivisible*; and to effect
> this, it is necessary to put to death the representatives of one half the
> republic, that the whole may be governed by the other half. Free-
> dom of debate is a constitutional right; but we must have a Paris mob
> to hiss down our enemies. (PS, 1283)

Webster quotes from another commentator on the French Revolution,
a "Mr. Neckar," to argue that the Jacobins succeeded in France by the
artful abuse of two words – "liberty" and "equality." "But the people
are to be acted upon only by reducing things to a small compass; it is
by restricting their ideas to the narrow circle of their feelings, and
absorbing their passions in a phrase, that we become their masters"
(PS, 1292). Webster then warns, "The emissaries of the Jacobins are
attempting to make themselves masters of the people in America by
the same means" (ibid.). Fear of the double-tongued deceiver – the
seducer of opinion that a logocracy summoned to the forum – was the
reigning fear of post-Revolutionary America.

To believe that a language has become corrupt or demoralized is to
acknowledge that a word is no more inherently virtuous, or no less
prey to corruption, than a politician. Just like a politician, words are
motivated by interests; they respond to constituencies of power; they
cannot be trusted to speak the same thing to different audiences. But
the American civil religion demands that we moralize the language of
the founding fathers. Once upon a time the words of the founders
were sacred, honest, trustworthy. Then we fell. The republic lost its
virtue. The letter lost its spirit. Politicians became actors. This is a
favorite fairy tale told by the party of memory. The party of hope tells
the same tale but ends it differently: the word will be redeemed.
Historians prefer to challenge the myth by demoralizing language in
their own way: moral terms are fists gloved in velvet. Nietzsche, who
is one of the guiding lights of this critical perspective, writes in *The
Will to Power*: "*Toward a critique of the big words*. – I am full of suspicion
and malice against what they call 'ideals.' . . . Christianity, the revolution, the abolition of slavery, equal rights, philanthropy, love of

peace, justice, truth: all these big words have value only in a fight; as flags: *not* as realities but as *showy words* for something quite different (indeed, opposite!)."[22] The French Revolution proved beyond a doubt to Webster what communist rule proved to Václav Havel: "The same word can, at one moment, radiate great hope; at another, it can emit lethal rays. The same word can be true at one moment and false the next, at one moment illuminating, at another, deceptive. On one occasion it can open up glorious horizons, on another, it can lay down the tracks to an entire archipelago of concentration camps."[23] The rhetoric of liberty spilled blood in America; the rhetoric of liberty spilled blood in France. That the blood spilled in America did not lead to the terror of the French Revolution made Webster and the Federalists no less suspicious of big words in the mid 1790s: what happened in France could happen here. The amount of confidence or distrust placed in the rhetoric of liberty became a measure of the difference between Republicans and Federalists, and by 1800 Webster was siding with distrust. Jefferson's rhetoric of reconciliation in his first inaugural address did anything but lessen this distrust.

For Webster, Jefferson was little else than an American Jacobin, duping the people with his claim that "we are all Republicans, we are all Federalists" (JLA, 493). In a letter addressed to Jefferson, Webster protests that his first inaugural address contains "a studied ambiguity of language, which seems to cover a spirit of conciliation, impartiality, and sound political morality."[24] To expose Jefferson, Webster joins verbal and political criticism. He asks, "What is meant by the indefinite and ambiguous term, 'anti-republican tendencies'?" And he later adds: "Is this the age of reason, Sir? . . . And are the people still so blind as to be the dupes of hypocritical professions? Will they not discover the clove foot? Will not they see that the public interest is a secondary consideration, and that all the zeal about republican principles and equal rights has been the smoke, under cover of which, bold, intriguing, hungry office-seekers, have taken possession of the best offices of government?" (MP, 16, 39). Ever the grammarian, Webster also informs Jefferson that "your writings are remarkable for incorrect language" (MP, 9).

Shortly after Jefferson's inauguration, the *New England Palladium* recorded its own response to the semantics of party politics: demagogues had obscured the meaning of words to appeal more readily to the "passions of their hearers," and "too many people have been made the dupes of mere verbal abuses." Countering any quick embrace of linguistic liberty, the writer adds, "Names, which formerly stood for distinct and known ideas, have had new applications, without the necessary definitions."[25] Rufus King, a leading Federalist, offered a similar dissent near the close of Jefferson's second term: "Words without meaning, or with wrong meaning have especially of late years done great harm. Liberty, Love of Country, Federalism, Republicanism, Democracy, Jacobin, Glory, Philosophy and Honor are words in the mouth of everyone and without any precision used by any one; the abuse of words is as pernicious as the abuse of things."[26] Violations of the linguistic contract and failure to adhere to Lockean remedies for the abuse of words, it was feared, was leading to the breakdown of the social order. "The abuse of language, or the substitution of names for realities," Warren Dutton declares in a Fourth of July oration in 1805, "is one of the most successful instruments ever wielded in the demolition of government." "If experience made the world wiser," he suggests, "it might be useful to compile a dictionary, containing a number of words and phrases, with the revolutionary explanations, designed particularly for the use of free governments." The prospectus for the dictionary that he then sketches is the prospectus for a "Devil's Dictionary" such as Ambrose Bierce later devised:

> Opening this book, and looking at the word "economy," we might read this explanation. A word used by demagogues in and out of office, to delude the multitude; the art of growing rich without revenue, and strong without force, – also the maintenance of courts without judges; the science of preventing war by tameness and submission. . . . "Political toleration," or equal and exact justice to all men; – a phrase often used by men new in office, to gain the confidence of the credulous, and dissipate the fears of those, who can be made easy by their hopes – also the punishment of political heresy. "Aristocrat" or "Federalist," a term of reproach, applied to the ablest and most virtuous men of a country to render them unpopular. "Independent Judiciary," a phrase not to be found in this dictionary.

Dutton concludes with the resignation that marked Johnson's reflections on his own labors as a lexicographer: "In popular governments such abuses will exist, in spite of all the power of argument, or the light of evidence."[27] The sounds of politicians are too subtle to be restrained by definition or by the instruction of schoolmasters. None of these writers, it seems, needed Wittgenstein to understand language games, or Nietzsche to tell them the value of big words in a power struggle, or Pocock to explain that a paradigm was shifting or under strain. Thanks in part to the debate over the French Revolution and the logomachy of the 1800 election, this period was the first sophistic of the United States democracy. Webster's dictionaries emerge from this sophistic.

Webster's essay on the French Revolution, his letter to Jefferson in 1801, and the *Compendious Dictionary of the English Language* he published in 1806 reveal a habit of thought that was common to his age and that he would advance by uncommon labors for the remaining forty years of his life. He made words and politicians the subject of his inquiry and criticism as he sought to provide the American people with clear ideas about the terms that others saw being abused, such as "liberty," "equality," and "republic," and about an enormous lexicon of other words. At the end of his study of the French Revolution, Webster cautioned his countrymen that the moment they quit the "sheet-anchor" of the Constitution, they would be "threatened every moment with ship-wreck" (PS, 1299). To help settle the course of the ship of state, Webster sought to settle its language. But his hopes for reform were tempered by doubt about a people's capacity to govern themselves by reason and words. In his later years, he distrusted both the vox populi and the words of the Declaration and the Constitution as a basis for government; he placed greater faith in obedience to the vox Dei, and what was as important to him as the definition of words was his quest to illuminate the meaning of God's Word.

The culmination of Webster's work defining words was the publication in 1828 of his two-volume *An American Dictionary of the English Language*, which contained 70,000 definitions, 12,000 more than any previous dictionary. The Webster who wrote the dictionary, however, was a man much different from the Webster who wrote the speller. Once a young revolutionary committed to republican principles, by 1828 he had renounced his early political beliefs as the follies of youth. In 1808 he had an emotional religious experience that led to his conversion to Calvinism and strengthened his emphasis on the need for strict discipline in the public world as well as in personal life.[28] The linguistic theory of the dictionary reveals the determining influence of his religious convictions. Certain of the truth of the biblical story of the tower of Babel, he disregarded the advances made in philology by Franz Bopp and Jacob Grimm, and, convinced that Chaldee was the original biblical language whose traces could still be found in modern languages, he compared twenty languages to prepare his etymologies, searching for what he termed the "radix" of words – their origin in Chaldee. The dictionary became Webster's single-handed and single-minded effort to redeem language from the curse of Babel.

Webster's 1828 dictionary has been considered as much a work of cultural nationalism as his speller. But if the speller was America's Declaration of Linguistic Independence, the dictionary was a linguistic Treaty of Paris wherein Webster maintains that while a difference of language between England and America is inevitable, a sameness is desirable. Webster included as few as fifty "Americanisms" in the dictionary and, tellingly, it was initially better received in England

than in America. Richard Rollins and Joseph Ellis have closely examined Webster's definitions, and they conclude that rather than the
work of a patriotic booster of the United States, the dictionary, in
Ellis's words, is "the life statement of a disillusioned republican who
hoped to shape the language and therefore the values of subsequent
generations in ways that countered the emerging belief in social
equality, individual autonomy, and personal freedom."[29] For instance,
Webster defines "people" as "The body of persons who form a
community. . . . The vulgar; the mass of illiterate persons. The com-
monality, as distinct from men of rank." This is a definition of
"people" that befits someone who in his later years advocated the
passage of a federal law requiring that men be denied the vote until
they were forty-five. "A republic," he wrote, referred to "Common
interest; the public." Then in brackets, he adds, *Not in use.* And
"virtue" was "Strength. . . . Bravery; valor." But again Webster
cannot resist weighting the language of the lexicographer with the
gravity of a satirist condemning a demoralized state. In brackets he
adds, "Meaning obsolete."[30] That the dictionary could be an armory
in the battle against misrepresentation is suggested by "Rhetor," who
in an 1833 essay entitled "The Abuse of Words" writes, "We think
that speech was given to some that they might utter falsehoods and
make misrepresentations, and to some, that they might conceal or
disgrace their ideas." After advocating the perusal of "Locke on the
Human Understanding" as one remedy, he also advises, "No man
should ever sit down to write without a copy of Webster's Dictionary
at his left elbow."[31]

In 1837, at the age of seventy-nine, Webster admitted in a letter to
Daniel Webster that he had "nearly lost all hope of benefiting my
country by correcting the disorders of our language."[32] But his despair
did not prevent him from lecturing in another letter the man who had
won wide respect as the "Defender of the Constitution" on the
meanings of words in the Declaration and the Constitution. Though
we do not have Daniel Webster's reaction, he might well have been
astonished by the lecture, for Noah Webster provides a verbal criticism of the Declaration that unsettles more than it defends the foundation documents of the American republic. He complains that the
misunderstanding of the words "*born free and equal*" and the "enjoyment
of *life* and *liberty*" have led to "radical errors in the opinions of our
citizens in regard to the principles on which a republican government
is to be founded and the means by which it is to be supported" (NWL,
482). To correct those errors, Webster tests those words against the
facts as he sees them. He begins with an analysis of the phrase "born
free and equal."

> The constitutions of government in the United States commence
> with a declaration of certain abstract principles of general and
> indefinite propositions, as that all men are *born free and equal* or all
> men are *created equal*. But as universal propositions, can they be true?
> In what sense are men *born free*? If they are born under a despotic
> government, they are not born *free*. But in any government, children
> are born subject to the control of their parents, and this by the
> express ordinance of the Creator. . . . The general proposition,
> then, that *all* men are *born free* is the reverse of the truth, for *no person
> is born free*, in the general acceptation of the word *free*. (Ibid.)

He then proceeds to examine the word "equal": "In what sense then
are men born *equal*? Is it true that all men are furnished with equal
force of constitution or physical strength? Is it true that all men are
endowed by the Creator with equal intellectual powers? No person
will contend for an affirmative answer to these questions" (ibid.).
"Equally indefinite," he adds, "is the proposition that all men are
entitled to the enjoyment of *life* and *liberty*" (ibid.). "They are entitled
to life," Webster explains, "unless it has been forfeited; but even life is
to be enjoyed under the conditions prescribed by law. . . . The
enjoyment of liberty is subject to a like restriction. No society can
exist without restricting the liberty of every member by the laws or
will of the community" (NWL, 482–3). With this analysis, Webster
claims to have "clearly proved that the general principles assumed by
the framers of our government are too indefinite to be the basis of
constitutional provision" (NWL, 483). He then adds a final observation and a prophecy: "It is believed . . . that the loose, undefined sense
in which the words *free* and *equal* are used in some of the American
constitutions has been and will be a source of immense evil to this
country. Illiterate men will mistake the just limitations of the words,
and unprincipled men will give them a latitude of construction incom-
patible with the peace of society" (ibid.). To restrain the power of
illiterate and unprincipled men, Webster believes the boundaries of
such words as "free" and "equal" must be fenced and guarded. For
Webster, as for Hobbes, loose definitions are a source of political evil,
and strict definitions are a means of establishing order. In the same
year, 1837, Webster registers another protest against the vagueness of
American political discourse. He argues that the language so often
repeated in America, that "the *people* can govern themselves and that a
democracy is of course a *free government*," should be carefully examined
rather than automatically accepted as "political axioms of unquestion-
able truth" (NWL, 504). He complains that the people who preach
these doctrines "have never defined what they mean by the *people*, or
what they mean by *democracy*" (ibid.).

In the late 1830s, Webster was invited by the board of directors of the New York Lyceum to deliver a set of lectures. Unable or unwilling to present the lectures, he prepared a pamphlet entitled "Observations on Language," which was published in 1839. Although he continued to revise various texts until his death in 1843, this pamphlet was his last formal discussion of language. When Webster composed the pamphlet, the criticism of American political discourse that he made to Daniel Webster could not have been far from his mind, because near the end he comments that "it is believed that a misapplication of terms, or the use of indefinite terms, sometime leads to serious mistakes, both in religion and government," and he adds, "It is obvious to my mind, that popular errors proceeding from a misunderstanding of words are among the *efficient causes of our political disorders*."[33] Though Webster at this point had become a bitter critic of American democracy who admitted that he never would have supported the Revolution if he had known that it would lead to the excesses and disorders he observed in his later years, this statement cannot be dismissed as the crankiness of a dyspeptic schoolmaster frustrated by a class who had never listened to his lectures. The connection Webster made so often in his career between political and linguistic disorders had become in the 1830s a political axiom, and American political debate in these years was preoccupied with the problem of settling the meanings of words or countering their force.

Daniel Webster: Schoolmaster of the Constitution

Daniel Webster was the preeminent gladiator in the forum of antebellum political debate. "Through his speeches," Edwin Whipple reports, "he seemed to be almost bodily present wherever the family, gathered in the evening around the blazing hearth, discussed the questions of the day."[34] Noah Webster might have chosen him to be the recipient of his lecture on the meanings of political terms precisely because he had devoted parts of his key political speeches in the early 1830s to the project of defining words and preventing the incorporation of solecisms in what he termed the "American political grammar" – the Constitution. His central place in antebellum politics as a lecturer on the law is suggested by a book published in 1854. Entitled *The Constitutional Text Book* (*The Union Text Book* in an 1860 edition), it was designed for students and dedicated to the governors of each state, and it consisted of selections from a wide range of Webster's speeches, along with the texts of the Declaration and the Constitution. In one speech in particular, "The Constitution Not a Compact Between Sovereign States," which he gave in February 1833 in reply to resolutions and a speech made by John Calhoun, Webster became at once a defender of the Constitution and a schoolmaster to America as he turned his speech into a lesson about political language and the politics of language.

Early in this speech, which Whipple characterized as "a verbal fortress constructed for the purpose of defense and aggression,"[35] Webster asks, "Was it Mirabeau . . . or some other master of the human passions, who has told us that words are things?" (DWW, VI, 186). No correct citation was necessary: Webster himself proved that equivalence to his contemporaries as he dominated, in Robert Ferguson's words, "every podium except the pulpit in an age when speech controlled thought and action."[36] Indeed, in what Whipple termed the "gladiatorial strife . . . of debate" where "brain [was] pitted against brain, and manhood against manhood," Webster showed that words are what he said they were in this address: "They are indeed things, and things of mighty influence, not only in addresses to the passions and high-wrought feelings of mankind, but in the discussion of legal and political questions also" (DWW, VI, 186). That equivalence between words and things, speech and action, definition and political decision became an American fact of life the moment the states ratified the Constitution. In America, the written law is a king, and its words are as much political actions as the sentences that had been proclaimed by a king whose royal "we" spoke for and ruled his subjects. If there were any problem interpreting the words of the Constitution or any substitution in its language, it could "have an important bearing on the happiness of millions," as one political commentator pointed out in 1833.[37]

During his reply to Calhoun's speech, Webster sought to reject not only mistaken definitions that could disrupt a sovereign people's pursuit of happiness but a brazen attempt to transform the fundamental vocabulary of American politics by unsettling the meanings of old words and adding new words that the founding fathers had never spoken or sanctioned. Webster's "verbal fortress" is built to defend the "plain sense and meaning" of the Constitution, and his offensive tactic is to attack through a Lockean analysis of words the Newspeak of Calhoun.[38] Like Paine's pamphleteering in 1776, his aim was to render the influential words of a political enemy impotent by proving that they did not stand for common sense while establishing his own definitions as standard according to history and correct usage.

Webster's debate with Calhoun hinged on the question of whether or not the Constitution was a compact between sovereign states, and he begins to refute Calhoun's argument by noting that the word "compact" never appears in the text of the document and by claiming that Calhoun's theory "degrades" the word "constitution" – and thus the thing itself – into "an insignificant, idle epithet, attached to *compact*" (DWW, VI, 185). He then elaborates this point in the terms of a schoolmaster conducting a grammar lesson (and we can almost see him rapping a pointer against a blackboard as he does so):

> Sir, I must say to the honorable gentleman, that, in our American political grammar, CONSTITUTION is a noun substantive; it imports a distinct and clear idea of itself; and it is not to lose its importance and dignity, it is not to be turned into a poor, ambiguous, senseless, unmeaning adjective, for the purpose of accommodating any new set of political notions. Sir, we reject his new rules of syntax altogether. We will not give up our forms of political speech to the grammarians of the school of nullification. By the Constitution, we mean, not a "constitutional compact," but, simply and directly, the Constitution, the fundamental law; and if there be one word in the language which the people of the United States understand, this is that word. (DWW, VI, 185–6)

Webster appeals in this passage to the linguistic principle that nouns are more important than adjectives, but his ultimate appeal is to the principle that popular usage is sovereign in both law and language, or to the maxim that Noah Webster cites in the frontispiece of his speller, *Usus est norma loquendi*. To use the word "constitution" as an adjective is to violate the people's way of speaking.

Webster makes a similar objection to Calhoun's notion that the states "acceded" to the Constitution. "The people of the United States," Webster explains, "have used no such form of expression in establishing the present government. They do not say they *accede* to a league, but they declare that they *ordain* and *establish* a Constitution" (DWW, VI, 187). For Webster, in short, the words "compact" and "accession" are "not constitutional modes of expression," but instead are a spurious vocabulary that Calhoun has attempted to foist on the people (ibid.). Thus, to justify his theory, Calhoun must say the thing which is not. He must abandon "the use of constitutional language for a new vocabulary" and "give new names to things" (DWW, VI, 190). But by imposing on Calhoun "the restraints of constitutional language," Webster seeks to brand his neologisms as injudicious or illegal (ibid.). And by seeking to maintain the bond between the words the people have spoken and the meanings the people have attached to them, Webster hopes to maintain the bond of union – a bond that had been ratified not only by the rational consent the people gave to its words but by their patriotic love for the Declaration that Washington and the other heroes of the Revolution fought for in 1776 and for the language that was framed in Philadelphia in 1787.

Near the end of his speech, Webster expresses his fear about the disorder that would occur if the language of the founding fathers was replaced by the Newspeak of the school of nullification. He declares that "if we are to receive the Constitution as the text, and then to lay down in its margin the contradictory commentaries which have been, and which may be, made by different states, the whole page would be a polyglot indeed. It would speak with as many tongues as the builders of Babel, and in dialects as much confused, and mutually as unintelligible" (DWW, VI, 196). In Webster's view, the states of the Union, though federated along one keel, were speaking or were threatening to speak in the many tongues that had been the curse of the old world, or in as many dialects as the "Isolatoes" on board the *Pequod* in *Moby-Dick*, a work Melville composed at the height of the constitutional crisis in the early 1850s. When Ahab's cabin boy Pip observes the varied interpretations that Ahab, Starbuck, and others place on the doubloon Ahab nails to the mast, he remarks, "I look, you look, he looks; we look, ye look, they look." One character comments that Pip must have been studying *Murray's Grammar*. Perhaps he had been studying commentaries on the "American political grammar"; for in this period the Constitution was the epitome of an open-ended text subject to the politics of interpretation.

In mid-nineteenth-century America, the quest to save the Union from shipwreck, which Daniel Webster directed in Congress, was in large part a quest to produce a unified reading of the Constitution, a quest that could be no more successful than an attempt to reconcile the multiple commentaries on Ahab's doubloon and Hester's scarlet letter; for in each case ambiguity arises not from the inherent indeterminacy of the sign, but from the political, economic, and religious differences that led shipmates on the *Pequod* and the townspeople of Boston in *The Scarlet Letter* and citizens in the 1850s to read texts with different motivations. *Moby-Dick* and *The Scarlet Letter* reflect a world of competing voices and contested interpretations not just because God's texts – the Book of Scripture and the Book of Nature – were seen to be ambiguous in antebellum America by religious commentators, such as Horace Bushnell, but because these novels were written in a political state united by the letter of the law – the words of the Constitution – but divided in spirit over its interpretation. Bushnell himself recognized that it was not just the language of religion that was ambiguous and necessarily inexact in its representations, as he explains in his profound commentary on language and interpretation in *God in Christ* (1849), for he later writes, in 1861, "It is a remarkable but very serious fact, not sufficiently noted as far as my observation extends, that our Revolutionary fathers left us the legacy of this war in the ambiguities of thought and principle which they suffered in respect to the foundations of government itself."[39] Language, he argues in *God in Christ*, "is only tropical, and the meanings, of course, indefinitely variable. . . . And yet it seems to be imagined that we can saddle mere forms of words, and ride them into necessary unambiguous conclusions!"[40] *God in Christ*, *The Scarlet Letter*, and *Moby-Dick* disrupt the logic of any reader who would ride words into dogmatic conclusions. Daniel Webster, with his inexorable logic, was one such horseman. He rode words as hard as any antebellum politician into "unambiguous conclusions" to defeat the verbal duplicity that was threatening the Union.

To counter the babel of political dialects, Webster venerated the Constitution more than any schoolmaster venerated grammar. Through his "magnificent idealization, or idolization, of the Constitution and the Union," he became "a poet," or so Whipple declares in his essay "Daniel Webster as a Master of English Style." Whitman, who wrote in 1836 that the Constitution is "the grandest piece of moral building ever constructed" and that "its architects were some mighty prophets and gods," has Webster as a precursor (WLA, 1318). Their eloquent idealization of the Constitution and the Union is the opposite side of the doubloon of Ahab's eloquent demonization of Moby-Dick: Webster's speeches, Whitman's *Leaves of Grass*, and Ahab's oratory are Orphic acts of speech that seek to counter subversion of the ship of state by federating diversity into unity. Melville's narrative in *Moby-Dick*, which opens with a subsublibrarian humbly federating together a polyglot of etymologies and extracts, presents through Ishmael's voice a different alternative for achieving *e pluribus unum*. His union with Queequeg, a bond that saves him from shipwreck, arises through open-mindedness and affection, through good will and good talk, and through Ishmael's remarkable capacity for listening to and learning from a strange tongue. This union, however, is but a separate peace that saves one person.

"We are now at a time in history," Richard Poirier declared in 1969, "when nearly all voices ask to be listened to." "This is a literary as well as a political problem," he adds, and he argues that the "great American writers are those who have sought to promote the elements of eccentricity in the sounds that make up America, while searching for a design that does an injustice to none of them."[41] *The Scarlet Letter*, *The House of the Seven Gables*, and *Uncle Tom's Cabin* promote eccentric voices – the voices of Hester, Holgrave, and Uncle Tom – but they also promote the incorporation of these voices into a more perfect union. But given the divided structure of the political union and of the constitutional text itself, paradox, ambiguity, and the play of differences could not be escaped. Not even the godlike Webster could compromise these differences. The symmetry of form attainable in fiction could not be attained in fact without committing grave injustices, as Melville teaches in *Billy Budd*. If the unity of the novel was a way of imagining and constituting the unity of a state for Hawthorne and Stowe, the disunity of the novel – a breakup of the symmetry of form, a creation of ragged edges, a silenced voice that leaves a story untold – was the way Melville imagines or reflects upon the disunity of the state and the limits of the Union. *The Scarlet Letter* and *Uncle Tom's Cabin* can also be read, however, to suggest the lesson of the Civil War: the symmetry of the Union and the Constitution could only be preserved by suppressing contradictory voices or by reconstructing them by force.

Antebellum Schoolmasters of the Language and the Bonds of Union

The Constitution was exalted by Webster (and Whitman) as no mechanical contrivance: it was an "organic compact" emanating from the people, bound to their soul, and as adhesive for the people of the Union as the English language in America was for Whitman. Whitman presents the English language as the model for unity overcoming diversity: it is the "free and compacted composition of all" and a "universal absorber, combiner, and conqueror" (WLA, 1165). In 1859 James P. Herron similarly describes the English language in America in *American Grammar: Adapted to the National Language of the United States* as a federated language: "We express our own free thoughts in *language* our own, adopted from the tongues of many nations, of our forefathers. . . . Consequently, language in the United States is *Polyglot* – national with our people – not borrowed from any one distinct tongue."[42] Language was to many antebellum grammarians what it was to Noah Webster – a bond of union – and it was their quest to sustain and diffuse a uniformity of language as much as Daniel Webster sought to sustain a standard language for the Constitution. Lindley Murray's *English Grammar, Adapted to Different Classes of Learners*, first published in 1795, sold over a million copies and by 1850 had been printed in more than three hundred editions. More than 250 different grammars were published between 1800 and 1850. The polyglot of American democracy would be melted down in the schoolroom and remolded by the speller, the grammar, and the dictionary. Language instruction was a means to promote a standardization that promised allegiance to the rule of a common language perhaps more than it promised an equality of voices unmarked by differences of class and region. Moral duty and civic duty united together in the study of grammar. Linguistic propriety, or a strict adherence to the laws of language, was allied with those other modes of mitigating the centrifugal forces of democracy that Tocqueville notes – an identity of custom and conformity to laws. Radical grammarians in antebellum America followed Noah Webster's early lead in proposing reforms that would rationalize and democratize the language, simplifying spelling and battling against the rule of custom that preserved the polite usage of the elite as standard. These grammars, however, never became popular.[43] Of the two grammars that were most successful in antebellum America – Murray's *English Grammar* and Samuel Kirkham's *English Grammar in Familiar Lectures* (1825) – the first was heavy on grammar as moral piety, the second on grammar as civic duty. Kirkham concludes his preface with a Fourth of July tribute to the fathers – "The mighty struggle for independence is over; and you live to enjoy the rich boon of freedom and prosperity which was purchased with the blood of your fathers" – and an invocation to the sons: "These considerations forbid that you should ever be so unmindful of your duty to your country, to your Creator, to yourself, and to succeeding generations as to be content to grovel in ignorance."[44] Writing in the third person for a campaign biography in 1860, Abraham Lincoln associates his separation from an illiterate father with his own study of grammar: "After he was twentythree, and had separated from his father, he studied English grammar, imperfectly of course, but so as to speak and write as well as he now does" (LLA, II, 162). In a speech that inaugurates Lincoln's political career, his 1838 address before the Young Men's Lyceum, he pays tribute to the fathers – "They *were* the pillars of the temple of liberty" – and he provides an invocation to the sons: "Let every man remember that to violate the law, is to trample on the blood of his father" (LLA, I, 36, 32). The grammar text Lincoln studied was Kirkham's, a text that concludes by offering a list of provincialisms by region (e.g., New England; Pennsylvania; Md. Va. Ky. Miss. & c.; Irish) that should be fought to create a uniformity of language.

In antebellum America, political differences became legal differences, legal differences became verbal differences, and grammarians (and statesmen), working backwards, sought to settle political differences by settling things at the verbal end. Politics in this age was reduced at times to a matter of stating (or finding) the obvious meaning of the letter of the law that others had mystified or purloined. But multiple demystifications of the Constitution rendered it as hieroglyphic as Ahab's doubloon. Just as antebellum literature provides a number of mirrors in which we can see reflected, sometimes quite darkly as in Poe's *Narrative of Arthur Gordon Pym* and "The Gold-Bug," an acute self-consciousness about verbal ambiguity and the obtuseness that could accompany the decoding of signs, so too do antebellum works of linguistic theory and grammatical reform manifest this self-consciousness. They share, in short, the lament of Montaigne: "The troubles of the world are grammatical." And grammarians became prescriptive about more than usage: they offered remedies for settling the language of the Constitution in the midst of a divided political state.

In 1838 James Brown called for a revolution in grammatical instruction that draws upon the words and tones of Paine's *Common Sense*. The introduction to his new system of grammar is entitled "An Appeal from the British System of English Grammar to Common Sense." But besides a ringing critique of English grammar, Brown devotes attention to the problem of language in the American republic. He complains that "lax phraseology, unmeaning descriptions, and obscure expressions pervade, and deform the works of our great men" because "the subjects of *truth*, and *definitions* are generally cast out of our seminaries of learning."[45] He notes in particular that the Constitution, which he calls the "*ark*" bearing the rights and liberties of America, cannot be understood by two impartial statesmen in the same way because of its "philological defectiveness" and "a want of *skill* in the language which is used" (xv, xvii). Thus one party believes that the Constitution sanctions the institution of a national bank while the other party seeks to demolish the bank with the same instrument. Continuing to locate the source of sectional and family rivalries in language, he writes that "Most of those difficulties which distract neighborhoods, and array even brother against brother, and carry both before a *judge* and *jury*" arise from "a want of *closely* defining the terms or conditions of their own contracts" (xvii). It thus becomes every man and woman, he counsels, "to understand the language of their own country" (xvii). "This Republic," he insists, "is not to be saved from the attacks of ambitions, by a *Junius* brandishing the crimson steel. The guardian power of America, must be sought for in her *constitution*" (xv). The guardian of that guardian would be the schools that instruct a people in their language. "Let the institutions in which our youth complete their education, give attention to our *own* language; . . . our statesmen must be acquainted with their *own* language, or our republic is of short duration" (xviii). What makes an American, Brown insists at the end, is not birth but conduct that accords "with the spirit of *our* laws, whose eye is upon *our* constitution" – and his grammar is designed to diffuse through the country an education in both the language and the spirit of that law (xxi).

In 1850 Samuel Gridley Howe reported to the trustees of the Perkins Institution and Massachusetts Asylum for the Blind the success he had

had teaching language skills to Laura Bridgman, a deaf, dumb, and blind woman. The lessons Howe learned from teaching Bridgman led him to propose a method of education that would in his view guard others from the error that Bridgman avoided in large measure but that most other people commit: "misunderstanding and perverting the true meaning of words."[46] Howe reports that while children never fully learn to comprehend a word in "all its bearings," Bridgman "was early taught that words must come to her as things bringing some meaning," and "if they do not show it at once, she challenges them and bids them answer" (AR, 72). Unlike Bridgman, who was trained "to observe carefully, not only what objects are denoted by names, but what attributes are connoted also," "most of us grow up," he complains, "with very vague and imperfect notions of what is meant by the words we use" because we have not been trained "to distinguish the attributes connoted" by words (AR, 76). He then makes a more general observation about the perils of faulty instruction in language:

> Any one who has had dealings with the world, and has thought upon the subject of language, will see how this vagueness of people's ideas about the meaning of the words they use becomes the source of misunderstanding and mischief without end. To say nothing of the intentional double-dealing of all, from the Pythoness at Delphi, to the pettifogger everywhere, who purposely keep the word of promise to the ear, while they break it to the hope, – what wars and fightings among nations, what disputes and quarrels among individuals, what polemics among divines, what protocols among statesmen, what speeches and fees among lawyers, might have been saved to the world, if certain words, written down hastily, had been clearly understood by the writers and by the readers! (AR, 76-7)

Howe then makes an observation about interpretation that applies particularly to the United States:

> Why is it so notoriously difficult for a man to give clear instructions to an agent, to draw up a contract, or even to write his own will, so that his wishes and his meaning shall be clearly understood, when he is not by to explain it? Partly because his ideas of the meaning of language are so vague, that, as soon as he has written down one word, he is obliged to write down others to explain its meaning. . . .
> It may be the same with the will and testament of a generation, expressed in the form of a constitution. The hands that deliberately wrote it are scarcely cold, before people are quarreling about its meaning. What a satire upon language is the fact, that the ablest men in our day and generation are employed in trying to teach the people to read understandingly, and succeed with only a few at the

head of the class! If our fathers had written down, with Decalogic
simplicity and terseness, Thus shall ye do, and thus shall ye not do,
where would have been the necessity of expounding their meaning?
(AR, 77–8)

Howe does not blame the class that reads the Constitution for misunderstanding a language lesson, nor does he fault the teacher. He
blames the founders for a verbal obtuseness that made the Constitution
less luminous than scripture. But he suggests that their obtuseness may
have been not negligence but a deliberate strategy: "Perhaps, however, the case is not a happy illustration of the principle; for sometimes
writers, being afraid or ashamed to show exactly where they are and
what they mean, scatter their ink about and make a cloud, after the
manner of a certain fish, seeking darkness rather than light" (AR, 78).
Judge Pyncheon in Hawthorne's *House of the Seven Gables* (1851) hides a
sin under the cloak of authority; the sin of Pierre Glendinning's father,
a model of virtue and the son of a hero of the Revolution, lies hidden
beneath the glory of the Glendinning name in *Pierre* (1852). The sins of
the fathers regarding slavery, cloaked in a euphemism in the Constitution, threatened the perpetuation of the Union in 1850, but unlike
Holgrave, Pierre, and Howe, the great triumvirate of antebellum
orators – Daniel Webster, John Calhoun, and Henry Clay – did
anything but cast aspersions on the integrity of the founding fathers
and the soundness of the constitutional foundation.

"Let us make our generation," Webster implored near the close of
his "Seventh of March" speech, "one of the strongest and brightest
links in that golden chain which is destined, I fondly believe, to
grapple the people of all the States to this Constitution for ages to
come" (DWW, X, 97). The Constitution was the principle of union
for Webster, and he tried to inculcate affection for its language and
for its creators throughout his career. In 1850, William Fowler, who
married one of Noah Webster's daughters, published *English Language
in Its Elements and Forms*, a textbook designed to grapple college
students to "the foundation-principles of the rules, the *leges legum* of
the language" (xii). Concerned that Americans, as they settled the
West, would unsettle the language or "break loose from the laws of
the English language," Fowler perceives a deeper threat in the possibility that Americans will "in their ready invention and adoption of
flash words and slang, so change and corrupt their mother tongue, that
they would speak, not the English, but an American language; while
among themselves great diversities would exist, as now exist in the
counties of England" (127). Though he recognizes that dialects and
slang cannot be repressed any more than can "the general activity of

the human soul," he urges that those linguistic variations, though as much a consequence of liberty to Fowler as factions were to Madison, should be discouraged for the sake of linguistic uniformity – and union: "And though we have our fears, yet we also have our hopes, that diversities, and vulgarisms, and slang will not greatly or permanently increase" (128). Fowler grounds his fervent hope that America will "remain one in language as one in government" on several mitigating factors: "the system of common school education, the use of the same textbooks in the institutions of learning, and of the same periodicals and reading-books in families," and on "the mighty power of the press, urged on by those who have drunk from the 'wells of English undefiled'" (128). Finally, he calls upon the "leading men in the greater or smaller communities, the editors of periodicals, and authors generally" to exercise "the same guardian care" over the language that "they do over the opinions which it is used to express" (127).

Just as Daniel Webster sought to guard the Constitution and honor its authors with undying gratitude, George Marsh in *Lectures on the English Language*, like Fowler, seeks to guard the English language and develop a studied respect for the authors of "great, lasting works of the imagination." The creators of the "*'volumes paramount'*" of a country's literature, Marsh argues, are "among the most potent agencies in the cultivation of the national mind and heart, the strongest bond of union in a homogeneous people, the surest holding ground against the shifting currents, the ebb and flow, of opinion and of taste" (ML, 17). Marsh singles out Chaucer, Spenser, Shakespeare, and Milton as the founding fathers of English literature, and to these writers "and to the dialect which is their medium," he insists, "the instinct of self-preservation impels us tenaciously to cling." He then adds, with all the pathos of recent critics (and government officials) who have protested the reconstruction of the canon, "When . . . these volumes cease to be authorities in language, standards of moral truth and aesthetical beauty, and inspiriters of thought and of action, we shall have lost the springs of national greatness" (ML, 19). Marsh concludes his plea with an analogy that makes explicit the political importance he attaches to the canon as a method for settling the language:

> We hear much, in political life, of recurrence to first principles, and
> startling novelties not unfrequently win their way to popular accep-
> tance under that disguise. With equal truth, and greater sincerity,
> we may say that, in language and in literature, nothing can save us
> from ceaseless revolution but a frequent recourse to the primitive

authorities and the recognized canons of highest perfection. (ML, 19–20)

More succinctly, Theodoric Beck asserts in 1829, "The standard writers of a language are, like the guardians of a well ordered state, its preservers from anarchy and revolution."[47]

Based on the success of *The Spy* (1821), a tale set in Revolutionary America, James Fenimore Cooper became in the 1820s one of the most popular novelists in the United States, and thanks largely to the Leatherstocking Tales, he became, in Beck's word, one of the standard writers of antebellum America. A pioneer in the United States of several literary genres – the historical romance, sea fiction, the Western – and the author also of a political treatise, *The American Democrat* (1838), and of *History of the Navy of the United States* (1839), Cooper manifests a remarkable versatility as a writer, but much of his work is united by a single concern. Like Brackenridge, he sought to guard the language of the United States – both the English language and the language of the law – from the subversive forces of American democracy. The most treacherous force of subversion in *The Spy* comes from the Skinners: "Men who, under the guise of patriotism, prowl through the community, with a thirst for plunder that is insatiable, and a love of cruelty that mocks the ingenuity of the Indian – fellows whose mouths are filled with liberty and equality, and whose hearts are overflowing with cupidity and gall – . . ."[48] The language of the Revolution becomes counterrevolutionary in the mouths of these marauding freebooters: patriotism sanctions plunder, liberty lawlessness, and equality greed. From *The Spy* through the last of his more than thirty novels, *The Ways of the Hour* (1850), Cooper writes to guard the language of the American Revolution from the abuse that occurs in the Thucydidean moment; the only thing that changes is the source of subversion. From *The Spy* through *The Ways of the Hour*, this source becomes less alien or less un-American: first the Skinners, next politicians ruled by pecuniary interest in *The Monikins* (1835), then the local press ruled by Steadfast Dodge in *Home as Found* (1838), later the vox populi manipulated by the press in *The Crater* (1847), and finally it is the institutions of law itself, the bulwark of the republic, that become treacherous to justice in *The Ways of the Hour*.[49] But Cooper does not just manifest in these works (and others) a particular concern about the abuse of political language: he confronts the forces shaping and abusing the English language as a whole.

One of Cooper's first explicit discussions of the English language in America occurs in *Notions of the Americans* (1828), wherein he defends American ways of speaking against English criticism. Claiming that "there is vastly more bad English, and a thousand times more bad grammar spoken in England than in America," he predicts that "in another generation or two, far more reasonable English will be used in this country than exists here and now." He also expresses a tolerance toward neologisms: "I think when words once get fairly into use, their triumph affords a sufficient evidence of merit to entitle them to patronage."[50] *Notions of the Americans*, which he wrote while living in Europe, has been taken as a sign of Cooper's confidence in American virtue and the future of the republic. Though his earliest novels are rife with intimations of subversive threats to the republic from inside and outside the United States, after his return to the United States in 1833 the local politics in his home town surrounding the challenge to the Cooper family's ownership of Three Mile Point and national political controversies refocused and heightened his fears for the country. Party politics, demagogues, a press that indulges the public, and a soulless public that desires indulgence become the bane of the republic. Written in the aftermath of the constitutional controversies surrounding the tariff and Nullification, *The Monikins* is a blunt political satire that is dull to read but has the virtue of blatantly revealing, like the last part of Melville's *Mardi*, what later works of art by the author make more dramatically complex: that the fate of political justice is inextricably tied to the fate of the "just value" of words. In Leaplow, words lose their value, a constitution is subverted, and justice is eclipsed as "pecuniary interest" prevails. A prominent orator in Leaplow, one of the godlikes who reign in the legislative assembly (and who could be modeled on Daniel Webster), is the primary figure who endeavors "to destroy words by words" (345). The assembly responds as pliantly as a flag in the wind. Though the Monikins in Leaplow insist that their strength lies in the phraseology of their constitution, known as the "Great and Sacred National Allegory," thanks largely to the verbal legerdemain of the one orator they underhandedly overturn a clause in their constitution, thus proving the linguistic philosophy of the orator: "Words were so many false lights to mislead, and . . . words would be, and were, daily moulded to suit the convenience of all sorts of persons" (344).

In 1838 Cooper offers a more direct remedy for the republic: the pill of satire is followed by a political treatise, *The American Democrat*, which is a dictionary of political terms writ large. Considering it the duty of every citizen "to acquire just notions of the terms" of the "bargain," or political contract, that rules them, Cooper packages a course in political literacy by defining in a series of essays such terms as "republic," "liberty," "equality," "the people," "democracy," "aristocracy," and "constitution." Penned within a year of Noah

Webster's insistence that "the misunderstanding of words" is among the *"efficient causes of our political disorders,"* the treatise is Cooper's attempt to establish the "just value" of key terms in America's political lexicon and to refute the many "popular errors . . . on the subject of the influence of the federal constitution on the rights and liberties of the citizen" that have "arisen from mistaking the meaning of the language of the constitution" (AD, 87). Cooper notes that the most suitable title for the book would have been "something like 'Anti-Cant'" (AD, 71), and this term crystallizes his intention to arm the people with a weapon to defend themselves from the sources of trouble that appear so frequently in his novels: the falsehoods of the press, the rumors of the public, and the cant of the demagogue who courts the people with flattery and pours the poison of "rotten diction" into their ears. Designed in part as a text for the New York public schools, *The American Democrat* seeks to provide elementary instruction about the elementary tasks of the citizen in a republic: people must learn to distinguish between the demagogue and the democrat, words and things. What the text seeks to prevent is the advent of the Thucydidean moment when, in Cooper's words, public opinion is so perverted "as to cause the false to seem the true, the enemy, a friend, and the friend, an enemy; the best interests of the nation to appear insignificant, and trifles of moment; in a word, the right the wrong, and the wrong the right" (AD, 207). *The American Democrat* is the quintessential act of the American artist as schoolmaster of the republic. What the text lacks is the drama of Cooper's best novels wherein the simple terms of political justice spoken by Natty Bumppo and the law language of Judge Temple are each rendered insufficient by themselves for the government of a fallen world.

Cooper devotes one essay in *The American Democrat* solely to the condition of language in the United States. The English language in America was suffering, in his estimation, from several "common faults." The specific faults that he indicts – an "ambition to effect," a "want of simplicity," a "turgid abuse of terms," "perversions of significations," and "a formality of speech" – are all faults that Natty Bumppo's vernacular voice counters (AD, 171). Though Cooper blames these faults for restricting the playfulness and weakening the power of language, he condemns them more seriously as abuses that "subvert things by names" (AD, 174). What was suffering from this subversion were the distinctions and values that he saw as integral to a social order: distinctions like those among a gentleman, a laborer, and a blackguard and between a lady and a less refined woman. He also denounces the substitution of "boss" for "master" and "help" for "servant" as verbal subterfuges that obscure the actual relationship between employer and employee and replace "long established words" with "new and imperfect terms" (AD, 175). Cooper, the political democrat, was a social aristocrat who sought to prevent the word "equality" from acting as an acid in the social realm, corroding status, refinement, and taste. "In all cases in which the people of America have retained the *things* of their ancestors," he counsels, "they should not be ashamed to keep the *names*" (ibid.). Melville, in contrast, notes in *Pierre* how the "empty air of a name is more endurable than a man." People retain the names of their ancestors when the things are gone. Whereas Melville counsels, "The magnificence of names must not mislead us as to the humility of things," Cooper insists that the magnificence of things must not be obscured by a democratization of terms.[51] Cooper guards a language of virtue, incarnate in an earlier era, against a republic losing its soul, its very definition of itself. Melville in *Pierre* and *Israel Potter* exposes the language of virtue spoken by the heroes of the Revolution as hypocrisy.

The representative figure of American misrepresentation in the Revolutionary era becomes for Melville, in *Israel Potter*, Benjamin Franklin. The representative figure of American attempts to unsettle the language becomes for Cooper, in *Satanstoe* (1845), Jason Newcome, a caricature in part of Noah Webster. Set in New York in the era just before the Revolution, *Satanstoe* is the first part of Cooper's Littlepage trilogy, a family saga that continues in *The Chainbearers* (1845) and *The Redskins* (1846). Newcome appears in the first two novels, and his grandson, Seneca Newcome, in the last. When Newcome first appears in *Satanstoe*, he is a mildly insufferable Yankee schoolmaster. Bearing the résumé and personality associated with Noah Webster – he was born in Connecticut and educated at Yale, and he possesses "over-weening notions of moral and intellectual superiority" – Newcome is a reformer of the language whose reforms are ridiculed by Cooper. Newcome insists on conforming pronunciation to spelling, but his own pronunciations do not conform to his rules, and his language is marked by Yankee provincialisms and sounds that are "decidedly vulgar and vicious."[52] Though he is a rank hypocrite who professes Puritanism but bows down to the golden calf, Newcome is little more than a bother at first. But after the Revolution, in *The Chainbearers*, he is no mere pedagogue attempting to reform the language by unsettling it with some idiosyncratic ideas: he is an insidious demagogue who abuses the language of republican principle – terms such as "natural rights," "freedom," and "equality of men under law" – to gain power for himself. Seneca Newcome is an even more despicable figure in *The*

Redskins, a lawyer of low cunning who plots an arson. What the Snopes are to Faulkner's family sagas the Newcomes are to the Littlepage trilogy.

Disrespect for a settled language in *Satanstoe* is the germ that ends up as the disease of demagoguery in the later life of Newcome in *The Chainbearers* and as an epidemic of disorder in *The Redskins*. Cooper compresses the same story into one novel in *The Crater* (1847). Mark Woolston's attempt to create a more perfect republic ends in the reign of demagogues as a combination of unscrupulous politicians, journalists, and clerics take advantage of an amendment provision in the constitution of a republic founded by Woolston to subvert that constitution and depose Woolston as governor. The fate of the republic in *The Crater* is implicated in the opening sentence of the first chapter: "There is nothing in which American Liberty, not always as much restrained as it might be, has manifested a more decided tendency to run riot, than in the use of names."[53] Mark Woolston prefers to pronounce his name "Wooster," but a Yankee schoolmaster pronounces it "Woolston" against tradition as well as Woolston's wishes. Just as this Yankee schoolmaster and members of the community try to change the Woolston name to suit their pronunciation, so too do the demagogues at the end of the novel try to change Woolston's constitution to suit the "public voice" which they have manipulated. American liberty, Cooper suggests, can run riot in changing fundamental laws as well as names. Cooper, however, has the last word, or he leaves the final word to God: the republic, subverted by demagogues, is destroyed by a volcano. The vox populi can overcome Mark Woolston and a constitution, but it cannot resist the force of the vox Dei.

For Cooper, then, guarding the American language from unsettling changes was a process closely connected to guarding the Constitution itself. The hero of Cooper's last complete novel, *The Ways of the Hour* (1850), is Thomas Dunscomb, a lawyer who argues that constitutional issues regarding the sovereignty of the states are the questions of the hour and of years to come. It is his mission to educate people about the principles of "the much neglected compact" while exposing the corrupt practices of liberty and justice in his state. But "talk and prejudice" usurp the place "of principles and facts," and Dunscomb abandons the profession of law. By 1850, Cooper, it seems, had lost his own faith that instruction of the public voice in the grammar of republican discourse such as he provides in his writings could counter the force of the "I say" of the demagogue and the "they say" of popular opinion – the two forces that masquerade as a "we say" and whose talk poses the greatest threat of subversion to the American republic. Though Cooper in his fiction presents himself as a guardian of the language and a spokesman for republican principles and offers criticism of schoolmasters of the language, such as Noah Webster, and schoolmasters of the law, such as Daniel Webster, who adapt the language and the law to their own vision (or their personal advantage), he does not seem to recognize the degree to which he becomes a version of Noah and Daniel Webster himself. The narrative voice of his fiction conforms less and less to republican conjugation. The "I" does not speak for a "we" that is willing to incorporate a "they." The "I" speaks for a section or a class, a privileged "we," against a "they." Cooper's best fiction arises not from a clash between the gentleman as the true schoolmaster against the demagogue as the false schoolmaster, but from the conflict between the schoolmaster and the truant when the truant is an ungrammatical voice but no demagogue, a violator of the letter of the law but not of its spirit, a defender of the land (or of the landed interests of the Native American) but no property holder, and when that truant voice – the voice of Natty Bumppo – is valued as a dialogical challenge, or as a necessary supplement, to the schoolmaster's letter.

Truants of the Schoolmaster; or, Obedience to the Higher Laws of Grammar

In *The Pioneers*, Natty Bumppo lives almost beyond the margins, barely within reach of the civil law, and beyond the correction of any schoolmaster. His lawbreaking is not the defiance that most disturbs Cooper, since Natty remains governed by natural law, and his grammar breaking is benign: it influences no one, not even Oliver Edwards, who lives with Natty. But in antebellum America ungrammatical voices or voices that could do the colloquial move more to the center in the realms of politics, religion, and literature, challenging notions of propriety and raising more than eyebrows. The election of 1828 is the watershed event. The ungrammatical Andrew Jackson, a military hero, defeats John Quincy Adams, who had served as the first Boylston Professor of Rhetoric and Oratory at Harvard. Disgusted that Harvard would honor Jackson with an honorary Doctor of Laws degree at the June commencement in 1833, Adams refused to attend the ceremony and confided in his diary that he "would not be present to witness [the college's] disgrace in conferring her highest literary honors upon a barbarian who could not write a sentence of grammar and hardly could spell his own name."[54] Robert Ferguson describes a configuration between law and letters in post-Revolutionary America that begins to break down around 1850. The configuration of the statesman–humanist that distinguished the Revolutionary era experiences a compound fracture with the 1828 election. In the same era when Jackson advances the democratization of politics and when Seba Smith entertains and instructs the public with the vernacular voice of the Jack Downing tales, Lorenzo Dow and Elias Smith revive the art of vernacular preaching and become significant participants in what Nathan O. Hatch has called the democratization of American Christianity.[55] Boston, the hub of the genteel style, becomes as well a hub of dissent as Harvard-educated Brahmins challenge the confinements of standard political morality and linguistic decorum. To protest the war with Mexico, Lowell turns to an imitation of folk speech (and mocks the paraphernalia of literary criticism) in *The Biglow Papers*, and he later opposes in an 1859 review in the *Atlantic Monthly* the "universal Schoolmaster" who "wars upon home-bred phrases, and enslaves" minds to "the best models of English composition" that lack "blood" and who fails to recognize that "no language . . . that cannot suck up the feeding juices secreted for it in the rich mother-earth of common-folk-talk, can bring forth a sound and lusty book."[56] And to protest slavery, Wendell Phillips forgoes, as did Paine in *Common Sense*, a tempered, harmonious rhetoric for a rhetoric that is more terse, pithy, and conversational – and much more abusive – than the oratory of Webster, Everett, and Choate.[57] Frances Wright, Frances Stewart, and Angelina Grimké break a social code that regulates speech not by developing a vernacular voice but because they dare as women to speak out in public on political issues.[58] Grammarians themselves revolt against the grammar of the schoolmasters. William Fowle, who rejected William Ellery Channing's offer to pay for his schooling at Harvard, writes a grammar, *The True English Grammar* (1827), wherein he claims that grammars "were invented to clip the wings of fancy, and shackle the feet of genius."[59] He lives in the Boston area, where he devotes his efforts to educating students in the common schools, and he follows Horace Mann as the editor of the *Common School Journal*, wherein he remarks in an 1849 issue, "All our people study grammar, but not one in ten thousand can write or speak the English language correctly, and with facility."[60] His antidote is to recommend that grammar should be taught not by drills but by practice in writing.

But the truants of the schoolmaster who might most have appalled Theodoric Beck and George Marsh because they did anything but defend adherence to a language settled by dictionaries and grammars were Emerson, Thoreau, and Whitman. Rather than guarding an old order of words against revolutionary change, they argued as did Jefferson for the right to create new words and new classifications and to unsettle the established language. Though Emerson preached the virtues of the vernacular more than he practiced it in his own writings, his preaching was more important than any practice, because he declared independence from the schoolmasters not just in such essays as "Self-Reliance" and "The Poet" but before the schoolmasters in the high citadels of culture. Addressing the Phi Beta Kappa Society at Harvard in 1837, he proclaimed in the "American Scholar" oration, "Life is our dictionary," and "The way to learn grammar" is not from colleges and books but from "frank intercourse with many men and women" and through direct engagement in the life of the fields and the work yard where language is made (ELA, 61–2). Thoreau agreed with his neighbor and friend. He complains that "American scholars," who have "little or no root in the soil," would "fain reject" all "the true growth and experience, the living speech . . . as 'American-isms.'" He adds, "It is the old error, which the church, the state, the school ever commit, choosing darkness rather than light, holding fast to the old and to tradition. A more intimate knowledge, a deeper experience, will surely originate a word."[61] And just as Thoreau rejects squabbling about the meanings of words in the Constitution as a way to settle the controversy over slavery and appeals instead directly to the laws of nature, he also rejects "hypercritical quarrel-ling about grammar and style, the position of the particles, etc., etc." and about whether "Mr. Webster" spoke "according to Mr. Kirk-ham's rule" and argues instead that "the first requisite and rule is that expression should be vital and natural." He adds, "Essentially your truest poetic sentence is as free and lawless as a lamb's bleat" (HTJ, XI, 386).[62] Fear of breaking linguistic as well as legal precedents is the hobgoblin of the little mind for Emerson and Thoreau. The mind they admire is the mind of the "liberating god" – the poet or any man who delights in what Emerson calls the "fluxional" and "transitive" nature of language (ELA, 463). They are the ones who find that words mean more than what they thought when they uttered them and are "glad to employ them again in a new sense" (JMN, V, 409). "They are free, and they make free" (ELA, 462).[63] The antithesis of poets would thus be the imprisoning devils who would fix the language or nail a word to one sense. They would subject us to their usages, their preferences, their definitions; they would make us all copyists, scriveners, Bar-tlebys – people condemned to read and pen dead letters.

Noah Webster spent much of a lifetime writing and revising spellers, grammars, and dictionaries. Whitman spent much of a life-time building and rebuilding *Leaves of Grass* and collecting words in his notebooks. Neither Webster early in his career nor Whitman was afraid to embrace the forces that unsettle, amend, and reconstruct a language. The language they call for is a language open to change and open to the idioms of the people. The democratization of language that Webster propounded is advanced by Whitman. They both agree that the speech of the people must govern the language, but Whitman differs from Webster by broadening and deepening the concept of the people, whose speech should be represented in spellers, grammars, and dictionaries. "I love to go away from books, and walk amidst the strong coarse talk of men as they give muscle and bone to every word they speak. – I say The great grammar, and the great Dictionary of the future must . . . embody [these]."[64] Whitman is at once the fulfillment of Noah Webster and the prophet of his transcendence. Like Webster, Whitman would write the speller, the grammar, and the dictionary that needed to be written to represent the people of the United States and constitute the country as a nation. But he would write them with a poet's license: "Drawing language into line by rigid grammatical rules is the theory of the martinet applied to the . . . processes of the spirit, and to the luxurant growth of all that makes art." "It is," he adds, "for small school-masters, not for great souls. – Not only the Dictionary of the English language, but the Grammar of it, has yet to be written."[65] Whitman's ambition is to be the greatest schoolmaster of the English language in America.

Whitman recognizes, however, that his politics as a schoolmaster of the language would make him not the friend but the foe of the small schoolmaster and the gentleman scholar. He takes issue with Noah Webster: "The spelling of words is subordinate. – Morbidness for nice spelling, and tenacity for or against some one letter or so, means dandyism and impotence in literature" (AP, 13). He takes issue with Lindley Murray: "[Murray] fails to understand . . . those points where the language [is] strongest, and where [the] developements should [be] most encouraged, namely in being *elliptic* and *idiomatic*. – Murray would make of the young men merely a correct and careful set of writers under laws. – He would deprive writing of its life – there would be nothing voluntary and insociant left."[66] He becomes an early critic of bad teaching in the United States: "The study of language, dictionaries, 'grammar,' etc., as pursued in the public and other schools of New York, Boston, Brooklyn, and elsewhere through the States is worth nothing but the scornful and unrestrained laughter of contempt."[67] He even takes issue with Emerson: "Suppose these books [Emerson's] becoming absorb'd, the permanent chyle of American general and particular character – what a well-washed and grammatical, but bloodless and helpless, race we should turn out!"[68] And just as Whitman proclaims that the "greatest tongue" must spurn the laws of grammar, he also takes issue with schoolmasters of the law who would adhere slavishly to precedent: "I know my words are weapons full of danger, full of death, / For I confront peace, security, and all the settled laws, to unsettle them" (WLA, 454). Whitman conceives of the poet as the transcendent politician who would be "the voice and exposition of liberty" (WLA, 17).

Like Jefferson, Whitman loves neology, and he opposes the "purism" that would retard the demands of the spirit. He is also more than a revolutionary critic of dead language and false representation; he is an architect, builder, and inventor who will reconstruct the language. "The Real Grammar," he proclaims in *An American Primer*, "will be that which declares itself a nucleus of the spirit of the laws, with liberty to all to carry out the spirit of the laws, even by violating them, if necessary," and "The Real Dictionary will give all words that exist in use, the bad words as well as any" (AP, 6). And just as he envisions the people as the fountain of power that should flush away and cleanse stagnant language, he also envisions them, as did Jefferson, as a cleansing force in politics. The Real Congress Whitman calls for in "The Eighteenth Presidency" (1856) would sweep clean the "limber-tongued lawyers" who are "very fluent but empty, feeble old men, professional politicians, dandies and dyspeptics" and replace them with "qualified mechanics and young men" who possess "bravery, friendship, conscientiousness, clear-sightedness, and practical genius," and his Real Presidency would replace the "deformed, mediocre, snivelling, unreliable, false-hearted men" of the past two presidencies with "some heroic, shrewd, fully-informed, healthy-bodied, middle-aged, beard-faced American blacksmith or boatman . . . from the West" (WLA, 1307, 1310, 1308).

Whitman is not a lexicographer per se, but his poetry is partly lexicography: it is a collection of American words, a representation of American speech, a clarification of the idioms that compose the United States. At the conclusion of *Lectures on the English Language*, Marsh devotes his attention to the threat posed by dialects: "In a state where the differences of speech are numerous and great, the community is divided into so many disjointed fragments, that the notion of a commonwealth can scarcely be developed" (ML, 676). Differences of speech in Italy, he notes, defeated the hopes of Italian patriots, and it is Marsh's hope that "one form of syntax, one standard of speech, one medium of thought" will spread through the United States through the sympathies and associations promoted by economic development, charities, the government, the printing press, and literature (ML, 680–4). Whitman agrees with Noah Webster and Marsh that a uniformity of language is essential for political harmony: "I should say that without . . . a uniform, spoken and written dialect, elastic, tough and eligible to all, and blind and enfolding as air – the Liberty and Union of these Thirty-Eight or Forty States representing so many diverse origins and breeds would not be practicable."[69] But his great scheme of representation to promote the Union was a poem – *Leaves of Grass* – whose form, syntax, and vocabulary would amalgamate diversity into a "community of speech" and thus provide the American people with an incarnate image of itself as an ensemble. What Whitman seeks to create through the representation and transfiguration of his poetic voice is the language that the United States needs to realize its revolutionary and democratic principles. *Leaves of Grass* conjugates together words and people in a startling new syntax. Whitman is the higher grammarian of American democracy.[70]

After the Civil War, in *Democratic Vistas*, Whitman calls again for a reconstruction of the language by the poet: he proposes "new law-forces of spoken and written language – not merely the pedagogue-forms, correct, regular, familiar with precedents, made for matters of outside propriety, fine words, thoughts definitely told out – but a language fann'd by the breath of Nature, which leaps overhead, cares mostly for impetus and effects, and for what it plants and invigorates to grow" (WLA, 992). Language is a spiritual force for Whitman because it is a democratic, pragmatic instrument; it is not God's gift, but the people's creation. As Whitman grows older, he becomes no less a populist. "Language, be it remember'd," he asserts in "Slang in America" (1885), "is not an abstract construction of the learn'd, or of dictionary-makers, but is something arising out of the work, needs, ties, joys, affections, tastes, of long generations of humanity, and has its bases broad and low, close to the ground. Its final decisions are made by the masses, people nearest the concrete, having most to do with actual land and sea" (WLA, 1166). The schoolmasters of the language and the law sought to bend a people to the word, but Whitman asserts, "If anything is to bend, they [words] must bend to the people; the attempt to bend the people to them is always distressing and laughable."[71] Natty Bumppo and Huck Finn hightail it away from people as well as from the schoolmaster; Whitman, keeping his ear close to the ground, is a city poet in blue jeans: the language of the street is his muse.

The truant affirms against the decrees of the schoolmaster that the word is mobile, that there is death in the dictionary, that no grammar can confine the interpretation of the letter against the license of the poet – or the adultress. Hester Prynne in *The Scarlet Letter* is marked by the letter "A" as a violator of the law, and she confirms the correspondence of the letter to her spirit when, in her own act of interpretation, she vaingloriously embroiders the letter. Later, when she is alone with Dimmesdale and Pearl in the forest, in another pronounced declaration of her independence she casts off the letter. Subsequently, however, her spirit seems to conform to the letter: she resumes wearing the letter and returns to the community. But neither the letter nor Hester remains the same. Her own spirit, revealed through her public acts of charity, helps amend and reconstruct the interpretation of the letter. The "A" becomes the sign of able and angel. *The Scarlet Letter* is a tale of sin, punishment, and redemption that offers a lesson that mediates a compromise between the schoolmaster's demand that one obey the letter and the truant's claim to license. The letter imposed (and interpreted) without the spirit of love is tyranny; the spirit of love (or liberty) unconfined by the letter is adultery or disunion.

The schoolmasters of the law in antebellum America demanded obedience to the letter of the Constitution. Truants such as Garrison and Thoreau gave their own sanction to disobedience of the letter by appealing to the higher grammar of the laws of nature and nature's God. But opposition to adherence to a common law and a uniform language did not necessarily make one a liberating god in antebellum America. George Fitzhugh, a Southern intellectual, advocated truancy to the schoolmaster as vehemently as did Emerson and Thoreau. "Grammar, lexicography, and rhetoric, applied to language," he argues, "destroy its growth, variety, and adaptability – stereotype it, make it at once essentially a dead language, and unfit for future use; for new localities, and changes of time and circumstances beget new ideas, and require new words and new combinations of words." "Genius, in her most erratic flights," he adds, "represents a higher Grammar than Dr. Blair or Lindlay Murray." Fitzhugh staunchly opposes the "centralization and cosmopolitanism" that would "furnish a common language from the center"; he champions instead "national and even State peculiarities." There is a catch, however, to this argument. This enemy of monoglossia and hegemony is an ardent defender of slavery: "Imitation, grammar, and slavery suit the masses. . . . Liberty for the few – Slavery in every form, for the mass!"[72]

The verbalization of politics prescribed by the Constitution became more pronounced in antebellum America. The fate of the Union and the future of slavery seemed to hang in the balance of how the language of the Constitution was conserved or changed, settled or unsettled. Subject to an intense gaze, the letter of the law was magnified in importance. The Constitution in this period became more evidently what Edgar Allan Poe's resuscitated Egyptian in "Some Words of a Mummy" (1845) declares to be the status of historical documents: "a kind of literary arena for the conflicting guesses, riddles, and personal squabbles of whole herds of exasperated commentators" (PLA, 816). Poe himself often leaves the reader what the founding fathers left the public: an ambiguous text that invites interpretation but exasperates the commentator searching for the definitive meaning – the intention that is wrapped inside a layer of words and that can never be unraveled except by reaching some other-worldly communion with the spirit of the dead (or absent) author. Poe displaces into the realm of art the preeminent problem of antebellum politics: the decipherment of signs. The schoolmaster of interpretation for the riddles of his tales becomes the detective, a figure of ratiocination who resembles in his wisdom Judge Temple and Thomas Dunscomb but whose inimitable genius sets the detective farther apart from the men of the crowd than Cooper sets the judge. (Cooper never sets Temple up so high that he is above learning a thing or two from Natty Bumppo, while Poe's master decoder in "The Gold-Bug," William Legrand, is struck only by the stupidity of Jupiter, his dialect-speaking black servant.) As politics became more of a literary arena, a forum for debating and defining the meanings of words, language became more of a political arena, magnifying the importance of the schoolmaster and perhaps encouraging in Poe's case the privatization of language that marks the symbolist attempt to create a pure realm of words, a literary language separate from a public language desecrated by the mob. Poe's "Some Words of a Mummy" appeared in the April 1845 issue of the *American Review*. Several months later in the same magazine an essayist comments upon the importance of studying language and words in an article entitled "Human Rights": "There is nothing which, at the present day, would be productive of greater advantages to moral, social and theological science, than the careful analysis of the common elementary terms employed in them. We refer, for example, to such words as nature, right, rights, duty, property, State, government, law, punishment, liberty, slavery, & c.; from the abuse, or rather, from the use of which in senses entirely different from what they have borne since the first origin of language, there is arising a confusion, threatening to throw all modern institutions into utter disorder."[73] Poe's mummy tells the account of how "wise men" from thirteen Egyptian provinces "concocted the most ingenious constitution," but their experiment ended in "the most odious and insupportable despotism that ever was heard of upon the face of the Earth" (PLA, 820). The mummy, in his last words, blames the despotism on "*Mob*"; the author of "Human Rights" fears the mobility of words, the loss of an original meaning.

In the age of manifest destiny, Poe is the artist of manifest decline. He writes of decay and death: the degeneration of the cosmos in *Eureka*, the fall of the house of Usher, the descent into a maelstrom, and the corruption of a literature that pursues a didactic or political agenda rather than literary concerns. Emerson, in contrast, is the essayist of affirmation. He writes in an optative mood of the possibilities of reform, regeneration, revolution. But the contrast is too simple.

Emerson shares with Poe (and with the author of "Human Rights" and a number of other antebellum commentators) not just a suspicion of the mob but a fear of corruption and a haunting sense of the loss of an original spirit – a loss that manifested itself in "rotten diction" and a loss that helped encourage Poe's and Emerson's own quest, conducted in different ways, for a more transcendent language, a language that would give, in the words of Mallarmé's tribute to Poe, a purer meaning to the language of the tribe ("donner un sens plus pur aux mots de la tribu").[74] Emerson less than Poe separated himself from the crowd. He was no party politician, and no bookish schoolmaster; he was a minister to the soul who was not afraid to contradict himself. He preached against a settled language, demanding "initiative, spermatic, prophesying, man-making words," but he also preached against the corruption of the word – the unsettling of language that led to the disunion between words and things, language and nature, the representative and the constituent: ". . . and that nothing remains but to begin at the beginning to call every man in America to counsel, Representatives do not represent, we must (now) take new order & see how to make representatives represent us" (JMN, VIII, 148; XIV, 423).

10

Corrupt Language and a Corrupt Body Politic, or the Disunion of Words and Things

Anselmo
We are a nation of word-killers: *hero, veteran, tragedy*, –
Watch the great words go down.

Carl
The language grows like that.

Anselmo
At least, it changes.

Ricardo
Corruption, too, is a kind of development – it depends on the
    view-point. It depends on whether
You are the word, or the worm; and whose is the ultimate
    society.

Edna St. Vincent Millay, "Conversation at Midnight"

Emerson's dictum in *Nature* – "The corruption of man is followed by the corruption of language" – is a commonplace (ELA, 22). George Marsh in *Lectures on the English Language* offers a variant of the commonplace that reorders the relationship Emerson posits: "The depravation of a language is not merely a token or an effect of the corruption of a people, but corruption is accelerated, if not caused by the perversion and degradation of its consecrated vocabulary" (ML, 647). The corruption Emerson describes merely affects the language: "new imagery ceases to be created" and "words lose all power to stimulate the understanding or the affections." The corruption Marsh describes is more ominous in its consequences: "Every human speech has its hallowed dialect, its nomenclature appropriated to the service of sacred things, the conscience, the generous affections, the elevated aspirations, without which humanity is not a community of speaking men, but a herd of roaring brutes" (ibid.). The corruption of language is followed by a return to violence and anarchy – to civil war. Marsh published his lectures in 1859.

Marsh's fear of the corruption of language precipitating a return to the violent state of nature Melville portrays in "The House-top" has often been captured in literature but never more sublimely than in the apocalyptic conclusion to Pope's *Dunciad*. In the fourth book, the corruption of language does not just follow the loss of order (as it does in Ulysses' speech on degree in Shakespeare's *Troilus and Cressida*); it actively leads people downwards to Chaos. In Pope's epic inversion, the reigning dunces seem to be led and sometimes pursued by the "Mob of Metaphors" they incite to riot. The uncreating word – the anti-Logos – gains sway. For some writers in mid-nineteenth-century America, it also appeared that the country was being ruled for the worse by misnomers and cant – or by a language that had lost its vital principle of union with common ideas and with the truth.

When Marsh writes in *Lectures on the English Language* on "corruptions of language" in a chapter devoted to the topic, he carefully distinguishes between two types of corruption: on the one hand, the changes by which "language continually adapts itself to the intellectual and material condition of those who use it, grows with their growth, shares in their revolutions, perishes in their decay"; and, on the other, changes that "tend to the deterioration of a tongue in expressiveness or moral elevation of vocabulary, in distinctness of articulation, in logical precision, or in clearness of structure" (ML, 644). Changes of the first type, he explains, are "connatural with man or constitutive of him" and participate in his mutations, while the latter "arise from extraneous or accidental causes, may be detected, exposed, and if not healed, at least prevented from spreading beyond their source, and infecting a whole nation" (ibid.). Language reformers in England and the United States persisted through the eighteenth and into the mid nineteenth century in attempts to arrest the first type of linguistic change (or corruption) by appeals to some higher authority than popular usage. But Marsh recognizes that no person, no academy, and no authority could preserve a language from mutability. William Whitney codifies a new paradigm for understanding linguistic change that became predominant in the mid nineteenth century when he argues in *The Life and Growth of Language* that the changes words undergo are part of an evolutionary process: words meet, mate, and produce hybrids; they grow, evolve, and leave fossils. Marsh insists, however, with Samuel Johnson's vehemence, that the second type of corruption arising from "extraneous or accidental causes" must be resisted as threats to subvert the constitution of a people: "To pillory such offences, to point out their absurdity, to detect and expose the moral obliquity which too often lurks beneath them, is the sacred duty of every scholar, of every philosophic thinker, who knows how nearly purity of speech . . . is allied with purity of thought and rectitude of action" (ML, 644–5).

Emerson, Pound, Eliot, Tate, Ellison, Ginsberg, Mailer, and Rich are widely divergent in their politics, but they share as writers and critics Marsh's sense of a religious mission for the writer and a sense of a political role that unites them with a wide range of authors in the United States (and in foreign countries). Their mission is to sustain faith in the word and defend it not just in acts of creative art but as critics. Their political role in the drama of democracy is to check and balance the sovereign words and representations of others with their own representations. Emerson's section on language in *Nature* provides a credo for this faith: "1. Words are signs of natural facts. 2. Particular natural facts are symbols of particular spiritual facts. 3. Nature is the symbol of spirit" (ELA, 20). The faith that word, nature, and spirit can correspond is a belief in the principle of the *logos*. But the correspondence is not a given for each person: "A man's power to connect his thought with its proper symbol, and so to utter it, depends on the simplicity of his character, that is, upon his love of truth, and his desire to communicate it without loss" (ELA, 22). Crystallizing principles developed in the classical rhetorical and republican traditions, Emerson outlines the forces that conspire to corrupt man and language, breaking the union not just between word and nature, thought and symbol, but between man and man:

> When simplicity of character and the sovereignty of ideas is broken up by the prevalence of secondary desires, the desire of riches, of pleasure, of power, and of praise – and duplicity and falsehood take place of simplicity and truth, the power over nature as an interpreter of the will, is in a degree lost; new imagery ceases to be created, and old words are perverted to stand for things which are not; a paper currency is employed, when there is no bullion in the vaults. In due time, the fraud is manifest. (ELA, 22)

Criticizing manifestations of the fraud and preaching against its root cause would be fundamental activities for Emerson – and for a host of other writers – in the antebellum era. What they observed in the political economy and culture of their age was a deviation from the correspondence between language and nature whose potential for correspondence was the promise of the United States, a country governed by the sovereign ideas of a Declaration and Constitution grounded in the laws of nature and nature's God.[1]

For Emerson, an original relation among word, nature, and spirit had been betrayed by the founding fathers in the construction of a constitution that sanctioned slavery. What the age demanded was an end to the blind worship of the fathers and a renewed vision of nature. In place of the building of "sepulchres" for the fathers and the honoring of the letter of the law of modern-day Pharisees, the letter had to be reformed by the spirit of nature, by a love of God. "Let us demand our own works and laws and worship" (ELA, 7). *Nature* is a guidebook to reform. The original relation of language to nature can be recovered: "wise men" can pierce "rotten diction" and "fasten words again to visible things" (ELA, 23). Let us create new words, new imagery, new allegories. Align oneself with nature, truth, God, the "divine aura" and become the instrument of "Original Cause," the agent of "proper creation" – an incarnation of the *logos* (ibid.).

The linguistic theory Emerson outlines in *Nature* provides the basis for more than an aesthetics of symbolism: it sets forth a politics of reform by symbolic action. The "facts" of language "may suggest," Emerson writes, "the advantage which the country-life possesses for a powerful mind, over the artificial and curtailed life of cities" (ibid.). Nature is the schoolmaster who teaches the lesson, and the "poet, the orator, bred in the woods" is the student who learns what will not be forgotten altogether when or if he ventures into "the roar of cities or the broil of politics" (ibid.). "Long hereafter," Emerson prophesies, "amidst agitation and terror in national councils, – in the hour of revolution, – these solemn images shall reappear in their morning lustre, as fit symbols and words of the thoughts which the passing events shall awaken" (ibid.). In the hour of revolution, at the "call of a noble sentiment," the Orphic poet, the orator – a Grey Champion whose weapon is words – will step out of the woods. Then the "rotten diction" that had buried the truths of nature will be uncovered; then new imagery will be created; then perhaps the "agitation and terror in national councils" will subside (ibid.). The representative words of the poet–orator will make him the acknowledged legislator of mankind. "And with these forms, the spells of persuasion, the keys of power are put into his hands" (ibid.).

The politics underlying Emerson's aesthetic of language become more visible when we recognize that several passages in *Nature* are incorporated from earlier entries in Emerson's journal when he is commenting on the political discourse of a leading figure in American politics who can be regarded as, in Harold Bloom's terms, the "strong poet" of American eloquence in the antebellum period: Daniel Webster. When, for instance, Emerson notes in his journal in 1835, "Good writing & brilliant conversation are perpetual allegories" (a phrase repeated word for word in *Nature*), he then adds, "Webster is such a poet in every speech" (JMN, V, 63). Earlier, in 1834, Webster again appears as Emerson's archetype of a poet when he makes in the journal a comparison between Edmund Burke and Webster: "Burke's imagery is much of it got from books & so is a secondary formation. Webster's is all primary. Let a man make the woods & fields his books then at the hour of passion his thoughts will invest themselves spontaneously with natural imagery" (JMN, V, 106). Webster also figures in the journal entry that sets forth the economic metaphor Emerson recycles in *Nature* when he links rotten diction and paper currency: "Webster's speeches seem to be the utmost that the unpoetic West has accomplished or can. We all lean on England[;] scarce a verse, a page, a newspaper but is writ in imitation of English forms, our very manners and conversation are traditional, and sometimes the life seems dying out of all literature & this enormous paper currency of Words is accepted instead" (JMN, IV, 297). To compose his theory of language in *Nature* Emerson creates abstractions from concrete references to the practice of American political oratory. Just as Whitman's poetic theory and practice must be seen as influenced not just by Emerson but by the preachers and orators whom he loved, such as Father Taylor and Elias Hicks ("Hearing such men sends to the winds all the books, and formulas, and polish'd speaking, and rules of oratory" [WLA, 1145]), Emerson's writings on the poet and on language must be read as part of a conversation with such orators as Webster, and during this conversation Webster may have the first word, but Emerson will not allow him to have the last. ("It was always the theory of literature," he notes elsewhere, "that the word of a poet was authoritative and final" [REW, IV, 143].)

Emerson describes conversation in "Circles" as a process wherein "each new speaker" who "strikes a new light" "emancipates us from the oppression of the last speaker" and "then yields us to another redeemer," who enables us again "to recover our rights, to become men" (ELA, 408). During the conversation Emerson held with American culture, he turns in the 1830s to Webster as the incarnation of the American poet–orator who will free the American scholar from the "courtly muses of Europe"; in 1841 he calls for every person to exercise self-reliance and generate "new and spontaneous" words and thus become "a word made flesh, born to shed healing to the nations" (ELA, 70, 264, 275); in 1850, Webster seals his displacement from the emancipatory conversation by his March 7 speech supporting the

Compromise of 1850, and in *Representative Men* Montaigne and Shake-speare figure as alternative exemplars of liberation through the word aligned to nature; then, during the Civil War, Lincoln, a "quite native, aboriginal man, as an acorn from an oak," redeems for Emerson the conversation that Webster had stifled: "We have recovered ourselves from our false position, and planted ourselves on a law of Nature" (REW, XI, 320).

After *Nature* appeared in 1836, more and more Americans began to pen warnings similar to Emerson's about the decay of language, and they began to attack "rotten diction" wherever they smelled it – usually in popular literature, newspapers, advertisements, and politi-cal speeches, and even in the Constitution. Like Emerson, these critics were partly reacting to what Edwin Whipple called in 1845 the "many queer developments of the cozenage of language" that can be found in the "everday world of books and men."[2] Wherever Americans turned, it seems, they could find such cozenages, and a glance at a few of these critiques can suggest the depth of concern about the state of the language in the mid nineteenth century.

Writing in 1840 for the *Democratic Review* on the Whig presidential campaign, an author describes in disgust how the true and natural titles, symbols, and slogans that attracted the people to Andrew Jackson had become the false signs and slogans of William Henry Harrison's "Log Cabin and Hard Cider" campaign:

> We have taught them how to conquer us! It was the dazzle of a military title that was the secret of General Jackson's inexplicable popularity – why, then, might not the name of General Harrison "tickle the ears of the groundlings" with the same charm that made that of the old hero of New Orleans such a tower of strength? The hickory-tree, too, played a conspicuous part in the old Jackson days, as a popular rallying cry of the friends of the stout and stalwart old man, of whose characteristic traits its uprightness, firmness, and excellent serviceable qualities, seemed to constitute it a natural symbol and representative – why, then, might not the watchword of a "Log Cabin and Hard Cider," however unmeaning and ridicu-lously inappropriate, answer a similar purpose of rousing the hurrah of a popular enthusiasm?[3]

Several months after Harrison's victory, Emerson comments in "Self-Reliance," "I am ashamed to think how easily we capitulate to badges and names" (ELA, 262). In 1841 Cooper publishes *The Deerslayer*, another novel in his Leatherstocking Tales, which feature as their hero Natty Bumppo, a figure named at one point in his life "Straight-tongue," who represents the virtues associated in Cooper's politics with the agrarian farmer of Thomas Jefferson's republicanism and the natural democrat of Andrew Jackson's populism. Just as Harrison is a simulacrum of Jackson for the *Democratic Review*, Hurry Harry March in *The Deerslayer* is a corrupt simulacrum of Natty. He too is an ungrammatical man of the woods, but his tongue speaks lies, his deeds are immoral, and he may be, as George Dekker suggests, Cooper's "caustic commentary" on the Whig election campaign of 1840, which began by starring Henry Clay, nicknamed "Harry of the West." "Hurry," George Dekker writes, "is an 1840 Whig – a man with a frank Western manner but with the conscience of a cut-throat city man."[4] The vernacular voice in *The Deerslayer* is no more a sign of uprightness than is Harrison's birth in a log cabin. Natty's admiration for the language of Native Americans who name places "by something reasonable and resembling," like Emerson's call in "Self-Reliance" to "speak the rude truth" in "our smooth times" and to stand alone rather than be recruited to the banner of Whig or Democrat, can be seen in part as Cooper's and Emerson's revulsion from the credit given to a paper currency of words that seemed to be worth more than bullion in winning votes in such political campaigns as the one that elected Harrison in 1840 (ELA, 262, 273).

From the Whig point of view, of course, it was the Democrats who had abused the potency of words. Calvin Colton, a leading penman for the Whig cause, protests in his *Junius Tracts* (1844) that the Democrats "have justified and sustained the President of the United States in the use of monarchical powers, we might say *absolute* powers . . . – all under the name of 'Democracy'!"[5] He explains that because "the people are honest, and take things by their *names*," the fraudulent word "Democracy" can mislead "the majority of the people" (95). In the election of 1840, Colton exults, the Democrats were defeated "because through the democratic symbols of 'Log Cabin and Hard Cider,' in connexion with the *facts* brought home to the people, the people saw on which side the true democracy was" (91). The Whigs, he insists, will not lay aside the symbols of "Log Cabin" or "Hard Cider" because the "poetry of symbols is the natural language of the heart – the first and everlasting altar of enthusiasm" (96). That natural symbols had the power to defraud as well as liberate was part of Emerson's argument in *Nature*, and in "The Poet," an essay included in the collection he published in 1844 (the same year that Colton's *Junius Tracts* appeared), he again investigates the power of symbols not just in poetry but in politics. "In our political parties," he remarks, "compute the power of badges and emblems. . . . Witness the cider-barrel, the log-cabin, the hickory-stick, the palmetto, and all the cognizances of party" (ELA, 454). The populace is as "intoxicated with their symbols" as the "schools of poets, and philosophers." "We are symbols, and inhabit symbols" (ELA, 454, 456). "Every actual State is corrupt," Emerson announces in "Politics," and against this corruption, and against the tyranny of bad laws and fixed symbols, he offers the poet as the genius who "repairs the decays of things" and who emancipates us as "liberating gods" (ELA, 463, 457, 462). That Lincoln displaced General Harrison as a more natural representation of the log-cabin candidate, just as Whitman's *Leaves of Grass* displaced in critical estimation Longfellow's *Hiawatha* as the poem that fulfilled more authentically Emerson's call for a poetry of natural symbols and his vision of America as a poem, may seem to prove Emerson's assertion in *Nature* that in due time the fraud of paper words would be manifest. But the popularity of *Hiawatha* and the success of Harrison's campaign suggest as well how potent the artifice of natural representation could be and how that potency could be tapped by poets and politicians with the ambition of Whitman or Lincoln.

For the editorial writer of the *National Intelligencer*, the capitulation to names and slogans which Emerson resists had become deadly serious. It had enslaved people into supporting a war designed to advance slavery. The writer complains in an 1848 essay entitled "Political Clap-Trap" that "through the force of a few perverted phrases" Americans had been captivated into fighting a war for the extension of slavery into new territories. The phrases the writer singles out for opprobrium are "Manifest Destiny," "Anglo-Saxonism," and "Our Country, right or wrong."[6]

Just as politics seemed rife with false advertising, advertising presented itself as full of political dangers to the author of an 1852 essay entitled "The Philosophy of Advertising." The author calls advertisers the latest in a long line of corrupters of language that begins with Satan and continues in a line of evolution that includes poets, historians, and politicians. "Reserved," the author writes, "for a more advanced stage of civilization," the advertisement is "the scientific application" of lying, for it works with cold calculation by preying upon a most impressionable substance – the human brain.[7] The author explains that the "natural inborn idea of the relation between words and facts compels a belief, even if qualified by doubt, in what is gravely and repeatedly asserted," and thus while the "reasoning few may resist the insinuating actions upon their brains," those "whose life is mainly sensuous" are without shield against the advertisement – that "engine of war that pours forth its missiles [i.e., words] with a certainty of aim, a rapidity and a continuity, compared to which all catapults, balistas, floating batteries and Perkins' steam-guns are mere trivial inventions of a coarse and material order" (122). The writer fears that whoever grasps "the gigantic lever of advertisement" will be more invincible than Napoleon. With his "battalions of words" he shall "conquer and subdue a world that shall render up its gold and its liberty" (122).

In the mid nineteenth century Edwin Whipple performed the calling that such later apostles of culture as T. S. Eliot and Ezra Pound would recommend for the man of letters: guardian of the culture of language. Whipple sought to guard the language not just from politicians and advertisers but from writers themselves. In an 1854 review of *Roget's Thesaurus* entitled "The Use and Misuse of Words," which appeared in the *North American Review*, Whipple declares that it is the "tendency of the time to divorce the body of words from the soul of expression, and to shrivel up language into a mummy of thought," and he blames the whipsters of rhetoric writing "the 'literature' of the day, so called" for the abuse.[8] Even a cursory glance over that literature will reveal, he asserts, "the peculiar form of marasmus under which the life of language is in danger of being slowly consumed" (221). It is not a pretty sight: "the chief characteristic" of the literature "is absence of restraint"; it "is developed according to no interior principle of growth" and "adapts itself to no exterior principle of art" (231). Whipple also explains that although "words and things" have "no vital principle of union" and can be easily "detached or unbound," perfection of expression "consists in identifying words with things, – in bending language to the form, and pervading it with the vitality, of the thought it aims to arrest and embody" (227, 225). The good writer, in other words, will establish his own "principle of union." Conversely, the misuse of words stems in his mind from a failure to exercise "any inward energy of thought on the thing to which they [the words] relate," and he accuses the hack writers of the day of an "ungoverned or ungovernable sensibility" that has led them to so sever "the connection between sign and thing signified" that they have threatened the "validity of all definitions" (229). Just as an anarchy of the intellect seemed to be threatening any definitive interpretation of the Constitution, an ungovernable sensibility was affecting the language. What is needed, in Whipple's opinion, to assist in literary composition is not a thesaurus but a "true philosophy of expression, founded on a knowledge of the nature and operations of the mind, and of the vital processes by which thought incarnates itself in words" (224). Only after attaining such knowledge will writers earn the right to use the words Roget puts at their disposal; only then, in his opinion, should a writer attempt to scale the heights that Chaucer, Shakespeare, Barlow, and Jonathan Edwards reached. They are the authors, he explains, who can ensoul words – the ones who can give words the life and meaning that they do not retain in their removal to dictionaries. In their writing "the moods seem to transcend the resources of language, yet they are expressed in common words, transfigured, sanctified, imparadised, by the spiritual vitality which streams through them" (225). This canon of writers – saints who have made the spirit flesh through the word – possess the inner constitution that governs the sensibility and allows them to forge living unions between words and things.

When Edwin Newman asked, "Will America Be the Death of the English Language?" in *Strictly Speaking* (1974), he greatly exaggerated death threats to the language, but this best-selling book helped make fears about the corruption of language a vogue concern in the mid 1970s. A century earlier, an essay entitled "Word-Murder" that appeared in the *Continental Monthly* voiced a similar concern. The author pens obituaries for a dozen words, citing exaggeration in newspapers as their cause of death. The old "intensifiers of meaning," he declares, "are as dead as herrings." To prevent further word murder, the author proposes the establishment of a new "Humane Society . . . for the prevention of cruelty to words" and a "judiciary department" with "full power to try *all* defilers of the well of English."[9] The next year another essay in the journal laments "the mere conventionality and utter arbitrariness of even our most important ethical terms."[10] These ethical terms, the writer says, were once "the innocent servants of truth," but now they have become "tools of falsehood and the abject instruments for the extinction of all honesty and nobleness."[11] Like the riverboat in Melville's *The Confidence-Man*, the American ship of state in this writer's view was seemingly packed full of knaves seeking to gull any passenger who still retained some confidence in the truth of verbal representation.

For these commentators on language, then, the American language was falling far short of fulfilling the manifest destiny proclaimed for it by Edward Everett in the early nineteenth century and by Whitman in the preface to *Leaves of Grass*. Instead of becoming the most pure and copious language, it had become glib and oily, debased by Gonerils and Regans – the politicians and other con men – who were willing to speak and purpose not for personal gain. Indeed, in the 1850s and 1860s, the high hopes of John Adams and his son for a renaissance of eloquence in the United States that would be coextensive with the pursuit of liberty, Noah Webster's dream of achieving political harmony through a uniform language, Everett's vision of America overcoming the confusion of Babel, and Whitman's conviction that "Americans are going to be the most fluent and melodious voiced people in the world – and the most perfect users of words" (AP, 2) all seemed to crumble as secondary desires – the desire for riches, for pleasure, for power, and for praise – gained sway over sovereign principles of justice and liberty.[12] Significantly, when Everett revised his 1824 Phi Beta Kappa address for publication in 1850, he made some alterations in both substance and style. In 1824 he asserted, "There is little doubt that the instrument of communication will receive great improvements; that the written and spoken language will acquire new force, and power; possibly, that forms of address, wholly new, will be struck out to meet the universal demand for energy."[13] In 1850 he wrote in a more chastened style, "The instrument of communication may receive some improvement; the written and spoken language acquire new vigor; possibly forms of address wholly new will be devised."[14]

For the author of an essay entitled "The Two Tongues," published in the *Atlantic Monthly* in 1860, the root cause for the corruption of language lies within the body politic. The author argues, "If the mind and heart of a nation become barbarized, no classic culture can keep its language from corruption. If its ideas are ignoble, it will turn to the ignoble and vulgar side of every word in its tongue, it will affix the mean sense it desires where it had of old no place."[15] Like Emerson, this author believes that the corruption of language occurs when the sovereignty of noble ideas is usurped by the pursuit of base self-interests. When a nation as a whole becomes corrupt in spirit, the letter will not be spared. The only possible cure, as this writer and Emerson suggest, is a change of heart and mind: a moral reform. What another dreamer, Stephen Pearl Andrews, proposes in 1864 is a utopian language. As part of his plan to form a New Universal or Planetary Government and a system of education that would unify the study of knowledge, he creates in 1864 a plan for a new "Scientific and Universal Language."[16] Besides new languages, a humane society for words, and moral reform, some other remedies are prescribed in the 1850s and 1860s for the corruption of language; they include such practical recommendations as increased criticism by scholars and the press, improved or stricter education, and the cultivation of linguistic skepticism.

Of the remedial actions proposed, the one that earned the highest respect from a number of writers was the study of language itself, or the practice of philology and etymology. For these writers, to study the turning and troping of the meaning of a word from a root sense to later branchings, flowerings, and rottings was to gain insight into the shiftiness of words and people. The growth and decay of words, their capacity for double meanings, were signs of a people's own history of advancement, degeneration, and duplicity. The author of an essay entitled "The Unity of Language and of Mankind" (1851) makes an early plea for a science of linguistics: the study of a word "in its origin, history, connections, relations, and significance" is at least "as worthy and useful an employment as the examination of a shell, a bug, or a worm." But he feels that the study of language is more than a science. It is a philosophical and moral discipline, for the study of words enables people to rise above the material and contemplate the spiritual: "Language itself, in its very structure and development, is the noblest and most characteristic, the most direct and perfect, manifestation of the human mind." Hence, "the study of language has a humanizing tendency; – it is the study of man, not indeed in his material and animal relations, but in his proper and peculiar character as an intellectual and logical, or rational, being."[17] The idea advanced in this essay that philology recapitulates ontology is one of the great truths of nineteenth-century linguistics. Philology in this age also recapitulated or refracted political concerns. Soon after the Civil War, the American Philological Association was born. Those who loved words would unite against the forces corrupting and otherwise disrespecting the language. In an 1867 address before the association, Edward Gould, its president (and later the author of *Good English*), predicts in a speech entitled "The Saxon Language – Its Eclipse and Relumination" that the world will "have a universal language, and that language will be, substantially, our own tongue." The mission of the association, in his vision, is to fulfill the prophecy "of sacred writ" that a "pure language" will be restored to the people: "The curse shall be removed; the babble, Babel, Babylon – in other words, the spirit of confusion – shall pass away, and the reign of peace and right, unanimity, order, beauty, truth, be everywhere consummated."[18] The American Philological Society, like the Royal Society of England, arises from the ashes of civil war and from a time when, in James Russell Lowell's phrase, the country was "weary of being cheated with plays upon words" (JLW, V, 52).

"Let me lay down the law upon the subject [of the pun question]," proclaims Holmes's Autocrat of the Breakfast-Table: "Life and language are alike sacred. Homicide and *verbicide* – that is, violent treatment of a word with fatal results to its legitimate meaning, which is its life – are alike forbidden. Manslaughter, which is the meaning of the one, is the same as man's laughter, which is the end of the other."[19] The pun is the most audible manifestation of a word's duplicity, and the autocrat, as Peter Gibian points out, can no more put an end to this duplicity or bring order to the babel of voices at the breakfast table than Daniel Webster or Judge Taney could bring order to the state of the Union by interpreting the Constitution.[20] The proclamations of the philologist and the words of literary critics could not match the force of the Supreme Court and the power of the vox populi in defining and interpreting the sacred words of American politics, and in some eyes those forces were not guarding but corrupting the consecrated vocabulary that makes a people, in Marsh's words, "a community of speaking men" rather than "a herd of roaring brutes" (ML, 647). Verbicide and homicide were linked in the equivocal sanction that the language of freedom gave to slavery.

For writers in both the North and the South, one of the most disturbing aspects of the political debate over slavery and related issues was the way in which the hallowed words that articulated and motivated the American Revolution became in their eyes and ears empty but dangerous sounds – words with their original reference frightened out of them. "Freedom is the name for a thing that is *not* freedom: this, a lesson never learned in an hour or an age," comments a character in Melville's *Mardi*.[21] "All statesmen," Emerson writes ". . . are sure to be found befriending liberty with their words, and crushing it with their votes" (REW, XI, 240). And in 1854 a writer in the *Southern Quarterly Review* comments upon "the many words which are working harm in the minds of men." He points out that

> "liberty" loses its rightful meaning, and breeds infection instead of sound sentiment; "the people" acquires a dangerous signification, and is used for evil purposes by designing men. . . . Words which were of good name once give currency to ideas that have become wrongfully attached to them, and work harm in proportion to the good they represented before. This tyranny of words, if it goes unchecked, misleads the mind of a whole nation. It is a dangerous enemy to correct thought, because it is subtle, insidious; it is of very slow growth, and none can trace its daily progress. But when the quiet ceaseless drift is detected, men find themselves far away from their true course, perhaps without the means of regaining it.[22]

This author sounds a tocsin against verbal inversion. The words representing the ideals of the American Revolution have become dangerously misrepresentative. The ship of state is drifting far off course on the fluency of language and is heading toward disaster. Emerson similarly remarks in his 1855 "Speech Against the Knownothings": "Certainly the social state, patriotism, law, government, will cover real ideas, though the words have wandered far from the things. . . . It was so once in this country when Washington, Adams, Jefferson, really embodied the ideas of Americans; but now we put obscure persons into the chairs, without character or representative force of any kind."[23] The next year Emerson reiterates the complaint in "Speech on Affairs in Kansas": "Language has lost its meaning in the

universal cant. *Representative Government* is really misrepresentative.
. . . the *adding of Cuba and Central America* to the slave marts is *enlarging
the area of Freedom. Manifest Destiny, Democracy, Freedom*, fine names for
an ugly thing. They call it otto of rose and lavender, – I call it bilge-
water. They call it Chivalry and Freedom; I call it the stealing all the
earnings of a poor man and the earnings of his little girl and boy, . . .
and the earnings of all that shall come from him, his children's
children forever" (REW, XI, 259–60). In Emerson's view, both political representatives and the representative signs of language have lost
their vital principle of union to things. Instead of becoming symbols of
natural fact or the spirit, they have become arbitrary signs; instead of
becoming the servants of the people, they have become their masters,
leading people into slavery. The bond between constituent and representative, forged by false representation, imprisons: "Our poor people, led by these fine words, dance and sing, ring bells and fire cannon
with every new link of the chain which is forged for their limbs by the
plotters in the Capitol" (REW, XI, 260).

On March 7, 1850, Daniel Webster became for Emerson the epitome of "rotten diction" and the archconspirator against liberty when
he used his magnificent oratory to support Henry Clay's compromise
bill (which included reinforcement of the Fugitive Slave Law of 1793).
On that date the curse of the country became the most eloquent man.
In 1834 Emerson had written in a poetic tribute to Webster that "when
the rising storm of party roared" "his clarion accents broke, / As if the
conscience of the country spoke," and when Webster "launched the
genuine word / It shook or captivated all who heard, / . . . And burned
in noble hearts proverb and prophecy" (REW, IX, 398–9). The distance
of Webster's fall into disgrace in Emerson's eyes can be measured by
two lines Emerson added to the poem in 1854: "Why did all manly
gifts in Webster fail? / He wrote on Nature's grandest brow, *For Sale*"
(REW, IX, 399). He also damned Webster after the March 7 speech in
his journal: "Webster truly represents the American people just as
they are, with their vast material interests, materialized intellect, &
low morals" (JMN, XI, 385). In a political state where the desire for
power, praise, and riches prevailed over the sovereignty of ideas,
Webster was the representative man: he was the corruption of representation and the representation of corruption.

That power could corrupt a political representative was no surprise.
What people could abide less was the corruption of transcendent
words. Not just representative men but the representative words of
the American Revolution were seen to have been corrupted by the
pursuit of self-interest and sectional interests, and this conviction,
enunciated more frequently and more passionately in the 1850s, pre-

pared people for the purification of holy war. The "greedy chase to make profit of the negro," Abraham Lincoln warns in an 1854 speech, threatened to transform the meaning and "tear to pieces" the Declaration itself: "Near eighty years ago we began by declaring that all men are created equal; but now from that beginning we have run down to the other declaration, that for SOME men to enslave OTHERS is a 'sacred right of self-government'" (LLA, I, 339). Condemning this betrayal of an "OLD for the NEW faith," Lincoln calls upon Americans to "repurify" the "republican robe" "in the spirit, if not the blood, of the Revolution" (LLA, I, 339–40). In an 1855 letter, Lincoln again condemns the degeneration that had turned the language of the Revolution into a Newspeak: "As a nation, we began by declaring that '*all men are created equal.*' We now practically read it 'all men are created equal, *except negroes.*' When the Know-Nothings get control, it will read 'all men are created equal, except negroes, *and foreigners, and catholics*'" (LLA, I, 363). Wendell Phillips similarly plotted American history along the lines of a progressively degenerate language. From the beginning of the United States, he argued in the late 1850s, compromises over slavery had compromised the language, producing a legacy of euphemisms, the homage of vice to virtue. "What a 'commodity of good names' this trouble of ours [slavery] has caused! 'Service and labor' was the Constitutional veil to hide the ugly face of slavery. Then, 'Peculiar Institution'! 'Patriarchal Institution'!! 'Domestic Institution'!!! And now, 'excluding foreigners from our soil'!!!!"[24] Frederick Douglass also chronicled for a lecture audience a legacy of misnomers stemming from attempts to veil the sin of slavery.

> Slavery has always sought to hide itself under different names. The mass of the people call it "our peculiar institution." There is no harm in that. Others call it (they are the more pious sort), "our Patriarchal institution." (Laughter.) Politicians have called it "our social system"; and people in social life have called it "our domestic institution." Abbot Lawrence has recently discovered a new name for it – he calls it "unenlightened labour." (Laughter.) The Methodists in their last General conference, have invented a new name – "the impediment." (Laughter.)[25]

The "climax of all misnomers," Douglass declared in *Narrative of the Life of Frederick Douglass*, was to call "the religion of this land Christianity," and his and Phillips's damnation of the discourse defending slavery belies all the prophetic hopes that Whitman would utter in *An American Primer* that Americans were to become "the most perfect users of words" (AP, 2). While Whitman declares, "Names are the turning point of all who shall be master" (AP, 34), Phillips and

Douglass reveal that euphemisms are the progeny of those who have become masters.

For James Russell Lowell, the culmination of the country's cheating with words was not a euphemism but the *Dred Scott* decision. He best sums up the outrage of the abolitionists over that judicial decision, which allowed the South to make cotton by unmaking men:

> With a representation, three fifths of it based on the assumption that negroes are men, the South turns upon us and insists upon our acknowledging that they are things. After compelling her Northern allies to pronounce the "free and equal" clause of the preamble to the Declaration of Independence . . . a manifest absurdity she has declared, through the Supreme Court of the United States, that negroes are not men in the ordinary meaning of the word. To eat dirt is bad enough, but to find that we have eaten more than was necessary may chance to give us an indigestion. (JLW, V, 20-1)

The Supreme Court defined the ordinary meaning of the word "man" to exclude the African-American in its *Dred Scott* decision. It was a triumph, in Lowell's view, of legal fiction over fact, of a bad opinion over common sense. Lowell himself would fight the pseudo-ordinary language of politics that sought to spread slavery through the war with Mexico and defend it in the *Dred Scott* decision with the ordinary-language philosophy of Hosea Biglow.

Shortly before the outbreak of the Civil War, Lowell issued a protest in his own voice against political discourse in an essay entitled "E Pluribus Unum." "The sporadic eloquence," he asserts, "that breaks out over the country on the eve of election, and becomes a chronic disease in the two houses of Congress, has so accustomed us to dissociate words and things, and to look upon strong language as an evidence of weak purpose, that we attach no meaning whatever to declamation" (JLW, V, 49-50). He then offers his own unmasking of Southern nomenclature: "Rebellion smells no sweeter because it is called Secession, nor does Order lose its divine precedence in human affairs because a knave may nickname it Coercion. Secession means chaos, and Coercion the exercise of legitimate authority. You cannot dignify the one nor degrade the other by any verbal charlatanism" (JLW, V, 53). Lowell resists the verbal reversals of the Thucydidean moment: a negative act must remain negative no matter what positive word may be employed to reverse the evaluation of it.

Change the angle of vision, cross the Mason–Dixon line, and observe a contrary reading of the sources of political and linguistic corruption. In direct contrast to Lowell, Jefferson Davis complains in 1866 that the words "rebellion and treason" were so "grossly misapplied and perverted" in the cant of the day before the outbreak of the Civil War "as to be made worse than unmeaning." For Davis, secession was not treason but the "assertion of the inalienable right of a people to change their government, whenever it ceased to fulfill the purposes for which it was ordained and established." "To term this action of a sovereign a 'rebellion,'" he adds, "is a gross abuse of language."[26] Secession was instead an exercise in the right of revolution that Jefferson had declared in 1776. Both North and South, as James McPherson points out, fought the Civil War in the name of the founding fathers and under the "Battle Cry of Freedom."[27]

In 1866 Melville concurred more with Lowell. He argues in the supplement to *Battle-Pieces*, his collection of Civil War poems, that the plotters of Secession had cajoled "the people of the South" into revolution "under the plea, plausibly urged, that certain inestimable rights guaranteed by the Constitution were directly menaced" (BP, 196–7). He continues, "Through the arts of conspirators . . . the most sensitive love of liberty was entrapped into the support of a war whose implied end was the erecting in our advanced country of an Anglo-American empire based upon the systematic degradation of man" (BP, 197). Seduced by a word, the people counter their ideal of liberty in the name of pursuing it. The great communicators in the South are great deceivers. They fulfill with a vengeance the conclusion of Melville's last novel, *The Confidence-Man*, published in 1857: "Something further may follow of this masquerade."[28] In one of his Civil War poems, "On the Slain Collegians," Melville laments how young, innocent men, as seemingly naive to the double meanings of words as Billy Budd proves to be, had sacrificed their lives all in the name of heaven. Melville holds two linguistic forces responsible for the Civil War: deceit and the "unfraternal denunciations" between North and South "which at last inflamed to deeds that ended in bloodshed" (BP, 189).

In 1865, at the conclusion of the Civil War, a writer in one of the first issues of the *Nation* provides a retrospective analysis of the verbal abuses that led up to the Civil War which bears a striking resemblance to Thucydides' own version of the connection between political and linguistic disorders in his description of the *stasis* at Corcyra. The author begins by complaining how people turned the Declaration of Independence into a "sophism," declaring it to be a "self-evident falsehood"; how extensive reading of Scott's novels promoted a "high toryism" that opposed the "old-fashioned notions of liberty and equality"; how various partisans claimed the "Protean word" "conservatism" as their peculiar property; and how slavery introduced the "most heterogeneous solecisms in our political language."[29] He continues,

> Kansas raids upon the ballot-box took the name of "law and order,"
> filibustering became conservative; the right of a slave state to de-
> clare a man *property*, and then to make him property in all the
> territories of the nation, this also was conservative and sound States'
> rights democracy; the right of a free State to make a man a *citizen*,
> and the claim that, by virtue of such citizenship and according to the
> express letter of the Constitution, he was a citizen everywhere, this
> was radicalism – yea worse than this, it was downright fanaticism.
> Property, the most questionable kind of property, was placed above
> citizenship. The lower thing was made the special charge of conser-
> vatism; the assertion of the highest of all State rights, and of its title
> to the respect in every other State; this was branded with the odious
> name. (72)

The author then describes the consequences of this mobility of terms.

> No wonder that our ideas, as well as practices, became terribly
> mixed up. Men began to call themselves "democratic conservative,"
> or "conservative democrat" – phrases which would have been in-
> comprehensible to Jefferson; and so, on the other hand, adherence to
> the fundamental ideas of the founders of the republic – a course
> which, in any other part of the world, would have been regarded as
> the soundest conservatism – was stigmatized as radical, until it
> became difficult to tell where we were, since words supposed to be
> the most fixed in political language seemed to have lost all meaning.
> What was worse than all, the famous Declaration of human right to
> which our fathers attached so much importance, came at last to be
> regarded as a mere rhetorical flourish, or a downright contradiction
> in terms. It was radicals and fanatics who quoted the fathers – it was
> the conservative, the "democratic conservative," who turned away
> from our national antiquity and poured contempt upon our heroic
> age. (72–73)

Just as in Thucydides' account of civil war, people here confound the
significance of the most hallowed words of their culture, and they
break the "civil charms" that subjected them "to a better sway / Than
sway of self" (BP, 89). Contemporary politics is presented as a fall,
morally and linguistically, from a past held sacred. A reconstruction is
necessary to restore a union that collapsed in a babel of words.

   In 1864 Emerson, Lowell, and Oliver Wendell Holmes met to
discuss Charles Sumner's proposal to establish a national academy of
letters in Washington, D.C. No longer truants of the language, the
three of them endorsed the plan, as Emerson reports in a letter to
Sumner: "We agreed on the general objects of such a society; as, for
the conservation of the English language; a constituted jury to which
questions of taste & fitness in literature might be carried; a jury to sit

upon abnormal pretensions to genius, such as puzzle the public mind
now & then. Custodians of sense & elegance – these colleagues are to
be, – in literature."[30] Sumner's bill for a national academy of literature and art, which he introduced on July 2, 1864, failed, but other
institutions began to foster the conservation of language. Under the
editorship of E. L. Godkin, the *Nation* in the early Reconstruction
period became a leader in publishing the "verbal criticism" that
became quite popular after the Civil War.[31] Corruptions of the language would be exposed and a people's tongue disciplined by a more
scrupulous attention to grammar. Verbal critics such as George Wakeman, who published a series of essays on language in the *Galaxy* in
1866, were searching for more than a means for a refined class of
gentlemen to oppose the corruptions of the vulgar. Wakeman wanted
to expose and mitigate "the confusions of our own tongue" – the
anomalies, inconsistencies, and ambiguities of speech that had produced "endless ill-feelings, dissensions, controversies, quarrels, enmi-
ties, and wars."[32] After the Civil War, the *Nation* also began a campaign against rhetorical excess. An 1866 editorial argued that
"Congressional debates" exercise "no influence on legislation" but
are "intended to amuse . . . the country people" and that "undue
importance is given in our colleges to the mere 'gift of gab.'" "The
art which we most need to cultivate among the young," the editorial
maintains, "is the art of having something to say, of saying it in clear,
pure, *unadorned* English."[33] No prose was more efficient in its plainness
than the prose of Ulysses S. Grant's *Personal Memoirs*, which became
one of the best-sellers of the Reconstruction era.

Lincoln's Gettysburg Address, Grant's *Memoirs*, the colloquial idiom
of Huckleberry Finn: these are landmarks in the chastening of prose
style associated with the post–Civil War era. The art of rhetorical
deflation has a long history in America, beginning with the Puritans'
quest to purify the Word of God of its excrescences. John Cotton pares
away the rhetoric of his sermons; Paine resorts to a low language in
Common Sense to cut down the claims of the British; and throughout
the course of American literature vernacular idioms have cut against
an inflated moral rhetoric.[34] Rhetoric was taken with the utmost
seriousness in the early republic: it was a dignified subject of study in
colleges; it was the dignified attribute of the statesman; and an oration
was the dignified ritual for the most serious of occasions – the death of
Washington, of Adams and Jefferson, and of the soldiers at Gettysburg. But rhetoric was also subject to ridicule. Before the Civil War
the bombast of Fourth of July orations was burlesqued, and the taller
the talk became of freedom, the quicker became the wit of the
colloquial. Rhetorical inflation and a distrust of moneyed men who

talk so fine but gloss over matters so smoothly led, at least in part, to the appeal of dialect speakers in such works as Lowell's *Biglow Papers* and to the cultivation of the vernacular voice in politics as practiced, for instance, by Andrew Jackson and Davy Crockett. It seemed that the farther one lived from Washington, D.C., the city of words, the closer one lived to the truth and the better one could hear and translate the voice of nature. In the period, language itself came under attack as a source of alienation; it separated people from nature and people from each other. "Speech is the sign of partiality, difference," Emerson notes in his journal (JMN, VII, 106). Another writer declares in 1860: "We cannot speak entire and unmixed truth, because utterance separates a part from the whole, and consequently in measure distorts and exaggerates and does injustice to other truths. The moment we speak we are one-sided and liable to be assailed by the reverse side of a fact."[35] Speech splits the world into parts and people into parties; it pollutes us with duplicity. The only escape is a retreat into nature or silence, the retreat Thoreau takes in *Walden*.

When Thoreau retreated from the public world to Walden pond, he did so not to escape America but to gain a vantage point from which he could measure the distance between what was good and bad and right according to his inner constitution and what was proclaimed good and bad and right by the public. In building a world elsewhere, Thoreau sought to juxtapose his ideal vision of America – the higher state of the mind – against a corrupt reality, just as he often juxtaposed the "corrupt" meaning of a word against its etymological root in the ground of a natural fact. And Thoreau, like Emerson, hoped to recall words and America back to an original relationship with nature: "Talk about learning our *letters* and being *literate*! Why the roots of *letters* are *things*" (HTJ, XII, 389).[36] Indeed, just as *Walden* itself moves, structurally and thematically, from corruption to purification and regeneration in nature, that movement is replicated as he progresses from a commentary on spoken and written language in the third chapter, "Reading," to the language of nature in the next chapter, "Sounds." While Emerson and Whitman appeal to the voice to transcend or uncorrupt the written, Thoreau moves in the opposite direction. He argues in "Reading" that the spoken language is "commonly transitory, a sound, a tongue, a dialect merely, almost brutish, and we learn it unconsciously, like the brutes, of our mothers" (TLA, 403). The written tongue, in contrast, is the "maturity and experience" of the spoken; it is the "father tongue, a reserved and select expression, too significant to be heard by the ear, which we must be born again in order to speak" (ibid.). The oral is the least pure: it is the ore, and books are the refinement, the "treasured wealth of the world and the fit inheritance of generations and nations" (TLA, 405). The "noblest written words," Thoreau writes, "are commonly as far behind or above the fleeting spoken language as the firmament with its stars is behind the clouds" (TLA, 404). Thoreau then links his preference for the written over the oral to a criticism of the orator. "The orator yields to the inspiration of a transient occasion, and speaks to the mob before him, to those who can *hear* him; but the writer . . . who would be distracted by the event and the crowd which inspire the orator, speaks to the intellect and heart of mankind, to all in any age who can *understand* him" (TLA, 404). Thoreau is as counteroratorical in *Walden* as Publius is in *The Federalist*. The orator, in their regard, is a prisoner of the times and of mobs, and just as the written Constitution counters the force of the vox populi for Madison, the authors of books act for Thoreau as "a natural and irresistible aristocracy in every society" (TLA, 405). But in "Sounds" Thoreau transcends the written: he moves from "particular written languages, which are themselves but dialects and provincial," to the language "we are in danger of forgetting," "the language which . . . alone is copious and standard" – the language of nature (TLA, 411). Reading in "the leaves of books" gives way to the higher act of contemplating "living poetry like the leaves of a tree" (TLA, 568). The first summer, Thoreau reports, "I did not read books . . . ; I hoed beans" (TLA, 411). *Walden* is composed of a series of refinements, of a sequence of passages from corruption to purification. Speech yields to writing, writing yields to nature, the "noise of contemporaries" to silence, the times to the eternities, luxury to simplicity, the laws of the state to the higher laws of nature, the speech of Webster to the "solid bottom," money to truth (TLA, 584, 585). Against the vox populi, Thoreau offers, in short, the "*lingua vernacula* of Walden Wood" (TLA, 538).

Thoreau's essays are essays in redefinition: the commonplace word is challenged or revised by an extravagant expression, the minority opinion of one man – Thoreau.[37] Emerson reports that Thoreau's "first instinct on hearing a proposition was to controvert it" and that his writings were marked by a "trick of rhetoric . . . of substitution for the obvious word and thought its diametrical opposite" (REW, X, 456, 479). "The greater part of what my neighbors call good," Thoreau confesses in *Walden*, "I believe in my soul to be bad" (TLA, 331). Thoreau challenges the corruption of a word by breaking the linguistic contract. He will expand or narrow the meaning of a word beyond its common sense, uprooting a word from its normal context and grounding it in new soil. But more than a schoolmaster, Thoreau is a minister. "The heroic books," he asserts, ". . . will always be in a language dead to degenerate times; and we must laboriously seek the meaning of each word and line, conjecturing a larger sense than common use permits out of what wisdom and valor and generosity we have" (TLA, 403). To end the corrupt use of words, or to end corrupt interpretations, there must be a regeneration of the spirit, an awakening, a change of soul. "There are also a great many words which are spurious and artificial, and can only be used in a bad sense, since the thing they signify is not fair and substantial, – such as the *church*, the *judiciary*, to *impeach*, etc., etc. They who use them do not stand on solid ground" (HTJ, X, 233). No verbal qualification, no precision, no clarity of style will uncorrupt these words: "It is in vain to try to preserve them by attaching other words to them as the *true* church, etc. It is like towing a sinking ship with a canoe" (ibid.). Thoreau's contempt for the artifice of these words matches the disgust felt by Frederic Henry in Ernest Hemingway's *Farewell to Arms*: "There were many words that you could not stand to hear and finally only the names of places had dignity. . . . Abstract words such as glory, honor, courage or hallow were obscene behind the concrete names of villages, the number of roads, the names of rivers, the numbers of regiments and the dates."[38] For Thoreau, the only remedy is to "work and wedge our feet downward through the mud and slush" of opinion–prejudice–tradition–delusion–appearance and right ourselves on solid ground (TLA, 400). Hemingway's heroes follow a similar path. When Nick Adams returns to the woods after the war in Hemingway's "Big Two-Hearted River," he registers his thoughts and experiences with as much attention to detail – to the concreteness of names, numbers, and dates – as Thoreau gives to the recording of his own experiences in nature. Neither Thoreau nor Hemingway is so naive as to believe that an Adamic right naming of nature will recover innocence or render peace in his time, but both do envision it as a therapeutic response to the nausea of untruth – and Hemingway in prose, like Ezra Pound in poetry, set an example for modern literature by putting into stylistic practice what Emerson and Thoreau preached.

Partly because the United States was a country governed by a written text and dependent upon representation as its vital principle, or partly because Emerson and Thoreau would have agreed with Ezra Pound that "your legislator can't legislate for the public good, your commander can't command, your populace . . . can't instruct its 'representatives,' save by language," they believed as strongly as did Pound that "when words cease to cling close to things, kingdoms fall, empires waver and diminish . . ."[39] After World War I, while he was constituting and amending *The Cantos*, Pound drew upon the founding fathers of American politics and poetry (e.g., John Adams, Emerson, and Whitman) (and upon the example of Confucius) to promulgate in prose works such as *How to Read*, *ABC of Reading*, and *Guide to Kulchur* a set of convictions about the interrelationship of linguistic, political, and economic corruption that shaped the methods and ends of his art – and these convictions provide an important corollary in literary history to Emerson's and Thoreau's own efforts to oppose linguistic corruption. They also provide a crucial perspective on the ideological limitations of such an effort.

Opposed to the bloated and effusive rhetoric of later-nineteenth-century poetry, Pound championed at the outset of the twentieth a new and more precise mode of poetic representation which he called *imagisme*. "The poetical reform between 1910 and 1920 coincided with the scrutiny of the word, the cleaning-up of syntax," Pound writes, and it is this practice of verbal scrutiny that he extends to the domain of politics and economics as part of his Emersonian quest to expose and reform corruptions not just in culture but in the state. "With the falsification of word everything else is betrayed," he asserts.[40] He also insists upon a corollary argument – "The *mot juste* is of public utility" – in a 1922 review of Joyce's *Ulysses* wherein he condemns a sequence of American presidents from Cleveland to Wilson for their failure to take an interest in "the public utility of accurate language." "A sense of style could have saved America and Europe from Wilson," he maintains.[41] Soon thereafter, in *How to Read*, a primer designed to cultivate the sense of style and clarity he found lacking in modern republics and that he hoped would serve as a weapon against the bogus language games and bullying tactics of propaganda, Pound again maintains that when the "very medium" of writers, "the very essence of their work, the application of word to thing goes rotten, i.e., becomes slushy and inexact, or excessive and bloated, the whole machinery of social and individual thought and order goes to pot." "This is a lesson of history, and a lesson not yet half learned," he adds, and this is the lesson Pound keeps teaching in the 1930s as he condemns the lies of arms dealers, businessmen, journalists, and politicians from Woodrow Wilson to Franklin Roosevelt.[42] His antidote to the Thucydidean moment is the rectification of names, the Confucian doctrine of *Cheng Ming*, which is the doctrine Pound proselytizes as the mission of the poet.[43] "As language becomes the most powerful instrument of perfidy, so language alone can riddle and cut through the meshes. Used to conceal meaning, used to blur meaning, to produce the complete and utter inferno of the past century . . . discussion of which would lead me out of the bounds of this volume . . . against which, SOLELY a care for language, for accurate registration by language avails."[44] The poet, in Pound's (and Eliot's) vision, is a conservator (or purifier) of the language of the tribe who guards the word hoard as carefully as Plato's ideal statesman guards the realm of Ideas and who challenges an earthly inferno of usurers and betrayers (as depicted, for instance, in Canto 38) by creating poetic paradisos, illustrations of the noble vernacular. "We are governed by words, the laws are graven in words, and literature is the sole means of keeping these words living and accurate," Pound insists.[45] The social function of the writer, Pound asserts, "has to do with the clarity and vigour of 'any and every' thought and opinion. It has to do with maintaining the very cleanliness of the tools, the health of the very matter of thought itself. Save in the rare and limited instances of invention in the plastic arts, or in mathematics, the individual cannot think and communicate his thought, the governor and legislator cannot act effectively or frame his laws, without words, and the solidity and validity of these words is in the care of the damned and despised *literati*."[46]

That Pound himself became one of the damned literati suggests the dubiousness of his claim that guardianship of the language belongs particularly to the poet. There is no more persuasive exposure of the fascism lying behind Pound's project of linguistic purification – the search for the perfectly representative word – than this poet's support for the politics of Mussolini. But while we can doubt the wisdom of the wise men who claim to pierce "rotten diction" and fasten words to things (Ahab was such a harpooner), we can also doubt that poets will refrain from doing battle against rotten diction and that they will abandon Whitman's hope that new words, even slang words, like new politicians, even uncouth ones from Springfield, Illinois, such as Abraham Lincoln, could revitalize representation and extend the capacity of common words to express what can unite a diverse people.[47]

11

Sovereign Words vs. Representative Men

They say that folks misuse words, but I see it the other way around, words misuse people. . . . Throw a kiss or hold out your arms and even a baby can understand you. But just try to say it in words and you raise up Babel and the grapes of wrath. If you nod your head and smile even folks who don't speak your language will get the idea, but you just whisper *peace* somebody will claim you declared war and will insist on trying to kill you. No wonder we have war! No wonder history is a bitch on wheels with wings traveling inside a submarine. Words are behind it all.

> Ralph Ellison, "A Song of Innocence"

"But we care not for men's words; we look for creeds in actions; which are the truthful symbols of the things within. He who hourly prays to Alma, but lives not up to world-wide love and charity – that man is more an unbeliever than he who verbally rejects the Master, but does his bidding. Our lives are our Amens."

> Herman Melville, *Mardi*

When John Quincy Adams delivers his inaugural lecture as the first Boylston Professor of Rhetoric and Oratory at Harvard, before he proclaims the glorious promise of eloquence in a republican America he explains that in Europe, "where the semblance of deliberative assemblies has been preserved, corruption . . . in the form of executive influence, [and] . . . in the guise of party spirit" has "crippled the sublimest efforts of oratory," so that in the old world "questions of magnitude to the interest of the nation" are decided "long before the questions themselves are submitted to discussion" (LR, I, 27). The politics of modern Europe have divorced what Pericles praises Athens and Adams praises the United States for integrating: word and action, deliberation and decision making, eloquence and liberty.

> Under governments purely republican, where every citizen has a deep interest in the affairs of the nation, and, in some form of public assembly or other, has the means and opportunity of delivering his opinions, and of communicating his sentiments by speech; where government itself has no arms but those of persuasion; where prejudice has not acquired an uncontroled ascendency, and faction is yet confined within the barriers of peace; the voice of eloquence will not be heard in vain. (LR, I, 30–1)

Across the Atlantic, at the time of Adams's oration, the classical rhetorical tradition had fallen into decline. The antirhetorical empiricism of the new science and Locke proved stronger than Sheridan and the elocution movement. Print culture displaced the tongue as the medium of political communication in the nation-state. The Romantic movement made rhetoric appear more artificial and the orator more imitative. The maneuvers of Walpole's politics and Napoleon's army and not the words of any orator (or any assembly of orators) represented the new order of the ages in Europe.[1] The United States was not immune to these developments, and the dependence of education on the "dead" classical languages was attacked by an ex-printer's devil, Benjamin Franklin, whose "principal Means of . . . Advancement," as he declares in his *Autobiography*, was not speech but "Prose Writing." But for John Quincy Adams, who continued to read Cicero for hours in the morning when he was a representative in Congress at the end of his career, the languages of ancient Athens and Rome were anything but dead for a son of Harvard with ambition: "Is there among you a youth," he asks at the close of his inaugural address,

> whose bosom burns with the fires of honorable ambition; who aspires to immortalize his name by the extent and importance of his service to his country; whose visions of futurity glow with the hope of presiding in her councils, of directing her affairs, of appearing to future ages on the rolls of fame, as her ornament and pride? Let him catch from the relics of ancient oratory those unresisted powers, which mould the mind of man to the will of the speaker, and yield the guidance of a nation to the dominion of the voice. (LR, I, 30)

Through eloquence alone the virtuous citizen could distinguish himself and rise through the ranks of society and fulfill his own aspirations by serving the country and directing its affairs. "In the flourishing periods of Athens and Rome," Adams asserts, "eloquence was POWER," and so it would be again in the United States (LR, I, 19). In lecture after lecture, in essay after essay, in a monotony of orations and manuals of elocution, the same truism was proclaimed (with Emerson himself declaring it twice in two different lectures on eloquence). But a revival of the "unresisted powers" from the relics of ancient oratory promised not just the return of the scourge of tyrants but the threat that oratory could become not a blessing but a curse, not the "benefactress of human kind" but the "pest of nations" (LR, I, 65). This threat leads Adams to affirm the importance of a rhetorical education: "Since eloquence is in itself so powerful a weapon, and since by the depravity of mankind, this weapon must, and often will be brandished for guilty purposes, its exercise, with equal or superior skill, becomes but the more indispensable to the cause of virtue" (ibid.). The eloquence of the corrupt must be countered and surpassed by the eloquence of the virtuous; the sovereign word must be tamed by the representative man.

The antebellum era became an era of oratorical politics.[2] The speeches of Webster, Clay, and Calhoun confirmed Adams's vision of eloquence as the medium of politics and Emerson's evaluation: the orator is the "true potentate," and the orator's speech "is not to be distinguished from action. It is the electricity of action. It is action, as the general's word of command or chart of battle is action" (REW, VII, 115). In paintings, histories, and school readers, political action was represented as verbal action: as oration, debate, talk, argument. The triumph of the politician was the triumph of the word: "Look at a Webster or a Calhoun," William Mathews writes, "when his mighty enginery of thought is in full operation; how his words tell upon his adversary, battering down the entrenchments of sophistry like shot from heavy ordnance!" (WMW, 14). The words of Webster, declares Edwin Whipple, "are thunder-bolts, which sometimes miss the Titans at whom they are hurled, but always leave enduring marks when they strike" (EWW, 180).

The classical conceptualization of politics as a military campaign and the orator's voice as the instrument of battle became something of a self-fulfilling prophecy in antebellum America, and it helped lead Whipple and others to envision the word itself as an independent power, a sovereign force. The "Lexicon" is the "true ruler" of the world, Whipple declares in 1845; each word is "a new element of servitude to mankind," and some have "exercised greater influence, and swayed with more absolute power, than Alexander or Napoleon" (EWW, 182). "Words," he adds, "head armies, overthrow dynasties, man ships, separate families, cozen cozeners, and steal hearts and purses" (EWW, 182). By the 1850s Whipple's opinion approaches the status of a critical commonplace. William Swinton collaborates with Whitman in writing *Rambles Among Words: Their Poetry, History and Wisdom* (1859), which gives tribute not just to the wisdom of words but to their militancy: "How titantic is the power which many words wield! . . . How are we under the sway of Words! They tyrannize over and terrify us."[3] Words are also described as "powerful engines in the cause of truth – flails with which shames and meannesses are castigated" (192). "Words and deeds are quite indifferent modes of the divine energy," claims Emerson (ELA, 450). Language for Mathews in *Words; Their Use and Abuse* is "the armory of the human mind, which contains at once the trophies of its past and weapons of its future conquests" (WMW, 14). He later adds: "Words . . . are excellent servants, but the most tyrannical of masters. Some men command them, but a vast majority are commended by them. There are words which have exercised a more iron rule, swayed with a more despotic power, than Caesar or the Russian Czar" (WMW, 73).

The age also witnesses the popular success of the political slogan, the sound bites of the past. "Log Cabin and Hard Cider," "Tippecanoe and Tyler, too," "Fifty-four forty or fight," "Free soil, free speech, free labor, and free men," "Fight on, fight ever" were probably among the "badges and names" Emerson had in mind when he computed the power of symbols in "Self-Reliance" and "The Poet." Mathews similarly comments in his book on the use and abuse of words that the slogans "'Free Trade and Sailors' Rights,' 'No More Compromise,' 'The Higher Law,' 'The Irrepressible Conflict,' 'Squatter Sovereignty,' and other similar phrases, have roused and moved the public mind as much as the pulpit and the press" (WMW, 77). Joshua Leavitt, a leader of the Liberty Party, is most blatant about the power of a slogan when he advises Samuel Chase in a letter that the Liberty Party must "make the most" of the term "*Slave Power*": "It is not necessary that they who use it should ever know who taught it to them – the name and the thing – but the incessant use of the term will do much to open the eyes and arouse the energies of the people. . . . Let it appear that it is the *Slave Power* which we wish to restrict and curtail."[4]

Every new trick of rhetoric and every slogan devised by a Southerner, Northerner, Whig, Republican, Democrat, or abolitionist seemed to contribute to the conviction that the controversies of the day were aided and abetted, if not caused by, the omnipotence of words. Viewed as an efficient mode of political actions, the word was also viewed as an efficient cause of political disorder. The keys to its power could be grasped by good and bad alike. Language could be the instrument of society and the revelation of the soul; it could be the instrument of the demagogue, Satan manifesting himself as an angel of light. "Words – so innocent and powerless as they are, as standing in a dictionary, how potent for good and evil they become," Hawthorne writes in his notebook, "in the hands of one who knows how to combine them" (NHW, VIII, 280). The "perfect writer," Whitman declares in *An American Primer*, would make words "sing, dance, do the male and female act, bear children, weep, bleed, rage, stab, steal, fire cannon, steer ships, sack cities, charge with cavalry or infantry, or do any thing, that man or woman or the natural powers can do" (AP, 16). Words can destroy; words can perform acts of union.

Confronted with the word as a sovereign power, political and literary critics offered the standard response, calling for precision and clarity and advocating judicious review of the word to check and balance its power. The writers who regularly reviewed political affairs in journal essays in the period resort to definition. Incessantly, they examine the history and meaning of the verbal representatives that possessed the most influence, such as "freedom," "democracy," "republic," "liberty," "the people," "states' rights." The watch-words of this criticism are a set of adjectives that affirm confidence in the rightness of their own words: "obvious," "correct," "plain," "true." Mathews counsels, for instance, that people need to form "definite conceptions" of what they mean by such expressions as "the sovereignty of the people" (WMW, 225). But he also points out the limits of clarity and definition when he asserts that we "must . . . keep constantly in mind the fact that language, when used with the utmost precision, is at best but an imperfect representation of thought" (WMW, 257). Whipple offers an additional piece of advice. He advocates that we should "look sharply at all axioms which seem to fix the significance of these little substantives and sovereigns" (EWW, 178). Rather than recommending more and better legislation by definitions, he advises readers to question the legislation itself and its guiding principles.

But all the words about words made people tired and frustrated with words. The word from this perspective was neither a sovereign nor a representative force; it was impotent. The word could do little to sustain the Union, and much to harm it. "The curse of this country is eloquent men," declared the preeminent eloquent man – Daniel Webster – in 1845. "Not only in our court-houses and representative halls," asserts Mathews, "but everywhere, we are literally deluged with words, – words, – words" (WMW, 154). "In the South," Whitman observes in 1856, "no end of blusterers, braggarts, windy, melo-dramatic, continually screaming in falsetto"; in the North, a "parcel of windy . . . liars are bawling in your ears the easily-spoken words Democracy and the democratic party," and "base political blowers and kept-editors . . . are raising a fog of prevarications" (WLA, 1309, 1315, 1316). Not just the sovereign power of words but their failure made for a crisis in representation that was the prelude to civil war. The turning point, as Emerson identified it, was March 7, 1850. A consummate irony during the debate over the Compromise of 1850, Robert Ferguson explains, is that "each of the Senate's three great orators" – Clay, Calhoun, and Webster – "rose in turn to condemn public speaking as a source of the nation's problem."[5] Then abolitionists in the North rose up to condemn Webster's prostitution of his own immense gift for oratory. The conclusion to be drawn from the Compromise and its reception was a lesson that countervailed the schoolmasters. "Oratory," Ferguson writes "no longer governed; it no longer led to consensus. . . . When speech failed, Stephen Douglas manipulated behind the scenes to create the Compromise of 1850."[6]

Soon after the Compromise of 1850, for every verbal action in the North there was, it seems, an equal and opposite – if not more belligerent – reaction in the South, and vice versa. Charles Sumner's brutal caning by Preston Brooks on the Senate floor in 1856, an attack provoked by Sumner's rhetorical abuse of Brooks's uncle during his "Crime Against Kansas" speech, immediately became an icon in the North of the South's inhumanity or of its unwillingness to conduct politics by the word; in the South, Sumner's uncivil tongue deserved the dishonor of a caning. Congress, designed as a sanctum for deliberation, had become the scene not just of logomachy but of violence itself. "Fiery words," George Marsh warned in 1859, "are the hot blast that inflames the fuel of our passionate nature" and only lead to hotter conflicts. "In a personal altercation," he adds, "it is most often the stimulus men give themselves by stinging words, that impels them to violent acts" (ML, 235).

The age of words culminates in *Representative Men, The Scarlet Letter, Moby-Dick, The House of the Seven Gables, Pierre, Uncle Tom's Cabin* (all published between 1850 and 1852), *Walden* (1854), and *Leaves of Grass* (1855). These works tap the energy of words charged by the political action of oratory to criticize and transcend oratory. Emerson and Whitman provide the theory that helps link these works together. They proclaim that the role of the poet and scholar is to be a representative voice for the American people, a voice that would challenge the misrepresentations of its politicians and amend the judgments of its judges. "The poet is . . . representative of man," Emerson asserts (ELA, 448). "I act as the tongue of you," says Whitman (WLA, 243). Whitman also declares, "The poets I would have must be a power in the state, and an engrossing power in the state," and Emerson comments in his journal, ". . . and to mend the bad world, we do not impeach Polk & Webster, but we supersede them by the Muse" (JMN, IX, 357). The American poet assumes in such a vision the ancient role of Orphic legislator and biblical prophet: the poet as lawgiver and name giver. Hawthorne and Melville, however, reveal their skepticism about the "tongues of flame" possessed by poets, reformers, and preachers as well as by politicians and judges. The modest, honest tongue of Ernest in "The Great Stone Face" and of Ishmael in *Moby-Dick*, as opposed to the oratory of "Stony Phiz" and Ahab, are the speakers of representative words for Hawthorne and Melville. Stowe makes a young girl and an old slave, Eva and Uncle Tom, representative voices of the Word of God, but beyond that faith, George Harris is an incarnation of the words and actions of the Revolution. *Uncle Tom's Cabin* reunifies through the dramatic action what Daniel Webster had split apart: the discourse of liberty and the deed of liberty. *Pierre* fractures them wider despite Pierre's best efforts at unification.

"In the village of Saddle Meadows," where Pierre is born and raised, "there was an institution, half common-school and half academy," and here the students were taught, Melville writes, "some touch of belles lettres, and composition, and that great American bulwark and bore – elocution" (278). "On the high-raised, stage platform of the Saddle Meadows Academy," he adds, "the sons of the most indigent day-laborers were wont to drawl out the fiery revolutionary rhetoric of Patrick Henry," but on "Saturdays, when there was no elocution and poesy, these boys . . . grow melancholy and disdainful over the heavy, plodding handles of dung-forks and hoes" (278–9). These boys are not John Quincy Adams's sons of Harvard; no matter how hard they practice Henry's orations, they will most likely never advance from wielding dung-forks to wielding power in political assemblies. Garrison was as much a lover of "bold, nervous, lofty language" as Melville, but he too grew disgusted with the inaction of talk, rhetoric, elocution. "O, the odious inconsistency of the American people!" he declares in an oration that was published in 1852. What he condemns is the failure of Americans to act consistently with their past: "When the news of the passage of the Stamp Act, and the tax on tea, by the mother country, was received by our fathers, . . . insurrections for liberty broke out in all parts of the colonies. . . . Then words, however huge, expostulations, however earnest, petitions, however importunate, assertions of rights, however bold and uncompromising in language, were deemed wholly inadequate to such a crisis."[7] The age of oratorical action had to give way to action plain and simple. Words had to become flesh. "An American State," Theodore Parker proclaims, "is a thing that must also be; a State of free men who give over brawling, resting on industry, justice, love, not on war, cunning, and violence – a State where liberty, equality, and

fraternity are deeds as well as words."[8] "These men are all talk," John
Brown muttered in disgust after attending a meeting of the New
England Anti-Slavery Society. "What is needed is action – action!"[9]

John Brown becomes Thoreau's representative man because his life
as well as his words are acts that represent the principles of Christ and
the American Revolution. Combining the heroic action of George
Harris and the martyrdom of Uncle Tom, Brown becomes in Thoreau's "Plea for Captain John Brown" (1859) the antithesis of John
Quincy Adams's vision of a republic sustained (and saved) by the
eloquent man. He is a truant free from the enslaving discourse of the
schoolmaster: "He did not go to the college called Harvard"; he
would say he knows "no more of grammar than one of your calves";
and "he would have left a Greek accent slanting the wrong way, and
righted up a falling man" (HTW, 113). Mimicking the language of the
schoolmaster to challenge its authority and to sanction Brown, Thoreau reports that Brown "went to the great university of the West,
where he sedulously pursued the study of Liberty, . . . and having
taken many degrees, he finally commenced the public practice of
Humanity in Kansas" (ibid.). Thoreau then puns upon or etymologizes
a word to reveal how Brown literalizes the spirit of the letter. "Such
were *his humanities*, and not any study of grammar" (ibid.). While
Thoreau calls Brown "the most American of us all," he describes him
as something different from a representative (HTW, 125). He wishes
he could call Brown the "representative of the North," but he cannot,
because Brown "was too fair a specimen of a man to represent the like
of us" (HTW, 125, 127). His constituency was not the people of the
North but truth. "Not yielding to a whim or transient impulse,"
Brown is the ideal representative because he represents the ideal, or
the eternities and not the times (HTW, 115). His transcendent representativeness as an actor corresponds to his linguistic practice: "He
was not in the least a rhetorician, was not talking to Buncombe or his
constituents any where" (ibid.). Brown then becomes for Thoreau in
his "Last Days of John Brown" (1860) a truant schoolmaster of the
language (and thus something of an uncle to Huck Finn): "This
unlettered man's speaking and writing are standard English. Some
words and phrases deemed vulgarisms and Americanisms before, he
has made standard American; such as '*It will pay.*' It suggests that the
one great rule of composition – and if I were a professor of rhetoric, I
should insist on this – is to *speak the truth*" (HTW, 151). Brown is also
for Thoreau the best minister to the people of the Word, for not only
do his words teach a pure, spiritual diction, but his actions are
incarnate words. He was "by far the greatest preacher of them all,
with the Bible in his life and in his acts" (HTW, 146). Brown was for

Thoreau a revival preacher who converted people in the North to "original perceptions"; "They saw that what was called order was confusion, what was called justice, injustice, and that the best was deemed the worst" (HTW, 147). Brown, in short, counters the corruption of the Thucydidean moment. He remoralizes words and a people demoralized by slavery by revealing to them how their positive terms had become euphemisms, veiling the sins of the fathers. The people had been taught too well by Daniel Webster and the other schoolmasters of the Constitution: they "remembered the old formula" (HTW, 148). But Brown gave them "the new revelation," and the people responded. "There was a slight revival of old religion. . . . This attitude suggested a more intelligent and generous spirit than that which actuated our forefathers" (HTW, 147). The ones who failed to recognize in Brown's language and actions "a wisdom and nobleness, and therefore an authority, superior to our laws" are, Thoreau puns, "constitutionally blind" (HTW, 148).

In 1838, Lincoln was as adamant a schoolmaster of the Constitution as Daniel Webster. He regarded it as more than a grammar that had to be obeyed; it was the creed of a "*political religion*" that had to be reverenced (LLA, I, 32). By the late 1850s, however, Lincoln had become more like Thoreau, grounding his political principles in the Declaration (though he was still as devoted to preserving the Union as Whitman). By the time of the Emancipation Proclamation, he had become more like Brown, willing to fight to free the slaves. And by the time of his assassination, he was Emerson's and Lowell's representative man. What he fought against with the lexicographical talents of Noah Webster and Cooper, the aphorisms of Emerson, the wit of Twain, the capability to redefine of Thoreau (and Bierce), the cadences in prose of Paine and Jefferson, the close reading and historical knowledge of Daniel Webster, and the religious vocabulary of Stowe were the betrayers of the word, such as Stephen Douglas, who had turned the Declaration into a Newspeak that sanctioned slavery, and the embalmers of the word, such as Justice Taney, who were willing to preserve the language of the Constitution as a dead letter. No president – and perhaps no American writer – has conducted politics by the word with more command and grace. Opposed to Taney, who argued that the Declaration's principle that "all men are created equal" was not intended to apply to black men and that the Constitution had to "be construed now as it was understood at the time of its adoption," Lincoln argues in a speech on the *Dred Scott* decision that the Supreme Court's decision reduces the Declaration to "mere rubbish – old wadding left to rot on the battle-field after the victory is won"

(LLA, I, 400).[10] He insists instead, in a remarkably condensed (and poetically cadenced) statement of a complex hermeneutics which embraces a bipolar relationship between strict and liberal construction, that the words of the Declaration should be "constantly looked to, constantly labored for, and even though never perfectly attained, constantly approximated, and thereby constantly spreading and deepening its influence, and augmenting the happiness and value of life to all people of all colors everywhere" (LLA, I, 398). Later he maintains, in his 1860 "Address at Cooper Institute," that we are not "bound to follow implicitly in whatever our fathers did" (LLA, II, 119). Lincoln's hermeneutics after the Dred Scott decision are guided in theory by a fundamental principle: the words of the founding fathers cannot become rotten diction or dead letters, and thus interpretation must resurrect the spirit of Jefferson. Construction should counter the corruption that subverts liberty and prohibits the pursuit of a more perfect union, and it is the people themselves who are ultimately responsible for governing the meaning of the Declaration and the Constitution. They are the ones who must uncorrupt words. "Are you really willing," he asks the people near the close of his speech opposing the Dred Scott decision, "that the Declaration shall be thus frittered away? – thus left no more at most, than an interesting memorial of the dead past? and thus shorn of its vitality, and practical value . . . ?" (LLA, I, 400). The question reposes interpretive authority not solely in the past but in the present generation of readers, and when Lincoln later defends a proposal of his to amend the Constitution a month before he issued the Emancipation Proclamation, he calls upon citizens to liberate themselves from the past as strongly as Emerson demands in *Nature* and "Self-Reliance": "The dogmas of the quiet past, are inadequate to the stormy present. . . . As our case is new, so we must think anew, and act anew. We must disenthrall ourselves, and then we shall save our country" (LLA, II, 415). We must also use words anew. Lincoln's own Gettysburg Address is a speech that renews as it rewrites a tradition: he misreads the fathers, as Garry Wills argues, to reconstruct their house.[11]

Lincoln achieves through his speeches and writings the highest honors as a schoolmaster of America. His preeminence stems in part from practicing a political pedagogy that abandons the dogmatism of lecture for the habit of conducting seminars that inquire into the meanings of words. On July 4, 1861, in a special message to Congress he chose to defend the Union against the secessionists who were claiming the revolutionary right of a state to declare its independence from a political bond that had become destructive of its liberty. For Lincoln, secession was treason and not justifiable revolution, but the

people of the South had been deluded to think otherwise by the
sophisms of their leaders. At the heart of his message to Congress is
thus an attempt to expose the verbal charlatanism lying behind "the
magical omnipotence of 'State rights.'"

> It might seem, at first thought, to be of little difference whether the
> present movement at the South be called "secession" or "rebellion."
> The movers, however, well understand the difference. At the begin-
> ning, they knew they could never raise their treason to any respect-
> able magnitude, by any name which implies *violation* of law. They
> knew their people possessed as much of moral sense, as much of
> devotion to law and order, and as much pride in, and reverence for,
> the history, and government, of their common country, as any other
> civilized, and patriotic people. They knew they could make no
> advancement directly in the teeth of these strong and noble senti-
> ments. Accordingly they commenced by an insidious debauching of
> the public mind. They invented an ingenious sophism, which, if
> conceded, was followed by perfectly logical steps, through all the
> incidents, to the complete destruction of the Union. The sophism
> itself is, that any State of the Union may, *consistently* with the
> national Constitution, and therefore *lawfully*, and *peacefully*, with-
> draw from the Union without the consent of the Union, or of any
> other State. . . .
>   With rebellion thus sugar-coated, they have been drugging the
> public mind of their section for more than thirty years. (LLA, II,
> 254–5)

Lincoln exposes the plotting that advances the Thucydidean moment:
a community's vocabulary of moral and political principle – its
pharmakon of words – is drawn upon to defend the indefensible. He
then offers a lesson about America's political grammar and ends with a
proposal for a new consensus about the meaning of a word.

> This sophism derives much – perhaps the whole – of its currency,
> from the assumption, that there is some omnipotent, and sacred
> supremacy, pertaining to a *State* – to each State of our Federal
> Union. Our States have neither more, nor less power, than that
> reserved to them, in the Union, by the Constitution – no one of them
> ever having been a State *out* of the Union. The original ones passed
> into the Union even *before* they cast off their British colonial depen-
> dence; and the new ones each came into the Union directly from a
> condition of dependence, excepting Texas. . . . Having never been
> States, either in substance or in name, *outside* of the Union, whence
> this magic omnipotence of "State rights," asserting a claim of power
> to lawfully destroy the Union itself? Much is said about the "sover-
> eignty" of the States; but the word, even, is not in the national
> Constitution; nor, as is believed, in any of the State constitutions.

> What is a "sovereignty," in the political sense of the term? Would it
> be far wrong to define it "A political community without a political
> superior?" Tested by this, no one of our States, except Texas, ever
> was a sovereignty. (LLA, II, 255-6)

To defeat the "magical omnipotence" of state rights, Lincoln becomes
a grammarian, a historian, a Socratic gadfly, and a Lockean linguist.
As a grammarian, he appeals to the standard language of the Constitution, just as Webster did in his debate with Calhoun in 1833. As a
historian, he examines the idea of the sovereignty of states in the
crucible of history and in the light of the Constitution. As a Socratic
gadfly, he questions the people and invites their collaboration. As a
Lockean linguist, he seeks to settle the meaning of a word through
rational analysis and common consent. The definition of sovereignty
that he advances for ratification becomes the touchstone that exposes
the magic of state rights to be as spurious as the alchemists' philosophers' stone. The language is gilded diction: there is no gold bullion
from the vault of the Declaration or silver from the Constitution
inside this verbal currency to guarantee and enrich this language.
Lincoln is also an Emersonian linguist.

At the end of this passage Lincoln is not lecturing in the declarative
mood. He is leading a seminar in the interrogative mood. This method
of address counters the manipulation of public opinion through the
flattery of the demagogue by prodding public opinion to become
informed consent, a practice he comments on directly in another 1861
speech that calls into question state rights:

> Now, I ask the question – I am not deciding anything – [laughter,] –
> and with the request that you will think somewhat upon that subject
> and decide for yourselves, if you choose, when you get ready, –
> where is the mysterious, original right, from principle, for a certain
> district of country with inhabitants, by merely being called a State,
> to play tyrant over all its own citizens, and deny the authority of
> everything greater than itself. [Laughter.] (LLA, II, 202)

Lincoln's questions are leading questions (hence the laughter): they seek
to draw out, in the root meaning of education (*e-ducere*), an answer from
the seeds of words planted in the minds of the audience. Those words
are not just the ones Lincoln plants; they are the leading words of the
founding fathers that Lincoln seeks to clarify and defend as a student of
the fathers. "All my political warfare," he remarks to an audience in
Philadelphia in 1861, "has been in favor of the teachings coming forth
from that sacred hall [Independence Hall]" (LLA, II, 212).

Often in his addresses Lincoln is not just a schoolmaster of the
language, but a vernacular preacher. No speech of his stands out as a

better example of how he performs this role than his 1864 address at the Sanitary Fair in Baltimore. Near the opening of his address he makes a remark about the unsettled state of the word "liberty" in America: "The world has never had a good definition of the word liberty, and the American people, just now, are much in want of one. We all declare for liberty; but in using the same *word* we do not all mean the same *thing*" (LLA, II, 589). Under the seeming unity of the word, there lurks a dualism of meaning, and Lincoln makes his audience alert to this duplicity.

> With some the word liberty may mean for each man to do as he pleases with himself, and the product of his labor; while with others the same word may mean for some men to do as they please with other men, and the product of other men's labor. Here are two, not only different, but incompatible things, called by the same name – liberty. And it follows that each of the things is, by the respective parties, called by two different and incompatible names – liberty and tyranny. (LLA, II, 589)

In an essay on Lincoln, Lowell complains how demagogues easily "confound the distinction between liberty and lawlessness in the minds of ignorant persons, accustomed always to be influenced by the sound of certain words, rather than to reflect upon the principles which give them meaning" (JLW, V, 200–1). Lincoln fights against this overinfluence of sound. To help people reflect upon the meanings of words, he illustrates underlying principles by resorting to a homespun parable:

> The shepherd drives the wolf from the sheep's throat, for which the sheep thanks the shepherd as a *liberator*, while the wolf denounces him for the same act as the destroyer of liberty, especially as the sheep was a black one. Plainly the sheep and the wolf are not agreed upon a definition of the word liberty; and precisely the same difference prevails to-day among us human creatures, even in the North, and all professing to love liberty. Hence we behold the processes by which thousands are daily passing from under the yoke of bondage, hailed by some as the advance of liberty, and bewailed by others as the destruction of all liberty. Recently, as it seems, the people of Maryland have been doing something to define liberty; and thanks to them that, in what they have done, the wolf's dictionary, has been repudiated. (LLA, II, 589–90)

The rhetorical tactics of this address are typical of Lincoln. Throughout his political career, he counters sophisms with logic, indefinite words with common sense, vituperative rhetoric with humor, inflated eloquence with the wit of a folk proverb, and corruption with the virtue of a parable. Opposed to the wolf's dictionary, Lincoln articulates a redemptive language– the sheep's lexicon – that draws upon the resources of the Bible and the "principles of Jefferson," which Lincoln terms the "definitions and axioms of free society" (LLA, II, 19).[12] The parable accomplishes what he praises the people of Maryland for doing: it defines liberty not by precept but through dramatic action (the illustration of a definition). Beyond lexicography, Lincoln's story preaches the golden rule as he praises the people for defending the sheep against the wolf.

If Lincoln's questions and definitions are aids to reflection worthy of Socrates, his parables and proverbs are worthy of Aesop and Twain – or Melville. The ease with which a sinister plot could masquerade behind such a righteous term as "liberty" is something that Melville also exposes in his commentary in *Battle-Pieces* on the origins of the Civil War. *The Confidence-Man*, which juxtaposes the word against the word, or an honest interpretation against a possible corrupt one, as Lincoln does in 1864, is the artist's treatment of the antebellum crisis in representation. A lamblike man speaks the language of the Bible, but his calls for charity and faith are suspected of being the work of a satanic figure, and whether this lamblike man is an avatar of the devil masquerading in sheep's clothing, and whether his words should be given a wolfish or a sheepish interpretation are questions that remain unanswered, for the end is inconclusive. Should we place confidence or distrust in the words that have been spoken by men (or a man) calling for confidence? Does the novel preach the word of charity on board the *Fidèle* to save us from shipwreck, as Winthrop did on the *Arbella*? Or does it preach the antiword of cynicism to save us from the wolf in sheep's clothing? Or does it teach the pragmatist's lesson that the value of a word should be determined by the consequence of accepting it as true (i.e., its cash value)?

Lincoln, like Melville, is more than a Jeremiah preaching against the corruption of the word. He too is a poet–critic who teaches us about the duplicity of language. But he resolves the ambiguities. Beginning with his 1838 speech "Perpetuation of Our Political Institutions," Lincoln defines his own ambition to be that of a countervoice to the demagogue: he will maintain the definitions, and particularly the distinction between liberty and lawlessness, that the demagogue blurs. "The greatest utterances of the Lincoln presidency," Robert Ferguson declares, "seek a solution to this problem, namely, the precise relation between liberty and law or how men will articulate the meaning and scope of liberty."[13] To attain this solution, Lincoln does more than propose definitions. He calls into question the prose of the world as he provokes reflection upon the politics of consent and interpretation that determine how and why such words as "liberty" represent principles or betray them.

Commenting on how pecuniary interests had supplanted higher principles in the debate over slavery, Lincoln observes, "The plainest print cannot be read through a gold eagle" (LLA, I, 403). Lincoln needs no jargon to offer this Aesopian lesson on hermeneutics that could serve as an epigraph for *The Confidence-Man*. By 1863 Lincoln attempts to read the Declaration and the Constitution not through a gold eagle or a doubloon but more from the perspective of Pip or in the same manner in which he is fighting the Civil War: in the name of an interest higher than the property interests of slaveholders. Legendary for the chaste plainness of his own style, Lincoln finds in the euphemisms of the Constitution concerning slavery not a fault but a virtue that enables him to read the text as plainly opposed to the principle of slavery. The fig leaf of the euphemism becomes for him the sign of a fortunate cover-up. The indirect "phraseology of the Constitution" provides proof of the founders' moral opposition to slavery (LLA, II, 142):

> In all matters but this of Slavery the framers of the Constitution used the very clearest, shortest, and most direct language. But the Constitution alludes to Slavery three times without mentioning it once! The language used becomes ambiguous, roundabout, and mystical. They speak of the "immigration of persons," and mean the importation of slaves, but do not say so. In establishing a basis of representation they say "all other persons," when they mean to say slaves – why did they not use the shortest phrase? In providing for the return of fugitives they say "persons held to service or labor." If they had said slaves it would have been plainer, and less liable to misconstruction. Why didn't they do it? We cannot doubt that it was done on purpose. Only one reason is possible, and that is supplied us by one of the framers of the Constitution – and it is not possible for man to conceive of any other – they expected and desired that the system would come to an end, and meant that when it did, the Constitution should not show that there ever had been a slave in this good free country of ours! (LLA, II, 142)

In 1863 in the person of Lincoln the democratic idiom of the straight-tongue of Hawkeye converges with the politics of democracy. He fights a war to edit the Constitution of its tortured language that sanctions slavery. The abolitionists were the catalysts, but Lincoln was the consummation of a remoralization of language that makes a time of civil war, surprisingly, a counter to the Thucydidean moment. The Civil War was "one of those periods of excitement," Lowell writes in a tribute to Lincoln, ". . . which, while they last, exalt and clarify the minds of men, giving to the mere words *country, human rights, democracy,* a meaning and a force beyond that of sober and logical argument" (JLW, V, 185–6). But Lincoln's great willingness to chasten the prose of the founding fathers is marred by his willingness to recolonize slaves in Liberia and thus erase their presence from the land of the United States as well as from the language of the Constitution.

Lecturing on "discoveries, inventions, and improvements" in 1859, Lincoln singles out speech and writing (along with steam power) as the great inventions that improved the condition of the world (LLA, II, 3–11). These inventions become, of course, Lincoln's own steam engine of power, his mode of liberation and advancement. Perhaps no one besides Frederick Douglass fulfills more successfully in antebellum America the emancipatory promise of eloquence as proclaimed by John Quincy Adams and limned in Lincoln's own commentary on literacy (LLA, II, 10).[14] Lincoln is the political apotheosis in America of the classical rhetorical tradition, just as Whitman is its poetic apotheosis. Through speech he rises from log cabin to the White House, and through metaphors, James McPherson writes, he wins the Civil War, thus fulfilling Adams's and Emerson's claim that eloquence is power.[15] But Lincoln presides over the death of classical political oratory. The place: Gettysburg. The time: November 19, 1863. Denigrating the significance of his own speech – "the world will little note, nor long remember what we say here" – and silently eschewing here (and throughout his career) the classical equation of word and action, speech and battle that Webster, Emerson, Thoreau, and Phillips all affirm, Lincoln pays sole tribute to the soldier (LLA, II, 536). The sword is mightier than the pen. Not words but death brings new life to the Declaration. (But Lincoln's words and the Reconstruction amendments give living meaning to those deaths.) Lincoln's speech, a consummate act of self-effacement, is not the electricity of action but a funeral panegyric; it is not the cause or the effect of deliberation but an afterword to the battle that monumentalizes the failure of American politics to be conducted by the word.

Charles Dudley Warner, coauthor with Mark Twain of *The Gilded Age*, offers his own eulogy in 1872 to the oratorical dreams that possessed him (and his culture) from the time of John Adams studying Cicero in the 1750s through the years when Emerson contemplated the siren charms of eloquence as a student at Harvard and when he later delivered and published two separate lectures on eloquence:

> Twenty-one years ago in this house I heard a voice, calling me to ascend the platform, and there to stand and deliver. The voice was

the voice of President North; the language was an excellent imitation of that used by Cicero and Julius Caesar. . . . To be proclaimed an orator, and an ascending orator, in such a sonorous tongue, in the face of a world waiting for orators, stirred one's blood like the herald's trumpet when the lists are thrown open. Alas! for most of us, who crowded so eagerly into the arena, it was the last appearance as orators on any stage.

The facility of the world for swallowing up orators, and company after company of educated men, has been remarked.[16]

The Gilded Age itself confirms the astuteness of Frederick Law Olmsted's observation made before the Civil War that the "valuable men at Washington are not speakers of Greek or aught else, but the diggers and builders of the committees, and the clerks of the departments, and the best of these are men trained in habits of business by the necessities of what is called private business, and who have been drawn directly from private business."[17] The age of oratory gives way to four years of war and then to the age of incorporation. The classical tradition with its Ciceronian ideal of the orator as the representative man is trumped by the art of the deal: captains of industry stifle the orator in most public realms save religion. The Dodges and Braggs and Newcomes of the world talk less and connive more: they become the robber barons of the Gilded Age. What counts in industrial capitalism and not just in pragmatism is the cash value of the word. The aesthetes of style seem to escape to Europe, where they appear in the fiction of Henry James or become expatriate poets writing about economic conspiracies and the wasteland. Greek becomes a deader language; Thucydides is forgotten by the statesman; Cicero is just a bust in the lawyer's office, No. — Wall Street, as in "Bartleby, the Scrivener." The most inspiring eloquence in post–Civil War America belongs to an ungrammatical juvenile delinquent – Huck Finn – created by the Lincoln of our literature.

Nathaniel Hawthorne's "Great Stone Face," published in 1850, the year of Daniel Webster's fall, offers a commentary on the oratorical tradition in America which Lincoln transformed by offering a prose that was more condensed, more cadenced, and more earnest or spiritual than Webster's. Hawthorne's tale is as much a political allegory (and commentary on language) as *The Confidence-Man*. It tells the story of a young man, Ernest, who comes to fulfill a local legend that some day "a child should be born hereabouts, who was destined to become the greatest and noblest personage of his time, and whose countenance, in manhood, should bear an exact resemblance to the Great Stone Face" – an immense rock formation on the side of a mountain in New Hampshire that bears the features of a human countenance (a natural Mount Rushmore) (HLA, 1069). In the course of Ernest's life, three other characters – Gathergold, General Blood-and-Thunder, and Old Stony Phiz – each come to be seen by the people as the Great Stone Face. But Ernest and then the other citizens perceive what makes each character a false representation of the face of nature. Gathergold is a "shrewd and active" merchant, endowed by Providence with luck, who makes an immense fortune and who seems to bear some resemblance to Benjamin Franklin as well as to the Great Stone Face (HLA, 1071). Old-Blood-and-Thunder, an illustrious military commander, disappoints Ernest because he expects the prophetic person to "appear in the character of a Man of Peace, uttering wisdom, and doing good, and making people happy" (HLA, 1076). Ernest's reservations are borne out, because, despite the general's "iron will," which makes him something of a figure for the military-hero-cum-president, such as Jackson, Harrison, and Taylor, he too fails as a personification of nature (ibid.). As Ernest becomes a local preacher whose "pure" thought manifests itself in "good deeds" and spoken "truths" that mold the "lives of those who heard him," Old Stony Phiz, who had taken up "the trades of law and politics" after leaving the valley, returns as a "wondrous man" whose "tongue" has proven mightier than Gathergold's wealth and Old-Blood-and-Thunder's sword (HLA, 1078). Hawthorne describes his eloquence in a passage that captures all the two-facedness of an oratorical tradition that glorifies the power of the word while acknowledging with a deep (and often muted) anxiety the dangers of that power:

> So wonderfully eloquent was he, that whatever he might choose to say, his auditors had no choice but to believe him; wrong looked like right, and right like wrong; for when it pleased him, he could make a kind of illuminated fog with his mere breath, and obscure the natural daylight with it. His tongue, indeed, was a magic instrument; sometimes it rumbled like the thunder; sometimes it warbled like the sweetest music. It was the blast of war – the song of peace; and it seemed to have a heart in it, when there was no such matter. (Ibid.)

The duplicitous power of Old Stony Phiz's tongue, as well as the description of his face as a visage marked by the "massive depth and loftiness" of his brow, makes him not the Great Stone Face but a caricature of Daniel Webster (HLA, 1080).

Ernest delights in sage conversation with a poet whom he also considers at one point to be the Great Stone Face. But the poet, whose words possess "a strain of the Divinity," denies that he can be the prophetic figure, because, as he admits in a line that links him to

Emerson, "I lack faith in the grandeur, the beauty, and the goodness, which my own words are said to have made more evident in nature and in human life" (HLA, 1085). The poet, however, is the first to acknowledge that Ernest "is himself the likeness of the Great Stone Face!" (HLA, 1086). Born in a log cottage, dutiful to his mother, educated by communing with nature, possessed of a loving heart, conversant with friends and seemingly with the angels, Ernest is a preacher who makes "great truths . . . familiar by his simple utterance of them" and whose words are a sovereign power because they are representative: they "accorded with his thoughts, and his thoughts had reality and depth, because they harmonized with the life which he had always lived" (HLA, 1084, 1086). Ernest thus stands in marked contrast not just to "Old Stony Phiz" but to that other preacher, Dimmesdale, whom Hawthorne also creates in 1850: "It was not mere breath that this preacher uttered; they were words of life, because a life of good deeds and holy love was melted into them" (HLA, 1086). Ernest may be also considered a version of Emerson's prophecy – the "man conversing in earnest" or "the poet, the orator bred in the woods" of *Nature* who represents the "Original Cause" and counters "rotten diction" (ELA, 23). But beyond that, Ernest is the legend of Lincoln before Lincoln becomes a legend.

At the end of the Civil War, Emerson and Lowell advance the rhetorical project they had begun in the antebellum era: the reconstruction of a more natural language and the regrounding of rhetoric's authority in the ethos or character of the orator. Words had to be made more representative or serve something beyond self-interest. Throughout his career, Emerson longed for a representative man – a person of earnest character – whose voice would counterbalance the materialism of America that had made the country a contradiction in terms. Whitman answered his call in 1855, but in 1865 Lincoln comes closest to becoming Emerson's – and Lowell's – Great Stone Face. In their view, when he portrayed his own ideas, he represented the whole; by perfecting his speech, he became a representative man. Lowell writes of Lincoln, "He forgets himself so entirely in his object as to give his *I* the sympathetic and persuasive effect of *We* with the great body of his countrymen. . . . [H]e is so eminently our representative man, that, when he speaks, it seems as if the people were listening to their own thinking aloud" (JLW, V, 208). And Emerson calls Lincoln "a plain man of the people" and "the true representative of this continent; an entirely public man; father of his country, the pulse of twenty millions throbbing in his heart, the thought of their minds articulated by his tongue" (REW, XI, 331, 335). Lincoln's language is regarded at once as sovereign and representative: his words lead the people by representing their ideals. "In the midst of fears and jealousies, in the Babel of counsels and parties," Emerson writes in praise of Lincoln, "this man wrought incessantly with all his might and all his honesty, laboring to find what the people wanted, and how to obtain that" (REW, XI, 334). Emerson describes the reception of Lincoln's Emancipation Proclamation as if it were an act of oratory that so transformed an audience through its "vibrating voice" announcing "grand human principles" that everyone became "a representative of mankind, standing for all nationalities" (REW, XI, 316). War and not speech reconfigured a babel of tongues into a nation, but the malice of war was transfigured by Lincoln's voice – by his Pentecostal gift of tongues that represented a spirit of charity. Robert Ferguson acknowledges this gift when he comments so fittingly at the end of *Law and Letters* on the closing paragraph of Lincoln's second inaugural address, wherein Lincoln switches, abruptly, from the voice of an Old Testament prophet invoking the wrathful judgment of a righteous God against a sinful people to the voice of the New Testament promising "charity for all": "The many voices of a national leadership speak as one here. All the sources of American thought recombine. Lincoln is the spiritual leader correcting and then blessing his congregation in benediction, the Ciceronian orator defining his country, and, not least, the lawyer–politician acting out his highest social role, that of peacemaker. One of these voices, and thereby all, reaches every American."[18]

Typical of his humility, Ernest in Hawthorne's story doubts his own likeness to the Great Stone Face. Lincoln too might have denied his representativeness, preferring to locate the power that healed the crisis of representation not in himself but in the face of all the dead who perished fighting for a rebirth of liberty and a more perfect union. Lincoln, that is, probably would have agreed with the authors of *Rambles Among Words*, William Swinton and his silent partner Walt Whitman, who place their faith in reform of a corrupt language not in the original genius of a representative man but in the people as a whole. Swinton writes that a "petrified and mechanical national mind will certainly appear in a petrified and mechanical language," but the "renovation of language is provided for, as the renovation of races is provided for, by a subtle chemistry" (11). The catalyst of renovation is the "sublime democracy of speech!": "When a tongue has become dead and effete, the mind walks out of it. With an advance in the national mind – with the influx of a nobler spirit, comes a renovation of its language: by a passionate propulsive movement it ejects its old dead speech, and rises to a larger and freer expression. Like the waters in spring, the rising spirit sweeps away the frozen surface of an effete society, literature, language and thought" (11). Swinton adopts the revolutionary and democratic postulate of Jefferson (and Whitman) that change in language, especially if it springs from below, is a source of regeneration. He also declares, "We . . . meet with numerous cases in which terms acquire burdens of significance which primitively and properly do not belong to them. The sons become stronger and wiser and wittier than their sires" (42). Just as Sidney George Fisher argues in the 1860s that the sons of the founding fathers could make the language of the Constitution stronger and wiser if they reconstructed the letter of 1789, Swinton endorses the development of an original meaning into something different.[19] The loss of an old meaning can be liberation, not corruption. Swinton thus approaches Ralph Ellison's argument that change in language is not just liberating but also conservative, because it keeps the constitution of language responsive to the vox populi. To keep literary standards high, Ellison argues, the artist in America must explore "new possibilities of language which would allow it to retain that flexibility and fidelity to common speech which has been its glory since Mark Twain."[20] Political representation, like literary representation, is also charged with this task of making provisional sense of the babel of tongues in a polity, of refining the multiplicity of voices into written forms of law and art while reminding us that any representation of the vox populi is necessarily misrepresentative and open to revision.

Writers as well as politicians in the early republic maintained, by and large, a faith that distinctions could be made between representation and misrepresentation, the proper use of a word and its abuse. The province of the schoolmaster was precisely to make such distinctions. Hawthorne's tantalizing phrase "Representative – misrepresentative" can serve to remind us, however, that the two concepts do not stand necessarily in contradiction to each other. Perhaps the two concepts are not stark alternatives but bipolar aspects of any act of language, the positive and negative poles that must inevitably be connected when we tap into the power of words in politics or art. This conclusion, unfortunately, gives no consolation to those who wish to protect the sheep by protesting the wolf's definition of words. Yet we can remind ourselves that if, in exercising our freedom to make a word represent whatever idea we wish, we make the word "liberty" represent the right to hunt, kill, or enslave, the same freedom allows us to create a counterstatement from the same sound, to define liberty, for instance, as the right of the sheep to graze unmolested in a field and the obligation of others to protect that right. Our words, Kenneth Burke argues, can be no more than a perspective on the truth. No voice, no act of language can speak for the whole. Yet a collection of voices, speaking, listening, revising together, multiplying perspectives, can enlarge or refine our understanding of the whole. Such an enlargement or refinement of the understanding is the end of political representation according to Madison and of speech according to Lincoln: "Speech . . . by enabling different individuals to interchange thoughts, and thereby to combine their powers of observation and reflection, greatly facilitates useful discoveries and inventions" (LLA, II, 6). Recognition of the limitations of any single language as a mode of representation invokes a call for the checking and balancing of representation by multiplying the modes of representation, and this is the call Burke makes in his "Dialectician's Hymn," wherein he presents democracy and dialectic – the fair and free competition of voices in the forum – as the last safe hope for overcoming misrepresentation:

> Hail to Thee, Logos,
> Thou Vast Almighty Title,
> In Whose name we conjure –
> Our acts the partial representatives
> Of Thy whole act.
>
> May we be Thy delegates
> In parliament assembled.
> Parts of Thy wholeness.
> And in our conflicts
> Correcting one another.
> By study of our errors
> Gaining revelation
>
> . . . .
>
> May we compete with one another,
> To speak for Thy Creation with more justice –
> Cooperating in this competition
> Until our naming
> Gives voice correctly.
> And how things are
> And how we say things are
> Are one.[21]

Between the Revolutionary era and the Civil War, Americans discovered for themselves what every era seemingly must rediscover: language is a political power that can be representative and misrepresentative, a force for freedom and a force for tyranny, a manifestation of individual liberty and a sign of one's bondage to others. In the act of speaking, we bear witness to our freedom, for there is nothing more common for a person than to combine words in new and unique ways.

At the same time, and without contradiction, we also bear witness to our lack of liberty and to our status as political animals, for our freedom of speech and capacity for self-expression depend to a large extent on our adherence to the rules of grammar and to the meanings of words established by the community. Our native language and thus an inherited scheme of representation comes to us as naturally as the milk (or formula) we drink as infants; yet it is nonetheless imposed upon us and limits us in countless ways – all the more subtly and irresistibly because it is assimilated before we can so much as begin to think for ourselves. The language we hear and learn as infants begins to govern our thoughts and develop our conscience just as much as the milk we drink helps develop the structure of our bodies. Language, in effect, constitutes us as much as we constitute language, or, as George Marsh says, "So truly as *language* is what man has made it, just so truly *man* is what language has made him" (ML, 647). We cannot nullify this constitution, but we can reconstruct it. "Words, like the physical world," Hugh Kenner writes, "are imposed upon the artist from without." He then elaborates, in a striking metaphor, how that imposition can be resisted: "Language is a Trojan horse by which the universe gets into the mind. The business of the artist is to be constantly aware that the horse houses armed warriors, even while admitting it to his mental citadel. He has then a chance of winning them over, upon their emergence, and cross-questioning them about the collective consciousness outside, of which they are the armed representatives."[22] What Plato understood is what Kenner suggests: by cross-questioning words and by testing them against experience, we can counter the advance of the Thucydidean moment when words bearing false witness mislead the judgment and usurp the citadel of the mind.

The sovereign words and the representations of politics in the United States between 1776 and 1865 convinced many citizens of the republic of letters in America that they should treat language as a Trojan horse, a weapon that had to be guarded against if the city of freedom was to be preserved, and a weapon that could be deployed if the walls of tyranny were to be overcome. Words were regarded as a standing army of representatives and thus a force that had to be checked by distrust and by an education in the potentials and liabilities of language to insure that their power served liberty-keeping and peacekeeping rather than house-invading or empire-building missions. And in this age of Newspeak and Peacekeeper missiles, perhaps an education in the uses and abuses of words along the lines of the lessons conducted by the schoolmasters and artists of the early republic (and by their classical and Enlightenment forebears) can help teach us how the language of the past can be used to defend ourselves from the Newspeak of the future, and how old words can serve as a mentor for instructing us how to revitalize the language the governs us, and how, finally, words can be used to supplant arms as the peacekeeping and liberty-keeping force in which we should place not only our distrust but our confidence. A "communication of grandeur & of freedom" must not be beyond our dignity, for when words fail, as *Billy Budd* reminds us, we are left with fighting peacekeepers and the muteness of violence.

Afterword

Jeremiads against the corruption of the word and visions of its redemption have persisted in American culture down to this day. I conclude with two recent versions of the counterpoint between perceptions of the corruption of language and visions of its redemption. The first is from Allen Ginsberg's "Wichita Vortex Sutra," and the second is from Reverend Tosamah's sermon in N. Scott Momaday's *House Made of Dawn*. Each passage offers as a remedy for the corruption something different from Emerson's (and Orwell's) prescription to be concrete, to be faithful to things, to stand by words. The poet and storyteller in these two passages are not schoolmasters of the language, seeking to purify the language of the tribe, but counterstaters, envisioning a more creative language, a therapy of verbal music and magic:

> The war is language,
>   language abused
>   for Advertisement,
>   language used
>   like magic for power on the planet[1]

Against this black magic, the poet offers his own magic, a spell of words chanted to call forth a vision of transcendence:

> I lift my voice aloud,
>   make Mantra of American language now,
>   I here declare the end of the War.[2]

For Cooper, for Thoreau, and now for Momaday, the language of the Native American stands as a rebuke to the language of foreigners to the land. Reverend Tosamah, in the midst of preaching upon the text *In principio erat Verbum*, comments upon the wasty ways of the contemporary white man's attitude toward words:

397

> In the white man's world, language, too – and the way in which the
> white man thinks of it – has undergone a process of change. The
> white man takes such things as words and literature for granted, as
> indeed he must, for nothing in his world is so commonplace. On
> every side of him there are words by the millions, an unending
> succession of pamphlets and papers, letters and books, bills and
> bulletins, commentaries and conversations. He has diluted and mul-
> tiplied the Word, and words have begun to close in upon him. He is
> sated and insensitive; his regard for language – for the Word itself –
> as an instrument of creation has diminished nearly to the point of no
> return. It may be that he will perish by the Word.[3]

Shipwreck by neglect of the word and its manipulation for advertisement and power replace shipwreck by neglect of God's Word as the
fear that cultivates the wisdom of new Jeremiahs and promotes new
language experiments that seek to recover or advance the potentialities of the word as medicine – the potentiality Momaday invokes in
House Made of Dawn:

> But it was not always so with him [the white man], and it is not so
> with you. Consider for a moment that old Kiowa woman, my
> grandmother, whose use of language was confined to speech. And be
> assured that her regard for words was always keen in proportion as
> she depended upon them. You see, for her words were medicine;
> they were magic and invisible. They came from nothing into sound
> and meaning. They were beyond price; they could neither be bought
> nor sold. And she never threw words away.[4]

Yet for all the hope we place in the potentialities of the word as a
remedy for the abuses of Power Superpower, perhaps what language
can do most importantly in this regard is represent its own unfaithful-
ness and duplicity – its potential for corruption. "Words that electrify
society with their freedom and truthfulness are r·atched," Václav
Havel writes, "by words that mesmerize, deceive, inflame, madden,
beguile, words that are harmful – lethal, even. The word as arrow."[5]
Momaday's telling and reading of the story of the Kiowa arrowmaker
in "The Man Made of Words" affirms the same lesson: the word is an
arrow. It can protect life; it can kill. The lesson Havel draws from his
own corner of the world in 1989 is one, he maintains, that has
universal application: "It always pays to be suspicious of words and to
be wary of them, and . . . we can never be too careful in this
respect."[6] If the events of 1939–89 in Berlin and Eastern Europe, like
the events of 1765–75 in the Colonies and the events of the *stasis* in
Corcyra in Thucydides' *History* and the events in Orwell's *1984*,
demand we heed that lesson, perhaps in contrast the civil rights

protests and successes of 1776, of 1863, of 1963–4 in the United States and of 1989 in Czechoslovakia can serve as a reminder that the "Bastille of a word" is not impregnable, and that the order of things that are in the saddle and ride humankind can be challenged and sometimes unseated by the words of the people and the representations of their dramatists and storytellers.

Notes

Introduction

1. Edwin P. Whipple, "Words," *American Review*, 1 (1845), p. 178. Subsequent references to this work (abbreviated EWW) are given parenthetically.
2. Protests against the corruption of language in the era of Vietnam and Watergate were legion. See, for example, Arthur Schlesinger, Jr., "Politics and the American Language," *American Scholar*, 43 (1974), pp. 553–62. The term "Nukespeak" is borrowed from Stephen Hilgartner, Richard Bell, and Rory O'Connor, *Nukespeak: Nuclear Language, Visions, and Mindset* (San Francisco: Sierra Club Books, 1982).
3. For a discussion of the classic status of Orwell's essay and for a much-needed critique of its limitations as a primer for analyzing and combating the abuse of language, see Harvey A. Daniels, *Famous Last Words: The American Language Crisis Reconsidered* (Carbondale: Southern Illinois University Press, 1983).
4. In China, the tradition connecting political disorder and linguistic corruption stretches back to *The Analects* of Confucius, wherein the Master asserts, "When names are not correct, what is said will not sound reasonable; when what is said does not sound reasonable, affairs will not culminate in success; when affairs do not culminate in success, rites and music will not flourish; when rites and music do not flourish, punishments will not fit the crimes; when punishments do not fit the crimes, the common people will not know where to put hand and foot" (trans. D. C. Lau [New York: Penguin, 1979], XIII.3, p. 118). The quest to oppose this corruption is the practice of *Cheng Ming*, the rectification of names, which the Master suggests should be the first action of a new administration.
5. Phrases such as "linguistic misrepresentation" and "corruption of words" should be read in the light of Gerald Graff's caution in *Literature Against Itself: Literary Ideas in Modern Society* (Chicago: University of Chicago Press, 1979) that "our ability to identify a perverse use of terms *as* perverse depends on the assumption that there is such a thing as calling things by their right names, and this in turn depends on the assumption that there is a common world and that language's relation to it is not wholly arbitrary"

(p. 90). I use these phrases to characterize or describe critical judgments made by those who did presume a common understanding or standard that enabled them to make distinctions between proper and corrupt uses of language.

6. Ralph Ellison, *Shadow and Act* (New York: New American Library, 1966), p. 42.

7. John Dos Passos, *The Big Money* (1936) (New York: New American Library, 1969), p. 468.

8. John Quincy Adams, *Argument of John Quincy Adams Before the Supreme Court of the United States in the Case of the United States, Appellants vs. Cinque, and Other Africans, Captured in the Schooner Amistad* (New York: S. W. Benedict, 1841), p. 39.

9. For versions of the American writer as an Adamic namer, see William Carlos Williams, *In the American Grain* (New York: New Directions, 1956), Introduction; Ellison, *Shadow and Act*, p. 257; and Ralph Waldo Emerson, "The Poet," in *Essays and Lectures*, ed. Joel Porte (New York: Library of America, 1983), p. 449. (Subsequent references to the last volume [abbreviated ELA] are given parenthetically.) On this Adamic impulse and the problems attending it in American literature, see Tony Tanner, *The Reign of Wonder* (Cambridge: Cambridge University Press, 1965) and *Scenes of Nature, Signs of Men* (Cambridge: Cambridge University Press, 1987). The phrase "fresh, green breast of the new world" is from the end of *The Great Gatsby*, and the phrase "city of words" is borrowed from Tony Tanner, *City of Words* (New York: Harper and Row, 1971).

10. Sacvan Bercovitch makes the compelling argument I am alluding to here that American Jeremiahs translate "the contradiction between history and rhetoric" into "a discrepancy between appearance and promise" and thus sustain the validity and vitality of American's governing rhetoric, in *The American Jeremiad* (Madison: University of Wisconsin Press, 1978). See esp. pp. 17–28.

11. The imagery of "promissory notes" and the phrase "the riches of freedom and the security of justice" come from Martin Luther King, Jr.'s "I have a dream" speech, in *A Testament of Hope: The Essential Writings of Martin Luther King, Jr.*, ed. James Melvin Washington (San Francisco: Harper and Row, 1986), p. 217.

12. The vision of America as a political Messiah is from Herman Melville, *White-Jacket, or the World in a Man-of-War*, ed. Harrison Heyford, Hershel Parker, and G. Thomas Tanselle (Evanston and Chicago: Northwestern–Newberry, 1970), p. 151.

13. Dos Passos, *The Big Money*, p. 468.

14. Bercovitch, *The American Jeremiad*.

15. Williams, *In the American Grain*, p. 63. The terms "soul-butter" and "hogwash" are those used by Huck Finn to describe the confidence games of the King and Duke in *The Adventures of Huckleberry Finn*.

16. The phrase "polyphonic oratory of reality" is from Ann Douglas, intro-

duction to Harriet Beecher Stowe, *Uncle Tom's Cabin* (New York: Penguin, 1981), p. 16.

17. Ibid.

18. Leo Marx has been one of the foremost guides in explaining the significance of the vernacular tradition in American culture. See "The Vernacular Tradition in American Writing" and "'Noble Shit': The Uncivil Response of American Writers to Civil Religion," repr. in *The Pilot and the Passenger* (New York: Oxford University Press, 1988). See also Richard Bridgman, *The Colloquial Style* (New York: Oxford University Press, 1966); Tanner, *The Reign of Wonder*; Houston A. Baker, Jr., *Blues, Ideology, and Afro-American Literature: A Vernacular Theory* (Chicago: University of Chicago Press, 1984); and Gayl Jones, *Liberating Voices* (Cambridge: Harvard University Press, 1991).

19. Douglas, introduction to *Uncle Tom's Cabin*, p. 34.

20. ELA, 10; James Madison, *Federalist* No. 37, in *The Federalist Papers*, ed. Clinton Rossiter (New York: New American Library, 1961), p. 229. Subsequent references to this volume (abbreviated FP) are given parenthetically.

21. Noah Webster, *Dissertations on the English Language* (Boston: Isaiah Thomas, 1789), p. 405. Subsequent references to this volume (abbreviated DEL) are given parenthetically.

22. Noah Webster, *Observations on Language, and on the Errors of the Class-Books: Addressed to the New York Lyceum* (New Haven, Conn.: Babcock, 1839), p. 31.

23. Alexander Pope, *The Dunciad*, IV, lines 501–2.

24. Dos Passos, *The Big Money*, p. 523.

25. Roger Williams, *The Bloody Tenet of Persecution, for Cause of Conscience in a Conference Between Truth and Peace*, in *Norton Anthology of American Literature*, ed. Nina Baym et al. (New York: Norton, 1989), I, 90.

26. Ralph Ellison, *Going to the Territory* (New York: Random House, 1986), p. 243.

27. Ibid., p. 8.

28. *The Centenary Edition of the Works of Nathaniel Hawthorne*, ed. William Charvat, Roy Harvey Pearce, and Claude M. Simpson, 20 vols. (Columbus: Ohio State University Press, 1965), VIII, 311. Subsequent references to these volumes (abbreviated NHW) are given parenthetically.

29. Oliver Wendell Holmes *The Autocrat of the Breakfast-Table* (Boston: Houghton Mifflin, 1892), p. 13; Whipple, "Words," p. 178.

30. Alexis de Tocqueville, *Democracy in America*, trans. Henry Reeve, ed. Arthur B. Fuller, 2 vols. (New York: Random House, 1945), I, 290. Subsequent references to these volumes (abbreviated DA) are given parenthetically.

31. Margaret Fuller Ossoli, *Woman in the Nineteenth Century* (Boston: John P. Jewett and Co., 1855), p. 27.

32. The quoted phrases are taken, respectively, from Charles Feidelson, Jr., *Symbolism and American Literature* (Chicago: University of Chicago Press,

1953), p. 4, and Philip F. Gura, *The Wisdom of Words* (Middletown, Conn.: Wesleyan University Press, 1981), p. 149.

33. The phrase "obliquity of signs" is from Millicent Bell, "The Obliquity of Signs: *The Scarlet Letter*," *Massachusetts Review*, 33 (1982), pp. 9–26.

34. Ossoli, *Woman in the Nineteenth Century*, p. 27.

35. Charles S. Peirce, *Selected Writings*, ed. Philip P. Wiener (New York: Dover, 1958), p. 103.

36. Pocock has explained his method for studying the history of political thought in several works. See J. G. A. Pocock, *Politics, Language, and Time: Essays on Political Thought and History* (New York: Atheneum, 1971); "Verbalizing a Political Act: Towards a Politics of Speech," *Political Theory*, 1 (1973); "The Reconstruction of Discourse: Toward the Historiography of Political Thought," *MLN*, 96 (1981), pp. 959–80; and his introduction, subtitled "The State of the Art," to a collection of his studies entitled *Virtue, Commerce, and History: Essays on Political Thought and History* (Cambridge: Cambridge University Press, 1985).

37. Gura, *The Wisdom of Words*; Dennis E. Baron, *Grammar and Good Taste: Reforming the American Language* (New Haven, Conn.: Yale University Press, 1982); David Simpson, *The Politics of American English, 1776–1850* (New York: Oxford University Press, 1986); Kenneth Cmiel, *Democratic Eloquence* (New York: Morrow, 1990); and Michael P. Kramer, *Imagining Language in America: From the Revolution to the Civil War* (Princeton, N.J.: Princeton University Press, 1992). See also Cynthia S. Jordan, *Second Stories: The Politics of Language, Form, and Gender in Early American Fictions* (Chapel Hill: University of North Carolina Press, 1989).

38. John Adams, *The Works*, ed. Charles Francis Adams, 10 vols. (Boston: Little, Brown, 1850–6), VII, 249. Subsequent references to these volumes (abbreviated JAW) are given parenthetically.

39. Whipple, "Words," p. 178.

40. Thomas Paine, *The Complete Writings of Thomas Paine*, ed. Philip S. Foner, 2 vols. (New York: Citadel, 1945), I, 287; John Locke, *An Essay Concerning Human Understanding*, ed. Alexander Campbell Fraser, 2 vols. (Oxford: Clarendon Press, 1894), II, 12; Horace Bushnell, *God in Christ: Three Lectures . . . with a Preliminary Dissertation on Language* (Hartford, Conn.: Brown and Parsons, 1849), p. 84. For the cultural and political context of Bushnell's linguistic study, see Michael P. Kramer, "Horace Bushnell's Philosophy of Language Considered as a Mode of Cultural Criticism," *American Quarterly*, 38 (1986), pp. 573–90.

41. Horace Bushnell, "The Doctrine of Loyalty," *New Englander*, 13 (1863), p. 560.

42. For an exposition of the concept of America's civil religion, see Robert N. Bellah, "Civil Religion in America," *Beyond Belief* (New York: Harper and Row, 1970), pp. 168–92.

43. Literary critics, historians, and political scientists in the twentieth century have increasingly developed terms and methods for studying the politics of language and the language of politics. In literary criticism, see,

for example, Mikhail Bakhtin, *The Dialogic Imagination*, trans. Caryl Emerson and Michael Holquist (Austin: University of Texas Press, 1981), and Kenneth Burke, *Attitudes Towards History*, 2d ed. (Los Altos, Calif.: Hermes, 1959). In history, see J. H. Hexter, "The Loom of Language and the Fabric of Imperatives: The Case of *Il Principe* and *Utopia*," *American Historical Review*, 69 (1964), pp. 945–68; the studies by Pocock cited above; Carroll Smith-Rosenberg, "Writing History: Language, Class, and Gender," in *Feminist Studies/Critical Studies*, ed. Teresa de Lauretis (Bloomington: Indiana University Press, 1986), pp. 31–54; and Daniel T. Rodgers, *Contested Truths: Keywords in American Politics Since Independence* (New York: Basic, 1987). In political science, see William E. Connolly, *The Terms of Political Discourse*, 2d ed. (Princeton, N.J.: Princeton University Press, 1983); Russell L. Hanson, *The Democratic Imagination in America* (Princeton, N.J.: Princeton University Press, 1985); and *Political Innovation and Conceptual Change*, ed. Terence Ball, James Farr, and Russell L. Hanson (Cambridge: Cambridge University Press, 1989). Such works of Michel Foucault's as *The Order of Things* (London: Tavistock, 1970) and *The Archaeology of Knowledge* (New York: Pantheon, 1972) could be placed in each of these categories.

44. Thucydides, *History of the Peloponnesian War*, 3.82–4. On the paradigmatic importance of this passage, see also James Boyd White, "Thinking About Our Language," *Yale Law Journal*, 96 (1987), p. 1966.

45. J. G. A. Pocock, *The Machiavellian Moment* (Princeton, N.J.: Princeton University Press, 1975), p. viii.

46. T. S. Eliot, "Four Quartets," *The Complete Poems and Plays, 1909–1950* (New York: Harcourt Brace and World, 1971), pp. 121–2; ELA, 22.

47. On the liberating potential of social and linguistic disorder, see Carroll Smith-Rosenberg, *Disorderly Conduct: Visions of Gender in Victorian America* (New York: Knopf, 1985), p. 44. For an illuminating series of case studies drawn from literature and politics about how change in the meanings of words can constitute or reconstitute communities, see James Boyd White, *When Words Lose Their Meaning: Constitution and Reconstitution of Language, Character, and Community* (Chicago: University of Chicago Press, 1984).

48. Foucault, for instance, asserts, "We must conceive discourse as a violence that we do to things, or, in all events, as a practice that we impose upon them" (*The Archaeology of Knowledge*, p. 229). See also Jacques Derrida, *Of Grammatology*, trans. G. C. Spivak (Baltimore: Johns Hopkins University Press, 1974), esp. the section entitled "The Violence of the Letter."

49. For key works studying the sovereignty of discourses in America, see Bernard Bailyn, *The Ideological Origins of the American Revolution* (Cambridge: Harvard University Press, 1967); Lance Banning, *The Jeffersonian Persuasion: The Evolution of a Party Ideology* (Ithaca, N.Y.: Cornell University Press, 1978); Marvin Meyers, *The Jacksonian Persuasion: Politics and Belief* (Stanford, Calif: Stanford University Press, 1960); Bercovitch, *The American Jeremiad*; and Edwin G. Burrows and Michael Wallace, "The Ameri-

can Revolution: The Ideology and Psychology of National Liberation,"
Perspectives in American History, 6 (1972), pp. 167–306. Various scholars have
recently extended or complicated these analyses of the languages of early
America to give us a greater sense of how people enacted or chose their
roles in history from different scripts or from competing and overlapping
idioms. See, for example, Gordon S. Wood, *The Creation of the American
Republic, 1776–1787* (Chapel Hill: University of North Carolina Press,
1969); Joyce Appleby, "Republicanism in Old and New Contexts,"
William and Mary Quarterly, 3d ser., 43 (1986), pp. 20–34; Isaac Kramnick,
"The 'Great National Discussion': The Discourse of Politics in 1787,"
William and Mary Quarterly, 3d ser., 45 (1988), pp. 3–32; Andrew Del-
banco, "The Puritan Errand Re-viewed," *Journal of American Studies*, 18
(1984), pp. 343–60; Jay Fliegelman, *Prodigals and Pilgrims: The American
Revolution Against Patriarchal Authority, 1750–1800* (Cambridge: Cambridge
University Press, 1982); Daniel T. Rodgers and Sean Wilentz, "Lan-
guages of Power in the United States," in *Language, History and Class*, ed.
Penelope J. Corfield (Oxford: Blackwell Publisher, 1991), pp. 240–63;
and the essays collected in *Conceptual Change and the Constitution*, ed.
Terence Ball and J. G. A. Pocock (Lawrence: University Press of Kansas,
1988). For a general critique of the "linguistic turn" in history, see Bryan
D. Palmer, *Descent into Discourse* (Philadelphia: Temple University Press,
1990).

Chapter 1. Political and Linguistic Representation: Confidence or Distrust?

1. James Fenimore Cooper, *The Last of the Mohicans; A Narrative of 1757*, ed.
   James Franklin Beard, James A. Sappenfield, and E. N. Feltskos (Albany,
   N.Y.: State University of New York Press, 1983), p. 12.
2. J. Hillis Miller, "Nature and the Linguistic Moment," in *Nature and the
   Victorian Imagination*, ed. U. C. Knoepflmacher and G. B. Tennyson (Berkeley and Los Angeles: University of California Press, 1977), p. 450.
3. F. O. Matthiessen, *The American Renaissance* (Oxford: Oxford University
   Press, 1941); Feidelson, *Symbolism and American Literature*; Gura, *The Wisdom of Words*; Tanner, *Scenes of Nature, Signs of Men*.
4. Tanner, *Scenes of Nature, Signs of Men*, p. 6.
5. Tanner, *City of Words*, p. 27.
6. Michael Paul Rogin, *Subversive Genealogy: The Politics and Art of Herman
   Melville* (New York: Knopf, 1983), p. 19.
7. James Fenimore Cooper, *The American Democrat*, ed. George Dekker and
   Larry Johnston (Baltimore: Penguin, 1969), p. 159.
8. Ibid., p. 236.
9. "Theory of Political Representation," *American Quarterly Review*, 20
   (1836), p. 187.
10. Bercovitch, *The American Jeremiad*.
11. *The Complete Works of Ralph Waldo Emerson*, ed. Edward Waldo Emerson,
    12 vols. (Boston: Houghton Mifflin, 1903–4), X, 530. Subsequent refer-
    ences to these volumes (abbreviated REW) are given parenthetically.

12. Herman Melville, *Mardi: and a Voyage Thither*, ed. Harrison Hayford, Hershel Parker, and G. Thomas Tanselle (Evanston and Chicago: Northwestern–Newberry, 1970), p. 528.
13. For a study of the rhetorical violence used to conquer a "savage wilderness," see Francis Jennings, *The Invasion of America: Indians, Colonialism, and the Cant of Conquest* (New York: Norton, 1976).
14. On the paranoid style, see Richard Hofstadter, *The Paranoid Style in American Politics* (New York: Knopf, 1964); *The Fear of Conspiracy*, ed. David Brion Davis (Ithaca, N.Y.: Cornell University Press, 1971); Robert S. Levine, *Conspiracy and Romance* (New York: Cambridge University Press, 1989).
15. Herman Melville, *Billy Budd, Sailor*, ed. Harrison Hayford and Merton M. Sealts, Jr. (Chicago: University of Chicago Press, 1962), p. 88. Subsequent references to this book (abbreviated BB) are given parenthetically.
16. Cooper, *The American Democrat*, p. 169.
17. Herman Melville, *The Battle-Pieces of Herman Melville*, ed. Hennig Cohen (New York: Thomas Yoseloff, 1963), p. 197. Subsequent page references in this volume (abbreviated BP) are given parenthetically.
18. John Taylor of Caroline, *An Inquiry into the Principles and Policy of the Government of the United States* (1814) (New Haven, Conn.: Yale University Press, 1950), pp. 483, 484.
19. Herman Melville, *The Confidence-Man: His Masquerade*, ed. Harrison Hayford, Hershel Parker, and G. Thomas Tanselle (Evanston and Chicago: Northwestern–Newberry, 1971), p. 236.
20. Quoted in Hannah Arendt, *On Revolution* (New York: Penguin, 1963), p. 251.
21. Edmund S. Morgan, "Government by Fiction: The Idea of Representation," *Yale Review*, 72 (1983), pp. 322–39. This article is incorporated in Morgan, *Inventing the People* (New York: Norton, 1988).
22. Quoted in Bernard Bailyn, *The Origins of American Politics* (New York: Random House, 1970), p. 85.
23. Quoted in Derrida, *Of Grammatology*, p. 297.
24. Quoted in ibid.
25. Wood, *The Creation of the American Republic*, pp. 162–88, 363–73, 596–600.
26. See ibid., pp. 471–518.
27. For an excellent discussion of this division of authority, see Bruce Ackerman, "The Storrs Lectures: Discovering the Constitution," *Yale Law Journal*, 93 (1984), p. 1013.
28. Taylor, *Inquiry into the Principles*, p. 171.
29. William Whitney, *The Life and Growth of Language* (New York: D. Appleton, 1875), p. 35.
30. Ibid., p. 110.
31. Ibid., p. 109.
32. Walt Whitman, *An American Primer*, ed. Horace Traubel (Boston: Small, Maynard and Co., 1904), pp. viii–ix. Subsequent references to this volume (abbreviated AP) are given parenthetically.
33. Ellison, *Going to the Territory*, p. 291.

34. For a discussion of Jackson as a natural symbol, see John William Ward, *Andrew Jackson – Symbol for an Age* (New York: Oxford University Press, 1962), p. 52 and passim.

35. For a discussion of Jefferson's affection for Sterne and his understanding of the Revolution as a sentimental journey away from England, see Garry Wills, *Inventing America: Jefferson's Declaration of Independence* (New York: Doubleday, 1978), pt. 4, esp. pp. 273-6.

36. Leslie Fiedler, *Love and Death in the American Novel* (New York: Criterion, 1960), p. xvii. For the intimate connections between the family concerns of the eighteenth-century novel and the politics of the American Revolution, see Fliegelman, *Prodigals and Pilgrims*.

37. Bakhtin, *The Dialogic Imagination*, pp. 22, 366–71.

38. Ibid., p. 67.

39. *The Mind of the Founder*, ed. Marvin Meyers (Hanover, N.H.: University Press of New England, 1981), p. 441.

40. Kerry C. Larson, *Whitman's Drama of Consensus* (Chicago: University of Chicago Press, 1988), p. xiv.

41. My argument here skims the surface of arguments about the relationship among the novel, the nation, and forms of discourse made by Benedict Anderson, *Imagined Communities* (London: Verso, 1983), and Timothy Brennan, "The National Longing for Form," in *Nation and Narration*, ed. Homi K. Bhabha (London: Routledge, 1990), pp. 44–70. See also Ellison's essays on the novel in *Going to the Territory* and Michael Warner, *The Letters of the Republic* (Cambridge: Harvard University Press, 1990).

42. Walter L. Reed, *An Exemplary History of the Novel: The Quixotic Versus the Picaresque* (Chicago: University of Chicago Press, 1981), p. 92.

43. Leo Braudy, *Narrative Form in History and Fiction: Hume, Fielding and Gibbon* (Princeton, N.J.: Princeton University Press, 1970), p. 148.

44. On multiple forms of representation in the novels of Hawthorne and Melville, see Richard H. Brodhead, *Hawthorne, Melville, and the Novel* (Chicago: University of Chicago Press, 1976), pp. 20–2.

45. Henry Fielding, *The History of Tom Jones* (New York: Penguin, 1966), p. 88.

46. Jones, *Liberating Voices*, p. 192.

47. For a development of the argument about linguistic skepticism in American fiction, see Tanner, *City of Words*, pp. 27–8. On the linguistic self-consciousness of antebellum American romances, see also Evan Carton, *The Rhetoric of American Romance* (Baltimore: Johns Hopkins University Press, 1985).

48. For the political circumstances surrounding Stowe's decision to write *Uncle Tom's Cabin* and countervail the eloquence of Daniel Webster, see Ann Douglas's introduction, p. 6.

49. King, *Testament of Hope*, p. 219.

50. Warner Berthoff, *Literature and the Continuances of Virtue* (Princeton, N.J.: Princeton University Press, 1986), p. 43.

51. Horace Bushnell, "The True Wealth and Weal of Nations," in *Representative Phi Beta Kappa Orations*, ed. Clark S. Northrup, William C. Lane, and John C. Schwab (Boston: Houghton Mifflin, 1915), p. 21.

52. Ellison, *Shadow and Act*, pp. 112–13.
53. Ralph Ellison, *Invisible Man* (New York: Random House, 1982), pp. xvi–xvii.
54. The phrase "a world elsewhere" alludes to Richard Poirier's study *A World Elsewhere: The Place of Style in American Literature* (New York: Oxford University Press, 1966).

Chapter 2. Language and Legal Constitutions: The Problem of Change and Who Governs

1. *The Writings of Thomas Jefferson*, ed. A. Lipscomb, 20 vols. (Washington, D.C.: Thomas Jefferson Memorial Association, 1903), XVIII, 391. Subsequent references to these volumes (abbreviated TJW) are given parenthetically.
2. Richard Grant White, *Words and Their Uses* (Boston: Houghton Mifflin, 1870), pp. 15–16.
3. *The Writings and Speeches of Daniel Webster*, 18 vols. (Boston: Little, Brown, 1903), VI, 185. Subsequent references to these volumes (abbreviated DWW) are given parenthetically.
4. Plato makes this assertion in *Cratylus*, 436b; Horace's dictum is in *Ars poetica*, line 72.
5. Baron provides a wealth of information about this effort to govern the American language in *Grammar and Good Taste*.
6. Christopher Looby, "Phonetics and Politics: Franklin's Alphabet as a Political Design," *Eighteenth-Century Studies*, 18 (1984–5), pp. 1–34.
7. Quoted in Linda K. Kerber, *Federalists in Dissent* (Ithaca, N.Y.: Cornell University Press, 1980), p. 89.
8. "The Union and the States," *North American Review* (1833), p. 245.
9. Theodoric Beck, "Notes on Mr. Pickering's 'Vocabulary of Words and Phrases, Which Have Been Supposed Peculiar to the United States,' with Preliminary Observations" (1829), in Mitford Mathews, *Beginnings of American English* (Chicago: University of Chicago Press, 1931), p. 79.
10. Quoted in Allen Walker Read, "American Projects for an Academy to Regulate Speech," *PMLA*, 51 (1936), p. 1160.
11. *Letters and Other Writings of James Madison*, 4 vols. (New York: R. Worthington, 1884), III, 172–3. Subsequent references to these volumes (abbreviated JML) are given parenthetically.
12. Cited in Mary Helen Dohan, *Our Own Words* (Baltimore: Penguin, 1974), p. 196.
13. George P. Marsh, *Lectures on the English Language* (New York: Scribner, 1859; rev. 1882), p. 637. Subsequent references to this volume (abbreviated ML) are given parenthetically.
14. Quoted in Edward C. Wagenknecht, *Nathaniel Hawthorne: Man and Writer* (New York: Oxford University Press, 1961), p. 26.
15. Raoul Berger, *Government by Judiciary: The Transformation of the Fourteenth Amendment* (Cambridge: Harvard University Press, 1977), p. 366.
16. *The Mind of the Founder*, p. 361.

17. John Taylor of Caroline, *New Views of the Constitution of the United States* (Washington, D.C.: Way and Gideon, 1823), p. 294. Subsequent references to this volume (abbreviated NV) are given parenthetically. For the context of Taylor's (and southern states' rights activists') outrage at *McCulloch v. Maryland*, see R. Kent Newmyer, "John Marshall and the Southern Constitutional Tradition," in *An Uncertain Tradition: Constitutionalism and the History of the South*, ed. Kermit L. Hall and James W. Ely, Jr. (Athens: University of Georgia Press, 1989), pp. 105–24.

18. William Leggett, *Democratick Editorials*, ed. Laurence H. White (Indianapolis: Liberty Press, 1984), pp. 238–9.

19. James Fenimore Cooper, *The Monikins* (New York: Putnam, 1896), p. 341.

20. Ibid., pp. 344, 337. The political context of *The Monikins* is also suggested by Cooper's A.B.C. Letters, which were published in the *Evening Post*. Protesting that Congress overstepped its authority when it censured Jackson's withdrawal of funds from the Second Bank, Cooper accuses Congress of violating constitutional checks and balances and insists upon a strict construction of the Constitution. See *The Letters and Journals of James Fenimore Cooper*, ed. James Franklin Beard, 6 vols. (Cambridge, Mass.: Belknap Press, 1960), III, 61–139.

21. Noah Webster, *A Collection of Papers on Political, Literary and Moral Subjects* (New York: Webster and Clark, 1843), p. 41.

22. Edwin P. Whipple, *Outlooks on Society, Literature, and Politics* (Boston: Houghton Mifflin, 1892), p. 172.

23. Sidney George Fisher, *The Trial of the Constitution* (Philadelphia: Lippincott, 1862), p. 71.

24. Ibid., p. 72.

25. For a perceptive reading of antebellum sea fiction and its political contexts, see Levine, *Conspiracy and Romance*, chap. 4.

26. Herman Melville, *Redburn*, ed. Harrison Hayford, Hershel Parker, and G. Thomas Tanselle (Evanston and Chicago: Northwestern–Newberry, 1969), pp. 155–7.

27. "Argument of John Quincy Adams Before the Supreme Court of the United States," p. 39.

28. Henry D. Thoreau, *Reform Papers*, ed. Wendell Glick, The Writings of Henry D. Thoreau (Princeton, N.J.: Princeton University Press, 1973), p. 103. Subsequent references to this volume (abbreviated HTW) are given parenthetically.

29. Wendell Phillips, *Speeches, Lectures, and Letters* (Boston: Walker, Wise, and Co., 1864), p. 265.

30. Frederick Douglass, *The Constitution of the United States: Is It Pro-slavery or Anti-slavery?* (1860), excerpted in *The Antislavery Argument*, ed. William H. Pease and Jane H. Pease (Indianapolis: Bobbs-Merrill, 1965), p. 354.

31. On the theory and politics of judicial interpretation in antebellum America, see in particular Robert M. Cover, *Justice Accused: Antislavery and the Judicial Process* (New Haven, Conn.: Yale University Press, 1975).

32. For the political context of the *Commentaries* and an excellent biography

of Story, see R. Kent Newmyer, *Supreme Court Justice Joseph Story: Statesman of the Old Republic* (Chapel Hill: University of North Carolina Press, 1985).

33. Joseph Story, *Commentaries on the Constitution of the United States* (Boston: Hilliard, Gray, 1833), p. 158.
34. Ibid., p. 145.
35. Owen M. Fiss, "Objectivity and Interpretation," *Stanford Law Review*, 34b (1981–2), p. 744. Subsequent page references in this article are given parenthetically.
36. Cover, *Justice Accused*, p. 126. Subsequent page references in this book are given parenthetically.
37. Francis Lieber, *Miscellaneous Writings*, Vol. II (Philadelphia: Lippincott, 1881), p. 142.
38. Joseph Story, *The Miscellaneous Writings, Literary, Critical, Judicial, and Political* (Boston: James Munroe and Co., 1835), p. 153.
39. *The Works of Rufus Choate*, ed. Samuel Gilman Brown, 2 vols. (Boston: Little, Brown, 1862), I, 436.
40. Warner, *Letters of the Republic*, p. 102.
41. Abraham Bishop, *Connecticut Republicanism: An Oration on the Extent and Power of Political Delusion* (New Haven, 1800), p. 31.
42. Quoted in Perry Miller, *The Life of the Mind in America* (New York: Harcourt Brace and World, 1965), p. 132.
43. Hugh Henry Brackenridge, *Modern Chivalry*, ed. Claude M. Newlin (New York: American Book, 1937), p. 639. Subsequent references to this volume (abbreviated MC) are given parenthetically.
44. Robert Rantoul, Jr., "Oration at Scituate," in Perry Miller, *The Legal Mind in America* (Ithaca, N.Y.: Cornell University Press, 1962), p. 224.
45. Alexander Bryan Johnson, *A Guide to the Right Understanding of Our American Union; or, Political, Economical and Literary Miscellanies* (New York: Darby and Jackson, 1857), p. 73.
46. For a reading of *The Scarlet Letter* which draws connections between the ambiguity of the scarlet letter and antebellum constitutional exegesis, see Jonathan Arac, "The Politics of *The Scarlet Letter*," in *Ideology and Classic American Literature*, ed. Sacvan Bercovitch and Myra Jehlen (Cambridge: Cambridge University Press, 1986), pp. 247–66.
47. Theodore Sedgwick, *A Treatise on the Rules Which Govern the Interpretation and Application of Statutory and Constitutional Law* (1857), in Miller, *The Legal Mind*, p. 305.
48. Barbara Foley, "From New Criticism to Deconstruction: The Example of Charles Feidelson's *Symbolism and American Literature*," *American Quarterly*, 36 (1984), p. 55. For a reading of the Constitution which illuminates how the text quarrels with itself, see John Leubsdorf, "Deconstructing the Constitution," *Stanford Law Review*, 40 (1987), p. 181.
49. "Judge Story's *Commentaries on the Constitution*," *American Quarterly Review*, 14 (1833), p. 327.
50. Herman Melville, *Pierre: or, The Ambiguities*, ed. Harrison Hayford, Her-

shel Parker, and G. Thomas Tanselle (Evanston and Chicago: Northwest-ern–Newberry, 1971), p. 342.

51. Stowe, *Uncle Tom's Cabin*, p. 391.

52. *Mind of the Founder*, p. 367.

53. Hermann Von Holst, *Constitutional and Political History of the United States* (New York: Lalor and Mason, 1881), p. 78.

54. James Russell Lowell, *The Works of James Russell Lowell*, 10 vols. (Boston: Houghton Mifflin, 1890), V, 276–7. Subsequent references to these volumes (abbreviated JLW) are given parenthetically.

55. Laurence H. Tribe, *Constitutional Choices* (Cambridge: Harvard University Press, 1985), pp. vii–viii.

56. John Hart Ely, *Democracy and Distrust: A Theory of Judicial Review* (Cambridge: Harvard University Press, 1980), pp. 74, 76.

57. Lawrence M. Friedman, *A History of American Law* (New York: Simon and Schuster, 1973), pp. 530–6.

58. Quoted in Jerome Frank, *Courts on Trial* (New York: Atheneum, 1966), p. 299.

59. Oliver Wendell Holmes, Jr., "The Path of the Law," in *Collected Legal Papers* (New York: Harcourt, Brace, 1921), p. 179.

60. For a similar argument, see James Boyd White, "Law as Rhetoric, Rhetoric as Law: The Arts of Cultural and Communal Life," *University of Chicago Law Review*, 52 (1985), p. 697.

61. Sanford Levinson, "The Specious Morality of the Law," *Harper's*, 254 (May 1977), p. 37.

62. Samuel Johnson, "Preface to the English Dictionary," in *Works of Samuel Johnson*, ed. Arthur Murphy, 12 vols. (London: Luke Hanford, 1806), II, 61. Subsequent page references in these volumes (abbreviated SJW) are given parenthetically.

63. Robert M. Cover, "The Folktales of Justice: Tales of Jurisprudence," *Capital University Law Review*, 14 (1985), p. 183; Brook Thomas, *Cross-examinations of Law and Literature* (New York: Cambridge University Press, 1987), "Reflections on the Law and Literature Revival," *Critical Inquiry*, 17 (1991), pp. 510–39, and *"Billy Budd* and the Untold Story of the Law," *Cardozo Studies in Law and Literature*, 1 (1989), pp. 49–70.

64. Max Lerner, "The Constitution and Court as Symbols," *Yale Law Journal*, 46 (1937), p. 1294.

65. Benjamin Cardozo, *The Nature of the Judicial Process* (New Haven, Conn.: Yale University Press, 1971), pp. 166–7. This passage and its significance were drawn to my attention by John P. McWilliams, Jr.'s essay "Innocent Criminal or Criminal Innocence: The Trial in American Fiction," in *Law and American Literature* (New York: Knopf, 1983), pp. 45–124.

66. White, *When Words Lose Their Meaning*, p. 278.

67. Horace Bushnell, *Life and Letters of Horace Bushnell*, ed. M. B. Cheney (New York: Harper, 1880), p. 209.

68. For the political context of Ahab's oratory, see Alan Heimert, *"Moby-Dick* and American Political Symbolism," *American Quarterly*, 16 (1963),

pp. 498–504, and Rogin, *Subversive Genealogy*, chap. 4. For an explication of Huck's struggle to free his voice (and thinking) from a dominant discourse – the language of the law – see Elizabeth Perry Hodges, "Writing in a Different Voice," *Texas Law Review*, 66 (1988), p. 629.

69. H. Jefferson Powell, "Parchment Matters: A Meditation on the Constitution as Text," *Iowa Law Review*, 71 (1986), p. 1432.

70. Lerner, "Constitution and Court as Symbols," p. 1319.

71. *Walt Whitman's Workshop: A Collection of Unpublished Manuscripts*, ed. Clifton Joseph Furness (Cambridge: Harvard University Press, 1928), p. 57.

72. William J. Brennan, Jr., "The Constitution of the United States: Contemporary Ratification," in *Interpreting Law and Literature*, ed. Sanford Levinson and Steven Mailloux (Evanston, Ill.: Northwestern University Press, 1988), p. 13.

73. Macaulay, quoted in Michael Kammen, *A Machine That Would Go of Itself: The Constitution in American Culture* (New York: Knopf, 1986), p. 17. Despite its wealth of information about cultural perception of the Constitution, Kammen's book slights the commentary on the Constitution in American literature.

74. Plato, *Phaedrus*, 275e, 521.

75. The metaphor of the law as a bridge between past and future, the actual and the ideal, or what is and what ought to be is borrowed from Robert M. Cover's essays on the law. See "Folktales of Justice" and "The Supreme Court, 1982 Term – Foreword: *Nomos* and Narrative," *Harvard Law Review*, 97 (1983), p. 4.

Chapter 3. The Classical Pattern: From the Order of Orpheus to the Chaos of the Thucydidean Moment

1. For arguments regarding resistance to unjust authority in *White-Jacket*, see, in particular, p. 145. Robert Levine in *Conspiracy and Romance* appropriately cautions us, however, that in *White-Jacket*, as in Melville's other sea narratives, "concerns about insurrectionary disorder lie submerged but present . . . and implicitly challenge the antiauthoritarian sentiments of these works" (p. 190).

2. In antebellum America, Melville was not alone in representing Orpheus's power as the power of law. In an essay entitled "The Conservative Force of the American Bar," Rufus Choate quoted the following passage from Coleridge's "The Friend": "This is the spirit of *LAW*, – the lute of Amphion, – the harp of Orpheus. This is the true necessity which compels man into the social state, now and always, by a still beginning, never ceasing, force of moral cohesion" (*Works*, I, 437).

3. Georges Gusdorf, *Speaking*, trans. Paul T. Brockelman (Evanston, Ill: Northwestern University Press, 1965), p. 9. For the humanist tradition of viewing Orpheus as an orator and founder of civilization, see Kirsty Cochrane, "Orpheus Applied: Some Instances of His Importance in the Humanist View of Language," *Review of English Studies*, 19 (1968), pp. 1–13.

4. On Emerson's Orphic aspirations, see R. A. Yoder, *Emerson and the Orphic Poet in America* (Berkeley and Los Angeles: University of California Press, 1978). For Emerson's own reading of the transformation of Greek culture by eloquence, see JMN, II, 104-5.

5. *Walt Whitman's Workshop*, pp. 31, 34-5. On Whitman's "oratorical impulse," see C. Carroll Hollis, *Language and Style in "Leaves of Grass"* (Baton Rouge: Louisiana State University Press, 1983), chap. 1.

6. On the imperialist implications of this Orphic vision of transforming rude and savage people through the civilizing word of the eloquent orator, see Eric Cheyfitz, *The Poetics of Imperialism* (New York: Oxford University Press, 1991), chap. 7 and passim.

7. *The Politics of Aristotle*, trans. Ernest Barker (New York: Oxford University Press, 1962), pp. 5-6.

8. Ibid., p. 6.

9. Henry James, *The Question of Our Speech: The Lesson of Balzac* (Boston: Houghton Mifflin, 1905), p. 10.

10. N. Scott Momaday, "The Man Made of Words," in *Indian Voices: The First Convocation of American Indian Scholars* (San Francisco: Indian Historian Press, 1970), p. 49.

11. The biological foundation for this view is developed by Jacques Monod in *Chance and Necessity*, trans. Austryn Wainhouse (New York: Random House, 1972), chap. 7. In a lighter vein, see the essays "Social Talk" and "Information" in Lewis Thomas, *The Lives of a Cell* (New York: Viking, 1974). In sociology, see Peter L. Berger and Thomas Luckmann, *The Social Construction of Reality* (Garden City, N.Y.: Doubleday, 1966). In philosophy, see Gusdorf, *Speaking*, chaps. 1 and 4, and Hans-Georg Gadamer, "Man and Language," in *Philosophical Hermeneutics*, trans. David E. Linge (Berkeley and Los Angeles: University of California Press, 1976), pp. 59-68. On the ramifications of this view for political theory and law, see Drucilla Cornell, "Toward a Modern/Postmodern Reconstruction of Ethics," *University of Pennsylvania Law Review*, 113 (1985), p. 291.

12. Fénelon, "Lettre a l'Académie," IV, quoted in Gusdorf, *Speaking*, p. 109.

13. For a discussion of the exclusion of women from the public speech of the agora and the philosophic speech of the symposia in ancient Greece and beyond, see Jean Bethke Elshtain, "Feminist Discourse and Its Discontents: Language, Power, Meaning," *Signs*, 7 (1982), pp. 603-2..

14. Quoted in Hannah Arendt, *The Human Condition* (Chicago: University of Chicago Press, 1958), p. 27.

15. See Hannah Arendt, *On Revolution* (New York: Penguin, 1963), pp. 103, 119-31. For a further development of this argument, see R. G. A. Buxton, *Persuasion in Greek Tragedy: A Study of Peitho* (Cambridge: Cambridge University Press, 1982).

16. Euripides, *Supplices*, lines 438-41, quoted in Paul A. Rahe, "The Primacy of Politics in Classical Greece," *American Historical Review*, 89 (1984), p. 282. Rahe examines the relationship between free speech and democracy in classical Greece, and I have drawn upon his analysis in this

section. See also Josiah Ober, *Mass and Elite in Democratic Athens* (Princeton, N.J.: Princeton University Press, 1989).

17. *Selections from Ralph Waldo Emerson*, ed. Stephen E. Whicher (Boston: Houghton Mifflin, 1960), p. 7.

18. Ibid.

19. Arendt, *The Human Condition*, pp. 26-7.

20. Aristotle's account of the birth of rhetoric is described in Cicero's *Brutus*, 12.46.

21. John Quincy Adams, *Lectures on Rhetoric and Oratory*, 2 vols. (Cambridge: Hilliard and Metcalf, 1810), I, 19. Subsequent references to these volumes (abbreviated LR) are given parenthetically.

22. Thomas Carlyle, *Heroes and Hero-Worship* (Lincoln: University of Nebraska Press, 1966), p. 164.

23. Cover, "*Nomos* and Narrative," p. 53. For an extension of Cover's argument about the jurispathic office of the judge and the nature of legal interpretation as the social organization of violence, see his article "Violence and the Word," *Yale Law Journal*, 95 (1986), p. 1601. Cover provides his own reading of *Billy Budd* in *Justice Accused*, pp. 2-7.

24. Max Byrd, *London Transformed* (New Haven, Conn.: Yale University Press, 1978), p. 69.

25. Isocrates, *Antidosis*, trans. George Norlin (New York: Loeb, 1929), II, 327, 329. Brian Vickers points out in *In Defence of Rhetoric* (Oxford: Clarendon Press, 1988) that Isocrates' tribute to language as an Orphic civilizing power was echoed by Cicero in *De inventione* and by Quintillian, and that these passages "played a major role in forming the image of the orator as a culture-hero" into the eighteenth century (p. 10). See Cicero, *De inventione* (1.2.2-3, 1.4.5) and *De oratore* (1.8.32-3) and Quintillian, *Institutio oratorio* (2.16.9-17, 2.20.9). After defending rhetoric as a civilizing power in *Antidosis*, Isocrates also offers a critique of the corruption of language in Athens that resembles Thucydides' diagnosis in his *History*. Isocrates asserts, "Athens has in many respects been plunged into such a state of topsy-turvy and confusion that some of our people no longer use words in their proper meaning but wrest them from the most honourable associations and apply them to the basest pursuits" (II, 341, 343). In another oration, *On the Peace*, Isocrates blames the Athenians and their desire for war (arising from a lust for the riches of empire) for corrupting oratory by "driving all the orators from the platform except those who support your desires" and who "practise and study, not what will be advantageous to the state, but how they may discourse in a manner pleasing to you" (II, 7, 9). Isocrates' idealization of the word in *Antidosis* should be seen as a reaction against political and linguistic corruption in Athens and not as a historical preface to such a fall.

26. Since the line that is translated "words lost their significance" in Adams's text is at the center of my discussion of this passage, and since it has received the attention of previous commentators who have differed in their interpretations of it, I shall note some of the other ways it has been

translated. "The received value of names imposed for signification of things, was changed into arbitrary," in *Hobbes's Thucydides*, ed. Richard Schlatter (New Brunswick, N.J.: Rutgers University Press, 1975), p. 222. "The customary meanings of words were changed as men claimed the right to use them as they would to suit their actions," in A. W. Gomme, *A Historical Commentary on Thucydides*, Vol. II. (Oxford: Clarendon Press, 1956), p. 384. "To fit in with the change of events, words, too, had to change their usual meanings," in *The Peloponnesian War*, trans. Rex Warner (Baltimore: Penguin, 1954), p. 242. "And they modified at their discretion the customary valences of names for actions," in W. Robert Connor, *Thucydides* (Princeton, N.J.: Princeton University Press, 1984), p. 100. "Words were forced to change their ordinary meaning and to assume a significance that distorted the extraordinary deeds now undertaken," in J. Peter Euben, "Political Corruption in Euripides' *Orestes*," in *Greek Tragedy and Political Theory*, ed. Euben (Berkeley and Los Angeles: University of California Press, 1986), p. 226. "Further, they exchanged their usual verbal evaluations of deeds for new ones, in the light of what they now thought justified; thus irrational daring was considered courage for the sake of the Party; prudent delay, specious cowardice," in John Wilson, "'The Customary Meanings of Words Were Changed' – Or Were They? A Note on Thucydides 3.82.4," *Classical Quarterly*, 32 (1982), p. 19. Wilson's translation is not the most elegant, but his argument is persuasive that Thucydides does not mean that words became meaningless or that people sought to change their customary meanings. Instead their old meanings were betrayed as schemers sought to apply the sanction of moral or positive terms to actions that in a previous light would have been considered immoral or negative. Through such application, which involves a new and to some a perverse estimation of actions, the positive meaning or moral valence of the word is retained rather than being lost or changed. But the retention of the positively charged word to describe a negative action can bring that word into such disrepute that it could be said to lose or change its customary meaning. The sanctioning of crime in the name of liberty or of war in the name of peacekeeping, for instance, calls into disrepute and thus changes the meaning of the popular evaluation of the words "liberty" and "peacekeeping."

27. The literal meaning of the word *stasis*, which has been translated as "civil war," "factional strife," "revolution" "class warfare," is "standing," an etymology that suggests the unwillingness or inability to shift ground, to compromise, to modify one's position which typifies the spirit of party or faction in republican ideology. The word "stalemate" is a modern approximation of the term. For a further discussion of the meaning of *stasis* and its significance for a study of Hobbes and *The Federalist*, see J. Peter Euben, "Corruption," in *Political Innovation and Conceptual Change*, ed. Ball, Farr, and Hanson, pp. 220–46. For two valuable studies of Thucydides' *History*, see Connor, *Thucydides*, and Peter R. Pouncey, *The Necessities of War: A Study of Thucydides' Pessimism* (New York: Columbia Univer-

sity Press, 1980). See also J. Peter Euben, "Creatures of a Day: Thought and Action," in *Political Theory and Praxis: New Perspectives*, ed. Terence Ball (Minneapolis: University of Minnesota Press, 1977).

28. Sallust, *The War with Catiline*, in *Sallust*, trans. J. C. Rolfe (New York: Loeb, 1931), p. 103. For a discussion of Thucydides' importance to Roman historians and of the connections between political and linguistic change and corruption in classical Rome, see Ronald Syme, "History and Language at Rome," *Diogenes*, 85 (1974), pp. 1–11. On the eve of World War II, Syme also discussed linguistic manipulation in Roman politics in a chapter entitled "Political Catchwords" in *The Roman Revolution* (Oxford: Clarendon Press, 1939).

29. Montaigne, *The Complete Essays of Montaigne*, trans. Donald M. Frame (Stanford, Calif.: Stanford University Press, 1968), p. 119. For a discussion of the significance of Thucydides' description to Montaigne and his contemporaries, see Timothy J. Reiss, "Montaigne and the Subject of Polity," in *Literary Theory/Renaissance Texts*, ed. Patricia Parker and David Quint (Baltimore: Johns Hopkins University Press, 1986), pp. 115–49.

30. Thomas Gordon, *The Works of Sallust. Translated into English. With Political Discourses upon That Author* (London, 1744), p. 157.

31. *The Adams–Jefferson Letters*, ed. Lester J. Cappon, 2 vols. (Chapel Hill: University of North Carolina Press, 1959), II, 295. Subsequent references to these volumes (abbreviated AJL) are given parenthetically. Jefferson notes his own fondness for Thucydides in an earlier letter to Adams (AJL, II, 291). For the general importance of classical writers to Adams, Jefferson, and their generation, see Meyer Reinhold, *Classica Americana: The Greek and Roman Heritage in the United States* (Detroit: Wayne State University Press, 1984), and H. Trevor Colbourn, *The Lamp of Experience: Whig History and the Intellectual Origins of the American Revolution* (Chapel Hill: University of North Carolina Press, 1965).

32. Choate, *Works*, I, 94–5; III, 453.

33. Letter from Francis Lieber to Oscar Lieber, dated November 2, 1860, quoted in Frank Friedel, *Francis Lieber: Nineteenth Century Liberal* (Baton Rouge: Louisiana State University Press, 1977), p. 301; Francis Lieber, *Manual of Political Ethics*, Vol. II (Philadelphia: Lippincott, 1911), pp. 262–3.

34. Quoted in Edmund Wilson, *Patriotic Gore* (New York: Farrar, Straus and Giroux, 1962), p. 754.

35. Adam Milman Parry, *Logos and Ergon in Thucydides* (New York: Arno, 1981), p. 61 and passim.

36. In his chapter on Thucydides' *History* in *When Words Lose Their Meaning*, James Boyd White argues similarly with Parry that what breaks down in the course of events is a "culture of argument" – the linguistic means by which Greeks "maintain and regulate their relations with each other" (p. 82).

37. Garry Wills, "Talking Ourselves Out of a Fight," *William and Mary Quarterly*, 3d ser., 44 (1987), p. 624.

38. John Wild, *Plato's Theory of Man: An Introduction to the Realistic Philosophy of*

Culture (Cambridge: Harvard University Press, 1946), p. 36. My discussion of the concept of *anatrope* in Plato's philosophy relies on the analysis and references provided in Michael Seidel's unpublished Ph.D. dissertation, *Satiric Theory and the Degeneration of the State: The Tyrant and the Mob in Satiric Literature of the Restoration and Early Eighteenth Century* (UCLA, 1970).

39. John Dos Passos, "The Changing Shape of Institutions," *Occasions and Protests* (Chicago: Regnery, 1964), pp. 201–2.

40. *The Collected Dialogues of Plato*, ed. Edith Hamilton and Huntington Cairns (Princeton, N.J.: Princeton University Press, 1961), p. 788; 560b–c. Subsequent references to *The Republic* are given parenthetically.

41. René Girard, *Violence and the Sacred*, trans. Patrick Gregory (Baltimore: Johns Hopkins University Press, 1977), p. 49.

42. V. N. Volosinov, *Marxism and the Philosophy of Language*, trans. Ladislav Matejka and I. R. Titunik (Cambridge: Harvard University Press, 1986), pp. 23–4. In the text I attribute this work to Bakhtin.

43. On the inversions of carnival time, see Mikhail Bakhtin, *Rabelais and His World*, trans. Helen Iswolsky (Cambridge: MIT Press, 1968). On the inversions of *communitas*, see Victor Turner, *The Ritual Process: Structure and Anti-Structure* (Ithaca, N.Y.: Cornell University Press, 1977). For a discussion of the dynamics of linguistic change and conflict that can accompany social restructuring, see Smith-Rosenberg, *Disorderly Conduct*, p. 44.

44. For another elaboration of this pattern of political and linguistic betrayal, see Melvin J. Lasky, *Utopia and Revolution* (Chicago: University of Chicago Press, 1976), pp. 155–6.

45. Jean-Paul Sartre, *What Is Literature?* trans. Bernard Frechtman (New York: Philosophical Library, 1949), pp. 280–1, 283–4.

46. Two highly influential schools of post–World War II literary criticism, the new criticism and deconstruction, have been described as efforts toward a form of "verbal hygiene" that arose in part as a reaction to the political corruption of language. On the new criticism, see Leo Braudy, "Succeeding in Language," in *The State of the Language*, ed. Leonard Michaels and Christopher Ricks (Berkeley and Los Angeles: University of California Press, 1980), pp. 490–1. On deconstruction, see Geoffrey Hartman, *Easy Pieces* (New York: Columbia University Press, 1985), pp. 214–18. Terence Ball suggests that political (and literary) theorists who have taken as their guides the work of Nietzsche or Foucault or Habermas have engaged in what he identifies in Habermas's idiom as the quest of Thucydides' own political theory: the quest to "expose, criticise and remove the sources of blocked or systematically distorted communication." See Terence Ball, "In the Shadow of Babel: The 'Scientific' Reconstruction of Political Discourse," in *Political Discourse*, ed. Bhiku Parekh and Thomas Pantham (New Delhi: Sage, 1987), p. 31.

47. By 1941, the foil for Burke's dialectical rhetoric is Hitler's demagoguery. See Burke's essay "The Rhetoric of Hitler's 'Battle,'" *The Philosophy of Literary Form* (Baton Rouge: Louisiana State University Press, 1967), wherein he maintains that in Hitler's politics "the wrangle of the parlia-

mentary is to be stilled by the giving of *one* voice to the whole people, this to be the 'inner voice' of Hitler, made uniform throughout the German boundaries'' (p. 207).

48. Kenneth Burke, *A Rhetoric of Motives* (New York: Prentice-Hall, 1950), p. 23. Subsequent page references are given parenthetically.

49. Wilson, *Patriotic Gore*, pp. xi–xii, xxxi.

50. Marcuse analyzes the "closing of the universe of discourse" in *One-Dimensional Man* (Boston: Beacon, 1964), chap. 2. Edwin Newman's best-seller *Strictly Speaking* (Indianapolis: Bobbs-Merrill, 1974) is typical of the 1970s schoolmaster's reproach to a perceived dissolution of standards in linguistic behavior.

51. Herbert Marcuse, *An Essay on Liberation* (Boston: Beacon, 1969), p. 8. See also pp. 34–6, 71–8. Subsequent page references are given parenthetically.

52. Norman Mailer, *The Armies of the Night* (New York: New American Library, 1968), p. 63. Subsequent page references are given parenthetically.

53. Ellison, *Going to the Territory*, pp. 124–5.

54. On the politics of obscenity in *The Armies of the Night*, see Marx, "'Noble Shit': The Uncivil Response of American Writers to Civil Religion." Mailer deploys the phrase "totalitarian prose" in his review of Lyndon Johnson's *My Hope for America*, which he reprints in *Cannibals and Christians* (New York: Dell, 1967), pp. 47–52.

55. Eric A. Havelock, *The Liberal Temper in Greek Politics* (New Haven, Conn.: Yale University Press, 1964), p. 193. The quarrel between the Sophists and Plato and its legacy in Western culture have been discussed by a number of scholars. See, for example, Ernst Cassirer, *The Philosophy of Symbolic Forms*, Vol. I (New Haven, Conn.: Yale University Press, 1953), chap. 1; Nancy S. Struever, *The Language of History in the Renaissance* (Princeton, N.J.: Princeton University Press, 1970); Terry Eagleton, *Walter Benjamin; or, Towards a Revolutionary Criticism* (London: Verso and NLB, 1981), chap. 2; Vickers, *In Defence of Rhetoric*, chaps. 2 and 3; Debora Shuger, *Sacred Rhetoric* (Princeton, N.J.: Princeton University Press, 1988), chap. 3.

56. The distinction between educative and economic models of discourse and politics was suggested to me by Terence Ball's discussion of models of democracy in *The Transformation of Political Discourse* (Oxford: Blackwell Publisher, 1988).

57. Vickers, *In Defence of Rhetoric*, p. 87.

58. Gorgias, "Encomium on Helen," in *Ancilla to the Pre-Socratic Philosophers*, trans. Kathleen Freeman (Oxford: Clarendon Press, 1948), p. 133.

59. Ibid. On Gorgias's concept of the power of words, see Charles P. Segal, "Gorgias and the Psychology of the *Logos*," *Harvard Studies in Classical Philology*, 66 (1962), pp. 99–155. See also Jacques Derrida, "Plato's Pharmakon," in *Disseminations* (Chicago: University of Chicago Press, 1981).

60. Gerald L. Bruns, "Language and Power," *Chicago Review*, 34 (1984), p. 29. On the connection between seduction and rhetoric in early American

culture and fiction, see Fliegelman, *Prodigals and Pilgrims*, pp. 235–41, and his introduction to Charles Brockden Brown, *Wieland and Memoirs of Carwin the Biloquist* (New York: Penguin, 1991).

61. For a discussion of Plato's challenge to the spellbinding power of the spoken word, see Jacqueline de Romily, *Magic and Rhetoric in Ancient Greece* (Cambridge: Harvard University Press, 1975), chap. 2, and Robert J. Connors, "Greek Rhetoric and the Transition from Orality," *Philosophy and Rhetoric*, 19 (1986), pp. 38–65.

62. Benjamin R. Barber, *Strong Democracy: Participatory Politics for a New Age* (Berkeley and Los Angeles: University of California Press, 1984), p. 193.

63. Sophocles, *Philoctetes*, lines 98–9, quoted in Pedro Lain Entralgo, *The Therapy of the Word in Classical Antiquity*, trans. L. J. Rather and John M. Sharp (New Haven, Conn.: Yale University Press, 1970), p. 68.

64. Michael A. Roberts, *Marlowe's "Tamburlaine": A Study of Verbalism in Drama* (Ph.D. diss., Yale University, 1970), pp. 10–11.

65. Ibid., p. 11. For an essay that documents how Roman figures posited this same connection between the decline of liberty and the decline of eloquence, see Harry Caplan, "The Decay of Eloquence at Rome in the First Century," in a collection of his essays, *Of Eloquence* (Ithaca, N.Y.: Cornell University Press, 1970).

66. For a classic version of this argument, see chap. 23, "Relationship of Languages to Government," in Jean-Jacques Rousseau, *On the Origin of Language*, trans. John H. Moran and Alexander Gode (New York: Ungar, 1966); Derrida's commentary on Rousseau in *Of Grammatology*; and J. Patrick Dobel, "The Role of Language in Rousseau's Political Thought," *Polity*, 18 (1986), pp. 638–58. Eagleton's phrase is quoted in Peter Goodrich, *Legal Discourse: Studies in Linguistics, Rhetoric and Legal Analysis* (New York: St. Martin's, 1987), p. 97.

67. Abigail Adams makes the same point in a 1776 letter to her husband when she quotes for him the following passage from Joseph Warton's *Essay on the Genius and Writing of Pope*: "In Monarchy there may be poets, painters and Musicians, but orators, Historians and philosophers can exist in a Republic alone. The Roman Nation by their unjust attempt upon the liberty of the World, justly lost their own, and with their liberty they lost not only their force of Eloquence, but even their Stile and language itself" (*Adams Family Correspondence*, ed. L. H. Butterfield, 4 vols. [New York: Atheneum, 1965], I, 404).

68. "Oration on Eloquence," in Caleb Bingham, *The Columbian Orator* (Boston, 1832), p. 33.

69. Tacitus, *A Dialogue on Oratory*, in *The Complete Works of Tacitus*, ed. Moses Hadas (New York: Random House, 1942), p. 768.

70. Cited in Abiel Abbot Livermore, *The War with Mexico Reviewed* (Boston: American Peace Society, 1850), p. 219. The passage is from *Agricola*, in *Complete Works of Tacitus*, p. 695. In a 1794 letter to Jefferson, John Adams also echoed this passage to compare the atrocities of the French revolutionaries to those of the Romans: "When will the Crisis of this fever in

human Nature be over, and in what State of Health will it be left? *Solitudinem faciunt, Libertatem appelant"* (AJL, I, 256).

Chapter 4. The Christian Typology: From Eden to Babel to Pentecost

1. Henry James, *Hawthorne* (New York: AMS Press, 1968), p. 144.
2. Cited in Daniel Aaron, *The Unwritten War* (New York: Oxford University Press, 1973), p. 75.
3. *Benjamin Franklin's Letters to the Press, 1758-1775*, ed. Verner W. Crane (Chapel Hill: University of North Carolina Press, 1950), p. 172; Andrew Lee, *Sin Destructive of Temporal and Eternal Happiness* (Hanover, N.H., 1776), p. 211.
4. *Selections from the Writings and Speeches of William Lloyd Garrison* (Boston: R. F. Wallcut, 1852), p. 249; Horace Mann, *Slavery: Letters and Speeches* (Boston: B. B. Mussey, 1851), p. 184.
5. Livermore, *The War with Mexico Reviewed*, p. 263.
6. See Levine, *Conspiracy and Romance*, for a study of the relationship between the conspiracy fears of history and the plotting of American romances by Brown, Cooper, Hawthorne, and Melville.
7. See, for instance, Ernest Lee Tuveson, *Redeemer Nation: The Idea of America's Millennial Role* (Chicago: University of Chicago Press, 1968), and Cushing Strout, *The New Heavens and New Earth: Political Religion in America* (New York: Harper and Row, 1973).
8. Cited in Aaron, *The Unwritten War*, p. 343.
9. "Our Language Destined to Be Universal," *United States Magazine and Democratic Review*, 4 (1855), p. 308.
10. Several other passages in the Bible refer to the tongue as a dangerous weapon, including Psalms 52:2, 57:4, and 64:3.
11. "Our Language Destined to Be Universal," p. 309.
12. Fliegelman, *Prodigals and Pilgrims*, chap. 8.
13. Cited in James Morton Smith, *Freedom's Fetters: The Alien and Sedition Laws and American Civil Liberties* (Ithaca, N.Y.: Cornell University Press, 1956), p. 99.
14. Abraham Bishop, *Proofs of a Conspiracy Against Christianity, and the Government of the United States*, in *Fear of Conspiracy*, ed. D. B. Davis, p. 62.
15. Abraham Bishop, *Connecticut Republicanism: An Oration on the Extent and Power of Political Delusion* (New Haven, Conn., 1800), pp. 1, 2, 26, 28, 56.
16. Edward Everett, *Orations and Speeches on Various Occasions*, 4 vols. (Boston: Little, Brown, 1850–68), I, 32.
17. On the significance of the "road to happiness" metaphor in Jefferson's work, see Harold Hellenbrand, "Roads to Happiness: Rhetorical and Philosophical Design in Jefferson's *Notes on the State of Virginia*," *Early American Literature*, 20 (1985), pp. 3–23.
18. James Madison, *Notes of Debates in the Federal Convention of 1787 Reported by James Madison*, ed. Adrienne Koch (New York: Norton, 1969), p. 210. Subsequent references to this volume (abbreviated NFC) are given parenthetically.

19. On Franklin's quest to offer himself as a representative man who subsumes the differences of Babel into the unity of consensus, see Mitchell Breitwieser, *Cotton Mather and Benjamin Franklin* (Cambridge: Cambridge University Press, 1984), pp. 1–2 and chap. 6.

20. *The Works of Joel Barlow*, 2 vols. (Gainesville, Fla.: Scholars' Facsimiles and Reprints, 1970), pp. 350–1.

21. Melville, *Redburn*, p. 160.

22. "Our Language Destined to Be Universal," p. 308.

23. Ibid.

24. Sacvan Bercovitch, "The A-Politics of Ambiguity in *The Scarlet Letter*," *New Literary History*, 19 (1988), pp. 639–54.

25. King, *A Testament of Hope*, p. 219.

26. Eliot, *The Complete Poems and Plays*, pp. 121, 122, 145.

27. Thomas Pynchon, *The Crying of Lot 49* (Philadelphia: Lippincott, 1966), pp. 58, 134–5.

28. Ibid., p. 87.

29. Herman Melville, *Moby-Dick; or, The Whale*, ed. Harrison Hayford and Hershel Parker (New York: Norton, 1967), pp. 136–7.

30. Carolyn L. Karcher, *Shadow over the Promised Land: Slavery, Race, and Violence in Melville's America* (Baton Rouge: Louisiana State University Press, 1980), p. 157.

31. Fisher, *The Trial of the Constitution*, p. 386.

32. Stephen Pearl Andrews, "A Universal Language: Its Possibility, Scientific Necessity, and Appropriate Characteristics," *Continental Monthly*, 5 (1864), pp. 532, 543. An earlier attempt by Andrews to promote reform through linguistic experiments involved his efforts to educate illiterate slaves by teaching them to read a phonetic alphabet and system of shorthand developed in England by Isaac Pitman. See Madeleine B. Stern, *The Pantarch: A Biography of Stephen Pearl Andrews* (Austin: University of Texas Press, 1968), chap. 5. She writes that because of Andrews's enthusiastic promotion of a "new alphabet of nature" "New Englanders were almost convinced they could overthrow the Tower of Babel" (p. 61). In 1845 Andrews formed and became president of the American Phonographic Society, whose aim as stated in the preamble of its constitution was to use "Phonography" to "universalize education" and promote "a free intercourse among the nations of the earth" (p. 62). William Lloyd Garrison, who was a member of its executive council, declared that Andrews's system of phonography "is perhaps next in importance to the discovery of printing" (p. 64).

33. Andrews, "A Universal Language," p. 543; Stephen Pearl Andrews, *The Primary Synopsis of Universology and Alwato* (New York: Dion Thomas, 1871), pp. 45, 46.

34. Cited in Frank, *Courts on Trial*, p. 294.

35. George Fitzhugh, *Cannibals All!* (1857; repr. Cambridge, Mass.: Belknap Press, 1960), pp. 59–60. Sheldon S. Wolin reminds us that "it is precisely because the men of Shinar have one language and a highly unified social

organization and thus have suppressed their differences that they are able to mobilize the power necessary to erect a tower" (*The Presence of the Past* [Baltimore: Johns Hopkins University Press, 1989], p. 124).

36. Whitney, *The Life and Growth of Language*, pp. 176-7.

37. Ibid., p. 178.

38. Cited in R. W. B. Lewis, *The American Adam* (Chicago: University of Chicago Press, 1955), p. 32.

39. Roman Jakobson, "The World Response to Whitney's Principles of Linguistic Science," in *Whitney on Language*, ed. Michael Silverstein (Cambridge: MIT Press, 1971), pp. xxviii, xxxiv. For more on Whitney's contributions to linguistics and the politics of his linguistic principles, see Julie Tetel Andresen, *Linguistics in America, 1769-1924* (London: Routledge, 1990), pp. 135-68.

40. *Whitney on Language*, p. xxxiv.

41. Ibid., pp. 99, 16.

42. Emerson himself talks about debate in the political forum in much the same terms he uses to describe the game of conversation in "Circles." See *Selections from Ralph Waldo Emerson*, p. 118. For a keen appreciation of the importance to democratic politics of what Emerson would call good conversation, see Benjamin R. Barber, "Political Talk – and 'Strong Democracy,'" *Dissent*, 31 (1984), pp. 215-22. Peter Gibian in *Oliver Wendell Holmes in the Conversation of His Culture* (Ph.D. diss., Stanford University, 1986) illuminates the connections between democracy and conversation and among linguistic theory, literature, and politics in the American Renaissance as he reveals the importance of reading Holmes for a fuller appreciation of that age.

43. Benjamin R. Barber, "The Compromised Republic," in *The Moral Foundations of the American Republic*, ed. Robert H. Horwitz (Charlottesville: University Press of Virginia, 1979), p. 27.

44. Ellison, *Going to the Territory*, p. 19; *Shadow and Act*, p. 122.

45. Ellison, *Going to the Territory*, pp. 20-1.

46. For a qualification regarding Whitman's pentecostal spirit, see David Simpson, "Destiny Made Manifest: The Styles of Whitman's Poetry," in *Nation and Narration*, pp. 77-96.

47. Roland Barthes, *The Pleasure of the Text* (New York: Hill and Wang, 1975), p. 4.

48. W. H. Auden, *Secondary Worlds* (New York: Random House, 1968), p. 134.

Chapter 5. Eloquence, Liberty, and Power: Civic Humanism and the Counter-Renaissance

1. Dante, *Literature in the Vernacular* (*De Vulgari Eloquentia*), trans. Sally Purcell (Manchester: Carcanet New Press, 1981), p. 27.

2. Thomas Jefferson in several of his letters views the American Revolution as an extension of the scientific revolution and the revolt against the "ignorance and barbarism" of the so-called Dark Ages. See, for instance, his August 1, 1816, letter to John Adams (AJL, II, 484). For a probing and

synthetic commentary on the implications of the Renaissance and the method of scientific reason for America and the "evolution of modern consciousness," see Richard N. Goodwin, *The American Condition* (New York: Doubleday, 1974), Part II.

3. Roberts, *Marlowe's "Tamburlaine,"* p. 66.

4. Quoted in Jerrold E. Seigel, *Rhetoric and Philosophy in Renaissance Humanism* (Princeton, N.J.: Princeton University Press, 1968), p. 34.

5. On how and why the humanists pursued eloquence, see Hanna H. Gray, "Renaissance Humanism: The Pursuit of Eloquence," *Journal of the History of Ideas*, 24 (1963), pp. 497–514.

6. Thomas Wilson, *The Arte of Rhetorique*, in *English Literary Criticism: The Renaissance*, ed. O. B. Hardison, Jr. (New York: Harper and Row, 1963), pp. 26–7.

7. For a study of the various interpretations of Orpheus in the Renaissance, see Thomas Cain, "Spenser and the Renaissance Orpheus," *University of Toronto Quarterly*, 52 (1970-1), pp. 24–47.

8. In *English Literary Criticism*, p. 27.

9. Henry Peacham, *The Garden of Eloquence*, 2d ed. (London, 1593), p. 49.

10. Michael Roberts, *Marlowe's "Tamburlaine,"* p. 75.

11. Quoted in Struever, *The Language of History in the Renaissance*, p. 40.

12. John Quincy Adams, *Lectures on Rhetoric*, I, 19.

13. Henri I. Marrou, *A History of Education in Antiquity*, trans. George Lamb (New York: New American Library, 1964), pp. 81–2.

14. Edward T. Channing, *Lectures Read to the Seniors in Harvard College* (Boston: Ticknor and Fields, 1856), p. 2.

15. Roger Ascham, *The Scholemaster* (Don Mills, Ont.: Dent, 1966), p. 111.

16. Peacham, *The Garden of Eloquence*, p. 121.

17. Channing, *Lectures*, p. 8.

18. *The Earliest Diary of John Adams*, ed. L. H. Butterfield, Wendell D. Garrett, and Marc Friedlaender (Cambridge, Mass.: Belknap Press, 1966), p. 74.

19. Quoted in Eugenio Garin, *Portraits from the Quattrocento* (New York: Harper and Row, 1963), p. 102.

20. *The Humanism of Leonardo Bruni: Selected Texts*, trans. Gordon Griffiths, James Hankins, and David Thomson, Medieval and Renaissance Texts and Studies, no. 46 (Binghamton, N.Y., 1987), pp. 124–5. For a guide to developments in political thought and concepts of liberty in the Italian city-states, see Quentin Skinner, *The Foundations of Modern Political Thought*, Vol. I (Cambridge: Cambridge University Press, 1978), chap. 1–4.

21. Struever, *The Language of History in the Renaissance*, p. 118.

22. *The Humanism of Leonardo Bruni*, p. 125.

23. Ibid., p. 126.

24. Quoted in Struever, *The Language of History in the Renaissance*, p. 40.

25. Quoted in Ephraim Emerson, *Humanism and Tyranny: Studies in the Italian Trecento* (Cambridge: Harvard University Press, 1925), p. 41.

26. Quoted in Struever, *The Language of History in the Renaissance*, p. 40.

27. Baron, *The Crisis of the Early Italian Renaissance*, chaps. 1 and 6.
28. Quoted in ibid., pp. 66–7, 479.
29. See Struever, *The Language of History in the Renaissance*, pp. 120–1, 166–7.
30. Lauro Martines, *The Social World of the Florentine Humanists, 1340–1460* (Princeton, N.J.: Princeton University Press, 1963), p. 302.
31. Quoted in Edward Hutton, *Pietro Aretino: The Scourge of Princes* (London: Constable, 1922), p. xiv.
32. Cicero, *Basic Works*, trans. Moses Hadas (New York: Random House, 1951), p. 240.
33. Juan Luis Vives, *Introduction to Wisdom*, trans. Alice Tobriner (New York: Columbia University Teachers College Press, 1968), p. 140.
34. *Collected Works of Erasmus*, ed. Elaine Fantham and Erika Rummel, Vol. XXIX (Toronto: University of Toronto Press, 1989), pp. 259–60.
35. Desiderius Erasmus, *The Complaint of Peace*, trans. T. Paynell (La Salle, Ill.: Open Court, 1974), pp. 5–6.
36. Marjorie O'Rourke Boyle, "Erasmus' Prescription for Henry VIII: Logo-therapy," *Renaissance Quarterly*, 31 (1978), p. 164. For a fuller discussion of Erasmus's faith in the civilizing power of the word, see her *Erasmus on Language and Method in Theology* (Toronto: University of Toronto Press, 1977), esp. chap. 2.
37. Cheyfitz, *The Poetics of Imperialism*, p. xx.
38. Hiram Hadyn, *The Counter-Renaissance* (New York: Harcourt Brace and World, 1950).
39. *Complete Essays of Montaigne*, p. 222. Subsequent page references in this volume are given parenthetically. For a suggestive discussion of Montaigne's work in the context of the French Wars of Religion, see Margaret M. McGowan, *Montaigne's Deceits* (Philadelphia: Temple University Press, 1974), chaps. 6 and 7.
40. *Emerson in His Journals*, ed. Joel Porte (Cambridge: Harvard University Press, 1982), pp. 240–1.
41. For an influential discussion of Don Quixote's madness in the context of Renaissance attitudes toward language, see Foucault, *The Order of Things*, chaps. 1 and 2. The transformation in linguistic attitudes in the Renaissance or between medieval and modern worlds has been treated from different angles in a number of studies. See, for instance, Timothy J. Reiss, *The Discourse of Modernism* (Ithaca, N.Y.: Cornell University Press, 1982); Maureen Quilligan, *The Language of Allegory* (Ithaca, N.Y.: Cornell University Press, 1979), chap. 3; Margreta De Grazia, "The Secularization of Language in the Seventeenth Century," *Journal of the History of Ideas*, 41 (1980), pp. 319–29; Terence Cave, *The Cornucopian Text: Problems of Writing in the French Renaissance* (Oxford: Oxford University Press, 1979); Richard Waswo, *Language and Meaning in the Renaissance* (Princeton, N.J.: Princeton University Press, 1987); John Bender and David J. Wellbery, "Rhetoricality: On the Modernist Return of Rhetoric," in *The Ends of Rhetoric*, ed. John Bender and David Wellbery (Stanford, Calif.: Stanford University Press, 1990), pp. 3–39; Debora Shuger, *Habits of*

Thought in the English Renaissance (Berkeley and Los Angeles: University of California Press, 1990).

42. For a fuller development of the argument that Shakespeare's plays participate with Montaigne and Bacon in a shift in linguistic attitudes that would lead to Locke, see Gayle Greene, "'The Power of Speech / To Stir Men's Blood': The Language of Tragedy in Shakepeare's *Julius Caesar*," *Renaissance Drama*, 11 (1980), pp. 67–93, and "Language and Value in Shakespeare's *Troilus and Cressida*," *Studies in English Literature*, 21 (1981), pp. 271–85. See also James L. Calderwood, *Shakespearean Metadrama* (Minneapolis: University of Minnesota Press, 1971).

43. Gerald Gillespie, "Scientific Discourse and Postmodernity: Francis Bacon and the Empirical Birth of Science," *boundary 2*, 7 (1979), p. 128.

44. Bakhtin, *Rabelais and His World*, pp. 470–1.

45. Walt Whitman, "America's Mightiest Inheritance," in *New York Dissected*, ed. Emory Holloway and Ralph Adimari (New York: Rufus Rockwell Wilson, 1936), p. 56.

46. *The Works of Francis Bacon*, ed. James Spedding, 8 vols. (New York: Garrett, 1968), IV, 61. Subsequent references to these volumes (abbreviated FBW) are given parenthetically.

47. Ascham, *The Scholemaster*, p. 101.

48. Ibid.

49. For more on the context of this passage in *The Scholemaster* and on the tradition of connecting virtue and good letters in English humanism, see Alvin Vos, "'Good Matter and Good Utterance': The Character of English Ciceronianism," *Studies in English Literature*, 19 (1979), pp. 3–18.

Chapter 6. The Enlightenment Project: Language Reform and Political Order

1. Bailyn, *Origins of American Politics*, p. 53. See also Bailyn, *The Ideological Origins of the American Revolution*; Wood, *The Creation of the American Republic*; Pocock, *The Machiavellian Moment*; and Robert Shalhope, "Republicanism and Early American Historiography," *William and Mary Quarterly*, 3d ser., 39 (1982), pp. 334–56.

2. John P. Diggins, *The Lost Soul of American Politics* (New York: Basic, 1984), p. 364.

3. Thomas L. Pangle, *The Spirit of Modern Republicanism* (Chicago: University of Chicago Press, 1988), p. 36.

4. John Locke, *Two Treatises of Government*, ed. Peter Laslett (New York: New American Library, 1965), p. 463.

5. *The English Writings of Abraham Cowley*, ed. A. R. Waller (Cambridge: Cambridge University Press, 1905), pp. 449–50.

6. James Thomson, "Summer," in *The Complete Poetical Works of James Thomson*, ed. J. Logie Robertson (Oxford: Oxford University Press, 1977), p. 110.

7. *Papers of John Adams*, ed. Robert J. Taylor, G. L. Lint, and C. Walker, 8 vols. to date (Cambridge: Harvard University Press, 1977–), I, 42; *The*

Mind of the Founder, p. 183. For Bacon's reputation and influence in nineteenth-century America, see Theodore Dwight Bozeman, *Protestants in an Age of Science: The Baconian Ideal and Antebellum Religious Thought* (Chapel Hill: University of North Carolina Press, 1977).

8. *The Farmer Refuted: or, A More Impartial and Comprehensive View of the Dispute Between Great Britain and the Colonies, Intended as a Further Vindication of the Congress* (New York: James Rivington, 1775), p. 7.

9. "Letter to the Lord Treasurer Burghley," in *Francis Bacon*, ed. Arthur Johnston (New York: Schocken, 1965), p. 208.

10. In ibid., p. 14.

11. Charles Whitney, *Francis Bacon and Modernity* (New Haven, Conn.: Yale University Press, 1986), pp. 38–9.

12. Kenneth Minogue, "Bacon and Locke: Or Ideology as Mental Hygiene," in *Ideology, Philosophy and Politics*, ed. Anthony Parel (Waterloo, Ont.: Wilfred Laurier University Press, 1983), p. 180.

13. *Hobbes' Thucydides*, ed. Schlatter, p. 222.

14. Thomas Hobbes, *Leviathan*, ed. C. B. MacPherson (Baltimore: Penguin, 1968), p. 728. Subsequent page references in this book (abbreviated L) are given parenthetically.

15. In *The English Works of Thomas Hobbes*, ed. Sir William Molesworth, 11 vols. (London: John Bohn, 1840), IV, 26. Subsequent references to these volumes (abbreviated THW) are given parenthetically.

16. Thomas Hobbes, *De Cive, or The Citizen*, ed. Sterling P. Lamprecht (New York: Appleton-Century-Crofts, 1949), p. 29. Subsequent references to this volume (abbreviated DC) are given parenthetically.

17. Sheldon S. Wolin, *Politics and Vision* (Boston: Little, Brown, 1960). See also Terence Ball, "Hobbes' Linguistic Turn," *Polity*, 17 (1985), pp. 739–60.

18. For a study of Hobbesian ideas in American politics, see Frank M. Coleman, *Hobbes and America: Explaining the Constitutional Foundations* (Toronto: University of Toronto Press, 1977).

19. Oliver Wendell Holmes, *The Autocrat of the Breakfast-Table*, p. 13.

20. For the connection between the rhetorical figure "amphibology" and the political figure the traitor in Renaissance England, see Steven Mullaney, "Lying like Truth: Riddle, Representation and Treason in Renaissance England," *ELH*, 47 (1980), pp. 32–47. For connections between equivocation and treason by Southern rebels, see JLW, V, 49–50, 276–7. Carwin and Claggart, traitors against the truth in, respectively, *Wieland* and *Billy Budd*, are also double-tongued equivocators.

21. Samuel Butler, *Hudibras*, ed. John Wilders (Oxford: Clarendon Press, 1967), p. 1. I was pointed to these sources by Ann Cline Kelly's article "After Eden: Gulliver's (Linguistic) Travels," *ELH*, 45 (1978), pp. 38–54.

22. Earl of Clarendon (Edward Hyde), *The History of the Rebellion*, Vol. I (Oxford: Clarendon Press, 1888), p. 2.

23. Thomas Sprat, *History of the Royal Society*, ed. Jackson I. Cope and Harold W. Jones (St. Louis: Washington University Press, 1958), p. 111.

24. Quoted in Richard Foster Jones, "The Attack on Pulpit Eloquence in the Restoration: An Episode in the Development of the Neo-Classical Standard for Prose," *Journal of English and Germanic Philology*, 20 (1931), p. 76.

25. Joseph Glanvill, *An Essay on Preaching* (London, 1703), pp. 19–20.

26. John Wilkins, *An Essay Toward a Real Character and a Philosophical Language* (London, 1668; repr. Menston: Scolar, 1968), "Epistle Dedicatory," n.p. On Wilkins's *Essay* and its context, see Sidonie Clauss, "John Wilkins' *Essay Toward a Real Character*: Its Place in the Seventeenth-Century Episteme," *Journal of the History of Ideas*, 43 (1982), pp. 531–54.

27. Samuel Shaw, *Words Made Visible* (London, 1679; repr. Menston: Scolar, 1972), p. 98.

28. William Mathews, *Words; Their Use and Abuse* (Chicago: S. C. Griggs, 1876), chap. 2. Subsequent references to this volume (abbreviated WMW) are given parenthetically.

29. Robert South, *Sermons Preached upon Several Occasions*, 4 vols. (Philadelphia: Sorrin and Ball, 1844), I, 176–7. Subsequent page references in these volumes are given parenthetically.

30. Lasky, *Utopia and Revolution*, p. 158; George Williamson, "The Restoration Revolt Against Enthusiasm," *Studies in Philology*, 30 (1933), pp. 571–603.

31. Ibid., p. 155.

32. Sprat, *The History of the Royal Society*, pp. 112, 113.

33. Ibid., pp. 131, 56. On the politics of the Royal Society's language reforms, see John Reed, "Restoration and Repression: The Language Projects of the Royal Society," in *Studies in Eighteenth-Century Culture*, Vol. 19 (Madison: University of Wisconsin Press, 1989), pp. 399–412.

34. For a study of these projects and proposals in the context of seventeenth-century theories of language, see Murray Cohen, *Sensible Words: Linguistic Practice in England, 1640–1785* (Baltimore: Johns Hopkins University Press, 1977); James Knowlson, *Universal Language Schemes in England and France 1600–1800* (Toronto: University of Toronto Press, 1975); and Hans Aarsleff, *From Locke to Saussure* (Minneapolis: University of Minnesota Press, 1982).

35. Jones's essays on science and stylistic reform are collected in *The Seventeenth Century: Studies in the History of English Thought and Literature from Bacon to Pope*, ed. Richard Foster Jones (Stanford, Calif.: Stanford University Press, 1969). On the connections between the language of politics and the politics of language in Restoration literature, see Steven N. Zwicker, *Politics and Language in Dryden's Poetry* (Princeton, N.J.: Princeton University Press, 1984).

36. On Thoreau's philological researches, which led him, under the influence of Charles Kraitsir's *Glossology: Being a Treatise on the Nature of Language and on the Language of Nature* (1852), to suppose a uniform language that corresponded to nature, see Gura, *The Wisdom of Words*, chap. 4. Kraitser's (and Thoreau's) philological beliefs can be seen as not just participating in a Romantic tradition but as similar in kind (and cause) to the universal and scientific language theories of the seventeenth century.

37. Wilkins, Epistle Dedicatory, *Essay Toward a Real Character*, n.p.

38. George Dalgarno, *Ars Signorum*, in *Works* (Edinburgh, 1834), p. 164.

39. George Dalgarno, *Didascalocophys* (Menston: Scolar, 1971), introduction, n.p.

40. Jonathan Swift, "A Proposal for Correcting, Improving and Ascertaining the English Tongue," in *The English Language: Essays by English and American Men of Letters, 1430-1839*, ed. W. F. Bolton (Cambridge: Cambridge University Press, 1966), pp. 112-13. On Swift's efforts to reform the language, see Ann Cline Kelly, *Swift and the English Language* (Philadelphia: University of Pennsylvania Press, 1988).

41. "The Abuse of Words," *New England Magazine*, 4 (1833), p. 58.

42. Henry F. May and David Lundberg, "The Enlightened Reader in America," *American Quarterly*, 26 (1976), pp. 262-72.

43. Hans Aarsleff, *The Study of Language in England, 1780-1860* (Princeton, N.J.: Princeton University Press, 1967).

44. Perry Miller, *Errand into the Wilderness* (New York: Harper and Row, 1964), p. 168. Philosophers of language who explicitly referred to or used Locke's language theory as the starting (or breaking-away) point for their own theory of language include Thomas Sheridan, Edmund Burke, Jeremy Bentham, John Horne Tooke, Dugald Stewart, Etienne Condillac, Horace Bushnell, Alexander Bryan Johnson, C. S. Peirce, Fritz Mauthner, and Ferdinand de Saussure.

45. Quoted in Neal Wood, *The Politics of Locke's Philosophy: A Social Study of "An Essay Concerning Human Understanding"* (Berkeley and Los Angeles: University of California Press, 1983), p. 26.

46. John Locke, *Two Tracts on Government*, ed. Philip Abrams (Cambridge: Cambridge University Press, 1967), p. 119.

47. Quoted in Lasky, *Utopia and Revolution*, pp. 408-9.

48. Quoted in ibid., p. 409.

49. Wood, *The Politics of Locke's Philosophy*, pp. 2, 5.

50. See Fliegelman, *Prodigals and Pilgrims*, for a development of the ramifications of this view for a study of Enlightenment politics and literature.

51. Quoted in Lord King, *The Life of John Locke with Extracts from His Correspondence, Journals and Commonplace Books*, Vol. I (London, 1830), p. 188.

52. John J. Richetti, *Philosophical Writing: Locke, Berkeley, Hume* (Cambridge: Harvard University Press, 1983), p. 86.

53. *The Autobiography of Benjamin Franklin*, ed. Leonard Labaree, Ralph L. Ketcham, Helen C. Boatfield and Helene H. Fineman (New Haven, Conn.: Yale University Press, 1964), p. 65. Subsequent references to this volume (abbreviated BFA) are given parenthetically.

54. Ibid., pp. 60, 64.

55. Quoted in *Supreme Court and Supreme Law*, ed. Edmond Cahn (New York: Simon and Schuster, 1954), p. 7.

56. Miller, *Errand into the Wilderness*, p. 169.

57. For the theme of the abuse of language in works by Swift, Pope, Fielding, Richardson, and Sterne, see, respectively, Martin Price, *To the Palace of*

Wisdom (Garden City, N.Y.: Doubleday, 1964), and Aubrey L. Williams, *Pope's "Dunciad"* (Baton Rouge: Lousiana State University Press, 1955); Glenn W. Hatfield, *Henry Fielding and the Language of Irony* (Chicago: University of Chicago Press, 1968); Terry Castle, *Clarissa's Ciphers* (Ithaca, N.Y.: Cornell University Press, 1982); John Traugott, *Tristram Shandy's World: Sterne's Philosophical Rhetoric* (Berkeley and Los Angeles: University of California Press, 1954), and Max Byrd, *Tristram Shandy* (London: Allen and Unwin, 1985).

58. Gordon S. Wood, "Conspiracy and the Paranoid Style: Causality and Deceit in the Eighteenth Century," *William and Mary Quarterly*, 3d ser., 39 (1982), p. 407. On the connections between Lockean epistemology and the fear of deceptive words and appearances in eighteenth-century literature and politics, see also Fliegelman, *Prodigals and Pilgrims*. For a study of how the vision of Augustan satirists informed the political vision of early republican statesmen and writers, see Kerber, *Federalists in Dissent*, and Robert Dawidoff, *The Education of John Randolph* (New York: Norton, 1979).

59. Peter Gay, *The Enlightenment: An Interpretation*, 2 vols. (New York: Knopf, 1966–9), I, 152.

60. Thomas Gordon, *Sallust*, p. 45. In this text Gordon also comments on Thucydides' *History* and provides what he calls a "summary account" of the "Civil Feuds and Outrages" that happened at Corcyra (pp. 156–8).

61. John Trenchard and Thomas Gordon, *Cato's Letters*, 4 vols. in 2 (New York: Russell and Russell, 1969), IV, 221. Subsequent page references in these volumes are given parenthetically.

62. Gordon, *Sallust*, excerpted in *The Classick Pages*, ed. Meyer Reinhold (University Park, Pa.: American Philological Association, 1975), pp. 103–4.

63. Trenchard and Gordon collaborated on another series of essays, *The Independent Whig* (London, 1721). The first number in that series, dated January 20, 1720, contains a similar argument about the power of words: "The majority of Mankind have always worshipped the Idols of Words and Sounds; and a Monosyllable has often done more than an Army, towards keeping them under Awe and Servitude. . . . This blindful Devotion to Names, so inconsistent with true Liberty, which shews itself in *Judging* as well as *Acting*, has also prevailed in this free Nation to a shameful and dangerous Degree. We know what terrible Lengths the words *Church*, *Clergy*, *Divine Right*, and the like undefined Nonsense, have gone towards enslaving us; and what a steady and ridiculous Reverence is still paid to them, even they are evidently apply'd to the most impious and tyrannical purposes. . . . Credulity and implicit Belief are equally as dangerous in Government as in Religion: They have made the World Slaves, and they keep it so. Every Party has its Pope" (pp. 6–7).

64. Bernard Mandeville, *The Fable of the Bees; or, Private Vices, Publick Benefits*, ed. F. B. Kaye, Vol. II (Oxford: Clarendon Press, 1924), p. 289.

65. Ben Jonson, *Timber; or, Discoveries*, in Bolton, *The English Language*, pp. 38–40.

66. John Barrell, *English Literature in History, 1730–80: An Equal, Wide Survey* (New York: St. Martin's, 1983), p. 113.

67. Ibid., p. 118.

68. Quoted in ibid., p. 132.

69. Lord Chesterfield, letter to the *World*, November 28, 1754, repr. in Susie I. Tucker, *English Examined* (Cambridge: Cambridge University Press, 1961), pp. 90–1.

70. Quoted in ibid., p. 89.

71. Scott Elledge, "The Naked Science of Language, 1747–1786," in *Studies in Criticism and Aesthetics: Essays in Honor of Samuel Holt Monk*, ed. Howard Anderson and John S. Shea (Minneapolis: University of Minnesota Press, 1967), pp. 266–95.

72. Barrell, *English Literature in History*, p. 128.

73. C. H. Knoblauch, "Coherence Betrayed: Samuel Johnson and the 'Prose of the World,'" *boundary 2*, 7 (1979), p. 256.

74. Joseph Priestley, *A Course of Lectures on the Theory of Language and Universal Grammar* (Menston: Scolar, 1970), pp. 168–9. Subsequent references to this volume are given parenthetically.

75. Joseph Priestley, *The Rudiments of English Grammar; Adapted to the Use of Schools with Observations on Style* (London, 1761), p. vii.

76. Ibid., p. vi.

77. Ibid., pp. vi–vii.

78. Oliver Goldsmith, "The Deserted Village," in *Collected Works of Oliver Goldsmith*, 5 vols. (Oxford: Clarendon Press, 1966), IV, 287–304.

79. Goldsmith, *Works*, I, 447.

80. William Warburton, *The Divine Legation of Moses*, 2 vols. (1741), II, 147.

81. W. Jackson Bate, *The Burden of the Past and the English Poet* (Cambridge: Harvard University Press, 1970), chap. 4.

82. Thomas Blackwell, *Enquiry into the Life and Writings of Homer* (London, 1735), pp. 58–9.

83. Robert Wood, *An Essay on the Original Genius and Writings of Homer* (1769) (London, 1824), p. 172.

84. For development of this argument, see Cohen, *Sensible Words*, pp. 125–7, and James H. Stam, *Inquiries into the Origin of Language* (New York: Harper and Row, 1976), chap. 3.

85. Johann Herder, "Essay on the Origin of Language," in *On the Origin of Language*, trans. John H. Moran and Alexander Gode (New York: Ungar, 1967), pp. 88, 91, 149. For a study of Herder's essay in the context of Enlightenment linguistic theory in Germany (and other European countries), see Stam, *Inquiries into the Origin of Language*, Part II.

86. Jean-Jacques Rousseau, "Essay on the Origin of Language," in *On the Origin of Language*, p. 11. For a study of Rousseau's work in the context of French linguistic theory in the eighteenth century, see Pierre Juliard, *Philosophies of Language in Eighteenth-Century France* (The Hague: Mouton, 1970).

87. Percy Bysshe Shelley, "Prometheus Unbound," lines 415–17, in *Selected Poetry and Prose* (New York: Random House, 1951), p. 125. For a study of the politics of language in the poetry and poetic theory of Wordsworth and other Romantic poets, see Olivia Smith, *The Politics of Language, 1791–*

1819 (Oxford: Oxford University Press, 1984), chap. 6, and Linda Dowling, *Language and Decadence in the Victorian Fin de Siècle* (Princeton, N.J.: Princeton University Press, 1986).

88. E. J. Hundert, "The Thread of Language and the Web of Dominion: Mandeville to Rousseau and Back," *Eighteenth-Century Studies*, 21 (1987–8), p. 188.

89. William Wirt, *Letters of the British Spy* (1803; repr. Chapel Hill: University of North Carolina Press, 1970), pp. 133–4.

90. Ibid., pp. 144, 146.

91. For studies of the British elocutionary movement and Sheridan's central role in it, see Wilbur Samuel Howell, *Eighteenth-Century British Logic and Rhetoric* (Princeton, N.J.: Princeton University Press, 1971), chap. 4, and G. P. Mohrmann, "The Language of Nature and Elocutionary Theory," *Quarterly Journal of Speech*, 52 (1966), pp. 116–24.

92. Thomas Sheridan, *British Education . . .* (London, 1756).

93. Thomas Sheridan, *A Rhetorical Grammar of the English Language* (Dublin, 1781), p. 163.

94. Thomas Sheridan, *A Discourse Being Introductory to His Course of Lectures on Elocution and the English Language* (London, 1759; repr. Los Angeles: Clark Memorial Library, 1969), pp. 5–6.

95. Thomas Sheridan, *A Course of Lectures on Elocution* (London, 1762; repr. New York: Benjamin Bloom, 1968), p. 206. Subsequent references to this volume are given parenthetically. This text appeared in the Harvard Library catalogue of 1765, and in 1767 it was withdrawn three times (which was more often than any other rhetorical text).

96. Between 1785 and 1827 nine rhetoric texts following the elocutionary patterns were published in America. For information on the importance of the elocutionary movement in America, see Ota Thomas, "The Teaching of Rhetoric in the United States During the Classical Period of Education," in *A History and Criticism of American Public Address*, ed. William Norwood Brigance (New York: McGraw-Hill, 1943), and Marie Hockmuth and Richard Murphy, "Rhetorical Education and Elocutionary Training in Nineteenth-Century Colleges," in *History of Speech Education in America*, ed. Karl R. Wallace (New York: Appleton-Century-Crofts, 1954), pp. 153–77.

97. Jay Fliegelman develops this argument in the unpublished "Jefferson and the Oratorical Ideal: Natural Language and Theatricality in Revolutionary Rhetoric" (which will appear in a much-revised form in Fliegelman's forthcoming book *Declaring Independence: Jefferson, Natural Language, and Cultural Performance* [Stanford University Press]). This essay revealed to me the significance of the elocutionary movement for an understanding of the practice and theory of rhetoric in the American Revolution, and I thank Professor Fliegelman for sharing it with me. He also treats the elocutionary movement in the context of his commentary on *Wieland*. See "Introduction," *Wieland*.

98. James Fenimore Cooper, *The Last of the Mohicans* (Albany: State University of New York Press, 1983), pp. 199–200, 324, 343–7.

Chapter 7. The Language of Revolution: Combating Misrepresentation with the Pen and Tongue

1. Oliver Wendell Holmes, *The Professor at the Breakfast-Table* (Boston: Houghton Mifflin, 1892), pp. 41–2.
2. Karl Marx, *The Eighteenth Brumaire of Louis Bonaparte* (New York: International Publishers, 1972), p. 15.
3. Ibid., pp. 5–6.
4. Whitman, *American Primer*, Foreword, n.p.
5. *Correspondence Between John Adams and Mercy Warren*, ed. Charles F. Adams (New York: Arno, 1972), p. 355.
6. *Adams: His Political Writings*, ed. George Peck, Jr. (Indianapolis: Bobbs-Merrill, 1954), p. 20.
7. For the argument, which I am drawing upon here, that classical political discourse was toppled during the construction of the United States, see Wood, *Creation of the American Republic*, chap. 15.
8. Gordon S. Wood, *Representation in the American Revolution* (Charlottesville: University Press of Virginia, 1969), p. 1.
9. Ibid.
10. Daniel Dulany, *Consideration on the Propriety of Imposing Taxes . . .*, in *Pamphlets of the American Revolution*, ed. Bernard Bailyn (Cambridge, Mass.: Belknap Press, 1965), p. 611. Subsequent references to this volume (abbreviated *PAR*) are given parenthetically.
11. Tony Tanner, *Adultery in the Novel* (Baltimore: Johns Hopkins University Press, 1979), p. 65.
12. For more on the philosophes' concept of ideology, see H. B. Acton, "The Philosophy of Language in Revolutionary France," *Proceedings of the British Academy*, 45 (1959), pp. 199–219.
13. Wood, *Creation of the American Republic*, p. 5.
14. Fliegelman, *Prodigals and Pilgrims*, p. 106.
15. Quoted in *PAR*, p. 209.
16. See Fliegelman, *Prodigals and Pilgrims*, chap. 1.
17. For Algernon Sidney's critique of titles and false naming, see *Discourses Concerning Government* (Indianapolis: Liberty Classics, 1990), chap. 1, sect. III, and chap. 3, sect. XII.
18. Cited in Michael P. Kramer, "Jonathan Mayhew," in *Dictionary of Literary Biography*, Vol. XXXI, *American Colonial Writers, 1735–1781*, ed. Emory Elliott (Detroit: Gale Research, 1985), p. 161.
19. Quoted in Wood, *Creation of the American Republic*, p. 290.
20. George Washington, "The Time of . . . Political Probation" (June 8, 1783), in *Colonies to Nation: 1763–1789*, ed. Jack P. Greene (New York: McGraw-Hill, 1967), pp. 483–9.
21. Peter Oliver, *Origin & Progress of the American Rebellion*, ed. Douglass Adair

and John Schutz (Stanford, Calif.: Stanford University Press, 1967), pp. 39–41. Page references to this volume are given parenthetically.

22. *The Writings of Samuel Adams*, ed. Harry Alonzo Cushing, 4 vols. (New York: Putnam, 1904–8), I, 240. Subsequent page references in these volumes (abbreviated SAW) are given parenthetically.

23. *The Poems of Alexander Pope*, ed. John Butt (New Haven, Conn.: Yale University Press, 1963), p. 775.

24. Cited in Bailyn, *Ideological Origins of the American Revolution*, p. 153.

25. For a discussion of the role of conversation and raillery as an antidote for linguistic dogmatism and political tyranny in eighteenth-century literature, see Peter M. Briggs, "Locke's *Essay* and the Strategies of Eighteenth-Century English Satire," *Studies in Eighteenth-Century Culture*, ed. Harry C. Payne (Madison: University of Wisconsin Press, 1981), X, 135–51; and Price, *To the Palace of Wisdom*, chap. 3.

26. In *Great Issues in American History*, Vol. I, *1765–1865*, ed. Richard Hofstadter (New York: Random House, 1958), p. 4.

27. Fliegelman, *Prodigals and Pilgrims*, p. 102.

28. Ibid.

29. For Franklin's protests against British misrepresentation and verbal abuse of the colonists as "Rebels, Knaves, Fools, Traitors, &c. &c.," see *Benjamin Franklin's Letters to the Press, 1758–1775*, ed. Verner W. Crane, pp. 214, 81–2, 216, 223–34.

30. Edmund S. Morgan and Helen M. Morgan, *The Stamp Act Crisis* (New York: Collier, 1962), p. 99.

31. Rowland Jones, *The Circles of Gomer* (London, 1771), pp. 43–4.

32. Soame Jenyns, *The Objections to the Taxation of Our American Colonies by the Legislature of Great Britain, Briefly Consider'd*, in *Sources and Documents Illustrating the American Revolution*, ed. Samuel Eliot Morison (New York: Oxford University Press, 1965), p. 18. Subsequent references to the pamphlet are given parenthetically.

33. Morgan and Morgan, *Stamp Act Crisis*, p. 352.

34. *The Writings of Benjamin Franklin*, ed. Albert Henry Smyth, 10 vols. (New York: Macmillan, 1905–7), IV, 413.

35. Pauline Maier, *From Resistance to Revolution* (New York: Random House, 1972), p. 148.

36. Quoted in ibid.

37. Quoted in *Colonies to Nation*, p. 151.

38. Pierre Marambaud, "Dickinson's Letters from a Farmer in Pennsylvania as Political Discourse: Ideology, Imagery, and Rhetoric," *Early American Literature*, 12 (1977), p. 65.

39. David Ramsay, *The History of the American Revolution* (1789), 2 vols. (New York: Russell and Russell, 1968), II, 319. Subsequent references to this volume (abbreviated DRH) are given parenthetically.

40. *The Writings of John Dickinson*, ed. Paul Leicester Ford (Philadelphia: Historical Society of Pennsylvania, 1895), p. 324. Subsequent page references are given parenthetically.

41. Locke, *Two Treatises of Government*, p. 463. Dickinson was also one of the coauthors of the "Centinel" pieces, which were written and published in 1768 in the *Pennsylvania Journal and Weekly Advertiser* to oppose a movement supported by Dr. Chandler to introduce an Anglican bishopric in the Colonies. The authors frequently protest the cant of Dr. Chandler, and in a passage that resembles Dickinson's warning in the *Letters from a Farmer in Pennsylvania* they assert: "The Doctor cannot have read so little either of Civil or Ecclesiastical History, or be so very little acquainted with Mankind as not to know the Magic of Words, and the blind Devotion to Names and Sounds. . . . terrible confusions and animosities have been raised in other Countries by the Words Church, Clergy, Divine Right, Uninterrupted Succession, Indelible Character and such like undefined Nonsense; we hope the like Game will never be played in America" (*The Centinel*, ed. Elizabeth I. Nybakken [Newark: University of Delaware Press, 1980], pp. 86-7).

42. James Wilson, "Vindication of the Colonies," in *American Eloquence*, ed. Frank Moore, 2 vols. (New York: D. Appleton, 1857), I, 68-9. Subsequent page references in these volumes are given parenthetically.

43. Fliegelman, *Prodigals and Pilgrims*, p. 83.

44. See Castle, *Clarissa's Ciphers*, pp. 22-4, 69-72, 96.

45. Ibid., p. 26.

46. Samuel Richardson, *Clarissa*, 8 vols. (Oxford: Blackwell Publisher, 1943), I, 110.

47. Thomas Hutchinson, *The History of the Colony and Province of Massachusetts-Bay* (Cambridge: Harvard University Press, 1936), p. 234.

48. Jonathan Boucher, *A View of the Causes and Consequences of the American Revolution in Thirteen Discourses, Preached in North America Between the Years 1763 and 1775; with an Historical Preface* (London, 1797; rept. New York: Russell and Russell, 1967), p. vi.

49. Ibid., pp. xix–xx.

50. Jonathan Boucher, *Reminiscences of an American Loyalist, 1738–1789* (Boston, 1925), p. 61. Subsequent references to this work are given parenthetically.

51. Boucher, *View of the Causes and Consequences of the American Revolution*, p. viii.

52. John Drinker, *Some Further Observations, &c.* (1774), p. 13.

53. Ibid., pp. 22, 18–19.

54. In *Colonies to Nation*, p. 266.

55. Jonathan Swift, *Gulliver's Travels and Other Writings*, ed. Ricardo Quintana (New York: Random House, 1958), p. 406.

56. In *Colonies to Nation*, p. 267.

57. Samuel Seabury, *Letters of a Westchester Farmer*, ed. Clarence H. Vance, Publications of the Westchester Historical Society, Vol. VIII (White Plains, N.Y.: The Society, 1930), p. 71. Subsequent references to this volume are given parenthetically. For a profile of Seabury which includes a moving account of his subjection to mob anger and a glowing tribute to

his style, see Moses Coit Tyler, *The Literary History of the American Revolution, 1763–1783*, 2 vols. (New York: Barnes and Noble, 1941; repr. of 1897 ed.), I, 334–55.

58. Quoted in Ross Harrison, *Bentham* (London: Routledge and Kegan Paul, 1983), p. 52. On Locke's influence on Bentham and his linguistic philosophy, see chap. 3 of Harrison's study and Douglas G. Long, *Bentham on Liberty* (Toronto: University of Toronto Press, 1977), chaps. 2 and 4.

59. Bentham Manuscripts, Library of University College, London (UCL, Box 69, p. 53), quoted in Long, *Bentham on Liberty*, p. 235.

60. John Horne Tooke, *The Diversions of Purley* (London, 1786), p. 75. John Adams quotes this passage in a letter he sent in 1814 to John Taylor of Caroline. He adds, "This wise saying of my learned friend [Tooke], is no more than every attentive, thinking, and reflecting mind sees, feels, and laments every day" (JAW, IX, 465).

61. Jeremy Bentham, "A Critical Declaration of the Declaration of Rights," in *Bentham's Political Thought*, ed. Bhiku Parekh (New York: Harper and Row, 1973), p. 269. Subsequent references to this volume are given parenthetically.

62. John Lind, "An Answer to the Declaration" (1776), in *A Casebook on the Declaration of Independence*, ed. Robert Ginsberg (New York: Crowell, 1967), p. 10. Bentham's contribution to this pamphlet can be studied by comparing Lind's pamphlet with the letter Bentham drafted to Lind, which is contained in *The Correspondence of Jeremy Bentham*, ed. Timothy L. S. Sprigge, Vol. I (London: Athlone, 1968), pp. 341–4.

63. My comments here rely on James Streintrager's study, *Bentham* (Ithaca, N.Y.: Cornell University Press, 1977), chap. 1. I thank Jay Fliegelman for directing my attention to Bentham's project to settle the "American dispute" by defining words.

64. Streintrager, *Bentham*, p. 26.

65. Manuscripts, UCL, Box 69, p. 62, quoted in Long, *Bentham on Liberty*, p. 60.

66. This phrase is quoted in Rodgers, *Contested Truths*, p. 21. In chap. 2 Rodgers discusses Bentham's political philosophy, his effort to demystify the language of politics, and his reception in America.

67. Kenneth Burke, *Permanence and Change* (New York: New Republic, 1935), p. 191.

68. Bentham's famous study of logical and rhetorical "fallacies," which existed in outline in 1806, was printed in 1816 under the title *Traites des sophismes politiques*.

69. Quoted in Streintrager, *Bentham*, p. 26.

70. Jeremy Bentham, *A Fragment on Government*, ed. F. C. Montague (Oxford: Clarendon Press, 1891), pp. 240–1.

71. Ibid., pp. 160, 93.

72. Heimert, *Religion and the American Mind*, pp. 21, viii.

73. Quoted in ibid., p. 21.

74. Emory Elliott, "The Puritan Roots of American Whig Rhetoric," in

Puritan Influences in American Literature, ed. Emory Elliott (Urbana: University of Illinois Press, 1979), p. 109; Bercovitch, *The American Jeremiad*, chap. 4; Donald Weber, *Rhetoric and History in Revolutionary New England* (New York: Oxford University Press, 1988). See also Harry S. Stout, Jr., *The New England Soul: Preaching and Religious Culture in Colonial New England* (New York: Oxford University Press, 1986), and Ruth H. Bloch, *Visionary Republic: Millennial Themes in American Thought, 1756-1800* (Cambridge: Cambridge University Press, 1985).

75. Elliott, "The Puritan Roots of American Whig Rhetoric," p. 113.
76. Kenneth Burke, "In Vague Praise of Liberty," *Hound and Horn*, 7 (1933-4), pp. 704-7.
77. Simeon Howard, "A Sermon Preached to the Ancient and Honorable Artillery Company in Boston" (1773), in *American Political Writing During the Founding Era, 1760-1805*, ed. Charles Hyneman and Donald S. Lutz, 2 vols. (Indianapolis: Liberty Press, 1983), pp. 195-208.
78. Levi Hart, "Liberty Described and Recommended: In a Sermon Preached to the Corporation of Freemen in Farmington" (1775), in *American Political Writing*, pp. 305-17.
79. Weber, *Rhetoric and History*, p. 13.
80. Ibid., pp. 63-4. On the political and religious dimensions of the rhetoric of liberty, see also Bloch, *Visionary Republic*, and Stout, *The New England Soul*.
81. John Tucker, "An Election Sermon" (1771), in *American Political Writing*, p. 172.
82. Simeon Howard, in *American Political Writing*, p. 204.
83. Gad Hitchcock, "An Election Sermon" (1774), in *American Political Writing*, pp. 294, 297, 304.
84. Heimert, *Religion and the American Mind*, p. 18.
85. Weber, *Rhetoric and History*, p. 151.
86. Heimert, *Religion and the American Mind*, pp. 20, 19.
87. Tyler, *Literary History of the American Revolution*, I, 9; Harry S. Stout, Jr., "Religion, Communication, and the American Revolution," *William and Mary Quarterly*, 3d ser., 34 (1977), pp. 519-41; Rhys Isaac, *The Transformation of Virginia, 1740-1790* (Chapel Hill: University of North Carolina Press, 1982), pp. 121-4, 243-69.
88. Quoted in Derrida, *Of Grammatology*, p. 244.
89. Miller, *Errand into the Wilderness*, p. 179.
90. Heimert, *Religion and the American Mind*, p. 18.
91. Derrida, *Of Grammatology*, p. 177.
92. Ibid.
93. Edmund Burke, *An Enquiry into the Origin of Our Ideas of the Sublime and Beautiful* (Notre Dame, Ind.: University of Notre Dame Press, 1968), p. 175. Subsequent references to this edition are given parenthetically.
94. On seduction, politics, and the novel, see Fliegelman, *Prodigals and Pilgrims*, and Cathy N. Davidson, *Revolution and the Word: The Rise of the Novel in America* (New York: Oxford University Press, 1986).

95. William Wirt, *Sketches of the Life and Character of Patrick Henry* (Philadelphia: Thomas, Cowperthwait and Co., 1841), p. 125. Subsequent references to this edition are given parenthetically.

96. Edmund Randolph in his *History of Virginia*, ed. Arthur H. Shaffer (Charlottesville: University Press of Virginia, 1970), makes a similar distinction between other Virginia orators and Henry: "In others rhetorical artifice and unmeaning expletives have been often employed as scouts to seize the wandering attention of the audience; in him the absence of trick constituted the triumph of nature" (p. 180).

97. Randolph similarly notes contempt for Henry's nonstandard style. See *History of Virginia*, p. 179.

98. Ibid., p. 179.

99. Ibid., p. 194; Isaac, *The Transformation of Virginia*, p. 268.

100. Joseph Warren, "Massacre Day Oration," in *The World Turned Upside Down*, ed. James H. Pickering (Port Washington, N.Y.: Kennikat Press, 1975). For a valuable discussion of the "highly rhetorical character" of the literature of the Revolution that treats Warren's oration in the context of developments in rhetorical strategy during the Revolutionary era, see Gordon S. Wood, "The Democratization of Mind in the American Revolution," in *Leadership in the American Revolution* (Washington, D.C.: Library of Congress, 1974). Barnet Baskerville also provides a helpful introduction to the oratory of the Revolutionary period in *The People's Voice* (Lexington: University Press of Kentucky, 1979), chap. 1.

101. Quoted in Baskerville, *The People's Voice*, p. 15.

102. Quoted in Peter Shaw, *The Character of John Adams* (Chapel Hill: University of North Carolina Press, 1976), p. 10.

103. *Correspondence Between John Adams and Mercy Warren*, p. 467.

104. *The Earliest Diary of John Adams*, pp. 66, 74. Subsequent references to this edition (abbreviated ED) are given parenthetically.

105. On the Ciceronian model for early-republic lawyers, see Robert A. Ferguson, *Law and Letters in American Culture* (Cambridge: Harvard University Press, 1984), pp. 20–1, 74–6. Ferguson also provides insightful commentary on the significance of oratory in post-Revolutionary American culture and politics; see esp. pp. 78–84.

106. Quoted in Shaw, *The Character of John Adams*, p. 98.

107. *The Spur of Fame: Dialogues of John Adams and Benjamin Rush, 1805–1813*, ed. John A. Schutz and Douglass Adair (San Marino, Calif.: Huntington Library, 1966), p. 43.

108. Ibid., pp. 59, 64.

109. Gordon E. Bigelow, *Rhetoric and American Poetry of the Early National Period*, University of Florida Press Monographs (Gainesville: 1960), p. 24. For additional information on rhetorical theory and practice in the colleges of colonial America, see the essays by Ota Thomas and Bower Aly and Grafton P. Tanquary in *A History and Criticism of American Public Address*, ed. William Norwood Brigance (New York: McGraw-Hill, 1943), Vol. I.

110. Bigelow, *Rhetoric and American Poetry*, p. 24.

111. Quoted in Albert Frank Gegenheimer, *William Smith: Educator and Churchman* (Philadelphia: University of Pennsylvania Press, 1943), pp. 60–1.

112. Boucher, *Reminiscences of an American Loyalist*, pp. 101–2.

113. For more information on changes in the colonial colleges that produced a greater emphasis on rhetoric, see Kenneth Silverman, *A Cultural History of the American Revolution* (New York: Crowell, 1976), pp. 55–7, 217–20, and Lawrence Cremin, *American Education: The Colonial Experience, 1607–1783* (New York: Harper and Row, 1970), chap. 15.

114. *Benjamin Franklin: Representative Selections*, ed. Charles E. Jorgensen and Frank Luther Mott (New York: Hill and Wang, 1962), p. 203.

115. Benjamin Rush, "Thoughts upon the Mode of Education Proper in a Republic," excerpted in *Colonies to Nation*, p. 403.

116. Boucher, *A View of the Causes of the American Revolution*, pp. 320–1.

117. Carlyle, *Heroes and Hero-Worship*, p. 164.

118. Bernard Bailyn, "The Most Uncommon Pamphlet of the Revolution: *Common Sense*," *American Heritage*, 25 (1973), p. 36.

119. On Paine and *Common Sense*, see esp. Eric Foner, *Tom Paine and Revolutionary America* (New York: Oxford University Press, 1976), chap. 3.

120. Rousseau, quoted in Derrida, *Of Grammatology*, p. 168.

121. Quoted in Bailyn, "The Most Uncommon Pamphlet," p. 39.

122. See Fliegelman, *Prodigals and Pilgrims*, and Burrows and Wallace, "The American Revolution: The Ideology and Psychology of National Liberation."

123. Henry Fielding, *Jonathan Wild* (New York: New American Library, 1961), p. 168.

124. For another version of this argument, see Wood, "The Democratization of Mind."

125. *Adams Family Correspondence*, I, 352, 363.

126. Randolph, *History of Virginia*, pp. 233–4.

127. Fliegelman, *Prodigals and Pilgrims*, pp. 230–67.

128. Laurence Sterne, *The Life and Opinions of Tristram Shandy, Gentleman*, ed. Melvyn New, Richard Davies, and W. G. Day, Vol. I (Gainesville: University Presses of Florida, 1978), p. 432. Subsequent page references are given parenthetically. For a valuable study of Sterne, see Byrd, *Tristram Shandy*. For many critics, Byrd writes, Sterne's "great moral point" is that "by our hearts (and gestures) alone do we free ourselves from the prison of language and establish true community" (p. 117). Jefferson, I believe, could be included among this group of critics.

129. See Wills, *Inventing America*, chap. 20, for a discussion of Jefferson's high appreciation of Sterne, and Parts III and IV of the book for the argument that the Declaration is a sentimental and moral (as well as scientific) paper addressed to the heart and the head.

130. Langston Hughes, "In Explanation of Our Times," *Selected Poems of Langston Hughes* (New York: Random House, 1974), pp. 281–3.

131. Richard Wright, *12 Million Black Voices* (New York: Viking, 1940), p. 40.
132. What Warner Berthoff has described as the "first *gran rifuto* in American letters" and what we might also describe as the first Hemingway-like or Twain-like or Lincoln-like turn from an artificial, overblown, declamatory rhetoric to a deflated, colloquial style occurred, in Berthoff's words, "several years in advance of the settlement of New England; it was the decision by John Cotton . . . not to continue preaching in the erudite and 'oratorious' manner which, according to his first biographer, had made him locally famous as 'another Xenophon, or Musa Attica'" ("Continuity in Discontinuity: Literature in the American Situation," in *American Literature*, ed. Boris Ford [Harmondsworth: Penguin, 1988], p. 660).
133. Wills, *Inventing America*, p. 47.
134. Quoted in Wood, *Creation of the American Republic*, p. 61.
135. Patrick Henry's famous cry of defiance (as reported by Wirt) – "I know not what course others may take; but as for me, give me liberty, or give me death" – can be read as a startling violation of republican grammar because of his willingness to stand apart from a consensus and brave an independent course.
136. For a further development of the argument regarding the consensual rhetorical strategy of the Declaration (and other literature of the founding era), see Robert A. Ferguson's fine essay "'We Hold These Truths': Strategies of Control in the Literature of the Founders," in *Reconstructing American Literature*, ed. Sacvan Bercovitch (Cambridge: Harvard University Press, 1985), pp. 1–28.
137. Anthony Ashley Cooper, Earl of Shaftesbury, *Characteristics of Men, Manners, Opinions, Times*, ed. John M. Roberston, 2 vols. in 1 (Indianapolis, Ind.: Bobbs-Merrill, 1964), I, 282. Subsequent references are given parenthetically.
138. John Diggins maintains in *The Lost Soul of American Politics* that neither the "classical nor the Scottish idea of virtue had any basis" in Paine's *Common Sense* and Jefferson's Declaration (p. 20). But Shaftesbury's (and the Scottish) sense of virtue, like Jefferson's concept of the moral sense and Paine's notion of our "unextinguishable feelings for good and wise purposes," links together the values of happiness, correspondence, kindness, and community. For a concise presentation of Shaftesbury's concept of virtue, see *Characteristics*, I, 388.
139. Barber develops the fundamental importance of strong affective talk in politics in *Strong Democracy*, pp. 173–98.
140. Anthologized in James C. Gaston, *London Poets and the American Revolution* (Troy, N.Y.: Whitson, 1979), p. 75.
141. Quoted in Janice Potter, *The Liberty We Seek: Loyalist Ideology in Colonial New York and Massachusetts* (Cambridge: Harvard University Press, 1983), p. 150.
142. Tyler, *Literary History of the American Revolution*, I, 521. For analysis of the literary character of the Declaration, see also Kenneth Silverman's

poetic reading of it in *A Cultural History of the American Revolution*, pp. 318–19; James Boyd White's nuanced interpretation of its tone and rhetorical strategies in *When Words Lose Their Meaning*; Carl L. Becker's commentary on Jefferson's revisions and his felicity of expression in *The Declaration of Independence: A Study in the History of Political Ideas* (New York: Knopf, 1942), pp. 194–223; and Robert Ginsberg, "The Declaration as Rhetoric," in *A Casebook on the Declaration of Independence*, pp. 219–44.

143. Neither *The Norton Anthology of American Literature* nor *The Harper American Literature* includes Jefferson's commentary on slavery in the section "Manners" in *Notes on the State of Virginia*. An essay in the *Columbia Literary History of the United States*, ed. Emory Elliott (New York: Columbia University Press, 1988), describes Jefferson's passage on slavery deleted from the final version of the Declaration as a "stirring" passage charging the king "with responsibility for the slave trade," but it never mentions Jefferson's charge that the king is stirring up the slaves to revolt (p. 145). These resources for students of American literature could present a less edited account of Jefferson's views on slavery. Conversely, *The Heath Anthology* accepts, without qualification, the claim that Jefferson was the father of children by a slave woman, Sally Hemmings, a claim that historians by and large have not accepted as fact.

144. Abraham Lincoln, *The Illinois Political Campaign: A Facsimile of the Printer's Copy of His Debates with Senator Stephen Arnold Douglas as Edited and Prepared for Press by Abraham Lincoln* (Washington, D.C.: Library of Congress, 1958), pp. 45–6. For a compilation of sequels to the Declaration that reveals how the text has served as a stencil for the declaration of rights by labor groups, farmers, women's rights advocates, socialists, and blacks, see *We, the Other People*, ed. Philip S. Foner (Urbana: University of Illinois Press, 1976).

145. Ellison, *Invisible Man*, p. 561.

146. Hughes, "Freedom's Plow," *Selected Poems*, pp. 291–7.

147. For Jefferson's schemes for improving study of the English language, see *Thoughts on English Prosody* and *An Essay on the Anglo-Saxon Language* (TJW, XVIII, 365–411, 415–57).

148. On Jefferson's complex pastoral vision, see Leo Marx, *The Machine in the Garden* (New York: Oxford University Press, 1964), chap. 3.

149. M. M. Mahood, *Shakespeare's Wordplay* (London: Methuen, 1957), p. 73.

150. The process by which a newly exalted vox populi is divested of a measure of its power by subordinating its rule to representative institutions and the grammar of a written constitution is a subsequent act in the drama of the word against the word, and it will be discussed in Chapter 8. For the importance of print culture in promoting the sovereignty of the written over the vox populi and for creating an autonomous realm of readers – or citizens – linked in union by print, see Warner, *The Letters of the Republic*.

Chapter 8. The Grammar of Politics: The Constitution

1. Alexander Hamilton, *A Letter from Phocion to the Considerate Citizens of New-York on the Politics of the Times in Consequence of the Peace* (New York: Samuel Loudon, 1784), p. 8.

2. *Correspondence and Public Papers of John Jay*, ed. Henry P. Johnston, 4 vols. (New York: Putnam, 1890–3), I, 217.

3. *The Complete Anti-Federalist*, ed. Herbert J. Storing, 7 vols. (Chicago: University of Chicago Press, 1981), VI, 229. Subsequent references to these volumes (abbreviated CAF) are given parenthetically.

4. David Humphreys, Joel Barlow, John Trumbull, and Dr. Lemuel Hopkins, *The Anarchiad*, ed. Luther G. Riggs (Gainesville, Fla.: Scholars' Facsimiles and Reprints, 1967), pp. 6–7.

5. Ibid., p. 61.

6. Wood, *Creation of the American Republic*, chap. 12.

7. Condillac, quoted in Aarsleff, *From Locke to Saussure*, p. 150.

8. Antoine Lavoisier, *Méthode de nomenclature chimique* (Paris, 1787), p. 12.

9. William F. Harris II, "Bonding Word and Polity: The Logic of American Constitutionalism" *American Political Science Review*, 76 (1982), pp. 34–45.

10. Edwin Meese, quoted in "Meese Again Attacks Judicial Activism," *Los Angeles Times*, November 16, 1985, Part I, p. 4.

11. Quoted in Kammen, *A Machine That Would Go of Itself*, p. 43.

12. *Authenticated Copy of the Last Will and Testament of George Washington of Mt. Vernon. . . .* (Washington, D.C.: A. Jackson, 1863), p. 28.

13. Quoted in *The States Rights Debate*, ed. Alpheus Thomas Mason (New York: Oxford University Press, 1972), p. 107.

14. *The Debates in the Several State Conventions on the Adoption of the Federal Constitution*, ed. Jonathan Elliot, 5 vols. (Philadelphia: Lippincott, 1936), IV, 185. Subsequent references to these volumes (abbreviated DSC) are given parenthetically.

15. Leonary Levy, *Constitutional Opinions: Aspects of the Bill of Rights* (New York: Oxford University Press, 1986), p. 232. Laurence H. Tribe similarly contends that "the Constitution is an intentionally incomplete, often deliberately indeterminate structure for the participatory evolution of political ideals and governmental practices" (*American Constitutional Law* [Mineola, N.Y.: Foundation Press, 1988], p. vii).

16. Brennan, "The Constitution of the United States: Contemporary Ratification."

17. See Robert A. Ferguson, "Ideology and the Framing of the Constitution," *Early American Literature*, 22 (1987), esp. pp. 158–9.

18. For a detailed account of the convention's compromises on the slavery issue, see Paul Finkelman, "Slavery and the Constitutional Convention: Making a Convenant with Death," in *Beyond Confederation*, ed. Richard Beeman, Stephen Botein, and Edward C. Carter II (Chapel Hill: University of North Carolina Press, 1987), pp. 188–225. Madison indicates in *Notes* that he preferred a euphemism for slavery in the Constitution because he "thought it wrong to admit in the Constitution the idea that

there could be property in men" (p. 534). On the cultural consequences of the founders' political acceptance and linguistic cover-up of slavery, see Ralph Ellison, "Perspective of Literature," *Going to the Territory*, pp. 321–38.

19. William Manning, *The Key of Libberty* (Billerica, Mass.: Manning Association, 1922), p. 21.

20. Wood, *Creation of the American Republic*, p. 521.

21. Significantly, critics of the Constitution in the ratifying conventions often acknowledged their limitations as speakers. Embarrassed by their own verbal inadequacy or intimidated by the eloquence of the Constitution's supporters, these speakers suggest that in the war of words over the Constitution the Antifederalists could muster neither the firepower nor the mobilizing skills of the Federalists. See, for instance, DSC, II, 102, 159; IV, 336. For a commentary on the Antifederalist critique of the Federalists as in part an "outcry against literate civility," see Albert Furtwangler, *The Authority of Publius* (Ithaca, N.Y.: Cornell University Press, 1984), chap. 4.

22. For Publius's defense regarding the ambiguity of these clauses, see *Federalist*, Nos. 33 and 41.

23. Cecelia M. Kenyon, "Men of Little Faith: The Anti-Federalists on the Nature of Representative Government," *William and Mary Quarterly*, 3d ser., 12 (1955), pp. 3–43.

24. Manning, *The Key of Libberty*, p. 39.

25. I thank Professor Michael P. Kramer for sending me a copy of his essay "Why Does Language Matter to *The Federalist?*," delivered in 1987 at an international symposium on *The Federalist*. This essay explains why language mattered so much to Madison and why the philosophy of the Enlightenment matters so much to an understanding of the political concerns of the Federalists and Antifederalists. A version of this essay appears in Kramer, *Imagining Language*, chap. 4.

26. Garry Wills, *Explaining America: The Federalist* (New York: Doubleday, 1981), p. 54.

27. For an excellent treatment of Madison the elder statesman speaking out on issues of constitutional interpretation through his private correspondence, see Drew R. McCoy, *The Last of the Fathers: James Madison and the Republican Legacy* (Cambridge: Cambridge University Press, 1989), esp. chap. 4.

28. For a more comprehensive study of Madison's theories of interpretation, see H. Jefferson Powell, "The Original Understanding of Original Intent," *Harvard Law Review*, 98 (1985), pp. 935–43.

29. Harris, "Bonding Word and Polity," p. 34.

30. *Collected Poems of Herman Melville*, ed. Howard P. Vincent (Chicago: Packard, 1947), p. 411.

31. Wood, *Creation of the American Republic*, p. 562. For an early scathing critique of the Federalist persuasion that exposes through verbal criticism how the Federalists "ingeniously constructed" or substituted a "federal

dialect" for a "consolidating dialect" in order to accommodate their plan to the public, see Taylor, *New Views of the Constitution of the United States*, pp. 49–52, 61, 112, and passim. In this brief for states' rights, which opens with a long section on the "meaning of primary words," Taylor recapitulates the Antifederalist attack on the Constitution's ambiguity and argues that "a national dialect cannot be proper for construing the constitution, since a federal dialect was necessary to procure its ratification" (p. 50).

32. On the democratization of leadership, see Wood, "The Democratization of Mind."

33. For the importance of Hume to Madison as Publius, see Douglass Adair, "'That Politics May Be Reduced to a Science': David Hume, James Madison, and the Tenth Federalist," *Huntington Library Quarterly*, 20 (1957), pp. 343–60, and Wills, *Explaining America*.

34. See *Federalist*, Nos. 6, 9, 8, 14, 38, 43, 55, 63. See also Hamilton's comments at the New York ratifying convention, in DSC, II, 253–4.

35. *The Mind of the Founder*, p. 64.

36. Ibid., p. 62.

37. For Publius's counterrevolutionary distrust of the affections and of enthusiasm and his insistence that "it is the reason, alone, of the public, that ought to control and regulate the government" (FP, 49. 317), see Daniel W. Howe, "The Political Psychology of *The Federalist*," *William and Mary Quarterly*, 3d ser., 44 (1987), pp. 485–507.

38. Neil Postman, *Amusing Ourselves to Death: Public Discourse in the Age of Show Business* (New York: Penguin, 1985).

39. Howe, in "The Faculty Psychology of Publius," elaborates the importance of the analogy Plato developed between the psychological state of man and the political order for an understanding of Publius's republican remedies.

40. In *Explaining America*, chap. 28, Wills elaborates an analogy between Jefferson's plan for "universal" education delineated in *Notes on the State of Virginia* and Madison's theory of representation.

41. On deliberation and representation as remedies for the disease of faction, see Cass R. Sunstein, "Interest Groups in American Public Law," *Stanford Law Review*, 38 (1985), p. 29, and Wood, *Creation of the American Republic*, chap. 11.

42. For Madison on Lycurgus and the honor of state building, see *Federalist* No. 38. On "the state-centered language of power" as a paradigmatic discourse, see Kramnick, "'The Great National Discussion.'"

43. Paul W. Kahn, "Reason and Will in the Origins of American Constitutionalism," *Yale Law Journal*, 98 (1989), p. 468.

44. Powell, "The Original Understanding of Original Intent," pp. 913–21.

45. *John Marshall's Defense of McCulloch v. Maryland*, ed. Gerald Gunther (Stanford, Calif.: Stanford University Press, 1969), p. 33.

46. Ibid.

47. White, *When Words Lose Their Meaning*, p. 260.

48. *John Marshall's Defense of McCulloch v. Maryland*, p. 34. My discussion of

Marshall's decision is indebted to White's commentary on it in the last chapter of *When Words Lose Their Meaning*, pp. 247–63.

49. Walter Benn Michaels, "Against Formalism: Chicken and Rocks," in *Interpreting Law and Literature*, ed. Levinson and Mailloux, p. 224.

50. E. L. Doctorow, "The People's Text: A Citizen Reads the Constitution," *Nation*, 244 (1987), p. 216.

51. Laurence H. Tribe, "The Idea of the Constitution: A Metaphor-morphosis," *Journal of Legal Education*, 37 (1987), p. 173.

52. Richard Wright, "How 'Bigger' Was Born," *Native Son* (New York: Harper and Row, 1966), pp. xix, xviii.

53. Ibid., p. 386.

54. I have borrowed the phrase "visionary compacts" from Donald Pease, *Visionary Compacts* (Madison: University of Wisconsin Press, 1987), who stresses the importance of the search for a more perfect union in American Renaissance literature. Strangely, he makes little mention of the Constitution itself. In contrast, Kerry Larson, in *Whitman's Drama of Consensus*, finds in the Constitution a model for explicating Whitman's democratic aesthetic and his poetics of union: a poetic that seeks to foster "a great aggregate Nation" at the moment when a politics of compromise and consensus was collapsing.

Chapter 9. The Unsettled Language: Schoolmasters vs. Truants

1. For Madison's reflections on the problem of naming and defining the political system of the United States, see also JML, IV, 85, 209.

2. William Fowler, *English Language in Its Elements and Forms* (New York: Harper Bros., 1873), p. xii.

3. James Fenimore Cooper, *Homeward Bound* (New York: Putnam, 1896), p. 230.

4. Fowler, *English Language in Its Elements and Forms*, p. xii.

5. The history of these early calls for a national language and attempts to republicanize or reform the language in the aftermath of the Revolution have been much studied. Besides the books cited earlier by Baron, Simpson, and Cmiel, see Alan Walker Read, "American Projects for an Academy to Regulate Speech," *PMLA*, 51 (1936), pp. 1141–79, and Shirley Brice Heath, "A National Language Academy? Debate in the New Nation," *Linguistics*, 189 (1977), pp. 9–43.

6. J. Hector St. John de Crèvecoeur, *Letters from an American Farmer* (New York: Penguin, 1981), pp. 69–70.

7. William Whitney, *Language and the Study of Language*, in *Whitney on Language*, ed. Michael Silverstein (Cambridge: MIT Press, 1971), p. 51.

8. Melville, *Moby-Dick*, p. 332.

9. On the politics of language and representation in *Modern Chivalry*, see in particular Mark R. Patterson, *Authority, Autonomy, and Representation in American Literature, 1776–1865* (Princeton, N.J.: Princeton University Press, 1988), chap. 2, and Davidson, *Revolution and the Word*, chap. 7.

10. Wood, "Democratization of Mind." See also Wood's commentary on *Modern Chivalry* and its historical context in "Interests and Disinterested-

ness in the Making of the Constitution," in *Beyond Federation*, pp. 69–109. For a study of *Modern Chivalry* in relation to Brackenridge's career, see esp. Joseph J. Ellis, *After the Revolution: Profiles of Early American Culture* (New York: Norton, 1979), chap. 4.

11. Ferguson, *Law and Letters*, p. 128.

12. Noah Webster, *On Being American: Selected Writings, 1783–1828*, ed. Homer D. Babbidge, Jr. (New York: Praeger, 1967), pp. 25–6. Subsequent references to this volume (abbreviated NW) are given parenthetically.

13. Johann David Michaelis, *A Dissertation on the Influence of Opinions on Language and of Language on Opinions* (New York: AMS Press, 1973), p. 78.

14. Ibid.

15. Noah Webster, "A Dissertation Concerning the Influence of Language on Opinions and of Opinions on Language," *American Magazine*, May 1788, p. 389.

16. *The Collected Works of Dugald Stewart*, ed. Sir William Hamilton, 11 vols. (Edinburgh: Constable, 1854), IX, 423.

17. For an account of this procession and a fuller description of the seal, see Baron, *Grammar and Good Taste*, pp. 18–20.

18. Ellis, *After the Revolution*, pp. 202–4.

19. On Webster's concerns about the social and linguistic disorders, see also Richard M. Rollins, *The Long Journey of Noah Webster* (Philadelphia: University of Pennsylvania Press, 1980), chap. 8.

20. *National Gazette*, December 12, 1972, quoted in Regina Ann Markel Morantz, *"Democracy" and "Republic" in American Ideology, 1787–1840* (Ph.D. diss., Columbia University, 1971), p. 143.

21. Noah Webster, "The Revolution in France" (1794), in *Political Sermons of the American Founding Era*, ed. Ellis Sandoz (Indianapolis: Liberty Press, 1991), p. 1264. Subsequent references to this volume (abbreviated PS) are given parenthetically.

22. Friedrich Nietzsche, *The Will to Power*, trans. Walter Kaufman and R. J. Hollingdale (New York: Random House, 1968), p. 50.

23. Václav Havel, *Open Letters* (New York: Knopf, 1991), pp. 383–4.

24. Noah Webster, *Miscellaneous Papers, on Political and Commercial Subjects* (New York: E. Belden, 1802; repr. New York: Burt Franklin Research and Source Works, 1972), pp. 17–18. Subsequent page references in this volume (abbreviated MP) are given parenthetically.

25. *New England Palladium*, March 24, 1800, quoted in Morantz, *"Democracy" and "Republic,"* pp. 140–1.

26. Rufus King, "Words," quoted in Kerber, *Federalists in Dissent*, pp. 196–7. Kerber's study, which includes a discussion of Federalist responses to Webster's linguistic reforms, is a valuable guide to the relationship between political and literary concerns in this era.

27. Warren Dutton, *An Oration, Pronounced July 4, 1805* (Boston: A. Newell, 1805), pp. 7–8.

28. For an account of this conversion and its significance, see Rollins, *The Long Journey*, chap. 7.

29. Ellis, *After the Revolution*, p. 211.

30. Ibid., pp. 211–12.

31. "The Abuse of Words," pp. 58, 59.

32. *The Letters of Noah Webster*, ed. Harry M. Warfel (New York: Library Publishers, 1953), p. 459. Subsequent references to this volume (abbreviated NWL) are given parenthetically.

33. Noah Webster, *Observations on Language, and on the Errors of the Class-books: Addressed to the New York Lyceum* (New Haven, Conn.: Babcock, 1839), p. 31.

34. Edwin Percy Whipple, *American Literature, and Other Papers* (Boston: Ticknor and Co., 1887), p. 144.

35. Ibid., p. 210.

36. Ferguson, *Law and Letters*, p. 209. On the poetics and politics of Webster's oratory, see chap. 8, and Paul D. Erickson, *The Poetry of Events: Daniel Webster's Rhetoric of the Constitution and Union* (New York: New York University Press, 1986).

37. "The Union and the States," *North American Review*, p. 245.

38. That Webster was familiar with Locke's *Essay* is suggested by Rufus Choate when he points out in his eulogy of Webster that his mentor in law was "irresistibly and instinctively . . . attracted" to the "conduct of what Locke calls the human understanding; the limits of human knowledge; the means of coming to knowledge of different classes of truth" (Choate, *Works*, I, 500).

39. Horace Bushnell, *Reverses Needed* (Hartford, Conn.: L. E. Hunt, 1861), p. 9.

40. Bushnell, *God in Christ*, p. 62.

41. Richard Poirier, *The Performing Self* (New York: Oxford University Press, 1971), p. 4.

42. Quoted in Baron, *Grammar and Good Taste*, p. 14.

43. For more on the radical grammarians, see Cmiel, *Democratic Eloquence*, pp. 74–80.

44. Samuel Kirkham, *English Grammar in Familiar Lectures* (Rochester, N.Y.: Wm. Alling & Co. 1837), p. 15.

45. James Brown, *An American System of English Syntax* (Philadelphia: T. K. and P. G. Collins, 1838), p. xvi. Subsequent references to this volume are given parenthetically.

46. Samuel Gridley Howe, *Eighteenth Annual Report of the Trustees of the Perkins Institution and Massachusetts Asylum for the Blind* (Cambridge, Mass.: Metcalf and Co., 1850), p. 73. Subsequent references to this volume (abbreviated AR) are given parenthetically.

47. Beck, "Notes on Mr. Pickering's 'Vocabulary of Words and Phrases,'" p. 79.

48. James Fenimore Cooper, *The Spy: A Tale of the Neutral Ground* (New York: Putnam, 1896), p. 302.

49. On the development of Cooper's thought in relation to his political concerns, see esp. John P. McWilliams, *Political Justice in a Republic: James*

Fenimore Cooper's America (Berkeley and Los Angeles: University of California Press, 1972); George Dekker, *James Fenimore Cooper: The American Scott* (New York: Barnes and Noble, 1967); and Levine, *Conspiracy and Romance*, chap. 2. On the languages of Cooper's fiction, see Simpson, *The Politics of American English*, chaps. 5 and 6.

50. James Fenimore Cooper, *Notions of the Americans: Picked Up by a Traveling Bachelor*, 2 vols. (Philadelphia, 1828), II, 178, 167.

51. Melville, *Pierre*, p. 9.

52. James Fenimore Cooper, *Satanstoe, or The Littlepage Manuscripts*, ed. Kay Seymour House and Constance Ayers Denry (Albany: State University of New York Press, 1990), pp. 43, 42.

53. James Fenimore Cooper, *The Crater, or Vulcan's Peak*, ed. Thomas Philbrick (Cambridge, Mass.: Belknap Press, 1962), p. 7.

54. *Memoirs of John Quincy Adams, Comprising Portions of His Diary from 1798 to 1848*, ed. Charles Francis Adams, 12 vols. (Philadelphia, 1876), VIII, 546. For a full account of this ceremony, its treatment by Seba Smith, and the portrayal of Jackson as a backwoodsman who was his own schoolmaster, see John William Ward, *Andrew Jackson – Symbol for an Age*, chaps. 4 and 5.

55. Nathan O. Hatch, *The Democratization of American Christianity* (New Haven, Conn.: Yale University Press, 1989), chap. 5.

56. James Russell Lowell, "Reviews and Literary Notices," *Atlantic Monthly*, 25 (1859), p. 638.

57. On Phillips's "eloquence of abuse," see Irving Bartlett, *Wendell Phillips* (Boston: Beacon, 1961), chap. 11.

58. On opposition to women orators in antebellum America, see Lillian O'Connor, *Pioneer Women Orators: Rhetoric in the Ante-Bellum Reform Movement* (New York: Columbia University Press, 1954), pp. 22–40.

59. William B. Fowle, *The True English Grammar* (Boston: Munroe and Francis, 1827), p. 25.

60. *Common School Journal*, 11 (1849), p. 258.

61. *The Journal of Henry David Thoreau*, ed. Bradford Torrey and Francis H. Allen, 14 vols. (Boston: Houghton Mifflin, 1906), XII, 389–90. Subsequent references to these volumes (abbreviated HTJ) are given parenthetically.

62. On Thoreau's advocacy and practice of lawless language, see Henry Golemba, *Thoreau's Wild Rhetoric* (New York: New York University Press, 1990).

63. On Emerson's advocacy of linguistic freedom, see Richard Poirier, *The Renewal of Literature* (New York: Random House, 1987), whose analysis needs to be supplemented by critics who have considered this advocacy more fully in the light of Emerson's biography and context.

64. Walt Whitman, *Daybooks and Notebooks*, ed. William White, 3 vols. (New York: New York University Press, 1978), III, 811.

65. Ibid., p. 666.

66. Ibid., pp. 666-7.

67. Walt Whitman, "America's Mightiest Inheritance," in *New York Dis-*

sected, ed. Emory Holloway and Ralph Adimari (New York: Rufus Rockwell Wilson, 1936), p. 59.

68. Quoted in Matthiessen, *American Renaissance*, p. 532.

69. Quoted in Michael Rowan Dressman, "Walt Whitman's Plans for the Perfect Dictionary," in *Studies in the American Renaissance*, ed. Joel Meyerson (Boston: Twayne, 1979), p. 469.

70. For the politics of Whitman's poetics and his linguistic theory, see, most recently, Allen Grossman, "The Poetics of Union in Lincoln and Whitman: An Inquiry Toward the Relationship of Art and Politics," in *The American Renaissance Reconsidered*, ed. Donald Pease and Walter Benn Michaels (Baltimore: Johns Hopkins University Press, 1985), pp. 183–208; Betsy Erkkila, *Whitman the Political Poet* (New York: Oxford University Press, 1989); Larson, *Whitman's Drama of Consensus*; Timothy Sweet, *Traces of War: Poetry, Photography, and the Crisis of the Union* (Baltimore: Johns Hopkins University Press, 1990), chap. 1.

71. "America's Mightiest Inheritance," p. 56.

72. Fitzhugh, *Cannibals All!*, pp. 59–60, 63.

73. "Human Rights," *American Review*, 2 (November 1845), p. 441.

74. On the theme of manifest decline in the period, see George B. Forgie, *Patricide in the House Divided* (New York: Norton, 1979), pp. 173–8. Stéphane Mallarmé, "Le tombeau d'Edgar Poe," in *Mallarmé*, ed. Anthony Hartley (Baltimore: Penguin, 1970), p. 90.

Chapter 10. Corrupt Language and a Corrupt Body Politic, or the Disunion of Words and Things

1. For a study of Emerson's concerns about the corruption of language in the context of his critique of trade and the social concerns of the mid 1830s, see Ian F. A. Bell, "The Hard Currency of Words: Emerson's Fiscal Metaphor in *Nature*," *ELH*, 52 (1985), pp. 733–53.

2. Whipple, "Words," p. 179.

3. *United States Magazine and Democratic Review*, 6 (1840), p. 486.

4. Dekker, *James Fenimore Cooper*, p. 176.

5. Calvin Colton, *The Junius Tracts* (New York: Greeley and McElrath, 1844), p. 89. Subsequent references to this volume are given parenthetically.

6. "Political Clap-Trap," *National Intelligencer*, January 15, 1848, p. 6.

7. "The Philosophy of Advertising," *American Review*, 16 (1852), p. 121. Subsequent references to this article are given parenthetically.

8. Edwin Whipple, "The Use and Misuse of Words," *Literature and Life* (Boston: Houghton Mifflin, 1896), p. 221. Subsequent references to this essay are given parenthetically.

9. "Word-Murder," *Continental Monthly*, 2 (1862), pp. 524, 527.

10. "The Wonders of Words," *Continental Monthly*, 3 (1863), p. 394.

11. Ibid.

12. On Whitman's hopes for the study and practice of language in America, see Kramer, *Imagining Language*, chap. 3.

13. Quoted in James Brown, "An Appeal from the Old Theory of English Grammar, to the True Constructive Genius of the English Language," preface to *English Syntithology* (Philadelphia: Grubb and Reazon, 1845), p. xvi.
14. Everett, *Orations and Speeches*, I, 21–2.
15. "The Two Tongues," *Atlantic Monthly*, 6 (1860), p. 673.
16. This plan became the foundation for Andrews's larger work *The Primary Synopsis of Universology and Alwato*, discussed in Chapter 4.
17. "The Unity of Language and Mankind," *North American Review*, 73 (1851), p. 165.
18. Edward Gould, *Good English* (New York: A. C. Armstrong, 1880), pp. 3, 25.
19. Holmes, *The Autocrat of the Breakfast-Table*, p. 11.
20. Gibian, *Oliver Wendell Holmes in the Conversation of His Culture*, chap. 1.
21. Melville, *Mardi*, p. 528.
22. "The People," *Southern Quarterly Review*, 25 (1854), pp. 32–3.
23. *The Works of Ralph Waldo Emerson*, 5 vols. (New York: Harper Bros., n.d.), II, 494.
24. *Wendell Phillips on Civil Rights and Freedom*, ed. Louis Filler (New York: Hill and Wang, 1965), p. xxvii. See also pp. 99–100.
25. *Frederick Douglass: The Narrative and Selected Writings*, ed. Michael Meyer (New York: Random House, 1984), p. 252.
26. Jefferson Davis, *The Rise and Fall of the Confederate Government*, 2 vols. (Cranbury, N.J.: Yoseloff, 1958), I, 183–4.
27. James M. McPherson, *Battle Cry of Freedom* (New York: Oxford University Press, 1988), pp. vii–viii.
28. Melville, *The Confidence-Man*, p. 251.
29. "Political Equality," *Nation*, 1 (1865), p. 72. Subsequent references to this essay are given parenthetically.
30. *The Letters of Ralph Waldo Emerson*, Vol. V, ed. R. L. Rusk (New York, 1939), pp. 395–6.
31. See Cmiel, *Democratic Eloquence*, chaps. 4 and 5.
32. George Wakeman, "Verbal Anomalies" and "The Confusion of Tongues," *Galaxy*, 2 (1866), pp. 443, 29.
33. "The Gift of Gab," *Nation*, 3 (1866), p. 75.
34. On the dialectical struggle between a high (inflated) moral rhetoric and a low style, see Marx, "'Noble Shit' and Civil Religion," and John P. Sisk, "The Devil and American Epic," *Hudson Review*, 40 (1987), pp. 31–47.
35. "Expression," *Atlantic Monthly*, 6 (1860), p. 573.
36. On the politics and philosophy of Thoreau's philology, see Michael West, "Scatology and Eschatology: The Heroic Dimensions of Thoreau's Word-play," *PMLA*, 89 (1974), pp. 1043–64; and Gura, *Wisdom of Words*, chap. 4.
37. For an analysis of Thoreau's tactic of corrective redefinition in "A Plea for Captain John Brown," see George P. Landow, *Elegant Jeremiahs: The Sage from Carlyle to Mailer* (Ithaca, N.Y.: Cornell University Press, 1986), pp. 120–4.

38. Ernest Hemingway, *A Farewell to Arms* (New York: Scribner, 1929), p. 185.
39. Ezra Pound, *ABC of Reading* (New York: New Directions, 1960), p. 32, and *Gaudier-Brzeska: A Memoir* (New York: John Lane, 1916), p. 136.
40. Ezra Pound, *Impact* (Chicago: Regnery, 1960), pp. 45, 99.
41. Ezra Pound, *Literary Essays of Ezra Pound*, ed. T. S. Eliot (New York: New Directions, 1944), p. 409.
42. Ezra Pound, *How to Read* (London: Desmond Harmsworth, 1931). pp. 17–18. For further prose commentary by Pound on the interrelationship of political and linguistic corruption, see *ABC of Reading*, pp. 32–4; *Gaudier-Brzeska*, pp. 136–42; *Guide to Kulchur* (New York: New Directions, 1970), pp. 15–17, 49–50, 57–9, 241–8.
43. For the ways in which Pound's linguistic criticism drew sustenance from the Chinese doctrine of Cheng Ming as well as from the Western tradition of connecting the decline of liberty to the decline of eloquence, see Pound's translation and commentary on *The Analects* in *Confucius* (New York: New Directions, 1951); *Guide to Kulchur*, pp. 15–17, 244; and his essays "Immediate Need of Confucius" and "A Visiting Card" in *Impact*.
44. Pound, *Literary Essays*, p. 77 (ellipses in original). On Pound's call for verbal rectitude and how he turned to the Confucian doctrine of Cheng Ming as a means to combat political and economic corruption, see Victor P. H. Li, "Philology and Power: Ezra Pound and the Regulation of Language," *boundary 2*, 15 (1986–7), pp. 187–210. See also Michael André Bernstein, *The Tale of the Tribe* (Princeton, N.J.: Princeton University Press, 1980), pp. 127–61.
45. Pound, *Literary Essays*, p. 409.
46. Pound, *How to Read*, p. 17.
47. On poetry's capacity to sustain a belief in language as a revitalizing force in our lives, see David St. John, "Poetry, Hope, and the Language of Possibility," *Antioch Review*, 48 (1990), pp. 269–73.

Chapter 11. Sovereign Words vs. Representative Men

1. For a fuller sketch of these developments, see Bender and Wellbery, "Rhetoricality: On the Modernist Return of Rhetoric," pp. 3–39. Unfortunately, they do not consider the persistence (and reinvigoration) of the classical rhetorical tradition in the early American republic.
2. On antebellum oratory, see, for a general survey, Baskerville, *The People's Voice*. On New England oratory and its relationship to American Renaissance literature, see, first and foremost, Lawrence Buell, *New England Literary Culture* (New York: Cambridge University Press, 1986), chap. 6, "New England Oratory from Everett to Emerson."
3. William Swinton, *Rambles Among Words: Their Poetry, History and Wisdom* (New York: Ivisan, Blakeman, Taylor, and Co., 1865; rev. 1872), pp. 50, 126. Subsequent references to this volume are given parenthetically.

4. Joshua Leavitt, cited in Eric Foner, *Free Soil, Free Labor, Free Men: The Ideology of the Republican Party Before the Civil War* (New York: Oxford University Press, 1970), p. 93.
5. Ferguson, *Law and Letters*, p. 229.
6. Ibid., pp. 229–30.
7. *Selections from the Writings and Speeches of William Lloyd Garrison*, pp. 317–24.
8. *Theodore Parker: An Anthology*, ed. Henry Steele Commager (Boston: Beacon, 1960), p. 182.
9. Quoted in J. C. Furnas, *The Road to Harpers Ferry* (New York: Sloan, 1959), p. 311.
10. Taney, quoted in *Supreme Court and Supreme Law*, ed. Edmond Cahn, p. 65.
11. Wills, *Inventing America*, Prologue.
12. On Lincoln's style, see Richard M. Weaver, "Abraham Lincoln and the Argument from Definition," *The Ethics of Rhetoric* (Chicago: Regnery, 1953), pp. 85–114; Roy P. Basler, *A Touchstone for Greatness: Essays, Addresses, and Occasional Pieces About Abraham Lincoln* (Westport, Conn.: Greenwood, 1973), pp. 53–100, 206–27.
13. Ferguson, *Law and Letters*, p. 312.
14. On Douglass's mastery of the master's eloquence (and the restrictions of that mastery), see Houston A. Baker, Jr., *The Journey Back: Issues in Black Literature and Criticism* (Chicago: University of Chicago Press, 1980), pp. 31–46; and Cheyfitz, *The Poetics of Imperialism*, pp. 33–40, 127–34.
15. James M. McPherson, "How Lincoln Won the War with Metaphors," *Abraham Lincoln and the Second American Revolution* (New York: Oxford University Press, 1990), pp. 93–112.
16. Charles Dudley Warner, "What Is Your Culture to Me?" *Scribner's Monthly*, 4 (1872), p. 470.
17. Quoted in Kenneth S. Greenberg, *Masters and Statesmen: The Political Culture of American Slavery* (Baltimore: Johns Hopkins University Press, 1985), p. 14.
18. Ferguson, *Law and Letters*, p. 317.
19. Fisher, *The Trial of the Constitution*, pp. vi, 18, 55, 65, 77, 96.
20. Ellison, *Shadow and Act*, pp. 164–5.
21. Burke, *The Philosophy of Literary Form*, pp. 448–9.
22. Hugh Kenner, "A Portrait in Perspective," in *James Joyce: Two Decades of Criticism*, ed. Sean Givens (New York: Vanguard, 1948), pp. 143–4.

Afterword

1. Allen Ginsberg, *Collected Poems, 1947–1980* (New York: Harper and Row, 1984), p. 401.
2. Ibid., p. 407.
3. N. Scott Momaday, *House Made of Dawn* (New York: New American Library, 1968), p. 89.
4. Ibid.
5. Havel, "Words on Words," p. 5.

6. Ibid. On the role of poetry and the literary artist as counters to the linguistic corruption of the Thucydidean moment, see also in particular Eduardo Galeano's essay "In Defense of the Word," trans. Bobbye S. Ortiz, in *Days and Nights of Love and War* (New York: Monthly Review Press, 1983), pp. 183–94, and Octavio Paz, *The Bow and the Lyre*, trans. Ruth L. C. Sims (Austin: University of Texas Press, 1987), and *The Other Voice*, trans. Helen Lane (New York: Harcourt Brace Jovanovich, 1990).

Index

Continued from the front of the book

The following books in the series are out of print: